**PRACTICE
MAKES
PERFECT®**

Complete Spanish All-in-One

PRACTICE MAKES PERFECT®

Complete Spanish All-in-One

Premium Second Edition

Gilda Nissenberg, PhD, Editor

New York   Chicago   San Francisco   Athens   London   Madrid
Mexico City   Milan   New Delhi   Singapore   Sydney   Toronto

3 4 5 6 7 8 9   LHS   23 22 21 20 19

ISBN   978-1-260-12105-6
MHID   1-260-12105-4

e-ISBN   978-1-260-12106-3
e-MHID   1-260-12106-2

Portions of this book were previously published under the titles of *Practice Makes Perfect: Complete Spanish Grammar*, *Practice Makes Perfect: Intermediate Spanish Grammar*, *Practice Makes Perfect: Spanish Conversation*, *Practice Makes Perfect: Spanish Problem Solver*, and *Practice Makes Perfect: Spanish Sentence Builder*.

Interior design by Village Bookworks, Inc.

McGraw-Hill Education products are available at special quantity discounts to use as premiums and sales promotions or for use in corporate training programs. To contact a representative, please visit the Contact Us pages at www.mhprofessional.com.

McGraw-Hill Education Language Lab App

Extensive streaming audio recordings and vocabulary flashcards are available to support your study of this book. Go to mhlanguagelab.com to access the online version of this application or to locate links to the mobile app for iOS and Android devices. (Note: Internet access is required to access audio via the app.)

Contents

Preface

Practice Makes Perfect: Complete Spanish All-in-One, aimed especially at self-taught learners, is designed to provide a user-friendly way to study at different levels. All language needs are covered, including vocabulary, conversation, pronunciation, and information about grammar, syntax, and spelling.

This book contains numerous ideas from the following five *Practice Makes Perfect* titles:

- *Practice Makes Perfect: Spanish Problem Solver* tackles many challenges for Spanish learners, including when to use confusing verbs pairs such as **ser** and **estar**, how to use double object pronouns, and how to spell words and enunciate properly in Spanish.
- *Practice Makes Perfect: Intermediate Spanish Grammar* provides clear explanations of verbs and tenses, such as how to conjugate present tense irregular verbs and how to use **gustar**. Numerous examples and exercises help users continue building competency to communicate in Spanish.
- *Practice Makes Perfect: Spanish Conversation* includes vocabulary for informal conversation and example dialogues with questions and responses. Expressions that do not always translate literally, such as **bueno** (well) and **Parece mentira** (It doesn't seem possible), are reviewed.
- *Practice Makes Perfect: Complete Spanish Grammar* may not include every grammatical rule but does provide a general overview of Spanish grammar, including many examples and practice exercises.
- *Practice Makes Perfect: Spanish Sentence Builder* covers the Spanish syntax needed to build sentence structure, along with spelling, punctuation, and many exercises.

Readers will gain more knowledge through informal Spanish conversation, vocabulary, and writing practice to communicate clearly with Spanish speakers. And new to this premium second edition, recordings of the answers to numerous exercises are provided via the McGraw-Hill Education Language Lab app. This streaming audio will help readers improve both listening and speaking skills.

Spelling, pronunciation, and punctuation

·1·

This chapter will show you how to reconcile written and spoken Spanish words so you can understand and read them aloud with accuracy. Students are sometimes confused about the rules and mechanics of writing in Spanish, which makes their written work difficult to follow. Since pre-college education includes less and less attention to grammatical issues, most students are adrift in misty confusion because they don't know how to name what they are confused about. This chapter, therefore, also contains some observations about the parts of speech and a bit of basic grammar terminology.

Correct punctuation and spelling are needed to communicate written messages effectively. Punctuation is an established system of standardized marks that separate structural units (sentences, quotes, paragraphs, etc.) and clarify the meaning of written language:

system of standardized marks → punctuation

Spanish and English conventions regarding punctuation are similar, but they vary in detail. In writing, we must adhere to the punctuation rules specific to a given language.

Sentences are based on their structures, word order, and punctuation. In this unit we will review and expand details regarding punctuation, building sentences, and building paragraphs.

one or more sentences dealing with one topic → paragraph

Accent marks and pronunciation

Spanish slowly emerged as a written language, consciously and clearly distinct from Latin, during the late Middle Ages. There were no rules, no one to guide its development. Most people were illiterate. English was in a similar condition when it emerged from the amalgam of languages that contributed to its development.

In 1728, more than one hundred years after the death of Cervantes, the Royal Academy of the Spanish Language was founded, and still exists today, to watch over the language and safeguard its transmission to future generations. (English has no such body, and this explains in part why there are so many differences in spelling throughout the English-speaking world.)

Some of the important features of Spanish spelling, known more formally as *orthography*, are that the Academy eventually dropped double consonants, such as *ss* and *tt* and simplified *ph* to *f* and *th* to *t*. Words with a *cc* in the middle are not considered a consonant pair because the first *c* ends the previous syllable and the second *c* begins the next, such as in **diccionario**. The famous double or trilled **rr**, as in **perro** (*dog*) as opposed to **pero** (*but*), actually represents a different sound and can be considered as if it were one letter. The good news here is that many English words are cognates with Spanish and only require you to understand a handful of rules in order to spell—and thus pronounce—them correctly. One example is sufficient to make this point. The English word *commission* is **comisión** in Spanish.

The only other small detail in this example has to do with the use of written accent marks. Over time, the Academy established more and more conservative rules about accent marks. There are four rules, and they can actually help you learn to pronounce words even if you've never seen or heard them before. Here's how the system works:

♦ Observing that a vast number of the words in Spanish end in a vowel, an **-n**, or an **-s**, and that these words are almost always pronounced by stressing the next-to-the-last syllable, the Royal Academy economically ruled that such words would not bear a written accent. What this means to you, as a learner of Spanish, is that when you see a word of more than one syllable, with no written accent and that ends in a vowel, an **-n**, or an **-s**, you should immediately know to pronounce it with the stress on the next-to-the-last syllable. It really is that simple. Open any dictionary, or **diccionario**.

♦ The Academy also noticed that the second largest number of words in Spanish end in a consonant other than **-n** or **-s** and that they are pronounced with the stress on the last syllable. They decided that these words also would not bear a written accent. All infinitives are examples of such words, as are all those ending in **-dad** or **-tud** (which are also, by the way, all feminine in gender). Other common examples include **animal**, stressed on the final **-a**, and **reloj**, stressed on the final **-o**.

♦ The next observation of the Royal Academy results in the third rule and is very important: all exceptions to the first two rules will be marked by a written accent. Remember, the exceptions are determined by how words are pronounced, speech being prior to any written system. Thus, we have many, many words ending in **-ión** (almost all feminine), such as **comisión** and **nación**, as well as others such as **fármaco, malévolo**, and **cónsul**. The point is, if you know these three rules and see a word in print, you should be able to correctly put the stress on the proper syllable of a Spanish word, even if you've never seen or heard the word before.

♦ The fourth and last rule about the use of written accents applies only to a means of distinguishing between two otherwise identical one-syllable words. These are known as *monosyllabic homonyms,* one-syllable words that sound alike but have different meanings. Examples of contrastive pairs include **tú** (*you*) and **tu** (*your*), **él** (*he*) and **el** (*the*, masculine singular) **té** (*tea*) and **te** (object pronoun corresponding to **tú**) **sé** (*I know*) and **se** (the third-person object pronoun).

Finally, there is only one group of words that stand outside these rules and cause difficulty. In English these words end in *-cy* and in Spanish they end in **-ia** or **-ía**. There is simply no way to predict whether they will be stressed on the final **i** or on the next-to-the-last syllable. The best strategy is to look them up—and pay attention as you read. Examples include **farmacia, malicia, farmacología**, and **alevosía**. You're in luck, of course, if you first encounter such words in print, since the presence or lack of a written accent will tell you where to place the stress when pronouncing them.

Pronunciation

A couple of general remarks may help you improve your Spanish pronunciation and make it closer to that of native speakers. First, vowels are pure. That means, for instance, that the (American) English vowel sounds as heard in *cat*, *set*, *sit*, *on*, and *up* are not found in Spanish—ever! Instead, the Spanish pronunciation of these vowels is more like those heard in the following (American) English words:

    a *father*
    e *weigh*
    i *seen*
    o *woe*
    u *moon*

It only takes a slight adjustment to these to get them right: The sound of the **e** should not glide up into the *i* sound in *weigh* or the *y* sound in *they*. Likewise, the pronunciation of **u** in Spanish, represented approximately by the *oo* in *moon*, should not glide into an *ee* sound at the end or glide from it at the beginning, as is sometimes heard in some dialects of U.S. English. I've heard this phenomenon most often in Western states, particularly in Southern California. Even Ronald Reagan's pronunciation had a touch of this!

Regarding consonants, the best advice I can give you here is to soften them. English speakers everywhere tend to explode the pronunciation of initial occlusive consonants in particular, such as are heard in *Carl*, *Tom*, and *Peter*. One way to practice this is to hold the back of your hand about an inch away from the your lips and practice saying these names in a normal volume and pitch, but without so much force, so that you no longer feel your breath on the back of your hand.

The next and last bit of guidance I offer about pronunciation is to listen and read much. But to whom should you listen and what should you read? The choice is yours, of course, but my advice is to remember that you will be judged by how you speak—in socio-economic and class terms. True, your Spanish-speaking listeners will realize that you are not a native speaker, but they will judge you anyway, because the way you speak will suggest to them the sort of company you keep. As the Spanish proverb goes: **Dime con quién andas y te diré quién eres.** (Literally, *Tell me with who you hang out with and I'll tell you who you are.*) For speech models, I often suggest that learners judiciously follow a character from a **telenovela** (*soap opera*) who is about their age and gender and who represents a respectable character. I've known more than one native speaker of Spanish who vastly improved his or her English by doing the same thing with American "soaps."

The one remaining question I often hear from forward-looking learners who may have specific career goals that could lead them in specific geographical directions is which dialect of Spanish they should emulate. Depending on how you define them, in simple, practical terms there are six or seven major dialectical regions in the Spanish-speaking world. Each, of course, can be further subdivided, but for my readers, as learners of Spanish, the contours I shall present will enable you to make some informed decisions about the dialect you select as your model.

In Spain, there are those who pronounce the letter **z** and the consonant-vowel combinations **ce-/ci-** as the *th* sound of the English word *thin* (often called *theta*, after the name of the Greek letter). There are others who do not follow this pattern and who pronounce these sounds approximately as an *s*. The dividing line is roughly north-south, the north being the zone of the *theta* pronunciation. The ancestors of most of the people of the New World were from the south of Spain, which largely explains why the pronunciation of Castile is not found in the Americas.

In the Americas, the major dialect groups are: Mexican, Caribbean (Cuba, Dominican Republic, Puerto Rico and coastal areas of Central America, Colombia and Venezuela), Central American (except Caribbean coastal areas), Andean (interior of Colombia, Peru, Ecuador, most of Chile, Bolivia and Paraguay), and finally the area known as the **Cono del Sur** or Southern Cone (Argentina, southern Chile, and Uruguay).

Spanish in the United States itself is evolving. In South Florida, New York, and New Jersey, you will find mostly Caribbean dialects. In Chicago, Minneapolis–St. Paul, and other Mid-western cities, as well as in most of the Western states, the Mexican dialect predominates. Interestingly, in the metropolitan area of Washington, D.C., the Salvadoran dialect predomi-nates, due to the presence of more than a hundred thousand immigrants who fled El Salvador in the 1980s.

No one dialect is superior to another. The Royal Academy has corresponding members in every corner of the world where Spanish is or ever has been a language of government. There are educated and non-educated speakers in each dialect, so if you have professional reasons for spending much time in any particular region, you should seek out people of your profession who are from there so you can fit in as easily as possible. This book, therefore, takes a neutral approach in its choice of vocabulary, a sort of *airport* dialect, if you wish.

The brief set of exercises that follow give practice in the use of the dictionary—to check spellings, accent marks, and proper classification according to part of speech. It is assumed that learners will also be pronouncing the words they find.

EJERCICIO
1·1

Indicate whether the following words correctly use accent marks or do not require one according to the following key: **correctly used**; **incorrectly placed** *(but needed on a different syllable);* **correct, with no accent mark**; **superfluous** *(placed on syllable that would be stressed anyway); or* **missing**.

1. organizacion _____

2. consul _____

3. lealtad _____

4. animál _____

5. camión _____

6. tecnologia _____

7. háblas _____

8. teorico _____

9. temeraria _____

10. primorosa _____

11. caracter _____

12. avíon _____

13. caracteres _____

14. vendio _____

15. ventána _____

16. vecino _____

17. frijoles _____

18. proyector _____

19. cortinas _____

20. teoría _____

Punctuation marks

The following punctuation marks are used in both Spanish and English sentences:

la coma	*comma*
las comillas	*quotation marks*
dos puntos	*colon*
el paréntesis	*parenthesis*
el punto y coma	*semicolon*
el punto	*period*
el signo de admiración	*exclamation point*
el signo de exclamación	*exclamation point*
el signo de interrogación	*question mark*

The period

Use a period (.) to indicate the end of a declarative sentence (a sentence that makes a statement), an indirect question, or a command (imperative) sentence:

Pablo sabe la verdad.	*Pablo knows the truth.*
Ana no sabe quién toca a la puerta.	*Ana does not know who is knocking at the door.*
Firmen la carta antes de enviarla.	*Sign the letter before you mail it.*

A period separates sentences in a paragraph structure. The first letter of the word that follows a period is capitalized:

Esta noche vamos a observar un eclipse lunar. Los telescopios están listos. Los miembros del equipo nos enviarán los detalles.	*Tonight we will watch a lunar eclipse. The telescopes are ready. The members of the team will send us the details.*

Note that in typing or keying in text, you should leave a single space between a period and a new sentence. When you write paragraphs that are part of a longer piece, indent the first sentence or line of each paragraph:

El gobernador del Estado de Aragua pronunciará un discurso acerca de las necesidades de los ciudadanos. Dos de sus consejeros le comunicaron las preocupaciones de algunos de sus compatriotas.

The governor of the State of Aragua will give a speech about the needs of the citizens. Two of his advisors told him about the concerns of some of his fellow citizens.

Abbreviations

Periods are also used in abbreviations and some acronyms (**siglas**). Not all abbreviations have equivalents in both English and Spanish. Some abbreviations have been used for a very long time, while others have or may become obsolete, falling out of favor for various reasons. Here are some frequently used abbreviations in Spanish:

a. de J.C.	*B.C.*
a.C.	*B.C.*
d.C.	*A.D.*
Dr.	*Dr.*
Dra.	*Dr.*
Drs.	*Drs.*
etc.	*etc.*
ONU	*UN*
pág.	*p. (page)*
P.D.	*P.S.*
S.A.	*Inc.*
Sr.	*Mr.*
Sra.	*Mrs.*
Srta.	*Miss*
FUNDÉU (La Fundación del Español Urgente)	
UE	*EU (European Union)*
EE.UU.	*US or U.S.*
JJ.OO. (Juegos olímpicos)	*Olympic Games*

In Spanish, note the repetition of the initial letters of each component of abbreviations that consist of plural nouns such as **EE.UU.** Also, note that **FUNDÉU** has an accent mark to indicate the stressed syllable.

Encontraron evidencias de una civilización de alrededor del año **200 a. de J.C.**

*They found evidence of a civilization dated around **200 B.C.***

La petición va dirigida al **Dr.** E. Santos.

*The petition is addressed to **Dr** .E. Santos.*

El Consejo de Seguridad de la **ONU** tiene una sesión de emergencia.

*The **UN** Security Council has an emergency meeting.*

La abreviatura **P.D.** viene de la frase latina "postdata".

*The abbreviation **P.S.** comes from the Latin phrase "postscriptum."*

Los **EE.UU** ganaron más medallas en los **JJ.OO.** de 2008.

*The **US** won more medals in the 2008 **Olympic Games**.*

En español. *Add the appropriate Spanish punctuation for the sentences below.*

1. Mr. Jiménez travels to the U.S.

2. He found artifacts (*artefactos*) from 200 B.C.

3. Dr. Melissa Marcos is an expert in old civilizations.

4. Miss Marcos, her daughter, helps her mother.

5. They will give a lecture in the EU.

1. _____

2. _____

3. _____

4. _____

5. _____

Acronyms

Acronyms are words created with the initial letter or letters of each of the components of names of institutions, organizations, etc. Some are international. Periods are not usually used with acronyms:

OEA (Organización de Estados Americanos)	*OAS*
ONG (Organización no Gubernamental)	*NGO (Non-Governmental Organization)*
ONU	*UN*
OTAN (Organización del Tratado del Atlántico Norte)	*NATO*
OVNI (Objeto volador no identificado)	*UFO*
La **ONG** defiende los derechos de los niños.	*The **NGO** defends children's rights.*
Revelaron la presencia de **dos OVNI** en California.	*They revealed the presence of **two UFOs** in California.*

Note the Spanish spelling of the plural of **OVNI**, with no final **s**, in the example above.

Comma

A comma (**,**) indicates a brief pause in a sentence. In Spanish, use a comma to separate the elements of a series, except for the element immediately preceded by the conjunctions **y** and **o**. In English, *and* and *or* in such a series are often preceded by a comma.

Vamos a necesitar **lápices, papel y sobres**.	*We will need **pencils, paper, and envelopes**.*
Vimos a **los alumnos, los maestros, los ayudantes, los voluntarios, etc**.	*We saw **the students, the teachers, the aides, the volunteers, etc**.*

The series may consist of a series of nouns, adjectives that are part of a subject, or direct and indirect objects:

Viven en una casa **destartalada, descuidada y viejísima.**	*They live in a **ramshackle, rundown, very old** house.*
Cati, Rosa, María Luisa y Nina son hermanas.	*Cati, Rosa, María Luisa, and Nina are sisters.*

Remember, the spelling of **y** (*and*) changes to **e** when preceded by a word that starts with **i-** or **hi-**:

Ana **e** Irene salieron.	*Ana **and** Irene left.*
En la cesta hay naranjas **e** higos.	*In the basket there are oranges **and** figs.*

Use the spelling **u** instead of **o** (*or*) when the word that follows the conjunction starts with **o-** or **ho-**:

Tiene siete **u** ocho millones de habitantes.	*It has seven **or** eight million people.*
Puedes freírlos **u** hornearlos.	*You can fry them **or** bake them.*

EJERCICIO 1·3

Las oraciones. *Reword the sentences with the appropriate spelling and punctuation.*

1. Alicia Luisa y Irene son disciplinadas trabajadoras pacientes y eficientes

    Alicia, Luisa y Irene son disciplinadas, trabajadoras, pacientes y eficientes

2. Hacen ejercicios montan en bicicleta levantan pesas y corren siete ó ocho millas

    Hacen ejercicios, montan en bicicletas, levantam pesas y corren siete ó ocho millas

3. Estas chicas también hacen yoga trabajos comunitarios sirven a la comunidad

    Estas chicas también hacen yoga, trabajos com y sirven a la comunidad.

4. Hacen campañas en EEUU para recoger (*raise*) fondos para niños y indigentes

    Hacen campañas en EEUU para recoger fondos para niños y indigentes.

5. Han recibido premios certificados y innumerables homenajes de varias organizaciones

    Han recibido premios certificados y innumerables homenajes de varias organizaciones

6. Ellas demuestran que la rutina es esencial para ser disciplinado cumplir metas y triunfar

    Ellas demuestran que la rutina es esencial para ser disciplinado, cumplir metas y triunfar.

Comma after vocatives, phrases, and transition words

A *vocative* is the person addressed in a message. A comma follows the vocative in English and Spanish:

Juan, abre la puerta para que tu hermano entre.	*Juan, open the door so that your brother may come in.*

A comma must be used to separate elements that introduce a sentence, such as infinitive phrases or phrases that express contrasts or similarities:

Al entrar en la tienda, encontré lo que buscaba.

Upon entering the store, I found what I was looking for.

Por otro lado, Alba es amable y generosa.

On the other hand, Alba is pleasant and generous.

Del mismo modo, Felipe coopera con todos sus colegas.

Likewise, Felipe works well with all his colleagues.

Commas are also used after *transition words or phrases*. Most transition words are adverbs. They add a point or idea, illustrate examples, arrive at a conclusion, etc.

consecuentemente	*consequently*
de hecho	*in fact*
no obstante	*nevertheless*
por consiguiente	*therefore*
por eso	*therefore*
sin embargo	*however* ,poném

Llovió muchísimo esa tarde. **Consecuentemente,** las carreteras se inundaron.

*It rained a lot that afternoon. **Consequently,** the roads were flooded.*

La policía cerró varias carreteras. **Por consiguiente,** el tráfico estaba muy congestionado.

*The police closed a few roads. **Therefore,** the traffic was very congested.*

A comma separates *parenthetical phrases* such as relative clauses or adverbial clauses that include added information that may not be essential to the sentence:

Estudiaron el artículo de la profesora, **cuya obra se extiende por tres décadas,** para comprender sus teorías pedagógicas.

*They studied the professor's article, **whose work stretches over three decades,** in order to understand her pedagogical theories.*

Commas separate geographical names in Spanish, as they do in English:

La Habana, Cuba
San Diego, California

Havana, Cuba
San Diego, California

**EJERCICIO
1·4**

Oraciones en español. *Create sentences with the appropriate word order, spelling, and punctuation.*

1. a / las ocho / regresa / esta / Carmen / noche

   Carmen regresa esta noche a las ocho

2. los / decidimos / al / escuchar / llegar / a casa / mensajes

   Al llegar a casa decidimos escuchar los mensajes

3. de hecho / paciencia / mucho / no tienes / enojas / porque / mucho / te

   De hecho no tienes paciencia porque te enojas mucho

4. una / recibieron / carta / San Antonio / de / Texas

   Recibieron una carta de San Antonio, Texas

5. tu / necesitaba / ayuda / amistad / tu / y / compañía / tu

Necesitaba tu ayuda, tu compañía y tu amistad

6. dice / documento / eres / Lima / este / que / de / Perú

Este documento dice que eres de Lima, Perú.

Colons and semicolons

Colons (:) indicate a pause to call attention to what follows in a sentence. The colon may also introduce a list of elements:

Subastaron tres piezas: **un cuadro de Picasso, una estatua italiana y un manuscrito del siglo XV.**
*They auctioned three pieces: **a painting by Picasso, an Italian statue, and a fifteenth-century manuscript.***

In Spanish, colons may bring a conclusion to an enumeration, which seems to reverse the order suggested in the previous examples:

Sanos, frescos y orgánicos: así deben ser todos los ingredientes.
Healthy, fresh, and organic: that is how all the ingredients should be.

Claro, conciso, al grano: **has listado las cualidades de un buen discurso.**
*Clear, concise, to the point: **you have listed the qualities of a good speech.***

Another function of a colon is to introduce textual quotes. Remember to include quotation marks. A capital letter usually starts the quote:

Lo decía el letrero: **"No fumar".**
*The sign said: **"No smoking."***

Colons are used after a salutation in both formal and informal letters in Spanish:

Querida Anita:
Dear Anita,
Estimado Sr. Martínez:
Dear Mr. Martínez:

A semicolon (;) indicates a pause longer than one that uses a comma, but not as long as one indicated by a period. Usually, a semicolon separates elements of complex enumerations. Elements separated by semicolons sometimes have their own internal punctuation; each may have a subject-verb combination of its own.

Las rosas necesitan el abono; los claveles, agua; las otras plantas, luz.
The roses need plant food; the carnations, water; the other plants, light.

Parentheses and quotation marks

Parentheses and quotation marks have similar uses in both English and Spanish. Parentheses enclose incidental information or a clarification. Remember that elements inside parentheses are independent from the sentence; always follow appropriate spelling rules.

Salieron de Cuba **(diciembre, 1957)** antes de la Revolución.
*They left Cuba **(December 1957)** before the Revolution.*

Debido a la lluvia **(copiosa y persistente)** cancelaron el concierto.
*Due to the rainfall **(abundant and persistent)** they canceled the concert.*

Los delegados negaron **(¿acaso no lo sabían?)** la inocencia del acusado.
*The delegates denied **(perhaps they didn't know it?)** the innocence of the accused.*

quizás

At times, quotations get complicated. For sentences at this level, let's consider the most common uses of quotation marks. Quotation marks are used to show spoken language, to quote from a written or spoken source, and sometimes to refer to titles of poems, newspaper articles, etc.:

El vendedor dijo: **"Vaya a la caja, por favor"**.

El artículo dice: **"El calentamiento global hace daño a todas las ballenas"**.

El poema **"Sólo el amor"** está en esta colección.

*The salesman said: **"Go to the register, please."***

*The article states: **"Global warming is harming all the whales."***

*The poem **"Love Alone"** is in this collection.*

Note the use of the periods in the following Spanish examples. After quotation marks, a period ends the sentence; a complete sentence within parentheses ends with a period inside the end parenthesis:

Y dijimos lo siguiente: **"No vamos"**.

No respondía. **(Era obvio que estaba acompañado.)**

*And we said the following: **"We will not go."***

*He wasn't answering. **(It was obvious he had company.)***

Words or phrases used ironically, as well as words and phrases from another language, are usually set in quotations:

Él dijo que estaban muy **"ocupados"**.

Es como un **"déjà vu"**.

*He said that they were very **"busy."***

*It's like having a **"déjà vu."***

EJERCICIO
1·5

¿Coma (,)? ¿Punto y coma (;)? ¿Dos puntos (:)? *Add the appropriate punctuation.*

1. Vamos a mudarnos a una casa más grande no tenemos suficiente espacio.

2. Los muebles de la sala los cuadros los platos de la cocina todo está listo.

3. Compramos cuatro aparatos nuevos una computadora un televisor HD un teléfono móvil y una aspiradora.

4. Cómoda amplia fresca y acogedora así es la casa nueva.

5. Una cocina debe ser lo mejor de una casa espaciosa bien equipada y llena de luz.

6. Ahora podemos quitar el letrero que dice Se vende casa.

Exclamation points and question marks

Question marks (¿?) and exclamation points (¡!) are needed both before and after questions and exclamatory sentences. Remember that with the appropriate punctuation, you can use declarative sentences, negative sentences, and questions to express an emphatic idea or extreme emotion. Don't forget that emphatic commands need exclamation points.

¡Las joyas desaparecieron!

¡No tenemos seguro!

¡Pero dónde estás!

¡Levántate!

The jewels disappeared!

We do not have insurance!

But where are you!

Stand up!

Correcciones. *Add parentheses, colons, semicolons, or quotation marks as needed.*

1. El primer día del verano 21 de junio en el hemisferio norte nos trae alegría.

2. Mi madre mujer muy sabia siempre me hablaba de sus experiencias cuando era niña.

3. Uno de sus consejos era El tiempo es oro.

4. Pensaba que mi madre era invencible ¡qué ilusión! cuando yo era niño.

5. Todas las mañanas cantábamos una canción La cucaracha.

6. ¡Qué risa me da ahora han pasado tantos años porque mi madre era divertida!

7. Y le gustaba en especial un poema La rosa blanca.

8. Raras veces era dura, pero su amenaza siempre era ¡A la cama!

9. Cuando no estaba de buen humor, yo sabía que estaba ocupada.

10. Y puedo repetir las palabras que decía mi padre para recordarla Corazón de oro.

Some considerations about spelling

Spelling, the sequence of letters that compose a word, is a system of written conventions of a specific language. For example, the English spelling rule "i *before* e *except . . .* " does not apply to correct spelling in Spanish. In this unit, we will review some of the uses of *capital letters* in Spanish and their role in building sentences.

Capital letters (**las mayúsculas**) are needed in the following situations: the first letter of a sentence, the first letter of a proper noun, the first letter after a period or other end punctuation, and all letters of an acronym:

¿Alida es tu hermana? No sabíamos eso.	*Is Alida your sister? We did not know that.*
La **UNICEF** ayuda a los niños de muchos países.	*UNICEF helps children in many countries.*

Proper nouns

A *proper noun* designates a specific person, place, institution, or thing and is usually capitalized in both Spanish and English. Common nouns are not capitalized.

Veo a María.	*I see María.*
Estuvimos en Guadalajara.	*We were in Guadalajara.*
Trabajo en el Instituto Miguel de Cervantes.	*I work at the Miguel de Cervantes Institute.*
Los chicos irán con nosotras.	*The boys will go with us.*
Son los Gómez de siempre.	*They are the same Gomez family (the same Gomezes).*

Note above that in the plural, Spanish surnames referring to a family or a couple are preceded by the definite article **los**; do not add an **-s** or **-es** ending to the name itself.

La ortografía apropiada. *Indicate the words that need capital letters.*

en la universidad de sevilla, un grupo de estudiantes norteamericanos estudian un curso avanzado de literatura hispanoamericana contemporánea. en la lista de lecturas, hay dos novelas de mario vargas llosa, cuentos de isabel allende y obras de autoras mexicanas. al final del semestre y después del examen, los estudiantes van a celebrar el fin de curso en casa belisa, un restaurante popular cerca del río.

Proper names of geographical places

Nouns that refer to mountains, rivers, deserts, oceans, seas, and other geographical proper names are preceded by a definite article (**el/la/los/las**) which indicates the gender (masculine or feminine) and number (singular or plural) of that noun:

La papa es originaria de **los Andes**.	*Potatoes are originally from **the Andes**.*
de **las Rocosas**	*from **the Rocky Mountains***
Hacen rafting en **el Colorado**.	*They go rafting on **the Colorado** (River).*
El Sahara está en el norte de África.	*The Sahara is in northern Africa.*
el Pacífico	*the Pacific (Ocean)*
las Malvinas (en **el Atlántico**)	*the Falkland Islands (in the Atlantic)*
la Bahía de Cochinos	*the Bay of Pigs*

A few proper names of regions, cities, and countries have "permanent" definite articles. In this case, the articles begin with a capital letter because they are part of the proper name:

La Habana	*Havana*
La Mancha	*La Mancha*
La Haya	*The Hague*
El Cairo	*Cairo*

For some countries, use of the definite article varies according to speech and local preferences; however, generally speaking, it is not often used:

Marcos nació **en Perú** pero vive **en la Argentina**.	*Marcos was born **in Peru** but lives **in Argentina**.*
En (el) Japón, la salsa es muy popular.	*In Japan, salsa is very popular.*

However, the definite article is always used when a phrase refers to a particular period of time in a country, continent, or region:

definite article + proper noun + complement(s)

la + **Rusia** + de los Zares	*the Russia of the Tzars*
la Salamanca del siglo XVI	*the Salamanca of the sixteenth century*
el México de Frida Kahlo	*Frida Kahlo's Mexico*
la Cuba de ayer	*yesterday's Cuba*

Keep in mind that nouns and adjectives that refer to the inhabitants of a country are *not* capitalized in Spanish:

Los venezolanos son amistosos.	***Venezuelans** are friendly.*
las chicas californianas	*California girls*

Ortografía. *For every word, review the first letter. If needed, indicate the appropriate capital or lowercase letter.*

A mi amiga marcia le gusta escribir cuentos. Por eso, todos los Lunes escribe durante tres horas. Está escribiendo ahora dos cuentos sobre la california de principios del siglo XX. Ella es la mujer con más imaginación que conozco. Viajó por áfrica y otros lugares exóticos pero para Ella, el lugar más interesante es el Suroeste de los estados unidos.

Days of the week and months of the year

In Spanish, unlike English, names of the days of the week and months of the year are *common nouns*. Thus, they are not capitalized. In the examples below, note the articles and adjectives that precede those nouns:

No trabajo **los domingos**.	*I do not work **on Sundays**.*
El viernes es mi día favorito.	***Friday** is my favorite day.*
La conferencia es **este martes**.	*The conference is **this Tuesday**.*
Todos los lunes empiezo a las seis.	***Every Monday** I start at six o'clock.*

The names of the months are not preceded by articles unless they are accompanied by modifiers, and they are not capitalized:

Voy a Guatemala en **enero**.	*I travel to Guatemala in **January**.*
Me encanta **agosto**.	*I love **August**.*
Recuerdo **el julio** de mis vacaciones.	*I remember **the July** of my vacation.*

Constellations, stars, and planets

Names of constellations, stars, and planets are capitalized in Spanish:

el Sol	*the sun*
la Osa Mayor	*the Big Dipper (Bear)*
la Osa Menor	*the Little Dipper (Bear)*
la Vía Láctea	*the Milky Way*
la Luna	*the moon*
la Tierra	*Earth*
Júpiter	*Jupiter*
Marte	*Mars*
Plutón	*Pluto*
Saturno	*Saturn*
Urano	*Uranus*
Venus	*Venus*

Astrological signs

Astrological signs are capitalized in Spanish, but individuals who fall under the sign are not:

Aries	*Aries*
Tauro	*Taurus*
Géminis	*Gemini*

Cáncer	Cancer
Leo	Leo
Virgo	Virgo
Libra	Libra
Escorpio	Scorpio
Sagitario	Sagittarius
Capricornio	Capricorn
Acuario	Aquarius
Piscis	Pisces
Mi signo zodiacal es **Libra**.	My sign is **Libra**.
Soy un **piscis**.	I am a **Pisces**.

(handwritten, right margin)
lunes — enero
martes — febrero
miércoles — marzo
jueves — abril
viernes — mayo
junio
julio
septiembre
~~octubre~~ octubre
noviembre
diciembre

Cardinal points

Use capital letters only when you refer to the cardinal points themselves. Otherwise, use lower-case letters.

La Estrella Polar señala **el Norte**.	The North Star points to **the North**.
El sol sale por **el Este**.	The sun rises in **the East**.
Viajaremos al **sur**.	We will travel **south**.

EJERCICIO 1·9

Te toca a ti. *Answer the questions in complete sentences.*

1. ¿Qué día de la semana prefieres?
   Prefiero lunes

2. ¿Cuándo vas de vacaciones? ¿En qué mes?
   Voy de vacaciones en Octubre.

3. ¿Qué día de la semana descansas?
   Yo descanso los sabados

4. ¿En qué idioma escribes mejor?
   Escribo mejor en Portugues

5. ¿Qué países te gustaría visitar?
   Me gustaría visitar Japon y Israel

6. ¿Cuándo vas al cine?
   No voy al cine porque no tengo tiempo

7. ¿Cuándo es tu cumpleaños, en marzo?
   No, mi cumpleaños es en Diciembre

8. Por último, ¿cuál es tu signo zodiacal?
   Mi zodiaco es sagitario

Subject pronouns and the present tense

In English and Spanish there are three grammatical persons—first, second, and third—in both singular and plural. Pronouns are used to replace the name of a person or object.

Subject pronouns

SINGULAR		PLURAL	
yo	*I*	**nosotros, -as**	*we*
tú	*you (fam.)*	**vosotros, -as**	*you (fam., masc., fem.)*
usted (Ud.)	*you (form.)*	**ustedes (Uds.)**	*you (form.)*
él	*he*	**ellos**	*they (masc.)*
ella	*she*	**ellas**	*they (fem.)*

The chart shows that, except the first person singular and the formal *you*, subject pronouns have both feminine and masculine forms. When a plural includes both masculine and feminine, the masculine form is used.

Marcos y Sandra son primos.	*Marcos and Sandra are cousins.*
Ellos son primos.	*They are cousins.*

The familiar plurals **vosotros** and **vosotras** are used in most regions of Spain; **ustedes** is the familiar plural used in most of the rest of the Spanish-speaking world. **Ud.** and **Uds.** are abbreviations of the formal subject pronouns. The context will clarify whether to use the familiar or the formal pronoun.

Señor López, ¿**usted** trabaja aquí?	*Mr. López, do you work here?*
Chicos, ¿**ustedes** salen ahora?	*Boys, are you leaving now?*

By addressing a man as **Señor**, you are showing this is a formal context. The word **chicos**, on the other hand, implies familiarity.

Subject pronouns are usually omitted in Spanish because the verb endings clarify both person and number. However, the subject pronoun is used if the subject is not clear, or if there is a need for emphasis.

¿Quién entra? ¿Ella o él?	*Who is coming in? She or he?*
No, **yo** entro ahora.	*No, I am coming in now.*

tu sales ahora?
ya te vas?

Subject pronouns are used as substitutes for nouns or noun phrases that have already been named or understood in context in order to avoid unnecessary repetition.

Carlos y Martín viajan a Perú. **Ellos** son mis hermanos.

Carlos and Martín travel to Peru. *They are my brothers.*

Mi madre trabaja aquí. **Ella** recibe un descuento.

My mother works here. She gets a discount.

When used as the subject in an indefinite sentence, *it* has no equivalent subject pronoun in Spanish.

Es hora de comer.

It is time to eat.

Now, practice what you have studied and learned about subject pronouns in Spanish.

EJERCICIO
2·1

Repaso. *Complete the sentence with the appropriate subject pronoun to replace the underlined words.*

1. <u>Mi hermana</u> no vive aquí. ___Ella___ vive en California.

2. <u>Las chicas</u> no son mexicanas, ___Ellas___ son panameñas.

3. Aquí está ya el <u>Sr. López</u>. ___El___ llega temprano, como siempre.

4. ¿Quién, <u>Carlos o Marta</u>? ___Ellos___ bajan la escalera.

5. <u>Marisa y yo</u> leemos siempre en la sala. ___Nosotros___ nos llevamos bien. (we get along)

6. ¡<u>Ana, Pedro</u>! ¡Hola! ¡___Ustedes___ pueden subir ya!

7. <u>María y Luis</u> son mis amigos. Por eso ___ellos___ me ayudan tanto.

8. <u>Usted y el Sr. López</u> pasan ahora al frente de la oficina. ___Ustedes___ deben esperar allí.

The present tense

There are three conjugations of verbs in Spanish with infinitives that end in **-ar**, **-er**, or **-ir**. To form the present tense, replace the infinitive ending with the appropriate personal ending:

-**ar** verbs: -**o**, -**as**, -**a**, -**amos**, -**áis**, -**an**

-**er** verbs: -**o**, -**es**, -**e**, -**emos**, -**éis**, -**en**

-**ir** verbs: -**o**, -**es**, -**e**, -**imos**, -**ís**, -**en**

The following are examples of regular verbs of each conjugation in the present tense. Irregular verbs, and verbs with changes in spelling and in the stem, are reviewed later.

	gastar *to spend*	**vender** *to sell*	**abrir** *to open*
yo	gast**o**	vend**o**	abr**o**
tú	gast**as**	vend**es**	abr**es**
usted	gast**a**	vend**e**	abr**e**
él/ella	gast**a**	vend**e**	abr**e**
nosotros	gast**amos**	vend**emos**	abr**imos**
vosotros	gast**áis**	vend**éis**	abr**ís**
ustedes	gast**an**	vend**en**	abr**en**
ellos/ellas	gast**an**	vend**en**	abr**en**

In the first person singular (the **yo** form), the ending is the same in all three conjugations. In **-er** and **-ir** verbs the endings are the same in the third person forms.

Luisa **come** frutas tropicales.	*Luisa eats tropical fruits.*
Pero ella **vive** en Quito.	*But she lives in Quito.*

EJERCICIO 2·2

En casa. *Complete the sentence with the appropriate form of the present tense of the verb in parentheses.*

1. Yo _____canto_____. (cantar)

2. Él _____escucha_____. (escuchar)

3. Ustedes _____bailan_____. (bailar)

4. Ellas _____descansan_____. (descansar)

5. Nosotras _____preparamos_____ la cena. (preparar)

6. Tú _____lavas_____ los platos. (lavar)

7. Tú no _____compartes_____ tus secretos. (compartir)

8. Yo _____confío_____ en ti. (confiar)

9. Ellas _____deciden_____. (decidir)

10. Ustedes _____responden_____. (responder)

11. Mi esposo _____entra_____. (entrar)

12. Nuestra hija _____recibe_____ un regalo. (recibir)
     _____presente_____

Traducción. *Use the present tense to translate each sentence. Include the subject pronoun if needed.*

1. You (*sing., fam.*) need to rest.

   Necesitas descansar

2. He talks, I listen.

   El habla, yo escucho

3. She studies Chinese and Spanish, too.

   Ella estudia chinos y español también

4. We (*masc.*) spend too much money.

   Nosotros gastamos ~~muy~~ mucho dinero

5. You (*pl., form.*) buy expensive shirts.

   Ustedes compran camisas caras

6. I work five days a week.

   Trabajo cinco días a la semana

7. They (*fem.*) dance every Saturday.

   Ellas bailan todos los sábados

8. My sister plays the piano, but I play the guitar.

   Mi hermana toca ~~la~~ piano pero yo toco la guitarra
   el

Conjugating verbs

To conjugate a verb in the present tense or in any other tense, you will need the root of a verb and the particular ending that expresses information about the action you wish to communicate. You will find the root (or radical) of the verb in its infinitive form. It is easy to spot an infinitive in English because it is preceded by the word to: to shop, to learn, to receive, etc. Infinitives in Spanish are not preceded by a particular word but can be recognized by one of three endings: **-ar**, **-er**, or **-ir**. The infinitive endings are attached to the root of the verb: **habl** + **ar**, **beb** + **er**, **decid** + **ir**.

The three groups of infinitives are called the first, second, and third conjugation, respectively. To conjugate a verb in Spanish, drop the **-ar**, **-er**, or **-ir** and replace it with the corresponding ending that agrees with the subject doing the action.

   Vendo pólizas de seguro.   *I sell life insurance.*

Because conjugation endings tell who the subject is, subject pronouns in Spanish are usually omitted. The **-o** of the form **vendo** reveals the subject is **yo** (*I*). But conjugated verb endings tell more than just who does the action. Usually, these endings tell the tense (or time) actions take place: the present, past, or future.

   Sales muy temprano.   *You leave very early.*

te vas muy temprano

Sales (*you leave*) is like **vendo** (*I sell*); each indicates an action in the present. The **-es** ending can only refer to the person **tú** in the present tense of the indicative mood. However, endings convey additional information. With **vendo** and **sales**, the speaker indicates that these actions are perceived as a fact or reality: *I sell*; *you leave*. This is called the indicative mood (**modo indicativo**) of the verb. The mood expresses the attitude of the speaker. The examples **vendo** and **sales** are in the indicative mood because these verbs communicate actions perceived as factual or real. Later on, you will study other moods, such as subjunctive, conditional, and imperative.

Thus, the endings attached to the stem of a verb hold a lot of information: who does the action, when it takes place, and the attitude or perception of the speaker.

Regular verbs in the present tense

To form the present tense, drop the **-ar**, **-er**, or **-ir** from the root (or radical) of the infinitive, and add the ending that corresponds to the subject. The following verbs can be used as models for all regular verbs in the present tense.

Comprar *to buy*

singular		plural	
compro	*I buy*	compramos	*we buy*
compras	*you (fam.) buy*	compráis	*you buy*
compra	*he/she/it buys, you (for.) buy*	compran	*they buy, you buy*

Aprender *to learn*

singular		plural	
aprendo	*I learn*	aprendemos	*we learn*
aprendes	*you (fam.) learn*	aprendéis	*you learn*
aprende	*he/she/it learns, you (for.) learn*	aprenden	*they learn, you learn*

Recibir *to receive*

singular		plural	
recibo	*I receive*	recibimos	*we receive*
recibes	*you (fam.) receive*	recibís	*you receive*
recibe	*he/she/it receives, you (for.) receive*	reciben	*they receive, you receive*

In the following conjugations, note the *subject pronouns*, as well as the English equivalents:

yo compro	*I buy, am buying, do buy*
tú compras	*you (familiar singular) buy, are buying, do buy*
él compra	*he buys, is buying, does buy*
ella compra	*she buys, is buying, does buy*
usted (Ud.) compra	*you (formal singular) buy, are buying, do buy*
nosotros compramos	*we (masculine) buy, are buying, do buy*
nosotras compramos	*we (feminine) buy, are buying, do buy*
vosotros compráis	*you (masculine plural) buy, are buying, do buy*
vosotras compráis	*you (feminine plural) buy, are buying, do buy*
ellos compran	*they (masculine) buy, are buying, do buy*
ellas compran	*they (feminine) buy, are buying, do buy*
ustedes (Uds.) compran	*you (formal plural) buy, are buying, do buy*

Study the conjugations above and remember that:

- the first-person singular **yo** has the same ending in all three conjugations.
- in the **-er** and **-ir** verb categories all three third-person singular forms have the same endings.
- the subject pronouns are usually omitted in Spanish. Verb endings give information about the subject.

Some commonly used regular verbs appear in the following lists.

-ar		-er		-ir	
bajar	to step down	**beber**	to drink	**compartir**	to share
cocinar	to cook	**comer**	to eat	**cubrir**	to cover
comprar	to buy	**comprender**	to understand	**decidir**	to decide
conversar	to talk	**correr**	to run	**discutir**	to discuss
cooperar	to cooperate	**creer**	to believe	**escribir**	to write
dibujar	to draw	**leer**	to read	**repartir**	to distribute
escuchar	to listen	**responder**	to answer	**subir**	to climb, to go up
limpiar	to clean	**romper**	to break	**sufrir**	to suffer
preparar	to prepare	**temer**	to fear	**vivir**	to live
sacar	to take out				
sumar	to add (up)				
trabajar	to work				

EJERCICIO
2·4

La familia Gómez. *Complete each sentence with the appropriate present tense form of the verb in parentheses.*

1. Pedro Gómez ___vive___ (vivir) con su familia en mi edificio de apartamentos.

2. Lucía, la esposa de Pedro, no ___trabaja___ (trabajar) todos los días.

3. La hija, Mercedes, ___estudia___ (estudiar) en la universidad.

4. Lucía y su esposo ___planean___ (planear) una visita a Mercedes esta semana.

5. Pedrito, el hijo, ahora ___sube___ (subir) a su apartamento.

6. Pedrito ___saca___ (sacar) a su perro a caminar todos los días.

7. Y tú, ¿ ___conversas___ (conversar) con los Gómez?

8. Pedro ___necesita___ (necesitar) una persona para cuidar su apartamento esta semana.

Práctica. *Translate the sentences into Spanish.*

1. I prepare dinner. *Yo preparo la cena*
2. The children climb the stairs. *los niños suben la escalera*
3. My cats drink milk. *Mis gatos beben leche*
4. The customer adds up the bill (**la cuenta**). *El cliente suma la cuenta*
5. Carli's mother talks to the reporter (**el/la reportero[a]**). *la madre de Carli habla*
   al reportero, a la reportera
6. The actress fears the critics. *la actriz teme a los críticos*
7. Your friends eat fajitas. *tus amigos comen fajitas*

When is the present tense used in Spanish?

The present tense is used in Spanish:

- to describe an action happening now. Often, it is translated with the *-ing* form in English.

Ahora, **veo** a Anna.	*Now I see Anna.*
Louis **llega** a la puerta.	*Louis is arriving at the gate.*

- to express actions that take place regularly, in a habitual way, although the actions may not be occurring in the present. Expressions of time and other adverbs are often used to indicate that these actions take place routinely in the present.

Normalmente, **compro** las frutas en el supermercado.	*Usually I buy fruit at the supermarket.*

- to describe events that will take place in the near future. A reference to the future may appear in the context or sentence.

Mañana discuto el plan con ustedes en la reunión.	*Tomorrow I will discuss the plan at the meeting.*
Este verano, **viajo** a Alemania.	*I will travel to Germany this summer.*

- to ask questions, especially questions requesting permission or someone's opinion or preference.

¿**Bebes** café o té?	*Do you drink coffee or tea?*
¿**Abro** la puerta?	*Shall I open the door?*
¿**Compramos** la casa?	*Do we buy the house?*

  Keep in mind the auxiliary verb *do* in English is not translated. In Spanish, an auxiliary verb is not needed to ask a question.

Often the context or words surrounding a verb help pin down information about the time the action takes place. The following are some expressions of time used frequently to refer to actions that take place customarily in the present:

no tiene arreglo = there's no solution

VOCABULARIO

al mediodía	*at noon*	**nunca**	*never*
de vez en cuando	*from time to time*	**por la mañana**	*in the morning*
el lunes, el martes, etc.	*on Monday,*		or *this morning*
	on Tuesday, etc.	**por la noche**	*in the evening*
esta semana	*this week*		or *at night*
este mes	*this month*	**por la tarde**	*in the afternoon*
hoy	*today*	**siempre**	*always*
los lunes, los martes, etc.	*on Mondays,*	**todos los días**	*every day*
	on Tuesdays, etc.		

EJERCICIO 2·6

Y en tu caso... *¿Es verdadero (V) o falso (F)?*

1. Desayuno a las ocho todos los días. ___F___

2. Miro los programas de noticias por el cable por la tarde. ___F___

3. Trabajo ocho horas. ___V___

4. Escribo mensajes electrónicos todos los días. ___V___

5. Preparo la cena de lunes a viernes. ___V___

6. Como muchas frutas y vegetales frescos. ___V___

EJERCICIO 2·7

En español. *Give the present tense for each answer.*

1. Today Martha and Linus are celebrating their anniversary. _____
   Hoy Martha y Linus celebran su anviersario

2. Their relatives (**los parientes**) arrive on time. _____
   Sus parientes llegan a tiempo

3. Some friends are talking in the living room. _____
   Varios amigas hablan en la sala

4. In the backyard, the children listen to Latin music. _____
   En el patio, los chicos escuchan musica latina.

5. The smell (**el olor**) of enchiladas circulates through the house. _____
   El olor (a) enchilada circula por toda la casa

6. The children drink lemonade. _____
   los niños beben limonada

Preguntas personales. *Give the present tense form for each answer.*

1. ¿Vives en el campo o en una ciudad? _Vivo en una ciudad_

2. ¿Lees novelas de misterio o de ciencia-ficción? _Leo_

3. ¿Hablas de política o de deportes con tus amigos? _Hablo de política con mis amigos_

4. ¿Bebes té o café? _Yo bebo té_

5. ¿Trabajas de día o de noche? _Trabajo de día_

6. ¿Compartes tu tiempo libre con tu perro o con tu gato? _Comparto mi tiempo libre con mi perro._

Other uses of the present tense

The present is also used:

♦ to tell facts considered unquestionable or universal truths.

Cinco más quince **son** veinte.   *Five plus fifteen **is** twenty.*

♦ to describe a past event, making it more vivid. This is called the historical present.

En 1969 el primer hombre **llega** a la luna.   *The first man **gets** to the moon in 1969.*

♦ to express hypothetical actions introduced by **si**.

Si llega el tren, salimos.   *If the train **arrives**, we leave.*

♦ to refer to possible consequences from an action that took place in the past with **casi...** (*almost*) and **por poco...** (*nearly*).

Sacó la pistola y casi me **mata**.   *He drew the gun and nearly **killed** (**kills**) me.*

One more use of the present tense

The present tense is used:

♦ to express actions that began in the past and continue in the present with the construction **hace** + expression of time + **que** + verb in the present tense.

Hace tres años que esperamos una respuesta.   ***We have been waiting** for an answer **for three years**.*

This construction has two other variations that carry the same meaning:

♦ verb in the present tense + **hace** + expression of time

Esperamos una respuesta **hace tres años**.   ***We have been waiting** for an answer **for three years**.*

♦ verb in the present tense + **desde hace** + expression of time

Esperamos una respuesta **desde hace tres años**.   ***We have been waiting** for an answer **for three years**.*

Note the following questions using each of these constructions. They all have the same meaning:

¿Cuánto tiempo hace que observas las estrellas?
¿Desde hace cuánto tiempo observas las estrellas?
¿Desde cuándo observas las estrellas?

How long have you been watching the stars?

Preguntas personales. *Give the appropriate present tense form for each answer.*

1. ¿Cuánto tiempo hace que estudias español? _Hace 5 días que Estudio Español_

2. ¿Desde hace cuánto tiempo usas la computadora? _Uso la computadora desde hace 30 años_

3. ¿Cuántos años hace que los Estados Unidos son una nación independiente? _____
Hace 500 anos que ...

4. ¿Cuánto tiempo hace que usamos la Internet? _Usamos la internet desde hace 10 anos_

5. ¿Desde cuándo escuchas música clásica? _Escucho musica clasica hace 30 anos_

Tu experiencia. *Complete each sentence with the present tense form* **yo.**

1. Hace una semana que _yo estudio Espanol._
2. Desde hace un año _que vivo nos EUA_
3. Hace diez días _que estoy (a) dieta._ ?
4. Desde hace un año, no _gasto dinero_.
5. Hace tres meses _que compré un auto_

The new technology. *¿Verdadero (V) o falso (F)?*

_____ 1. Usamos la Internet desde el siglo (*century*) pasado.

_____ 2. Enviamos mensajes de texto (*text messages*) desde hace cincuenta años.

_____ 3. Desde hace dos décadas usamos el teléfono.

_____ 4. Hace más de dos siglos que existe el telescopio Hubble.

_____ 5. Viajamos en avión de los Estados Unidos a otros continentes desde hace casi un siglo.

Irregular verbs in the present tense

Many Spanish verbs do not follow the patterns of the regular verbs you have just studied. Instead, they change the root (or radical) of the verb, the conjugation endings, or both. Because they follow different patterns, they are considered *irregular* verbs. Since irregular verbs are so commonly used, a good strategy to identify and learn them is to focus on similarities, grouping them into patterns. Study the following groups of irregular verbs in the present:

◆ Verbs with irregular first-person singular only; all other forms in the present are regular.

caber	*to fit*	**quepo**	**saber**	*to know*	**sé**
caer	*to fall*	**caigo**	**salir**	*to leave*	**salgo**
dar	*to give*	**doy**	**traer**	*to bring*	**traigo**
estar	*to be*	**estoy**	**valer**	*to be worth*	**valgo**
hacer	*to do*	**hago**	**ver**	*to see*	**veo**
poner	*to put*	**pongo**			

Práctica. En español.

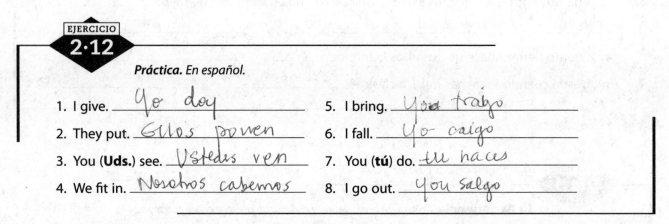

1. I give. _Yo doy_
2. They put. _Ellos ponen_
3. You (**Uds.**) see. _Ustedes ven_
4. We fit in. _Nosotros cabemos_
5. I bring. _Yo traigo_
6. I fall. _Yo caigo_
7. You (**tú**) do. _tu haces_
8. I go out. _yo salgo_

Compound verbs are easy to spot because they show a prefix (**des-**, **dis-**, **com-**, **con-**, etc.) preceding the radical. Here is a list of frequently used compounds of **hacer**, **poner**, and **traer**:

componer	*to compose*	**compongo**	**proponer**	*to propose*	**propongo**
deshacer	*to undo*	**deshago**	**rehacer**	*to remake*	**rehago**
disponer	*to arrange*	**dispongo**	**reponer**	*to replace*	**repongo**
distraer(se)	*to distract*	**distraigo**	**suponer**	*to suppose*	**supongo**

En español.

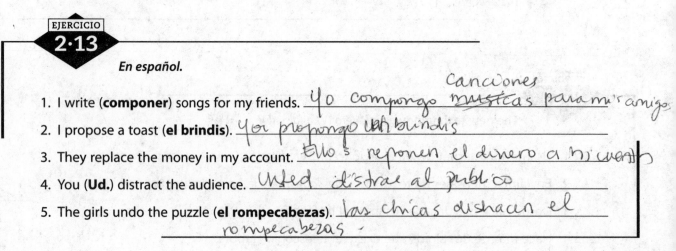

1. I write (**componer**) songs for my friends. _Yo compongo músicas canciones para mis amigos_
2. I propose a toast (**el brindis**). _Yo propongo un brindis_
3. They replace the money in my account. _Ellos reponen el dinero a mi cuenta_
4. You (**Ud.**) distract the audience. _Usted distrae al público_
5. The girls undo the puzzle (**el rompecabezas**). _las chicas dishacen el rompecabezas._

Pareados. *Choose the letter that best completes each sentence.*

b 1. Sé   a. a mis compañeros de trabajo.

a 2. Distraigo   b. que trabajas mucho.

h 3. No quepo   c. música para mis canciones.

c 4. Compongo   d. en esa trampa (*trap*) a menudo.

f 5. Propongo   e. de la conferencia ahora.

g 6. Pongo   f. una solución para tu problema.

e 7. Salgo   g. el agua en un vaso.

d 8. Caigo   h. en estos pantalones.

Other verbs with irregular forms in the first person

◆ Verbs that end in a vowel followed by **-cer** and **-cir** change **c** to **zc** in the first-person singular only. They are conjugated like **conocer**.

Conozco muy bien a Margo.   *I know* Margo very well.

-er verbs like *conocer*		
agradecer	*to thank, to be grateful*	**agradezco**
aparecer	*to appear*	**aparezco**
complacer	*to please*	**complazco**
crecer	*to grow*	**crezco**
establecer	*to establish*	**establezco**
merecer	*to deserve*	**merezco**
ofrecer	*to offer*	**ofrezco**
padecer	*to suffer*	**padezco**
permanecer	*to remain*	**permanezco**
pertenecer	*to belong*	**pertenezco**
reconocer	*to recognize*	**reconozco**

-ir verbs like *traducir*		
traducir	*to translate*	**traduzco**
conducir	*to drive, to lead*	**conduzco**
producir	*to produce*	**produzco**

EJERCICIO 2·15

Práctica. *Complete each sentence with the appropriate present tense verb in parentheses.*

1. Yo _conduzco_ (conducir) el coche.
2. Marta y tú _salen_ (salir) de casa juntos (*together*).
3. Yo no _conozco_ (conocer) a esa familia.
4. ¿Quién _ofrece_ (ofrecer) más por este cuadro?
5. ¡Yo no _merezco_ (merecer) este regalo!
6. Las asistentes del director _obedecen_ (obedecer) sus órdenes.

EJERCICIO 2·16

Traducción. ¿Y yo? *Translate the sentences from English to Spanish with the present tense.*

1. I deserve a raise. _Yo merezco un aumento de sueldo_
2. Do I go out now? _Yo salgo ahora?_
3. I am grateful for your friendship. _Yo soy Agradezco tu amistad_
4. I do not belong to this group. _Yo No pertenezco a este grupo_
5. I translate the instructions. _Yo traduzco las instrucciones_
6. I seldom impose my ideas! _Rara vez impongo mis ideas_
7. I remain quiet (**callado**[a]). _Permanezco callado_

Other frequently used verbs with irregular forms in the present tense

Study the conjugations of the verbs that follow. They have irregular forms in the present tense:

decir *to say*	
digo	**decimos**
dices	**decís**
dice	**dicen**

ir *to go*	
voy	**vamos**
vas	**vais**
va	**van**

oír *to hear*	
oigo	oímos
oyes	oís
oye	oyen

ser *to be*	
soy	somos
eres	sois
es	son

tener *to have*	
tengo	tenemos
tienes	tenéis
tiene	tienen

venir *to come*	
vengo	venimos
vienes	venís
viene	vienen

Compounds of tener have the same irregular forms.

Verbs like tener

contener	*to contain*	contengo
detener	*to detain*	detengo
mantener	*to maintain*	mantengo
obtener	*to obtain*	obtengo
retener	*to retain*	retengo
sostener	*to sustain*	sostengo

EJERCICIO 2·17

¡Mira quién baila! Complete each sentence with the appropriate present tense form of the verbs in parentheses.

1. Mi amiga Alicia __está__ (estar) en el estudio para ver el programa *¡Mira quién baila!*

2. Aquí, en el estudio, __hay__ (haber) muchos aficionados (*fans*) al baile.

3. Todos los aficionados __llegan__ (llegar) al estudio para ver esta competencia de baile.

4. Marcos __es__ (ser) uno de los participantes y yo __digo__ (decir) que Marcos va a ganar hoy.

5. Muchas personas __vienen__ (venir) para escuchar la música.

6. Marcos __tiene__ (tener) a su hermana aquí y baila con ella.

7. Si vienes al programa, tú __oyes__ (oír) los comentarios de los jueces.

8. ¡Todos ustedes __van__ (ir) a querer bailar aquí, en el estudio!

Verbs with spelling changes in the present tense

In the present tense, certain verbs have spelling changes. These are determined by Spanish rules of pronunciation to preserve the sound appearing in the infinitive. The following groups of verbs have spelling changes before the verb ending -**o**, in the **yo** form only.

- ◆ Verbs ending in -**ger** or -**gir** change **g** to **j** before the -**o** ending.

coger *to catch, grab*

cojo	cogemos
coges	cogéis
coge	cogen

exigir *to demand*

exijo	exigimos
exiges	exigís
exige	exigen

Verbs like coger

encoger	*to shrink*	**encojo**
escoger	*to choose*	**escojo**
proteger	*to protect*	**protejo**
recoger	*to pick up*	**recojo**

Verbs like exigir

dirigir	*to direct*	**dirijo**
fingir	*to pretend*	**finjo**

Other -**gir** verbs have stem changes as well. Check the sections on stem-changing verbs in Unit 2.

- ◆ Verbs ending in -**guir** change **gu** to **g** before the -**o** ending.

distinguir *to distinguish*

distingo	distinguimos
distingues	distinguís
distingue	distinguen

Verbs like distinguir

extinguir	*to extinguish*

- ◆ Verbs ending in -**cer** and -**cir** change **c** to **z** before the -**o** ending.

convencer *to convince*

convenzo	convencemos
convences	convencéis
convence	convencen

Verbs like convencer

ejercer	*to practice (a profession)*	**ejerzo**
vencer	*to overcome*	**venzo**

Some -**cer** and -**cir** verbs may have stem changes as well: **e** changes to **i** and **o** to **ue**.

elegir	*to correct*	**elijo**
torcer	*to twist*	**tuerzo**

"Yo también..." Write the present tense of the **yo** form of the verb in italics.

1. *Exige* una explicación. _____Exijo_____
2. *Escoge* los colores. _____Escojo_____
3. *Extingue* el fuego. _____Extingo_____
4. *Recoge* los periódicos. _____Recojo_____
5. *Vence* los obstáculos. _____Venzo_____
6. *Protege* sus derechos (*rights*). _____Protejo_____
7. *Convence* a sus amigos. _____Convenzo_____
8. No *finge*. _____finjo_____

Dar, haber, hacer, and tener in expressions with a special meaning

In this unit, you studied **dar**, **haber**, **hacer**, and **tener**, verbs with irregular forms in the present. These verbs appear frequently in idiomatic expressions. Many are formed with a conjugated verb + an infinitive, called **formas perifrásticas** or **perífrasis verbales** in Spanish.

Other idiomatic verbal expressions will appear in other units. Learn them as lexical (vocabulary) items.

Note the use of the present tense in the examples with **dar**, **haber**, **hacer**, and **tener** that follow. Keep in mind that, in different contexts or surrounded by expressions of time referring to the past or the future, these idioms may also be used in other tenses.

◆ **Dar**
dar un abrazo *to hug, to embrace*

Le da un abrazo a su amigo.	*He hugs his friend.*

dar gritos *to shout*

La multitud da gritos.	*The crowd screams.*

dar la hora *to strike the hour*

El reloj da la una.	*The clock strikes one.*

◆ **Haber**
hay que + infinitive *to be necessary* (to express obligation)

Hay que estudiar para aprender.	*It is necessary to study in order to learn.*

haber sol *to be sunny*

Hay sol por la mañana.	*It is sunny in the morning.*

haber neblina *to be foggy*

Hay neblina esta mañana.	*It is foggy this morning.*

Note that **haber** is also irregular. One meaning of **haber** is *to have*. However, in the present as well as in other tenses, **haber** is more frequently used as an impersonal verb in the third-person singular form. The present tense form is **hay**. It means *there is* and *there are*.

Hay tres sillas en la sala.	***There are*** three chairs in the living room.
Hay una posibilidad solamente.	***There is*** only one possibility.

EJERCICIO 2·19

Traduccion. *Translate with the appropriate present tense form of the verbs* **dar, haber, hacer,** *and* **tener.**

1. It is not foggy this morning. *No hay neblina esta mañana*
2. The clock strikes ten thirty. *El reloj da las dez y media*
3. It is sunny now. *Hay sol ahora / Hace sol ahora*
4. The audience screams at the stadium. *El publico da gritos en el estadio*
5. The captain gives a hug to the goalkeeper (**portero**). *El capitán le da un abrazo al portero* ✳ *golero*

EJERCICIO 2·20

Amigos. *Create five sentences using* **hay que** *to make friends.*

1. *Hay que ser amable para hacer amigos*
2. *Hay que ser generoso para hacer amigos*
3. *Hay que ser bueno para hacer amigos*
4. *Hay que ser sociable para hacer amigos*
5. *Hay que salir a hacer amigos*

- **Hacer** in expressions that refer to weather conditions

hacer calor, hacer fresco *to be hot, to be cool*

Hace fresco, no hace calor.	*It is cool; it is not hot.*

hacer viento *to be windy*

Hace viento.	*It is windy.*

hacer un viaje *to take a trip*

Lina hace un viaje a las Bahamas.	*Lina takes a trip to the Bahamas.*

- **Hacer** in other expressions

hacer una visita *to pay a visit*

Marcus hace una visita a su tío.	*Marcus visits his uncle.*

hacer daño *to harm, damage*

Beber mucha agua no te hace daño.   *Drinking a lot of water does not harm you.*

→ **hacer caso a** *to notice, pay attention (to)*

Los niños no hacen caso al maestro.   *The children do not pay attention to the teacher.*

hacer el papel de *to play the role of*

El actor hace el papel de Hamlet.   *The actor plays the role of Hamlet.*

◆ **Tener**
To express obligation with a conjugated verb use the formula **tener** + **que** + infinitive.

Tenemos que salir.   *We must leave.*

tener frío *to be cold*

Tengo frío.   *I am cold.*

tener hambre *to be hungry*

¿Tienes hambre?   *Are you hungry?*

tener miedo *to be afraid*

No tienen miedo a las serpientes.   *They are not afraid of snakes.*

tener razón *to be right*

Yo tengo razón.   *I am right.*

tener sed *to be thirsty*

¿Tienes sed?   *Are you thirsty?*

tener prisa *to be in a hurry*

Mi esposo tiene prisa.   *My husband is in a hurry.*

tener la culpa (de) *to be to blame*

El sospechoso tiene la culpa de este accidente.   *The suspect is to blame for this accident.*

→ **tener lugar** *to take place*

La reunión tiene lugar los domingos.   *The meeting takes place on Sundays.*

EJERCICIO
2·21

Y en tu caso... ¿Es verdadero (V) o falso (F)?

__F__ 1. Tengo miedo a los fantasmas (*ghosts*).

__F__ 2. Nunca tengo prisa.

__V__ 3. Tengo que hacer la cama todos los días.

✓ 4. Hago caso a las buenas sugerencias de mis amigos.

✓ 5. No tengo mucho sueño ahora.

✓ 6. Siempre hago una visita a mi familia en diciembre.

2·22

En español.

1. Are you (**tú**) hungry? _¿Tienes hambre?_

2. We are thirsty. _Tenemos sed_

3. Lori pays a visit to her cousin. _Lori hace una visita a su primo_

4. Mario hugs his friend. _Mario (le) da un abrazo (a) su amigo_

5. They are in a hurry. _Tienen prisa_

6. You (**tú**) are right this time. _(Usted) tienes razón esta vez_

7. I am not afraid. _No tengo miedo_

8. Are you (**Ud.**) cold? _¿Ustedes tiene frío?_

EJERCICIO
2·23

Conecta la letra. Use the appropriate letter to complete each sentence.

e 1. ¡Quiero dos hamburguesas!   a. Tengo razón.

b 2. Obedezco a mi médico.   b. Hago caso.

h 3. Bebo dos vasos de agua.   c. Hago una visita.

a 4. Estoy en lo cierto.   d. Tengo prisa.

d 5. Tengo diez minutos nada más.   e. Tengo hambre.

f 6. Quiero dormir.   f. Tengo sueño.

c 7. Voy a ver a mi amigo.   g. No tengo la culpa.

g 8. Soy innocente.   h. Tengo sed.

Present tense irregular verbs

Chapter 2 shows that many frequently used verbs in Spanish are considered irregular. In this chapter, the verbs in the present tense are considered irregular verbs that undergo a change in the last vowel of the stem.

Verbs with stem changes in the present tense

The vowel change in the stem of the present tense does not affect the personal endings, which remain the same. The stem change holds for all forms except the **nosotros/nosotras** and **vosotros/vosotras** forms.

Siempre **pienso** en mis amigos.	*I always think about my friends.*
Nosotros **preferimos** las sillas azules.	*We prefer the blue chairs.*

Stem change e → ie

The conjugations of -**ar**, -**er**, and -**ir** verbs that change the stem vowel **e** to **ie** are as follows:

pensar to think	**querer** to love	**preferir** to prefer
pienso	quiero	prefiero
piensas	quieres	prefieres
piensa	quiere	prefiere
pensamos	queremos	preferimos
pensáis	queréis	preferís
piensan	quieren	prefieren

VOCABULARIO

Here are some verbs with the **e → ie** stem change that you may use for the exercises that follow.

-AR VERBS		-ER VERBS		-IR VERBS	
atravesar	*to cross over*	**ascender**	*to promote*	**advertir**	*to notify, warn*
cerrar	*to close*	**defender**	*to defend*	**convertir**	*to convert*
comenzar	*to start*	**descender**	*to go down*	**divertir**	*to have fun*

35

confesar	*to confess*	encender	*to light up*	herir	*to hurt*
despertar	*to wake up*	encerrar	*to lock in*	hervir	*to boil*
empezar	*to start*	entender	*to understand*	mentir	*to lie*
fregar	*to scrub*	perder	*to lose, miss*	presentir	*to sense*
gobernar	*to govern, rule*			sentir	*to feel*
negar	*to deny*				
recomendar	*to advise*				
sentar	*to sit*				

EJERCICIO
3·1

La rutina de Julia en la casa. *Complete each sentence with the appropriate present tense* **ella** *form of the verb in parentheses.*

1. Todos los días, Julia _desciende_ las escaleras. (descender)

2. Después, _despierta_ a su esposo. (despertar)

3. Luego _enciende_ la luz de la cocina. (encender)

4. _Empieza_ a preparar el café. (empezar)

5. También, _hierve_ el agua para el té de su esposo. (hervir)

6. _friega_ los platos y las tazas. (fregar)

7. Entonces _atraviesa_ el pasillo para ir a su oficina. (atravesar)

8. _Comienza_ su trabajo en la oficina en su casa. (comenzar)

9. Después _sienta_ a su gato en una silla cerca de la computadora. (sentar)

10. Quiere silencio y _cerra_ la puerta de la oficina. (cerrar)

EJERCICIO
3·2

Un programa de radio. *First underline the verb in parentheses that best fits the meaning of each sentence. Then fill in the appropriate present tense form of the verb.*

Modelo   Nosotros (sentar / negar) la noticia.

Nosotros _____ la noticia. (sentar / negar)

Nosotros negamos la noticia.

1. Ahora _comienza_ el programa de noticias. (comenzar / convertir)

Ahora comienza el programa de noticias

2. La presentadora _divierte_ a los oyentes (*listeners*). (confesar / divertir)

La presentadora divierte a los oyentes.

3. Los oyentes ___*sienten*___ una voz agradable. (referir / sentir)

Los oyentes sienten una voz agradable

4. Los oyentes comentan y ___*defienden*___ sus ideas. (defender / encender)

Los oyentes comentan y difienden sus ideas

5. Los anuncios ___*recomiendan*___ muchos productos naturales. (fregar / recomendar)

Los anuncios recomiendan muchos productos naturales

6. A veces, ___*empieza*___ una canción antes de otras noticias. (empezar / perder)

A veas empienza una cancion antes de otras noticias

7. ¡Noticia de última hora! La emisora ___*advierte*___ una tormenta de nieve. (advertir / querer)

La emisora advierte una tormenta de nieve

8. Las autoridades ___*cierran*___ las autopistas (*expressways*) mañana. (encerrar / cerrar)

Las autoridades cierran las autopistas mañana.

Stem change o → ue

The conjugations of -**ar**, -**er**, and -**ir** verbs that change the stem vowel **o** to **ue** are as follows:

contar to count, tell	**poder** to be able, can	**dormir** to sleep
c**ue**nto	p**ue**do	d**ue**rmo
c**ue**ntas	p**ue**des	d**ue**rmes
c**ue**nta	p**ue**de	d**ue**rme
contamos	podemos	dormimos
contáis	podéis	dormís
c**ue**ntan	p**ue**den	d**ue**rmen

VOCABULARIO

Below you find verbs with the **o → ue** stem change, mostly -**ar** and -**er** verbs. Use them for the exercises that follow.

-**AR** VERBS		-**ER** VERBS		-**IR** VERBS	
almorzar	*to eat lunch*	**conmover**	*to move, to touch*	**morir**	*to die*
aprobar	*to approve*	**devolver**	*to return*		
colgar	*to hang*	**doler**	*to hurt*		
costar	*to cost*	**llover**	*to rain, pour*		
demostrar	*to prove*	**morder**	*to bite*		
encontrar	*to find*	**mover**	*to move*		

mostrar	*to show*	**oler**	*to smell*
recordar	*to remember*	**resolver**	*to solve*
rogar	*to beg*	**revolver**	*to stir*
soñar (con)	*to dream*	**volver**	*to return*
sonar	*to ring, sound*	**soler**	*to tend to*
volar	*to fly*		

The verb **oler** also adds an **h** to all forms *except* **nosotros** and **vosotros**: **huelo**, **hueles**, etc.

No **huelo** las flores.   *I do not smell the flowers.*
Vosotros **oléis** los pasteles.   *You smell the pastries.*

Note also that in the verb **jugar**, the **u** in the stem changes to **ue** in all forms *except* **nosotros** and **vosotros**.

Yo **juego** tenis los sábados.   *I play tennis every Saturday.*
Jugamos al ajedrez.   *We play chess.*

Mis amigos Bernardo y José. Traducción.

1. Bernardo and José tend to help their friends.

   Ellos suelen ayudar a sus amigos

2. When it rains, José picks me up at my office.

   Cuando llueve, Jose recoge me en mi oficina

3. Bernardo remembers my birthday every year.

   él recuerda mi cumpleaños todos los años

4. I eat lunch with José frequently.

   Almuerzo con Jose frecuentemente

5. They play golf on Sundays.

   Ellos juegan golf los domingos.

6. When I play with them, I count the points for the score (**el resultado**).

   Cuando juego con ellos, yo cuento los puntos para el resultado.

7. José flies to Costa Rica every summer.

Jose vuela a Costa Rica todos los veranos

8. He usually returns to Albuquerque after one week.

El usualmente vuelve a Albuquerque después de una semana

Usa la lógica. *Write in the letter of the phrase that best completes each sentence.*

1. __h__ Duerme
2. __i__ Devuelve casi siempre
3. __c__ Cuelga la ropa
4. __d__ Demuestra su mejor característica:
5. __f__ Huele el perfume
6. __e__ Resuelve sus problemas porque
7. __b__ Muerde
8. __g__ Recuerda mucho,
9. __j__ Cuenta
10. __a__ Juega todos los domingos y

a. gana siempre contra sus amigos.
b. una manzana; tiene hambre.
c. en el ropero de su habitación.
d. la generosidad a su comunidad.
e. piensa mucho y toma decisiones.
f. de una rosa en la terraza.
g. tiene buena memoria.
h. en el sofá de la sala.
i. los regalos de sus amigos.
j. el dinero en el banco.

Stem change e → i

The conjugation of **-ir** verbs with the **e → i** stem vowel change is as follows:

pedir *to ask for, request*	
pido	pedimos
pides	pedís
pide	piden

VOCABULARIO

Now, review the list of commonly used verbs with the **e → i** stem change that may be useful for the exercises that follow:

competir	*to compete*	**medir**	*to measure*
conseguir	*to get, obtain*	**perseguir**	*to pursue, follow*
decir	*to say, tell*	**reír**	*to laugh*

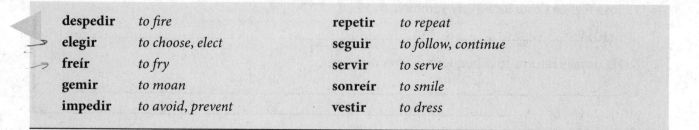

despedir	*to fire*	repetir	*to repeat*
elegir	*to choose, elect*	seguir	*to follow, continue*
freír	*to fry*	servir	*to serve*
gemir	*to moan*	sonreír	*to smile*
impedir	*to avoid, prevent*	vestir	*to dress*

Some verbs in this list have additional spelling changes and a written accent.

◆ **Seguir, conseguir: u** follows **g** where needed to maintain the hard **g** sound: **sigues, sigue, siguen**; consigues, consigue, consiguen.

Siempre tú **sigues** las reglas de la clase.	*You always follow the class rules.*
Juan **consigue** un trabajo excelente.	*Juan gets an excellent job.*

◆ All forms of **reír** and **sonreír** have a written accent on the stem vowel **í**.

Mis amigos **ríen** cuando terminan su trabajo.	*My friends laugh when they finish their work.*
¿Por qué no **sonríen** los chicos?	*Why don't the children smile?*

◆ In addition to the stem vowel change, the **yo** form of **elegir** is **elijo**, and the **yo** form of **decir** is **digo**.

Elijo estos libros.	*I choose these books.*
No siempre **digo** la verdad.	*I do not always tell the truth.*

Vowel changes in verbs ending in -uir

For verbs ending in **-uir** not preceded by **g**, **y** is inserted after the **u**, except in the **nosotros** and **vosotros** forms.

concluir *to conclude, to finish*	
concluy**o**	concluimos
concluyes	concluís
concluye	concluyen

VOCABULARIO

This is a short list of commonly used verbs ending in **-uir** *not* preceded by a **g**.

construir	*to build, construct*	huir	*to flee, run away*
contribuir	*to contribute*	incluir	*to include*
destruir	*to destroy*	influir	*to influence*
distribuir	*to distribute*	sustituir	*to substitute*

En el banco. *Complete each sentence with the appropriate present tense form of the verb in parentheses.*

1. En el banco, un cliente_____ una hipoteca (*mortgage*). (conseguir)

2. La cajera (*teller*)_____ un documento de identidad (*ID card*) a los clientes. (pedir)

3. Los empleados saludan a los clientes y_____. (sonreír)

4. Todos los empleados_____ las reglas de la oficina. (seguir)

5. Un joven_____ café a los clientes. (servir)

6. Este banco_____ con otros bancos en mi barrio. (competir)

7. Al final del día, el guardia_____ un robo. (impedir)

8. El ladrón_____ en su auto. (huir)

9. ¡Qué pena! El gerente_____ a dos empleados hoy. (despedir)

10. El día de trabajo_____ a las seis de la tarde. (concluir)

Y en tu caso, ¿verdadero (V) o falso (F)?

1. _____ Gimo cuando siento dolor en una muela.

2. _____ Mido mis palabras cuando hablo con mi jefe.

3. _____ Río cuando escucho chistes.

4. _____ Visto a mi perro con un suéter cuando salimos al parque.

5. _____ Repito palabras en español en voz alta.

6. _____ Sirvo té a mis colegas en la oficina.

7. _____ Elijo a buenos candidatos en las elecciones de mi país.

8. _____ Pido sal cuando como en un restaurante.

Irregular verbs

As you have learned, many frequently used irregular verbs change their forms in different ways. With some (e.g., **ir**) all forms are irregular, in others (e.g., **tener**) only some forms change, and in many verbs only the **yo** form is irregular.

Frequently used irregular verbs

Irregular forms in the following frequently used verbs are printed in bold.

ir *to go*	oír *to hear*	ser *to be*	tener *to have*	venir *to come*
voy	**oigo**	**soy**	**tengo**	**vengo**
vas	**oyes**	**eres**	**tienes**	**vienes**
va	**oye**	**es**	**tiene**	**viene**
vamos	oímos	**somos**	tenemos	venimos
vais	oís	**sois**	tenéis	venís
van	**oyen**	**son**	**tienen**	**vienen**

Verbs that are irregular in the **yo** form only

Many verbs that end in -**cer** or -**cir** preceded by **e**, **o**, or **u** add **z** in the **yo** form only.

agradecer	*to be thankful*	**agradezco**
aparecer	*to appear*	**aparezco**
conocer	*to know*	**conozco**
conducir	*to drive*	**conduzco**
crecer	*to grow*	**crezco**
desaparecer	*to disappear*	**desaparezco**
establecer	*to establish*	**establezco**
merecer	*to deserve*	**merezco**
obedecer	*to obey*	**obedezco**
ofrecer	*to offer*	**ofrezco**
pertenecer	*to belong*	**pertenezco**
producir	*to produce*	**produzco**

Some -**er** verbs add **g** before the present tense endings.

caer	*to fall*	**caigo**
hacer	*to do*	**hago**
poner	*to put*	**pongo**
salir	*to leave*	**salgo**
traer	*to bring*	**traigo**
valer	*to be worth*	**valgo**

Other commonly used verbs also are irregular in the **yo** form only.

caber	*to fit*	**quepo**
dar	*to give*	**doy**
estar	*to be*	**estoy**
saber	*to know*	**sé**

The addition of prefixes **com-**, **des-**, **dis-**, **pro-**, **-re**, **-su**, and so on does not change the irregular forms of the verbs **hacer**, **poner**, **tener**, and **traer**.

hacer

deshacer	*to undo*	**deshago**
rehacer	*to remake*	**rehago**

poner

componer	*to compose*	**compongo**
disponer	*to arrange*	**dispongo**
proponer	*to propose*	**propongo**
reponer	*to replace*	**repongo**
suponer	*to suppose*	**supongo**

tener

contener	*to contain, hold*	**contengo**
entretener	*to distract, entertain*	**entretengo**
retener	*to keep, retain*	**retengo**
sostener	*to hold up, support*	**sostengo**

traer

atraer	*to attract*	**atraigo**
distraer	*to distract*	**distraigo**
sustraer	*to subtract*	**sustraigo**

EJERCICIO
3·7

En la oficina. *Complete each sentence with the appropriate present tense form of the verb in parentheses.*

1. Yo nunca miento, siempre_____ la verdad. (decir)

2. Marta no_____ veinte años, ¡treinta! (tener)

3. En la oficina, yo_____ mi cartera en la gaveta. (poner)

4. Yo_____ los nombres de todos los países europeos. (saber)

5. Carlos_____ mañana de Argentina. (venir)

6. Yo_____ las gracias a mis amigos. (dar)

7. Luisa_____ puertorriqueña. (ser)

8. Ahora yo_____ aquí, delante de la computadora. (estar)

9. Yo no_____ mucho dinero a la oficina. (traer)

10. Brenda y yo_____ música cuando trabajamos. (oír)

11. Pedro siempre_____ su trabajo. (hacer)

12. Pedro propone un restaurante para almorzar pero yo_____ otro. (proponer)

EJERCICIO
3·8

Preguntas personales.

1. ¿A qué hora sales de casa por la mañana?

_____

2. ¿Conduces un auto nuevo o viejo?

_____

3. ¿Perteneces a un partido político en tu país?

_____

4. ¿Qué traes a casa cuando vas al mercado?

_____

5. ¿Haces tareas en español o alemán?

_____

6. ¿Mereces un descanso después de este ejercicio? ¿Sí o no?

_____

Uses of the irregular verbs saber and conocer

Remember both **saber** and **conocer** are irregular in the present and both mean *to know*. However, in Spanish they are used in different contexts.

◆ **saber**: *to know information and facts, to know how*

Ellos saben los detalles del accidente.	*They know the details about the accident.*
Lola sabe que vivo en la Florida.	*Lola knows that I live in Florida.*
Sé tocar la guitarra.	*I know how to play the guitar.*

◆ **conocer**: *to be familiar with a person, a place, or a location; to meet a person*

Conozco a Juan.	*I know Juan.*
No conocemos ese museo.	*We are not familiar with that museum.*
Es un gusto conocer a su hijo.	*It is a pleasure to meet your son.*

Una conversación. ¿Conocer o saber? *Complete the following sentences using the* **yo** *form of the present tense of* **saber** *or* **conocer** *as appropriate.*

1. _____ a Sebastián, el hijo de Martina.

2. _____ dónde vive Sebastián.

3. No_____ este lugar muy bien.

4. _____ algunas tiendas excelentes aquí.

5. No_____ los nombres de las estaciones de trenes tampoco.

6. _____ que Buenos Aires es una ciudad muy cosmopolita.

7. _____ a muchas personas en México.

8. Y_____ buenas playas en ese país.

The near future, nouns, and articles

As previously observed, the present tense is used to indicate actions or situations that are going on at this moment, activities and routines that take place regularly, and actions that will take place in the near future.

The present and the near future

Spanish tends to use the present tense rather than the future tense for actions that will occur within a short time. There are two ways to do this.

◆ The present tense plus adverbs or adverbial phrases that indicate when the action will take place

El próximo lunes regresamos.   *Next Monday we will go back.*

◆ The verb **ir** (*to go*) + **a** + the infinitive, as in English you could say *I am going to*. All present tense forms of **ir** are irregular.

ir *to go*	
voy	vamos
vas	vais
va	van

Voy a ayudar a mi tía en su oficina.   *I am going to help my aunt in her office.*
Mis amigos van a viajar mañana.   *My friends are going to travel tomorrow.*

VOCABULARIO

These are some of the adverbial expressions that pinpoint the time when an action will take place in the near future.

el año que viene	*next year*	**mañana**	*tomorrow*
el mes que viene	*next month*	**mañana por la mañana**	*tomorrow morning*
esta noche	*tonight*	**mañana por la noche**	*tomorrow night*
esta tarde	*this afternoon*	**mañana por la tarde**	*tomorrow afternoon*
la semana que viene	*next week*	**más tarde**	*later on*
la semana siguiente	*the following week*	**pasado mañana**	*the day after tomorrow*

EJERCICIO
4·1

Traducción.

1. Tomorrow morning we are going to visit a museum in Madrid.

   _____

2. Later I am going to walk around the city.

   _____

3. Tomorrow afternoon Laurita is going to see her friends from Barcelona.

   _____

4. Next week Laurita and I will travel to Seville.

   _____

5. The following week you and Laura (*pl., fam.*) will return to California.

   _____

6. My parents are going to move from Los Angeles to Miami next year.

   _____

EJERCICIO
4·2

Y en tu caso, ¿verdadero (V) o falso (F)?

1. _____ El año que viene voy a estudiar alemán.

2. _____ Voy a celebrar mi cumpleaños con mis padres.

3. _____ Este fin de semana voy a ir de vacaciones.

4. _____ El próximo verano voy a graduarme de una universidad.

5. _____ Mañana vamos al cine mi novio/novia y yo.

6. _____ Voy a ir a un restaurante mexicano esta noche.

7. _____ Pasado mañana voy a jugar basquetbol.

8. _____ Mañana por la noche voy a bailar en una discoteca.

9. _____ Voy a tomar un autobús para regresar a mi casa esta semana.

10. _____ Voy a terminar estos ejercicios más tarde.

Gender of nouns in Spanish: Endings of nouns

Nouns designate people, places, actions, things, events, concrete or abstract ideas, and so on. In Spanish, nouns are either **feminine** or **masculine**, grammatically speaking. Sometimes this classification will not make sense to the English-speaking learner of Spanish. **La mesa** (*table*) is not viewed as an object with a "feminine" nature, but as an inanimate object that is feminine because the ending in **-a** is an indication of grammatical gender: most nouns that end in **-a** are feminine in Spanish.

In Spanish, there are some general rules, which are not absolute, about the gender of nouns. In the examples that follow, the masculine article **el** and the feminine article **la** are placed before the nouns to indicate the gender. **El** and **la** are equivalent to the English definite article *the*.

Masculine nouns and their endings in Spanish

The general rule states that all nouns in Spanish are masculine or feminine. The gender is associated with specific word endings. The following endings generally indicate the masculine gender:

- Nouns that designate male beings generally (but not always) end in **-o**.

el cartero	*mailman, mail carrier (m.)*
el general	*general (military) (m.)*
el hombre	*man*
el profesor	*(male) professor or teacher*

- Most nouns ending in **-o** referring to animals, things, or ideas are masculine.

el año	*year*	**el queso**	*cheese*
el caballo	*horse*	**el zapato**	*shoe*
el catálogo	*catalogue*		

- However, some nouns that end in **-a** are masculine. Note that the following groups with the endings **-al**, **-el**, **-ía**, **-ma**, **-ama**, **-ema**, and **-oma** include many nouns that are cognates, that is, words that have similar spelling and meaning in English and Spanish.

el aroma	*aroma, fragrance*	**el mantel**	*tablecloth*
el clima	*weather, climate*	**el pastel**	*cake*
el crucigrama	*crossword puzzle*	**el poema**	*poem*
el delantal	*apron*	**el problema**	*problem*
el día	*day*	**el programa**	*program*
el dilema	*dilemma*	**el sistema**	*system*
el diploma	*diploma*	**el tema**	*theme*
el fantasma	*ghost, phantom*	**el tranvía**	*trolley (car)*
el idioma	*language*		

Other groups of masculine nouns are:

- nouns with the endings **-ambre** and **-aje**.

el calambre	*cramp*	**el paisaje**	*landscape*
el equipaje	*luggage*	**el pasaje**	*passage, (train, bus) fare*
el mensaje	*message*	**el personaje**	*character*
		el salvaje	*savage*

◆ nouns that end in **-or** and **-án**.

el amor	*love*	**el rencor**	*hate*
el calor	*heat*	**el sudor**	*sweat*
el imán	*magnet*	**el volcán**	*volcano*
el refrán	*saying, proverb*		

Spanish has two contractions: **al** and **del**. They are both combinations of the prepositions **a** or **de** + the article **el**. **El** is the only form of the article that contracts with **a** or **de**. The contractions are not used if the article **el** is part of a proper noun.

No vamos **al cine** los lunes por la noche.	*We do not go **to the movies** on Monday nights*
Éste es el juguete **del niño**.	*This is the **child's** toy.*

Notice the absence of the contraction in the next example; the article is part of the noun.

Le escribieron **de El Pardo**, una población cerca de Madrid.	*They wrote to him/to her **from El Pardo**, a community near Madrid.*

EJERCICIO
4·3

Práctica. Use an M to indicate masculine endings: an X if the ending is not masculine.

_____ 1. dolor (*pain*)

_____ 2. avión (*plane*)

_____ 3. maquillaje (*makeup*)

_____ 4. suspiro (*sigh*)

_____ 5. cabeza (*head*)

_____ 6. viaje (*trip*)

_____ 7. rumor (*rumor*)

_____ 8. visión (*vision*)

_____ 9. mensaje (*message*)

_____ 10. virtud (*virtue*)

_____ 11. síntoma (*symptom*)

_____ 12. belleza (*beauty*)

EJERCICIO
4·4

Sustantivos. Are the following nouns masculine (Y) or not (N)?

1. _____ casa

2. _____ mensaje

3. _____ cama

4. _____ profesora

5. _____ televisor

6. _____ mantel

7. _____ tristeza

8. _____ taza

9. _____ niño

10. _____ dirección

11. _____ diagrama

12. _____ canción

13. _____ clima

14. _____ delantal

15. _____ dilema

16. _____ tema

17. _____ exposición

18. _____ calor

19. _____ libertad

20. _____ sección

Feminine nouns and their endings in Spanish

The following endings generally identify feminine nouns:

- Nouns that identify female beings generally end in **-a**.

la enfermera	*(female) nurse*	**la profesora**	*(female) professor*
la hija	*daughter*	**la yegua**	*mare (horse)*

- Nearly all other nouns ending in **-a** are also feminine.

la cocina	*kitchen*	**la pelota**	*ball*
la guitarra	*guitar*	**la piscina**	*pool*
la maleta	*suitcase*		

- A few nouns ending in **-o** are feminine. With the exception of **la mano**, the other examples in this list are abbreviations of compound feminine nouns.

la foto (la fotografía)	*photo, photograph*
la mano	*hand*
la moto (la motocicleta)	*motorcycle*

- Nouns that end in **-ción** and **-sión** are feminine. These are often near cognates with English; note the similarities in spelling and meaning with the English equivalents.

la canción	*song*	**la exposición**	*exposition, exhibit*
la dirección	*address; direction*	**la inyección**	*injection*
la división	*division*	**la misión**	*mission*
la estación	*station; season*	**la pasión**	*passion*

- Nouns that have endings **-dad** and **-tad** are usually feminine. Many English equivalents are nouns ending in *-ty*.

la amistad	*friendship*	**la dignidad**	*dignity*
la ciudad	*city*	**la libertad**	*liberty, freedom*
la dificultad	*difficulty*	**la voluntad**	*will*

- Endings **-ie**, **-eza**, **-sis**, and **-itis** are generally feminine.

la crisis	*crisis*	**la riqueza**	*richness, riches*
la dermatitis	*dermatitis*	**la serie**	*series*
la dosis	*dosage, dose*	**la sinusitis**	*sinusitis*
la especie	*species*	**la tristeza**	*sadness*

- Nouns that end in **-tud** and **-umbre** are feminine. Many of these nouns designate abstract ideas. Most abstract nouns are feminine in Spanish.

la certidumbre	*certainty*	**la esclavitud**	*slavery*
la costumbre	*custom, tradition*	**la exactitud**	*exactness, precision*
la cumbre	*summit, mountaintop*	**la virtud**	*virtue*

El artículo y el género apropiado. Use the ariticle **el** or **la** to indicate the gender of the noun.

_____ 1. enfermedad (*illness*)	_____ 5. sociedad	_____ 9. eternidad
_____ 2. pureza (*purity*)	_____ 6. explosión	_____ 10. decencia
_____ 3. distracción	_____ 7. temor (*fear*)	
_____ 4. pereza (*laziness*)	_____ 8. tranvía	

Vocabulario. Complete each sentence with the appropriate noun.

el equipaje	la fealdad	la estación
el tenor	la dermatitis	la dosis

1. _____ es una inflamación de la piel.

2. Debo tomar _____ apropiada de este medicamento.

3. _____ espera una ovación después del concierto.

4. Debes colocar _____ en el baúl (*trunk*) del auto.

5. El tren llega a _____ a las siete en punto.

6. _____ es lo opuesto de la belleza.

Other endings to consider for the gender of nouns

Some nouns do not fit into any of the previous groups. Memorization and frequent practice will help you learn their gender.

- ◆ Nouns ending in **-e** or in consonants not included in previous lists of noun endings may be either feminine or masculine.

el antifaz	*mask*	**la clase**	*class*
el cine	*movies, movie house*	**la cruz**	*cross*
el examen	*exam*	**la mente**	*mind*
el lápiz	*pencil*	**la miel**	*honey*
el merengue	*meringue (baked egg white);*	**la vejez**	*old age*
	merengue (dance)	**la vez**	*turn; time*
el mes	*month*		

◆ Nouns designating professions and individuals may end in **-a**, **-ante**, **-e**, or **-ista**, and in general they may designate either a male or a female person. The article and adjectives, if expressed, normally agree in gender and number with the noun.

el/la atleta	*athlete*	**el/la pediatra**	*pediatrician*
el/la cantante	*singer*	**el/la periodista**	*journalist*
el/la gerente	*manager*	**el/la poeta**	*poet*
el/la intérprete	*interpreter*	**el/la turista**	*tourist*

◆ Nouns of professions, of people in general, and names of some animals that end in **-és**, **-n**, **-ón**, and **-or** are masculine. They add **-a** to create the feminine form and drop the accent mark (in the case of **-on**).

el campeón/la campeona	*champion*
el director/la directora	*principal, director*
el león/la leona	*lion*
el profesor/la profesora	*professor, teacher*
el francés/la francesa	*Frenchman, Frenchwoman*

◆ Some nouns are spelled the same for the masculine and feminine, and only the article changes.

el joven/la joven	*young man/young woman*
el modelo/la modelo	*male model/female model*
el testigo/la testigo	*(male) witness/(female) witness*
el turista/la turista	*(male) tourist/(female) tourist*

El juez interrogó a **la testigo**.	*The judge interrogated the (female) witness.*

In English, the gender of this type of noun would be clarified by the context.

◆ Other nouns referring to people change both the ending and the article in the masculine and feminine forms.

el muchacho/la muchacha	*boy/girl*
el niño/la niña	*boy/girl/child*
el novio/la novia	*fiancé/fiancée*

◆ Some nouns are **invariable**; that is, they designate both male and female individuals. Some of these end in **-a**, **-ente**, and **-ista**; others have a variety of endings. The article *does not* change with invariable nouns. "Invariable" or "inv." will be noted in dictionary entries.

el ángel	*angel*	**la estrella**	*star*
el personaje	*character*	**la víctima**	*victim*
el ser	*being*		

Tu hermana es **un ángel**.	*Your sister is **an angel**.*
Bob es **la estrella** de este espectáculo.	*Bob is **the star** of this show.*

◆ Feminine nouns that begin with a stressed **a-** or **ha-** are feminine but, for purposes of pronunciation, take a masculine definite article in the singular form. Because they are feminine nouns, the feminine forms of the adjective are used to modify them.

el agua (*f.*)	*water*	**el arpa** (*f.*)	*harp*
el águila (*f.*)	*eagle*	**el aula** (*f.*)	*classroom*

el alma (*f.*)	*soul*	**el hacha** (*f.*)	*ax*
el arma (*f.*)	*weapon*	**el hambre** (*f.*)	*hunger*

El agua fría es refrescante.   ***Cold water*** *is refreshing.*

Más vocabulario. Complete each sentence with the appropriate article and noun.

el águila	el arpa	el marqués	el hacha
la gerente	la campeona	la estrella	el mes

1. _____ : instrumento musical de cuerdas.

2. _____ : herramienta (*tool*) para cortar árboles.

3. _____ : deportista que gana en las olimpiadas.

4. _____ : persona que dirige una empresa.

5. _____ : símbolo de los Estados Unidos.

6. _____ : cuerpo celestial que brilla por la noche.

7. _____ : título aristocrático.

8. _____ : cada una de las doce partes en que se divide el año.

Other nouns and their gender

Certain groups of nouns are *masculine*:

◆ days of the week and months of the year. Note that they are not capitalized in Spanish.

El martes es mi cumpleaños.   ***Tuesday*** *is my birthday.*
Éste ha sido **un diciembre** muy frío.   *This has been* ***a very cold December***.

◆ compound nouns. Note that these compounds usually consist of a verb + a noun. They end with an **-s** but are singular nouns.

el abrelatas	*can opener*	**el paraguas**	*umbrella*
el lavaplatos	*dishwasher*	**el sacacorchos**	*corkscrew*
el parabrisas	*windshield*	**el salvavidas**	*lifeguard*

◆ nouns that name colors.

el amarillo	*yellow*	**el naranja**	*orange*
el azul	*blue*	**el negro**	*black*
el blanco	*white*	**el rojo**	*red*
el lila	*lilac*	**el rosado**	*pink*
el morado	*purple*	**el verde**	*green*

♦ infinitives used as nouns. English equivalents are usually in the *-ing* form.

El comer y **beber** mucho no son recomendables.

Eating and drinking a lot is not advisable.

♦ names of rivers, seas, and oceans.

El río Mississippi está en los Estados Unidos.

The Mississippi River is in the United States.

El mar Mediterráneo tiene playas fabulosas.

The Mediterranean Sea has fabulous beaches.

Note: The names of islands are *feminine*.

Las Malvinas están en el Atlántico y **las Galápagos** en el Pacífico.

The Malvinas are in the Atlantic and the Galápagos in the Pacific.

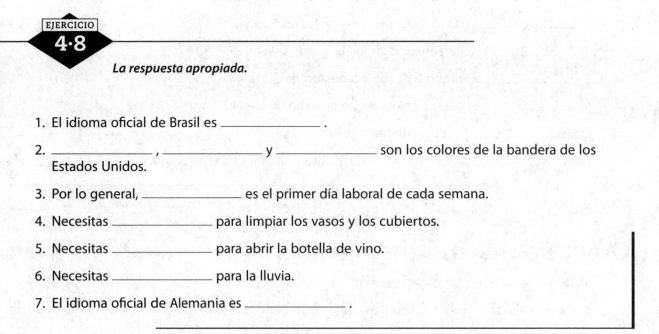

EJERCICIO
4·8

La respuesta apropiada.

1. El idioma oficial de Brasil es _____ .

2. _____ , _____ y _____ son los colores de la bandera de los Estados Unidos.

3. Por lo general, _____ es el primer día laboral de cada semana.

4. Necesitas _____ para limpiar los vasos y los cubiertos.

5. Necesitas _____ para abrir la botella de vino.

6. Necesitas _____ para la lluvia.

7. El idioma oficial de Alemania es _____ .

One useful strategy to learn the gender of Spanish nouns is to study them in two ways: first, nouns with specific endings that indicate either feminine or masculine, and second, whole groups of nouns that are either masculine or feminine.

Two more groups deserve attention, especially because they include some very common words. These lists show a selected number of words from these categories. Use them as a reference tool.

♦ Some nouns referring to people or animals may have different forms for the masculine and feminine. The articles, of course, change with the gender. Note the similarities of some of the English equivalents.

el actor/la actriz	*actor/actress*
el caballo/la yegua	*horse/mare*
el conde/la condesa	*count/countess*
el emperador/la emperatriz	*emperor/empress*
el héroe/la heroína	*hero/heroine*

el hombre/la mujer	man/woman
el marido, esposo/la esposa	husband/wife
el padre/la madre	father/mother
el príncipe/la princesa	prince/princess
el rey/la reina	king/queen
el varón/la hembra	male/female
el yerno/la nuera	son-in-law/daughter-in-law

◆ Some nouns have a different meaning if used with the masculine or the feminine article. Grammatical gender changes the meaning even though the word is spelled the same.

el capital/la capital	capital (money)/capital (city)
el cometa/la cometa	comet/kite
el corte/la corte	cut/court
el cura/la cura	priest/cure
el editorial/la editorial	newspaper editorial/publishing house
el frente/la frente	front/forehead
el guía/la guía	guide/female guide, telephone guide, or guidebook
el orden/la orden	order (in a sequence)/order (command)
el Papa/la papa	the Pope/potato
el policía/la policía	police officer/the police force

EJERCICIO
4·9

Más vocabulario. Give the feminine article and noun.

1. el profesor _____

2. el maestro _____

3. el periodista _____

4. el rey _____

5. el pintor _____

6. el actor _____

7. el padre _____

8. el gerente _____

9. el caballo _____

10. el comandante _____

11. el artista _____

12. el bailarín _____

EJERCICIO
4·10

En tu opinion, ¿sí? o ¿no?

_____ 1. La médica probablemente trabaja en el hospital.

_____ 2. Muchos turistas necesitan una guía.

_____ 3. El francés es la lengua oficial de Alemania.

_____ 4. El orden es lo opuesto al desorden.

_____ 5. Las guerras son conflictos.

En español.

1. the female student _____

2. the lion (*m.*) _____

3. the female lawyer _____

4. the apple tree _____

5. the pear _____

6. the empress _____

7. the husband _____

8. the son-in-law _____

9. the hero (*f.*) _____

10. the female tourist _____

11. the victim _____

12. the potato _____

Plural of nouns

The plural of nouns in Spanish is formed by adding the plural endings **-s** or **-es**. A definite article, **los** before masculine nouns and **las** before feminine nouns, indicates the plural of nouns. Follow these guidelines:

◆ For nouns that end in a vowel, add **-s**.

el café/los cafés	*café/cafés*	**la casa/las casas**	*house/houses*
el caso/los casos	*case/cases*	**la fruta/las frutas**	*fruit/fruits*
el vino/los vinos	*wine/wines*	**la niña/las niñas**	*girl/girls*

◆ For nouns that end in a consonant, add **-es**.

el papel/los papeles	*paper/papers; role/roles*
el reloj/los relojes	*clock/clocks*

Some spelling changes need to be observed:

◆ Singular nouns ending in **-z** change to **-ces** in the plural.

el lápiz/los lápices	*pencil/pencils*
la matriz/las matrices	*matrix/matrices*

◆ Nouns ending in **-í** and **-ú** add **-s** or **-es** and keep the accent mark in the plural. There are only a few nouns in this group.

el manatí/los manatís/los manatíes	*manatee/manatees*
el rubí/los rubís/los rubíes	*ruby/rubies*
el tabú/los tabús/los tabúes	*taboo/taboos*

◆ Nouns with accent marks on the last syllable lose the accent mark in the plural.

el camión/los camiones	*truck/trucks*
el francés/los franceses	*Frenchman/Frenchmen*
el león/los leones	*lion/lions*
el marqués/los marqueses	*marquis/marquises*

El plural. Give the plural article and noun.

1. el señor _____
2. la reina _____
3. el alma _____
4. el avión _____
5. la leona _____
6. la flor _____
7. la cárcel (*prison*) _____

8. el restaurante _____
9. la carne _____
10. el agua _____
11. la guía _____
12. el padre _____
13. el temor _____
14. el domingo _____

Mas plurales. Fill in the blanks with the plural article and noun.

1. sopa _____
2. residencia _____
3. pasaje _____
4. mujer _____
5. reloj _____
6. española _____

7. bebé _____
8. mantel _____
9. rubí _____
10. canción _____
11. luz _____
12. región _____

More about the plural of nouns in Spanish

Some groups of nouns and their corresponding plurals are exceptions to the rules we have just studied. Note the plural of the following nouns:

◆ Nouns that end in **-s** do not change their spelling in the plural, if the final syllable is not stressed.

el miércoles/los miércoles	*Wednesday/Wednesdays*
el paraguas/los paraguas	*umbrella/umbrellas*
la tesis/las tesis	*thesis/theses*

All days of the week except **sábado** and **domingo** end in **-s**. The **los** form of the article identifies the plural form of **lunes**, **martes**, **miércoles**, etc.

Los lunes son siempre largos.   *Mondays are always long.*

◆ For compound words formed with two nouns, add the plural ending to the first element only.

el coche cama/los coches cama	*sleeping car/sleeping cars*
el hombre rana/los hombres rana	*(deep-sea) diver/divers (frogmen)*

◆ Some nouns are always plural in Spanish.

las afueras	*the outskirts*	**las vacaciones**	*vacation*
las cosquillas	*tickling*	**los binoculares**	*binoculars*
las gafas	*eyeglasses*	**los gemelos**	*twins; cuff links*
las tijeras	*scissors*	**los lentes**	*eyeglasses; lenses*

EJERCICIO 4·14

En español.

1. My vacation ends on Sunday. _____

2. I'm going to see the panthers (**panteras**) at the zoo tomorrow. _____

3. Now Lina and I put on our sunglasses. _____

4. This hotel is on the outskirts of Madrid. _____

5. We travel at night and rest in a sleeping car. _____

6. Lina never brings an umbrella. _____

EJERCICIO 4·15

Escoge. Complete each sentence with the appropriate article and noun.

las gafas	las tijeras	los domingos
las tesis	los binoculares	los gemelos

1. Pablo compra _____ de rubí para su camisa elegante.

2. Muchas personas no trabajan _____.

3. Desde su casa, Berta puede espiar a sus vecinos con _____ .

4. No me gustan _____ que defienden mis enemigos.

5. Necesito _____ para cortar los papeles.

6. ¿Dónde están _____ ? No veo bien.

Definite articles

The definite articles (**artículos definidos**) have appeared in most of the examples and exercises in this unit. You are already familiar with their gender and number forms. The definite article introduces the noun it precedes and it agrees with it in gender and number. In English, *the* is the equivalent of four different forms in Spanish. English equivalents of Spanish nouns in context do not always include *the*.

- ◆ feminine forms.

    la   las

    La luna es un satélite.   ***The** moon is a satellite.*
    ¡Las vacaciones son siempre agradables!   *Vacations are always pleasant!*

- ◆ masculine forms.

    el   los

    El amor es maravilloso.   ***Love** is wonderful.*
    Los tigres están en la jaula. ***The tigers** are in the cage.*

EJERCICIO
4·16

*¿Qué hacen estas personas? Give the appropriate article **el, los, la, las**.*

1. _los_ músicos prefieren _la_ música pop.
2. _los_ niños no piden _los_ espárragos. (asparagus)
3. _los_ orangutanes duermen en _las_ árboles.
4. _el_ senador enfrenta _la_ crítica de sus opositores.
5. _los_ meteorólogos estudian _las_ tormentas.
6. _las_ investigadoras escriben _las_ reportajes.
7. _las_ bailarines interpretan _el_ ballet.

When are definite articles used in Spanish?

As we have already noted, in many instances where the definite article is necessary in Spanish, it is omitted in English.

        Las mujeres están presentes aquí.   ***Women** are present here.*

Using Spanish articles will take practice, since quite a few situations require their use in Spanish, but not in English. At times, it may appear that the use or omission of these articles is contrary to their use in the other language.

Use the definite articles in Spanish:

- with nouns used in a general sense.

  La comida española es deliciosa. *Spanish cuisine is delicious.*

- with days of the week. The English equivalent in this case is the preposition *on*.

  El martes tenemos un examen. ***On Tuesday**, we have an exam.*
  No trabajamos **los domingos**. *We do not work on **Sundays**.*

- with names of languages, except after **hablar**. Names of languages are not capitalized.

  El alemán y **el inglés** no son lenguas romances. ***German** and **English** are not Romance languages.*
  No hablo **alemán**. *I do not speak **German**.*

- with parts of the body, items of personal hygiene, and clothing. In English, the possessive adjective is used in these situations.

  Me duele **la muela**. ***My tooth** hurts.*

- to tell time.

  Es **la una**. *It is **one o'clock**.*
  Son **las diez y media**. *It is **ten thirty**.*

EJERCICIO
4·17

Un mensaje. Give the appropriate definite article (**el**, **la**, **los**, **las**).

1. _____ sección "Salud es vida", publicada todos 2. _____ martes, dice que

3. _____ espárragos son saludables. Si no hablas 4. _____ español, puedes leer

5. _____ artículos traducidos en la página escrita en 6. _____ inglés. ¿Te duele

7. _____ cabeza? Descansa, ya son 8. _____ seis de la tarde. ¿Te molesta

9. _____ luz? Cierra 10. _____ persianas y descansa en 11. _____ sofá de la sala.

EJERCICIO
4·18

En español.

1. Today I have an appointment at nine thirty in the morning. _____

_____

2. The assistant to the dentist speaks Portuguese and Spanish. _____

_____

3. My wisdom tooth (**la muela del juicio**) hurts. _____

4. Cavities may cause pain. _____

5. On Friday, I always get home late. _____

6. I go home around (**a eso de**) ten o'clock. _____

7. I need to rest! _____

More about the uses of definite articles in Spanish

The definite articles in Spanish are also required:

- with names and titles.

    El doctor Perdomo va a presentar a   *Dr. Perdomo* will introduce the guests.
    los invitados.
    El director cerrará la sesión.   *The director* will close the session.

- with nouns that refer to weights and measurements. Note that the English equivalent takes the *indefinite* article.

    Los huevos cuestan a un dólar   *Eggs cost one dollar **a dozen**.*
    la docena.
    Y la harina se vende a cincuenta   *And flour is sold at fifty cents **a pound**.*
    centavos **la libra**.

- with nouns designating specific people and things.

    Vi **el programa** que me recomendaste.   *I saw **the program** you recommended.*

- with last names referring to the members of a family in the plural, or referring to people who possess qualities associated with the people who bear those last names. Note that the proper names in this construction remain singular, while the articles are pluralized.

    Los Martínez y **los López** no vienen   *The Martinezes and the Lopezes are not coming*
    a la fiesta.   *to the party.*
    Estos artistas son los **Dalí** y **Miró** del   *These artists are the Dalís and the Mirós of*
    futuro.   *the future.*

- with nouns that refer to geographic places like rivers, mountains, bays, some cities, regions, and others.

    El Amazonas está en Suramérica.   *The Amazon River is in South America.*
    Los Pirineos son las montañas en la   *The Pyrenees are mountains on the border*
    frontera entre Francia y España.   *between France and Spain.*
    La Bahía de Cochinos está en el sur   *The Bay of Pigs is in the south of Cuba.*
    de Cuba.
    La Mancha es famosa por el personaje   *La Mancha is famous for the character*
    Don Quijote.   *Don Quixote.*

- with an infinitive functioning as a noun. The English equivalent is the present participle, with its -*ing* ending. The infinitive is usually used alone, but the definite article may be added for emphasis or style.

    Dormir (**El dormir**) mucho no es bueno.   *Sleeping a lot is not good.*

Frases en español. If necessary, give the appropriate definite article (*el, la, los, las*).

1. a dime a dozen _____

2. the Goyas of today _____

3. the Lopez _____

4. the United States _____

5. twelve dollars a yard _____

6. working hard _____

7. the Galapagos Islands _____

8. President Roosevelt _____

9. eating and drinking _____

When are definite articles omitted in Spanish?

In a very few cases the Spanish definite article is not used. Omit the definite article:

◆ with titles when addressing the person, or with **San**, **Santo**, **Santa**, **Don**, and **Doña**.

Sra. Almendro, pase por favor.	*Mrs. Almendro, please come in.*
Santo Domingo es una ciudad caribeña.	*Santo Domingo is a Caribbean city.*
Aquí viene **Don Pedro**.	*Here comes Don Pedro.*

◆ with nouns that refer to academic subjects.

Estudia **matemáticas** y **sicología**.   *He/She studies **mathematics** and **psychology**.*

◆ ordinal numbers used in titles.

Felipe **II** (**Segundo**)   *Philip **the Second***

◆ when stating someone's occupation following a form of the verb **ser**.

Paulina **es terapeuta**.	*Paulina is **a therapist**.*
José **era maestro**.	*José was **a teacher**.*

El artículo definido, ¿se usa o no? Give the appropriate definite article as needed. Use **X** if an article is not necessary.

1. Entrega estos documentos a _____ directora de finanzas.

2. ¡Qué caras (*expensive*)! Rosas a diez dólares _____ docena.

3. Necesitamos _____ hoja de papel.

4. _____ Morales llegaron al aeropuerto.

5. Las uvas cuestan un dólar _____ libra.

6. ¿Estudian Uds. _____ geometría?

7. Marcos es _____ enfermero.

8. ¿Las galletas (*cookies*) cuestan tres dólares _____ docena?

Indefinite articles

The indefinite article refers to one individual out of a general group. English has two forms: *a* and *an*. (*A* is used before words beginning with a consonant and *an* before words beginning with a vowel sound.) In Spanish indefinite articles have the same function but have two genders:

◆ feminine forms.

una *a, an*   **unas** a few, some

Una pera es **una** fruta.   *A pear is **a** fruit.*
Unas canciones, **una** guitarra y   *A **few** songs, **a** guitar and we have **a** party.*
tenemos **una** fiesta.

◆ masculine forms.

un *a, an*   **unos** *a few, some*

Tengo **un** abrigo nuevo.   *I have **a** new overcoat.*
Compramos **unos** sobres.   *We bought **a few** envelopes.*

EJERCICIO
4·21

Los artículos indefinidos. *Fill in the blanks with the appropriate indefinite article.*

1. _____ vez   5. _____ hospital   9. _____ escalera

2. _____ temblor   6. _____ crisis   10. _____ manatí

3. _____ verdad   7. _____ rubí   11. _____ capitán

4. _____ pasaje   8. _____ sofá   12. _____ pensión

EJERCICIO
4·22

Ahora, los plurales. *Give the plural indefinite article and noun from Ejercicio 4–21.*

1. _____   5. _____   9. _____

2. _____   6. _____   10. _____

3. _____   7 _____   11. _____

4. _____   8 _____   12. _____

When are indefinite articles used in Spanish?

In some situations the use of the indefinite articles in English and Spanish is equivalent. Use the indefinite articles:

◆ to refer to one individual in a general group.

Una sinfonía es **una obra de arte**.   *A symphony is **a work of art**.*

That is, among many works of art, **una sinfonía** stands out as an example.

◆ to identify a person with a noun indicating his or her personal qualities.

Eres **un ángel**.   *You are **an angel**.*
Ellos siempre han sido **unos cobardes**.   *They have always been **cowards**.*

◆ to indicate an approximate amount with numbers and quantities.

La bolsa cuesta **unos cincuenta euros**.   *The bag costs **about fifty euros**.*
En esta caja hay **unas tres docenas**   *There are **about three dozen** roses in this box.*
de rosas.

Note: Feminine nouns that begin with a stressed **a** or **ha** (**agua**, **águila**) take a masculine indefinite (or definite) article in the singular form. However, because they are feminine nouns, they take feminine adjectives.

Un arma siempre es peligrosa.   ***A weapon** is always dangerous.*

EJERCICIO
4·23

¿Verdadero (V) o falso (F)?

_____ 1. Un ángel es una persona generosa.

_____ 2. El helado es un alimento bajo en calorías.

_____ 3. Un cobarde enfrenta a sus enemigos.

_____ 4. El gato es un animal doméstico.

_____ 5. Hay una frontera entre Estados Unidos y Canadá.

_____ 6. En una fábrica se usan maquinarias.

_____ 7. Un total es la suma de sus partes.

_____ 8. En unos desiertos hay camellos.

_____ 9. Una escultura es una obra musical.

_____ 10. Un coche alemán de lujo cuesta un ojo de la cara.

_____ 11. Romeo y Julieta son unos personajes de la novela Don Quijote.

When are indefinite articles not used in Spanish?

Remember *not* to use the indefinite articles:

- with nouns designating a nonspecific amount of material or materials.

    ¿Pones **tomate** en la paella?   *Do you put **a (any) tomato** in the paella?*

- with nouns of professions and occupations, nationality, or religion after **ser**. If the noun is modified by an adjective or adjective phrase, the indefinite article is used.

    Somos **electricistas**.   *We are **electricians**.*
    Raúl es **un excelente carpintero**.   *Raúl is **an excellent carpenter**.*
    Todos ellos son **venezolanos**.   *They are all **Venezuelans**.*
    Son **judíos** de Grecia.   *They are **Jews** from Greece.*

    Remember nouns and adjectives of nationality and religion are *not* capitalized in Spanish.

- when the noun is preceded by the following words **cierto(a)**, **medio(a)**, **mil**, **otro(a)**, **qué**, or **tal(-es)**. Note the English equivalents in these examples.

    Cierta persona te visita a menudo.   ***A certain person*** *visits you often.*
    Salimos en **media hora**.   *We will leave in **a half hour**.*
    Perdieron **mil dólares** en la apuesta.   *They lost **one thousand dollars** on the bet.*
    Compra **otro ramo** de flores.   *Buy **another bunch** of flowers.*
    ¡Qué mala suerte!   ***What bad luck!***
    No me cuentes **tal cosa**.   *Don't tell me **such a thing**.*

EJERCICIO 4·24

El artículo indefinido, ¿se usa o no? Give the appropriate indefinite article if needed. Use **X** if one is not necessary.

1. _____ amigos de Mandy llegaron al aeropuerto.

2. Necesitamos _____ cita con el dentista.

3. Compré _____ revistas extranjeras.

4. Manuel, ¡ _____ qué inteligente eres!

5. Entrega estas cartas a _____ empleado de esa oficina.

6. Antonio Lázaro es _____ buen electricista.

7. Me lo dijo _____ cierta persona.

8. Yo no dije _____ tal cosa.

9. Marcos es _____ enfermero con mucha experiencia.

10. Lola, dame _____ otro helado.

·5· Gustar, ser, and estar and expressing opinions

Gustar and verbs like gustar

The Spanish verb **gustar** is used to express likes and dislikes.

Me gusta la música mexicana.	*I like Mexican music.*
No me gustan los platos picantes.	*I do not like spicy dishes.*

Gustar, and verbs like it, are used in the third person singular and plural *only*, and are preceded by an indirect object pronoun. That is, the subject is a person, an animal, or an item that is pleasing to the indirect object.

SPANISH	ENGLISH
indirect object + **gustar** + subject	subject + *to like* + direct object
Me **gusta** el programa.	*I like the program.*

The translation of **gustar** is *to like, to please*. In Spanish the word order is not rigid—the preceding example could be changed to **El programa me gusta** (*The program is pleasing to me*). Placing the subject first in a sentence with **gustar** stresses what it is that is pleasing to the indirect object **me** (*me*)—**el programa**. Note that any negative words precede the indirect pronoun. See Chapter 12 for more about indirect object pronouns.

No me gustan los colores claros.	*I do not like light colors.*
No les gusta una paella con alcachofas.	*They do not like a paella with artichokes.*
No nos gustan las novelas largas.	*We do not like long novels.*

Use the singular form if one or more infinitives follow **gustar**.

¿Te **gusta ir** al museo y **comprar** regalos allí?	*Do you like to go to the museum and buy gifts there?*
No nos **gusta lavar y planchar**.	*We do not like to wash and iron.*

The preposition **a**, followed by a pronoun or noun, is commonly used with **gustar** to clarify who is, or is not, pleased. The indirect noun or pronoun usually precedes the object pronoun.

A Juanita le gusta la pintura barroca.	*Juanita likes Baroque paintings.*
A él le gustan los cuadros de Dalí.	*He likes Dalí's paintings.*
Le gusta al guardia ese cuadro.	*The custodian likes this painting.*

Verbs like gustar

Many verbs follow the same pattern as **gustar**—that is, they are used with an indirect object pronoun.

VOCABULARIO			
aburrir	*to bore*	**fascinar**	*to fascinate, to love*
agradar	*to please*	**hacer falta**	*to miss, to need*
angustiar	*to worry*	**importar**	*to matter, to care about*
apasionar	*to excite, to thrill*	**interesar**	*to be interesting, appealing*
bastar	*to be enough*	**molestar**	*to annoy, to bother*
disgustar	*to upset*	**preocupar**	*to worry*
doler	*to hurt, to ache*	**quedar**	*to fit, to remain*
encantar	*to like thoroughly, to love*	**sobrar**	*to be left over*
faltar	*to lack, to be missing*	**tocar**	*to be one's turn*

Me aburre esta sinfonía.	*This symphony bores me.*
A Uds. les faltan diez euros.	*You are missing ten euros.*
Nos basta este dinero.	*This money is enough for us.*
¿Cómo **le queda a Ud.** la chaqueta?	*How does the jacket fit you?*

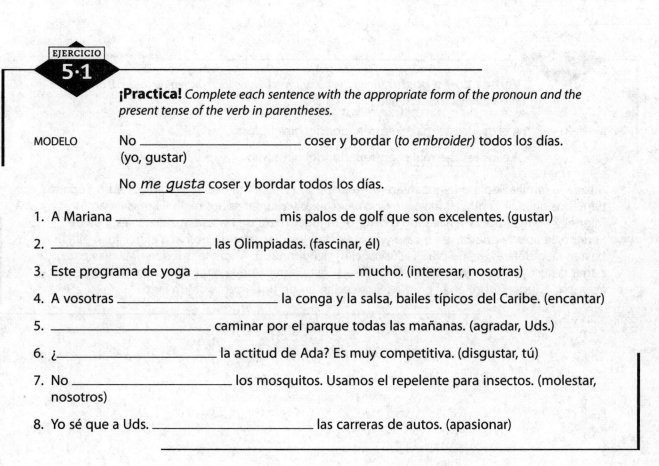

EJERCICIO

5·1

¡Practica! *Complete each sentence with the appropriate form of the pronoun and the present tense of the verb in parentheses.*

MODELO   No _____ coser y bordar (*to embroider*) todos los días.
(yo, gustar)

No *me gusta* coser y bordar todos los días.

1. A Mariana _____ mis palos de golf que son excelentes. (gustar)

2. _____ las Olimpiadas. (fascinar, él)

3. Este programa de yoga _____ mucho. (interesar, nosotras)

4. A vosotras _____ la conga y la salsa, bailes típicos del Caribe. (encantar)

5. _____ caminar por el parque todas las mañanas. (agradar, Uds.)

6. ¿_____ la actitud de Ada? Es muy competitiva. (disgustar, tú)

7. No _____ los mosquitos. Usamos el repelente para insectos. (molestar, nosotros)

8. Yo sé que a Uds. _____ las carreras de autos. (apasionar)

¡Practica! *Complete each sentence with the appropriate present tense form of the verb in parentheses.*

1. Me _____ los pies. Voy a comprar esos zapatos para caminar. (doler)

2. ¿Te _____ el precio de estas camisas? Yo tengo doscientos dólares en mi bolsillo. (preocupar)

3. A nosotros nos _____ solamente dos horas para elegir (*to choose*) los trajes. (quedar)

4. A Mara le _____ el dinero para comprar los esquís y los guantes. (sobrar)

5. Ahora les _____ a Uds. el turno y pueden pagar la tabla hawaiana. (tocar)

6. Sí, pero nos _____ también los bañadores, la sombrilla y el bronceador. (hacer falta)

7. ¿Les _____ a Uds. la opinión de la dependiente de la tienda? (importar)

8. A ellos les _____ cincuenta dólares para comprar los patines de ruedas (*roller skates*). (bastar)

Verbos como *gustar*. *Read the paragraph below, then underline the verb and the indirect object preceding it.*

Modelo   A ellos les cae mal el entrenador del gimnasio.

                 A ellos <u>les cae mal</u> el entrenador del gimnasio.

A toda la familia Sedano le encantan los deportes y las actividades al aire libre. Pedro Sedano tiene dos hijos. A Pablo, el mayor, le fascina esquiar y patinar sobre hielo. El más joven es Miguel y no le importa si hace frío o calor para jugar fuera de la casa. A Julia, la esposa de Sedano, le aburre quedarse en casa y le molestan los días cuando no hace ejercicio. A ella le bastan cien dólares al año para la suscripción del gimnasio. Ahora le quedan diez días para pagar la suscripción. Hoy le duele la cabeza. A esta familia no le hace falta una excusa para acampar o jugar fútbol en el parque. Se quedan en un hotel cerca de un lago.

Read the paragraph in Ejercicio 5-3 again and answer the questions below in complete sentences.

1. ¿Qué actividades le gustan a la familia Sedano?

   _____

2. Y a Pablo, ¿qué le fascina?

   _____

3. ¿Le importa a Miguel si hace frío o calor?

   _____

4. ¿Qué le aburre a Julia?

   _____

5. ¿Qué le duele hoy a Julia?

   _____

Similarities and differences between **ser** and **estar**

◆ Learning the different uses of **ser** and **estar** in Spanish may present some challenges for the English speaker. Both **ser** and **estar** are equivalent to the English *to be*, and they are frequently used in daily communication. A comparison of **ser** and **estar** will help highlight some similarities and differences.

◆ Both **ser** and **estar** are irregular verbs in some tenses. For the sake of comparison, let us look at the present tense forms.

ser *to be*		**estar** *to be*	
soy	somos	estoy	estamos
eres	sois	estás	estáis
es	son	está	están

See the Verb Tables at the back of this book for the other tenses of **ser** and **estar**.

◆ Both **ser** and **estar** are used as the main verb in a sentence.

| **Soy** de los Estados Unidos. | *I am from the United States.* |
| **Estoy** en Washington. | *I am in Washington.* |

◆ Both are used as auxiliary verbs. **Ser** is used in the passive voice; and **estar** helps conjugate the progressive forms (equivalent of *-ing* in English).

| El caso **fue estudiado** por las autoridades. | *The case **was studied** by the authorities.* |
| **Estamos considerando** tu propuesta. | *We are considering your proposal.* |

But **ser** and **estar** are very different both in meaning and in usage. Later in this chapter you will review the passive voice.

Let's start with a key distinction: **ser** is used to describe permanent or more lasting situations, while **estar** indicates location and what are considered temporary situations.

Soy Graciela.	*I am Graciela.*
Ahora, **estoy** en Madrid.	*I am in Madrid now.*

Trying to reason out what is permanent and what is temporary will not help us in all situations where either **ser** or **estar** may be used. The initial, basic distinction between permanent and temporary conditions is not absolute, and, on occasion, may appear somewhat confusing. Sometimes the uses of these two verbs seem to defy logic:

¡**Está** muerto!	*He is dead!*

Is death not permanent? As you become familiar with their uses, it will be easier to choose which of these two verbs you will need to communicate your meaning.

When is **ser** used in Spanish?

Use **ser** to indicate:

- the identity of the subject (person, thing, or event).

Soy Pedro.	*I am Pedro.*
Éste **es** el mercado.	*This is the market.*
El 4 de julio **es** el Día de la Independencia de los Estados Unidos.	*The Fourth of July is the Independence Day of the United States.*

- someone's occupation or profession.

Raúl **es** dentista.	*Raul is a dentist.*
Somos estudiantes.	*We are students.*

Note that the indefinite article **un**, **una**, **unos**, or **unas** is omitted in Spanish when stating a profession following the verb **ser**. The indefinite article is used if an adjective modifies the occupation.

Eres **un buen** estudiante.	*You are **a good** student.*

- essential or inherent qualities not likely to change such as nationality, moral attributes, and religion.

El guacamole **es** un plato mexicano.	*Guacamole is a Mexican dish.*
Felicia **es** cubana.	*Felicia is Cuban.*
El señor Benigno **es** muy honrado.	*Mr. Benigno is very honest.*
La familia de Delia **es** católica.	*Delia's family is Catholic.*

Remember that adjectives and nouns of nationalities are not capitalized in Spanish.

- characteristics of physical appearance and personality. They may also be considered inherent. A person's appearance may change: one's hair may be colored, for instance, but the results are considered lasting if not permanent.

Charley **es** alto, rubio y simpático.	*Charley is tall, blond, and pleasant.*
Antes, Rosa **era** pelirroja. Ahora, **es** rubia.	*Before, Rosa **used to be** a redhead. Now she is a blond.*

- relationships. Even after the death or dissolution of someone or something, a relationship is expressed with a form of **ser**. Relationships are examples of identity.

Ellas **son** mis hermanas.	*They **are** my sisters.*
John **es** su ex-marido.	*John **is** her ex-husband.*
¡Tú **eres** mi amigo!	*You **are** my friend!*

◆ time. The singular form **es** is used to refer to *it is* for *one o'clock*. Use the plural **son** for all other hours.

Es la una y media.	***It is** half past one.*
Son las ocho y cuarto.	***It is** eight fifteen.*

◆ place and date of an event.

Mañana **es** mi cumpleaños.	*Tomorrow **is** my birthday.*
Las reuniones **son** en el salón de conferencias.	*The meetings **are** in the conference room.*
Hoy **es** el primero de mayo.	*Today **is** May 1.*

◆ origin, possession, and the materials objects are made of, with the preposition **de**.

Estos zapatos **son de** Italia.	*These shoes **are** from Italy.*
La casa **es de** Lucy.	*The house **is** Lucy's.*
Mi reloj no **es de** oro.	*My watch **is** not (made of) gold.*

◆ quantity and price.

Cuatro por tres **son** doce.	*Four times three **is** twelve.*
—¿Cuánto **es**?	*"How much **is it**?"*
—**Son** doce euros.	*"**It is** twelve euros."*

◆ with the passive voice construction **ser** + participle (+ **por**).

Las playas **son admiradas por** los turistas.	*The beaches **are admired by** the tourists.*
El libro **será publicado** en San Juan.	*The book **will be published** in San Juan.*

Note that in the passive voice construction with **ser**, the past participle of the verb functions as an adjective and must agree in gender and number with the subject.

◆ with impersonal expressions.

¡**Es urgente** llamar a tu casa ahora!	***It is urgent** to call your house now!*

EJERCICIO
5·5

¿Verdadero (V) o falso (F)?

_____ 1. La luna es un planeta.

_____ 2. Picasso es un científico famoso.

_____ 3. Cuatro por cinco son veinte.

_____ 4. La biología es una ciencia.

_____ 5. Buenos Aires es la capital de Ecuador.

_____ 6. Una hora es una medida de tiempo.

En español.

1. This is Manuel Ortiz. _____

2. He is from Puerto Rico. _____

3. This is his assistant, Leticia. _____

4. She is Ecuadorian. _____

5. They are our friends. _____

6. Manuel is an excellent athlete. _____

La graduación de mi amigo Hernán. Match the letter that best answers each question.

_____ 1. ¿De dónde es Hernán?   a. Es cómico y simpático.

_____ 2. ¿Cómo es Hernán?   b. Es a las 10 de la mañana.

_____ 3. ¿Cuándo es la graduación?   c. Es en el auditorio de la escuela.

_____ 4. ¿A qué hora es?   d. Es gratis.

_____ 5. ¿Dónde es la ceremonia?   e. Es de San Diego, California.

_____ 6. ¿Cuánto es cada entrada?   f. Es el 25 de mayo.

When is estar used in Spanish?

You learned that **estar** is used mainly to indicate location and temporary situations or conditions. Use **estar** to express:

♦ location—permanent, temporary, or short term, real or imaginary.

La ciudad de Miami **está** en la Florida.	*The city of Miami **is** in Florida.*
Estoy en la sala ahora.	*I **am** in the living room now.*
Estaré afuera en dos minutos.	*I **will be** outside in two minutes.*
Ella **está** en la luna.	*She **is** lost.*

♦ temporary physical conditions.

Los chicos **están** enfermos.	*The children **are** ill.*

Remember that temporary conditions are not characteristics. A temporary condition could indicate a short-lived state, as is the case with **están enfermos**. The condition described with **estar** could also indicate the result of a previous action.

La sesión **está cancelada**.	*The session **is cancelled**.*

- temporary mental conditions and moods.

¡Yo **no estoy** loca!	*I am not crazy!*
¡**Estás** deprimida!	*You are depressed!*

- temporary traits or qualities. **Estar** emphasizes a short-term condition or a basis for a comparison with a previous state or condition.

Hombre, **estás** delgado.	*Listen, you are (you look) thin.*
Para su edad, **están** muy maduros estos chicos.	*For their age, these kids are very mature.*

- a temporary situation with the preposition **de**.

Luisa **es** ingeniera pero ahora **está de** camarera en un restaurante muy fino.	*Luisa is an engineer but now she is a server at a fancy restaurant.*

- with the **-ando**, **-iendo** forms or the **gerundio** in the present progressive construction.

Estamos buscando trabajo.	*We are looking for work.*
Los bailarines **están saliendo** al escenario.	*The dancers are coming out to the stage.*

EJERCICIO 5·8

¿Ser o estar? Complete each sentence with the appropriate present tense form of **ser** or **estar**.

1. _____ las once de la mañana y Patricia _____ tomando el sol en su traje de baño.

2. Ella _____ lista para nadar una milla de estilo libre (*freestyle*).

3. Patricia _____ en muy buena forma (*good shape*).

4. Ella usa una crema y _____ muy buena para proteger la piel.

5. Los ejercicios de calentamiento (*warm-up*) _____ a las ocho de la mañana.

6. Patricia _____ una deportista dedicada.

EJERCICIO 5·9

¿Por qué? Go back to Ejercicio 5–8 and indicate the reason for using **ser** or **estar**.

1. _____

2. _____

3. _____

4. _____

5. _____

6. _____

Adjectives that change their meaning when used with either **ser** or **estar**

Ser or **estar** determine the meaning of some adjectives. The ideas they convey are different, as you can see in the following examples. Keep in mind that your choice of **ser** or **estar** will strongly affect your message.

ser		estar	
ser aburrido(a)	*to be boring*	**estar aburrido(a)**	*to be bored*
ser bueno(a)	*to be good*	**estar bueno(a)**	*to be fine, tasty*
ser listo(a)	*to be clever*	**estar listo(a)**	*to be ready*
ser malo(a)	*to be bad*	**estar malo(a)**	*to be ill*
ser orgulloso(a)	*to be conceited, vain*	**estar orgulloso(a)**	*to be proud*
ser pálido(a)	*to be pale complexioned*	**estar pálido(a)**	*to be pale*
ser rico(a)	*to be rich*	**estar rico(a)**	*to be tasty*
ser seguro(a)	*to be safe*	**estar seguro(a)**	*to be sure, certain*
ser viejo(a)	*to be old*	**estar viejo(a)**	*to look old*
ser vivo(a)	*to be sharp*	**estar vivo(a)**	*to be alive*

EJERCICIO
5·10

¿Ser o estar? Choose the appropriate verb.

1. Arturo quiere bailar. Él (es | está) listo para la fiesta.

2. ¡Ay! ¡Alicia tiene solamente treinta años pero en la foto (es | está) vieja!

3. Yo necesito saber la respuesta. Quiero (ser | estar) seguro.

4. Voy a comprar estos quesos. (Son | Están) frescos.

5. Los empleados (son | están) orgullosos de su trabajo.

6. Ella siempre ayuda a sus amigos. (Es | Está) atenta y servicial.

EJERCICIO
5·11

En español.

1. I am depressed but I am not crazy. _____

2. These are not my shoes. _____

3. Why are you (**Uds.**) here? _____

4. You (**Uds.**) are not sure! _____

5. Well, I am hungry and tired. _____

6. Are we ready to leave? _____

7. The game is at the university stadium. _____

Expressions with estar

Estar appears in common expressions used in everyday communication in Spanish. Note the English equivalents of the examples.

estar a + date *to be a certain date*

    Estamos a cuatro de mayo.   *It is May 4.*

estar a punto de + infinitive *to be just about to*

    Estoy a punto de acabar.   *I am just about to finish.*

estar de acuerdo (con) *to agree with*

    Estamos de acuerdo con María.   *We agree with María.*

estar para + infinitive *to be about to*

    Estoy para salir.   *I am about to leave.*

estar por + a noun *to be in favor of*

    Estoy por la reducción de los impuestos.   *I am in favor of cutting taxes.*

estar conforme (con) *to agree, be in agreement (with)*

    ¿Están conformes con nuestra decisión?   *Do you agree with our decision?*

estar de vacaciones *to be on vacation*

    Eva López **está de vacaciones** en Los Ángeles.   *Eva López is on vacation in Los Angeles.*

estar de vuelta *to be back*

    Todos **están de vuelta.**   *They are all back.*

EJERCICIO
5·12

Traducción.

_____ 1. It's April 25.	a. Está a punto de terminar.
_____ 2. She is about to finish.	b. Estamos por la paz.
_____ 3. We are all for peace.	c. El jefe está de vuelta.
_____ 4. Do you (**tú**) agree with me?	d. Están de vacaciones.
_____ 5. They are on vacation.	e. ¿Estás de acuerdo conmigo?
_____ 6. The boss is back.	f. Estamos a veinticinco de abril.

Confusing verb pairs

Students often have difficulty distinguishing the differences in usage of many pairs of verbs.

Ser and estar

The first verb pair they encounter, and the most notorious, is **ser** vs. **estar**, a pair of verbs that truly has only one English counterpart, the verb *to be*. The other confusing pairs often have alternative English translations that turn out to be better than the first-level dictionary entries. The mental hand-wringing over the other confusing verb pairs is often a result of not digging a bit deeper, as you will see. First, let's deal head-on with **ser** and **estar**.

The verb pair of **ser** and **estar** can be treated under three main subdivisions. In the majority of cases, which I call the 90 percent rule, **estar** is used for health and location and **ser** is used for everything else. If you understand and remember these two uses of **estar**, you can save yourself the trouble of having to memorize the uses of **ser**, although it is still useful and important to review them. There is only one use of **ser** that seems to contradict the use of **estar** for dealing with location. The verb **ser** is used to speak of where an event takes place. Most students find it helpful to consider this an example of *identifying* a location rather than saying where that place is (as in an address), as the last three examples show if you read them as a short dialogue.

¿Cómo **estás**?	*How are you?*
Mi oficina **está** en la ciudad.	*My office is in the city.*
¿Dónde **es** la fiesta de María?	*Where is Mary's party?*
Es en casa de José.	*It's at Joe's house.*
¿Dónde **está** la casa de José?	*Where is Joe's house?*

Let's review what is meant when I say that **ser** is used for "everything else." The verb **ser** is used to *identify* a person, place, thing, abstraction, and so forth. Thus, it is the verb needed to identify a person's profession, nationality, race, and religion. It is also used with **de** to show origin, material composition (what something is made of), and possession, corresponding to the English use of *apostrophe + s*. (Note that English uses an indefinite article in the following examples, but Spanish does not.)

Juan **es** médico.	*John is a doctor.*
Elena **es** estudiante.	*Helen is a student.*
Patricio **es** irlandés.	*Patrick is Irish.*
Iván **es** de Rusia.	*Ivan is from Russia.*
Mi suéter **es** de lana.	*My sweater is made of wool.*
Estos libros **son** de mi hermano.	*These books are my brother's.*

The second subdivision involves the use of both **ser** and **estar** as auxiliary or helping verbs. The use of the verb **estar** as a helping verb is often introduced early in many textbooks as the verb that, used with the gerund of another verb, forms the progressive aspect. In English, the progressive is also formed with the *be* verb, plus the English gerund, easily recognized as the *-ing* form. The endings **-ando** (for **-ar** verbs) and **-iendo** (for **-er/-ir** verbs) correspond to the *-ing* form of English, insofar as these are used to form the progressive. Note that the progressive is not used as much in Spanish as it is in English.

The progressive is used in Spanish when one emphasizes the immediacy of an ongoing action (in any tense). If used in the wrong circumstance, it can communicate a sense of urgency that the English usage does not communicate in the same circumstance.

Mi caballo **está cojeando**.	*My horse is limping.*
Esta tarde a las tres, **estaré preparando** la cena.	*This afternoon at three, I will be fixing dinner.*

Now consider this phone conversation. In English, the progressive is used quite routinely. However, if the progressive is used in Spanish, its use would communicate a sense of urgency.

Hola. ¿Qué **estás haciendo**?	*Hi. What are you doing (right now)?*
No mucho, pero, ¿qué pasa?	*Not much, but what's wrong?*

To avoid misunderstandings like this, simply use the present: **¿Qué haces?** This conveys no sense of urgency, as when English speakers casually ask *What are you doing?*

The passive voice

The verb **ser** is used to form the passive voice, which is not used nearly as much in Spanish as it is in English. Most verbs form their passive participles, also known as past participles, quite regularly. The -**ar** verbs drop the infinitive ending and append -**ado** and the -**er** and -**ir** verbs drop their infinitive endings and add -**ido**.

hablar	→hablado
comer	→comido
vivir	→vivido

However, there are a handful of common verbs whose passive participles are irregular:

abrir	abierto	morir	muerto
absolver	absuelto	poner	puesto
cubrir	cubierto	romper	roto
decir	dicho	ver	visto
escribir	escrito	volver	vuelto
hacer	hecho		

Another handful of verbs has two endings: the passive participle, formed regularly and used with **haber** to form the perfect tenses, and an irregular adjectival function. These verbs are:

	VERBAL	ADJECTIVAL
bendecir	bendecido	bendito
confesar	confesado	confeso
convertir	convertido	converso
elegir	elegido	electo
expresar	expresado	expreso
freír	freído	frito
imprimir	imprimido	impreso
reducir	reducido	reducto
suspender	suspendido	suspenso

The following examples contrast the use of the passive and active voice, which is preferred for most situations in Spanish as well as the **se** construction. Spanish frequently employs the **se** construction, also commonly called the pseudo-passive, instead of the true passive voice.

As the following examples show, the active voice reflects the reality in which a subject performs an action, while the passive voice makes the object of the action a grammatical subject and turns the "real" subject into a passive player in the sentence (using the preposition *by*). The **se** construction focuses solely on the action and does not mention the real world subject at all. In addition, note that the passive voice requires the agreement of the participle with its grammatical subject, since it is a *predicate adjective*. It helps to remember that the term *participle* indicates that it sometimes *participates* as a verb, sometimes as an adjective. The last example shows the passive participle in its role as an adjective (i.e., when it is not being used in passive constructions).

Active voice:

Los niños **rompieron** las ventanas.	*The boys broke the windows.*
Él **escribió** la novela.	*He wrote the novel.*

Passive voice:

Las ventanas **fueron rotas** por los niños.	*The windows were broken by the boys.*
La novela **fue escrita** por él.	*The novel was written by him.*

Se construction:
Se rompieron las ventanas.   *The windows broke/got broken.*
Se escribió la novela.   *The novel was written.*

You will learn more about the passive voice in Chapter 18.

Use with adjectives

The third subdivision regarding the usage of **ser** and **estar** deals with the use of these verbs with adjectives. There is one very mistaken idea that I would not mention were it not for the fact that it does not seem to go away in the world of Spanish teaching and learning. I refer to the notion that "**ser** is used with permanent characteristics and **estar** is used with temporary ones." This is misleading and simply not true. Consider the following examples. Their meanings prove the foregoing "rule" to be false:

Jacob Marley **está muerto**.   Jacob Marley is dead.
Juan **es soltero**.   John is single.
María **está casada**.   Mary is married.

Obviously, death is plenty permanent and yet **estar** is the proper verb to use. Then again, although marriages can end in death or divorce, **estar** once again is the proper verb to use when describing someone with regard to these characteristics. It might seem as if the often repeated but incorrect rule has something of a ring of truth about it and the examples above must simply be exceptions, but it is simply missing something important—almost everything changes over time. Over-thinking the choice of verb and trying to use this misleading notion will bring on headaches—and mistakes in Spanish (some of which can be humorous or embarrassing).

Compared with English, Spanish has fewer pure adjectives. The lack is made up by using passive participles, often with **estar** or **tener.** In the following examples, observe how the participles agree with the nouns they modify.

Las tres cartas, **escritas** en español,   *The three letters, written in Spanish, are on*
    están en la mesa.   *the table.*
Mi tío tenía dos carros, **hechos** en   *My uncle had two cars, made in Japan.*
    el Japón.

Ser is used with characterizing adjectives when those adjectives describe something or someone in a normative or identifying way, such as one's physical features, social and economic status, and nationality.

Ellos **son** italianos.   *They are Italians.*
El Sr. Acero **es** mentiroso.   *Mr. Acero is a liar.*
Su hermano **es** comilón.   *His brother is a big eater.*
La nieve **es** blanca.   *Snow is white.*
Juanita **es** pelirroja.   *Jane is a redhead.*
Esos atletas **son** altos y fuertes.   *Those athletes are tall and strong.*

By over-thinking the problem, I refer to the fact that people can change their nationality or their character, habits, or hair color. Snow on the street turns black. Tall athletes will probably not lose much in the way of height over time, but there will come a day when they no longer will be considered robust. Yet the adjectives are considered normative, characterizing and identifying features of the subjects, and therefore **ser** will be used when the adjectives are meant to point to these features as identifying marks.

The verb **estar** is used with adjectives intending to show a *change of state or condition*. In fact, the word *state* derives from the same Latin root as the Spanish verb **estar**, a fact that might help you remember what follows. Thus, when we say **María está casada**, we are showing that the civil status she was born with (single) has changed; it also explains why **ser** is used when we say someone is single—that is everyone's civil status until they change it. Thus:

Juan **es** soltero.	*John is single.*
Ella **está** divorciada.	*She is divorced.*

Now let's consider some other examples of normal usage that are often a bit more challenging: social and economic status, and life and death.

Los gladiadores **están** muertos.	*The gladiators are dead. (the resultant state of combat)*
La Sra. Martínez **es** viuda.	*Mrs. Martínez is a widow. (her social condition)*

But if one says . . .

La Sra. Martínez **está** viuda (ahora).	*Mrs. Martinez is a widow (now).*

. . . it is because her husband has just died and the speaker is showing this recent change of her status. How long will the same speaker use **estar** when describing Mrs. Martínez as a widow? Until he or she comes to think of Mrs. Martínez's new social condition as a settled matter.

The verb **estar** is also used to indicate surprise or an unexpected observation. Imagine the following examples to be about a customer's reaction to the soup in a restaurant. The difference between using this verb and **ser** is that, with **estar**, the speaker is not expecting the soup to be as good as it is; when **ser** is used, he is reporting what he has come to know habitually.

¡La sopa **está** rica!	*The soup is delicious!*
La sopa **es** rica.	*The soup is delicious.*

This usage can also be applied to people. In the next example, imagine that the speaker is an older relative of a young boy whom she has not seen for a couple of years. She shows her surprise at how tall he is. Certainly, his height is not going to revert to what she remembers—the use of **estar** is simply to register her surprise. Soon, she will settle into using **ser** to describe this characteristic.

¡Ay, Jaimito, pero qué grande **estás**!	*Oh my, Jimmy, but how you've grown!*

Now for life and death:

Soy vivo.	*I am alive (as in I am a living person).* or *I am sharp (quick-witted).*

Likewise:

Es un muerto.	*He's a dead man.*

In the previous example, the speaker is identifying someone (a male) as a dead person (i.e., he is among the dead). Watch out though, because in some situations, this is a death threat! Certainly it would be if one said **¡Eres hombre muerto!**, or **¡Eres muerto/a!** You are a dead man/ woman!

But what of this next example?

Estoy vivo.	*I'm alive.*

You would say this if something had threatened that condition, even if you're being humorous, after having a rough day at the office, for instance. It can be used in the same situations as when in English one says "I'm hanging in there."

Finally, some adjectives are used with either **ser** or **estar**—but their meaning changes as a consequence of that choice. Consider these examples:

Juan **está** casado.	*John is married. (a mere observation of his civil status—without any implications at all)*
Juan **es** casado.	*John is a married guy. (he doesn't cheat on his wife)*
Marta **está** cansada.	*Martha is tired.*
Marta **es** cansada.	*Martha is boring.*
El viejo **está** enfermo.	*The old man is sick.*
El viejo **es** enfermo.	*The old man is sickly.*
Juan, ¡**estás** loco!	*John, you've lost your mind!*
Julio **es** loco.	*Julio is a crazy guy (the life of the party).*

Finally, many students find the problem of choosing between **ser** and **estar** compounded when they also face the choice of preterit vs. imperfect. Use the preterit of **estar** when a *specific* time frame or clock time is mentioned. In all other cases, if **estar** is the proper choice, then you'll need the imperfect.

¿Dónde **estabas** cuando te llamé?	*Where were you when I called?*
Estaba de compras cuando me llamaste.	*I was out shopping when you called.*
Ellos **estuvieron** en el museo por tres horas.	*They were in the museum for three hours.*
Estuve trabajando tres días sin dormir.	*I was working for three days without sleep.*
Fui a buscarte en la tienda a las tres pero no estuviste.	*I went to the shop to pick you up at three but you weren't there.*

Saber and conocer

The verb pair **saber** vs. **conocer** deals with *to know*, but in what sense? **Saber** is *to have knowledge of, to possess a command of facts or a body of information*, while **conocer** is *to have familiarity with*, or *to be acquainted with a person, place, or ideas*.

Conozco bien la ciudad de Seattle.	*I know Seattle well.*
Quisiera conocer mejor las obras de Espronceda.	*I'd like to know Espronceda's works better.*
No la **conozco** a ella.	*I don't know her.*
Ella **sabe** la letra de todas las canciones populares.	*She knows the lyrics of all the pop tunes.*

In the preterit, **saber** means *to find out* and **conocer** means *to meet*—not because of anything peculiar about the verbs but because the preterit views past action as an event at a point in time in the past. Hence, if one compresses the notion of knowing facts to a moment, it focuses upon the moment when they became found out. Likewise, if being familiar with someone is compressed to a moment in the past, it can only refer to the moment when the two people met.

| ¿**Conociste** a mi hermano en el baile? | *Did you meet my brother at the dance?* |
| Cuando **supe** lo que el Sr. Acero había hecho, puse el grito en el cielo. | *When I found out what Mr. Acero had done, I hit the ceiling.* |

Additionally, the verb **saber**, when followed by the preposition **a**, means to taste like:

| Esto **sabe** a canela. | *This tastes like cinnamon.* |

Finally, **saber** may be a helping verb. Followed by an infinitive, it means *to know how to do something*. Note that **cómo** is *not* used, although many native speakers of Spanish, if they have been contaminated by English, will often use it. It is proper to use **cómo** when asking how something is done.

Ella **sabe** tocar el piano.	*She knows how to play the piano.*
¿**Sabes** cómo se abre esta lata de anchoas?	*Do you know how to open this can of anchovies?*

Pedir and preguntar

The verb pair **pedir** and **preguntar** causes confusion only because they are too often introduced as meaning *to ask*. Instead, **pedir** means *to ask for* and **preguntar** means *to ask a question*. The whole muddle could be avoided from the outset if **pedir** is introduced as meaning *to request* or *to order* and **preguntar** as meaning *to question*. Interestingly, in Spanish there is no simple verb for *to borrow*, but rather **pedir prestado** (*to ask for something to be lent*).

Después de leer el menú, **pedí** langosta y una copa de champán.	*After reading the menu, I ordered lobster and a glass of champagne.*
Mi hermano me **pidió prestado** cinco dólares.	*My brother borrowed five dollars from me.*
Los chicos le **preguntaron** a su padre por qué el cielo es azul.	*The children asked their father why the sky is blue.*

Criar and crecer

The verb pair **criar** and **crecer** frequently cause confusion even for more advanced learners. This is partly because they sound so much alike, but more importantly because in various ways they involve the notions of growing: growing up, growing physically, and being cared for.

It may seem comical, but the following distinctions seem to help students avoid errors most of the time, even though they are not mutually exclusive differences. For children and animals, the verb to use is **criar**, which means *to raise*. If by *to grow up* you mean *to be raised*, you need **criar**, because *to grow up* doesn't focus on the physical maturing of a person.

Of course, children, animals, and plants also increase in stature, so in such cases, **crecer** is the verb to use. Related to **crecer**, particularly when speaking of plants (but also of a person's education), is the verb **cultivar**. It also is a friendly cognate.

Los padres de Juanito lo **criaron** bien, pues tiene buenos modales.	*Johnny's parents raised him well, he has such good manners.*
El maíz **crece** muy rápido en los calurosos meses del verano.	*Corn grows very quickly in the hot summer months.*
Los adolescentes parecen **crecer** ante los ojos.	*Teenagers seem to grow before your eyes.*
En Hawaii, se **cultivan** orquídeas exóticas.	*In Hawaii, they grow exotic orchids.*
Es importante descubrir y **cultivar** los talentos naturales.	*It is important to discover and cultivate your innate talents.*

Salir and dejar

The verb pair **salir** and **dejar** are often introduced with the primary meanings of *to leave* and *leave behind*. It is best, however, to translate **salir** as *to exit*. It is always followed by the preposition **de**, which helps recall its meaning as *to exit from*. Moreover, **dejar**, followed by an infinitive, means *to allow* (to do something). These two verbs also form an interesting constellation of uses, in part due to associated uses of the curious auxiliary verb **acabar de** + infinitive, which translates as *to have just*, and also to the uses of **dejar de** + infinitive which means *to quit* (doing something). Let's examine the various uses of these verbs.

Mi amigo **salió** del cuarto de baño.	*My friend came out of the restroom.*
Mi amigo **dejó** sus llaves en el cuarto de baño.	*My friend left his keys in the restroom.*
Los padres de mi amigo no lo **dejaron** ir a la fiesta de Juana.	*My friend's parents didn't let him go to Jane's party.*
Mi amigo **dejó** de fumar.	*My friend quit smoking.*
Mi amigo **acaba** de salir del cuarto de baño.	*My friend just came out of the restroom.*

Finally, just as we've seen how there is no simple Spanish verb for *to borrow*, there is no simple verb meaning *to drop*. The phrase **dejar caer** is used—literally, *to allow to fall*.

Cuando abrió la puerta, mi amiga **dejó caer** los libros.	*When my friend opened the door, she dropped the books.*

Mover(se) and mudarse

Finally, the verbs **mover(se)** and **mudarse** are often confused because **mover** is a false cognate when one refers to changing abodes. The verb **mover** means *to move*—but in the sense of moving an object, such as a pencil. In the reflexive, it means *to move about*, as in doing exercises or dancing.

The verb for changing one's residence is exclusively **mudarse**—and it is always reflexive in this usage. The verb **mudar** is often used with the preposition **de** when referring to changing one's clothes, opinions, and so forth. It is also the verb used to refer to a reptile *moulting* (changing skin) and even for when a child *changes* his or her baby teeth for permanent ones: **mudar los dientes**—and it is *not* reflexive when used in these latter senses.

**EJERCICIO
5·13**

Match each English verb with its corresponding Spanish translation.

_____ 1. to request/order   a. estar

_____ 2. to know (math)/find out/taste like   b. mover

_____ 3. to move (residence)   c. cultivar

_____ 4. to leave/exit   d. dejar

_____ 5. to know/meet   e. mudarse

_____ 6. to be (a doctor, a student)   f. ser

_____ 7. to raise (a child or animals) g. crecer

_____ 8. to leave behind/allow   h. pedir

_____ 9. to question   i. saber

_____ 10. to be (well/in a place)   j. conocer

_____ 11. to raise (corn)/develop (a talent)   k. preguntar

_____ 12. to move (a box)   l. criar

_____ 13. to grow   m. salir

Translate the following sentences from Spanish to English.

1. Mi amigo ruso sabe mucho de la física y la astronomía.

   _____

2. Ese libro fue impreso en Barcelona.

   _____

3. El centro comercial no está precisamente en el centro de la ciudad.

   _____

4. En este momento, estoy sentado ante la computadora, escribiendo esto.

   _____

5. Ya tengo la carta escrita para el jefe.

   _____

6. ¿Estás bien, chico? Te ves preocupado.

   _____

Translate the following sentences from English to Spanish.

1. Do you know Mary well?

   _____

2. He's boring.

   _____

3. José is Mexican.

   _____

4. This is a silk (**seda**) dress.

   _____

5. The party is on the beach.

   _____

6. This is my father's car.

   _____

7. Are you tired? (**Uds.**) (*don't* use **sueño**)

_____

8. Julius Caesar is dead.

_____

9. You have just finished this exercise. (**tú**)

_____

Expressing opininions, likes, and dislikes

First let's look at a sample dialogue that talks about expressing opinions.

Conversation: Getting acquainted

LAURA: Hola, ¿eres Sara? Soy Laura.¡Por fin nos conocemos! **Como** vamos a compartir el apartamento este semestre, **espero que** seamos compatibles.

Hi, are you Sara? I'm Laura. Finally we meet! Since we're going to share the room this semester, I hope we'll get along OK.

SARA: Yo también lo espero. Veo por tu camiseta que eres aficionada de béisbol, pues ¡yo también!

I hope so, too. I see from your tee shirt that you're a baseball fan—I am too!

LAURA: Bueno, la camiseta me la regaló mi hermano, que es beisbolista. Mira que en la parte de atrás, tiene la foto de todos los jugadores de su equipo. Imagínate que ganaron el campeonato de nuestra ciudad este verano.

Well, the tee shirt was a present from my brother, who's a baseball player. Look on the back—it has a photo of all the players on his team. They actually won the city championship this summer.

SARA: ¡Fantástico! Te digo que aunque no soy muy atlética, **me encanta** ver béisbol, **ya sea** un partido entre dos escuelas o uno profesional. Soy más bien una espectadora que deportista. Y tú, ¿juegas algún deporte?

Fantastic! I tell you, although I'm not very athletic, I love to watch baseball, whether it's a game between two schools or a professional one. I'm more of a spectator than an athlete. And you, do you play a sport?

LAURA: Sí, juego al tenis. **De hecho** tengo una beca y voy a jugar para la universidad. Ahora dime tú, ¿qué más **te gusta** hacer?

Yes, I play tennis. As a matter of fact, I have a scholarship and I'm going to play for the university. Now, tell me, what else do you like to do?

SARA: Lo que más **me gusta** es bailar. Soy estudiante de baile clásico, pero también **me gustan** la salsa y el merengue y claro, todo lo que se baila en las discotecas.

What I like to do best is dance. I'm studying classical ballet, but I also like salsa, merengue, and of course, everything you dance at the discos.

LAURA: Entonces, tendremos que salir este mismo fin de semana para explorar los clubs de la ciudad.

Then we have to go out this weekend to check out the clubs in this city.

SARA:	¡Y los restaurantes! **A propósito** de eso, ¿tienes hambre? Dicen que hay una excelente cocina internacional aquí. ¿**Qué te parece** si vamos ahora mismo al restaurante mexicano en la esquina para probar los tacos y charlar más?	*And the restaurants! Speaking of which, are you hungry? They say there's wonderful international cuisine here. How about going right now to the Mexican restaurant on the corner to try their tacos and talk some more?*
LAURA:	Ah, me encantaría. A mí **me gusta** mucho la cocina mexicana, sobre todo la picante. En realidad, me fascinan todas las comidas de otros países.	*Oh, I'd love to. I like Mexican food a lot, especially the hot stuff. Actually, I love all ethnic food.*
SARA:	Parece que nos vamos a llevar muy bien. ¡No te imaginas lo contenta que estoy!	*It looks like we're going to get along really well. You can't imagine how happy I am!*

Más tarde:

SARA:	Laura, ¿**qué te parece** la decoración de nuestro cuarto?	*Laura, what do you think of the décor of our room?*
LAURA:	**Para serte sincera**, realmente no **soporto** ese color oscuro de las paredes. Prefiero los tonos claros. **Por otra parte**, quisiera cambiar la alfombra y las cubrecamas. ¿A ti **te gustan**?	*To be honest, I really can't stand that dark color on the walls. I prefer light colors. Plus, I'd like to change the rug and the bedspreads. Do you like them?*
SARA:	No, estoy de acuerdo contigo. Con una buena pintura y unos pequeños cambios, este cuarto estará mucho más cómodo y acogedor.	*No, I agree with you. With a good paint job and a few changes, this room will be much more comfortable and cozy.*

Esperar que

Esperar que followed by the subjunctive means *to hope that something happens* or *somebody else does something.*

Esperamos que nuestro equipo gane el partido.	*We hope our team wins the game.*
Ella **espera que** vayas a la reunión.	*She hopes you go to the meeting.*

When someone hopes to do something himself or herself, use an infinitive after **esperar** instead of the subjunctive.

Esperamos ganar el partido.	*We hope we win the game.*
Espero ir a la reunión.	*I hope to go to the meeting.*

Other verbs used like this include **querer**, **preferir**, **necesitar**, **gustar**, **molestar**, and others.

Quiero que me acompañes.	*I want you to go with me.*
No **quiero** ir sola.	*I don't want to go alone.*
Prefieren que no hablemos.	*They would rather that we didn't talk.*
Prefieren hablar ellos.	*They prefer to talk./They would rather do all the talking.*
Me gusta que siempre llegues a clase a tiempo.	*I like it that you always come to class on time.*
Me gusta ir a tu casa.	*I like to go to your house.*

Necesitamos que nos ayudes.	*We need you to help us.*
Le molesta que hagan ruido.	*It bothers him that they make noise.*

Esperar can also mean *to wait.*

Espérame aquí.	*Wait for me here.*

Como

Como means *since* in the sense of *because.*

Como eres muy joven, no puedes ir con nosotros.	*Since you're so young, you can't come with us.*

Como has a number of other meanings.

◆ It is translated as *how* when used with **estar** and action verbs.

¿**Cómo** estás?	*How are you?*
No sé **cómo** haces eso.	*I don't know how you do that.*

◆ It is translated as *what . . . like* when used with **ser**.

¿**Cómo** eres?	*What are you like?*

◆ It can mean *like* in the sense of *approximately/about/more or less.*

Ella tiene **como** treinta años.	*She's like thirty years old./She's about thirty years old.*

◆ And it can mean *just like.*

Eres **como** una hermana para mí.	*You're just like a sister to me.*

Desde

Desde means *since* in the sense of time.

Te estoy esperando **desde** las siete.	*I've been waiting for you since seven o'clock.*

Ya sea

Sea is the present subjunctive form of **ser**. With **ya,** it can be translated as *whether*, in the sense of *whatever, whenever, whoever, however.*

Me puedes visitar cuando quieras, **ya sea** por la mañana, por la tarde o por la noche.	*You can visit me when(ever) you want, whether it's in the morning, in the afternoon, or at night.*
Invita a quien quieras, **ya sea** un chico o una chica.	*Invite whomever you wish, whether it's a boy or a girl.*

O sea

This is a common expression—so common that it is often used as a "crutch," like *you know* or *I mean*. But it has a real function as well—to put something in different words to make it clearer.

Vengan temprano, **o sea,** a las ocho o las nueve.

Come early, in other words, at eight or nine.

De hecho

De hecho is one of a number of conversational markers that can be translated as *actually* or *as a matter of fact*. However, its function is limited to introducing a fact that serves as an example of what was just said. It's easy to translate this into English, but much trickier use it correctly in Spanish. Think of **de hecho** as meaning *as proven by the fact that . . . .*

Mi papá es muy generoso conmigo. **De hecho,** puedo comprar toda la ropa que quiera.

My dad is very generous with me. As a matter of fact, I can buy all the clothes I want.

Ella es como parte de la familìa. **De hecho,** celebra todos los festivos con nosotros.

She is like family. As a matter of fact, she celebrates all the holidays with us.

A propósito

This expression is used to add information to a conversation that relates to something said, but in a different context. It can be translated as *speaking of which . . . .*

Tenemos que ir de compras para buscar un regalo para Carlos. Su fiesta de cumpleaños es mañana.

We have to go shopping to get a present for Carlos. His birthday party is tomorrow.

A propósito, ¿sabes si los niños están invitados?

Speaking of which, do you know if the kids are invited?

¿Qué te parece?

This is a way of asking someone's impression, feeling, or opinion about something. Literally it's *How does this seem to you?*

¿Qué te/le parece este cuadro?

What do you think of this painting?

(A mí) me gusta mucho/no me gusta/ me encanta/me parece muy feo.

I like it/I don't like it/I love it/I think it's really ugly.

¿Qué te parece si... ? can be translated as *How about if we . . ./Do you think it would be a good idea to . . . ?*

¿Qué te parece si llamamos a Carolina?

How about if we call Carolina?

¿Qué te parece si le compramos un osito de peluche?

Do you think it would be a good idea to buy her a Teddy bear?

Gustar and similar verbs

A number of verbs are used in Spanish with indirect object pronouns to indicate the effect of something or someone on somebody else. To use these verbs correctly, think about their literal translations into English, rather than their more natural translations. Remember that the subject of the sentence is the person or thing that *causes* the opinion or feeling, and the verb conjugation agrees with this subject. The person affected is indicated by the indirect object pronoun.

Me gusta la casa.

The house appeals to me. (I like the house.)

Me gusta Fernando.

Fernando appeals to me. (I like Fernando.)

A Ana le importan sus estudios.	*Her studies are important to Ana. (Ana cares about her studies.)*
A Ana le importas tú.	*You are important to Ana. (Ana cares about you.)*
Le fascinan las comedias.	*Comedies fascinate him. (He loves comedies.)*
Me fascinan Fernando y Tomás.	*Fernando and Tomás fascinate me. (I'm fascinated by Fernando and Tomás.)*

When the subject is a *thing* (rather than a *person*), it requires an article, whether it is singular or plural.

Me gusta **el** chocolate.	*I like chocolate.*
Me gustan **los** chocolates.	*I like chocolates.*

When using these verbs, a subject pronoun (**yo, tú, él, ella, nosotros, ustedes, ellos**) can replace the subject if it is a person or people, but it is omitted when the subject is a *thing*. Never use direct object pronouns with these verbs. (**Lo** and **la** can mean *it* in other places, but not here!)

Te gusta **el chocolate**?	*Does chocolate appeal to you?*
Sí, me gusta.	*Yes, it appeals to me. (Yes, I like it.)*
¿Te gusta **Fernando**?	*Does Fernando appeal to you?*
Sí me gusta **él.**	*Yes, he appeals to me. (Yes, I like him.)*

You can use the third person singular of this type of verb plus an infinitive to indicate that you *like to, love to,* or *don't like to* do something.

Me gusta esquiar.	*I like to ski. (Skiing appeals to me.)*
Me encanta tocar la guitarra.	*I love to play the guitar. (Playing the guitar enchants me.)*
No me gusta levantarme temprano.	*I don't like to get up early. (Getting up early doesn't appeal to me.)*

Other verbs used like this include:

molestar	*bother*
fastidiar	*annoy*
impresionar	*impress*
importar	*be important to*
doler	*hurt*
entristecer	*sadden*
aburrir	*bore*

Para serte sincero, -a

This expression is used to preface a statement that may seem a little uncomfortable, exactly like *to be honest with you.*

Tengo dos entradas para el concierto esta noche. ¿Quieres ir?	*I have two tickets to the concert tonight. Do you want to go?*
Para serte sincero, no soy aficionado de ese grupo. No me gusta su música.	*To be honest, I'm not a fan of that group. I don't like their music.*

Soportar

This is a real **falso amigo**—it does not mean *to support*, but rather *to tolerate*.

No quiero ir a la reunión. **No soporto** la actitud de ciertos colegas nuestros.

I don't want to go to the meeting. I can't stand the attitude of some of our coworkers.

To support can be expressed by several different verbs, each with a different function: **mantener, apoyar,** and **sostener.**

Mantener

Mantener means *to provide a living for someone.*

No sé cómo esa mujer **mantiene** a su familia con tan poco dinero.

I don't know how that woman supports her family on so little money.

Apoyar

Apoyar means *to provide moral or physical support.*

Mis padres **apoyan** mi decisión.
Apóyame, por favor. Se me ha torcido el tobillo.

My parents support my decision.
Hold me up, please. I've twisted my ankle.

Sostener

Sostener can mean *to give physical support,* and also *to maintain a position on something.*

Esta silla antigua **no sostiene** tanto peso.
El alcalde **sostiene** que los profesores merecen un incremento de sueldo.

This old chair won't support that much weight.
The mayor maintains that teachers deserve a salary increase.

Por otra parte

Por otra parte is used to give additional back-up to a positive argument. It can be translated as *in addition, plus,* or *furthermore.*

Esta casa es perfecta para nosotros. Tiene mucho espacio, un jardín lindo y está cerca del centro. **Por otra parte,** está en un buen distrito escolar.

This house is perfect for us. It has a lot of space, a nice yard, and it's close to town. Plus, it's in a good school district.

If you want to give the meaning of *on the other hand*—indicating a contrasting argument—you need to precede it with **pero**.

Me gusta la casa y estoy de acuerdo en que tiene muchas ventajas. **Pero por otra parte**, está muy lejos de mi trabajo.

I like the house and I agree that it has a lot of advantages. On the other hand, it's a long way from where I work.

Quisiera

Quisiera is an imperfect subjunctive form (see the Verb Tables) that can be used instead of **quiero** for the sake of politeness or to indicate a wish that may seem impossible.

Quisiera una reservación para el 12 de marzo.	*I would like a reservation for the 12th of March.*
Quisiéramos ir en un crucero al Caribe.	*We would like to go on a Caribbean cruise.*

Another way to express this is by using the conditional form (see the Verb Tables) of **gustar**, **encantar**, or **fascinar**.

Nos gustaría/encantaría ir en un crucero al Caribe.	*We would like/love to go on a Caribbean cruise.*
Cómo **me encantaría** volver a mi país para los festejos.	*Oh, how I'd love to go back to my country for the holidays.*
A mi mamá **le fascinaría** esta película.	*My mother would love this movie.*

This form is a polite way of making an invitation—or accepting one.

¿Le gustaría bailar?	*Would you like to dance?*
Sí, **me encantaría.**	*Yes, I'd love to.*

EJERCICIO
5·16

*Choose between **como** and **desde** to complete the following.*

1. Estudio español _____ hace cinco años.

2. _____ hablas tan bien español, ¡vamos a México!

3. Tenemos _____ una hora para hacer las compras.

4. ¿_____ es tu amiga?

5. ¿_____ cuándo trabajas en esta empresa?

6. ¿Sabe usted _____ se dice eso en inglés?

7. Ella baila _____ una caribeña.

8. _____ que vivo aquí, tengo trabajo.

9. _____ vivo aquí, voy a buscar trabajo.

10. Estaré aquí _____ a las ocho.

EJERCICIO
5·17

Choose from the following combinations of words to complete each sentence.

para ti o para tu amiga

aquí o en tu país

con un hombre o con una mujer

hoy o mañana

1. Llámame cuando quieras, ya sea _____.

2. Quiero vivir donde tú estés, ya sea _____.

3. Venga a la boda con quien quieras, ya sea _____.

4. Compra lo que te guste, ya sea _____.

Circle the most appropriate word or expression to complete each sentence.

1. Sus padres apoyan su plan de estudiar medicina, _____ van a mantenerlo mientras estudia.

   por otra parte   a propósito   de hecho   para serte sincero

2. Pepe, estoy muy emocionada con la idea de comprar la casa que vimos hoy.

   Cariño, _____, no me gusta esa casa.

   o sea   para serte sincero   de hecho   por otra parte

3. Lo que no me gusta de esa casa es que me parece pequeña, necesita muchas reparaciones

   y _____, está muy lejos de la ciudad.

   por otra parte   de hecho   para serte sincero   o sea

4. A mí me encanta el grupo Los Cuates. _____ de eso, ¿te gustaría ir a verlos?

   Por otra parte   A propósito   O sea   Para serte sincero

5. Somos muy buenas amigas, _____, ella es como una hermana para mí.

   para serte sincera   a propósito   o sea   por otra parte

Fill in each blank with the correct pronoun.

1. A mí _____ encantan estos guantes.

2. ¿A ti _____ gusta mi nuevo vestido?

3. A mis padres no _____ molesta el ruido.

4. A mi prima y a mí _____ fascina el cine.

5. ¿A ustedes _____ parece una buena idea ir al cine?

6. ¿A vosotros _____ parece una buena idea ir al cine?

7. A tus hermanos _____ gustan estas galletas.

8. A Carlos no _____ gustan las clases de baile.

Gustar, **ser**, and **estar** and expressing opinions   **91**

Fill in each blank with the correct form of the verb indicated.

1. A Carmen le (encantar) _____ los bailes.

2. No nos (parecer) _____ justo.

3. A mí no me (gustar) _____ las ensaladas que sirven aquí.

4. ¿Qué les (parecer) _____ estas fotos?

5. ¿Te (gustar) _____ los dulces?

6. Creo que a Jorge le (gustar) _____ tú.

7. Tú me (importar) _____ mucho.

8. ¿Te (importar) _____ yo?

Match all the possible items from the right column that can complete the expressions in the left column.

1. _____ Me gusta _____.   a. bailar

2. _____ Le fascinan _____.   b. el ruido

3. _____ Nos encantan _____.   c. la música

4. _____ Les molesta _____.   d. las fiestas

5. _____ Me importas _____.   e. la clase

6. _____ ¿Te gustan _____?   f. muy bonito

7. _____ ¿Les gusta _____?   g. tú

8. _____ ¿Te importo _____?   h. mi hermano

9. _____ Me parece _____.   i. las flores

                                                                     j. él

                                                                      k. yo

                                                                      l. viajar

¿Cómo se dice en inglés? *Translate each sentence into English.*

1. Su actitud me molesta.

_____

2. Les encanta jugar básquetbol.

_____

3. ¿Qué les parece?

_____

4. ¿Te gusta ir al cine?

_____

5. Le fastidian los niños.

_____

6. Me entristece la noticia.

_____

7. Nos aburre la clase.

_____

8. Tú me importas mucho.

_____

¿Cómo se dice en español? *Translate each sentence into Spanish.*

1. I love to go to the beach.

_____

2. His ideas fascinate her.

_____

3. She doesn't like the noise.

_____

4. She likes you.

_____

5. His classes bore him.

_____

6. I love guitar music.

_____

7. We like horror movies.

_____

8. They love to go shopping.

_____

9. I think it's ugly. (It seems ugly to me.)

_____

10. We like it.

_____

Circle the most appropriate word to complete each sentence.

1. No estoy trabajando ahora, así que mis padres me _____.
   soportan   mantienen   apoyan   sostienen

2. Ella tiene muchos datos que _____ su tesis.
   sostienen   soportan   mantienen   apoyan

3. Mis padres _____ mi decisión de hacer un semestre en el extranjero.
   mantienen   soportan   apoyan   sostienen

4. No me gusta esa película porque yo no _____ la violencia.
   mantengo   soporto   apoyo   sostengo

Adjectives, adverbs, and comparisons

Adjectives

Adjectives have different functions according to the role they play relative to the word they modify. One function is to limit or determine a noun. Adjectives in this category are demonstrative and possessive adjectives.

Mi reloj no funciona.	*My watch is not working.*
Esta rosa tiene un perfume fuerte.	*This rose has a strong fragrance.*

Another function associated with adjectives is complementing nouns, completing their meanings with various characteristics and qualities.

¿No quieres ese bolso **grande** y **barato**?	*Don't you want that **big**, **inexpensive** bag?*

Sometimes the role of adjectives is to specify the noun.

Quiero un auto **alemán**.	*I want a **German** car.*

The meaning of **auto** is made more precise by the adjective of nationality **alemán**. Note that, with some exceptions, descriptive adjectives in Spanish generally follow the nouns they modify. You will learn more about the placement of adjectives later in this unit.

Gender and number of adjectives in Spanish

Adjectives must agree in gender and number with the noun or pronoun they modify; therefore, adjectives are either feminine or masculine, singular or plural, according to the nouns they modify. Here are some gender and number rules for adjectives:

◆ Masculine adjectives that end in **-o** drop the **-o** and add **-a** for the feminine forms. To form the plural, both masculine and feminine, add **-s** to the singular ending.

SINGULAR	PLURAL
buen**o**, buen**a** (*good*)	buen**os**, buen**as**
perezos**o**, perezos**a** (*lazy*)	perezos**os**, perezos**as**
precios**o**, precios**a** (*precious*)	precios**os**, precios**as**

95

Esta camisa **negra** es de Italia. *This **black** shirt is from Italy.*
Los zapatos **rojos** son de España. *The **red** shoes are from Spain.*

♦ Numerous adjectives in Spanish have a single form for the masculine and feminine. If the adjective ends in **-e**, add **-s** for the plural. If it ends in a consonant, add **-es**.

SINGULAR	PLURAL
débi**l** (*weak*)	débile**s**
perseverant**e** (*persevering*)	perseverante**s**

una personalidad *agradable*	*a pleasant personality*
un cuento *interesante*	*an interesting story*
películas *populares*	*popular movies*
un vino *francés* **y pasteles** *franceses*	*French wine and French pastries*
un auto *veloz* **y unos botes** *veloces*	*a fast car and some fast boats*

A few spelling rules: Note that some adjectives may drop or add an accent mark when they are changed from singular to plural and vice versa. Adjectives of nationality are not capitalized. Remember to change **z** to **c** before adding the -**es** plural ending.

Here are some adjectives that have the same form in the masculine and feminine.

agradable	*pleasant*	**feliz**	*happy*	**natural**	*natural*
azul	*blue*	**fuerte**	*strong*	**optimista**	*optimistic*
carmesí	*red*	**gris**	*gray*	**pesimista**	*pessimistic*
difícil	*difficult, hard*	**inferior**	*inferior*	**realista**	*realistic*
fácil	*easy, simple*	**interesante**	*interesting*	**triste**	*unhappy*
fatal	*fatal*	**mediocre**	*mediocre*	**verde**	*green*

EJERCICIO
6·1

Práctica. ¿Masculino o femenino? Give the appropriate form of the adjective in parentheses.

1. dolor (agudo) _____

2. patio (grande) _____

3. avión (viejo) _____

4. casa (fabuloso) _____

5. viaje (interminable) _____

6. suspiro (*sigh*) (profundo) _____

7. mesa (redondo) _____

8. rumor (malicioso) _____

EJERCICIO
6·2

¿Masculino o femenino? ¿Singular o plural? Give the appropriate form of the adjective in parentheses.

1. Tina prefiere la ropa _____ (elegante).

2. Manuel compra unas camisas _____ (raro).

3. Hay programas _____ (violento) en la tele.

4. Estos actores _____ (popular) no quieren firmar autógrafos.

5. Venden pendientes (*earrings*) _____ (azul).

6. ¿No has visto mi foto _____ (preferido)?

7. Prefiero el clima _____ (cálido).

8. Siempre me regalan corbatas _____ (feo) el día de mi cumpleaños.

En español. Translate each phrase into Spanish and place the adjective where it belongs.

1. a beautiful day _____

2. a sad morning _____

3. a big hand _____

4. a pleasant aroma _____

5. a long song _____

6. a deep sleep _____

7. a sincere friend (*f.*) _____

8. a dedicated nurse _____

9. an interesting city _____

10. a difficult language _____

11. a terrible explosion _____

12. a brave soldier _____

More about adjectives and their endings

◆ To form the feminine of adjectives ending in **-án**, **-dor**, and **-ón**, add **-a** to the masculine form.

Note that the accent mark is not used in the feminine endings **-ana** and **-ona**. The plural of these adjectives is formed by adding **-es** to the masculine forms and **-s** to the feminine ending.

SINGULAR	PLURAL
charlat**án**/charlat**ana** (*talkative*)	charlatan**es**/charlatan**as**
glot**ón**/glot**ona** (*gluttonous*)	gloton**es**/gloton**as**
pelead**or**/pelead**ora** (*feisty, aggressive*)	peleador**es**/peleador**as**

Mi hermana es muy **habladora**.   *My sister is very **chatty**.*

◆ Adjectives of nationality that end in **-o** drop the masculine ending and add **-a** to the feminine form. They are not capitalized in Spanish.

SINGULAR	PLURAL
mexican**o**/mexican**a** (*Mexican*)	mexican**os**/mexican**as**
peruan**o**/peruan**a** (*Peruvian*)	peruan**os**/peruan**as**

- Many adjectives of nationality have other endings such as **-a**, **-án**, **-és**, **-ense**, and **-í**. These endings are both feminine and masculine.

Estos chocolates son **belgas**.	*These chocolates are **Belgian**.*
El idioma **catalán** se habla en Cataluña.	*The **Catalan** language is spoken in Catalonia.*
La nación **costarricense** es admirada por su tradición democrática.	*The **Costa Rican** nation is admired for its democratic tradition.*

- Use the masculine plural for an adjective that modifies a group of two or more nouns where at least one noun is masculine and one or more is feminine.

¿Adónde vas con el vestido y la chaqueta **viejos**?	*Where are you going with the **old** dress and jacket?*

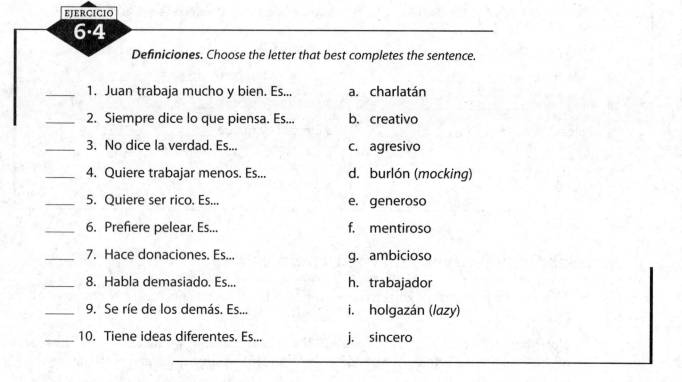

EJERCICIO
6·4

Definiciones. Choose the letter that best completes the sentence.

_____ 1.	Juan trabaja mucho y bien. Es...	a. charlatán
_____ 2.	Siempre dice lo que piensa. Es...	b. creativo
_____ 3.	No dice la verdad. Es...	c. agresivo
_____ 4.	Quiere trabajar menos. Es...	d. burlón (*mocking*)
_____ 5.	Quiere ser rico. Es...	e. generoso
_____ 6.	Prefiere pelear. Es...	f. mentiroso
_____ 7.	Hace donaciones. Es...	g. ambicioso
_____ 8.	Habla demasiado. Es...	h. trabajador
_____ 9.	Se ríe de los demás. Es...	i. holgazán (*lazy*)
_____ 10.	Tiene ideas diferentes. Es...	j. sincero

Where are adjectives placed in Spanish?

The position of adjectives in Spanish is related to the information they provide about the noun they modify. Adjectives that add information or describe qualities generally *follow* the noun. However, there are exceptions to this rule:

- Descriptive adjectives that emphasize intrinsic characteristics are placed before the noun.

El **fiero** león pasea por la selva.	*The **ferocious** lion wanders in the jungle.*

These adjectives stress certain inherent qualities. They appear more frequently in written Spanish and in literary style.

- Limiting adjectives, adjectives that indicate numbers and amounts, and possessive and demonstrative adjectives are placed before the noun.

Queremos **dos** helados.	*We want **two** ice creams.*
Hoy hay **menos** nieve.	*Today there is **less** snow.*

Mis problemas no son **tus** problemas.   *My problems are not **your** problems.*
Este edificio tiene **cuatro** ascensores.   *This building has **four** elevators.*

See Chapter 13 for the study of possessive and demonstrative adjectives and Chapter 23 for numbers.

Adjectives that indicate numbers and amounts are called indefinidos when they do not designate specific numbers or amounts of things, people, or ideas.

Here is a list of common adjectives of quantity, with their corresponding gender and number forms. Note that some have the same ending for both masculine and feminine.

algún/alguna/algunos/algunas	*some*
bastante/bastantes	*enough*
cuanto/cuanta/cuantos/cuantas	*as much*
mucho/mucha/muchos/muchas	*many*
ningún/ninguna/ningunos/ningunas	*no, not any*
poco/poca/pocos/pocas	*few*
suficiente/suficientes	*sufficient*
varios/varias	*various, few*

EJERCICIO
6·5

Place the adjective that appears in parentheses before or after the noun is needed.

1. El director trae _____ informes _____ para sus empleados. (algún)

2. El director y el productor hablan de _____ temas _____. (filosófico)

3. No vamos a tomar _____ decisiones _____ antes de las cinco. (mucho)

4. En esta película, Cenicienta no compra _____ zapatillas _____ para ir a la fiesta. (ningún)

5. Esta película no va a ganar _____ premio _____ en el festival de cine. (ningún)

6. Esto va a ser un _____ proyecto _____ para nosotros. (difícil)

Here is another group of adjectives that usually *precede* the noun:

◆ Adjectives that change meaning according to their position relative to the noun they modify. Placing these adjectives before the noun usually underscores an opinion, whether or not it is shared by others. Compare the change of meaning in the following examples:

Don Quijote es una **gran** novela.   Don Quixote *is a **great** novel.*
Viven en una casa **grande**.   *They live in a **large** house.*

Few would doubt calling *Don Quixote* a great novel. Placing the adjective before the noun emphasizes the significance of this work of art. In the second example, **grande**, following the noun, describes the size of the house. If we placed **grande** before **casa**, the meaning would change, and we would perceive a great house, adding the idea of "wonderful" or "famous" to the notion of size.

The following list includes other commonly used adjectives that change meaning according to their position with respect to the noun they modify:

ADJECTIVE	ENGLISH EQUIVALENT	
	BEFORE A NOUN	AFTER A NOUN
antiguo, -a, -os, -as	former	ancient
cierto, -a, -os, -as	(a) certain	sure
cualquier	any	any (old) . . .
grande	great	large
mismo, -a, -os, -as	same	himself, herself
nuevo, -a, -os, -as	different	new
puro, -a, -os, -as	nothing but	pure
simple	simple, easy	unsophisticated
único, -a, -os, -as	only	unique
viejo, -a, -os, -as	an old (time) . . .	old

Use **gran** and **cualquier**, the shortened forms of **grande** and **cualquiera**, before singular feminine and masculine nouns.

EJERCICIO
6·6

En español.

1. This comedy is unique; it is outstanding (**fuera de serie**)! _____

_____

2. My old friend Manolito writes the script (**el guión**). _____

_____

3. A former colleague comes to the theater to watch the comedy. _____

_____

4. The main character (**el protagonista**) is a simple man. _____

_____

5. Manolito always uses new ideas. _____

_____

6. Any person who comes to the theater will pay five dollars. _____

_____

Other adjective forms used before nouns: The shortened forms

When they precede the noun, certain adjectives have shortened forms, that is, the masculine forms of several adjectives drop the **-o** ending when they are immediately followed by a masculine noun.

Si me ayudas eres un **buen amigo**.
Eres un **amigo bueno** si me ayudas. } *If you help me, you are a **good friend**.*

The following list includes the basic adjectives and their shortened forms in context:

alguno (*some*)	**algún libro** (*some book*)
bueno (*good*)	**buen consejo** (*good advice*)
malo (*bad*)	**mal ejemplo** (*bad example*)
ninguno (*no, not any*)	**ningún soldado** (*no soldier*)
primero (*first*)	**el primer capítulo** (*the first chapter*)
tercero (*third*)	**el tercer año** (*the third year*)
uno (*a, an, one*)	**un poema** (*a poem*)

Note the accent mark on the shortened forms **algún** and **ningún**. Remember that **cien** and **ciento** are adjectives of quantity:

- ◆ **Cien** is used for the number *one hundred* before a plural noun (masculine or feminine).

Tengo solamente **cien dólares** en el bolsillo.	*I only have **one hundred dollars** in my pocket.*
La Casa de Representantes quiere **cien mil millones**.	*The House of Representatives wants **one hundred billion**.*

- ◆ **Ciento** appears in numbers 101 and higher.

Hay **ciento noventa y nueve** sillas en este salón.	*There are **one hundred and ninety-nine** chairs in this room.*

- ◆ **San**, the shortened form of the adjective **Santo**, is used with all masculine names of saints. Exceptions are **Santo Domingo** and **Santo Tomás**.

San Francisco es una ciudad en California.	***San Francisco** is a city in California.*

EJERCICIO
6·7

Y en tu caso... ¿Verdadero (V) o falso (F)?

_____ 1. Celebro el primer día del año, el Año Nuevo, en mi casa.

_____ 2. Ahora tengo ciento cincuenta dólares en mi billetera.

_____ 3. Hay algunos extraterrestres entre nosotros.

_____ 4. Si los padres fuman delante de los niños dan un mal ejemplo.

_____ 5. No termino de leer el primer capítulo si la novela es aburrida.

¿Dónde están los adjetivos? *Identify the adjectives in each sentence.*

1. El viajero portugués trae un pasaporte vencido (*expired*).

2. El tercer año en la universidad es difícil y largo.

3. Han pasado tres meses.

4. Pablo Neruda, el gran poeta chileno, es un personaje curioso en una película italiana.

5. ¿Quién es el cantante famoso de San Juan?

Preguntas personales. *In your answers, place the adjectives in the appropriate place.*

1. ¿Tienes algunos amigos en otros países? _____

2. ¿Cuantas ciudades de los Estados Unidos conoces? _____

3. ¿Qué programas cómicos te gustan? _____

4. ¿Tienes un(-a) poeta favorito(a)? ¿Cómo se llama? _____

5. ¿Has visitado el Viejo San Juan, en Puerto Rico? _____

6. ¿Quieres un coche nuevo o un nuevo coche? _____

Other considerations about the position of adjectives

More than one adjective can modify a noun. The rules for placement you have already learned still apply.

◆ Two or more adjectives may follow the noun and are usually linked by a conjunction or separated by a comma.

No es **impaciente o consentida**.	*She is not **impatient or spoiled**.*
Tiene un perro **simpático y pequeño**.	*He/She has a **pleasant, small** dog.*
El viaje fue **largo, tedioso**.	*The trip was **long, tedious**.*

◆ If, according to the rules, one of the adjectives precedes the noun, it remains in place. This applies to shortened forms or an adjective that conveys a different meaning when placed before the noun.

Vivían en un **gran** castillo **medieval**.	*They used to live in a **grand medieval** castle.*

En español. Place the adjectives in their appropriate places.

1. He is courteous and generous. _____

2. We hear a loud and clear noise. _____

3. This chair costs three hundred dollars. _____

4. A glass of cold milk, please. _____

5. His office is on a long and narrow street. _____

6. There are some new stores on the first floor of this shopping center. _____

7. Elly wants a brand new bicycle. _____

Words that function as adjectives

Other parts of speech can function as adjectives:

◆ A noun + a preposition + another noun.

Rompí **la copa de cristal**.	*I broke the **crystal stem glass**.*
¿Te gusta mi **collar de perlas**?	*Do you like my **pearl necklace**?*

◆ Most past participles can complement a noun and function as adjectives. Remember that the regular past participles end in **-ado** and **-ido** and that many commonly used verbs have irregular participles. Consult the Verb Tables at the back of this book for past participles.

Las islas **situadas** al oeste de Ecuador son las Galápagos.	*The islands **situated** west of Ecuador are the Galápagos Islands.*
El plato **roto** está en la basura.	*The **broken** dish is in the garbage.*
La puerta está **cerrada**.	*The door is **closed**.*

En español.

1. the diamond earrings _____

2. the open door _____

3. a summer dress _____

4. the broken records _____

5. some plastic bags _____

6. three paper baskets _____

7. a crystal dish _____

8. the written letter _____

9. my gold ring _____

10. the lost men _____

En tu opinión... ¿Verdadero (V) o falso (F)?

_____ 1. Las pulseras de esmeraldas son valiosas.

_____ 2. El pollo asado es mi comida favorita.

_____ 3. Conviene tener una casa de verano.

_____ 4. En el invierno no uso ropa de algodón.

_____ 5. Una fina caja de chocolates es un regalo apropiado para una novia.

_____ 6. Patino en el lago congelado (_frozen_) en el invierno.

_____ 7. Siempre tengo un ramo de flores en mi sala.

_____ 8. Los zapatos de piel de cocodrilo son muy elegantes.

_____ 9. Hoy, he recibido tres cartas de amor.

_____ 10. Los cuentos de misterio me irritan.

Adverbs

An adverb is a modifier or a word that modifies other elements in a sentence: a verb, an adjective, or another adverb. Adverbs answer questions such as _how? how long? how much? when?_ and _where?_ They are easy to spot: certain adverbs in English are made by adding _-ly_ to an adjective. They emphasize the meaning of the verb: _I can **really** do it well. He spoke **softly**._

In Spanish, there are several adjectives that may function as adverbs. When they are adverbs, they do not agree in number or gender. An example is **demasiado** (_too much_), an adverb of manner. In this example, it shows _how_ the subject _works_ (**trabaja**):

Ustedes trabajan   _You work **too much**._

However, in the following example, **demasiadas** agrees with the noun that follows it. In this sentence, as an adjective, it modifies **preguntas**.

Lola hace **demasiadas preguntas**.   _Lola asks **too many questions**._

With all adverbs and adjectives in Spanish, it is important to understand the function of the words you choose and to select their appropriate forms.

Adverb forms in Spanish

Adverbs appear in a wide variety of forms. They can be:

◆ a single word.

Los chicos llegan **ahora**.   _The boys are arriving **now**._
¿Hablamos **luego**?   _Shall we talk **later**?_
Todavía no he terminado.   _I have not **yet** finished._

◆ a compound word.

Salieron **anteayer**.   _They left **the day before yesterday**._

Ahora, luego, and todavía are single words. Anteayer is a compound of two adverbs, antes and ayer. Note that, unlike in English, the adverb todavía does not come between the auxiliary verb and the participle in the compound tenses (he terminado). Compound tenses cannot be separated in Spanish.

The following list includes frequently used adverbs referring to place, time, quantity or measure, and manner:

PLACE		TIME	
abajo	down, downstairs	ahora	now
acá	over here	anteanoche	the night before last
afuera	out; outside	anteayer	the day before yesterday
ahí	there	ayer	yesterday
allá	over there	después	later
aquí	here	luego	then, later
arriba	up, upstairs	nunca	never
cerca	near	siempre	always, all the time
debajo	under	tarde	late
delante	in front	temprano	early
detrás	behind	todavía	still
lejos	far	ya	already, right now

QUANTITY		MANNER	
bastante	enough	bien	well
demasiado	too much	mal	badly
mucho	much, a lot		
poco	little		
suficiente	enough		

EJERCICIO
6·13

El adverbio apropiado. Complete each sentence with the appropriate adverb.

todavía	cerca	bien	nunca
lejos	poco	debajo	mal

1. No voy a la playa porque vivo _____ de la costa.

2. ¡Uds. _____ están listos para salir a tiempo!

3. Me siento _____ , fantástico, y tengo ganas de nadar dos millas.

4. Vivo muy _____ de mi tía, a una milla, más o menos.

5. No puedo salir de casa _____ porque tengo que terminar mi trabajo.

6. Yo pongo el dinero _____ del colchón (*mattress*) para no perderlo.

7. ¿Te sientes _____? Siéntate en el sofá y descansa.

8. ¿Tienes _____ dinero? Necesitas un aumento de sueldo.

Preguntas personales.

1. ¿Prefieres despertarte tarde o temprano? _____

2. ¿Qué haces por la noche? _____

3. ¿Guardas tu dinero siempre en el banco? _____

4. ¿Crees en los cuentos de hadas (*fairy tales*) todavía? _____

5. ¿Qué haces siempre los lunes? _____

6. ¿Tienes bastante confianza en tus ideas? _____

7. ¿Estás ya listo(a) para irte a dormir? _____

8. ¿Bebes café después de cenar? _____

9. ¿Qué haces antes de salir de casa? _____

10. ¿Te gustan mucho o poco las películas de ciencia-ficción? _____

Así soy yo. En español.

1. There is always a reason to be happy. _____

2. I never have enough money. _____

3. I still have hopes to win the lottery. _____

4. Well, I dream a lot. _____

5. I expect too much from my friends. _____

6. Also, I have headaches frequently. _____

7. Besides, I don't complain (**quejarse**) often. _____

8. Later, I am going to take two aspirins. _____

9. But not yet, I want to wait. _____

10. Then I will continue to talk about my personality. _____

Compound adverbs

Compound adverbs in Spanish are formed as follows:

◆ The feminine singular form of adjectives + the suffix **-mente**, equivalent to the English *-ly*.

Los estudiantes trabajan **lentamente**.   *The students work **slowly**.*

- Adjectives with a single form for the feminine and masculine + the suffix -**mente**. Such adjectives usually end in -**e** or a consonant (**fácil** [*easy*]). -**Mente** is added directly to the adjective.

Eso se hace **fácilmente**.	*This is **easily** done.*
La niña ríe **ruidosa y alegremente**.	*The girl laughs **loudly and happily**.*

Note: If the basic adjective has a written accent mark, the accent remains in place (**fácilmente**). If two or more adverbs ending in -**mente** are connected by conjunctions such as **y**, **ni**, or **pero**, only the final adverb in the series adds the suffix -**mente** (in the example above: **ruidosa y alegremente**). Certain adverbs ending in -**mente** are more commonly seen in written language.

Los niños cantaron **alegremente**.	*The children sang **happily**.*
Finalmente, termina este programa.	*This program is **finally** ending.*

In everyday language, **alegremente** would likely be replaced by the adverbial expression **con alegría**, and **finalmente** by **por fin**. You will study such adverbial expressions later in this unit.

EJERCICIO 6·16

*Práctica. Change adjectives to adverbs. Each adverb will end in -**mente**.*

1. ansioso _____
2. definitivo _____
3. lento _____
4. tímido _____
5. ágil _____
6. fácil _____
7. dulce _____
8. desgraciado _____
9. profundo _____
10. inmediato _____
11. total _____
12. obvio _____
13. claro _____
14. hábil _____
15. alegre _____
16. desafortunado _____
17. violento _____
18. completo _____
19. fuerte _____
20. rápido _____

EJERCICIO 6·17

Y en tu caso... ¿Verdadero (V) o falso (F)?

_____ 1. Probablemente recibiré una sorpresa agradable hoy.

_____ 2. Como lentamente.

_____ 3. Aprendo español rápidamente.

_____ 4. Trabajo tranquilamente en mi casa.

_____ 5. Hago mis ejercicios aeróbicos rápidamente.

_____ 6. Siempre duermo profundamente.

_____ 7. A menudo, me visto muy elegantemente.

_____ 8. Prefiero trabajar cómodamente en mi jardín.

_____ 9. Siempre saludo amablemente a todos mis vecinos.

_____ 10. Claramente sigo las instrucciones de mi médico.

En español.

1. We do the exercises slowly. _____

2. Do you (**Uds.**) follow instructions carefully? _____

3. Usually, we do not like to work on weekends. _____

4. Obviously, this dog does not protect your (**Uds.**) house. _____

5. Unfortunately, you (**Uds.**) do not have too many jewels (**joyas**). _____

6. You (**Uds.**) can easily protect your house with an alarm (**alarma**). _____

7. Lisa speaks slowly and clearly. _____

8. She also speaks briefly. _____

9. Frankly, I do not like waiting. _____

10. Fortunately, I do not have much homework. _____

Other adverb forms: Adverbial expressions

Groups of words may serve as adverbial expressions (**frases adverbiales**). Prepositions often tell where something or someone is; thus, many adverbial expressions consist of a preposition followed by other elements or parts of speech.

Here are the typical patterns:

- Preposition + an adjective.

  El auto salió **de repente**.   *The car left **suddenly**.*
  Tengo que ir al dentista **de nuevo**.   *I have to go to the dentist **again**.*

- Preposition + a noun.

  Llegaron **de día**.   *They arrived **in the daytime**.*
  Lo investigaron **a fondo**.   *They investigated it **thoroughly**.*

Here is a selected list of commonly used fixed expressions:

a menudo	*frequently, often*	**de nuevo**	*again*
a veces	*sometimes*	**de pronto**	*suddenly*

al fin	*finally*	**de repente**	*suddenly*
al mismo tiempo	*at the same time*	**por desgracia**	*unfortunately*
con alegría	*happily*	**por fin**	*finally*
con facilidad	*easily*	**por suerte**	*fortunately*
con frecuencia	*frequently*	**por supuesto**	*of course*
con rapidez	*quickly*	**por último**	*finally*
con tristeza	*sadly*	**sin duda**	*without a doubt*
de día	*in the daytime*	**sin razón**	*without (a) reason*
de noche	*at night*		

EJERCICIO
6·19

En español. Complete each sentence with the adverbial phrase in parentheses.

1. Barbara va al gimnasio _____ (*at night*).

2. No puede ir _____ (*in the daytime*) porque está muy ocupada.

3. Ella monta en bicicleta y habla por teléfono _____ (*at the same time*).

4. _____ (*Fortunately*) la bicicleta está cerca de la ventana y la recepción es buena.

5. Barbara va _____ (*frequently*) a la cafetería dentro del gimnasio.

6. _____ (*Sometimes*) ella pasa mucho tiempo charlando por teléfono.

7. _____ (*Without a doubt*) Barbara prefiere hablar, no hacer ejercicio.

8. Hoy, ella está _____ (*again*) practicando una rutina de aeróbicos.

EJERCICIO
6·20

Y en tu caso... ¿Verdadero (V) o falso (F)?

_____ 1. Por suerte, tengo muchos días feriados (*holidays*).

_____ 2. Por desgracia, no tengo suerte en la vida.

_____ 3. Siempre me despido con tristeza del Año Viejo.

_____ 4. Puedo viajar con rapidez en mi motocicleta.

_____ 5. Prefiero trabajar de día en mi computadora.

_____ 6. Me enseñaron que no debo hablar y comer al mismo tiempo.

_____ 7. A veces llego tarde a mis citas (*appointments*).

_____ 8. No puedo dormir bien de noche.

More adverbial expressions

In adverbial expressions, prepositions precede adjectives and nouns, and they may also precede verb forms or other adverbs.

Pedro regresó **al amanecer**.			*Pedro came back **at daybreak**.*
No puedo hacer dos cosas **al mismo tiempo**.			*I cannot do two things **at the same time**.*

Al amanecer is a combination of the contraction **al** + an infinitive. **Al mismo tiempo** consists of the contraction **al** + adjective + noun. Both are adverbial expressions of time. Consider the following lists as fixed expressions to be learned as lexical items. You will encounter them elsewhere in this program.

The following adverbial expressions are formed with verb forms and other adverbs:

acá abajo	*down here*	**de ahora en adelante**	*from now on*
al anochecer	*at nightfall*	**de veras**	*really, truly*
al frente de	*in front of*	**de vez en cuando**	*once in a while*
al parecer	*apparently*	**desde aquí**	*from here*
al salir el sol	*at sunrise*	**desde entonces**	*since then*
allá arriba	*up there*	**hasta aquí**	*up to here*
cerca de	*near (to)*	**por lo visto**	*apparently, evidently*

EJERCICIO

6·21

***En español.** Use one of the adverbial expressions listed above.*

1. Apparently, we want a better life. _____

2. Once in a while, we need to consider that life is short. _____

3. Really, I cannot find an apartment! _____

4. From now on, we are going to change our lifestyle (**estilo de vida**). _____

5. We are not going to get up at sunrise. _____

6. At nightfall we can relax and forget about tomorrow. _____

7. From here we have a view of the river. _____

8. Up to now (here), this plan is boring. _____

9. Do we really have to change our lifestyle? _____

10. From now (today) on, we cannot complain any more. _____

Comparisons

Before you can compare any two (or more) people, things, or ideas, you have to be able to describe them. Doing that, as you know, requires knowledge of adjectives.

The positive degree

When an adjective is used to describe one person, thing, or idea, it is said to be in the *positive degree. Positive*, in this case, is simply a grammatical term and includes both good and bad qualities. The following three examples are simple statements in which the predicate adjectives attribute some quality—good, neutral, and bad, respectively.

Roberto es **alto**.	*Robert is **tall***.
Esta manzana es **roja**.	*This apple is **red***.
El Sr. Acero es **mentiroso**.	*Mr. Acero is a **liar***.

These examples are clearly not comparisons. Another person or thing needs to be introduced for comparison with these subjects with respect to the different qualities.

The comparative degree

A comparison of two (or more) people, things, or ideas, whether they are equal or unequal comparisons, is called the *comparative degree*. The structure of a comparative sentence is very much like a mathematical equation: $X > Y$ (X is *greater* [than] Y) in which the word *than* is expressed by the conjunction **que**. The word **menos** can also be used, in which case it means $X < Y$ (X is *less* [than] Y). This mathematical abstraction suggests that the structure of unequal comparisons in English and Spanish is very similar.

Roberto es **más alto** que Enrique.	*Robert is taller than Henry.*
Esta manzana es **más roja** que la otra.	*The apple is redder than the other one.*
El Sr. Acero es **más mentiroso** que el diablo.	*Mr. Acero is a bigger liar than the devil.*
Hay **menos tráfico** en Acapulco que en Guadalajara.	*There is less traffic in Acapulco than in Guadalajara.*

Comparisons can be made with respect to *nouns*, *adjectives*, or *adverbs*, whether of equality or inequality. This can be seen in the following examples of comparisons of inequality.

Tengo **más libros** que ella.	*I have more books than she.*
Ella es **menos talentosa** que sus colegas.	*She is less talented than her colleagues.*
Él corre **más rápido** que yo.	*He runs faster than I.*

There are several adjectives in Spanish whose comparative forms are, or may be, irregular, depending on their meaning. Note that **más bueno** and **más malo** are used when speaking of character, as in the examples below.

POSITIVE DEGREE	COMPARATIVE DEGREE
bueno	más bueno *or* mejor
grande	más grande *or* mayor
joven	más joven *or* menor
malo	más malo *or* peor
mucho	más
pequeño	más pequeño *or* menor
poco	menos
viejo	más viejo *or* mayor

The forms **mejor** and **peor** are used when they refer to any quality other than moral ones, such as skills, talents, or other abilities. Likewise, **más grande** and **más pequeño** can refer to size or age, while **más joven** refers to age only. The form **menor** performs double duty, meaning either *younger* (particularly when referring to people) or *smaller* (referring to people or things). The comparative **más viejo** can be applied to people or things, while **mayor** refers always to age and mostly is used when comparing people's ages, such as siblings.

Yo soy **mayor** que mi prima.	*I am older than my cousin.*
La hermana de Jorge es **menor** que él.	*George's sister is younger than he.*

There are also two common adverbs that are used for description: **bien** (*well*) and **mal** (*badly* or *poorly*). Their comparative forms are the same as the irregular forms for **bueno** and **malo**— **mejor** and **peor**, respectively. The identical forms may lead a few learners to incorrectly use **bueno**, in particular, as an adverb.

Juan escribe **bien**.	*John writes well. (positive degree)*
Miguel escribe **mejor** que Juan.	*Michael writes better than John. (comparative degree)*
Mi hermano es **más grande** que yo.	*My brother is bigger than I am.*

In this last example, **más grande** also could mean *older*, unless clarified. Regional preferences exist with regard to the choice of **mayor/más grande** and **menor/más pequeño**.

Yo soy **mayor** que mi hermano.	*I am older than my brother.*

If these two statements are combined, any ambiguity of the first example is eliminated:

Mi hermano es **más grande** que yo, pero soy **mayor** que él.	*My brother is bigger than I am, but I'm older than he.*

The sentence structure for comparisons of equality is also similar in English and Spanish. Once again, comparisons are made with respect to nouns, adjectives, and adverbs. Note that when the comparison involves adjectives or adverbs, **tan** is used. The singular form **tanto** (**tanta**), which means *as much*, is used with what are called non-count nouns—things that are not being or cannot be counted. The plurals—**tantos** and **tantas**—mean *as many*, and are used with things that are or can be counted. Consider the following examples:

Mis padres tienen **tanto dinero** como mis tíos.	*My parents have as much money as my uncle and aunt. (money is not being counted)*
Yo tengo **tantos dólares** como tú.	*I have as many dollars as you. (money is being, or could be counted)*
Elena es **tan guapa** como su hermana.	*Ellen is as pretty as her sister.*
Ella no juega al baloncesto **tan bien** como su hermano.	*She doesn't play basketball as well as her brother.*

The superlative degree

The third degree of comparison is called the *superlative degree*. It is used when there are at least three people, things, or ideas being compared and one among them stands out with respect to some quality. Three things should be noted in the following examples. First, the definite article is used before the words **más** and **menos** in order to set apart the person(s), thing(s), or idea(s) that stand out among the members of a group being compared with one another. Second, the preposition **de** is used where English uses *in* or *on*. Third, the irregular forms of the adjectives of the comparative degree are used in the superlative.

Tomás es **el más alto** de la clase.	*Thomas is the tallest in the class.*
Juana es **la más lista** de la familia.	*Jane is the smartest in the family.*
Miguel y Pablo son **los peores jugadores** del equipo.	*Michael and Paul are the worst players on the team.*
Mi hija es **la mejor cantante** del coro.	*My daughter is the best singer in the chorus.*

The absolute superlative

Spanish also has what is known as the absolute superlative. It is a one-word adjective form, built from the adjective of the positive degree by appending **-ísimo**, **-ísima**, **-ísimos**, or **-ísimas**. Although it existed in Latin, Spanish did not use it until the late 15th century when Italian poetry took the poetic world by storm and Spanish poets began incorporating many forms and styles from Italy. Because of pop culture, this form is probably familiar to most English speakers whether they have studied Spanish or not. It does not have a precise English translation and so the same idea is often conveyed with tone or hyperbolic (exaggerated) language. It is used when a person, thing, or idea is so beyond compare that mentioning any other person, thing, or idea with similar qualities would seem fruitless.

Goliat fue **altísimo**.	*Goliath was tall.*
La modelo de París fue **bellísima**.	*The Parisian model was drop-dead gorgeous.*
Algunas mujeres creen que Paul Newman fue **guapísimo**.	*Some women think that Paul Newman was a real hunk.*

When an indefinite pronoun is used to conclude a comparative construction, the negative form of the indefinite is used. In English, the positive form is used.

Ese hombre es **más corrupto que** nadie.	*That man is more corrupt than anyone.*
Más que nada me encanta cocinar.	*More than anything, I love to cook.*

Más and menos with numbers

To conclude this section on comparatives, let's examine the use of **más** and **menos** with numbers. The standard rule that most texts give is to use **de** in comparisons with numbers. Some texts comment on the use of **que** in comparisons involving numbers when the statement is negative. The best way to clear the air on this issue is to offer examples presenting all the possible combinations.

Más

Hay **más de** cinco libros en la mesa.	*There are more than five books on the table.*
No hay **más de** cinco libros en la mesa.	*There are no more than five books on the table. (there could be fewer, but five is the max)*
No hay **más que** cinco libros en la mesa.	*There are but five books on the table. (not four, not six, but exactly five)*

Menos

Hay **menos de** cinco libros en la mesa.	*There are fewer than five books on the table.*
No hay **menos de** cinco libros en la mesa.	*There are no fewer than five books on the table. (five is the minimum)*

Note: It is incorrect to use **menos que** with *numbers*, whether in an affirmative or negative sentence.

*Recompose these dehydrated sentences. Using the elements given, create comparative
sentences. You will have to supply missing words and conjugate the verbs correctly. You will
also have to supply some verbs!*

1. Tú/más alto/Tomás.

   _____

2. Mi hermano/correr/tan/rápido/ellos.

   _____

3. Su hermana/tener/dinero/como yo.

   _____

4. Hoy/hacer/menos/frío/ayer.

   _____

5. Llover/más/aquí/en Arizona.

   _____

6. El Sr. Acero/tan malo/diablo.

   _____

7. Juana/alumna/más lista/clase.

   _____

8. Haber/menos/cinco libros/mesa.

   _____

9. ¡Padres/siempre/mayores/sus hijos!

   _____

10. Pedro/químico/más preparado/equipo.

    _____

11. María y Teresa/bailar/mejor/yo.

    _____

12. Estos dos/peores platos/menú.

    _____

13. Me gusta/postre/más/el otro.

    _____

14. ¡jugador/baloncesto/altísimo!

    _____

15. Juanito/tener/tantos/juguetes/su hermanita.

_____

16. Haber/menos nieve/esta montaña/la otra.

_____

17. Carro/más costoso/otro.

_____

18. Ella/leer/revistas/como yo.

_____

19. Esa muchacha/más/interesante/de todas.

_____

20. La oveja/no beber/tanta agua/como el camello.

_____

EJERCICIO
6·23

Translate the following sentences from Spanish to English.

1. Los chicos no duerman tantas horas como yo.

_____

2. Mi novia tiene el cabello tan largo como su mamá.

_____

3. Esa chica es guapísima.

_____

4. ¿Eres tan popular como él?

_____

5. ¿Tienes tantos amigos como yo?

_____

6. Creo que Juan es menor que tú.

_____

7. ¿Cómo se llama el mayor de tus hermanos?

_____

8. No hay más que cinco jugadores en un equipo de baloncesto.

_____

9. Ella es tan llorona como su tía.

_____

10. ¿Cuál es el país más grande del mundo?

_____

11. Puerto Rico es menos grande que Cuba.

_____

12. Nueva York no tiene tantos habitantes como México, D.F.

_____

13. Hay menos de cuatro pizzas en el refrigerador.

_____

14. Eres tan amable como me dice mi hermana.

_____

15. A Jorge le gusta jugar al tenis tanto como mirar películas.

_____

16. A mí me encanta nadar en el mar más que en los lagos.

_____

17. Estos dos son los más atléticos del grupo.

_____

18. Ella no tiene tanta energía como esperábamos.

_____

19. En la mesa hay tantos bolígrafos como lápices.

_____

20. Más que nada, le interesa fabricar pescaditos de oro.

_____

EJERCICIO
6·24

Translate the following sentences from English to Spanish.

1. Who is the most important person in your life? (**tú**)

_____

2. What do your friends like to do more than anything else? (**Ud.**)

_____

3. She is the richest woman in the world.

_____

4. Do you have as many shirts as you have socks? (**Uds**.)

_____

5. She is the best swimmer on the team.

_____

6. She paints as much as he does.

_____

7. There are no fewer than one thousand books in this collection.

_____

8. Her mother sells more than I do.

_____

9. Which lake in the United States is the deepest?

_____

10. The Atlantic is smaller than the Pacific.

_____

11. His brother is younger than you. (**tú**)

_____

12. We are not the tallest players on the team.

_____

13. This watch costs as much as that one.

_____

14. Who has as many shoes as she?

_____

15. We are the best chefs in town.

_____

16. Venus can shine as brightly as an airplane's light.

_____

17. There are more fish in this lake than in that one.

_____

18. He is the worst chess player in the school.

_____

19. He goes to the movies as often as I do.

_____

20. She writes as well as she sings.

_____

Describing people, places, and things

Let's look at a dialogue that shows description.

Conversation: Discussing roommates

PACO: Dime, Carlos, ¿cómo es tu nuevo compañero de cuarto?

Tell me, Carlos, what's your new roommate like?

CARLOS: Bueno, si tienes todo el día libre, te lo puedo describir. Es **un tipo bastante** raro.

Well, if you have all day, I can describe him. He's a very strange character.

PACO: **Mira**, todo el día no tengo, pero en general, ¿**se llevan** bien?

Look, I don't have all day, but in general, do you get along?

CARLOS: Imagínate que nos llevamos muy bien porque no nos vemos casi nunca. El **tipo** duerme durante el día. A veces se levanta sólo para ir a sus clases y luego vuelve al cuarto y **se queda** dormido hasta las diez de la noche. Luego **vuelve a** levantarse y estudia toda la noche.

Actually, we get along really well because we hardly see each other. The guy sleeps during the day. Sometimes he gets up just to go to his classes, then he comes back to the room and stays asleep until ten P.M. Then he wakes up again and studies all night.

PACO: Entonces, no comen juntos.

You don't eat together, then.

CARLOS: **La verdad**, no sé cuándo come él, ni dónde.

The truth is, I don't know when he eats, or where.

PACO: Entonces, al menos no ensucia la cocina.

Then at least he doesn't leave the kitchen dirty.

CARLOS: ¡No! Es un tipo increíblemente pulcro. **Incluso deja** el baño limpio todos los días y parece no tener ropa sucia. Es casi un fantasma.

No! The guy is incredibly neat. He even leaves the bathroom clean every day, and he doesn't seem to have dirty clothes. He's like a ghost.

PACO: Amigo, ¡creo que tienes el compañero de cuarto perfecto!

Man, I think you have the ideal roommate!

CARLOS: ¿Y el tuyo? ¿Cómo es?

And yours? What's he like?

PACO: Bueno, es **todo lo contrario** del tuyo, pues **tenemos mucho en común** y estamos juntos casi todo el día. **Es decir**, tenemos dos clases juntos y estamos en la misma asociación de estudiantes, así que somos muy buenos amigos.

Well, he's the exact opposite of yours. We have a lot in common and we're together all day. That is, we have two classes together and we're in the same fraternity, so we're really good friends.

CARLOS: Entonces, también tienes el compañero ideal...

Then you have the ideal roommate too . . .

PACO: Pues, sí—y no. El mío es un desastre en la casa. En primer lugar, siempre **deja** la cocina sucia, **no** lava los platos **ni** saca la basura. Además, tira su ropa por todos lados, **ni hablar** de cómo deja el baño...

Well, yes—and no. Mine is a disaster in the house. In the first place, he always leaves the kitchen dirty, he doesn't wash the dishes or take out the trash. Plus, he throws his clothes all over the place, not to mention how he leaves the bathroom . . .

CARLOS: **Vamos**, Paco—en todo eso **se parece** mucho a ti. ¡**Con razón** se llevan tan bien!

Come on, Paco—he sounds a lot like you. No wonder you get along so well!

Mira

This is a way to get someone to understand your situation or point of view.

¿Me puedes ayudar?	*Can you help me?*
Mira, me gustaría pero hoy no tengo tiempo.	*Look, I'd like to, but today I don't have time.*

Llevarse

This verb, used with reflexive pronouns, means *to get along with each other*. In Chapter 11 you will find more information about reflexive verbs and reflexive pronouns.

Me llevo muy bien con mi hermana.	*I get along really well with my sister.*
Mi hermana y yo **nos llevamos** muy bien.	*My sister and I get along really well.*
Él **se lleva muy mal** con sus padres.	*He doesn't get along with his parents.*
Él y sus padres **se llevan muy mal**.	*He and his parents don't get along.*

El tipo/la tipa

This is a way to refer to someone in a slightly deprecating or impersonal manner.

El amigo de Sergio me invitó a cenar, pero no quiero salir con **ese tipo.**	*Sergio's friend invited me to dinner, but I don't want to go out with that jerk.*
El tipo del garaje acaba de llamar para avisarte que tu carro está listo.	*The guy from the garage just called to tell you that your car is ready.*

In Spain, this is popularly shortened to **tío/tía**. (And of course it doesn't mean *uncle* in this sense!)

Bastante

This is an adverb, meaning *quite/rather/pretty*, when it precedes an adjective.

Soy **bastante** alto.	*I'm pretty tall.*

Other adverbs that describe adjectives include:

poco	*not very*
muy/bien/realmente	*very*
excesivamente/demasiado	*excessively*

Note that **bien** in this context has a very different meaning from its other uses.

Esa tipa es **bien** rara.	*That girl is really strange.*

Also note that **demasiado,** which is often translated as *too*, does not necessarily have a negative meaning, as *too* does in English.

Es posible que sea rara, pero yo creo que es **demasiado bonita.**	*She may be strange, but I think she's absolutely gorgeous.*

When **bastante** modifies a verb, it is translated as *quite a bit*.

Estudiamos bastante.	*We study quite a bit.*

Quedarse

This verb, used with reflexive pronouns, means *to stay/to remain/to keep* and can be followed by an adjective.

Cuando ella está con él, **se queda tranquila**.	*When she's with him, she keeps quiet.*
Los jóvenes **se quedan dormidos** hasta después de mediodía.	*The young ones stay asleep until after noon.*

When not followed by an adjective, it means *to stay/to remain* in a place.

No voy a mi casa esta noche. Quiero **quedarme** aquí con ustedes.	*I'm not going home. I want to stay here with you all.*

Volver a + infinitive

This construction is used to mean *do something again*.

Si no contesto el teléfono, **vuelve a llamarme**.	*If I don't answer the phone, call me again.*
Quiero **volver a verte** muy pronto.	*I want to see you again soon.*

La verdad

La verdad means *the truth*. It can also be used to preface something you might feel uncomfortable saying.

¡Vamos a la casa de Cristina! **La verdad,** ella y yo no nos llevamos muy bien.	*Let's go to Cristina's house! The truth is/Actually, she and I don't get along very well.*

Incluso

Incluso can indicate that what follows it seems a bit out of the ordinary.

Su mamá le plancha toda la ropa, **incluso** los calcetines.	*His mother irons all his clothes for him—even/including his socks.*

Dejar

When **dejar** is followed by an adjective, it means *to leave something in that condition*.

No dejes el piso **mojado**.	*Don't leave the floor wet.*

When followed by a noun, it means *to leave something or someone*.

Ella **deja los platos** sucios en el fregadero.	*She leaves the dirty dishes in the sink.*
El papá **deja a los niños** con una niñera.	*The father leaves the children with a babysitter.*

When followed by an indirect object, it means *to allow/to let someone do something*.

Papá, **déjame** comprar el videojuego.	*Dad, let me buy the video game.*

When followed by the preposition **de**, it means *to stop doing something*.

El médico me dice que tengo que **dejar de** tomar café.	*The doctor tells me I have to stop drinking coffee.*

Verbs that mean *to leave (a place)* include:

salir (de)

Salimos (de la oficina) a las cinco.	*We leave (the office) at five.*

partir (de)

Parten (de Bogotá) mañana por la mañana.	*They leave (Bogotá) tomorrow morning.*

irse/marcharse

Me voy./Me marcho.	*I'm leaving.*
¿A qué hora **te vas?/te marchas?**	*What time are you leaving?*

Todo lo contrario

This expression means *exactly the opposite/quite the contrary*.

Dicen que te vas a casar pronto.	*They say you're getting married soon.*
Es todo lo contrario. Acabo de romper con mi novio.	*It's quite the contrary. I just broke up with my boyfriend.*

Tener en común

This means *to have in common*.

Creo que **tenemos mucho en común**.	*I think we have a lot in common.*

The opposite is **no tener nada en común/no tener nada que ver**.

Ella **no tiene nada que ver** contigo.	*She is nothing like you.*

Es decir

This is used to explain something you have just said in more detail.

Ella está bastante ocupada. **Es decir**, aparte de su trabajo, también estudia y cuida a su familia.	*She's quite busy. That is, besides her job, she also studies and takes care of her family.*

No... ni

This combination expresses *neither . . . nor*.

Él **no fuma ni toma** alcohol.	*He neither smokes nor drinks./ He doesn't smoke or drink.*

Ni hablar

¡Ni hablar! is a way of saying *Nothing compares to it!* When it is followed by **de** + an object, it is better translated as *not to mention*.

Y la cocina de mi abuela, **¡ni hablar!**	*And my grandmother's cooking—there's nothing like it!*
Hay mucho que disfrutar en México: la gente amistosa, la música, **¡ni hablar de la cocina!**	*There's a lot to enjoy in Mexico: the friendly people, the music, not to mention the food!*

Adjectives, adverbs, and comparisons   **121**

Vamos

Vamos means *we're going/we go* but it can also be used like *Come on . . .* to get someone to accept or admit a situation, or at least be a little more realistic.

No voy al partido con ustedes, pues no tengo dinero.
I'm not going to the game with you guys because I don't have any money.

Vamos, Jorge, tú tienes más dinero que nadie.
Come on, Jorge, you have more money than anybody.

Parecerse

This verb, used with reflexive pronouns, means *to be like something or someone else.*

Tu apartamento **se parece** al mío.
Your apartment is like mine.

Carolina **se parece** a su mamá.
Carolina looks like her mother.

Con razón

Literally, *with reason*, this expression is better translated as *No wonder.*

¿Ya tienes novia? ¡**Con razón** no tienes dinero!
Now you have a girlfriend? No wonder you don't have any money!

EJERCICIO
6·25

Choose the most appropriate word to fill in each blank.

1. Mi compañera de cuarto es _____.

| simpático | bien | contentas | irresponsable |

2. Nuestro equipo de básquetbol tiene muchos jugadores _____.

| altas | buenos | mal | enérgicas |

3. La gente de esta ciudad es _____.

| amistosa | serio | malo | bien |

4. El nuevo profesor me parece _____.

| seria | exigente | interesantes | buena |

EJERCICIO
6·26

*Fill in each blank with the correct form of **ser** or **estar**, as appropriate.*

1. Llévame al médico, por favor. No _____ bien.

2. Mi hermana _____ enferma, también.

3. Los chicos _____ peor.

4. Los chicos _____ peores.

5. Todos mis amigos _____ simpáticos.

6. Él _____ un médico muy bueno.

7. Nuestros jugadores _____ mejores que los suyos.

8. Las chicas de esa clase _____ muy inteligentes.

EJERCICIO
6·27

Complete each of the following sentences with a logical comparison.

Diego mide 5 pies, 10 pulgadas. Arturo mide 6 pies.

1. Arturo es _____.

2. Diego es _____.

3. Diego no es _____.

Yo tengo 10 dólares. Mi hermano tiene 12 dólares.

4. Mi hermano tiene _____ 10 dólares.

5. Yo tengo _____ 15 dólares.

6. Mi hermano es _____ rico _____ yo.

7. Yo no soy _____ rico _____ mi hermano.

Berta tiene 10 libros. Ana tiene 7 libros.

8. Berta tiene _____.

9. Ana no tiene _____.

EJERCICIO
6·28

Use one of the following words in each blank to complete each sentence.

bastante   muy   bien   demasiado

1. María tiene 85 puntos en el examen. Ella es _____ lista.

2. Alejandra tiene más de 100 puntos porque tiene crédito extra. Ella es _____ lista.

3. Susana tiene 90 puntos. Ella es _____ lista.

4. Julia tiene 95 puntos. Ella es _____ lista.

Compare the girls in Exercise 6-28.

1. Julia es _____ lista _____ Susana.

2. Alejandra es _____.

3. María no es _____ Susana.

4. Julia es _____ María.

Use the appropriate form of one of the following verbs to fill in each blank.

dejar   salir   irse   marcharse   partir

1. Mi compañero de cuarto quiere _____ de fumar.

2. ¿A qué hora _____ (tú) del trabajo?

3. No quiero estar sola. ¡No me _____ (tú)!

4. Es una buena fiesta. ¿Por qué _____ (ustedes)?

5. El tren _____ a las seis.

6. Su mamá no le _____ ver televisión después de las ocho.

Fill in each blank with the most appropriate word or expression.

1. ¿Me vas a acompañar a la fiesta?

   _____, mi mamá está enferma y la tengo que visitar.

   Es decir   Vamos   Con razón   Mira

2. Mi profesor es bien exigente, _____, da exámenes difíciles y asigna muchos trabajos escritos.

   todo lo contrario   es decir   mira   la verdad

3. Tengo dos entradas para el ballet. ¿Quieres ir conmigo?

   _____, no me gusta el ballet.

   La verdad   Mira   Ni hablar   Vamos

4. A veces creo que nadie me quiere.

   _____, eres la chica más popular de la escuela.

   La verdad   Mira   Vamos   Es decir

5. Mi mamá prepara ricos tacos, frijoles, enchiladas, ¡_____ de sus tamales!

con razón   es decir   ni hablar   vamos

6. Tu hijo es muy exitoso. ¡_____ estás tan orgullosa!

La verdad   Con razón   Ni hablar   Vamos

7. Esa chica me parece muy floja.

Es _____, trabaja mucho.

ni hablar   la verdad   todo lo contrario   mira

EJERCICIO
6·32

Add your own words in the blank spaces to complete the following sentences. Have a Spanish-speaking friend check your answers.

1. Germán siempre saca muy buenas notas. ¡Con razón _____!

2. _____. Es todo lo contrario—es muy simpática.

3. Beatriz es una chica bastante egoísta, es decir, _____.

4. ¿Quieres leer este libro? La verdad, _____.

5. Amigo, todos vamos a la playa para el fin de semana. ¿Puedes ir tú? Mira, _____

_____

6. La playa lo tiene todo: el sol, las olas del mar, ¡ni hablar de _____

_____!

7. No quiero hacer la fiesta en mi apartamento, pues es bien pequeño. Vamos, ¡_____

_____!

EJERCICIO
6·33

¿Cómo es tu mejor amigo? Write at least eight sentences that describe your best friend. Use the present tense. Ask a Spanish-speaking friend to check your work.

_____

_____

_____

_____

_____

_____

The preterit tense

Regular verbs in the preterit

The preterit is one of several past tenses used in Spanish. As you study how to narrate and communicate in the past, you will be able to distinguish these past tenses by their endings and the specific functions they perform in context.

The preterit of regular verbs is formed by dropping the **-ar**, **-er**, and **-ir** of the infinitives and adding the following endings:

nadar to *swim*		**comer** to *eat*		**vivir** to *live*	
nad**é**	nad**amos**	com**í**	com**imos**	viv**í**	viv**imos**
nad**aste**	nad**asteis**	com**iste**	com**isteis**	viv**iste**	viv**isteis**
nad**ó**	nad**aron**	com**ió**	com**ieron**	viv**ió**	viv**ieron**

Note the following:

◆ The first- and third-person singular forms of the preterit have a written accent mark.
◆ The **nosotros** form of **-ar** and **-ir** verbs is the same in the preterit and the present.

The context (words surrounding the conjugated verb) will give you the clues necessary to identify and use the appropriate tense. In the examples that follow, each of the first two statements expresses an habitual action in the present with the help of the expressions **todos los días** (*every day*) and **siempre** (*always*). The present tense is appropriate in these examples.

Llegamos a las doce **todos los días**.	*We arrive at noon every day.*
Siempre viajamos a California los veranos.	*We always travel to California in the summer.*

On the other hand, the expressions of time **ayer... a la una y media** (*yesterday . . . at one thirty*) and **el año pasado** (*last year*) change the context of the statements, pointing to actions or events that took place at specific times in the past.

Ayer llegamos a la una y media.	*Yesterday we arrived at one thirty.*
El año pasado viajamos a Venezuela.	*Last year we traveled to Venezuela.*

These expressions of time provide context and help determine when the actions take or took place.

Noticias de ayer. *Complete each sentence with the appropriate preterit tense form of the verb in parentheses.*

1. Dos hombres _____ (robar) dos cuadros de Frida Kahlo en una galería.

2. La galería _____ (perder) sus pinturas más famosas.

3. Yo _____ (correr) detrás de un sospechoso (*suspect*) pero desapareció.

4. Los guardias de la galería no _____ (disparar) (*shoot*) las armas.

5. Marcelo y yo _____ (sospechar) que los guardias cooperaron con el robo (*robbery*).

6. ¿_____ (escuchar, tú) la noticia del robo por la radio?

7. Una agente de policía _____ (salir) en un carro de patrulla para buscar a los ladrones.

8. ¿_____ (comprar) ustedes el periódico para leer esa noticia?

When is the preterit used in Spanish?

Verb endings in Spanish indicate which noun or pronoun is doing the action. In addition, they provide details about the time and the circumstances under which the action takes place. As you describe experiences, events, or situations in the past, remember that different past tenses communicate different ideas. Thus, you must choose the tense that fits the message you want to convey. You have already seen some examples of uses of the preterit and expressions of time used with this tense.

The preterit is used to express:

♦ an action that was totally completed in the past.

  Ellos **viajaron** el mes pasado.   *They **traveled** last month.*

♦ an action completed at a definite, specific moment in the past.

  Mi suegro **regresó** a las cuatro.   *My father-in-law **came back** at four o'clock.*

Key time expressions help us establish the meaning of each sentence. **El mes pasado** and **a las cuatro** point out the time the actions took place and signal the use of the preterit. Sometimes these signals or expressions may not be stated literally. A single word such as **Salí** is equivalent to *I left*, communicating a simple action completed in the past. Learn the following expressions, which indicate a specific or fixed point in the past, or when an action began or ended, so that you may use the preterit clearly.

VOCABULARIO			
a esa hora	*at that time*	**el año pasado**	*last year*
anoche	*last night*	**el (lunes) pasado**	*last (Monday)*
anteanoche	*the night before last*	**el mes pasado**	*last month*
anteayer	*the day before yesterday*	**en ese momento**	*at that moment*
ayer al mediodía	*yesterday at noon*	**hace (diez) años**	*(ten) years ago*
ayer por la mañana	*yesterday morning*	**hoy por la mañana**	*this morning*
ayer por la noche	*yesterday evening*	**la semana pasada**	*last week*
ayer por la tarde	*yesterday afternoon*		

EJERCICIO
7·2

En español. Use the previous list of expressions to translate the sentences in Spanish.

1. The night before last, Ana returned home. _____

2. This morning, Pilar sent three e-mails to the bank. _____

3. Roberto traveled to San Antonio last month. _____

4. Ten years ago I moved to this building. _____

5. Detective Rojas and his assistant solved (**resolver**) the case last week. _____

6. At eight o'clock this morning, the doctor visited his new patient. _____

EJERCICIO
7·3

Y en tu caso... ¿Verdadero (V) o falso (F)?

_____ 1. Anoche, salí de casa a las ocho.

_____ 2. Tomé dos tazas de café por la mañana.

_____ 3. Compré dos billetes de lotería.

_____ 4. Visité un museo en la ciudad.

_____ 5. Regresé a casa por la tarde.

_____ 6. Leí mis mensajes en Internet.

Other uses of the preterit

The preterit is also used to communicate other actions in the past, such as:

♦ an action or event that lasted for a specific period of time. If you can determine how long the action took place, use the preterit.

Esperó dos horas en el consultorio del Dr. Bernal.

She waited two hours at Dr. Bernal's office.

♦ a series of actions or events completed in the past. Note that you may not be able to determine when these actions took place or for how long; yet you can identify a series of specific actions in the past.

Yo llegué a la oficina, **preparé** un café, **me senté** y **llamé** a un cliente.

I arrived at the office, prepared a cup of coffee, sat down, and called a client.

♦ actions or events that are not usually repeated, such as:

cumplir años	*to turn a specific age*	**descubrir**	*to discover*
darse cuenta de	*to realize*	**graduarse**	*to graduate*
decidir	*to decide*	**morir**	*to die*

Usually it is easy to establish that the action was completed at a certain point in the past or to determine the specific time it occurred, making the use of the preterit logical.

Mi hermano **cumplió** treinta años.	*My brother **turned** thirty.*
Los gemelos **se graduaron** hace varios años.	*The twins **graduated** a few years ago.*
Ella **murió** a los noventa años.	*She **died** at ninety years of age.*

**EJERCICIO
7·4**

Momentos importantes de la vida de Paco. Indicate the order of events with the numbers 1 to 5.

_____ 1. Estudió cuatro años en la escuela secundaria.

_____ 2. Trabajó en un proyecto de arquitectura por tres años.

_____ 3. Decidió cambiar de profesión.

_____ 4. Nació en una ciudad pequeña.

_____ 5. Se graduó de arquitecto de la Universidad de Madrid.

**EJERCICIO
7·5**

Carlos y yo pasamos el fin de semana juntos. En español.

Carlos y yo...

1. bought a TV to watch movies. _____

2. ate Mexican food, drank a soda, and washed the dishes. _____

3. visited my aunt Matilde. _____

4. arrived at 3:00 and chatted with my aunt. _____

5. realized that Matilde's dog is very ugly. _____

EJERCICIO
7·6

En español. Describe what you did yesterday.

1. Por la mañana _____, _____ y _____.

2. Al mediodía, yo _____ y_____ .

3. Por la tarde _____, _____ y también yo _____.

4. Por la noche _____, _____ y _____.

Verbs with spelling changes in the preterit

Verbs that end in -**car**, -**gar**, and -**zar** have a spelling change in the preterit in the **yo** form *only* to maintain the sound of the final consonant of the stem. Below are listed some frequently used verbs with this spelling change. Study these verbs before you read and answer the exercises in this chapter.

◆ Verbs ending in -**car** change **c** to **qu**

arrancar	*to start*	→ yo arran**qué**
buscar	*to look for*	→ yo bus**qué**
clarificar	*to make clear*	→ yo clarifi**qué**
colocar	*to place*	→ yo colo**qué**
dedicar	*to dedicate*	→ yo dedi**qué**
desempacar	*to unpack*	→ yo desempa**qué**
empacar	*to pack*	→ yo empa**qué**
equivocarse	*to make a mistake*	→ yo me equivo**qué**
explicar	*to explain*	→ yo expli**qué**
pescar	*to fish*	→ yo pes**qué**
sacar	*to take out*	→ yo sa**qué**
tocar	*to touch*	→ yo to**qué**

◆ Verbs ending in -**gar** change **g** to **gu**

apagar	*to turn off*	→ yo apa**gué**
cargar	*to load*	→ yo car**gué**
colgar	*to hang*	→ yo col**gué**
encargar	*to order goods*	→ yo encar**gué**
jugar	*to play*	→ yo ju**gué**

llegar	to arrive	→ yo lle**gué**
pagar	to pay	→ yo pa**gué**
pegar	to beat	→ yo pe**gué**

♦ Verbs ending in -**zar** change **z** to **c**

abrazar	to hug	→ yo abra**cé**
alcanzar	to catch up	→ yo alcan**cé**
almorzar	to eat lunch	→ yo almor**cé**
comenzar	to begin	→ yo comen**cé**
empezar	to begin	→ yo empe**cé**
lanzar	to throw	→ yo lan**cé**
realizar	to fulfill	→ yo reali**cé**
rezar	to pray	→ yo re**cé**
tropezar	to stumble	→ yo trope**cé**

EJERCICIO
7·7

Traducción.

1. Yesterday I lost a gold ring and I looked for it in my apartment.

   _____

2. I made a mistake.

   _____

3. Where did I place my ring?

   _____

4. I started to look for my ring in the living room.

   _____

5. I prayed for a few minutes.

   _____

6. Then I turned off the light and I left my living room.

   _____

7. I took out a suit and a pair of pants from my car.

   _____

8. Later, I hung them in a closet.

   _____

9. Then I stumbled against a big suitcase.

   _____

10. I touched something on the floor and I found my ring.

   _____

11. I started to feel much better.

   _____

12. Then I unpacked my suitcase.

   _____

Preguntas personales.

1. ¿Empacaste tu ropa en una maleta el verano pasado para hacer un viaje?

   _____

2. ¿Colocaste la maleta en el maletero del auto de un amigo?

   _____

3. ¿Tocaste la guitarra, el violín o el piano ayer?

   _____

4. ¿Saliste temprano ayer de tu casa para ir al trabajo?

   _____

5. ¿Jugaste en uno de los equipos de deporte en tu escuela secundaria?

   _____

6. ¿Qué almorzaste ayer? ¿Y anteayer?

   _____

7. ¿Comenzaste un plan de dieta para mejorar tu salud?

   _____

8. ¿Dedicaste varias horas la semana pasada para aprender vocabulario en español?

   _____

Other spelling changes in the preterit

Other verbs have spelling changes in the preterit. Observe the conjugations of **leer**, **oír**, and **construir**.

leer *to read*		oír *to hear*		construir *to build*	
leí	leímos	oí	oímos	construí	construimos
leíste	leísteis	oíste	oísteis	construiste	construisteis
leyó	leyeron	**oyó**	oyeron	construyó	construyeron

Observe that:

◆ **leer**, **oír**, and **construir** change **i** to **y**, but only in the third-person singular and plural forms. All the forms of **leer** and **oír** have accent marks on the endings except the **ellos/ellas** form.

◆ other verbs frequently used in Spanish follow the patterns of **leer**, **oír**, and **construir**.

Read and study the following lists.

VERBS LIKE **LEER**		VERBS LIKE **OÍR**		VERBS LIKE **CONSTRUIR**	
caer(se)	*to fall*	**desoír**	*to ignore*	**concluir**	*to finish*
creer	*to believe*			**contribuir**	*to contribute*
poseer	*to own, possess*			**distribuir**	*to distribute*
				huir	*to flee*
				incluir	*to include*
				intuir	*to feel, have a sense*

EJERCICIO
7·9

En español.

1. Alfonso read a gothic novel by Ruiz Zafón. _____

2. Her brother fell out of the chair. _____

3. We heard (**oír**) his screams! _____

4. Their dogs barked (**ladrar**) and contributed to the noise. _____

5. The cat fled from the house. _____

6. Alfonso built this home many years ago. _____

7. I had a feeling (**intuir**) that this family is crazy. _____

EJERCICIO
7·10

Un misterio. Give the appropriate preterit tense of the verb in italics.

1. El detective Martínez *lee* una carta anónima. _____

2. En la carta, el autor *incluye* noticias acerca de un caso muy misterioso y difícil. _____

3. Martínez *intuye* la identidad del autor de la carta. _____

4. Sus asistentes *distribuyen* copias de la carta a los oficiales. _____

5. La carta *contribuye* a resolver un caso muy complicado. _____

6. Todos *concluyen* que Martínez siempre gana. _____

Stem-changing verbs in the preterit

As in the present tense, there is a pattern of stem changes in the Spanish preterit. Remember that:

◆ -**ar** verbs with stem changes in the present tense *do not* have stem changes in the preterit.

◆ -**ir** verbs with stem changes in the present tense also have stem changes in the preterit.

The changes in the preterit for -**ir** verbs are as follows: **e** changes to **i** and **o** changes to **u**, *only* in the third-person singular and plural forms.

pedir *to ask for*		dormir *to sleep*		preferir *to prefer*	
pedí	pedimos	dormí	dormimos	preferí	preferimos
pediste	pedisteis	dormiste	dormisteis	preferiste	preferisteis
pidió	pidieron	durmió	durmieron	prefirió	prefirieron

Study the following verbs conjugated like **pedir**, **dormir**, and **preferir**.

VERBS LIKE **PEDIR**		VERBS LIKE **DORMIR**		VERBS LIKE **PREFERIR**	
conseguir	*to get*	**morir**	*to die*	**divertir(se)**	*to have fun*
convertir	*to change*			**mentir**	*to lie* (tell a
reír	*to laugh*				falsehood)
repetir	*to repeat*			**sentir**	*to feel; to be sorry*
seguir	*to follow*				
servir	*to serve*				
sonreír(se)	*to smile*				
vestir(se)	*to get dressed*				

Observe the conjugation of **reír** and **sonreír** in the preterit. All the forms except the third-person plural of **reír** and **sonreír** have a written accent mark.

reír *to ask laugh*		sonreír *to smile*	
reí	reímos	sonreí	sonreímos
reíste	reísteis	sonreíste	sonreísteis
rió	rieron	sonrió	sonrieron

EJERCICIO
7·11

Celebraron su aniversario en Cancún. Complete each sentence with the appropriate preterit form of the verb.

1. Hace un mes, Mario y Pola _____ (conseguir) una oferta excelente en un hotel en Cancún.

2. Mario _____ (preferir) pagar más por una habitación con un balcón de cara a (*facing*) la playa.

3. Anoche, ellos _____ (dormir) en El Palacio de Cancún, un hotel de lujo.

4. Esta mañana el gerente del hotel les _____ (sonreír) y los saludó.

5. Entraron a la piscina y en el bar _____ (pedir) dos limonadas.

6. En pocos minutos, el camarero _____ (servir) la limonada.

7. Pola _____ (reírse) mucho con los comentarios y los chistes (*jokes*) del camarero.

8. Mario salió de la piscina y _____ (vestirse) para jugar minigolf.

9. Muchos de los visitantes _____ (pedir) una sombrilla para sentarse al frente de la playa.

10. En verdad, Mario y Pola _____ (divertirse) y (disfrutar) mucho en Cancún.

¿Qué pasó? En español.

1. At the gym, Marisa managed (**conseguir**) to finish her exercises early. _____

2. She got dressed and arrived at the movies at 6:00 P.M. _____

3. She bought a ticket and ordered (**pedir**) a soda. _____

4. A young girl served her the drink and smiled. _____

5. In the theater, she sat and watched the commercials. _____

6. So many commercials! She paid to see a movie, not boring commercials! _____

7. Marisa slept for one hour. _____

8. She woke up twenty minutes before the end of the movie. _____

Irregular verbs in the preterit

Many common verbs have irregular forms in the Spanish preterit. These verbs have irregular stems and are easy to group according to their patterns of stem changes and endings. Instead of the regular preterit verb endings they have a distinctive set of endings. Note that they are without accent marks: **-e, -iste, -o, -imos, -isteis, -ieron**.

Study the following patterns of irregular verbs.

- Verbs with **uv** in the stem:

andar	*to walk*	**anduv-**	anduve, anduviste, anduvo, anduvimos, anduvisteis, anduvieron
estar	*to be*	**estuv-**	estuve, estuviste, estuvo, estuvimos, estuvisteis, estuvieron
tener	*to have*	**tuv-**	tuve, tuviste, tuvo, tuvimos, tuvisteis, tuvieron

- Verbs with **u** in the stem:

caber	*to fit*	**cup-**	cupe, cupiste, cupo, cupimos, cupisteis, cupieron
haber	*must, to be*	**hub-**	hube, hubiste, hubo, hubimos, hubisteis, hubieron
poder	*to be able*	**pud-**	pude, pudiste, pudo, pudimos, pudisteis, pudieron
poner	*to put*	**pus-**	puse, pusiste, puso, pusimos, pusisteis, pusieron
saber	*to know*	**sup-**	supe, supiste, supo, supimos, supisteis, supieron

EJERCICIO
7·13

Traducción. *Use the preterit tense to translate the sentences.*

1. Alberto could not. _____

2. Last night Rita put the keys on the table. _____

3. The suitcase did not fit in the car trunk. _____

4. Yesterday there was a meeting. _____

5. They were here. _____

6. I put the fork in the drawer (**gaveta**). _____

7. We had to go to the store. _____

8. Were you (**Uds.**) at the party? _____

9. My friends had an accident. _____

- Verbs with **i** in the stem:

hacer	*to do*	**hic-**	hice, hiciste, hizo, hicimos, hicisteis, hicieron
querer	*to want*	**quis-**	quise, quisiste, quiso, quisimos, quisisteis, quisieron
venir	*to come*	**vin-**	vine, viniste, vino, vinimos, vinisteis, vinieron

Note that, because of a spelling change, the third-person form of **hacer** is **hizo**.

- Verbs that have **j** in the stem:

atraer	*to attract*	**atraj-**	atraje, atrajiste, atrajo, atrajimos, atrajisteis, atrajeron
decir	*to say*	**dij-**	dije, dijiste, dijo, dijimos, dijisteis, dijeron
producir	*to produce*	**produj-**	produje, produjiste, produjo, produjimos, produjisteis, produjeron
traer	*to bring*	**traj-**	traje, trajiste, trajo, trajimos, trajisteis, trajeron
traducir	*to translate*	**traduj-**	traduje, tradujiste, tradujo, tradujimos, tradujisteis, tradujeron

Note that the third-person plural ending of this last group of verbs is **-eron**.

EJERCICIO
7·14

Más práctica. *Use the preterit tense to translate the sentences.*

1. I did not tell a lie. _____

2. She brought a cake. _____

3. They translated the exercises. _____

4. We did the work. _____

5. You (**tú**) came late. _____

6. Tim did the homework. _____

7. Did they come? _____

Now that you have learned irregular verbs in the Spanish preterit you will be able to conjugate and use compound verbs.

Many compound verbs are formed with a prefix plus an irregular verb. These compounds follow the conjugation patterns of the basic verbs. Here are some examples:

COMPOUNDS OF **PONER**		COMPOUNDS OF **HACER** AND **VENIR**	
componer	*to repair; to compose*	**deshacer**	*to undo*
disponer	*to arrange; to dispose*	**rehacer**	*to make over; to rebuild*
suponer	*to assume*	**convenir**	*to agree*

COMPOUNDS OF **DECIR**, **PRODUCIR**, AND **TRAER**	
desdecir	*to disagree*
predecir	*to predict*
reproducir	*to reproduce*
atraer	*to attract*
distraer	*to distract*

More irregular verbs in the preterit

◆ **Dar**, **ser**, and **ir** are irregular.

dar *to give*		**ser** *to be and* **ir** *to go*	
di	dimos	fui	fuimos
diste	disteis	fuiste	fuisteis
dio	dieron	fue	fueron

Note that:

◆ **dar** takes the regular -**er**, -**ir** preterit endings.

◆ **ser** and **ir** forms in the preterit are the same for both verbs. The context (the words surrounding the verb) will help you guess their meaning.

| Ellos **no fueron** a la playa el domingo. | *They **did not go** to the beach on Sunday.* |
| Ellos **fueron** los campeones del torneo de golf. | *They **were** the champions of the golf tournament.* |

In the first example, **ir** is the logical guess because the preposition **a** follows: **a la playa**. In the second example, **fueron**, a preterit form of **ser**, links the pronoun **ellos** and the noun **campeones**. For better understanding, always try to read or listen to the entire sentence or meaningful group of words.

La semana pasada. Give the appropriate preterit tense of the verbs in parentheses.

1. El lunes, Ana _____ (hacer) todo su trabajo.

2. La Srta. Simpson _____ (traer) unos paquetes para las secretarias.

3. La secretaria le _____ (dar) un informe a su jefe.

4. Paula y yo _____ (ir) al departamento de finanzas.

5. El miércoles yo _____ (poner) un aviso en el boletín (newsletter).

6. El vicepresidente de la compañía _____ (venir) a saludar a los trabajadores.

7. El jueves, los anuncios en la página de la Web _____ (producir) buenos resultados.

8. Ana y yo _____ (proponer) una campaña para la tele.

9. El viernes yo no _____ (poder) ir a la oficina.

10. Mi jefe _____ (suponer) que yo estaba enfermo.

Verbs with a special meaning in the preterit

Some verbs change their basic meaning when conjugated in the preterit. Remember the following special meanings in the preterit:

◆ **conocer** (*to meet*)

    Conocí al director de la escuela ayer.   *I **met** the school principal yesterday.*

◆ **saber** (*to find out, discover*)

    Supo la verdad.   *He **found out** the truth.*

◆ **poder** (*to manage*)

    No **pudieron** terminar.   *They **did not manage** to finish.*

◆ **querer** (*to refuse* [*in negative sentences*])

    Yo **no quise** salir a tiempo.   *I **refused** to leave on time.*

◆ **querer** (*to try*)

    Marta **quiso** ayudarme.   *Marta **tried** to help me.*

◆ **tener** (*to receive, get*)

    Tuve noticias hoy.   *I **got** (**received**) news today.*

En español. *Translate the sentences using the preterit.*

1. Yesterday I met Lily, the new secretary. _____

2. I found out she speaks three languages. _____

3. But she did not manage to finish her first task on time. _____

4. She refused to work after five o'clock. _____

5. Lily translated three documents. _____

6. She did a great job. _____

7. I read the documents. _____

8. We found out the news the next day. _____

9. Lily left before five and did not come back the next day. _____

10. I refused to believe it. We need a new secretary! _____

The progressive tenses

The progressive tenses are formed with the present participle. They express an action in progress in the present, the past, or the future. The English equivalent of these constructions consists of a form of the auxiliary verb *to be* followed by a present participle, the *-ing* form of the verb.

> *The detective **is searching** for the victim.*
> *She **was singing** when I came in.*
> *I **will be waiting** before you get to the station.*

In the three examples above, the action is in progress, not yet completed, and it is taking place at that moment, whether in the present, the past, or the future. In Spanish it is made up of a form of **estar** plus the participle (**Estoy leyendo**, *I am reading*).

The forms of the present participle in regular, irregular, and stem-changing verbs

With their **-ndo** ending, the Spanish participle forms are easy to spot.

Regular verbs

For regular verbs you will:

♦ drop the **-ar**, **-er**, or **-ir** from the infinitive, and add the corresponding ending, **-ando** for **-ar** verbs and **-iendo** for **-er** and **-ir** verbs.

sacar	*to take out*	**sacando**
beber	*to drink*	**bebiendo**
sufrir	*to suffer*	**sufriendo**

Remember that **-er** and **-ir** verbs have the same ending.

El autobús **está llegando** a la estación.	*The bus **is arriving** at the station.*
Estoy aprendiendo a cocinar con Hernán.	*I am learning to cook with Hernan.*
Ahora **ellos están escribiendo** el contrato.	*Now **they are writing** the contract.*

Actividades en el invierno. *Give the appropriate form of the present tense + participle of the verbs in parentheses.*

1. Una chica _____ (patinar) en la pista de hielo (*ice skating rink*).

2. Mis padres _____ (beber) una taza de chocolate caliente.

3. Gisela y yo _____ (esquiar) en la montaña.

4. Marta _____ (aplaudir) a los patinadores.

5. ¿Tú _____ (jugar) en la nieve otra vez?

6. Yo _____ (sacar) fotos aquí, en la terraza.

7. Los jugadores de hockey sobre hielo _____ (discutir) la última jugada.

8. ¿Ustedes _____ (compartir) las fotos de la nevada (*snowfall*)?

Present participle endings in -yendo

Verbs with stems that end in a vowel have slightly different present participle forms.

◆ For -**er** and -**ir** verbs with stems ending in a vowel, add -**yendo**.

| Lara **está leyendo** las instrucciones en la receta. | Lara **is reading** the instructions in the recipe. |

The following is a list of commonly used present participles that end in -**yendo**:

VERBS ENDING IN -ER			VERBS ENDING IN -IR		
atraer	to attract	**atrayendo**	**construir**	to build	**construyendo**
caer	to fall	**cayendo**	**contribuir**	to contribute	**contribuyendo**
creer	to believe	**creyendo**	**destruir**	to destroy	**destruyendo**
leer	to read	**leyendo**	**huir**	to flee	**huyendo**
traer	to bring	**trayendo**	**incluir**	to include	**incluyendo**
			influir	to influence	**influyendo**
			oír	to hear	**oyendo**

Un poco de lógica. *From the previous list of present participles choose the one that fits the meaning of each of the following sentences.*

1. La chica está _____ la radio.

2. El criminal está _____ de la policía.

3. El huracán está _____ los árboles.

4. En la playa, los niños están _____ un castillo de arena.

5. ¡El pastel está _____ las moscas!

6. Tus comentarios están _____ a complicar la situación.

Stem-changing verbs

Verbs with stem changes in the present have the following present participle forms:

◆ Some -**ir** verbs change the stem vowel **o** to **u**. Two verbs in this group are:

dormir	*to sleep*	**durmiendo**
morir	*to die*	**muriendo**

¿Quién **está durmiendo** en mi sofá?   *Who is sleeping on my sofa?*

◆ Some -**ir** verbs change the stem vowel **e** to **i**. For example, for **repetir**:

El maestro **está repitiendo** las   *The teacher is repeating the instructions*
instrucciones a los alumnos.   *to the students.*

Here is a list of commonly used verbs with the **e** to **i** change in the present participle:

advertir	*to warn*	**advirtiendo**	**reñir**	*to fight*	**riñendo**
competir	*to compete*	**compitiendo**	**repetir**	*to repeat*	**repitiendo**
conseguir	*to get*	**consiguiendo**	**seguir**	*to follow*	**siguiendo**
decir	*to say*	**diciendo**	**sentir**	*to feel*	**sintiendo**
hervir	*to boil*	**hirviendo**	**servir**	*to serve*	**sirviendo**
mentir	*to lie*	**mintiendo**	**sugerir**	*to suggest*	**sugiriendo**
pedir	*to ask for*	**pidiendo**	**venir**	*to come*	**viniendo**
reír	*to laugh*	**riendo**			

Note: You may want to review stem-changing verbs in the third-person singular of the preterit tense (Chapter 7). They mirror the changes in the present participle.

Irregular present participles

◆ The verbs **ir** and **poder** have irregular present participle forms:

ir	*to go*	**yendo**
poder	*to be able*	**pudiendo**

EJERCICIO
8·3

Decide. *From the list of verbs, choose the one that fits, and write the present participle to complete the meaning of each of the following sentences.*

competir	hervir	seguir
decir	reñir	servir

1. El camarero está _____ la cena.

2. El agua está _____.

3. Las autoridades están _____ al criminal.

4. ¿Por qué siempre estás _____ con tus vecinos?

5. Todos los atletas están _____ en los juegos preliminares del estado.

6. Ahora, la profesora está _____ que vamos a tener un examen.

When is the present progressive used in Spanish?

The present progressive, as its name states, indicates an action in progress in the present. In the previous exercises and examples you have seen its Spanish form expressed with the present tense of **estar** followed by the -**ando** or -**iendo** verb forms.

Chris **está preparando** la cena.	Chris **is preparing** dinner.
Juan **está aprendiendo** a usar el nuevo programa de la computadora.	Juan **is learning** to use the new computer program.

The present progressive in Spanish is used:

◆ to express an action that is in progress now.

Laura **está leyendo** una novela ahora.   *Laura **is reading** a novel now.*

Note that the action is not finished: Laura is not done reading a novel.

◆ to say that an action is continuing in the present.

Estoy aprendiendo a manejar.   ***I am learning** to drive.*

This example also indicates an action in progress, but the process is gradual. It takes time to learn to drive.

The present progressive is not used in Spanish as frequently as it is in English. Spanish normally uses the present tense—*not* the present progressive—to describe an action happening now. However, the English equivalent of the simple Spanish present is often a progressive form:

Traigo las manzanas en la bolsa.   ***I am bringing** the apples in my bag.*

Note: In Spanish, as in English, there are progressive forms of all tenses.

Ayer Pedro **estuvo buscando** algunos documentos.	*Yesterday, Pedro **was searching** for some documents.*

EJERCICIO
8·4

*¿Qué están haciendo ahora? Complete each sentence using **estar** + the participle of the verb in parentheses.*

1. El ladrón _____ (esconder) la evidencia del robo (*robbery*).

2. El reloj _____ (dar) las ocho.

3. ¿Quiénes _____ (gritar) en el pasillo (*corridor*)?

4. Los hermanos Díaz _____ (esperar) el autobús para ir a Málaga.

5. ¿Y Marlo? ¿ _____ (dormir) la siesta?

6. Andy _____ (vivir) una pesadilla (*nightmare*).

En español. Use *estar* + the participle.

1. The fans (**fanáticos**) are watching a good game. _____

2. It is not raining now. _____

3. The team is playing well. _____

4. The trainer (**entrenador**) is encouraging (**animar**) his players (**jugadores**). _____

5. A beer vendor (**vendedor**) is climbing up the stairs. _____

6. He is yelling: "Peanuts, beer!" _____

7. Now the band is playing music. _____

8. The fans are having fun. _____

9. The other team is losing the game. _____

Una película. Describe the scene. Write the present tense of *estar* + the present participle of the verb in parentheses.

1. Carlos (buscar) una silla para sentarse. _____

2. Marta y Raúl (rellenar) una planilla (*form*). _____

3. La secretaria (escribir) una nota. _____

4. Las telefonistas (responder) a los clientes por teléfono. _____

5. El cajero (*teller*) (recibir) los depósitos de los clientes. _____

6. Dos señoras (hacer) unas preguntas en el pasillo. _____

7. Yo (cambiar) euros por dólares. _____

8. El director de finanzas (tomar) un café. _____

9. Marta (leer) un libro en la fila (*line*). _____

En español. Answer the following questions.

1. ¿Qué estás haciendo ahora? _____

2. ¿A qué amigos estás invitando esta noche para cenar? _____

3. ¿Qué libro estás leyendo? _____

4. ¿Con quién estás hablando por teléfono? _____

5. ¿Qué estás escribiendo, una carta o un mensaje de texto por teléfono?

_____

Verbs of motion in progressive tenses

The progressive tenses formed with the present participle (-**ando**, -**iendo** forms) are used with the verbs **seguir** and **continuar** and with verbs of motion such as **andar**, **ir**, and **venir**. As with **estar**, they emphasize an action that continues, is repeated, or is not finished.

Sigue trabajando para la misma compañía chilena.	*He/She is still working* for the same Chilean company.
Ando buscando trabajo.	*I am looking for* a job.
Van diciendo que somos una pareja.	*They are going around saying* we are a couple.
Vienen caminando.	*They come walking*.

These forms are also used in other tenses. The first example is in the future using **ir** and the second example is using the preterit.

¿Irás camiando o en un auto?	*Will you go walking* or by car?
Thomas **anduvo buscando** a su hermana.	*Thomas was looking for* his sister.

EJERCICIO
8·8

En español. *Translate using the verbs in parentheses.*

1. Miriam *continues* singing the same song. (seguir) _____

2. My son *is* looking for a job. (andar) _____

3. Who *continues* making noise (**ruido**)? (continuar) _____

4. We'll *go* searching for an answer. (ir) _____

5. They will not *continue* lying. (seguir) _____

6. She *is* losing hope. (estar) _____

Present participle: Spanish compared to English

We have studied -**ando**, -**iendo** forms in uses equivalent to the English progressive tenses. In that role, the present participle in Spanish is equivalent to the English present participle.

There are three other considerations regarding the present participle:

◆ As the equivalent of the English present participle, used in a phrase *without* an auxiliary verb such as **estar**.

Meneando la cola, el gato se sentó en el sofá.	*Swaying its tail, the cat sat down on the sofa.*
Los huéspedes, **esperando** pacientemente en la fila, hablan del tiempo.	*The guests, **waiting** patiently in line, talk about the weather.*

Note the phrases above followed or enclosed by commas. In English these are called participial phrases.

The Spanish infinitive, and not the participle, is used in sentences as a noun.

Bailar es divertido.	*Dancing is fun.*

In the previous example, literal translation into the **-ando**, **-iendo** Spanish forms is not possible.

◆ In Spanish, always use the infinitive after prepositions.

Después de desayunar, ya estaba corriendo por el barrio.	*After having breakfast, he/she was running around the neighborhood.*

◆ **Al** + infinitive is equivalent to *upon* + present participle in English.

Al escuchar sonar el teléfono, se levantaron.	*Upon hearing the phone ring, they got up.*

EJERCICIO
8·9

En la piscina. *Give the appropriate participle or infinitive of the verbs in parentheses.*

1. Ando _____ (buscar) a mis amigos.

2. Quiero encontrarlos para _____ (ir) a la piscina.

3. _____ (nadar) es un ejercicio excelente y muy relajante.

4. Por fin, después de _____ (encontrar) a Marcos, estamos ya en la piscina.

5. ¡Hay mucha gente _____ (disfrutar) esta mañana aquí!

6. Delia está _____ (broncearse) al sol.

7. Pedro está _____ (flotar) en el agua.

8. Alina y Tony siguen _____ (dormir).

Questions, answers, and exclamations

Interrogative sentences

When you need information about a matter or a person, you use a question, that is, an *interrogative sentence*. In English and Spanish there are several ways to create questions. In the first example below, the verb form is **sabes**. Unlike Spanish, the English equivalent requires a form of the auxiliary verb *to do* to pose the question in the present tense:

¿**Sabes** la respuesta?   ***Do you know** the answer?*

In English an interrogative sentence with a verb in the past tense may include the past form *did* or a form of the auxiliary verb *to have*:

¿**Salió** Marcos?   ***Did** Marcos **leave**?*
¿**Has visto** a mi hermana?   ***Have you seen** my sister?*

Consider another question with a verb in the future tense that uses a form of the verb **ir**, *to go*:

¿**Irás** a la fiesta?   ***Will you go** to the party?*

A third type uses a form of the verb **estar**, *to be*, and no auxiliary in the English equivalent:

¿**Está** Juan en su casa?   *Is Juan at home?*

One way to create an interrogative sentence in Spanish is to use a declarative sentence that ends with a rising inflection. The intonation communicates a question in spoken language. Spanish question marks precede and follow all interrogative sentences in writing.

¿ + **declarative sentence** + ? → **interrogative sentence**

The message of a declarative sentence changes when it is used to create a question:

La tienda está cerrada.   *The store is closed.*
¿**La tienda está cerrada?**   ***The store is closed?***

Preguntas. *Indicate where question marks are needed.*

1. Llegas tarde.

_____

2. María ya está lista.

_____

3. Tiene poca paciencia.

_____

4. Esperamos hasta las cinco.

_____

5. Hay un taxi en la esquina.

_____

6. Hace calor en la calle.

_____

7. Lloverá esta noche.

_____

8. Llegaremos al cine a tiempo.

_____

Interrogative sentences and negative sentences

If you add question marks to a negative declarative sentence you will have an interrogative sentence:

¿ + negative declarative sentence + ? → interrogative sentence

No estás trabajando para esa compañía.	*You are not working for that company.*
¿**No estás** trabajando para esa compañía?	*Are you not (Aren't you) working for that company?*

The type of construction described above is used when the questioner expects an affirmative answer or an affirmation. When followed by **no**, some adverbs change their meaning and can be used to build similar interrogative sentences:

ya no	*no longer*
todavía no	*not yet*
aún no	*not yet*

Add the appropriate question marks to form an interrogative sentence:

Ya no trabajan aquí.	*They do **not** work here **any longer**.*
¿Ya no trabajan aquí?	*They do **not** work here **any longer**?*
Todavía no has terminado.	*You have **not** finished **yet**.*
¿Todavía no has terminado?	*Have you **not** finished **yet**?*
No tienes la respuesta **aún**.	*You **still** do **not** have the answer.*
¿No tienes la respuesta **aún**?	*You **still** do **not** have the answer?*

EJERCICIO
9·2

Create another question with negative words.

1. ¿Te gusta tu trabajo?

   No _____

2. ¿Ganas mucho dinero?

   Todavía no _____

3. ¿Estudias en una universidad?

   Ya no _____

4. ¿Estás listo/a para un ascenso (*promotion*)?

   No _____

5. ¿Tienes novio/a?

   Todavía no _____

6. ¿Estás enamorado/a?

   Ya no _____

Interrogative sentences and word order

Here is a frequently used structure to build interrogative sentences in Spanish:

¿ + verb + subject + other predicate elements + ?

¿Conoce tu hermano a María?	***Does** your brother know María?*

Consider the previous English sentence. It includes the helping or auxiliary verb *does*, followed by the subject and the verb *know*. The Spanish sentence does not need an auxiliary verb. A form of the auxiliary, *do* or *does* in the present, *did* in the past, and *will* in the future tense, always precedes the verb in English. Remember that these words do not translate into Spanish.

¿Viven tus hermanos en Miami?	***Do** your brothers live in Miami?*
¿Veis (vosotros) este programa?	***Do** you watch this program?*
¿Recibieron los chicos el paquete?	***Did** the children receive the package?*
¿Vendrá el cartero mañana?	***Will** the mail carrier come tomorrow?*

There are exceptions to this rule in English. One is the English verb *to be*.

¿**Eres** la amiga de Ana?	*Are you Ana's friend?*
¿**Está** Julián en casa?	*Is Julián at home?*

Some constructions in English use the auxiliaries *to have* and *can*:

¿**No tienes** vergüenza?	*Have you no shame?*
¿**Puedes** ayudarme?	*Can you help me? / Are you able to help me?*

Of course in Spanish sentences, the subject may not always be explicit. The verb ending helps you identify the subject. Look at the following examples:

¿Hab**las** alemán?	*Do you speak German?*
¿Compr**aron** esa casa?	*Did they buy that house?*
¿Llover**á** esta noche en Asturias?	*Will it rain tonight in Asturias?*

EJERCICIO
9·3

Pregunta. *Create a question using appropriate word order.*

1. profesora / es / tu / de matemáticas / ella

_____

2. aprecian / los conocimientos de la profesora / los alumnos

_____

3. ella / tiene / un hermano / en esta facultad

_____

4. eres / su alumna / preferida

_____

5. sus colegas / a / admira / disciplinas / otras / de

_____

6. ella / responde / tus preguntas

_____

7. explicó / la profesora / teoría / la

_____

Polite questions and word order

Some situations require us to be polite when making a request, particularly when we don't know the person or persons of whom we're asking the favor. The personal pronouns **Ud.** (*you*, formal singular) and **Uds.** (*you*, both familiar and formal plural) follow the verb when the circumstances require a polite tone:

¿ + verb + subject pronoun + object + ?

¿ + Desea + **Ud.** + un café + ?

¿Desea **Ud.** un café?	*Would **you** like some coffee?*
¿Sabe **Ud.** la hora de la salida?	*Do **you** know the departure time?*
¿Necesitan **Uds.** otro recibo?	*Do **you** need another receipt?*

EJERCICIO
9·4

Traducción. *For each polite question give the pronoun in parentheses.*

1. Do you (**Ud.**) need help?

   _____

2. Do you (**Uds.**) see the children?

   _____

3. Did you (**Uds.**) arrive yet?

   _____

4. Did you (**Ud.**) give (**hacer**) a donation?

   _____

5. Did you (**Uds.**) return (**entregar**) the car?

   _____

6. Do you (**Ud.**) want a seat near a window?

   _____

Polite phrases in interrogative sentences

Another to way to communicate a polite question is to use a phrase, such as **por favor**, before the question:

Con permiso	*Pardon me / Excuse me*
Por favor	*Please*
Disculpe	*Pardon me / Excuse me*
Perdón	*Pardon me / Excuse me*

Notice the punctuation:

polite phrase + , + ¿ + verb + subject pronoun + object + ?

Perdón, ¿tiene Ud. el boleto?	***Excuse me**, do you have your ticket?*
Por favor, ¿pueden Uds. abrir la puerta?	***Please**, could you open the door?*

EJERCICIO
9·5

En español. *Give the polite form for each question.*

1. Do you want this dress? _____

2. Do you prefer this pair of shoes? _____

3. Do you need new glasses? _____

4. Are you tired? _____

5. Are you ready to pay? _____

6. Did you pay with a credit card? _____

Alternative questions

Alternative questions are very similar in nature to the simple questions or *yes/no* interrogatives. Alternative questions offer a choice, that is, two or more alternate answers. Note the pattern and the punctuation:

¿Prefieren té **o** café?	*Do they prefer coffee **or** tea?*
¿Hoy es sábado **o** domingo?	*Is today Saturday **or** Sunday?*
¿Fueron a la playa, a la tienda **o** al cine?	*Did they go to the beach, the store, **or** the movies?*

EJERCICIO
9·6

Preguntas. *Create a question with the present tense form of the verb.*

MODELO   tener (tú) favorable / un comentario / desfavorable
            ¿Tienes un comentario favorable o desfavorable?

1. preferir (tú) / un refresco de limón / una cola / una cerveza

   _____

2. llegar (vosotros) esta tarde / mañana

   _____

3. desear (ellos) / ir a la playa / nadar en la piscina

   _____

4. comprar (nosotros) la corbata / el sombrero / un libro

   _____

5. querer (Uds.) ver una película / cenar conmigo

   _____

6. dormir (Ud.) en la hamaca / en el sillón

_____

7. vivir (él) en la ciudad / en el campo

_____

Tag questions

Another way of forming a question, in both English and Spanish, is to add a *tag question* to the end of a declarative sentence:

declarative sentence + , + ¿ + tag + ? → tag question

Tienes dinero, **¿no?**   *You have some money, **don't you?***

Tag questions are used in informal spoken communication. Most likely, the person posing a tag question expects agreement, but a *no* answer is also possible. Here are the most common "tags" added to create these questions:

¿no?	*isn't, aren't?*
¿cierto?	*is it not?, isn't it?, are they not?, aren't they?*
¿no es cierto?	*is it not (isn't it) true?*
¿verdad?	*right?*
¿no es verdad?	*is it not (isn't it) true?*
¿no crees?	*don't you think?*
La gerente es inteligente, **¿no?**	*The manager is smart, **isn't she?***
Esta bufanda es cara, **¿verdad?**	*This scarf is expensive, **right?***
Martín nada muy bien, **¿cierto? / ¿no es cierto?**	*Martin swims very well, **doesn't he / right?***
La chica tiene talento, **¿no es verdad?**	*The girl has talent, **doesn't she / isn't it true?***

EJERCICIO
9·7

Add a tag question for each sentence.

1. Lucía ve muchos programas dramáticos. (no)

_____

2. Pedro prefiere los documentales del canal de cable. (no es verdad)

_____

3. Carla y Marcos van a un concierto de un grupo mexicano. (no es cierto)

_____

4. En el concierto venderán copias del último CD. (verdad)

_____

5. Después del concierto irán a cenar todos juntos. (no es cierto)

_____

6. Celebran la ocasión especial del cumpleaños de Lucía. (no es verdad)

_____

Questions with short answers

Answers to *yes/no* questions frequently include phrases that stress the answers. The following phrases are used in both informal and formal situations, mostly to add emphasis. Exclamation points are added:

¡Claro, claro que sí!, ¡claro que no!	*Of course; of course not!*
¡Cómo no!	*Sure!*
¡Desde luego!	*Indeed!*
¡Naturalmente!	*Naturally!*
¡Por supuesto (que no)!	*Absolutely (not)!*
¡Qué va!	*No way!*
¡Ni modo!	*No way!*
—¿Vas a ir a la biblioteca esta tarde?	*—Are you going to the library this afternoon?*
—¡Claro que no!	**—*Of course not!***
—¿Prefieres ir a ver a Ana?	*—Do you prefer to go see Ana?*
—¡Por supuesto!	**—*Sure!***

EJERCICIO
9·8

Respuestas. *Use one of the following expressions to answer the questions.*

1. ¿Estados Unidos están en el hemisferio sur? _____

2. ¿El Río Amazonas atraviesa Canadá? _____

3. ¿La capital de Chile es Santiago? _____

4. ¿El Mar Caribe está cerca de Panamá? _____

5. ¿España es parte de Sur América? _____

Questions and answers

Earlier in this chapter, you learned how to ask basic questions. Now we will continue practicing more types of questions to get precise information.

¿Dónde están mis llaves?	***Where** are my keys?*
¿Quién es este señor?	***Who** is this gentleman?*

Specific information questions

Questions that expect more specific information than a simple choice answer or a straightforward *yes/no* response are information questions. They start with an *interrogative pronoun*, an *interrogative adverb*, or any other *interrogative word or phrase*.

Questions with interrogative words

Interrogative words are adverbs used to ask for specific information. In general, interrogative words are followed by the regular word order in interrogative sentences. Note that these are not *yes/no* questions.

> **¿ + interrogative word + verb + subject + complement + ? → complex question**
>
> ¿**Qué** hace Ana con su salario?   ***What** does Ana do with her salary?*

You will need some of the following interrogative words to get the information needed. Note that in Spanish they all have a written accent mark:

¿Adónde?	*Where to?*
¿Cómo?	*How?*
¿Cuál?, ¿Cuáles?	*Which?*
¿Cuándo?	*When?*
¿Cuánto?, ¿Cuánta?	*How much?*
¿Cuántos?, ¿Cuántas?	*How many?*
¿Dónde?	*Where?*
¿Qué?	*What?*
¿Quién?, ¿Quiénes?	*Who?*

Here are some example sentences:

¿**Qué** hora es?	***What** time is it?*
¿**Quién** llegó?	***Who** has arrived?*
¿**Dónde** está tu hermana?	***Where** is your sister?*
¿**Cómo** trabajan ellas?	***How** do they work?*

Answers to question words

Certain adverbs are used to answer the following specific questions. Here is a short list of questions and possible answers. Note that some are set or fixed expressions:

¿Cómo?	How?
así así	*not so great, so-so*
bien	*well*
bastante bien	*rather well*
mal	*badly*
mejor	*better*
peor	*worse*
—¿**Cómo** te sientes?	—***How** do you feel?*
—**Así así.**	—***Not so great.***

¿Cuándo?	When?
anoche	*last night*
ayer	*yesterday*
después	*later*
de vez en cuando	*once in a while*

en seguida	right away
mañana	tomorrow
nunca	never
—¿**Cuándo** vas a la playa?	—**When** do you go to the beach?
—**De vez en cuando.**	—**Once in a while.**

¿Dónde?	**Where?**
aquí	here
adentro	inside
debajo	under
cerca	near, close to
por allí	over there
por acá	over here
—¿**Dónde** están las fotos?	—**Where** are the pictures?
—**Aquí** tengo las fotos.	—I have the pictures **here**.

You may want to review adverbs and their uses in Chapter 6.

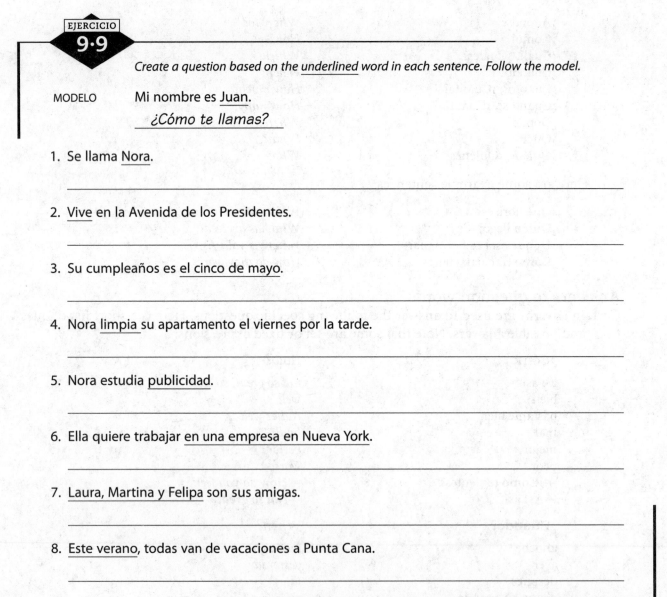

EJERCICIO
9·9

Create a question based on the underlined word in each sentence. Follow the model.

MODELO   Mi nombre es Juan.
           ¿Cómo te llamas?

1. Se llama Nora.

   _____

2. Vive en la Avenida de los Presidentes.

   _____

3. Su cumpleaños es el cinco de mayo.

   _____

4. Nora limpia su apartamento el viernes por la tarde.

   _____

5. Nora estudia publicidad.

   _____

6. Ella quiere trabajar en una empresa en Nueva York.

   _____

7. Laura, Martina y Felipa son sus amigas.

   _____

8. Este verano, todas van de vacaciones a Punta Cana.

   _____

Choose the interrogative word needed in each question.

1. ¿Cuál / Qué regalo prefieres, el cuadro o la fotografía?

2. ¿Cuál / Quién es la opinión de la madre?

3. ¿Quiénes / Cuáles son los colores preferidos del cliente?

4. ¿Qué / Cuál es la fecha para terminar el trabajo?

5. ¿Qué / Cuál día es hoy, tu aniversario?

6. ¿Cuál / Qué hay en la caja?

Complex questions with prepositions + interrogative words

Certain prepositions followed by a question word are used to elicit concrete or fuller responses to a question:

¿preposition + interrogative word + verb + subject + complement(s)?

¿**Desde** + **cuándo** + vive + Ana + en San Diego?
Since when does Ana live in San Diego?

Here is a list of *prepositions* followed by a question word used to create complex questions:

¿A quién / A quiénes?	*(To) Whom?*
¿Con quién / quiénes?	*With whom?*
¿De dónde?	*From where? / Where from?*
¿Desde cuándo?	*Since when?*
¿Hacia dónde?	*Toward where?*
¿Hasta cuándo?	*Until when?*
¿Para dónde?	*To(ward) where?*
¿Para qué?	*What for?*
¿Para quién / quiénes?	*For whom?*
¿Por dónde?	*Through where?*
¿Por qué?	*Why?*
¿Por quién / quiénes?	*For whom?*
¿**A quién** llamaste?	***Whom** did you call?*
¿**Desde cuándo** eres novia de Aldo?	***Since when** are you (have you been) Aldo's girlfriend?*
¿**Hasta cuándo** vas a trabajar?	***Until when** will you work?*
¿**Para qué** compras esta maleta?	***What** are you buying this suitcase **for**?*
¿**Por qué no** estudias matemáticas?	***Why** don't you study math?*

En español. *Answer the questions using the present tense* **tú.**

1. Where are you from?

_____

2. Where are you going?

_____

3. Since when do you study (have you been studying) Spanish?

_____

4. When are you going to finish this exercise?

_____

5. Until when are you going to wait?

_____

6. To whom do you write most of your e-mails?

_____

7. Who is knocking (**tocar a**) at the door?

_____

8. Where are you?

_____

Limiting questions

Some interrogatives are used to ask limiting or partial questions. Some elicit a specific answer about a noun: *how much?, how many?, which?*

¿Cuál? (*sing.*), ¿Cuáles? (*pl.*)	*Which?*
¿Cuánto? (*masc. sing.*); ¿Cuánta? (*fem. sing.*)	*How much?*
¿Cuántos? (*masc. pl.*); ¿Cuántas? (*fem. pl.*)	*How many?*
¿**Cuáles** son tus colores preferidos?	***Which** are your favorite colors?*
¿**Cuánto** dinero necesitas?	***How much** money do you need?*
¿**Cuántos** regalos vas a comprar?	***How many** gifts are you going to buy?*

EJERCICIO
9·12

Entrevista. *Complete each question using the words given. Follow the model.*

MODELO   quién / con / aprendió / guitarra / tocar / a / la

¿Con quién aprendió a tocar la guitarra?

1. países / ha visitado / cuántos

   _____

2. decidió / que / cuándo / quería / cantante / ser

   _____

3. su / será / próximo / concierto / dónde / su

   _____

4. voz / cómo / la / ensaya (*rehearse*) / conciertos / para / los

   _____

5. decidió / por / dedicarse / qué / música / a / la

   _____

6. son / sus / cantantes / cuáles / favoritos

   _____

7. quiere / hacer / futuro / qué / el / en

   _____

8. vacaciones / serán / cuándo / próximas / sus

   _____

EJERCICIO
9·13

Diez preguntas. *Read the paragraph and focus on the underlined phrases. Create a question with the interrogative words given.*

cuándo / cuántos / cómo / dónde / para qué / por qué / qué / quiénes

Abel Ruiz, a sus 19 años, es un gran atleta. Cuando era niño jugaba al fútbol y esa experiencia todavía lo inspira. Su padre lo llevaba a ver los partidos de fútbol. Abel quiere ser famoso, como sus ídolos, y jugar con un equipo profesional en los Estados Unidos. Ahora, Abel juega para el equipo de la universidad. Abel es muy disciplinado: siempre va a las prácticas y hace ejercicios para mantenerse en buena forma física. Tal vez Abel será un jugador famoso en unos cinco años.

1. a sus diecinueve años, _____

2. jugaba al fútbol _____

3. Su padre lo llevaba _____

4. Abel quiere ser famoso _____

5. en los Estados Unidos _____

6. para el equipo de la universidad _____

7. Abel es muy disciplinado _____

8. hace ejercicios para mantenerse en buena forma física _____

9. Abel será un jugador famoso _____

10. en unos cinco años _____

Responding to a question with another question

Frequently, a question is answered with another question if more information is needed or desired to answer the initial question:

—¿Dónde están los papeles?　　　　　—*Where are the papers?*
—**¿Qué papeles?**　　　　　　　　　　—***What papers?***

In a conversation, a question that follows a previous question may express surprise, interest, or another emotion:

—¿Conoces al novio de Lupita?　　　—*Do you know Lupita's boyfriend?*
—**¿Lupita tiene novio?**　　　　　　—***Lupita has a boyfriend?***
—**¿No lo sabías?**　　　　　　　　　—***You did not know that?***
—**¿De veras?**　　　　　　　　　　　—***Really?***

EJERCICIO
9·14

Preguntas y más preguntas. *Complete each sentence with the appropriate question word.*

1. —¿Recibiste mi mensaje? —¿_____ mensaje?

2. —¿No sabes que Ana está de viaje por Ecuador? —¿_____ fue Ana?

3. —Pero, ¿tú no recuerdas que hablamos de Ana? —¿_____ hablamos, ayer?

4. —¿Ayer? ¿No hablamos esta mañana? —¿A _____ hora?

5. —¿Por qué no te acuerdas?¿Tienes amnesia? —¿Amnesia yo? ¿De _____ hablas?

6. —¿Es esa una pregunta retórica? —¿A _____ de las preguntas te refieres?

7. —¿Quieres volverme loco? —¿_____ dices?

8. —¿Estás sorda (*deaf*)? —¿_____ ?

Exclamations

When we want to communicate strong feelings, emotions, or a sense of urgency, we use exclamations. These sentences are common in informal speech; the speaker adds facial expressions and voice modulation to stress his or her emotions. As we write in Spanish we may use an exclamation point both at the beginning and the end of the sentence:

¡Hace mucho frío!	*It is very cold!*
¡La cena está deliciosa!	*Supper is delicious!*

Exclamatory sentences

With the appropriate punctuation, you can use declarative sentences to express strong feelings. In both English and Spanish, an exclamatory sentence is a forceful, declarative sentence that shows strong emotion. Remember the inverted exclamation point that precedes exclamatory sentences and the regular exclamation point that ends them.

¡ + declarative sentence + ! → exclamatory sentence

Exclamatory sentences have several possible word orders. You can use the *subject + verb + object* word order. The exclamation points add emphasis: an element of surprise, astonishment, admiration, or happiness. Note the difference in these examples:

El hombre ganó la lotería.	*The man won the lottery.*
¡El hombre ganó la lotería!	*The man won the lottery!*

There are other possible patterns for exclamatory sentences, depending on which word or words the speaker chooses to stress:

¡ + verb + subject + object + !

¡**Ganaron** + el partido + los chicos!
*The boys **won** the match!*

¡ + adverb + verb + subject + object + !

¡**Muy lindo** + canta + Marla + esa canción!
*Marla sings that song **beautifully**!*

Exclamatory sentences and negative declarative sentences

Negative declarative sentences, with added exclamation marks, can also be the starting point for building an exclamatory sentence:

¡ + negative declarative sentence + ! → exclamatory sentence

¡ + Lula **no** hizo la tarea + !
*Lula did **not** do her homework!*

EJERCICIO
9·15

En español. *Add exclamation marks.*

1. There is a beautiful moon! _____

2. We (*fem.*) are going to walk on the beach! _____

3. It is very hot outside! _____

4. The lemonade is cold! _____

5. Lucy is so tired! _____

6. Now we (*fem.*) are ready to rest! _____

7. I am not going to sleep! _____

8. I agree (**estar de acuerdo**)! _____

Te toca a ti. *Describe yourself. Complete each sentence using exclamation marks in Spanish.*

1. Soy muy aburrido/a. _____

2. Bailo mucho en las fiestas. _____

3. Tengo muchos amigos. _____

4. Me gusta mi trabajo. _____

5. Tengo mucho dinero. _____

6. Ahorro dinero todos los meses. _____

7. Tengo mucha suerte en el amor. _____

8. Soy muy feliz. _____

Exclamation words and word order in exclamatory sentences

Exclamation words express the attitude and emotions of the speaker. A formal exclamatory sentence, used in writing, is one that begins with an exclamation word such as **¡Qué... !** (*What . . . !*), **¡Cómo... !** (*How . . . !*), as well as others. In Spanish, exclamation words, like question words, have a written accent mark:

¡Cómo!	*How!*
¡Cuán!	*How!*
¡Cuánto/a!	*How much!*
¡Cuántos/as!	*How many!*
¡Cuánto!	*How!*
¡Qué!	*What!*
¡Quién! / ¡Quiénes!	*Who!*

These exclamation words underscore the quantity, quality, nature, or intensity of the noun, adjective, adverb, or verb that follows:

¡Qué mentiras dices!	***How many** lies you tell!*
¡Qué ruido hace!	***What** noise it/he/she makes!*
¡Qué caro es!	***How** expensive it is!*

| ¡**Qué** mal toca la niña la guitarra! | *How badly the girl plays the guitar!* |
| ¡**Cómo** llueve! | *It is raining **so** hard! / **How** hard it's raining!* |

¡Así es la vida! *Create sentences with appropriate punctuation.*

1. cuanto cuestan estos zapatos _____

2. que largo es el vestido _____

3. como ha subido el precio de la vida _____

4 cuanto ganan _____

5. que amable es el camarero _____

6. cuantas entradas vendieron para el concierto _____

7. que bien hacen la paella en este restaurante _____

8. cuanta belleza hay en este lugar _____

Exclamation words in colloquial expressions

Some exclamations are used only in colloquial language, typical of informal conversation. The exclamations emphasize admiration, praise, or their opposite, ironically: contempt, disdain, scorn, dislike, etc. Note the following constructions and what they emphasize. These exclamations may have several meanings.

◆ ¡**Qué** + ... **que**... !

    ¡**Qué** auto **que** tienes!   *What a car you have!*

    ¡**Qué auto que tienes!** could praise the size, value, or qualities of the car; or the context may suggest the car is ugly, old, or small. A similar construction with similar meanings uses the interjection **vaya**:

◆ ¡**Vaya** + ... **que**... !

    ¡**Vaya** casa **que** tienes!   *What a great house you have!*
                                      or *What a horrible house you have!*

◆ The adjectives **menudo, menuda, menudos, menudas** (*small*) and **valiente** (*brave*) communicate an ironic or opposite sense, different from the usual meaning:

◆ ¡**Menudo** + ... **que**... !

    ¡**Menuda** mentira **que** dices!   *Some big lie you tell!*
    ¡**Valiente** trabajo **que** has hecho!   *Some work you have done!*
                                     or *What a disaster you have made!*

Choose the appropriate reaction.

1. _____ Francisco lava su ropa él mismo.

    a. ¡Qué disciplinado que es!

2. _____ Su padre le regaló un auto.

    b. ¡Qué listo que es!

3. _____ Juega a la baraja y siempre gana.

    c. ¡Menuda suerte que tiene!

4. _____ Siempre pide un descuento en la tienda.

    d. ¡Qué generoso que es!

5. _____ Va al gimnasio cuatro días a la semana.

    e. ¡Qué limpio que es!

Interjections and exclamatory sentences

Interjections are words or phrases that add emotion to the delivery of a sentence. These utterances frequently appear in exclamatory sentences to express a reaction to what we perceive around us, what we remember, feel, or wish. Interjections are usually separated by a comma in writing:

¡**Ah**, el concierto empieza a las ocho!	*Oh, the concert starts at eight!*
¡**Ay**, tengo dolor de cabeza!	*Ouch, my head hurts (I have a headache)!*

Some interjections are euphemisms, inoffensive expressions that replace expressions that may offend the listener or that allude to something perceived as unpleasant. They are more common in speech:

¡**Diantre**, el examen es difícil!	*Darn, the exam is hard!*

The English equivalents of interjections in a new language can be difficult to determine, because their meaning depends on the context: **¡ay!** may communicate pain, surprise, or delight. Nouns, adverbs, and verbs are also used as interjections. Here is a list of frequently used interjections in Spanish. Note the exclamation points:

¡Ah!	*Oh!*	¡Eh!	*Hey!*
¡Aj!	*Yuck!*	¡Fo!	*Ugh!*
¡Anda!	*Oops!*	¡Hala!, ¡Hale!	*Go!, Do it!, Hurry!*
¡Arre!	*Giddyup!*	¡Hola!	*Hi!*
¡Aupa!	*Up!* (especially with children)	¡Huy!	*Ouch!*
		¡Oh!	*Oh!, Oh really!*
¡Ay de mí!	*Poor me!*	¡Ojalá!	*I wish!, Let's hope!*
¡Ay!	*Oh!, Ouch!*	¡Olé, olé!	*Bravo!*
¡Bah!	*No way!*	¡Puaj!	*Yuck!*
¡Bravo!	*Bravo!*	¡Pobre!, ¡Pobre de mi!	*Poor thing!, Poor me!*
¡Caramba!	*Good grief!*		
¡Caracoles!	*Good grief!*	¡Pst!	*Hey!*
¡Caray!	*Oops!*	¡Puf!	*Yuck!, Hmm!*
¡Chist!	*Hey!*	¡Quia!	*No way!*
¡Chitón!	*Hush!, Quiet!*	¡Uf!	*Phew!* (tiredness), *Ugh!* (dislike, repugnance)
¡Cielos!	*Good heavens!*		
¡Córcholis!	*Good grief!*		
¡Diantre!	*Heck!*	¡Vale!	*Bye!, OK!*
¡Ea!	*Go!*	¡Vaya!	*Great!*

EJERCICIO
9·19

En español.

1. Hush, there is too much noise!

_____

2. Heavens, the lecture starts at eight o'clock!

_____

3. Hey, we are here!

_____

4. Poor me, I have no time!

_____

5. Let's hope, I need to win!

_____

6. Oh, the watch is beautiful!

_____

EJERCICIO
9·20

¡Usa la lógica! _Choose the logical reaction for each sentence._

1. _____ Marta siempre gana.   a. ¡Oh, fue terrible!

2. _____ Su esposo tuvo un accidente.   b. ¡Ah, qué suerte que tiene!

3. _____ La comida no sabe bien.   c. ¡Uf, tiene mucha suerte!

4. _____ Su padre le regaló doscientos euros.   d. ¡Puaj, es un desastre!

5. _____ Mario sabe muchos chistes.   e. ¡Qué cómico que es!

Questions, answers, and exclamations   **165**

The imperfect tense

The indicative imperfect tense in Spanish is used to communicate actions that happened [in the] past: actions, events, or situations that took place at a nonspecific time, or that happene[d sev]eral times or continuously in the past.

Camila **visitaba** a su familia en Colombia.	*Camila used to visit her family in Colombia.*
Su familia **vivía** cerca de Cali.	*Her family lived near Cali.*

Now, let's review the three conjugations of regular verbs in the imperfect tense.

Regular verbs in the imperfect

Almost all Spanish verbs are regular in the imperfect tense. To form the imperfect, dr[op the] infinitive endings -**ar**, -**er**, or -**ir** and add the following endings:

-**ar** verbs: -**aba**, -**abas**, -**aba**, -**ábamos**, -**ábais**, -**aban**

-**er** verbs: -**ía**, -**ías**, -**ía**, -**íamos**, -**íais**, -**ían**

-**ir** verbs: -**ía**, -**ías**, -**ían**, -**íamos**, -**íais**, -**ían**

contar *to count, tell*	**vender** *to sell*	**abrir** *to open*
cont**aba**	vend**ía**	abr**ía**
cont**abas**	vend**ías**	abr**ías**
cont**aba**	vend**ía**	abr**ía**
cont**ábamos**	vend**íamos**	abr**íamos**
cont**ábais**	vend**íais**	abr**íais**
cont**aban**	vend**ían**	abr**ían**

Note that the **nosotros** and **vosotros** forms of -**ar** verbs take a written accent. The endi[ngs of] -**er** and -**ir** verbs are the same throughout, and they all take a written accent.

Irregular verbs in the imperfect

Only three verbs are irregular in the imperfect tense: **ser**, **ir**, and **ver**.

ser *to be*	ir *to go*	ver *to see*
era	iba	veía
eras	ibas	veías
era	iba	veía
éramos	íbamos	veíamos
erais	ibais	veíais
eran	iba	veían

Los hábitos de Lulú. *Complete each sentence with the appropriate imperfect tense form of the verb in parentheses.*

1. Lulú y tú (*pl.; fam.*) casi siempre _____ a pasear los domingos cerca de tu casa. (ir)

2. Casi todos los días de la semana Lulú _____ muy tarde. (despertarse)

3. Sin embargo, ella _____ todos los días al trabajo. (ir)

4. Lulú y su hermana Alina _____ juntas. (vivir)

5. Lulú y yo _____ muy buenas amigas. (ser)

6. ¡Qué pena! Muchas veces las compañeras de trabajo _____ el cansancio en su cara. (ver)

7. A menudo Lulú _____ el pelo desarreglado. (llevar)

8. A veces, también ella _____ la camisa al revés (*inside out*). (ponerse)

9. En aquellos días yo _____ mucha pena por ella. (sentir)

10. Ella no _____ dormir porque _____ de insomnio. (poder, padecer)

11. Todos nosotros en la tienda _____ los problemas de Lulú. (conocer)

12. ¡Todos sus colegas _____ regalarle un despertador! (querer)

13. ¿Esto _____ una buena idea para un buen regalo o para una broma? (ser)

14. No, yo _____ que algunos _____ reírse de Lulú. (saber, querer)

Uses of the imperfect tense

The imperfect tense is used to express the following:

♦ A customary or habitual action, or an action that used to happen often in the past; the English equivalent is *used to* or *would*.

Nina **nadaba** en la piscina **los sábados**.	*Nina used to swim in the pool on Saturdays.*
Lisa **acompañaba** a Nina **a menudo**.	*Lisa would go often with Nina.*

♦ An action, a situation that was happening or was in progress in the past. There is no reference to when the action began or ended. English uses the verb *to be* + the gerund (*-ing* form of the verb) to translate this sense of the imperfect. Adding *-ing* to a verb in English indicates an action in progress.

Los chicos **jugaban** en el parque.	*The children were playing in the park.*

♦ A description of people, things, or events in the past

Ali **tenía** el pelo largo y los ojos verdes.	*Ali had long hair and green eyes.*
Las calles **estaban** resbalosas.	*The streets were slippery.*
El concierto **incluía** dos orquestas cubanas.	*The concert included two Cuban orchestras.*

♦ The time of day, the day of the week, or a date in the past

Eran las cuatro de la tarde.	*It was four o'clock in the afternoon.*
La reunión siempre **era los lunes**.	*The meeting was always on Monday.*
Era el primero de mayo.	*It was the first of May.*

♦ The age of a person or animal

Pablo **tenía cuarenta años**.	*Pablo was forty years old.*
Mi gato **tenía dos años**.	*My cat was two years old.*

♦ A state of mind in the past with **creer, pensar, querer, esperar,** or **saber**

Yo **pensaba** en ti todos los días.	*I used to think about you every day.*
Queríamos una casa con tres baños.	*We wanted a home with three bathrooms.*
Esperábamos el autobús cerca de mi casa.	*We used to wait for the bus near my house.*
Sabías que tenías problemas.	*You knew you had problems.*

♦ A physical sensation with **doler, sentir,** or **molestar**

Le **dolía la cabeza**.	*He had a headache.*
No **se sentía** bien.	*He did not feel well.*
¿Te **molestaba** el ruido?	*Did the noise bother you?*

EJERCICIO
10·2

Traducción.

1. When I was sixteen years old I used to live in a small town.

_____

2. My brother and I would run to a lake near our home.

_____

3. During the summer many of our friends used to swim in the lake.

_____

4. The lake was beautiful but the water was always cold.

_____

5. I always wanted to sleep under a tree.

_____

6. I felt comfortable and safe there.

_____

7. My brother and I always wanted to enjoy a long and delightful summer.

_____

Mi familia y yo. *First read the sentences. Then choose the letter that indicates the rule for the use of the imperfect tense.*

1. _____ Mi primo Alberto siempre salía temprano por la mañana.

2. _____ Se despertaba temprano porque le dolía la espalda.

3. _____ Era alto, tenía arrugas (*wrinkle*) en la cara y también era calvo (*bald*).

4. _____ Sal, mi hermano, quería una casa lejos de la ciudad.

5. _____ También deseaba comprar un auto nuevo.

6. _____ Sus hijas gemelas, Lola y Sarita, tenían 25 años en el año 2010.

7. _____ Mis tíos eran muy amables.

8. _____ Yo tenía dolor de cabeza.

9. _____ Mis padres tomaban café con leche todos los días.

10. _____ Mis primos pensaban en mí.

a. a physical sensation

b. a habitual action

c. a description

d. a person's age

e. a state of mind in the past

Una descripción en el pasado. *Complete each sentence with the appropriate form of the imperfect of each verb in parentheses.*

Cuando Juan 1. _____ (tener) quince años, todavía

2. _____ (dibujar) monigotes (*doodle*) en el cuaderno en la escuela.

Juan 3. _____ (ir) a casa y no 4. _____ (hacer) la

tarea. Su habitación 5. _____ (tener) dos ventanas y

6. _____ (haber) periódicos viejos en el piso. Cuando Juan

7. _____ (entrar) a su dormitorio, 8. _____ (escuchar) canciones, 9. _____ (ver) programas en la tele y

10. _____ (leer) las tiras cómicas (*comic strip*) en los periódicos. Juan

11. _____ (querer) resolver todos los problemas del mundo y

12. _____ (pensar) que la risa era la solución de muchos problemas.

¡Qué optimista 13. _____ (ser) Juan!

Phrases used with the imperfect

Previous examples included phrases that gave the context for the use of the imperfect. These phrases describe the frequency of repetitive and ongoing past actions and nonspecific time.

EJERCICIO
10·5

Traducción.

1. My parents and I usually visited several cities in the United States when I was a young girl.

_____

2. Every year we traveled to places like Fresno, St. Augustine, and other cities.

_____

3. Many times my father rented a big car.

_____

4. In those days I loved to stay a couple of days in different cities.

_____

5. Sometimes I met new friends like Fernando.

_____

6. Every week I wanted to talk to Fernando.

_____

7. He was so funny! Several times I wrote his name and drew a heart on a piece of paper.

_____

8. Fernando used to send me many letters.

_____

9. I always felt happy reading his letters.

_____

10. Fernando and I got married and now we remember those days when we were young.

_____

Imperfect or preterit?

Having dealt with the forms of the imperfect and the preterit, you are now ready to observe how these two aspects of the past are used. (You may want to review the preterit tense in Chapter 7.) Among teachers and students, there are many, many analogies, explanations, and mnemonic acronyms to help students conceptualize the use of these two tenses. So this is the proper moment to start at the conceptual level with the broadest, one-word label for what each of these tenses is about and then begin narrowing it:

- The imperfect is descriptive.
- The preterit is narrative.

When we say that the imperfect is *descriptive*, we refer to its role in setting a stage and giving background information about how a situation was. It is *not* used to tell what happened, but rather for telling what was going on or how things appeared, what conditions were. This is why time of day and one's age are always expressed in the imperfect. Weather phenomena in the past (what the day was like), are also expressed in the imperfect (unless you're telling about some phenomenon starting or stopping, or summing it up—functions of the preterit). Time is always flowing, and the imperfect reflects that in all its usages. The imperfect invites amplification and detail in terms of action—but that is the function reserved for the preterit. Consider the imperfect as you would stage directions that tell a set designer what to build and where to place items on a stage. The action is what goes on there. When the imperfect is used, one is in the middle of that flow, not at its beginning or end.

César **era** dictador.	*Caesar was a dictator.*
Era un día claro y hacía sol.	*It was a clear, sunny day.*
Mi tía **tenía** seis años en esta foto.	*My aunt was six years old in this photo.*
Eran las cuatro de la tarde...	*It was four in the afternoon . . .*

By contrast, and as its complement, the preterit is *narrative*. It tells or summarizes what happened at a particular moment. The preterit is used to tell when actions started and ended, and, when it summarizes, it can enclose even long periods of time. It treats time as an expandable or contractible parenthesis.

El siglo diecinueve **fue** el siglo de la clase media.	*The nineteenth century was the century of the middle class.*

Compare the following sentences. The first is in the preterit and the second in the imperfect.

Dejó de llover.	*It stopped raining.*
Dejaba de llover.	*The rain was letting up.*

The Spanish imperfect is almost always used when English uses *were + gerund (-ing)* to express an action already in progress or as *used to + verb*, to express habitual or repeated actions in the past. It also is used whenever *would + verb* can be substituted for *used to + verb*—but beware: it is *not* used in any other instances where *would + verb* is used in English. The other uses of *would* in English will require either the *conditional* or the *imperfect subjunctive*, when the English use of *would* is anticipatory. If you remember these observations as well as the use of the imperfect for time of day and telling a person's age in the past, then you'll be right more than 90 percent of the time.

The following examples illustrate uses of *would* with different Spanish tenses.

Cuando era niño, **jugaba** con mi perro.	*When I was a boy, I would play with my dog.*
Ella esperaba que Juan le **pidiera** la mano.	*She was hoping that John would ask her to marry him.*
Si tuviera más tiempo libre, lo **pasaría** con mi hija.	*If I had more free time, I would spend it with my daughter.*

As for the preterit's equivalent in English, the general rule of thumb is that it is used when English uses a simple, one-word past tense. But this rule is not as reliable as the observations about when the imperfect is used, particularly where the verb *to be* is used in English (**ser** and **estar** in Spanish) or when the action of the verb is qualified in some way by an adverb. Compare the following two sentences, the first of which is in the preterit, the second in the imperfect. These two sentences alone should suffice to demonstrate that often, the choice between using the preterit or the imperfect is not a matter of grammar, but rather of what one intends to communicate.

Fuimos a la playa.	*We went to the beach.*
Íbamos a la playa mucho.	*We went to the beach a lot.*

Now let's examine four verbs that, when used in the preterit, do not mean what the dictionary typically gives as the primary meaning of their infinitive forms. These verbs are **saber** and **conocer**—the two verbs that mean *to know* (but in very different senses)—and the auxiliary verbs **querer** (*to want*) and **poder** (*to be able*). Since the preterit focuses on a moment in time when an action occurs, these verbs are used in the preterit to mean, respectively, *to find out*, *to meet*, *to try* (or, in the negative, *to refuse*) and *to succeed* (or, in the negative, *to fail*). When their primary meanings are needed in the past, the imperfect is used. Observe the following contrastive examples.

¿Cuándo **supiste** que él falsificó la documentación?	*When did you find out that he falsified the documents?*
Yo ya **sabía** que el tipo era mentiroso.	*I already knew the guy was a liar.*

Yo **conocí** a la francesa en una fiesta.	*I met the French woman at a party.*
Goethe **conocía** bien la ópera *Die Zauberflöte*.	*Goethe was very familiar with the opera Die Zauberflöte.*
Ellos **quisieron** abrir la caja fuerte.	*They tried to open the safe.*
No **quería** que nadie descubriera su crimen.	*He didn't want anyone to discover his crime.*
Por fin, **pude** escalar la montaña.	*Finally, I succeeded at scaling the mountain.*
No la **pudieron** abrir.	*They failed to open it.*
En el colegio, Juan no **podía** correr tan rápido como su hermano.	*In high school, John couldn't run as fast as his brother.*

The glorious thing about these two aspects of the past is their ability to create vivid verbal cinema. Examine the following sentences in light of what this chapter has observed about how they conceptualize action in the past.

El intruso **abría** la ventana con cuidado y mientras **observaba** al señor que **leía**, no **advirtió** que éste **ocultaba** un revólver ya armado en su regazo.	*The thief opened the window cautiously and, as he observed the gentleman reading, he failed to notice that the fellow was hiding in his lap a revolver already cocked.*
Me **dijeron** que **sabían** que el galeón **estaba** a docenas de metros debajo de la superficie del mar, pero que **quisieron** subirlo porque **había** varios millones de dólares en piezas de a ocho en el suelo submarino.	*They told me they knew the galleon was dozens of meters below the surface, but they tried to raise it, because there was several millions of dollars' worth of pieces of eight on the sea floor.*
Cuando **supe** lo que el Sr. Acero me **hacía**, **decidí** denunciarlo ante todos.	*When I found out what Mr. Acero was doing to me, I decided to denounce him before all.*
Mientras **conversaban** en el pasillo sobre los pasteles que **horneaban** los fines de semana, yo **seguí escribiendo**.	*While they chatted in the hallway about the cakes they were baking on weekends, I kept writing.*

The following exercises will test your ability to properly conjugate verbs in the imperfect and preterit, as well as to determine which form to use in various contexts.

EJERCICIO
10·6

Give the proper form of the verb in the imperfect, according to the subject pronoun in parentheses.

1. (él) mirar _____

2. (tú) comer _____

3. (Ud.) tener _____

4. (yo) ver _____

5. (nosotros) haber _____

6. (ellas) hacer _____

7. (vosotros) trabajar _____

8. (yo) querer _____

9. (ellos) poder _____

10. (Uds.) deber _____

11. (ella) ser _____

12. (Ud.) ver _____

13. (tú) ir _____

14. (yo) poder _____

15. (él) ser _____

16. (ella) ir _____

17. (Uds.) establecer _____

18. (nosotros) leer _____

19. (yo) escribir _____

20. (tú) creer _____

Give the proper form of the verb in the preterit, according to the subject pronoun in parentheses.

1. (yo) ver _____

2. (tú) sentir _____

3. (Ud.) saber _____

4. (ellos) caber _____

5. (yo) dar _____

6. (ella) viajar _____

7. (Uds.) vivir _____

8. (yo) traer _____

9. (nosotros) trabajar _____

10. (ella) querer _____

11. (yo) entretener _____

12. (tú) conducir _____

13. (yo) tener _____

14. (vosotros) haber _____

15. (ellos) hablar _____

16. (yo) poner _____

17. (ella) estar _____

18. (tú) comer _____

19. (ellos) poder _____

20. (tú) hacer _____

Translate the following sentences from Spanish to English.

1. Mientras mis hermanas hablaban, yo tocaba la guitarra.

   _____

2. Cuando salió la película *La guerra de las galaxias*, yo tenía 22 años.

   _____

3. Había varios hombres en la esquina cuando el auto se resbaló y se chocó contra la pared.

   _____

4. Cuando estábamos de vacaciones, mis amigos y yo esquiábamos e íbamos a restaurantes.

   _____

5. ¿Dónde estabas tú y qué hacías cuando ocurrió el eclipse total de sol?

   _____

6. Comimos, descansamos y miramos la tele un rato, luego decidimos ir a la playa.

   _____

7. No me gustó cuando preparaba la cena y sonó el teléfono.

   _____

8. Los niños jugaban en el patio cuando llegó la abuela.

   _____

9. Se despertaba Elena cuando su papá llamó.

   _____

10. Eran las cuatro de la tarde y llovía cuando salí del cine.

   _____

11. Mi hermana tenía cuatro años cuando nací.

_____

12. ¿Qué tiempo hacía cuando iban al lago para esquiar?

_____

13. Mis padres se mudaron a otra casa cuando yo tenía dos años.

_____

14. El perro se echó a correr tras el conejo tan pronto como lo vio.

_____

15. A las tres en punto estuve esperando en la entrada de la biblioteca.

_____

16. Cuando dejó de llover, regresamos a la carpa.

_____

17. La cena salió bien ya que la comida estuvo rica.

_____

18. Ese año, nevó mucho en la ciudad.

_____

19. Cuando me di cuenta de que no tenía acceso a la red, decidí marcharme.

_____

20. La banda tocaba y la gente bailaba, pero me sentía solo.

_____

EJERCICIO
10·9

Translate the following sentences from English to Spanish.

1. When I arrived, the dog was sleeping.

_____

2. While you were eating, our brother was working. (**tú**)

_____

3. She left when he arrived.

_____

4. Alexandra was three years old when we moved to Seattle.

_____

5. After we got in the taxi, it began to rain.

_____

6. Yesterday was a very cold day for Seattle.

_____

7. He was fixing the table when he hurt his hand.

_____

8. Were you trying to call me yesterday? (**tú**)

_____

9. It was five in the afternoon, and raining, when my friends decided to come to visit me.

_____

10. I was preparing roast beef while I wrote this exercise.

_____

11. While I was setting the table, my friend was downstairs packing for his trip.

_____

12. Three birds were sitting on a wire when, suddenly, the cat tried to climb up to eat one.

_____

13. Her mother sat down when she heard the news.

_____

14. Mr. Acero was gossiping, everyone was listening to him, but only a few believed him.

_____

15. She wanted to go to bed but had too much work due the next day.

_____

16. The plane landed while it was snowing.

_____

17. When the train stopped, the passengers got off.

_____

18. While the ship was coming into port, customs agents detained it.

_____

19. While my grandmother knitted, we and the dog would play.

_____

20. Her friends bought her the gift while she was eating lunch.

_____

Preterit or imperfect? Fill in the blanks with the proper form of the verbs in parentheses.

Cuando Juan y María (1) _____ (ser) pequeños todavía, su familia (2) _____ (vivir) en el campo. Un día, su papá (3) _____ (aceptar) un puesto con una compañía extranjera que le (4) _____ (exigir) mudarse a Chile. Aunque su esposa no (5) _____ (saber) hablar español, a ella le (6) _____ (parecer) una muy buena e importante oportunidad para que los hijos lo aprendieran. Así que ella (7) _____ (aceptar) la idea con entusiasmo.

Mientras ellos (8) _____ (prepararse) para la mudanza y (9) _____ (hacer) las maletas y (10) _____ (empacar) todo, le (11) _____ (llegar) los boletos de avión. Juan y María (12) _____ (alegrarse) mucho porque nunca habían volado.

(13) _____ (Llegar) el día tan esperado. (14) _____ (Llover) cuando la familia (15) _____ (salir) de casa, pero todos (16) _____ (estar) muy contentos porque (17) _____ (ir) a tener una experiencia agradable: un viaje en avión y una nueva casa en otro país. (18) _____ (Ser) las ocho de la noche cuando ellos (19) _____ (abordar) el avión. Ellos (20) _____ (tener) que hacer muchas escalas—en México, D.F., en Panamá y en Lima. Cuando por fin el último vuelo (21) _____ (aterrizar) en Santiago, ellos (22) _____ (bajar) del avión y los niños (23) _____ (sorprenderse) porque (24) _____ (hacer) calor. ¡Las estaciones (25) _____ (estar) al revés y (26) _____ (ser) invierno en Estados Unidos!

Los problemas de la vida. Traducción. *Use the words in the* **Vocabulario útil** *for your translation.*

VOCABULARIO ÚTIL

annoying	**fastidioso, -a**	*pedestrian*	**el peatón / la peatona**
euphoric	**optimista**	*such bad luck!*	**¡qué mala suerte!**
holiday	**el día feriado**	*traffic lights*	**el semáforo**
luckily	**por suerte**	*to snore*	**roncar**
news	**las noticias**	*to stretch*	**estirar**
Oh, my God!	**¡Ay, Dios mío!**	*to yawn*	**bostezar**

This morning I woke up late. I yawned many times, I was happy, I felt optimistic. Then I opened the window in my bedroom and stretched my arms. The traffic lights were not working. Luckily, there was not much traffic on the street and I saw very few pedestrians. I went out to pick up my newspaper. I did not open it. I did not read the horrible news. I went to the kitchen and prepared my breakfast. I wanted to sleep and snore. Suddenly the alarm clock went off and I woke up. Oh, my God! It was not Saturday, not Sunday. It was not a holiday. Such bad luck! It was a dream.

_____

_____

_____

_____

_____

_____

_____

_____

_____

Reflexive verbs and reflexive pronouns

Reflexive verbs and reflexive pronouns in Spanish are used frequently in daily routines. As learners and speakers of a language become fluent, they increasingly rely on pronouns.

The subject of a reflexive verb both performs and receives the action.

Me seco el pelo con la secadora.	*I dry my hair with a hairdryer.*

In this example, the reflexive pronoun **me** precedes the verb **seco**.

A negative word precedes the reflexive pronoun in Spanish.

No me levanto tarde.	*I do not get up late.*

If there is an infinitive verb or a present participle, the reflexive pronoun may either be placed before the conjugated verb or be attached to the infinitive.

Se quiere afeitar. / Quiere **afeitarse**.	*He wants to shave.*

A written accent is placed on the stressed vowel of the present participle when the reflexive pronoun is attached to it.

Se está **despertando**. / Está **despertándose**.	*She is waking up.*
Estamos **vistiéndonos**.	*We are getting dressed.*
Ella está **levantándose**.	*She is getting up.*

Reflexive pronouns

The reflexive pronouns are as follows.

SUBJECT PRONOUN	REFLEXIVE PRONOUN	SUBJECT PRONOUN	REFLEXIVE PRONOUN
yo	**me**	nosotros, -as	**nos**
tú	**te**	vosotros, -as	**os**
Ud.	**se**	Uds.	**se**
él/ella	**se**	ellos/ellas	**se**

In English, reflexive pronouns end in *-self* or *-selves* (*myself, ourselves*) and are the object of the verb.

Me miro en el espejo.	*I see **myself** in the mirror.*

In a nonreflexive construction, the subject is placed first followed by the verb (in this example the ending **-o** indicates the subject is **yo**).

Seco las toallas en la terraza.	*I dry the towels on the terrace.*

VOCABULARIO

Reflexive verbs are used to express or describe personal care and routines. This list includes reflexive verbs in the infinitive with the attached reflexive pronoun **se**. Verbs may have stem changes; some are irregular.

acostarse (o → ue)	*to go to bed*	**levantarse**	*to get up, stand up*
afeitarse	*to shave oneself*	**maquillarse**	*to put on makeup*
arreglarse	*to dress up*	**peinarse**	*to comb one's hair*
bañarse	*to bathe oneself*	**ponerse**	*to put on*
cepillarse	*to brush one's hair/teeth*	**quitarse**	*to take off*
despertarse (e → ie)	*to wake up*	**secarse**	*to dry oneself*
desvestirse (e → i)	*to undress oneself*	**verse**	*to see oneself*
dormirse (o → ue)	*to fall asleep*	**vestirse (e → i)**	*to dress oneself*
ducharse	*to take a shower*		
lavarse	*to wash oneself*		

Alina **se cepilla** los dientes.	*Alina brushes her teeth.*
Marian **se viste** rápido.	*Marian dresses quickly.*

In English, personal items are used with possessive pronouns; in Spanish, with its reflexive construction, the definite article is used.

Me quito el pijama y **me pongo** el vestido.	*I take off my pajamas and put on my dress.*

EJERCICIO
11·1

¡Práctica! *Complete each sentence with the appropriate reflexive pronoun and the present tense form of the verb in parentheses.*

1. Laura _____. (levantarse)

2. Sara entra al baño y _____. (ducharse)

3. Lorena y Cati _____ los dientes después de desayunar. (cepillarse)

4. Carmen y yo _____ todos los días. (maquillarse)

5. Juanito y tú _____ antes de bañarse. (desvestirse)

6. Y Uds., ¿_____ el pelo todas la mañanas? (secarse)

Traducción.

1. I go to bed early every night.

   _____

2. Before I go to bed I get undressed.

   _____

3. Then I put on my pajamas.

   _____

4. I fall asleep around (**a eso de**) ten o'clock at night.

   _____

5. At six o'clock in the morning I wake up.

   _____

6. But I get up from bed half an hour later.

   _____

7. Then I take a cold shower.

   _____

8. I dry my hair.

   _____

9. I do not shave.

   _____

10. I brush my teeth in the morning at home.

    _____

11. I put on a bit of makeup.

    _____

12. I look at myself in the mirror.

    _____

13. I get dressed before eight from Monday to Friday.

    _____

14. Finally, I wash my hands and I am ready.

    _____

Preguntas personales. *Answer the following questions in complete sentences.*

1. ¿Te levantas a la misma hora los fines de semana? ¿Por qué?

   _____

2. ¿Te disgusta despertarte temprano los lunes? Explica.

   _____

3. ¿Prefieres ducharte o bañarte?

   _____

4. ¿Cómo te vistes cuando vas al trabajo?

   _____

5. ¿Te tiñes (*to dye hair*) el pelo tú mismo?

   _____

6. Yo me corto el pelo. ¿Y tú?

   _____

In Spanish many verbs can be used as either reflexive or nonreflexive, for a subtle change in meaning. Some are irregular or have stem changes in the indicative present tense.

VOCABULARIO

Nonreflexive		Reflexive	
aburrir	*to bore someone*	**aburrirse**	*to become bored*
caer	*to fall*	**caerse**	*to fall down*
enojar	*to bother*	**enojarse**	*to get angry*
despertar (e → ie)	*to wake someone up*	**despertarse (e → ie)**	*to wake up*
dormir (o → ue)	*to sleep*	**dormirse (o → ue)**	*to fall asleep*
ir	*to go*	**irse**	*to go away*
llevar	*to carry*	**llevarse**	*to get along*
parecer	*to seem*	**parecerse**	*to resemble*
poner	*to place, put*	**ponerse**	*to put on; to become*
quitar	*to take away*	**quitarse**	*to take off*

Reflexive verbs may be used in all tenses, both simple and compound.

Lisa **se despertó** a la medianoche.   *Lisa woke up at midnight.*

Juan Carlos **se levantaba** temprano   *Juan Carlos used to wake up early*
todos los sábados.   *every Saturday.*

The reflexive pronoun is usually placed before the auxiliary verb in compound tenses (see Chapter 17 for the uses of the compound tenses).

Carlos **se ha escondido** detrás de   *Carlos has hidden (himself) behind*
un árbol.   *a tree.*

Pablito **se había caído** de la cama.   *Pablito had fallen from his bed.*

EJERCICIO
11·4

¡Práctica! *Complete each sentence with the appropriate present tense form of the verb in parentheses.*

1. Beni _____ cuando está solo. (aburrirse)

2. Él y sus hermanos _____ mucho. (parecerse)

3. Hoy, Beni _____ a la casa de sus abuelos. (ir)

4. Antonia y Luis, los abuelos, no _____ cuando Beni va a su casa. (dormir)

5. A ellos les _____ que Beni es un fanático de la música del Caribe. (parecer)

6. Antonia _____ un canal hispano en la televisión y escuchan corridos mexicanos. (poner)

7. Luis _____ mientras Beni y Antonia hablan y escuchan el programa. (dormir)

8. Pero _____ furioso cuando lo despiertan para cantar con ellos. (ponerse)

9. Hoy _____ a visitarlos. (ir)

10. Beni _____ una guitarra para cantar con ellos. (llevar)

EJERCICIO
11·5

Traducción.

1. Your comments bore me.

_____

2. I am bored when I am alone.

_____

3. I am going to sleep now.

_____

4. You are bothering my dog.

_____

5. Money does not fall from the sky.

_____

6. My friend Alex wakes his children.

_____

7. I am going to take my mother to the dentist.

_____

8. I usually do not wake up late on weekends.

_____

9. I get angry if I do not sleep well.

_____

10. I take off my shoes and put on my slippers.

_____

11. I get along very well with my boss.

_____

12. When are you (*sing., fam.*) going away?

_____

13. I think you are going to visit Mila.

_____

14. I put my towels in the bathroom.

_____

15. I take my dogs to the park every day.

_____

Reflexive verbs and prepositions

As you have already seen, some verbs that are used in the reflexive form in Spanish are not usually reflexive in English. Many of these verbs are followed by a specific preposition.

VOCABULARIO

acordarse de	*to remember*	**morirse de**	*to die of*
atreverse a	*to dare*	**negarse a**	*to refuse to*
arrepentirse de	*to regret*	**olvidarse de**	*to forget about*
darse cuenta de	*to realize*	**parecerse a**	*to resemble*
burlarse de	*to make fun of*	**quejarse de**	*to complain about*
enterarse de	*to find out about*	**reírse de**	*to make fun of*
fijarse en	*to take notice*	**sorprenderse de**	*to be surprised*

Me quejo de mi jefe.	*I complain about my boss.*
¿Te burlas de mí?	*Are you making fun of me?*
Nos negamos a pagar la multa.	*We refuse to pay the fine.*
Uds. se olvidan de devolver los libros.	*You forget to return the books.*

EJERCICIO
11·6

¡Práctica! *Complete each sentence with the appropriate present tense form of the verb in parentheses.*

1. Jorge _____ y _____ de sus amigos. (burlarse, reírse)

2. Él no _____ de sus errores. (darse cuenta)

3. Nosotras _____ a limpiar este cuarto. (negarse)

4. Elli _____ de su jefe. (quejarse)

5. Uds. _____ a jugar este juego peligroso. (atreverse)

6. Marcos y yo siempre _____ de tu apellido. (olvidarse)

7. Siempre _____ de tus ideas fabulosas. (sorprenderse, yo)

EJERCICIO
11·7

Traducción.

1. Do you remember my friend Carlos?

_____

2. I make fun of my sister's boyfriend!

_____

3. I do not regret my comments.

_____

4. Now we find out about your lies.

_____

5. I do not complain about your questions.

_____

6. I am surprised because you are here!

_____

7. I realize that my car is not in the garage.

_____

8. I am dying of thirst!

_____

9. I do not dare to play golf with your father.

_____

10. I forget about everything!

_____

11. We refuse (**negarse**) to move to another city.

_____

EJERCICIO
11·8

Los buenos y los malos hábitos. Traducción. *Use the words in the* **Vocabulario útil** *for your translation.*

VOCABULARIO ÚTIL

according to	**de acuerdo a**	*lazy*	**haragán, -a; vago, -a**
nutritionist	**el/la nutricionista**	*past*	**el pasado**
need	**la necesidad**	*future*	**el futuro**

According to my nutritionist, we need to write two lists.

    A list of good habits: to go to bed early and sleep eight hours, to get up early and to give thanks for a new day, to dare to change our daily routine, to forget about the past and think about the future, to find out about our friends' needs, to refuse to be lazy, and to remember life is short.

    And a short list of bad habits: to complain about everything, not to realize our good fortune, to make fun of other people's habits, and to forget tomorrow is another day.

_____

_____

_____

_____

The uses of se

The use of **se** is frequently presented in standard textbooks either with or before direct object pronouns. More importantly, **se** is almost always presented before students learn about indirect object pronouns. There is nothing wrong with this; much of the confusion about object pronouns is unavoidable. (You will find more information on direct and indirect object pronouns as well as double object pronouns in Chapter 12.) The human, real-time learning curve to absorb what is presented and be able to use it properly is longer than the academic calendar.

The pronoun **se** may refer to a third-person as a reflexive pronoun, as seen previously. It can appear as the form it must assume when **le** or **les** would otherwise precede the direct, third-person object pronouns **lo**, **la**, **los**, or **las**. This is one of the difficulties of what is usually labeled _double object pronouns_, when both an indirect and a direct object pronoun are used in a sentence. Note that the indirect always appears first. Any of the indirect object pronouns in the table here may be followed by any of the direct object pronouns in the right-hand column.

INDIRECT	DIRECT
me	lo
te	la
nos	los
os	las
se	

Just as it did as a reflexive object pronoun, **se** may refer to six grammatical persons as indirect objects: **a él**, **a ella**, and **a ustedes** when **se** is derived from **le**, and **a ellos**, **a ellas**, and **a ustedes** when **se** is derived from **les**. One way to accept that this arrangement is reasonable is to recognize that reflexive objects are simply a special case of indirect objects in which the receiver of the action also happens to be the subject of the verb.

The pronoun **se** may also function to form what is known as the pseudo-passive construction that can only translate into English either as a passive construction or, more colloquially, as employing some use of _get_ or _got_. When translated literally, this third-person construction makes it appear as if things did something to themselves. This of course is silly (see parentheses in the examples below), but it can actually help some learners recognize this structure when they hear or see it and thus absorb and use it correctly.

Se rompió la ventana.	_The window was broken._
	The window got broken.
	(The window broke itself.)
Se abrieron las ventanas.	_The windows were opened._
	The windows opened up.
	(The windows opened themselves.)

There is another way in which this structure is used. You may have encountered it in your textbook as a way to express unexpected occurrences or as a way to show that a person is affected by an action. Here's how it works: The indirect object pronoun of the person affected is placed between **se** and the verb. In the following example, a literal translation of **se ... perdió** makes it appear that the glove lost itself. The presence of **me** in between shows that I am the person affected by the loss (and furthermore, deflects any responsibility or carelessness on my part!). If the third-person pronoun is used to show the person affected, then a clarifier is frequently needed, as shown in the second example. Note that **se ... descompuso** still makes it appear that the car broke itself and **le**, clarified in the second example by **A Juan**, tells us who owns the car and who was impacted by the event. The third example shows how this construction works by presenting one instance in which everything is plural. The fourth example has a parallel in colloquial English, shown by the second translation.

Se me perdió un guante.	*My glove got lost.*
A Juan **se le descompuso** el carro.	*John's car broke down.*
A Tere y Marta **se les quemaron** los pasteles.	*Tere's and Marta's cakes got burned.*
Al granjero **se le murió** la vaca.	*The farmer's cow died.*
	The farmer's cow up and died on him.

The pronoun **se** also forms what is known as the impersonal **se** construction, corresponding roughly to *one does this or that* or to what is sometimes called the "editorial or impersonal you" in English. It is common in ads and other forms of signage. The one most familiar to English speakers is the first example. The last one, which I picked up from a bulletin board in a northern Virginia shooting range, is from a real wanted poster issued by Colombia in the mid 1990s for the notorious leader of the Medellín drug cartel.

Se habla español aquí.	*Spanish spoken here.*
Se vende carro.	*Car for sale.*
Se alquila.	*For rent.*
Se busca. Emilio Escobar.	*Wanted: Emilio Escobar.*

Finally, when it comes to the Spanish pronoun system, the third person is where nearly all the troubles lie. There can be, as noted with **se**, six possible persons (three singular and three plural) to whom a third-person pronoun might refer. Let's ignore the other persons and numbers for a moment and isolate the forms of all pronouns in the third person.

The first difficulty was addressed in the chapter about forms of address: the fact that **usted** and **ustedes** are second person in meaning but take the third-person verb forms. Their corresponding object pronouns follow the third person.

Subject Pronouns

SINGULAR	PLURAL
él	ellos
ella	ellas
usted	ustedes

Reflexive Object Pronouns

SINGULAR	PLURAL
se	se

Indirect Object Pronouns

SINGULAR	PLURAL
le	les

Le and **les** become **se** before **lo**, **la**, **los**, and **las**, as was summarized and explained previously when dealing with double object pronouns.

Juan **se lo** dio a María.	*John gave **it to Mary**.*
Se lo dijimos ayer.	*We said **it to them** yesterday.*

Direct Object Pronouns

SINGULAR	PLURAL
lo	los
la	las

Direct object pronouns replace previously mentioned nouns and, when in the third person, show the gender and number of the nouns. Observe in the following examples how the direct object nouns are replaced by direct object pronouns.

Compré dos manzanas.	**Las** compré.	*I bought them.*
Vendió los carros.	**Los** vendió.	*He/She/You sold them.*

Observe how an indirect object is added to show someone receiving the direct objects:

Juan **me** dio las manzanas.	*John gave me the apples. (indirect object pronoun, but direct object noun)*
Juan **me las** dio.	*John gave them to me. (both objects expressed as pronouns)*
Juan **le** dio las manzanas (a Marta).*	*John gave the apples to Marta.*
Juan **se las** dio (a Marta).*	*John gave them to her.*

When the third-person finds itself an object of a preposition, the subject form is used, except when reflexive, as in the second example. The first- and second-person singular forms are more problematic, ironically.

In the first- and second-person singular, the forms of the object of a preposition are **mí** and **ti** (note the orthographical accent in **mí**, to distinguish it from the possessive adjective **mi**). When the preposition **con** is used, these become **conmigo** and **contigo**, respectively, as shown by the last two examples.

Juan fue **con ella**.	*John went with her.*
María se lo llevó **consigo** misma.	*Mary took it with her (herself).*
¿Quieres ir **conmigo** al cine?	*Do you want to go to the movies with me?*
¡Por supuesto! Siempre me gusta ir **contigo**.	*Of course! I always like going with you.*

EJERCICIO
11·9

Identify the English translations on the right that match the Spanish sentences on the left. Focusing on the pronoun usage as well as the verbs will help you sort them out.

_____ 1. Se lo dio a su papá.

_____ 2. Se necesita valor para ir allá.

_____ 3. Después de vestirse, se fue.

a. He will fall into his own trap.

b. The house burned down.

c. They awarded it to her.

*****a Marta** would only be used to avoid confusion.

_____ 4. Se busca. Gato perdido.   d. They fell in love.

_____ 5. Se cayó la lámpara.   e. He'll be charged as a criminal.

_____ 6. El carro se resbaló.   f. His dad gave it to my cousin.

_____ 7. La casa se incendió.   g. A great idea came to me.

_____ 8. Ella se enamoró de él.   h. They kissed after the ceremony.

_____ 9. La billetera se le perdió.   i. The lamp fell down.

_____ 10. Se lo otorgaron.   j. Old people die of old age.

_____ 11. Ellos se enamoraron.   k. The houses were painted blue.

_____ 12. Para aprender, se tiene que estudiar.   l. The car skidded.

_____ 13. Se me ocurrió una idea fantástica.   m. The meeting slipped our mind.

_____ 14. Los viejos se mueren de viejos.   n. He lost his wallet.

_____ 15. Se pintaron las casas de azul.   o. Lost cat.

_____ 16. Se besaron tras la ceremonia.   p. To learn, you have to study.

_____ 17. Él se caerá en su propia trampa.   q. He gave it to his dad.

_____ 18. Se le acusará de ser criminal.   r. She fell in love with him.

_____ 19. Su papá se lo regaló a mi primo.   s. You need courage to go there.

_____ 20. Se nos pasó la cita por completo.   t. After getting dressed, he left.

EJERCICIO

11·10

Translate the following sentences from Spanish to English.

1. ¿Sabe Ud. si se alquila un piso en este edificio?

   _____

2. Juan y María se fueron corriendo cuando oyeron el estallido de la bomba.

   _____

3. Por varias horas después del incidente, no se oía nada.

   _____

4. ¿La tarea? Se la comió el perro.

   _____

5. Ay, ¡tómate la medicina y ya!

   _____

6. Este anillo antiguo me lo regaló un amigo.

_____

7. El Sr. Martínez se levantó, tomó la propuesta de la mesa y se la llevó consigo mismo.

_____

8. ¿Se lo dijiste a ellos? Pero, hombre—¡Era un secreto!

_____

9. Se nos descompuso el auto en la carretera y tuvimos que llamar a mi tío.

_____

10. ¿La postal? Se la mandé ayer a nuestros papás.

_____

11. ¿Cómo se prepara una buena ensalada, mamá?

_____

12. Un regalo para ti. Fui con mi hermano para comprártelo.

_____

13. El jefe necesita el martillo, préstteselo, pues.

_____

14. El mecánico tiene las manos sucias. Se las va a lavar antes de usar el teléfono.

_____

15. ¿Qué hago yo día tras día? Pues, nada menos que lo que se tiene que hacer.

_____

16. ¿La factura para Don Tomás? Estoy preparándosela ahorita.

_____

17. ¿Quieres ver esa película conmigo o con él?

_____

18. Los novios se miraban todo el tiempo.

_____

19. Ese tipo parece loco—todo el tiempo se habla a sí mismo.

_____

20. El Sr. Acero no se avergüenza ni cuando se revelan sus mentiras.

_____

EJERCICIO

11·11

Translate the following sentences from English to Spanish.

1. How do you make a good salad?

   _____

2. The baby fell down.

   _____

3. The plate got broken.

   _____

4. She put on a new pair of shoes.

   _____

5. The dog licked his paws.

   _____

6. He got well quickly.

   _____

7. They went straight up the mountain!

   _____

8. The sweater came apart before she could finish knitting it.

   _____

9. They promised to love each other.

   _____

10. We were looking for each other all day.

    _____

11. We gave them (plates) to her.

    _____

12. They became teachers.

    _____

13. She combed her hair and put on makeup.

    _____

14. I sold it (painting) to them.

    _____

15. The shirt was hung on a hanger.

    _____

Reflexive verbs and reflexive pronouns   **193**

16. She was glad you had called her.

_____

17. In Macondo, the houses were not painted red.

_____

18. He was surprised by the noise.

_____

19. This letter was written in the nineteenth century.

_____

20. The stockings were hung by the chimney with care.

_____

EJERCICIO
11·12

Use all the elements in each series of words to create grammatically correct sentences in Spanish. You'll have to add some details such as articles and prepositions. Note that only the dictionary forms of nouns, verbs, and adjectives are supplied, so be careful with agreement rules and pay attention to clues for the tense of the verbs.

1. Él/mirarse/espejo/ayer.

_____

2. Ellos/comprarse/regalos/anoche.

_____

3. Zapatos/perderse/esta mañana/playa.

_____

4. Anoche/vino/derramarse/mesa.

_____

5. Ese día/campanas/repicarse/celebrar la paz.

6. Sr. Acero/condenarse/pronto.

_____

7. Ellas/creerse/lo máximo.

_____

8. Niños/dormirse/las ocho/ayer.

_____

9. Ella/levantarse/las siete/mañana.

_____

10. Ellos/enojarse/tú/no hacer/tarea/ayer.

_____

11. Bebé/tomarse/leche/ahora.

_____

12. Juan y María/abrazarse/anoche/parque.

_____

13. Mientras/ella/vestirse/anoche/ellos/dormirse/sofá.

_____

14. Anoche/yo/escribir/carta/ellos. (*Use object pronouns. Make a four word sentence*)

_____

15. Juan/enojarse/irse.

_____

16. Hansel/no perderse/bosque/nunca.

_____

17. Mantequilla/derretirse/si/no ponerse/nevera.

_____

18. Perderse/juicio/Don Quijote.

_____

19. Cómo/escribirse/su nombre?

_____

20. Él/ir a esquiar/ayer/rompérsele/pierna.

_____

·12·

Direct and indirect object pronouns, commands, and double object pronouns

In order to communicate more clearly and to avoid redundancy, we use pronouns—words that take the place of nouns. Direct object pronouns receive the action of a verb, whereas indirect object pronouns point *to whom* or *for whom* the action is done.

Direct and indirect object pronouns

Let's review the direct and indirect object pronouns.

DIRECT OBJECT PRONOUN		INDIRECT OBJECT PRONOUN	
me	*me*	**me**	*to/for me*
te	*you* (fam.)	**te**	*to/for you* (fam.)
lo *you* (form.)	**los** *you* (form.)	**le** *to/for you* (form.)	**les** *to/for you* (form.)
lo *him,* **la** *her*	**los, las** *them*	**le** *to/for him/ her*	**les** *to/for them*

◆ Both direct and indirect object pronouns precede the conjugated verb.

Alicia ayuda **a Luis. Lo** ayuda.	*Alicia helps Luis. Alicia helps him.*
Ada trae el café **para Ana.** Ada **le** trae el café.	*Ada brings the coffee to Ana. Ada brings her coffee.*
No tienen **dinero.** No **lo** tienen.	*They don't have money. They don't have it.*
No doy regalos **a los chicos.** No **les** doy regalos.	*I don't give presents to the kids. I don't give them presents.*

◆ Direct and indirect object pronouns used with an infinitive or a present participle may either be attached to or precede the conjugated verb.

Lo quieres revisar. / Quieres revisar**lo**.	*You want to review it.*
Te debo responder la pregunta. / Debo responder**te** la pregunta.	*I should reply to your question.*

196

In order to keep the original stress, an accent is required on the stressed vowel when object pronouns are attached to a present participle.

Los estamos viendo. / Estamos viéndo**los**.   *We are watching them.*

Los estoy lavando. / Estoy lavándo**los**.   *I am washing them.*

EJERCICIO
12·1

Pronombres. *First replace the underlined words with the appropriate direct object pronoun. Then rewrite the sentence using this direct object pronoun.*

MODELO   Manolo lee <u>la biografía de Vargas Llosa</u>.

la; Manolo la lee.

1. Rosa recita <u>dos poemas</u>.

_____

2. Manolita está componiendo <u>sus canciones</u>.

_____

3. Mari no lleva <u>los cuadernos</u> a María José.

_____

4. Almodóvar hace reír <u>a los actores</u>.

_____

5. Yo llevo <u>el agua</u> para Marcela.

_____

6. Martín no quiere conocer <u>a María Elena</u>.

_____

7. Gustavo toca <u>el piano y la guitarra</u>.

_____

8. ¿Vas a incluirnos <u>a nosotras</u> en la lista?

_____

EJERCICIO
12·2

Pronombres y verbos reflexivos. *First replace the underlined words with the appropriate indirect object pronoun. Then rewrite the sentence using the indirect object pronoun in the appropriate position.*

MODELO   Voy a prestar una guitarra <u>a mis vecinos</u>.

les; Voy a prestarles una guitarra. / Les voy a prestar una guitarra.

Direct and indirect object pronouns, commands, and double object pronouns   **197**

1. Ángel está comprando creyones <u>para los niños necesitados</u>.

   _____

2. Ali está llevando regalos <u>a los ancianos</u>.

   _____

3. Raquel va a distribuir la comida <u>a los pobres</u>.

   _____

4. Lalo y María no van a cantar canciones mexicanas <u>para los adultos</u>.

   _____

5. Lola nunca puede prestar atención (*pay attention*) <u>a su colega Mario</u>.

   _____

6. Margarita no quiere recitar sus poemas <u>a la audiencia</u> en el ayuntamiento (*city hall*).

   _____

Double object pronouns

It is important to review the order of pronouns when both direct and indirect object pronouns are used in the same sentence.

♦ The indirect object pronoun precedes the direct object pronoun

   subject + indirect object pronoun + direct object pronoun + verb
   Junior **me lo** regala.   *Junior gives it to me.*

♦ Change **le** and **les** to **se** when they are followed by **lo**, **la**, **los**, or **las**

   Carmen **le** da (a Ud.) **la nota**.   *Carmen gives the note to you.*
   Carmen **se** la da.   *Carmen gives it to you.*
   Ramón **le** pinta **un retrato**.   *Ramón paints a portrait for him.*
   Ramón **se lo** pinta.   *Ramón paints it for him.*

Prepositional pronouns

Pronouns that follow a preposition are formed as follows.

SINGULAR		PLURAL	
mí	*me*	**nosotros, -as**	*we*
ti	*you* (fam.)	**vosotros, -as**	*you* (fam.)
usted (Ud.)	*you* (form.)	**ustedes (Uds.)**	*you* (form.)
él	*him, it*	**ellos**	*they*
ella	*her, it*	**ellas**	*they*

El regalo es **de él** para Lidia.   *The gift is from him to Lidia.*

There is also the emphatic prepositional pronoun (*yourself, himself, herself, itself; yourselves, themselves*).

Joel está fuera **de sí**.   *Joel is beside himself.*

Prepositional pronouns are used to emphasize or clarify a message, especially when double object pronouns are used.

Le doy **los cupones** de descuentos a Bella.   *I give Bella the discount coupons.*
Se los doy **a ella**, no **a ti**.   *I give them to her, not to you.*

EJERCICIO
12·3

Dos pronombres en una oración. *First replace the underlined words with the appropriate direct and indirect object pronouns. Then rewrite the sentence using these pronouns in the appropriate position.*

MODELO   Pedro lleva los postres a la familia.

                los, le; Pedro se los lleva.

1. Carmen compra dos almohadas a sus hijos.

_____

2. Ella prepara platos mexicanos a sus amigos.

_____

3. Pedrito da agua a su hermana.

_____

4. Raúl plancha las camisas para nosotros.

_____

5. Carmen y Raúl están dando a los niños sus regalos de cumpleaños.

_____

6. Marta compra libros a sus amigos.

_____

7. ¿Marcos envió dos tarjetas a Uds.?

_____

8. Manuel trae malas noticias a mí.

_____

9. Yo compro las medicinas a mi tía.

_____

10. Martín está enviando estas cartas a sus empleados.

_____

Commands

When you need to give an order, advice, or a strong suggestion, you give commands directly to another person (*you*, singular or plural) using the imperative mood. Let's review how commands are formed and how to use them.

Regular affirmative **tú** commands

You give the familiar **tú** command to your family members, friends, classmates, or colleagues. To form the **tú** commands, use the third person singular (**él**, **ella**, **usted**) form of the present indicative. Note that some commands may include exclamation marks for emphasis. In Spanish, an inverted exclamation mark is placed at the beginning of the command.

Compra.	*Buy.*
Vende.	*Sell.*
¡Pide!	*Ask!*

Regular negative **tú** commands

To form familiar **tú** commands in the negative, use the first person singular (**yo**) form of the present tense, and replace the -**o** ending with -**es** for -**ar** verbs, and -**as** for -**er** and -**ir** verbs.

- -**ar** verbs   **mirar**   **mir**-o   **mir** + **es**

    No mires a esa persona.   *Don't look at that person.*

- -**er** verbs   **beber**   **beb**-o   **beb** + **as**

    No bebas el agua.   *Don't drink the water.*

- -**ir** verbs   **escribir**   **escrib**-o   **escrib** + **as**

    ¡No escribas la carta!   *Don't write the letter!*

Some verbs have spelling changes in the stem. In the following, the final consonant of the stem must be changed in order to preserve pronunciation.

- **c → qu**

    marcar, marc-a   No mar**ques** el número incorrecto.   *Don't dial the incorrect number.*

- **z → c**

    empezar, empiez-a   No empie**ces** a trabajar tarde.   *Don't start to work late.*

- **g → gue**

    colgar, cuelg-a   No cuel**gues** el teléfono.   *Do not hang up the phone.*

¡Órdenes! *Write the affirmative and negative familiar* **tú** *commands for each verb.*

1. cambiar _____; no _____

2. pedir _____; no _____

3. viajar _____; no _____

4. volver _____; no _____

5. dormir _____; no _____

6. pensar _____; no _____

7. correr _____; no _____

8. sufrir _____; no _____

9. leer _____; no _____

10. vender _____ no _____

Traducción. *Write the appropriate affirmative or negative familiar* **tú** *command.*

1. Use the new computer.

_____

2. Do not erase my notes.

_____

3. Put the paper in the printer.

_____

4. Please don't answer the phone.

_____

5. Go to your office now!

_____

6. Put away (**guardar**) these papers, please.

_____

7. Do not use these old keys.

_____

Direct and indirect object pronouns, commands, and double object pronouns   **201**

Irregular tú commands

A few verbs have irregular commands in the familiar **tú** form.

		AFFIRMATIVE COMMAND	NEGATIVE COMMAND
decir	*to say, tell*	**di**	**no digas**
hacer	*to do, make*	**haz**	**no hagas**
ir	*to go*	**ve**	**no vayas**
poner	*to put, place*	**pon**	**no pongas**
salir	*to leave, go out*	**sal**	**no salgas**
ser	*to be*	**sé**	**no seas**
tener	*to have*	**ten**	**no tengas**
venir	*to come*	**ven**	**no vengas**

EJERCICIO
12·6

Traducción. *Use the appropriate informal* **tú** *command.*

1. Put the bag on the floor.

   _____

2. Leave at eight thirty today.

   _____

3. Be careful (**tener cuidado**) because it's raining.

   _____

4. Come early to class.

   _____

5. Be (**ser**) courteous.

   _____

6. Go to the market and buy bread.

   _____

7. Tell the truth now.

   _____

8. Do your work carefully.

   _____

Traducción. *Use the appropriate informal* **tú** *command.*

1. Do not put your bag on my seat.

   _____

2. Do not leave the papers on the floor.

   _____

3. Don't have problems with your friends.

   _____

4. Do not come late to the theater.

   _____

5. Don't be ridiculous!

   _____

6. Do not go to the beach now.

   _____

7. Don't tell lies!

   _____

8. Do not make inappropriate comments.

   _____

Regular affirmative and negative formal **usted** commands

Use the formal **usted** command for people whom you address with respect, especially those you do not know well.

Suba usted, por favor.	*Go up, please.*
Hablen ustedes al gerente.	*Please speak to the manager.*

The regular **usted** commands are the same in both affirmative and negative. To form the **usted** commands, take the first person singular **yo** form of the present tense and replace the -**o** ending with -**e** for -**ar** verbs, and -**a** for -**er** and –**ir** verbs.

- -**ar** verbs **bailar** **bail**-o **bail** + **e**

Baile en la terraza.	**No baile** en la terraza.
Dance on the terrace.	*Don't dance on the terrace.*

- -**er** verbs **comer** **com**-o **com** + **a**

¡**Coma** chocolate!	¡**No coma** chocolate!
Eat chocolate!	*Don't eat chocolate!*

◆ -ir verbs   **abrir**   **abr**-o   **abr** + a

Abra la carta.   **No abra la carta.**
Open the letter.   *Don't open the letter.*

◆ Irregular **usted** commands

Only three verbs have irregular formal **usted** commands.

INFINITIVE	USTED COMMAND
saber	**sepa**
ser	**sea**
ir	**vaya**

EJERCICIO
12·8

En la oficina. *Write the appropriate affirmative and negative formal* **usted** *commands for each verb.*

1. (leer) las noticias   _____ ; _____

2. (contestar) las llamadas   _____ ; _____

3. (usar) las instrucciones   _____ ; _____

4. (recibir) a los clientes   _____ ; _____

5. (asistir) a la reunión esta mañana   _____ ; _____

6. (ir) al aeropuerto   _____ ; _____

7. (ser) amable   _____ ; _____

8. (descansar) durante el almuerzo   _____ ; _____

Regular affirmative and negative formal **ustedes** commands

To form the plural formal **ustedes** commands, simply add an **-n** to the singular formal **usted** command.

Viajen a las montañas.   *Travel to the mountains.*
No traigan los cupones vencidos.   *Do not bring the expired coupons.*
Salgan ya. **No vayan** muy tarde.   *Leave now. Do not go too late.*

Remember that the plural **ustedes** is used for both formal and familiar commands in most of the Hispanic world. The subject pronouns **usted** or **ustedes** sometimes may follow the verb as a sign of politeness.

Sí, por favor, **entre Ud.**   *Yes, please, come in.*
No **salgan Uds.** ahora.   *Do not leave now.*

Traducción. *Use the appropriate affirmative formal* **ustedes** *command.*

1. Turn to the right.

   _____

2. Follow the directions.

   _____

3. Find exit 45 on the turnpike (**autopista de peaje**).

   _____

4. Drive two miles after the exit.

   _____

5. Get to (**llegar**) Olmedo Street, number 114.

   _____

6. Park in front of our apartment building.

   _____

7. Ring the bell at the building entrance.

   _____

Affirmative and negative familiar **vosotros** commands

The familiar **vosotros** form is used only in peninsular Spanish. For affirmative commands of regular verbs, replace the final **-r** of the infinitive with **-d**. The only exception is with reflexive verbs: replace the final **-r** of the infinitive with the reflexive pronoun.

NONREFLEXIVE VERBS		REFLEXIVE VERBS	
Levantad el sofá.	*Lift the sofa.*	**Levantaos.**	*Stand up.*
Poned la ropa allí.	*Put the clothes there.*	**Poneos** la ropa.	*Put on your clothes.*
Vestid las muñecas.	*Dress the dolls.*	**Vestíos** ahora.	*Get dressed now.*

Negative **vosotros** commands for regular verbs are formed as follows.

-ar verbs:	**contar**	cont-	**cont + éis**	**No contéis** el dinero.
				Don't count the money.
-er verbs:	**temer**	tem-	**tem- + áis**	**No temáis.**
				Don't be afraid.
-ir verbs:	**ecribir**	escrib-	**escrib + áis**	**¡No escribáis** la carta!
				Don't write the letter!

Direct and indirect object pronouns, commands, and double object pronouns   **205**

Again, only three verbs have an irregular form of the negative **vosotros** commands.

saber	**No sepáis** las contraseñas.	*Do not know the passwords.*
ser	**¡No seáis** tacaños!	*Do not be stingy!*
ir	**No vayáis** por esa calle.	*Do not go down that street.*

Stem-changing -**ir** verbs again change **e** to **i** and **o** to **u**.

competir	**No compitáis.**	*Do not compete.*
dormir	**No durmáis.**	*Do not sleep.*
medir	**No midáis.**	*Do not measure.*
morirse	**No os muráis.**	*Do not die.*

EJERCICIO
12·10

En España. *Write the affirmative and negative* **vosotros** *commands for the following verbs.*

1. leer _____; no _____

2. dormir _____; no _____

3. sufrir _____; no _____

4. pensar _____; no _____

5. viajar _____; no _____

6. vivir _____; no _____

7. caminar _____; no _____

8. conseguir _____; no _____

9. hacer _____; no _____

Pronouns with commands

Where do we place pronouns with commands?

◆ The direct and indirect object pronouns are always attached to the affirmative commands.

Cierra la puerta. Ciérra**la**.	*Close the door. Close it.*
Abra la clase para Miguel.	*Open the classroom for Miguel.*
Ábra**le** la clase.	*Open it for him.*

◆ The direct and indirect object pronouns are placed immediately before the verb in negative commands.

No cierres la puerta. No **la cierres**.	*Don't close the door. Do not close it.*
No abras el banco para Miguel.	*Do not open the bank for Miguel.*
No **lo abras**.	*Do not open it.*

To use the double object pronouns, follow the structure for affirmative and negative commands.

◆ affirmative command + indirect object pronoun + direct object pronoun

Regálame tu blusa. ¡**Regálamela**!   *Give me your blouse. ¡Give it to me!*

Devuelvan el regalo a José.   *Return the gift to José. Return it to him.*
Devuélvanselo.

◆ negative word + indirect object pronoun + direct object pronoun + negative command

No **me** digas **una mentira**.   *Don't tell me a lie.*

No **me la digas**.   *Do not tell it to me.*

EJERCICIO
12·11

¡Órdenes son órdenes! *Replace the underlined words with the appropriate direct and indirect object pronouns. Then rewrite the sentence using the direct and indirect object pronouns in the appropriate position.*

MODELO   Responde las preguntas a tus amigos.

las, les; Respóndeselas.

1. Lee el poema a tus amigos.
   _____

2. Anita, escribe la lista de los regalos a tu mamá.
   _____

3. Da el dinero a tu amiga.
   _____

4. No compren los vegetales para mí.
   _____

5. Digan sus nombres a la secretaria.
   _____

6. Sra. Blanco, cuente Ud. sus problemas a su familia.
   _____

7. Abran la puerta a esos señores.
   _____

8. No envíen la invitación a mis hermanos.
   _____

Double object pronouns

If you are like most students, you were probably exposed to indirect object pronouns without their being identified as such. In an early chapter of most textbooks, students are often taught a few phrases involving the verb **gustar** to provide them with some groundwork for using Spanish in class. When most texts introduce object pronouns in a deliberate manner, they start with the direct object pronouns. This is fine, but, since students learn the direct object pronouns first, they may become confused later when they have to learn to use both types in one verb phrase. As a result, they often put the direct object first.

Besides that, at a more cognitive level, there are two other obstacles. First, students tend not to perceive the different functions of these two classes of object pronouns. Secondly, the forms of all but the third-person indirect and direct pronouns are identical. The object pronoun **me**, for instance, can be either direct or indirect:

Marta **me** vio.	Marta saw **me**. (**me** is a direct object pronoun)
Marta **me** dio una galleta.	Marta gave **me** a cookie. (**me** is an indirect object)

Object pronouns, especially direct object pronouns, are used when the noun they refer to has already been mentioned and need not be repeated—just as English uses *it* or *them*. Direct objects are the people, things, or even ideas that are acted upon directly. The question to ask in order to identify a direct object is "what?" As shown by the following example, using a noun as the direct object, the question to identify the direct object would be "What did I buy?"

Compré una rosa.	*I bought a rose.*

Thus, *what* did the subject (**yo**) buy? **Una rosa**. Therefore **una rosa** is the direct object of the verb **comprar** (*to buy*). Next, let's change the direct object noun into a direct object pronoun and observe what happens. Note first of all that the listener would have to know what **la** refers to—it would have been previously mentioned, just as is true when English uses *it* as a direct object.

La compré.	*I bought it.*

An indirect object shows *to whom* or *for whom* an action is performed, either to help or hurt them. Indirect object pronouns are generally not optional if there is a receiver mentioned. When the receiver is **le** or **les** and followed by a direct object pronoun, a clarifier is often used, such as **a él** or **a ustedes**, to make it clear to whom the indirect object is referring. Since no confusion can happen with the first and second-person indirect objects, they do not require any clarifiers—and when they are used, such as **a mí**, it is for emphasis. It is easy to identify an indirect object when you ask the question *to* or *for whom* was the action performed? For the following example, the question needed to identify the indirect object would be specifically formulated as *For whom did I buy a rose?* You can quickly see that the person *for whom* the subject (**yo**) bought a rose is the person spoken to, as revealed by the use of the indirect object pronoun **te**. Note that when **para** is used to indicate a receiver (i.e., the indirect object, noun, or pronoun), the indirect object pronoun is omitted.

Yo **te compré** una rosa.	*I bought you a rose.*
	I bought a rose for you.
Yo compré una rosa **para ti**.	*I bought a rose for you.*
	I bought you a rose.
Yo compré una rosa **para ella**.	*I bought her a rose.*
	I bought a rose for her.

The most condensed way to express that last example, when all objects are contextually clear to the listener, is to say:

Se la compré.   *I bought it for her.*

As you shall see shortly, object pronouns often can be placed in either of two positions. However, when there is only one conjugated verb involved, the indirect object pronoun must always be placed before the direct object pronoun, followed by the verb. If the sentence is negative, the negating word **no** comes before the object pronouns. The second translation of the example below is not the best English, but is common enough to admit, and, since it puts the objects in the same order as Spanish, it can be a useful starting point for understanding this in Spanish.

Te la compré.   *I bought it for you.*
                                               I bought you it.

Before proceeding to summarize and exemplify all the placement rules in outline form, let's look at all the indirect and direct object pronouns. Once again, we shall observe one of the functions of the object pronoun **se**, touched upon in the previous chapter.
    The indirect object pronouns are:

me	nos
te	os
le/se	les/se

The direct object pronouns are:

me	nos
te	os
lo, la	los, las

As was stated in the previous chapter, most of the morphological (form) confusion experienced by learners faced with the Spanish pronoun system seems to reside in the third-person forms. When learners are confused about the other forms (**me**, **te**, **nos**, and **os**), it inevitably has to do with understanding the differences in grammatical functions among indirect, reflexive, and direct objects. For users of this volume who may not be proceeding linearly through the chapters, but instead using it as a reference work, what was said in the previous chapter about the use of **se** bears repeating, beginning with the chart that shows the possible combinations of **se**, which *must* be used whenever **le** or **les** otherwise would precede **lo**, **la**, **los**, or **las**:

INDIRECT	DIRECT
me	lo
te	la
nos	los
os	las
se	

The pronoun **se** may refer to six persons when it, of necessity, replaces **le** or **les**, which are indirect object pronouns. This can be confusing if not viewed analytically. Spanish has a way of dealing with the ambiguity which, of course, exists even when **le** or **les** are used. The grammatical mechanism whereby this is achieved is known as a *clarifying clause*, which begins with the preposition **a** (*to*). The following examples will demonstrate and model the use of clarifiers, using only **le** or **les**, and showing how they refer to all three possible uses of each of these indirect object pronouns. The second translations in each example show the way in which the English preposition *to* is used to mark the indirect object, or recipient, as a clarifier of **le** and **les**, just as the preposition **a** does in Spanish. At the same time, however, notice that the first translation reflects the Spanish word order with regard to the use of double object pronouns, which we shall soon examine in more detail.

Clarifiers of le

Yo **le** di el libro **a Juan**.	*I gave John the book.*
	I gave the book to John.
Yo **le** di el libro **a Juana**.	*I gave Jane the book.*
	I gave the book to Jane.
Yo **le** di el libro **a usted**.	*I gave you the book.*
	I gave the book to you.

Clarifiers of les

Ella **les** vendió un carro nuevo **a Tomás y María**.	*She sold Tom and Mary a new car.*
	She sold a new car to Tom and Mary.
Ella **les** vendió un carro nuevo **a María y Marta**.	*She sold Mary and Martha a new car.*
	She sold a new car to Mary and Martha.
Ella **les** vendió un carro nuevo **a ustedes**.	*She sold you a new car.*
	She sold a new car to you.

Now that we have seen how **le** and **les** are clarified, we can examine what happens when the noun phrases **el libro** and **un carro nuevo**, functioning as direct objects, are changed to a direct object pronoun. In this case **lo** is the pronoun used since the nouns are third-person, singular, and masculine. By using **lo**, and retaining the clarifying clauses, we can produce a useful synopsis of the various meanings that **se** has as an indirect object pronoun when used with any of the remaining third-person direct object pronouns: **la**, **los**, and **las**. Notice how, when English uses both pronouns, there is no mechanism for further identifying the true third-person recipient—*him*, *her*, or *them*—by name.

When **se** is used before a third-person verb (singular or plural) and is not followed by **lo**, **la**, **los**, or **las**, the use of **se** is either: reflexive, pseudo-passive, or impersonal, as explained in the previous chapter. When **se** is followed by **lo**, **la**, **los** or **las**, its function is that of an indirect object pronoun, replacing **le** or **les**. In the following examples, only the masculine singular direct object **lo** (*it*) is used following **se**. The direct object noun that **lo** represents is indicated in parentheses.

Clarifiers of se when it must replace le

Yo **se** lo di **a Juan**.	*I gave him it (the book).*
	I gave it (the book) to him.
Yo **se** lo di **a Juana**.	*I gave her it (the book).*
	I gave it (the book) to her.
Yo **se** lo di **a usted**.	*I gave you it (the book).*
	I gave it (the book) to you.

Clarifiers of se when it must replace les

Ella **se** lo vendió **a Tomás y María**.	*She sold them it (a new car).*
	She sold it (a new car) to them.
Ella **se** lo vendió **a María y Marta**.	*She sold them it (a new car).*
	She sold it (a new car) to them.

Ella **se** lo vendió **a ustedes**.	*She sold you it (a new car).*
	She sold it (a new car) to you.

Now that we've seen all the permutations involving **se**, let's examine where object pronouns can be placed in modern Spanish. There are four scenarios, two of which have options and two of which do not:

- ◆ **Scenario One (no options)**: When a single conjugated verb is used, any and all object pronouns must precede the verb. If the sentence is negative, the word **no** will appear before the object pronoun or pronouns.

Juan **me lo vendió** ayer.	*John sold it to me yesterday.*
El Sr. Acero **no me lo** dijo honestamente.	*Mr. Acero did not say it to me honestly.*

- ◆ **Scenario Two (two options)**: When a verb phrase involving the auxiliary (helping) verb **estar** (or any other verb that can form progressives) and a gerund (-**ando** and -**iendo** endings) is used, pronouns may either precede the conjugated helping verb or be appended (added to the end) of the gerund, as the following examples show.

Juan **estaba vendiéndomelo** ayer.	*John was selling it to me yesterday.*
Juan **me lo estaba vendiendo** ayer.	

  When pronouns are added to the gerund, a written accent is placed on the vowel of the stressed syllable of the gerund, to preserve the stress on that syllable.

- ◆ **Scenario Three (two options)**: When a verb phrase involving an auxiliary verb and an infinitive is used, pronouns may either precede the conjugated helping verb or be appended to the infinitive, as the following examples show.

Juan **quería vendérmelo** ayer.	*John wanted to sell it to me yesterday.*
Juan **me lo quería vender** ayer.	

  When pronouns are added to the gerund, a written accent is placed on the vowel of the stressed syllable of the infinitive, to preserve the stress on that syllable. Since these are infinitives, the stress would fall on -**ár**, -**ér**, or -**ír**.

- ◆ **Scenario Four (no options)**: With regard to commands or imperative forms, pronouns must be appended to the end of affirmative commands and the accent mark placed on the stressed syllable.

¡Véndamelo!	*Sell it to me!*

  When pronouns are appended to the end of any verb form, an accent mark must be placed on the syllable that is stressed before they are added in order to indicate the preservation of its original pronunciation. However, when the command is negative, the object or objects must be detached and precede the verb, following the word **no**.

¡No **me lo venda**!	*Don't sell it to me!*

Now that we have seen how pronouns must or can be placed with respect to verbs in modern Spanish, we can examine the placement of object pronouns as found in older literature, features which still find their way into modern, formal writing and oratory.

In older literature and still often in formal oratory, editorials, and in many proverbs, you'll find object pronouns appended to the end of verbs. The tenses in which this phenomenon takes place most often are the present, the preterit, the imperfect, and the simple future.

Dígolo en serio.	*I say it in all seriousness.*
Fuese corriendo.	*He took off running.*

Viome, acobardóse y **huyóme**, rabo entre las piernas.		*He saw me, turned coward, and fled from me, tail between his legs.*
Érase una vez...		*Once upon a time . . .*
Dirételo de una vez...		*I'll tell it to you all at once . . .*

EJERCICIO
12·12

Match the English sentences with the Spanish; the cues in parentheses will help identify what direct object nouns are meant by the direct object pronouns in Spanish.

_____	1. They gave it (dress) to her.	a.	¡Escríbesela!
_____	2. She sold them (horses) to him.	b.	Se la quería traer.
_____	3. You're giving them (photos) to them.	c.	Espera contárselas.
_____	4. She wants to bring it (food) for her.	d.	¿Cuándo vas a mandársela?
_____	5. They couldn't send it (book) to him.	e.	Se la compró.
_____	6. Write him (a letter)!	f.	¡No se las vendan!
_____	7. He ought to repair it (car) for her.	g.	Estás dándoselas.
_____	8. He wanted to bring it (magazine) to her.	h.	¿Necesita llevárselos?
_____	9. I wanted to give it (coat) to her.	i.	Ella se los vendió.
_____	10. Don't sell them (tables) to her!	j.	Se la quiere traer.
_____	11. He hopes to tell them it (news).	k.	No pudieron enviárselo.
_____	12. When will you send her it (bill)?	l.	Debería arreglárselo.
_____	13. Buy them (flowers) for her!	m.	Quería dárselo.
_____	14. Don't read it (newspaper) to them!	n.	¡Présteselo!
_____	15. She bought it (necktie) for him.	o.	¡No se los compres!
_____	16. Loan them (the car)!	p.	Se la abrirán.
_____	17. Don't buy them (pencils) for her!	q.	Se los pidió.
_____	18. Does she need to take her them (plates)?	r.	¡Cómpraselas!
_____	19. They will open it (door) for her.	s.	¡No se lo lea!
_____	20. He ordered them (toys) for her.	t.	Se lo dieron.

Translate the following sentences into Spanish, using object pronouns for all noun objects of verbs.

1. She's washing his hands.

   _____

2. We want to buy her a watch.

   _____

3. Bring me the soap! (**tú**)

   _____

4. She was hoping to find him some shoes.

   _____

5. Don't send me the box!

   _____

6. He should record the news for her.

   _____

7. They are giving me gifts.

   _____

8. He gave us wine for Christmas.

   _____

9. They sent you the information yesterday. (**Ud**.)

   _____

10. He will send them their photo.

    _____

11. We want to make a web page for you. (**Uds**.)

    _____

12. She didn't want to knit him a sweater.

    _____

13. They brought us the tomatoes.

    _____

14. She prepared the meal for them.

    _____

15. We want to buy you a hat. (**tú**)

    _____

16. They are building them a house.

_____

17. Don't buy me the shirt! (**tú** command)

_____

18. I should give the painting to him.

_____

19. Do you want to send them a postcard? (**tú**)

_____

20. We will not send you a bill. (**Ud.**)

_____

EJERCICIO
12·14

Use all the elements in each string to create grammatically correct sentences in Spanish, using only object pronouns for all noun objects of verbs. You'll have to add some details in most cases (e.g., articles and prepositions). When the position rules allow for more than one solution, show them both. Then translate them into English! Note that only the dictionary forms of nouns, verbs, and adjectives are supplied, so be careful with agreement rules and pay attention to clues for the tense of the verbs.

1. tú/querer/mandar/(libros)/(a él)/ahora.

_____

2. yo/tener/comprar/(blusa)/(para ella)/anoche.

_____

3. Nosotros/ir/vender/(coche)/(a Ud.)/la semana pasada.

_____

4. Ellos/no deber/servir/(cerveza)/(a los menores de edad).

_____

5. Tú/estar/escribir/(cuento)/(para ella)/en este momento.

_____

6. ¡Arreglar/(computadora)/(para nosotros)! (**tú** command)

_____

7. Él/traer/(teléfono)/(a mí) ayer.

_____

8. Yo/ir/poner/(demanda)/(al Sr. Acero)/pronto.

_____

9. Ella/hacer/(maleta)/(para mí)/esta mañana.

_____

10. Uds./querer/dar/(regalos)/(a los niños)/el fin de semana pasado.

_____

11. Los niños/romper/(ventana)/(a mí)/el domingo pasado.

_____

12. Ella/ir/pedir/(favor)/(a ellos)/mañana.

_____

13. ¡No/mandar/(carta)/(a ella)! (**Uds**. command)

_____

14. Nosotros/no poder/enviar/(mensaje)/(a ti)/ahora.

_____

15. Ella/querer/dar/(beso)/(a él)/anoche.

_____

16. Tú/deber/mostrar/(colección)/(a nosotros)/ahora.

_____

17. ¡Dar/(dinero)/(ellos)! (**Ud**. command)

_____

18. Yo/querer/pedir/(libros)/(a Ud.).

_____

19. Ella/ir/enviar/(cajas)/(a él)/esta tarde.

_____

20. Él/querer/escribir/(carta)/(a ella)/la semana pasada.

_____

Other ways to command with **nosotros**

The **nosotros** commands are not actually a form of the imperative. They are in fact the **nosotros** form of the present subjunctive. *Let us* or *Let's* is used in English to express this idea. This form is used to invite or urge others to do or not do something, often when we ourselves may play a part. You may often find it in slogans, commercials, and so on.

Hablemos con los clientes ahora.	*Let us speak to the clients now.*
Toquemos la guitarra y **bailemos**.	*Let's play the guitar and let's dance.*
¡No volvamos aquí jamás!	*Let's not come back here ever again!*

The **nosotros** command form can also be derived from the present indicative. To form the **nosotros** commands of regular verbs, use the **yo** form of the present indicative:

♦ Drop the **-o** or **-oy** of the ending.

♦ Add the corresponding endings, as follows:

INFINITIVE	**NOSOTROS** COMMANDS
levant**ar** (*to raise*)	levant**emos**
le**er** (*to read*)	le**amos**
recib**ir** (*to receive*)	recib**amos**

♦ Add **no** before the verb to make a negative command.

No leamos esta revista.   *Let's not read this magazine.*

EJERCICIO
12·15

Un ensayo (rehearsal) *en el teatro*. *Complete each sentence with the present tense form of nosotros.*

1. _____ (cambiar) los papeles.   5. _____ (tomar) fotos.

2. _____ (recitar) las líneas.   6. _____ No (enojar) al director.

3. _____ (hablar) en voz alta.   7. _____ (comprar) disfraces.

4. _____ (repasar) el final.   8. _____ No (olvidar) nada.

Remember the following rules regarding the **nosotros** form of the command:

♦ Spelling changes affect verbs ending in **-car**, **-gar**, **-zar**; as in other forms, they change to **qu**, **gu**, and **c** respectively.

Eduquemos a nuestros jóvenes.   *Let us educate our youth.*
Carguemos estos paquetes.   *Let's pick up the packages.*
Comencemos este capítulo.   *Let us begin this chapter.*

♦ Only **-ir** stem-changing verbs show these changes in the **nosotros** command form, as follows:

Verbs like **dormir** change **o** to **u**: d**u**rmamos
Verbs like **mentir** change **e** to **i**: m**i**ntamos
Verbs like **seguir** change **e** to **i**: s**i**gamos

Durmamos aquí esta noche.   *Let's sleep here tonight.*
No mintamos acerca de este asunto.   *Let's not lie about this matter.*
Sigamos este camino.   *Let's follow this road.*

♦ Attach pronouns as you would with other affirmative commands. Note that reflexive verbs drop the **-s** from the ending **-mos** of the verb before adding the reflexive pronoun **nos** to it: **probemos nos** (*let us try on*) turns into **probémonos**.

Levantémonos.   *Let's get up.*
Sirvámonos la cena.   *Let us serve ourselves dinner.*

- The verbs **ir** and the reflexive **irse** are irregular in the affirmative command. Here are the forms:

  ¡Vamos! ¡Vámonos!   *Let's go! Let's go!*

  The negative form is **No vayamos**.

- Frequently, **ir a** (in the **nosotros** form of the present indicative) + the infinitive substitutes for the affirmative command.

  ¡Vamos a nadar!   *Let's swim! (Let's go swimming!)*

EJERCICIO
12·16

*Información. Give the **nosotros** form of the verb in parentheses.*

1. _____ (navegar) (*surf*) en la Web.

2. _____ (investigar) esta noticia.

3. _____ (empezar) a trabajar.

4. _____ (buscar) las respuestas.

5. No _____ (hacer) comentarios ridículos.

EJERCICIO
12·17

Preparémonos para el concierto. Replace the italicized direct objects with object pronouns and attach them to the verb.

1. Alquilemos *el teatro*. _____

2. Dibujemos *los carteles*. _____

3. Compongamos *nuevas canciones*. _____

4. Incluyamos *mi canción favorita*. _____

5. Vendamos *las entradas*. _____

Pleading

Imperative sentences are also used to plead or make an appeal or exhortation:

Den sangre. *Give blood.*
Protege el medio ambiente. *Protect the environment.*

The message in these sentences directs a person or sways or convinces someone to follow an idea or path. The speaker may be included as part of the implied subject in such an exhortation. Use the forms of the *first-person plural* (**nosotros**) of the subjunctive for this type of imperative:

first person plural subjunctive + predicate → exhortation

Seamos pacientes. *Let's be patient.*
Ayudemos a estas señoras. *Let us help these ladies.*
Cenemos en la cocina. *Let's have dinner in the kitchen.*

*Complete each sentence with the **nosotros** form, appropriate punctuation, and exclamation marks.*

1. usar el diccionario _____

2. hacer preguntas a la maestra _____

3. viajar a México _____

4. ver telenovelas colombianas _____

5. repasar la gramática _____

6. escuchar las canciones españolas _____

Imperative sentences and word order

You know that an imperative sentence may consist of a single verb in the imperative mood. You have already been using sentences that include a direct and/or indirect object. The word order of sentences with noun or pronoun objects in Spanish also applies to imperatives: direct objects and indirect objects follow the verb, in that order.

verb + direct object noun + indirect object noun

Lleven + **el correo** + **a la secretaria**.
*Take **the mail** to the secretary.*
¡Escuchen **este programa**! *Listen **to this program**!*
Devuelve **el dinero al dependiente**. *Return **the money to the salesperson**.*

Vas a dar una fiesta. *Give your friends affirmative commands (Uds.).*

1. el salón / preparar _____

2. limpiar / las mesas _____

3. comprar / las bebidas _____

4. enviar / las invitaciones _____

5. envolver / los regalos _____

6. traer / las flores _____

En la cocina. *Change the word order if needed.*

1. Marta, ponga la carne en la nevera. _____

2. La cebolla corte. _____

3. La botella abra de aceite. _____

4. Felipe, lave los platos en la fregadora. _____

5. Las cervezas sirva a los invitados. _____

6. Prepare el café, Mario. _____

Word order in imperative sentences with object pronouns

With affirmative commands, object pronouns are attached to the verb. Exclamation marks are used to indicate a sense of urgency.

affirmative command + object pronoun

¡Haz + **la**!
*Do **it**!*
¡Haz **la tarea**!   *Do **the homework**!*
¡Hazla!   ***Do it!***

Some sentences have more than one object pronoun. If there are two pronouns, the indirect object pronoun *precedes* the direct object pronoun: IO + DO.

A written accent mark appears on the stressed vowel of the imperative verb form when it is followed by one or two object pronouns. To place the accent, count back *three* vowels from the end of the imperative plus pronouns, and add the accent. (When an imperative verb form of more than one syllable has two object pronouns, count back *four* vowels, and add the accent mark.)

affirmative command + indirect object pronoun + direct object pronoun

Dá + **me** + **lo**
¡Dá**melo**!
*Give **it** to me!*

Dame el cuaderno, ¡**dámelo**!	***Give me** the notebook, **give it to me**!*
Chicos, **llévenselo**.	*Boys, **take it with you**.*
Escribamos **la lista**.	*Let's write **the list**.*
Escribámosla.	***Let's write it**.*
Lleva la taza **a Lisa**.	*Take the cup **to Lisa**.*
Llévale la taza.	***Take her** the cup.*
Tráeme la tarea.	***Bring me** the homework.*
Tráemela.	***Bring it to me**.*

With negative commands, object pronouns are placed *immediately before the verb* in a Spanish sentence. Again, if there are two pronouns, the indirect object pronoun precedes the direct object pronoun.

negative word + object pronoun(s) + verb

¡**No** + **lo** + hagas!
¡**No lo** hagas!
Don't do it!

¡No leas **el periódico**!	*Do not read **the newspaper**!*
No **lo** leas.	*Do not read **it**.*
No **me** des **las malas noticias**.	*Do not give **me the bad news**.*
No **me las** des.	*Do not give **it to me**.*

EJERCICIO 12·21

En español. *Substitute the underlined noun with the correct direct object pronoun. Then create a sentence using the* **tú** *command form.*

1. Call <u>Diana</u>! _____

2. Get (**recoger**) <u>the tickets</u>! _____

3. Buy the sodas <u>for us</u>! _____

4. Tell <u>me</u> <u>the time</u>! _____

5. Read <u>me</u> <u>the program</u>! _____

6. Wait <u>for me</u>! _____

Follow the model. *Complete each sentence with the* **tú** *command form of the infinitive. Place the pronouns in correct order and use exclamation marks.*

MODELO   ¿Las llaves? / buscar / las / cajón / el / en

           ¿Las llaves? Búscalas en el cajón.

1. ¿La ventana? la / cerrar / mismo / ahora

_____

2. ¿Tus zapatos? los / al / no / tirar / suelo

_____

3. ¿El perro? lo / no / molestar

_____

4. ¿Tus amigos? los / su / llamar / a / casa

_____

5. ¿Las toallas? las / buscar / en el dormitorio

_____

6. ¿El auto? llevar / lo / al mecánico

_____

7. ¿Las manzanas? las / lavar / antes / comerlas / de

_____

8. ¿Las luces? no / las / apagar

_____

9. ¿Los vegetales? comprar / los / en / mercado / el

_____

10. ¿Los ejercicios? los / entregar / no

_____

Imperative sentences with reflexive object pronouns

Reflexive verbs are conjugated with reflexive pronouns. Imperative sentences with reflexive verbs have the same word order you have already studied for object pronouns: the pronoun is attached to the affirmative command, but it precedes the verb in negative commands. Add a written accent mark on the stressed syllable of the verb form.

¡Láva**te** la cara!	*Wash **your** face!*
¡No **te** laves las manos!	*Do not wash **your** hands!*
¡Levánten**se**!	*Get up!*
¡No **se** levanten!	*Do not get up!*

EJERCICIO 12·23

Complete each sentence with the imperative affirmative or negative verb form as needed.

1. ¡_____ temprano! (despertarse)

2. ¡_____ antes de las ocho! (levantarse)

3. ¡_____ pronto! (prepararse)

4. ¡_____ la cara antes de salir! (lavarse)

5. ¡_____ los dientes! (cepillarse)

6. ¡No _____! (desanimarse)

7. ¡No _____ en el espejo! (mirarse)

8. ¡_____ la chaqueta! (ponerse)

9. ¡_____ ya! (sentarse)

10. ¡_____ tranquilos! (quedarse)

Using pronouns

A pronoun replaces an element that is either named or understood in a sentence or a larger context. Everyone involved must know which elements (or *referents*) the pronouns refer to. Notice how the referent of the pronoun **ellos** (*they*) needs to be clarified in the following dialogue:

—**Ellos** hablan dos idiomas.　　　—***They*** *speak two languages.*
—¿Luis y Fernando?　　　　　　　—*Luis and Fernando?*
—No, mis hermanos. Ellos hablan　—*No, my brothers do.* ***They*** *speak*
　francés.　　　　　　　　　　　　*French.*

Now, let's break a short paragraph into five sentences. Note that the proper noun **Marta** and the common noun **alumnos** (*students*) must be repeated in each sentence:

Marta era la maestra de español.　***Marta*** *was the Spanish teacher.*
Marta trabajaba en la escuela　　***Marta*** *used to work at the secondary*
　secundaria.　　　　　　　　　　　*school.*
Los chicos adoraban a **Marta**.　　*The kids adored* ***Marta***.
Todos agradecieron a **Marta** su　*Everyone thanked* ***Marta*** *for her*
　dedicación.　　　　　　　　　　　*dedication.*
Sus alumnos y **mis alumnos**　　***Her students*** *and* ***my students*** *went*
　fueron a su casa.　　　　　　　　*to her house.*

In the sentences that follow, let's look at which pronouns replace the proper noun **Marta** and where they are placed. The first sentence establishes who **Marta** is. In grammatical terms, **Marta** is the *subject* and also the *referent* or noun the paragraph refers to.

Marta era la maestra de español.　***Marta*** *was the Spanish teacher.*

In the second sentence, **Ella** is a pronoun that takes the place of the subject noun:

Ella trabajaba en la escuela secundaria.	*She used to work at the secondary school.*

In the third sentence, the pronoun **la** replaces the proper noun **Marta**. Now either **Marta** or **la** is the *direct object* of the verb.

Los chicos **la** adoraban.	*The kids loved her.*

In the fourth sentence the *indirect object pronoun* **le** represents **Marta**, the person *to whom* or *for whom* the action of the verb is done. Notice the *indirect object* **le** and the *direct object* **la** in the previous sentence. Both correspond to the English pronoun *her*, which follows the verb in the English sentences.

Todos **le** agradecían su dedicación.	*Everyone thanked **her** for her dedication.*

In the fifth and last sentence **alumnos** is replaced by **los míos**, to avoid repetition.

Sus alumnos y **los míos** fueron a su casa.	***Her students** and **mine** went to her house.*

These are examples of pronouns, small but powerful words loaded with meaning. Now read the sentences combined in a short paragraph:

> **Marta** era la maestra de español. **Ella** trabajaba en la escuela secundaria. Los chicos **la** adoraban. Todos **le** agradecían su dedicación. **Sus alumnos** y **los míos** fueron a su casa.

Pronouns are *substitutions* that make sentences run smoother, make them less clunky, and help avoid tedious repetition.

Pronouns that replace the subject

The pronouns that replace subject nouns are called *subject pronouns*, because they do the action of the verb. The usual word order of a sentence or clause with subject pronouns is the same as that of a sentence with the *subject-noun* word order:

subject pronoun + predicate

Ellos + protegen el medio ambiente.
They protect the environment.

In previous units you learned that the subject in Spanish sentences can also follow the verb in interrogatives and in exclamatory and declarative sentences. The same is true for subject pronouns:

—¿Conoce él a la novia de Juan?	—*Does **he** know Juan's girlfriend?*
—¡Sí, sí, él la conoce!	—*Yes, **he** knows her!*

Let's review the Spanish subject pronoun forms, their gender, their number, and their uses.

SINGULAR SUBJECT PRONOUNS		PLURAL SUBJECT PRONOUNS	
yo	*I*	nosotros, -as	*we*
tú	*you (familiar)*	vosotros, -as	*you (familiar)*
usted (Ud.)	*you (polite)*	ustedes (Uds.)	*you*
él	*he*	ellos	*they*
ella	*she*	ellas	*they*

Keep in mind the following tips when using subject pronouns in Spanish to build your sentences:

- As a general rule *subject pronouns* are not often used in Spanish because the verb endings identify the subject.
- Use *subject pronouns* only when you need to *clarify* or *emphasize* the subject in a sentence.

    Clarify if you need to differentiate between **él** or **ella,** or **ellos** and **ellas:**

Eso, **ellos** son los culpables.	*That's it, **they** are the guilty ones.*

    Emphasize if you need or want to stress the difference between two subjects, even when the verb is clearly understood. The second subject may be implied:

Yo no quiero trabajar hoy.	*I do not want to work today.*

    Show politeness by adding **usted** (**Ud.**) and **ustedes** (**Uds.**):

¿Son **ustedes** los padres de Lolita?	*Are you Lolita's parents?*
Pase **usted**, por favor.	*Come in, please.*

- **Tú** is used to address friends and family.
- **Vosotros/as** is used in most of Spain, but *not* in the rest of the Spanish-speaking world; it is a familiar form for addressing friends and family.
- **Usted** and **ustedes** are polite forms throughout most of the Hispanic world; **Ud.** and **Uds.** are abbreviations.
- **Ustedes** is the plural of the informal **tú**, except in Spain (**vosotros**).

EJERCICIO
12·24

En español. *If needed, reorder each sentence with pronouns.*

1. Marcos, he is Marta's brother. _____

2. He works with Marta. _____

3. He is the chef, not Marta. _____

4. I know Marta well. _____

5. I want to go to the movies tonight; not Marta. _____

6. Do you want to go to the movies? _____

EJERCICIO
12·25

¿Tú o usted? *Use the appropriate pronoun to address each person.*

1. la Dra. Balerdi _____

2. Don Augusto, el gerente de la compañía _____

3. tu primo _____

4. el alcalde (*mayor*) de tu ciudad _____

5. el director de la escuela _____

6. tus padres _____

7. los abuelos de tus amigos _____

8. un viejo amigo _____

En español. *Use the subject pronouns to emphasize communication. Note that the verbs are not always in the same tense.*

1. They (*masc.*) wanted to eat.

   _____

2. You sing (*sing., familiar*) but she plays the guitar.

   _____

3. They (*fem.*) can finish their homework!

   _____

4. You (*pl., polite*) started at ten but we finished early.

   _____

5. Now, you (*sing., familiar*) rest while I wash the clothes.

   _____

Pronouns that replace object pronouns and word order

Direct and *indirect object pronouns* replace the direct and indirect object nouns in a sentence. The following charts and examples will give you a quick review of direct and indirect object pronouns:

DIRECT OBJECTS

SINGULAR		PLURAL	
me	*me*	nos	*us*
te	*you*	os	*you*
lo/la	*him, her, you, it*	los/las	*them, you*

INDIRECT OBJECTS

SINGULAR		PLURAL	
me	*me*	nos	*us*
te	*you*	os	*you*
le	*him, her, you, it*	les	*them, you*

Let's look at some examples:

—¿Luisa conoce a **Jacobo**?   —*Does Luisa know **Jacobo**?*
—Sí, **lo** conoce.   —*Yes, she knows **him**.*
—Y **le** regaló una corbata.   —*And she gave **him** a tie.*
—**Me lo** dijo mi hermana.   —*My sister told **me** (**it**).*

These pronouns normally precede the conjugated verb in *affirmative* and *negative* sentences that have a single verb. Consider the position of one object pronoun:

Laura + **la** + compró.   *Laura bought **it**.*
Mayra + no + **la** + quiere.   *Mayra does not want **it**.*
Laura + **me** + dio + la billetera.   *Laura gave **me** the wallet.*

Note the word order in sentences with two object pronouns:

indirect object pronoun + direct object pronoun + verb

Laura + **me** + **la** + compró.
*Laura bought **it for me**.*

An important detail to remember: the third-person singular and plural *indirect* object pronouns **le** and **les** change to the form **se** when followed by a direct object pronoun that begins with the letter **l**: **la, lo, las,** or **los**.

Laura **se la** compró.   *Laura bought **it for him/her/them**.*
Marcos **se las** regaló.   *Marcos gave **them to him/her/them**.*

EJERCICIO
12·27

En el juzgado (*court*). *Substitute the underlined items with direct and indirect pronouns as needed. Follow the model.*

MODELO   El hombre saludó <u>a su amigo</u>.

Pronombre <u>lo</u>

El hombre lo saludó.

1. La policía encontró <u>al criminal</u>.

Pronombre _____

_____

2. Llevaron <u>a la víctima</u> al hospital.

Pronombre _____

_____

3. La víctima no reveló <u>su nombre</u>.

Pronombre _____

_____

4. El médico diagnosticó un trauma leve <u>a la víctima</u>.

Pronombre _____

_____

5. La enfermera llevó <u>un calmante</u> <u>a la víctima</u>.

Pronombre _____

_____

6. El noticiero local comunicó <u>el incidente</u> <u>a la comunidad</u>.

Pronombre _____

_____

7. Al día siguiente la policía investigó <u>los detalles del asalto</u>.

Pronombre _____

_____

8. El criminal recibirá <u>su sentencia</u>.

Pronombre _____

_____

The redundant use of indirect object pronouns in Spanish

In Spanish, it is not unusual for *both* the indirect noun *and* the indirect pronoun to appear in the same sentence. We see a similar structure with the use of the stressed pronouns (**mí, ti, usted, él, ella, nosotros/as, vosotros/as, ustedes, ellos, ellas, sí,** placed after **a**) that repeat the indirect object pronoun. At first, this may seem unnecessary. That is why we refer to these pronouns as *redundant*. One explanation: since the third-person indirect object pronouns **le** (*to him, to her, to you*) and **les** (*to them, to you*) are ambiguous, the redundancy clarifies who the receiver is.

a + indirect object noun or stressed pronoun → redundant indirect object

Ana **le** dio mi recado **a su hermana**.	*Ana gave my message **to her sister**.*
Ana **le** dio mi recado **a ella**.	*Ana gave **her** my message.*
Le regalé una camisa roja **a Ana**.	*I gave **Ana** a red shirt.*
Y **le** compré un libro **a su hermano**.	*And I bought a book **for her brother**.*

Another reason to add the redundant, stressed indirect object pronoun (after **a**) is the need, at times, to put emphasis on the indirect object:

Laura **me** llamó **a mí**.	*Laura called **me**.*
Raúl **nos** invitó **a nosotros**.	*Raúl invited **us**.*

EJERCICIO
12·28

En español. *Use* **a** + *indirect object or* **a** + *the stressed pronoun at the end of each sentence.*

1. I gave a note <u>to her</u>.

_____

2. We asked (**pedir**) <u>her brother</u> a favor.

_____

3. They brought a new computer to us.

   _____

4. Luis y Ana asked their boss for a raise.

   _____

5. Marcela sent flowers to them.

   _____

6. You prepared the reception for us.

   _____

7. Cindy told a few jokes (**chistes**) to my brother.

   _____

8. Robert announced his retirement (**jubilación**) to his friends.

   _____

En orden. *Create sentences with correct word order.*

1. devolvieron / los clientes / los zapatos / le

   _____ al empleado.

2. el empleado / otro modelo / mostró / les

   _____ a los clientes.

3. compraron / ese par de zapatos / le

   _____

4. la tienda / les / un descuento / dio

   _____ a los clientes.

5. los clientes / gastaron / más dinero

   _____

6. una comisión / el jefe / dio / le

   _____ al empleado.

7. los clientes / la amabilidad / agradecieron / les

   _____ a los empleados de la tienda.

Gustar, indirect object pronouns, and word order

In Spanish, **gustar** is a frequently used verb to communicate *to like*. In English, the word order in a sentence with *to like* is the usual *subject + verb + object*: *We like cool weather.* The subject is the person or persons who *like* something or someone. In the previous example, the subject is *we*. In Spanish (see the following example), the subject is the thing or person that is *pleasing to someone*, in this case *music*.

If you focus on the notion of *to someone*, the preposition *to* tells you how to build your sentence in Spanish: it always requires an *indirect object*. Word order in sentences or clauses with **gustar** is the following:

> **indirect object pronoun + a form of gustar + subject**
>
> **Nos** + **gusta** + la música.
> *We **like** music.*

In this structure, the form of **gustar**, the verb determined by a following subject, is always *third-person* singular or plural.

Me gustan las esculturas de Botero.	*I **like** Botero's sculptures.*
No me gusta la última película de Almodóvar.	*I **do** not **like** Almovodar's last movie.*

Infinitives that refer to actions can also be the subject of a sentence with **gustar**. Note (in the last example here) that the English element *it* does not translate into Spanish:

¿**Te gusta** correr o nadar?	*Do you **like** running or swimming?*
No **le gusta** ni trabajar ni estudiar.	*He/she **does** not **like** to work or study.*
—¿**Les gusta** bailar?	*—**Do you** (pl.) **like** dancing?*
—Sí, **nos gusta**.	*—Yes, we **like** it.*

For emphasis or clarification, the preposition **a**, followed by a noun or a *stressed or prepositional pronoun*, may precede the indirect object:

> **a + noun or stressed pronoun + indirect object pronoun + a form of gustar + subject**
>
> **A** + **nosotros** + **nos** + **gusta** + la música.
> *We **do** like music.*

EJERCICIO 12·30

Sondeo (survey) **de opinión.** *Create a question with the noun and use the appropriate indirect object pronoun plus the* **usted** *or* **ustedes** *form of* **gustar**.

MODELO   la comida japonesa

      ¿Les gusta la comida japonesa?

      Sí, nos gusta la comida japonesa.

1. el té

_____

No me gusta, prefiero el café.

2. la comida mexicana

_____

Sí, efectivamente, nos gusta la comida mexicana.

3. correr

_____

¡Claro!, me gusta correr por la playa.

4. nadar

_____

¡Ah, no! No nos gusta mucho nadar en la piscina. Preferimos la playa.

5. los programas cómicos o dramáticos

_____

A mí, particularmente me gustan más los programas cómicos.

6. esta encuesta

_____

Sí, nos ha gustado esta encuesta (*survey*). ¡Gracias!

Other verbs with indirect object pronouns

Here are some frequently used verbs that behave in the same manner as **gustar**. They will be useful for building sentences:

agradar	*to please*
bastar	*to suffice, to be enough*
caer bien (mal)	*to like (to dislike)*
doler	*to hurt*
encantar	*to love someone or something*
faltar	*to be lacking in, to be in need of*
fascinar	*to be fascinating to*
hacer(le) falta (a alguien)	*to need*
importar	*to be important to*
interesar	*to be interesting to*
molestar	*to be bothersome to*
parecer	*to seem to*
sobrar	*to be in surplus/excess*
tocar(le) (a alguien)	*to be someone's turn*

Mi vida. *Complete each sentence with the appropriate first person singular form of the present tense verb. Follow the* **modelo.**

MODELO   (tocar) la cancha de tenis a las tres

Me toca la cancha de tenis a las tres.

1. (fascinar) las novelas de misterio

_____

2. no (interesar) las biografías, son aburridas

_____

3. (doler) la cabeza y tomo una aspirina

_____

4. (hacer falta) dinero y voy al banco

_____

5. (bastar) con poco, soy modesto/a

_____

6. (caer mal) Carolina; es antipática

_____

7. (caer bien) Nina porque es agradable

_____

8. (faltar) diez dólares

_____

9. (tocar) descansar porque he terminado el ejercicio

_____

10. (encantar) estudiar español

_____

Reflexive object pronouns and word order

The function of reflexive object pronouns is not the same as that of other object pronouns: reflexive object pronouns always stay with their subject. In English, the reflexive object pronoun is compounded with *-self*. Note that the subject and object of the verb always refer to the same person, animal, or entity.

Let's compare this sentence in Spanish and in English:

Lucía **se** lava **los pies.**   *Lucia washes **her feet**.*

In Spanish, the reflexive pronoun **se** precedes the verb. It indicates that the *subject* receives the action of the verb. It is not translated in the English equivalent. (The reflexive pronoun *myself* is not needed in English because the possessive adjective *her* is used with *feet*.) In Spanish, because of the reflexive form, we understand that Lucía is washing her own feet. Note also that a form of the definite article (**el/la; los/las**) usually appears in the Spanish sentence with a part of the body. The word order is:

subject + reflexive pronoun + verb

Ana + **se** + peina.
*Ana is combing **her** hair.*

In the next example, the verb is *not* reflexive. The *indirect object pronoun* **le** indicates who receives the action of the verb, in this case, a person other than the subject.

Lucía **le** lava los pies **a su niña**.   *Lucía washes **her daughter's feet**.*

Reflexive pronouns in Spanish are closely related to *direct and indirect object pronouns* in that they follow the same word order and use many of the same forms.

SINGULAR		PLURAL	
me	*myself*	nos	*ourselves*
te	*yourself*	os	*yourselves*
se	*himself, herself, yourself*	se	*themselves, yourselves*

In Spanish, many verbs are classified as *reflexive*. Many of those describe routines we follow every day, in grooming, for example. However, almost all Spanish verbs can be turned into reflexives, which often changes the meaning of the verb. In this construction, the *reflexive pronoun* is always placed before the verb, whether in affirmative, negative, or interrogative sentences.

Carlos **no se despierta** temprano.   *Carlos **does not wake up** early.*
¿Por qué **te peinas los cabellos** otra vez?   *Why **are you combing your hair** again?*
Se ponen las botas.   *They **put on their boots**.*

EJERCICIO
12·32

La rutina y los verbos reflexivos. *Select the appropriate reflexive pronoun.*

me / te / se / nos / os / se

1. Juan _____ acuesta a las ocho cada día.

2. Nosotros _____ ponemos el pijama para dormir.

3. Luisa y Ana _____ duermen mirando la tele.

4. Ustedes siempre _____ enojan con los niños.

5. Yo _____ voy a dormir.

6. Tú _____ miras siempre en el espejo.

7. Vosotros _____ preparáis para descansar.

8. Yo siempre _____ lavo los dientes después de comer.

El orden de los pronombres. *Reword the paragraph replacing the underlined words with a direct or indirect pronoun.*

Eduardo Benítez dirige una agencia de publicidad. Eduardo dirige (1) esa empresa con éxito. El año pasado dobló las ganancias. Y logró (*achieve*) (2) las ganancias con su esfuerzo. Los inversionistas (*investors*) agradecen (3) a Eduardo su perseverancia. Eduardo asegura (4) a los inversionistas que el año próximo doblará las ganancias: más dinero. Y van a ganar (5) más dinero porque hay una gran demanda en el mercado internacional. Eduardo conoce muy bien (6) ese mercado.

_____

_____

_____

_____

_____

_____

Word order of direct, indirect, and reflexive pronouns with more than one verb

Now let's concentrate on sentences with more than one verb. This construction usually consists of a conjugated verb followed by an *infinitive* (-**ar**, -**er**, -**ir** ending) or a *present participle*, -**ndo** (the English *-ing* form).

◆ Pronouns may be placed *before the conjugated verb*:

direct object + conjugated verb + infinitive
Te + **quiere** + **ver**.
He/she wants to see you.

indirect object + conjugated verb + present participle
Paco **les** + **está** + **hablando**.
Paco is speaking to them.

Melisa **lo** quiere ver.	*Melisa wants to see **him/it**.*
Melisa no **te** quiere ver.	*Melisa does not want to see **you**.*
¿**Te** quiere ver Melisa?	*Does Melisa want to see **you**?*

◆ Spanish object pronouns may also be attached to *infinitives* and *present participles*:

conjugated verb + infinitive (pronoun)
Quiere + **verte**.
*He wants **to see you**.*

Queremos **visitarte** en Guadalajara.	*We want **to visit you** in Guadalajara.*

conjugated verb + present participle (pronoun)
Viene + **riéndose**.
*He comes along **laughing**.*
Estaba **cantándote** una canción.   *He was **singing you** a song.*
Estaba **cantándotela**.   *He was **singing it to you**.*

Note the written accent mark on the next-to-last syllable of the present participle, when one or more syllables have been added by attaching pronouns.

Otra posibilidad. *Create a sentence attaching the pronoun to the verb.*

MODELO   Necesita un libro en español. Lo va a buscar.
       Está buscándolo.

1. Es una pintura famosa. La estoy admirando. _____

2. Buscan unas notas. Las van a encontrar. _____

3. Necesitas un préstamo. (*loan*) Lo vas a pedir. _____

4. No tiene ayuda. No la va a tener. _____

5. ¿Quieren ellos dejar el auto? ¿Lo quieren dejar? _____

6. Vamos a terminar este ejercicio. Lo vamos a terminar. _____

Demonstrative and possessive adjectives and pronouns

Formerly you learned about adjectives and how to use them in Spanish to describe qualities, appearances of a person or objects, and quantities. However, demonstrative and possessive adjectives and pronouns have different functions, as we'll now review.

Demonstrative adjectives

Demonstrative adjectives point to the position of specific persons or things to which a speaker is referring. They precede the noun, with which they must agree in gender and number. In Spanish there are three demonstrative adjectives: **este**, **ese**, and **aquel**, and all their forms.

◆ **este** points out people or objects that are close to the speaker

      Este ejercicio es fácil.   *This exercise is easy.*

◆ **ese** indicates people or objects that are closer to the listener than to the speaker

      Esa computadora está muy cara.   *That computer is very expensive.*

◆ **aquel** shows people or objects that are far from both speaker and listener

      Aquellos monitores cuestan poco.   *Those monitors do not cost a lot.*

These three demonstrative adjectives decline as follows.

MASCULINE	FEMININE		MASCULINE	FEMININE	
este	**esta**	*this*	**estos**	**estas**	*these*
ese	**esa**	*that*	**esos**	**esas**	*those*
aquel	**aquella**	*that* (over there)	**aquellos**	**aquellas**	*those* (over there)

¿Necesitas **estas instrucciones**?	*Do you need these instructions?*
Quiero viajar en **ese auto**.	*I want to travel in that car.*
Luis trabaja en **aquella tienda**.	*Luis works in that store over there.*

En ese parque precioso. *Complete the paragraph below with the appropriate form of the demonstrative adjectives in parentheses.*

1. _____ (Este) verano voy a 2. _____ (ese) parques tranquilos con mi perro Max. Max corre alrededor de 3. _____ (aquel) dos lagos con 4. _____ (ese) patitos pequeños. 5. _____ (Aquel) peces tienen colores brillantes. Con 6. _____ (este) telescopio grande observo las estrellas y 7. _____ (aquel) planetas Venus y Marte. Escucho 8. _____ (aquel) cotorras (*parrot*) que hablan mucho. 9. _____ ¡(Este) vistas son impresionantes. 10. ¡_____ ¡(Este) parques son maravillosos!

En la joyería. Traducción.

1. This jewelry store is empty.

   _____

2. Oh, these diamond rings must cost a fortune!

   _____

3. Those earrings (**el arete**) are not cheap.

   _____

4. Use (*pl., fam.*) that elevator over there to go to the second floor.

   _____

5. In that shop window (**el escaparate**) they have pearls and emeralds.

   _____

6. Those gentlemen over there love watches from Switzerland.

   _____

7. I am ready to buy that gold bracelet.

   _____

Possessive adjectives

In Spanish, the preposition **de** is used to express ownership. (In Chapter 15 you will learn more about prepositions.)

| la casa **de Alfonsina** | *Alfonsina's house* |
| los juguetes **de Pepito** | *Pepito's toys* |

We use possessive adjectives to express the same idea of possession or ownership. There are two types of possessive adjectives in Spanish, short forms and long forms rather than the single form in English. The short forms agree in number but not gender with the object possessed, except for the **nosotros/vosotros** forms. All the long forms of possessive adjectives agree in gender and number with the object that someone or something owns.

SHORT FORMS		LONG FORMS	
mi *my*	**mis** *my*	**mío,-a** *my*	**míos,-as** *my*
tu (fam.) *your*	**tus** *your*	**tuyo, -a** (fam.) *your*	**tuyos, -as** (fam.) *your*
su *your*	**sus** *your*	**suyo, -a** *yours*	**suyos, -as** *yours*
su *his, her, its*	**sus** *his, her, its*	**suyo, -a** *his, her, its*	**suyos, -as** *his, her, its*
nuestro, -a *our*	**nuestros, -as** *our*	**nuestro, -a** *our*	**nuestros, -as** *our*
vuestro, -a *your*	**vuestros, -as** *your*	**vuestro, -a** *your*	**vuestros, -as** *your*
su *your*	**sus** *your*	**suyo, -a** *your*	**suyos, -as** *your*
su *their*	**sus** *their*	**suyo, -a** *his, her, its*	**suyos, -as** *their*

Now, let's review the position of these two possessive forms.

◆ The short forms are placed before the noun.

| **mi** calendario | *my calendar* |
| **nuestras** tradiciones | *our traditions* |

◆ The long forms are placed after the noun; they are used to express *of yours*, *of theirs*, etc.

un tío **tuyo**	*an uncle of yours*
los colegas **míos**	*colleagues of mine*
¡Ay, Dios **mío**!	*Oh, my God!*

◆ **Su, sus, suyo, suya, suyos,** and **suyas** have several meanings. It may sound repetitive, but to clarify the meaning of these forms, use this structure: article + noun + **de** + subject pronoun (**el** + **auto** + **de** + **ella**).

| un amigo **de ellos** | *their friend, a friend of theirs* |
| los parientes **suyos** | *your relatives, relatives of yours* |

EJERCICIO
13·3

Traducción. *Write the appropriate short form of the possessive adjective.*

1. my car _____

2. your (*sing., fam.*) bicycle _____

3. his skates_____

4. her taxi _____

5. our motorcycle _____

6. their fences (**la cerca**) _____

7. your (*pl., fam.*) neighbors _____

8. your (*pl., fam.*) garden _____

9. my trees _____

10. our building _____

Un viaje. *Write the long form of the possessive adjective to replace the underlined words.*

1. Aquí está <u>mi mapa</u>. _____

2. ¿Este es <u>tu calendario</u>? _____

3. Juan busca <u>su boleto</u>. _____

4. Alicia no encuentra <u>su mochila</u> (*backpack*). _____

5. Esos son <u>nuestros asientos</u>. _____

6. Julio tiene aquí <u>sus maletas</u>. _____

7. <u>Nuestro auto</u> está en el aparcamiento. _____

8. Aquí tenéis <u>vuestros sombreros</u>. _____

Demonstrative pronouns

The use of pronouns allows efficient, concise communication. Demonstrative pronouns are used to point at something that has been previously mentioned: *this, that one, that one over there,* and *these, those, those ones over there.* They have the same forms as the demonstrative adjectives, and reflect the gender and number of the noun they replace. Written accents are used only if it's necessary to distinguish the meaning.

SINGULAR			PLURAL		
masculine	feminine		masculine	feminine	
este	**esta**	*this one*	**estos**	**estas**	*these ones*
ese	**esa**	*that one*	**esos**	**esas**	*those ones*
aquel	**aquella**	*that one over there*	**aquellos**	**aquellas**	*those ones (over there)*

Tengo dos camisas. ¿Prefieres **esta** o **esa**?	*I have two shirts. Do you prefer this one or that one?*
Estos zapatos son caros pero **aquellos** son más baratos.	*These shoes are expensive but those ones are cheaper.*

The three demonstrative pronouns, **esto**, **eso**, and **aquello**, point to situations, ideas, etc., that are not clear or specified.

¿Por qué tienes **esto**?	*Why do you have this?*
Eso es un verdadero misterio.	*That is a real mystery.*
Y **aquello**, ¿qué es?	*And what is that over there?*

EJERCICIO
13·5

¡Práctica! *Write in the appropriate form of the demonstrative pronoun in parentheses that would replace each noun.*

1. los caminos _____ (este)
2. las salidas _____ (aquel)
3. los pueblos _____ (ese)
4. las avenidas _____ (esta)
5. el almacén _____ (aquel)
6. la calle _____ (aquel)
7. la estación _____ (ese)
8. los autobuses _____ (este)
9. el chofer _____ (aquel)
10. las motos _____ (esta)

EJERCICIO
13·6

Traducción.

1. Why do you want this?

_____

2. This is my umbrella and that one is Manuel's umbrella.

_____

3. I have a raincoat but I like this one.

_____

4. Molly does not have a hat. She needs that one over there.

_____

5. And that over there, what is it?

_____

Possessive pronouns

The possessive pronouns have the same forms as the long forms of possessive adjectives. They agree in gender and number with the noun they replace. Note that the Spanish possessive pronoun is always preceded by the definite article **el, la, los,** or **las**.

	SINGULAR	PLURAL
mine	**el mío, la mía**	**los míos, las mías**
yours (fam.)	**el tuyo, la tuya**	**los tuyos, las tuyas**
yours	**el suyo, la suya**	**los suyos, las suyas**
his, hers, its	**el suyo, la suya**	**los suyos, las suyas**
ours	**el nuestro, la nuestra**	**los nuestros, las nuestras**
yours	**el vuestro, la vuestra**	**los vuestros, las vuestras**
theirs	**el suyo, la suya**	**los suyos, las suyas**

No tengo mi cámara. Necesito **la tuya**.

I do not have my camera. I need yours.

Nuestra tienda abre a las ocho pero **la suya** no abre hasta las nueve.

Our store opens at eight but yours does not open until nine.

VOCABULARIO

Review this vocabulary before doing the exercises that follow.

la almohada	*pillow*	**el maquillaje**	*make-up*	**el peine**	*comb*
el despertador	*alarm clock*	**la navaja de afeitar**	*razor*	**la toalla**	*towel*
el espejo	*mirror*	**la pasta de dientes**	*toothpaste*	**la sábana**	*sheet*

EJERCICIO 13·7

¿De quién es? *Write in the appropriate form of the possessive pronoun.*

MODELO   ¿Ese peine? Es _____. (*mine*)

Es *el mío*.

1. ¿Estas toallas? Son _____. (*ours*)

2. ¿Y esta pasta de dientes? ¿Es _____, Marisa? (*yours*)

3. ¿De quién son estas sábanas? Estas son _____, de Marta y mía. (*ours*)

4. ¿Y este despertador? Ah, es _____. (*yours,* **Ud.**)

5. ¿Este maquillaje? Creo que es _____. (*hers*)

6. ¿Estos espejos? ¿Estos son _____, Laurita y Sara? (*yours,* **vosotros**)

7. ¿Estas dos almohadas? Sí, son _____. (*theirs*)

8. ¿La navaja de afeitar? Pues, es _____. (*ours*)

Neuter pronouns

There are a handful of neuter pronouns in Spanish. You may wonder why Spanish would need such a thing, since either the masculine or feminine genders are attached to every noun in the language. They exist because often we speak of more abstract things to which no noun is attached, for instance, a body of information such as is contained in a speech or article. In English, we often address these phenomena using verbal formulae such as "all that which was said" or colloquially, "all that" or even "all that stuff." Spanish has five neuter pronouns, shown as follows. The most common English translations are shown as well. Among these five forms, **ello** is found in somewhat formal writing (and even formal speech); despite occasional protestations that its use is rare, I frequently find it in newspapers from both sides of the Atlantic, so it is worth recognizing.

aquello	*that*
ello	*it*
eso	*that*
esto	*this*
lo	*it*

Most uses of neuter pronouns have to do with references to speech acts either in the present or the past. So the same observations about distance in space or time apply with regard to the forms that resemble the demonstrative adjectives and pronouns: **esto**, (something in the immediate present), **eso** (something in the immediate past or even in the present), and **aquello** (something more remote in the past that requires some recollection).

Pues, no entiendo **esto**.	*Well, I don't understand this.*
¿Escuchaste **eso**?	*Did you hear that?*
No entendí **aquello** que explicaba el profe la semana pasada.	*I didn't understand that stuff the prof was explaining last week.*
Los portavoces de la administración se negaron a elaborar sobre **ello**.	*Administrative spokespersons refused to elaborate about it.*

Using lo

The neuter pronoun **lo** is quite interesting, useful, and important. As you know, there is no subject pronoun in Spanish that corresponds to the English word *it* when *it* is used as a subject pronoun. In other words, to say *It is snowing*, you simply say **Está nevando** or even just **Nieva**. Likewise, *It is interesting* is simply **Es interesante**.

However, the word **lo**, placed before an adjective, creates an abstract, singular subject in the third-person, but only in combination with the adjective. This little device makes it possible to start a sentence by saying, for instance, **Lo interesante**, which means *The interesting thing*. Often, an adverb is inserted between **lo** and the adjective to intensify it.

Lo más triste de todo eso es que perdió su billetera.	*The saddest part in all that is that he lost his wallet.*
Lo menos divertido fue el viaje por el desierto.	*The least fun part was the trip through the desert.*
Lo mejor es que mi esposa podrá acompañarme.	*The best thing is that my wife will be able to come with me.*

Translate the following short phrases into Spanish.

1. these two (female) students _____

2. this hat _____

3. this first mountain _____

4. those paintings _____

5. that light (in the distance) _____

6. this museum _____

7. those old books _____

8. this antique mirror _____

9. that box of books (way over there) _____

10. this friendly dog _____

11. this red shirt _____

12. that thin woman _____

13. that class _____

14. these pretty dresses _____

15. these brown shoes _____

16. those soccer players _____

17. that man over there _____

18. that sailboat yonder _____

19. these six brand new cars _____

20. this old house _____

Select the Spanish translation that is both grammatically correct and best reflects the meaning of the following English sentences.

1. These are the books Dr. Ramírez was talking to us about last night.

   a. Éstos son los libros de los cuales nos hablaba el Dr. Ramírez anoche.

   b. Esos libros son los de que el Dr. Ramírez nos habló anoche.

   c. El Dr. Ramírez nos habló de aquellos libros anoche.

2. I didn't understand any of that.

    a. No entiendo esto para nada.

    b. Yo no entendí nada de eso.

    c. Nada entiendo de aquello.

3. That despicable guy burns me up.

    a. Ese hombre me cae mal.

    b. El tipo ese me cae gordo.

    c. Aquel hombre me da asco.

4. I don't even want to lay eyes on that woman.

    a. Ni siquiera deseo verla.

    b. A la mujer esa no la quiero ver ni en pintura.

    c. No quiero ver a esa mujer más.

5. Didn't you see that movie with your girlfriend?

    a. ¿Fuiste al cine con tu novia para ver esa película?

    b. ¿No viste esa película con tu novia?

    c. ¿No fueron tú y tu novia a ver esa película?

6. Those were different times.

    a. Esos tiempos eran diferentes.

    b. Aquélla fue otra época.

    c. Esos fueron tiempos diferentes.

7. This guy is a great friend of mine.

    a. Este señor es mi buen amigo.

    b. Éste es gran amigo mío.

    c. Éste es mi amigo grande.

8. For *that*, it's important to research the subject in detail.

    a. Para ello, es importante investigar la materia a fondo.

    b. Para realizarlo, es importante investigar la materia a fondo.

    c. Por eso, es importante investigar la materia a fondo.

9. The professor's presentation was the best part of the conference.

    a. La presentación del profesor fue la mejor parte de la conferencia.

b. La presentación del profesor es la parte que más me gustó de la conferencia.

c. La presentación del profesor fue lo mejor de la conferencia.

10. The most fun part was when that woman tried to dance the tango.

a. Lo más divertido fue cuando esa mujer quiso bailar el tango.

b. La parte más divertida fue cuando esa mujer trató de bailar el tango.

c. El momento más divertido fue cuando la mujer esa intentó bailar el tango.

11. Well, I don't know. This is a mystery.

a. Bueno, no sé. Es misterioso.

b. Pues, no sé. Esto es un misterio.

c. Esto, pues, no lo sé; es misterioso.

12. Don't say anything about what happened yesterday.

a. No digas nada sobre ayer.

b. No hables nada sobre lo que pasó ayer.

c. No digas nada sobre lo de ayer.

13. I told the whole thing to the lawyer, which seemed to him a scandalous matter.

a. Se lo conté todo al abogado y le pareció un escándalo.

b. Le conté todo al abogado, lo cual le pareció un asunto escandaloso.

c. Le dije todo al abogado y eso le pareció escandaloso.

14. Here's the one (woman) I told you about that night a while back.

a. Aquí está ésa de quien te hablé aquella noche.

b. Aquí, es la mujer de quien te hablé esa noche.

c. Allí está esa mujer de quien te hablé aquella noche.

15. Let's see the guest list . . . is this woman here?

a. A ver la lista de los invitados ... ¿Está ésta?

b. Pásame la lista de los invitados ... ¿Es ésta?

c. Veamos la lista ... ¿Dónde está ésta?

Using adjectives

When we write sentences to communicate thoughts, ideas, beliefs, feelings, or opinions, we often include *adjectives*. They specify and clarify nouns; for example, they state how many (*some*, *many*) we want to emphasize. Adjectives also describe the origin or material of an object or the color, size, age, or shape of nouns (persons, places, or things).

Adjectives modify all nouns: nouns used as subjects, as direct or indirect objects, as prepositional phrases, and so on.

adjective → describes or limits a noun

Consider the following sentences, the relationship of the adjectives to the nouns, and the position of nouns and adjectives:

Diez científicos **españoles** investigan regiones **montañosas**.	*Ten Spanish scientists are doing research in **mountain** regions.*
Estudian cambios **climáticos** en **varias** áreas.	*They are studying **climatic** changes in **several** areas.*
Es **necesario** comprender los cambios del medio **ambiente**.	*It is **necessary** to understand changes in the environment.*
Estudian las **antiguas** épocas **climáticas**.	*They study **remote climatic** eras.*
Este estudio incluye la adaptación a escenarios **futuros**.	*This study includes adaptation to **future** scenarios.*
Los científicos quieren comunicar **sus** ideas a la población.	*The scientists want to communicate **their** ideas to the public.*

The previous words in boldface are all adjectives. They fall into several categories. In the first sentence, two adjectives refer to the same plural masculine noun, **científicos**: **diez** is a *limiting adjective of quantity* that determines the *number* of the noun **científicos**, while **españoles** denotes the origin of the noun.

The adjective **climáticos** describes **cambios**; **varias** determines the number of **áreas**. The adjective **necesario** is part of the impersonal expression with **es,** or another form of **ser,** that indicates the necessity of what is to follow. **Ambiente** is part of the fixed expression **medio ambiente** (in English, a single word, *environment*). **Antiguas** denotes the age of **épocas**. And the demonstrative adjective **este** determines the noun **estudio**; that is, *this study*, not another. Finally, **sus**, a possessive adjective, shows that the ideas belong to the scientists working on this project.

The words discussed in the previous paragraph are all adjectives: words that *describe, modify,* or *limit* the name of a person, being, or thing appearing in a sentence.

Let's go back to the first sentence in the previous examples. If we eliminate the adjectives in the first sentence, the message is not complete; it is rather vague:

Científicos investigan regiones.	*Scientists are doing research in regions.*

Completed by its adjectives, the sentence is clearer and more informative.

Note that adjectives agree in *number* and *gender* with the nouns they modify. However, the adjective **diez**, like most other Spanish numerals, does not change with number or gender of the noun. Impersonal expressions with adjectives always use the masculine singular form of the adjective: **es necesario**, **es bueno**, etc.

Adjectives and gender and number

Let's review the gender formation of adjectives. Adjectives ending in **-o** change the ending to **-a** in the feminine. Adjectives of nationality often *add* an **-a** in the feminine when the masculine ends in a consonant (**español/española**, **irlandés/irlandesa**).

El chico es **pequeño** pero la nena no es **pequeña**.	*The boy is **little**, but the girl is not **little**.*
El periódico **francés** y la revista **francesa** son de Alba.	*The **French** newspaper and the **French** magazine are Alba's.*

Most adjectives ending in a consonant have the same singular form for both genders:

El reguetón es **popular**; y también es **popular** la salsa.

Reguetón is **popular**; *and salsa is* **popular** *too.*

El trabajo parece **difícil**, pero esta actividad es muy **fácil**.

The job seems **difficult**, *but this activity is very* **easy**.

The *plural* of adjectives ending in a vowel is formed by adding -**s**:

Las **rosas rojas** alegran la sala.

The **red roses** *cheer up the room.*

Compré los **zapatos caros**.

I bought the **expensive shoes**.

The plural of adjectives ending in a consonant is formed by adding -**es**:

Los estudiantes **alemanes** viajarán al Perú.

The **German** *students will travel to Peru.*

Adjectives ending in -**z**, such as **feliz**, change the -**z** to -**c** before adding the -**es** plural ending.

Me acuerdo de esos días **felices**.

I remember those **happy** *days.*

EJERCICIO 13·10

En el zoológico. *Indicate the adjectives that describe nouns in the paragraph.*

El zoológico de San Diego, California, está entre los más famosos del mundo. El área de los trópicos incluye bellas cascadas de agua y zonas elevadas, imitando las montañas africanas donde viven los gorilas. La sección de los gorilas, gigantes vegetarianos que viven en una sociedad muy compleja, tiene gorilas jóvenes y ágiles que se deslizan (*tumble down*) rápidamente para ir a observar a la gente curiosa. Cerca, están otros simios, monos inteligentes y simpáticos que divierten a los visitantes. Hay rocas enormes, palmas tropicales. ¡Es como si estuvieras en África!

EJERCICIO 13·11

Choose the appropriate adjective and correct form from the list.

rápido / fiel / incapacitado / cariñoso / humano / simpático / inteligente / agresivo / hablador / tropical / anfibio

1. Los perros _____ pueden ayudar a las personas _____.

2. Las cotorras (*parrots*) _____ me parecen cómicas.

3. Los peces _____ tienen una gran variedad de colores bonitos.

4. ¿Tienes un tigre en tu casa? Los tigres son _____

   pero _____.

5. Dos características de la mascota ideal: _____ y _____.

6. Los gorilas tienen características casi _____.

7. Las gacelas son _____.

8. La rana (*frog*) es un animal _____.

¿Cómo eras? *Describe your intellectual abilities and physical appearance.*

Tu descripción física

1. Soy _____, _____, _____
   y _____.

2. Mis ojos _____, un poco _____.

3. Mi nariz _____ pero _____.

4. La forma de mi cara es _____ y _____.

5. Mi pelo no es _____ sino _____ _____.

6. Me gusta(n) mi(s) _____ porque _____.

Ahora, tu personalidad y características intelectuales

7. Soy una persona _____ porque puedo _____.

8. Creo que soy _____ y además _____.

9. Mis amigos me aprecian porque _____.

10. En el futuro, puedo cambiar y ser más / menos _____.

Adjectives and word order

The nature of an adjective determines its place in a sentence. Most combinations with *descriptive* adjectives follow this order in Spanish:

> **noun + adjective → descriptive adjective combination**
> una rosa **amarilla**
> a *yellow* rose

Limiting adjectives are demonstratives, possessives, and adjectives of number and quantity. Limiting adjectives precede the noun in Spanish:

> **adjective + noun → limiting adjective combination**
> **mis cuatro** perros
> *my four* dogs

Adjectives that follow nouns

In English, with some exceptions, descriptive adjectives usually appear immediately before the noun they modify. In Spanish, descriptive adjectives are usually placed *after* the noun:

Los libros **interesantes** deleitan a los lectores.	***Interesting*** *books delight their readers.*
Una montaña **alta** separa las provincias.	*A **tall** mountain separates the provinces.*

Descriptive adjectives may appear in a sequence, separated by commas:

Alto, **delgado**, **musculoso** y a**tractivo**.	***Tall**, **slender**, **muscular**, and **attractive**.*
Tienes una colega **leal**, **lista**, **persistente**.	*You have a **loyal**, **sharp**, **persevering** colleague.*

Adjectives that precede nouns

Descriptive adjectives can be placed *before* the noun when the adjective underscores or contains an innate or inherent quality of the noun it modifies. In the first example below, the writer focuses on **duras**, placing the adjective immediately before the noun. In the second sentence, **valientes** serves a similar purpose:

Las **duras** experiencias fortalecen el carácter.	***Tough*** *experiences build character.*
Los patriotas son recordados por sus **valientes** hazañas.	*Patriots are remembered for their **courageous** deeds.*

Demonstrative adjectives, possessive adjectives, and adjectives of number and quantity *precede* the nouns they modify:

Este chico es un amigo de **mi** hermano Luis.	***This*** *young man is a friend of **my** brother Luis.*
Tus amigos y **mis** hermanos se reúnen mañana.	***Your*** *friends and **my** brothers are meeting tomorrow.*
Quieren ver **tres** películas argentinas en la tele.	*They want to see **three** Argentinean movies on TV.*
Muchas veces salen a cenar juntos.	***Many*** *times they go out to dinner together.*
Algunos amigos de Luis son italianos.	***Some*** *of Luis's friends are Italian.*

Note that the following adjectives of quantity are frequently used in the plural form:

algunos/as	*some*
muchos/as	*many*
ningunos/as	*none, not any*
pocos/as	*few*
unos/as	*some*
varios/as	*several*

EJERCICIO
13·13

Select the appropriate adjective and give it in the correct form: masculine or feminine; singular or plural.

1. _____ largo _____

2. _____ bello _____

3. _____ dulce _____

4. _____ fuerte _____

5. _____ destructivo _____

6. _____ suave _____

a. flores   d. bebida
b. dolor   e. huracán
c. piel   f. pelo

Go back to Ejercicio 13–13. Use the nouns and adjectives to create complete sentences using the present tense verb. Follow the **modelo.**

MODELO   interesante pasajes
                Me gustan los pasajes interesantes de la novela El juego del ángel.

1. _____

2. _____

3. _____

4. _____

5. _____

6. _____

Position and meaning of adjectives

In Spanish, some adjectives change their meaning according to their position *before* or *after* a noun:

ADJECTIVE	BEFORE A NOUN	AFTER A NOUN
antiguo/a	*former*	*old*
cierto/a	*certain*	*sure*
gran(de)	*great*	*big*
mismo/a	*same*	*himself/herself*
pobre	*unlucky*	*poor*
viejo	*old time*	*old*

La madre de mi amiga es una **señora vieja**.   *My friend's mother is an **old woman**.*
Me encanta charlar con mis **viejos amigos**.   *I love to chat with my **old friends**.*
¿Quieres ver la **misma película**, otra vez?   *Do you want to see the **same movie** again?*
¡Bueno, lo hicieron **ellas mismas**!   *Well, **they themselves** did it!*

Shortened adjective forms

Some adjectives drop the -o (or the -e) ending when they precede a masculine noun (**buen amigo**, **gran hombre**):

alguno, algún	*some*
bueno, buen	*good*
grande, gran	*big, great*
malo, mal	*bad*
ninguno, ningún	*no, not any*
primero, primer	*first*
tercero, tercer	*third*

Algún día entenderás a tus padres.	*__Someday__ you will understand your parents.*
Carlos se porta como un **buen estudiante**.	*Carlos behaves like a __good student__.*
No me gusta el **primer día** de clases.	*I do not like the __first day__ of school.*
Ese plato me dejó **mal sabor** en la boca.	*This dish left me with a __bad taste__ in my mouth.*

Here are more uses of the shortened adjectives:

◆ **Cien** is used when it precedes all nouns, except the numbers 1 to 99:

Cien años es un siglo.   *__One hundred__ years is a century.*

◆ **Grande** is also shortened when it precedes a feminine singular noun:

Gloria Fuertes era una **gran poeta**.   *Gloria Fuertes was a __great poet__.*

◆ **San**, the shortened form of the title **Santo**, is used before the names of all male saints, *except* those whose names start with the letters **Do-** or **To-**:

Santo Tomás y **Santo Domingo** son venerados.   *__Saint Thomas__ and __Saint Dominick__ are revered.*

EJERCICIO
13·15

En Quito. *Complete each sentence with the appropriate adjective in parentheses.*

1. Mi _____ amigo Franklin vive en Quito con su esposa Susi. (bueno, buen)

2. Creo que _____ día lo voy a visitar en su casa. (alguno, algún)

3. Tenemos una _____ amistad. (grande, gran)

4. Tuve un _____ sueño anoche: Franklin se había caído de la moto. (malo, mal)

5. Nunca conocí a _____ hombre más fanático de las motocicletas. (ninguno, ningún)

6. Hace dos años, Franklin tuvo su _____ accidente en la moto. (primer, primero)

7. Y este año tuvo su _____ problema con la moto: ¡se la robaron! (tercero, tercer)

8. ¡Pobre Franklin! El seguro le pagará solamente _____ dólares por la moto. (ciento, cien)

En español. *Translate into Spanish.*

1. Yesterday my brother went to visit his old friend, Mario.

2. Mario told me himself that he admires my father.

3. He believes our father is a great influence in his own life.

4. Mario's father is very old and he is ill.

5. Mario's father used to live in an old house in Guatemala.

6. One day, he decided to move to New Mexico.

7. Mario's family was not poor.

8. An old friend (*fem.*) of mine met Mario and his father, Don Julián.

9. Poor Don Julián, he is too ill now to go back to Guatemala.

1. _____

2. _____

3. _____

4. _____

5. _____

6. _____

7. _____

8. _____

9. _____

Words that function as adjectives

Past participles may function as adjectives in both English and Spanish. In Spanish, they must agree with the noun they modify in gender and number. Remember that Spanish past participles are formed by dropping the **-ar**, **-er**, and **-ir** infinitive endings of a verb and adding **-ado** or **-ido**.

Alina encontró las joyas **robadas** en su habitación.	*Alina found the **stolen** jewels in her room.*
¿No estuviste en Chile la semana **pasada**?	*Didn't you go to Chile **last** week?*
Suenas como un disco **rayado**.	*You sound like a **broken** record.*
¿No has encontrado los libros **perdidos**?	*Haven't you found the **lost** books?*

Remember that some common verbs have irregular past participle forms:

abrir	*to open*	abierto	*opened*
escribir	*to write*	escrito	*written*
hacer	*to do*	hecho	*done*
imprimir	*to print*	impreso	*printed*

morir	to die	muerto	dead
romper	to break	roto	broken
volver	to turn	vuelto	returned; turned over

Prefixes such as **en-**, **re-**, **des-**, and others can be added to the infinitive of some of these verbs, changing their meaning. Their irregular past participles are like those of the original verbs:

envolver	to wrap	envuelto	wrapped
desenvolver	to unwrap	desenvuelto	unwrapped
revolver	to stir	revuelto	stirred
deshacer	to undo	deshecho	undone
rehacer	to redo	rehecho	redone
reescribir	to rewrite	reescrito	rewritten

Son promesas **rotas**.	They are **broken** promises.
Lleva los paquetes **envuelto**s al correo.	Take the **wrapped** packages to the post office.
¿Donde está la versión **impresa**?	Where is the **printed** version?

EJERCICIO
13·17

Un día terrible ayer. *Complete each sentence with the appropriate past participle.*

MODELO   Llegué a casa y encontré los papeles _revueltos y deshechos_.

desenvuelto / muerto / revuelto / roto / impreso / reescrito / desecho / abierto

1. Entré en mi dormitorio y vi las ventanas _____ .

2. Fui al patio y encontré dos lagartijas (*lizards*) _____ .

3. En la cocina, había varios platos _____ .

4. Los paquetes _____ de los regalos del cumpleaños de Alicia estaban en el comedor.

5. Una extraña hoja con mi nombre _____ estaba en la mesa.

6. ¡El documento _____ en mi computadora estaba alterado!

7. ¡Toda mi casa _____ me daba miedo!

8. Comprendí las promesas _____ de mi sobrino: no me había ayudado a cuidar la casa en mi ausencia.

Declarative sentences and word order

Sentences and phrases are different in nature and serve different purposes to communicate ideas and thoughts.

What is a phrase?

A phrase consists of more than one word. It does not have the *subject* + *predicate* organization of a sentence.

one or more words → phrase

Some phrases are formulas used frequently in social situations. Note that they do not have a subject and a verb:

Buenos días.   *Good morning.*
Hasta luego.   *Bye for now.*

Other phrases may be clichés or proverbs that apply to specific situations. They are rarely translated word for word.

La niña de sus ojos.   *The apple of his eye.*
El alma de la fiesta.   *The life of the party.*

Other types of phrases are classified as *prepositional phrases*, **con su hermano** (*with his brother*), or *adverbial phrases*, **a través de los años** (*throughout the years*), that add information to your sentences. Later you will study these phrases and incorporate them into your writing practice.

What is a sentence?

Unlike a phrase, a *sentence* is defined as a grammatical unit:

subject + predicate → sentence

To build this unit in Spanish you need nouns, a verb, object pronouns, adverbs, etc., elements you have previously learned. Think of these elements as the blocks that help you build a structure. A Spanish sentence includes a *subject*, a word or a group of words that tell you what or whom the sentence is about, and a *predicate*, a word or words that tell us something about the subject. A capital letter is required to start a sentence and a period indicates the end of the message.

Declarative sentences

A *declarative sentence* (from the Latin **declarare**) makes a statement. A statement communicates information; it does not ask a question, it does not express exclamations or give a command. A declarative sentence consists of the following elements:

subject + predicate
El piloto + aterriza el avión.
El piloto **aterriza** el avión.   *The pilot **lands (is landing)** the plane.*
El piloto **aterrizó** el avión.   *The pilot **landed** the plane.*
El piloto **aterrizará** el avión.   *The pilot **will land** the plane.*

The verb in each of the three previous examples is in the *indicative* mode. The verb can be in the present, **aterriza**; the past, **aterrizó**; the future, **aterrizará**; or in compound tenses such as **ha aterrizado**, *has arrived*.

EJERCICIO 13·18

¿Es una oración o es una frase? *Indicate* **O** *(oración) for a sentence or* **F** *(frase) for a phrase.*

1. _____ Luisa y yo.

2. _____ La mesa está servida.

3. _____ Leemos el periódico.

4. _____ Buenas noches.

5. _____ De nada.

6. _____ Esto es cierto.

Práctica y repaso. *Reword each sentence with the appropriate verb form.*

1. Mi hermano Marcos está en Buenos Aires.

   PRETÉRITO _____

   FUTURO _____

2. Él vive en Argentina.

   PRETÉRITO _____

   FUTURO _____

3. Tiene un apartamento en el centro de la ciudad.

   PRETÉRITO _____

   FUTURO _____

4. Trabaja en una oficina del gobierno.

   PRETÉRITO _____

   FUTURO _____

5. Marcos viaja a Santiago también.

   PRETÉRITO _____

   FUTURO _____

Word order in declarative sentences

In English, the natural word order of the parts of a sentence is: *subject + verb + object*. This is also the most frequent word order in Spanish:

> **subject + verb + object**
>
> Mario contestó el teléfono.   *Mario answered the phone.*

Unlike English, Spanish allows a bit more flexibility in word order. Here are other possibilities:

> **verb + subject + object or other elements**
>
> Vino un hombre con Lucía.   *A man came with Lucia.*
> Se aproximan los coches.   *The cars are getting closer.*

There are other possibilities in the word order:

Anoche cenamos en "Casa Paco".
A Luisa la vimos en el restaurante.
Con mucho entusiasmo, el músico toca el piano.

Last night we dined at "Casa Paco."
We saw **Luisa** at the restaurant.
The musician plays the piano **with a lot of enthusiasm**.

In the previous examples, the Spanish sentences begin with an adverb (**Anoche**), a direct object (**A Luisa**), or a phrase (**Con mucho entusiasmo**). Note the comma between the phrase and the rest of the sentence in the third example.

Remember that in Spanish the subject is not always explicit. Verb endings indicate *who* does the action. Let's look at some examples where the subject is implicit or understood:

Encont**ramos** los zapatos.
Viv**o** en Argentina.
Sal**ieron** a las cuatro y media.
Escrib**es** una lista larga.

We found the shoes.
I live in Argentina.
They left at four-thirty.
You write a long list.

EJERCICIO
13·20

Reword each sentence in this word order: subject + verb + other elements.

1. vive / Pedro Gómez / en ese edificio _____

2. es / Lucía / la esposa / de Pedro _____

3. la noticia / leímos / de su boda / en el periódico _____

4. tienen / en la playa / una casa _____

5. salieron / Lucía y su esposo / de luna de miel _____

6. en Barcelona / nacieron / Pedro y Lucía _____

7. estudiaron / mis hermanos / con ellos _____

8. anoche / de Pedro / recibimos / un email _____

EJERCICIO
13·21

Mi rutina. *Choose one of the following phrases to complete each sentence.*

día tras día / cuando necesito comunicarme / en la piscina olímpica / con sólo un billete / en diez minutos / en el autobús camino a casa / cuando hago mucho ejercicio / con frecuencia

1. Escribo cartas en español _____.

2. Voy a mi oficina _____.

3. Tengo hambre _____.

4. Practico la natación _____

5. Corro casi una milla _____.

6. Voy a ganar la lotería _____.

7. Visito la biblioteca _____.

8. Leo el periódico _____.

Sentences with direct and indirect objects

To express ideas clearly in your sentences, you must arrange the words in a proper and logical order in Spanish. A sequence of words cannot always be translated word for word. Let's consider sentences that contain direct and/or indirect objects.

Direct object nouns

In Spanish, the direct object usually follows the verb:

       subject + verb + direct object

       El juez dictó **la sentencia**.   *The judge pronounced **the sentence**.*

In the previous sentence, these syntactical elements can be identified:

- **El juez** is the *subject* of the verb, in this case a person who does the action of the verb.
- **Dictó** is the *verb*. It is in the past tense and tells what the subject did.
- **La sentencia** is the *direct object*. The direct object receives the action of the verb.

EJERCICIO
13·22

       ¿Hay un complemento directo? *Indicate where direct object pronouns appear.*

1. Celebramos el cumpleaños de Laura.

2. Sus amigos hicieron una fiesta en la casa de Dora.

3. A las seis, llegaron los invitados.

4. Todos felicitaron a Laura en el día de su cumpleaños.

5. Sirvieron la cena en la terraza de Dora.

6. Luego saqué mi guitarra.

7. Canté dos rancheras a mis amigos.

8. Entró una chica encantadora.

9. Ahora sé su nombre.

El complemento directo. *Choose the appropriate noun to complete each sentence.*

un presidente / una reacción / un recuento / una solución / un problema /
una pregunta / una campaña / un proyecto

1. La noticia provoca _____ favorable para el candidato.

2. Todos los ciudadanos (*citizens*) quieren _____ honesto.

3. La campaña presidencial crea _____ para el partido de la oposición.

4. Una candidata exige (*demands*) _____ de los votos electorales.

5. El periodista hace _____ difícil a los dos candidatos.

6. Los expertos predicen _____ larga y dura.

7. Muchos jóvenes prefieren _____ rápida a sus problemas económicos.

The personal a with direct object nouns

This is a quick review of the use of the *personal* **a.** This preposition is placed before the *direct object* if the direct object is a definite or specific person or persons. The contraction **al** (**a** + **el** = **al**) is used if the masculine article **el** (*the*) follows the preposition.

> **subject + verb + personal a + direct object**

Recibimos **a** Roberto.	*We greeted Roberto.*
Vimos **a** tu hermana.	*We saw your sister.*
Reconocimos **al** tío de Ana.	*We recognized Ana's uncle.*

The *personal* **a** is also used with the following direct objects:

◆ Domestic animals and pets. This shows emotions or attachment for these animals:

Luisa quiere **a su perro** con locura.	*Luisa loves **her dog** to death.*
La niña baña **a su gatito**.	*The girl bathes **her kitten**.*

◆ Objects or entities that involve a degree of emotional attachment:

Amo **a mi patria**.	*I love **my country**.*
La niña adora **a su osito de peluche**.	*The girl adores **her teddy bear**.*

◆ Indefinite pronouns that refer to a person: **alguien** (*someone*), **alguno/a** (*someone*), **nadie** (*no one*), **ninguno/a** (*no, no one*):

Vieron **a alguien** en el teatro.	*They saw **someone** in the theater.*

◆ Countries, cities, and geographical names *not* preceded by a definite article *may* sometimes have the *personal* **a**:

Extraño **a Barcelona**.	*I miss **Barcelona**.*
Extraño **Barcelona**.	*I miss **Barcelona**.*

Note that the personal **a** is *not* used when the direct object is a person following a form of the verb **tener**:

Tenemos dos tíos.   We **have** two uncles.
Juanita **tiene** amigos en Perú.   *Juanita **has** friends in Peru.*

EJERCICIO 13·24

*Use the preposition **a** where necessary. If it's not needed use **X**.*

1. Mis hijos tienen _____ paciencia.

2. Las chicas saben _____ la verdad.

3. Conozco _____ tu jefe.

4. Sara tiene _____ sus amigos y su apoyo (*support*).

5. Invitamos _____ la familia García.

6. Saludamos _____ la bandera.

7. Amo _____ mi perrito y mi gata.

8. Extraño _____ Pedro.

EJERCICIO 13·25

En español.

1. Melissa works at the bookstore.

_____

2. She sees her boss (**jefe**) at the bus stop every morning.

_____

3. I know her boss.

_____

4. He drinks four cups of coffee in the morning.

_____

5. Melissa prefers tea.

_____

6. I saw her boss last week.

_____

7. He wears old clothes.

_____

8. Melissa's boss needs a new jacket.

_____

Direct and indirect object nouns in a sentence

When a sentence contains both a direct and an indirect object noun, the *direct object precedes the indirect object* in Spanish and both are placed after the verb:

subject + verb + direct object + indirect object

El chico comprará **ese libro a su padre**.   *The boy will buy **this book for his father**.*

- ◆ **El chico** is the subject of the verb.
- ◆ **Comprará** is the verb. It is in the future tense.
- ◆ **Ese libro** is the direct object. It receives the action of the verb.
- ◆ **A su padre** is the indirect object. It receives the action (done for him).

A few more examples follow. Note that, in these sentences, the preposition **a** is not the personal **a**; here, it introduces the *indirect object*. The English equivalent is *to*.

La Internet ofrece **oportunidades a nuestros estudiantes**.   *The Internet offers **opportunities to our students**.*

La bolsa de valores disminuyó **el capital a los inversores**.   *The stock market decreased **the wealth for the investors**.*

El doctor Benítez recetó **un antibiótico a su paciente**.   *Dr. Benítez prescribed **an antibiotic for his patient**.*

EJERCICIO
13·26

¿Entiendes el mensaje? *Put the words in correct order starting with the subject.*

1. alquiló / Paula / a su hermana Ana / un apartamento

_____

2. ella / la llave / tiene / del apartamento

_____

3. la hermana / ayuda / necesita

_____

4. en la universidad / inglés / Ana / estudia

_____

5. un trabajo mejor / ella / encontrará

_____

6. saludos / Ana y su hermana / envían / a sus amigos

_____

7. a sus primos / invitan / a su apartamento

_____

Negative declarative sentences

Declarative sentences are not all affirmative; some are negative. Not all affirmative sentences require an affirmative word. However, negative sentences *must* include negative words. These negative words are *adverbs* that modify the action of the verb. In Spanish, a simple way to turn an affirmative sentence into a negative sentence is to place the word **no** directly before the verb:

subject + no + verb (affirmative sentence) → negative sentence

Mario trabaja en aquella oficina.   Mario **no** trabaja en aquella oficina.
Mario works in that office.   *Mario does **not** work in that office.*

Other negative adverbs may be used to build negative declarative sentences. The negative words **nunca** (*never*), **jamás** (*never*), **tampoco** (*neither, nor*), and **ni** (*neither, nor*) appear before the verb in the following examples:

Nunca salimos de noche.   *We **never** go out at night.*
Jamás dice mentiras.   *She **never** tells lies.*
Tampoco niega la verdad.   *She does not deny the truth, **either**.*
La secretaria **ni** terminó la carta.   *The secretary did not **even** finish the letter.*

EJERCICIO
13·27

Te toca a ti. *Change the affirmative sentences to negative. Use* **nunca**, **jamás**, **tampoco** *or* **ni** *to substitute for the underlined words.*

1. Digo mentiras <u>siempre</u>.

_____

2. Falto (*miss*) a mi trabajo <u>a menudo</u>.

_____

3. Duermo hasta tarde <u>todos los días</u>.

_____

4. <u>Casi todos los días</u> termino el desayuno.

_____

5. Ahorro (*save*) agua <u>con frecuencia</u>.

_____

6. <u>A veces</u> gasto todo mi salario en la tienda.

_____

7. <u>Casi siempre</u> recibo un bono por Navidad.

_____

Remember that in Spanish two or three negative words may be used in the same sentence. If a negative word (**nunca**, **jamás**) follows a verb, the verb must also be preceded by a negative.

Nunca jamás te voy a ayudar con tu tarea.	*I will **never ever** help you with your homework.*
Elisa **no** viaja **nunca**.	*Elisa **never** travels.*
Yo **no** viajaré **jamás** contigo.	*I will **never** travel with you.*
Lucy **no** quiere **nada**.	*Lucy **does not** want **anything**.*

You may use redundant negative elements in a sentence, especially in informal conversations. Note that neither the auxiliary English verb *does* nor *did* is translated if the Spanish verb is in the past tense. Likewise, the auxiliary English verb *will* is not translated in the Spanish future tense.

Marta **no** vendrá **nunca jamás**.	*Marta will **never ever** come.*
Lucy **no tiene** tiempo **nunca**.	*Lucy **does not ever** have time.*

Complete each sentence with negative words. Follow the **modelo**.

MODELO   Mi cuenta de ahorro aumenta.

     no... nunca   *Mi cuenta de ahorro no aumenta nunca* .

     no... jamás   *Mi cuenta de ahorro no aumenta nunca jamás* .

1. Los políticos mienten.

     no... nunca _____.

     no... jamás _____.

2. Los periodistas redactan noticias optimistas.

     no... nunca _____.

     no... jamás _____.

3. Los vendedores respaldan (*back up*) sus productos.

     no... nunca _____.

     no... jamás _____.

4. Los camareros sirven a los clientes con amabilidad.

     no... nunca _____.

     no... jamás _____.

5. Los maestros asignan poca tarea a sus estudiantes.

no... nunca _____.

no... jamás _____.

6. Los marineros tienen miedo al mar.

no... nunca _____.

no... jamás _____.

Negative declarative sentences with negative pronouns

Note that the subject of the following sentences is a negative pronoun: **nadie** (*no one*), **ninguno/a** (*no one*), or **nada** (*nothing*). These pronouns appear with other negative words in the same sentence:

Mañana **no** viene **nadie**.   Tomorrow **no one** will come.
No hay **ningún** problema.   There is **no** problem.
Ninguno salió de su casa.   **No one** left their homes.

¡Más énfasis! *Add another negative word (**nadie** / **nunca** / **jamás** / **nada**) to each sentence.*

1. _____ jamás vamos a tener un año tan próspero.

2. No vemos _____ desde aquí.

3. Julia _____ invita a nadie a su casa.

4. No llames a Felipe _____.

5. Nunca viene _____ a esta clase.

6. Nunca dice _____ a nadie.

The future tense

The future is a simple tense in Spanish. Unlike its English equivalent, it does not include an auxiliary verb such as *will* or *shall*. The future tense indicates and describes actions or events that will take place at some future date.

Algún día mis padres **vivirán** conmigo.

Some day my parents will live with me.

Leeré mi horóscopo mañana.

I shall read my horoscope tomorrow.

Regresaremos el mes que viene.

We will come back next month.

Regular verbs in the future tense

In Spanish most verbs are regular in the future tense. The endings are the same for all three conjugations: **-é, -ás, -á, -emos, -éis, -án.** They are added to the full infinitive. Remember that all endings, except the **nosotros** form, carry a written accent.

hablar *to speak*	**comer** *to eat*	**abrir** *to open*
hablar**é**	comer**é**	abrir**é**
hablar**ás**	comer**ás**	abrir**ás**
hablar**á**	comer**á**	abrir**á**
hablar**emos**	comer**emos**	abrir**emos**
hablar**éis**	comer**éis**	abrir**éis**
hablar**án**	comer**án**	abrir**án**

Me **llevarán** a tu oficina y **hablaremos**.

They will take me to your office and we will talk.

¿Dónde **comeremos** el sábado?

Where will we eat on Saturday?

Abrirás la carta en tu correo electrónico.

You will open the letter in your electronic mail.

The word *will* in English may indicate either an action in the future or someone's willingness or eagerness to do something. In Spanish the future tense is not used to express intent; for this, Spanish uses **querer** + an infinitive.

¿Quieren Uds. ayudar al candidato?   *Will they help the candidate?*
Queremos ayudar, claro que sí.   *We will help, of course.*

EJERCICIO
14·1

Y en tu caso, ¿verdadero (V) o falso (F)?

1. _____ Recibiré mi salario este fin de semana.

2. _____ Votaré en las próximas elecciones presidenciales.

3. _____ Mi equipo de fútbol favorito perderá este año.

4. _____ Gastaré menos dinero y ahorraré más.

5. _____ Subiré las escaleras y no usaré el ascensor para hacer ejercicio.

6. _____ Mañana decidiré los planes para mis vacaciones.

7. _____ De ahora en adelante veré el programa «La ruleta de la suerte» en español.

8. _____ Practicaré el español con un amigo.

9. _____ Correré cinco millas este fin de semana.

10. _____ El sábado que viene descansaré todo el día.

EJERCICIO
14·2

El pronóstico del tiempo. *Complete each sentence with the appropriate future tense form of the verb in parentheses.*

1. Mañana _____ a caer mucha agua en nuestra ciudad. (empezar)

2. El sábado no _____ un día soleado. (ser)

3. La temperatura _____ a 90 grados. (bajar)

4. Una tormenta _____ muchos árboles en nuestra área. (destruir)

5. La meteoróloga _____ los mapas en la pantalla. (mostrar)

6. Los televidentes _____ los nuevos pronósticos de la tormenta. (oír)

7. Un satélite no _____ en el Océano Atlántico. (caer)

8. Los bañistas no _____ hacer surfing en las playas. (deber)

9. Los agentes de la policía _____ a la comunidad. (proteger)

10. El martes _____ el tiempo. (mejorar)

Preguntas personales.

1. ¿Dónde celebrarás tu próximo cumpleaños?

   _____

2. ¿A quiénes invitarás para celebrar tu cumpleaños?

   _____

3. Imagina que tus amigos te regalarán doscientos dólares. ¿Qué comprarás con el dinero?

   _____

4. ¿Cuántos años cumplirás este año?

   _____

5. ¿Qué harás el fin de semana que viene?

   _____

6. Y por último, ¿adónde irás de vacaciones el verano próximo?

   _____

Irregular verbs in the future tense

The irregular verbs in the future are grouped into three categories according to the stem change. The endings are the same as for regular verbs, but are added to the irregular stem rather than the full infinitive.

♦ The stem drops the vowel of the infinitive and the endings are added to the irregular stem.

caber *to fit*	**cabr-**	cabré, cabrás, cabrá, cabremos, cabréis, cabrán
haber *to have (auxiliary)*	**habr-**	habré, habrás, habrá, habremos, habréis, habrán
poder *to be able to*	**podr-**	podré, podrás, podrá, podremos, podréis, podrán
querer *to want*	**querr-**	querré, querrás, querrá, querremos, querréis, querrán
saber *to know*	**sabr-**	sabré, sabrás, sabrá, sabremos, sabréis, sabrán

Remember that **haber** in an impersonal sense is used in the third person singular only.

¿**Habrá** una fiesta mañana?	*Will there be a party tomorrow?*
Habrá cien mil personas en el estadio.	*There will be one hundred thousand people in the stadium.*

♦ The infinitive stem drops the vowel of the infinitive and replaces the vowel with the consonant **d**; the endings are added to this irregular stem.

poner *to place, put*	**pondr-**	pondré, pondrás, pondrá, pondremos, pondréis, pondrán
salir *to leave*	**saldr-**	saldré, saldrás, saldrá, saldremos, saldréis, saldrán
tener *to have, hold*	**tendr-**	tendré, tendrás, tendrá, tendremos, tendréis, tendrán
valer *to be worth, cost*	**valdr-**	valdré, valdrás, valdrá, valdremos, valdréis, valdrán
venir *to come*	**vendr-**	vendré, vendrás, vendrá, vendremos, vendréis, vendrán

◆ The verbs **decir** and **hacer** are irregular; the stems are shortened and the endings are added to the changed stem.

| decir *to say, tell* | **dir-** | diré, dirás, dirá, diremos, diréis, dirán |
| hacer *to do* | **har-** | haré, harás, hará, haremos, haréis, harán |

EJERCICIO
14·4

En el circo. *Complete each sentence with the appropriate future tense form of the verb in parentheses.*

1. Un circo _____ aquí en esta ciudad por seis semanas. (estar)

2. Nosotros _____ la oportunidad de disfrutar ese espectáculo con muchos amigos. (tener)

3. Los boletos no _____ mucho. (costar)

4. Muchos payasos _____ reír a los niños y a las personas mayores también. (hacer)

5. Juan y Martín _____ temprano el domingo para sentarse cerca de los payasos. (venir)

6. Un mago _____ trucos (*trick*) con un sombrero y dos conejos. (hacer)

7. ¡Una domadora (*tamer*) _____ la cabeza en la boca de un león! (poner)

8. Mis sobrinos no _____ perderse ese espectáculo. (querer)

9. Ellos _____ la oportunidad de compartir ese día con sus amiguitos. (tener)

10. _____ mucha gente en el circo este domingo. (haber)

11. _____ la pena reír y disfrutar allí, en el circo. (valer)

Tu horóscopo. *Complete each sentence with the* **tú** *form of the future tense of the verb in parentheses.*

1. Cuidado: _____ visitar a tu médico. Es la época de la gripe. (deber)

2. _____ mucha suerte en el amor. (tener)

3. ¡_____ a la pareja ideal de tu vida! (conocer)

4. No _____ mucho dinero este mes. (ganar)

5. Pero luego, buenas noticias: _____ información de un viejo amigo. (encontrar)

6. _____ su recomendación para trabajar en una corporación con mucho éxito. (recibir)

7. _____ trabajar desde tu casa varios días a la semana. (poder)

8. _____ tiempo y dinero. (ahorrar)

9. Si vas al casino _____ mucho dinero en las tragamonedas (*slot machine*). (perder)

You may already know some of the verbs in the following Vocabulario. It shows verbs that are formed with a prefix (such as **com-**, **sos-**, **su-**, **dis-**) that precedes an irregular verb **tener**, **poner**, **hacer**, or **venir**. Note that some are used with a reflexive pronoun.

VOCABULARIO

abstenerse de	*to abstain from*	**mantener**	*to maintain*
atenerse a	*to depend on*	**obtener**	*to obtain, get*
componer	*to compose*	**oponerse a**	*to be opposed to*
contener	*to contain, hold*	**proponer**	*to propose*
convenir en	*to agree*	**rehacer**	*to remake*
deshacer	*to undo*	**reponer**	*to replace*
detener	*to arrest, detain*	**sostener**	*to hold up, support*
disponer de	*to have (at one's disposal)*	**suponer**	*to suppose*

EJERCICIO

14·6

Noticias de mi barrio. *Complete each sentence with the appropriate future tense form of the verb in parentheses.*

1. ¿_____ a las ideas de tus amigos? (oponerse, tú)

2. Mis amigos _____ un trofeo porque ganarán el torneo de tenis. (obtener)

3. Yo _____ de mucho dinero porque el caballo de mi abuelo ganó una carrera en Kentucky. (disponer)

4. Todos mis vecinos _____ que ganamos la lotería. (suponer)

5. Pero mi esposo y yo _____ el mismo estilo de vida: ahorramos, no gastamos mucho. (mantener)

6. Un ladrón robó a una pobre vecina. La comunidad _____ el dinero que ella necesita. (reponer)

7. Pronto el departamento de policía _____ a ese criminal. (detener)

8. Esta investigación _____ mucha información para ayudar a la policía. (obtener)

The future tense to express probability in the present

Another use of the future tense is to express wonder or probability at the present time. The equivalent in English is *I wonder, probably, must be, can be.*

¿Cuánto **costará** este sofá?	*I wonder how much this sofa costs.*
¿Qué hora **será**?	*I wonder what time it is.*
Serán las cuatro.	*It is probably four o'clock.*

EJERCICIO 14·7

Probabilidades. *Complete each sentence with the appropriate future tense form of the verb in parentheses. Remember that some of the verbs may be irregular.*

1. Julián _____ ya aquí en el aeropuerto. (estar)

2. Miriam, ¿ya _____ muy tarde para llamar a tu casa? (ser)

3. Mira, ¿cómo _____ esta persona? No recuerdo su nombre. (llamarse)

4. Esta señora _____ ser la madre de Mari. (poder)

5. ¿Qué opinas? ¿Ella _____ unos cincuenta años de edad? (tener)

6. Oye, hay un bolso en un asiento vacío. ¿A quién le _____ este bolso? (pertenecer)

7. ¿Cuánto _____ esta maleta tan grande? (costar)

8. _____ mucho en Tampa porque el vuelo está retrasado. (llover)

9. ¿Oyes gritos? Esas personas _____ mal. (sentirse)

10. Talvez porque ellos no _____ perder el vuelo de conexión en San Juan. (querer)

11. El auxiliar de vuelo, ¿nos _____ colocar esta maleta debajo del asiento? (dejar)

Un cuento de hadas. Traducción. *Use the words in the* **Vocabulario útil** *for your translation.*

VOCABULARIO ÚTIL

ballroom	**la sala de baile**	*godmother*	**el hada madrina**
by heart	**de memoria**	*stepmother*	**la madrastra**
carriage	**el carruaje**	*stepsister*	**la hermanastra**
Cinderella	**Cenicienta**	*to drop*	**dejar caer**
fairy tale	**el cuento de hadas**	*wand*	**la varita mágica**
glass slipper	**la zapatilla de cristal**		

Mila will be five years old soon. Tonight her grandmother Alina will read Mila's favorite fairy tale, Cinderella. Mila will fall asleep and she will dream of Cinderella. Mila knows this story by heart. Cinderella will help her mean stepsisters and she will follow the rules of her stepmother. Then her stepsisters will go to the ballroom in the palace. Luckily, Cinderella will have the help of her fairy godmother: with a magic wand she will create (**hacer**) a beautiful dress, a pair of glass slippers, and a luxurious carriage to go to the palace. Cinderella will meet the prince and will dance with him. At a quarter to twelve, she will go back home. Cinderella will drop (**dejar**) one of her glass slippers. And then the prince will find her and they will get married.

_____

_____

_____

_____

_____

_____

Prepositions, phrases, and conjunctions

Prepositions

Prepositions are used to indicate the relationship between words. The word itself ("pre-position") tells us it is placed before other words. Think of **preposiciones** as connectors, linking a noun, a pronoun, or a phrase to other words.

Observe the relationship or connection established by the highlighted prepositions in the following examples:

Ellos trabajan **para mí**.	*They work **for me**.*
Mi casa está **cerca de la mansión**.	*My house is **close to the mansion**.*

Para and **de** introduce objects of prepositions. The words or phrases that follow the preposition are called the object of the preposition.

Spanish prepositions can present a challenge to English speakers. You will need to acquire them gradually. **Viajan** *por* **España** means *They are traveling **through** Spain*. If you change the preposition **por** to **para**, you alter the meaning of the sentence: **Viajan** *para* **España**. (*They are traveling to Spain.*)

Spanish speakers face similar challenges in learning English. *Get in*, *get in with*, and *get through* are only a few of the distinctions they must master. Note the Spanish equivalents: **entrar**, **quedar bien con**, **atravesar**. (A comedian, joking about the regional uses of words in the United States, objected to being told to *get on* the plane instead of to *get in* the plane. Getting *in* does sound more logical and safer than getting *on* a plane.) Significant changes in meaning can take place with a preposition.

As you study, it will be useful to group the common Spanish prepositions according to their form and meaning.

Frequently used prepositions in Spanish

Lists of prepositions, including verbs used with certain prepositions and idiomatic expressions with prepositions, appear in this chapter. You may choose various study strategies. Memorizing may be helpful as well as becoming aware of fixed expressions in context. The lists are provided as reference tools.

One-word (simple) prepositions

Prepositions appear in different forms. Here is a list of simple, or one-word, prepositions and their basic meaning:

a	to, at	hacia	toward
ante	before, in the presence of	hasta	until
bajo	under	para	for, in order to, to
con	with	por	for, by, through
contra	against	según	according to
de	of, from	sin	without
desde	from, since	sobre	over, above
en	in, on, into	tras	after
entre	between, among		

Práctica. *Choose the appropriate preposition.*

desde	por	hacia	sin	con
sobre	ante	según	entre	en

1. Vamos a hacer este trabajo _____ tú y yo.

2. Si quiere, Ud. puede pagar la multa _____ una tarjeta de crédito.

3. La abogada defendió a su clienta _____ el juez.

4. El ladrón entró a la casa _____ la ventana.

5. Elena habla _____ un asunto muy interesante.

6. Viajamos _____ el norte, ¿verdad?

7. Pablo me saludó _____ la puerta de su casa.

8. Los niños no pueden ir a la fiesta _____ el permiso de los padres.

9. Mira, Carlos está _____ la sala de urgencia.

10. _____ Carmen, su hermano sale del hospital mañana por la mañana.

¿Verdadero (V) o falso (F)? Historia y geografía.

_____ 1. El Día de la Independencia de México es el cinco de mayo.

_____ 2. La Estrella Polar indica el Sur.

_____ 3. México es un país independiente desde hace dos siglos.

_____ 4. Según los historiadores, los indígenas de América Central construyeron pirámides.

_____ 5. Hasta el siglo XVI, los aztecas dominaron lo que hoy es México.

_____ 6. Hacia finales del siglo XVI, Cristóbal Colón llegó a las islas del Caribe.

_____ 7. Para llevar los tesoros de América a España, había que atravesar el mar Pacífico.

En español.

1. Luisa cannot live without Jacob. _____

2. Jacob sent Luisa a card from Lima. _____

3. Jacob was traveling to Ecuador. _____

4. From the airport, he called Luisa. _____

5. He did not arrive in Quito until midnight. _____

6. Jacob found a coin under his pillow. _____

7. According to Luisa, he is superstitious. _____

8. With luck, Jacob will sell many of his products in Quito. _____

_____

Compound prepositions

There are numerous compound prepositions (made up of two or more words). In English you will be familiar with prepositional phrases, which are similar. Here are some Spanish prepositional phrases:

a cargo de	*in charge of*	**de vez en cuando**	*from time to time*
a causa de	*because of*	**debajo de**	*beneath, under*
a favor de	*in favor of*	**delante de**	*in front of*
a fines de	*at the end of*	**dentro de**	*within, inside (of)*
a mediados de	*around*	**desde luego**	*of course*
a partir de	*from*	**después de**	*after*
a pie	*walking*	**detrás de**	*behind*
a tiempo	*on time*	**en cambio**	*on the other hand*
a través de	*through*	**en (diez) días**	*in (ten) days*
además de	*besides*	**en efecto**	*in fact*
al norte de	*to the north of*	**en (una semana)**	*in (one week)*
al sur de	*to the south of*	**en vez de**	*instead of*
alrededor de	*around*	**encima de**	*above, on top of*
antes de	*before*	**enfrente de**	*in front of*
cerca de	*near*	**frente a**	*in front of*
de ahora en adelante	*from now on*	**fuera de**	*outside of*
de pie	*standing*	**lejos de**	*far from*

EJERCICIO
15·4

Práctica. *Complete the sentences with the appropriate prepositional phrase.*

| en una semana | a pie | además de | en cambio |
| de ahora en adelante | en vez de | a cargo de | a tiempo |

1. Estoy en La Habana y voy a regresar _____ a mi casa en Miami.

2. Quiero disfrutar más con mi familia _____ regresar a casa y trabajar.

3. Yo estoy _____ mi oficina, y puedo tener más tiempo de vacaciones.

4. _____, mis empleados tienen que trabajar todos los días mientras yo disfruto mis vacaciones.

5. También, quiero visitar las playas, _____ pasar tiempo con mis primos.

6. Creo que yo, _____, voy a tener mucho más contacto con mis familiares.

7. Mis primos y yo vamos a ir _____ desde la casa a Centro Habana.

8. Nosotros debemos llegar _____ a una tienda para comprar regalos.

EJERCICIO
15·5

Preguntas personales.

1. ¿Terminas tu trabajo a tiempo? _____

2. ¿Qué haces típicamente a mediados de la semana? _____

3. ¿Estás a favor de una causa especial? ¿Qué causa? _____

4. ¿Qué pones debajo de la cama? _____

5. ¿Vas a pie a tu trabajo o a la escuela? ¿Por qué? _____

6. ¿Qué hay cerca de tu casa? _____

7. ¿Qué vas a hacer a fines de este verano? _____

EJERCICIO
15·6

En español. *Translate the sentences using the appropriate prepositional phrases.*

1. The stores are far from our house. _____

2. My car is outside the garage. _____

3. Instead of sugar, the recipe (**receta**) says honey (**miel**). _____

4. From time to time, I run ten miles. _____

5. This meeting ends within an hour. _____

6. There are around fifteen birds in that tree. _____

Relationships of commonly used prepositions and compound prepositions

Note that the same preposition may express a different relationship in different contexts.

Si vas **a** la fiesta, llámame. (movement)	*If you go **to** the party, call me.*
La fiesta es **a** las nueve. (time)	*The party is **at** nine o'clock.*

As part of adverbial phrases, prepositions can modify a verb. Simple and compound prepositions can be classified and learned according to the relationships (of movement, place, time . . .) they establish. Remember that the same preposition can appear in a variety of adverbial phrases.

- Movement. Prepositions of movement indicate a position or the direction where someone or something is going.

Van **a** la biblioteca.	*They go **to** the library.*
Ellos caminan **hacia** el edificio.	*They walk **toward** the building.*
No podemos correr **hasta** tu casa.	*We cannot run **to** your house.*
El avión sale **para** Londres.	*The plane leaves **for** London.*

- Location. These prepositions or prepositional phrases tell where someone or something is in relation to other people or things.

El gimnasio está **a la derecha** del auditorio.	*The gym is **to the right** of the auditorium.*
Los papeles están **en** mi oficina.	*The papers are **in** my office.*
Están **sobre** mi escritorio.	*They are on **top of** my desk.*
Mi oficina no está **lejos de** aquí.	*My office is not **far from** here.*
Voy a caminar **por** el barrio.	*I am going to walk **around** the neighborhood.*

- Time. Most of these prepositions are used for other functions as well.

El concierto es **a** las ocho.	*The concert is **at** eight.*
No abren **antes de** las siete.	*They do not open **before** seven.*
¿**Hasta** cuando vas a esperar?	***Until** when will you wait?*
Llegan **para** fines de semana.	*They arrive **by** the weekend.*

- Other relationships. Most of these express relationships among people, things, or abstract ideas. They may establish a connection of means, company, etc.

Siempre sale **con** sus hermanas.	*She always goes out **with** her sisters.*
¡Sales **sin** la maleta otra vez!	*You're leaving **without** your bag again!*
El paciente habló **acerca de** sus síntomas.	*The patient talked **about** his symptoms.*

EJERCICIO
15·7

¿Cuál? *Choose the appropriate preposition or prepositional phrase to complete each sentence.*

1. Los turistas viajan (por | sin) la ciudad.

2. No quieren llegar (antes de | junto a) las diez al hotel.

3. Hay más de cuarenta personas (encima del | dentro del) autobús.

4. El grupo pasa (a favor de | a través de) una región de la costa.

5. Comen en un restaurante (debajo de | al lado de) la salida de la autopista.

6. Deciden explorar la costa (en vez de | enfrente de) regresar al hotel.

7. Por fin, van al hotel (dentro de | alrededor de) la medianoche.

8. Todos caminan (hacia | según) su cuarto.

9. Muchos duermen (contra | hasta) el mediodía.

10. Todos los turistas salen (sobre | contra) las dos.

EJERCICIO
15·8

¿En tu caso... ¿Es verdadero (V) o falso (F)?

_____ 1. No me levanto antes de las diez de la mañana los domingos.

_____ 2. Nunca voy al cine sin mis amigos.

_____ 3. Prefiero poner mis zapatos debajo de la cama.

_____ 4. Estoy a favor de la libertad de expresión para todos.

_____ 5. En mi casa, yo estoy a cargo de las compras en el supermercado.

_____ 6. De vez en cuando voy a un restaurante mexicano.

EJERCICIO
15·9

Indicate the letter that shows the relationship of the preposition or prepositional phrase: **M** *(movement),* **T** *(time),* **L** *(place), or* **O** *(other).*

_____ 1. Salen de la clase *antes de* las seis.

_____ 2. Podemos salir *hacia* el gimnasio.

_____ 3. ¿Pones tus cosas *en* la maleta?

_____ 4. Voy a cambiar *a partir de* hoy.

_____ 5. ¿Estás a *cargo de* lavar la ropa?

_____ 6. No caminan *alrededor de* la plaza.

_____ 7. Voy a votar *a favor de* esta candidata.

_____ 8. Estudio francés *en lugar de* español.

_____ 9. Van *a* la tienda.

_____ 10. Caminamos *a lo largo de* la playa.

The preposition a and the personal a

One of the basic functions of the preposition **a** is to indicate movement. Here are examples of some other functions of the preposition **a**.

Study these examples and describe the different functions of **a**.

Prefiero ir **a pie**.	*I prefer to go **on foot**.*
Estamos **a cuatro millas** del aeropuerto.	*We are **four miles** from the airport.*
Los mejillones son **a dos dólares** la docena.	*Mussels are **two dollars** a dozen.*

In the examples above, the preposition **a** appears in adverbial expressions indicating ways or means to do something (**a pie**), distance (**a cuatro millas**), and price (**a dos dólares**). Later in this unit you will find a list of verbs that require **a** + an infinitive when they follow a conjugated verb. Here are some examples:

Vienen **a ayudar**.	*They come **to help**.*
¿Quieren **aprender a preparar** tacos?	*Do you want **to learn to prepare** tacos?*

A appears with other verbs in idiomatic expressions. Some examples are **sonar a** (*to sound like*) and **saber a** (*to taste like*).

¡Este postre **sabe a** ron!	*This dessert **tastes like** rum!*
Sus palabras **suenan a** amenaza.	*Her words **sound like** a threat.*

The "personal **a**" (different from the preposition **a**) is required in the following contexts:

◆ before a noun if that direct object noun is a specific person or persons. Remember that **a** followed by the article **el** will result in the contraction **al**.

Llamo **a las chicas**.	*I am calling **the girls**.*
Veo **al cartero**.	*I see **the mail carrier**.*

Note: One exception to the use of the personal **a** before a direct object noun is the verb **tener**. Do not use the personal **a** after **tener** followed by a specific person or persons.

Tenemos parientes en San Francisco.	*We have relatives in San Francisco.*

◆ with pronouns like **alguien**, **nadie**.

No veo **a nadie** en este restaurante.	*I do not see **anyone** in this restaurant.*

◆ with domestic animals, highlighting the bond of affection between human beings and pets.

La nena adora **a su gatito**.	*The little girl adores **her kitten**.*

En español. *Use the preposition **a** in your translation.*

1. This house smells like fish. _____

2. Are you calling Rosa or Manuel? _____

3. I love my canary! _____

4. They do not invite anyone to their anniversary (party). _____

5. My soup tastes like parsley (**perejil**). _____

6. Do you (**Uds.**) know anyone in this class? _____

7. The flowers are three dollars a dozen. _____

8. The train station is ten miles from my house. _____

9. Luisa takes care of (**cuidar**) my cat. _____

Uses of prepositions and their English equivalents

A preposition may combine with other parts of speech as follows:

◆ A noun + a preposition (often **de** or **para**) + another noun may modify a noun or a pronoun. The resulting phrase functions as an adjective. In English, a noun alone can serve as an adjective.

Lee compra **la bandeja de cerámica**.	*Lee buys **the ceramic tray**.*
Es **un tiesto para flores**.	*It is **a flowerpot**.*

◆ A preposition + a noun modifies a verb. The result is an adverbial expression.

Pelea **sin cuidado**.	*He fights **carelessly** (without care).*
Trabajo **con paciencia**.	*I work **patiently** (with patience).*

◆ Certain prepositions followed by an infinitive are equivalent to the present participle (-*ing* form) in English. Remember to use the Spanish infinitive form after these prepositions.

Al regresar a Italia, fueron a Nápoles.	***Upon returning** to Italy, they went to Naples.*
¿Cómo entras al cine **sin pagar**?	*How do you go into the movie theater **without paying**?*

The following prepositions are used in front of infinitives in this way:

al	*upon*	**en lugar de**	*instead of*
antes de	*before*	**en vez de**	*instead of*
con	*with*	**hasta**	*until*
de	*of*	**sin**	*without*
después de	*after*		

En español. *Translate the phrases in parentheses into Spanish.*

1. Preferimos descansar _____ (*instead of walking*).

2. _____ (*After entering*) a la sala, puedes sentarte en el sofá.

3. _____ (*Upon finishing*) la merienda (*snack*), vamos a ver el programa de noticias.

4. Voy a cerrar la ventana _____ (*without making*) ruido (*noise*).

5. Marta hace sus tareas _____ (*with speed*).

6. En cambio, Ruth no sabe hacer nada _____ (*in peace*).

7. Tomamos café _____ (*upon arriving*) a la cafetería.

8. _____ (*Instead of washing*) la ropa, prefiero escuchar la radio.

The uses of para and por

For is the basic English equivalent of both **para** and **por**. However, these two prepositions change meaning in context. If you choose **para** or **por** incorrectly, you may cause confusion.

If you say **trabajo** *por* **Marco**, the listener will understand that you are taking over Marco's responsibilities and you are working *instead of* him. If you say **trabajo** *para* **Marco**, you mean that you do some work for Marco or he is your boss. The distinction between **para** and **por** is sometimes rather subtle in Spanish.

Use **para** to indicate the following relationships:

◆ Purpose. **Para** indicates the *purpose* of an action or goal, equivalent to the English phrase *in order to*. It may indicate the purpose or the use of an action, an event, or an object.

Comemos **para** vivir.	*We eat (**in order) to** live.*
Bill estudia **para** enfermero.	*Bill studies **to be** a nurse.*
La reunión es **para** comentar el libro.	*The meeting is **to** discuss the book.*
Necesito una caja **para** mis cosas.	*I need a box **for** my things.*

◆ Comparison. **Para** indicates the *contrast* of an idea, person, object, or situation in order to distinguish it from others in the same group or category.

Para una revista de modas, es muy cara.	*For a fashion magazine, it is very expensive.*
Es precoz **para ser** un niño de siete años.	*He is precocious **for** a seven-year-old boy.*

◆ Deadlines. **Para** indicates date, time, and deadlines in the future. Some English equivalents are *for*, *by*, or *on*.

La cita es **para** el martes por la mañana.	*The appointment is **for** Tuesday morning.*
Termina el informe **para** las diez.	*Finish the report **by** ten o'clock.*

◆ Destination. The intended destination preceded by **para** may be a place or a person.

¿Éste es el libro **para** el profesor?   *Is this the book **for** the professor?*
¿Sale ella **para** África?   *Is she leaving **for** Africa?*

EJERCICIO
15·12

Complete the sentences by matching the appropriate letter.

_____ 1. Hay que gastar mucho   a. para la señora.

_____ 2. Tienen que estudiar más   b. para tener solamente diez años.

_____ 3. Deben salir ahora   c. para tener más espacio.

_____ 4. Habla muy bien el alemán   d. para el lunes a las cuatro en punto.

_____ 5. El taxi es   e. para comprar este auto nuevo.

_____ 6. Necesitas una casa grande   f. para llegar a tiempo.

_____ 7. Este trabajo es   g. para ser español.

_____ 8. Estás muy alta   h. para pasar el examen.

EJERCICIO
15·13

En español. *Translate each sentence using the preposition para.*

1. For a liberal, he has traditional ideas. _____

2. Are you (**tú**) training for the Olympic games? _____

3. I need a lamp for my bedroom. _____

4. They must be here by four o'clock. _____

5. This coffee is for us. _____

6. Lucille reads the newspaper in order to find an apartment. _____

7. Is this letter for Susan? _____

8. We are leaving for San Francisco. _____

9. What do you need this money for? _____

10. I need the money for a new computer. _____

Use **por** to indicate the following relationships:

◆ Exchange. **Por** expresses the idea "in exchange for."

¡Compra los zapatos **por** $20!	*Buy the shoes **for** $20!*
Quiero cambiar mi auto **por** tu moto.	*I want to exchange my car **for** your motorcycle.*

◆ Moving through. **Por** indicates the action of moving through a space.

Corrieron **por** el parque.	*They ran **through** the park.*

◆ Duration of time. **Por** expresses how long something took.

Estudiaron **por** tres horas.	*They studied **for** three hours.*

◆ Expressions of time. **Por** is found in the fixed expressions of time: **por la tarde, por la mañana, por la noche**, etc.

Nos vamos **por la mañana**.	*We leave **in the morning**.*

◆ Movement. **Por** is used to talk about transportation, as the equivalent of *by means of.*

El turista viene **por** tren.	*The tourist comes **by** train.*

◆ Reason. **Por** points out a reason or rationale, as the equivalent of *because of.*

Por no jugar bien no vas a ganar el partido.	***Because** you do not play well, you are not going to win the game.*

◆ To introduce the agent of the passive voice.

El caso fue estudiado **por** los especialistas.	*The case was studied **by** the specialists.*

◆ To express the equivalent of *per.*

¿Escribes sólo veinte palabras **por minuto**?	*You can type only twenty words **per minute**?*

◆ To express the equivalent of *for* when it follows these verbs: **enviar** (*to send*), **ir** (*to go*), **preguntar** (*to ask*), **venir** (*to come*), **regresar** (*to come back*), and **volver** (*to come back*).

Lo **envío por** correo aéreo.	*I send it **by** air mail.*
Regresamos por los paquetes.	*We came back **for** the packages.*
Pregunten por Manuel.	*Ask **for** Manuel.*

◆ To indicate *to be about to do something* or *to be in favor of something or someone* with **estar** + **por** + infinitive.

Estamos por terminar.	***We are about** to finish.*
Ellos están por un aumento de sueldo.	***They support** a pay raise.*

EJERCICIO
15·14

Preguntas para un amigo. *Translate using the preposition **por** and the present tense familiar form **tú**.*

1. Do you go to work by train or by car? _____

2. Are you about to finish your work now? _____

3. Do you send your greetings by e-mail? _____

4. Do you run through the park often? _____

5. Good heavens! (**caramba**), did you buy those shoes for three hundred dollars? _____
_____

6. Do you drive on the highway at sixty-five miles per hour? _____
_____

7. Do you return home in the afternoon or in the evening? _____

8. And finally, are you for the liberals or for the conservatives? _____
_____

Por in common idiomatic expressions

Por appears in commonly used idiomatic expressions. This list is provided as a reference.

por ahí, allí	*around there*	**por lo general**	*generally*
por ahora	*for now*	**por lo menos**	*at least*
por aquí	*this way*	**por lo visto**	*apparently*
por cierto	*by the way*	**por poco**	*almost*
por Dios	*for God's sake*	**por separado**	*separately*
por ejemplo	*for example*	**por si acaso**	*just in case*
por eso	*that is why*	**por supuesto**	*of course*
por favor	*please*	**por último**	*finally*
por fin	*finally*		

EJERCICIO
15·15

Una conversación entre dos amigos. *Choose the appropriate idiomatic expression to complete the sentence.*

1. Oye, Pedro, (por ejemplo | por ahí) viene Antonio.

2. (Por lo visto | Por favor), ¿puedes prestarme tus lentes de sol?

3. ¡(Por separado | Por supuesto)! Pero, ¿por qué necesitas mis lentes?

4. (Por lo visto | Por separado) no sabes que le debo dinero a Antonio.

5. ¿De verdad? (Por lo general | Por cierto), tú me debes a mí veinticinco dólares.

6. ¡(Por ejemplo | Por Dios)! Yo no recuerdo eso.

7. (Por lo general | Por lo menos) no digas mentiras. Sabes la verdad.

8. ¡Ay!, (por favor | por si acaso), ten un poco de paciencia.

9. (Por ahí | Por fin) dices la verdad.

10. Sí, pero (por eso | por poco) ayúdame. No quiero que Antonio me vea aquí.

EJERCICIO
15·16

¿Por o para?

1. El avión sale _____ México en dos horas.

2. Los estudiantes van a estar en Acapulco _____ diez días.

3. Allí, no van a poder encontrar un hotel _____ poco dinero.

4. _____ ser jóvenes, son muy responsables.

5. _____ la mañana, quieren tomar el sol.

6. _____ el viernes, ya podemos llamarlos a Tijuana.

7. Van a pasar _____ la casa de unas amigas de Carmen.

8. Espero que ellos nos llamen _____ teléfono.

EJERCICIO
15·17

En español. *Use **por** or **para** according to the context.*

1. We work instead of Lidia. _____

2. They pass through the tunnel. _____

3. He has at least two cars. _____

4. Because of her illness (**enfermedad**), she is not here. _____

5. My friend comes by my office. _____

6. He comes by train. _____

7. He will be here by four o'clock. _____

EJERCICIO
15·18

Y en tu caso... ¿Verdadero (V) o falso (F)?

_____ 1. Debes tener 21 años para votar en los Estados Unidos.

_____ 2. Puedes recibir una multa (ticket) si conduces a ochenta millas por hora.

_____ 3. Trabajas mejor por la mañana y no por la tarde.

_____ 4. Tienes que terminar un proyecto especial para el sábado.

_____ 5. Entras a tu casa por la puerta del garaje.

_____ 6. Sales para México la semana que viene.

_____ 7. Siempre llevas un cepillo para el pelo.

EJERCICIO
15·19

Explica por qué. _Explain why either_ **por** _or_ **para** _is used in each of the following sentences. Indicate destination, movement, exchange, etc. in your answers._

1. Salen para Moscú esta tarde. _____

2. Viajan por avión. _____

3. Van a llegar para las cuatro. _____

4. Pagaron trescientos euros por los billetes. _____

5. Para un viaje tan largo, el billete es barato. _____

6. Viajan para asistir a un congreso. _____

7. Viajan por el oeste de Europa. _____

8. Viajan por necesidad. _____

9. Van a estar en Moscú por una semana. _____

10. Por último, van a visitar a unos amigos. _____

Verbs that require the preposition a or de + an infinitive in Spanish

In Spanish, some conjugated verbs always require **a**, **de**, or another preposition when followed by an infinitive (**Me decido a salir.** _I decide to go out._). Other conjugated verbs are followed directly by the infinitive (**Querríamos comer** ahora. _We would like to eat now._).

Whether or not they are followed by infinitives, prepositions often determine the meaning of Spanish verbs: **regresar** means _to return_. **Regresar a** means _to return to_ with the intention of doing something, while **regresar de** implies _to return from_.

Regresaron a terminar el trabajo.	_They returned to do the work._
Elisa **regresó de San Pedro** anoche.	_Elisa returned from San Pedro last night._

The following lists of commonly used verbs are provided for vocabulary study and as a reference tool. Entries in a good all-Spanish or bilingual dictionary will show prepositions used with verbs, often in examples. Consult your dictionary for verbs not found here.

Some verbs may be categorized according to the preposition they require. The following list includes verbs followed by the preposition **a**, either before an infinitive and/or before a predicate noun. Context will tell you if an infinitive or a noun is appropriate. (Stem-changing verbs are indicated in parentheses.)

acercarse a	to approach, come close to	montar a	to ride
aprender a	to learn to	oler a (o > ue)	to smell of
asistir a	to attend	oponerse a	to oppose, be opposed to
atreverse a	to dare to	ponerse a	to start to
comenzar a (e > ie)	to start to	quedarse a	to stay, remain (back) to
convidar a	to invite to	regresar a	to go back to
correr a	to run to	resistirse a	to resist
decidirse a	to decide to	saber a	to taste like
empezar a (e > ie)	to begin to	salir a	to go out to
enseñar a	to teach to	sonar a (o > ue)	to sound like
inspirar a	to inspire to	venir a	to come to
invitar a	to invite to	volver a (o > ue)	to return (something) to; to (do something) again
ir a	to go to		
llegar a	to arrive to/at; to succeed in		

EJERCICIO
15·20

¿**Cuál es la respuesta?** *Complete the sentences in Spanish. Use the appropriate present tense verb in parentheses followed by the preposition a.*

1. Mi habitación _____ (*smells like*) rosas.

2. Esas palabras _____ (*sound like*) mentiras (*lies*).

3. Gandhi me _____ (*inspires to*) buscar soluciones pacíficas.

4. Muchas personas no _____ (*dare to*) aprender una lengua extranjera.

5. No quiero aprender a _____ (*to ride*) caballo con un pony.

6. Sus padres _____ (*are opposed to*) su matrimonio con Carla.

Verbs with other prepositions

The prepositions **de, con,** and **por** also connect conjugated verbs with an infinitive or with a predicate noun. Learn the following verbs along with their prepositions.

acabar de	to have just
acordarse de (o > ue)	to remember (someone or something)
alegrarse de	to be glad about
alegrarse por	to be happy for
amenazar con	to threaten with
casarse con	to marry
consentir en (e > ie)	to consent to
consistir en	to consist of
dejar de	to stop (doing something)
insistir en	to insist on
olvidarse de	to forget about (something or someone)
soñar con (o > ue)	to dream of, about
terminar de	to finish (doing something)

Choose the appropriate preposition.

1. Carla está enamorada (con | de) Juan.

2. Laura se casa (con | a) Martín.

3. Yo sueño (de | con) ver a mis amigos en Colorado.

4. La profesora insiste (con | en) estos datos acerca de la comunidad hispana.

5. Paula, deja (con | de) hablar y empieza a trabajar ya.

6. Nos alegramos (de | para) verlos aquí.

7. ¿Vienen Uds. (en | a) el mes de mayo?

8. El meteorólogo se olvidó (de | por) dar el pronóstico del tiempo para mañana por la tarde.

Verbs that require a preposition in English but not in Spanish

Note that some Spanish verbs that *don't* require a preposition have English equivalents that do. Anglophones will be tempted to try to translate these verbs literally, adding a preposition where it doesn't exist. Learn this list of Spanish verbs without prepositions by picturing them in context (**bajar las escaleras**, *to go down the steps*).

In context, the verbs in this list are all followed by a direct object noun (or preceded by a direct object pronoun). Don't forget to include the personal **a** when the direct object noun is a specific person (**Busco a Carlos.** *I am searching for Carlos.*).

apagar	*to turn off (a light)*	**esperar**	*to wait for*
bajar	*to go down*	**mirar**	*to look at*
borrar	*to cross out*	**pagar**	*to pay for*
botar	*to throw away*	**poder**	*to be able to*
buscar	*to look for*	**poner**	*to turn on (an appliance)*
caerse	*to fall down*	**quitar(se)**	*to take off*
colgar (o > ue)	*to hang up*	**sacar**	*to take out*
encender (e > ie)	*to light up*	**salir**	*to go out*
escuchar	*to listen to*	**subir**	*to go up*

Las noticias. *Translate into Spanish and use the* **vocabulario.**

I go down the steps, I go into the living room, turn on the TV, and I listen to the news. I dream of a day full of good news. For example, foreign leaders do not threaten with a new international conflict, the financial experts do not report dreadful details about the economy, and I stop thinking of the world's problems. I am not selfish, for God's sake. I only want one day of peace and happy thoughts. What news do I want to hear? For example, that we are all for peace and against war, that we are glad to have the simple things in life. Today, I am going to turn off the television, and I am going to look for my shovel to work in the garden.

_____

_____

_____

_____

_____

_____

_____

_____

_____

_____

_____

VOCABULARIO

detail	**el detalle**	*news*	**las noticias**
dreadful	**horrible**	*peace*	**la paz**
financial	**financiero(a)**	*selfish*	**egoísta (m. and f.)**
foreign	**extranjero(a)**	*shovel*	**la pala**
full	**lleno(a)**	*thought*	**el pensamiento**
leader	**el líder**	*to report*	**reportar**

Idioms and special phrases

Native speakers understand idiomatic phrases in their own language; however, often they may not be clear to language learners, since idioms and idiomatic phrases do not translate word-for-word from one language to another. Idiomatic expressions and phrases often combine words, creating different meanings from their dictionary definitions.

¿**Te das cuenta** de lo que pasa?	***Do you realize*** *what is going on?*
¡El libro no **está disponible**!	*The book **is not available**!*

Darse cuenta de (*to realize*) is an idiomatic expression. At first glance, you might think it means *to give* a *sum* or an *account*. Note that *going on* is an idiomatic expression in English. Sometimes an idiom is used in a context that appears to have little to do with the situation at hand. Note the following exchange between an employee and a manager:

—¿Vamos a firmar el nuevo contrato?	*Are we going to sign the new contract?*
—No estamos **seguros**.	*We are not sure.*
—Entonces, ¿no recibiremos un bono?	*So, we will not get a bonus?*
—No está **el horno para galletitas**.	*This is not **the right time**.*

If you translate the last Spanish sentence literally it says *the oven is not (ready) for (baking) cookies.* What would *an oven ready to bake cookies* have to do with a discussion about contracts and bonuses? **No está el horno para galletitas** is a special phrase that fits the dialogue, hinting clearly that most probably there will not be a bonus. Idiomatic phrases in Spanish, learned carefully and practiced consistently, will help you communicate effectively and avoid awkward situations or misunderstandings. Think of this type of phrase as:

a combination of words that creates a different meaning from common definitions → idiomatic phrase

Some idioms may be complete sentences, proverbs, or sayings. Note the idiomatic English equivalents:

A la tercera va la vencida.	*Three strikes, you're out.*
A buena hambre, no hay pan duro.	*Beggars can't be choosers.*
El casado, casa quiere.	*Married people need a home of their own.*
A palabras necias, oídos sordos.	*Take no notice of (turn a deaf ear to) thoughtless words people say.*

Other idioms are adverbial phrases. You may wish to go back to Chapter 6 to review adverbial phrases. Remember that most of these phrases, functioning as adverbs, are formed with a preposition plus a noun, an adjective, or an infinitive. They are idiomatic since they do not translate literally into other languages. Note the following prepositional phrases and their English equivalents:

a cuentagotas	*in dribs and drabs*
a toda vela	*full speed ahead*
de mala gana	*unwillingly, reluctantly*
en esas condiciones	*in such condition(s)*
en mi opinión	*in my book*
en resumen	*in a nutshell*
Vamos **a toda vela**.	*We are moving **full speed ahead**.*
Nos dan las noticias **a cuentagotas**.	*They give us the news **in dribs and drabs**.*
No volverán a esta casa nunca **en esas condiciones**.	*They will never return to this house **in (under) those conditions**.*
Los chicos limpian su dormitorio **de mala gana**.	*The kids clean their room **reluctantly**.*

Many idioms, such as **soportar** (*to stand, to take*), are specific, idiomatic uses of verbs:

No soporta una broma.	***He can't take** a joke.*

The context for these messages is often informal. A paragraph such as the following may appear in a conversation, a short e-mail, or a message you may find on your answering machine:

Hice unos recados. Fui al supermercado que **da al este, di con** los ingredientes que buscaba. Luego llamé a Carla pero **no dio la cara**.	*I ran a few errands. I went to the supermarket **facing east, I found** the ingredients I was looking for. Then I called Carla, **but she did not (refused to) answer me**.*

In a somewhat different tone, the following paragraph might appear in a Spanish newspaper. Note the highlighted idiomatic phrases:

La comisión creada por el Presidente, **llevará a cabo** la investigación del secuestro, sin **perder de vista** las necesidades de los ciudadanos. El Presidente ha manifestado que para los secuestrados, su situación **es un asunto de vida o muerte.** También, ha comunicado la necesidad de **mantener la calma** y **estar alertas** ante cualquier situación sospechosa.

The commission created by the President **will carry out** *the investigation of the kidnapping,* **without losing sight** *of the needs of the citizens. The President has declared that, for the kidnap victims, their situation* **is a matter of life and death.** *He also emphasized the need* **to keep calm** *and* **be on the alert** *for any suspicious situations.*

Idiomatic expressions are used:

◆ To express the accurate equivalent of a word or phrase that does not have a literal translation:

No soporto sus comentarios.

I cannot stand his/her/their comments.

◆ To clarify the meaning of what is being communicated:

Estás débil y tienes que **guardar cama** por unos días.

You are weak and you have to **stay in bed** *for a few days.*

◆ To further explain or emphasize ideas:

No durmieron anoche; **pasaron la noche en blanco.**

They did not sleep at all; **they did not sleep a wink.**

Common phrases with verbs

Many common idiomatic phrases consist of a verb + another verb, a noun, or a preposition, followed by other elements. Here are some frequently used verbal expressions:

atar cabos	*to put two and two together*
dejar caer	*to drop*
dejar pasar la ocasión	*to miss the opportunity, to miss the boat*
deshacerse en lágrimas	*to burst into tears*
estar en ayuno, quedarse en ayuno	*to fast (not eat); to be unable to understand something*
guardar cama	*to stay in bed*
llevar a cabo	*to carry out, to realize*
llover a cántaros	*to rain cats and dogs*
meterse a alguien en el bolsillo	*to have someone eating out of one's hand, to buy someone off*
meterse en un lío	*to be in a pickle, to be between a rock and a hard place*
pasar la noche en blanco	*to not sleep a wink*
sacar una foto	*to take a picture / photo*
salir adelante	*to make headway / progress*
salirse con la suya	*to get one's way*
ser hombre muerto	*to be a marked man*
ser un asunto de vida o muerte	*to be a matter of life and death*
tirar la casa por la ventana	*to spend money excessively / left and right*
valer la pena	*to be worth it*

venderse como pan caliente	*to sell like hotcakes*
volverse + *adjective*	*to become*
Atando cabos, descubrieron las pistas.	***They put two and two together*** *and found the clues.*
Laura **dejó caer** el jarrón chino.	*Laura **dropped** / **let fall** the Chinese vase.*
Al ver la cara de su hija, la madre de Laura **se deshizo en lágrimas**.	*Upon seeing her daughter's face, Laura's mother **burst into tears**.*
Juan tiene fiebre y debe **guardar cama**.	*Juan has a fever and must **stay in bed**.*
Anoche estaba nervioso y **se pasó la noche en blanco**.	*Last night he was nervous and **could not sleep a wink**.*
Se preocupa porque su esposa **tira la casa por la ventana**.	*He is concerned because his wife **spends money excessively**.*
Pero **no vale la pena** preocuparse tanto.	*But **it is not worth** worrying so much.*

EJERCICIO
15·23

Un cuento. *Select the phrase that best communicates the message. Then create a new sentence with the appropriate past tense form of the verb.*

1. _____ El detective hizo un excelente trabajo. _____

2. _____ No durmió en toda la noche. _____

3. _____ Afuera, caía mucha agua. _____

4. _____ Entendió todo lo que había pasado. _____

5. _____ No quería perder una oportunidad. _____

6. _____ Hizo una foto del sospechoso (*suspect*). _____

7. _____ Para el detective, el caso era muy importante. _____

8. _____ El sospechoso estaba enfermo. _____

9. _____ Pero el sospechoso no podía ganar. _____

10. _____ El detective iba a ganar (*win*). _____

11. _____ El trabajo no fue en vano (*in vain*). _____

a. atar cabos	g. valer la pena
b. llover a cántaros	h. ser un asunto de vida o muerte
c. sacar una foto	i. guardar cama
d. salirse con la suya	j. ser hombre muerto
e. pasar la noche en blanco	k. llevar a cabo
f. dejar pasar la ocasión	

Idiomatic use of verbs in certain expressions

Some verbs appear in idiomatic expressions more often than others. The following list shows verbs frequently used in such expressions. Notice how words are combined in these expressions with **dar**:

verb + preposition

dar + con

No dimos con el edificio.   *We could not find the building.*

verb + preposition + infinitive

dar + a + conocer

Dieron a conocer la noticia.   *They revealed the news.*

verb + noun

hacer + preguntas

Les **hicieron preguntas**.   *They asked them questions.*

verb + article + noun

perder + la + calma

No pierdan la calma.   *Stay calm. (Don't lose your cool.)*

Verbs and idiomatic expressions

A few common Spanish verbs are particularly used in idiomatic expressions.

Verbal expressions with dar

If you open a Spanish-Spanish dictionary, the first definition of **dar** you will see is **donar** (*to give, to donate*) or **entregar** (*to turn in*). Keep looking under the same entry, **dar**, and a rather long list of verbal phrases appear. This is not the case for all verbs, but some (such as **dar, tener**, and **hacer**) are the bases of a rich list of idiomatic expressions. Here are some of the idiomatic verbal expressions that include **dar**. Note how they vary in meaning:

dar a conocer	*to reveal*
dar ánimo	*to encourage*
dar con	*to find*
dar cuerda	*to wind (a clock)*
dar gritos	*to scream*
dar la cara	*to face (up to) someone or something*
dar la hora	*to strike the hour*
dar la mano	*to shake hands*
dar las gracias	*to thank*
dar por hecho	*to take for granted*
dar un abrazo	*to embrace, to give a hug*
dar un paseo	*to take a walk; to go for a ride*
dar una bofetada	*to slap on the face*
dar una mano	*to give / lend a hand*
dar una vuelta	*to take a walk*
darse cuenta de	*to realize*
darse prisa	*to hurry*
La víctima **dio gritos**.	*The victim **screamed**.*
En ese momento, el reloj **dio las tres**.	*At that moment, the clock **struck three**.*
Un testigo **dio por hecho** que estaba loco.	*A witness **took for granted** that he was insane.*
Mi hermano **dio testimonio** bajo juramento.	*My brother **testified** under oath.*
Los miembros del jurado **se dieron cuenta** de su inocencia.	*The members of the jury **realized** that he was innocent.*
Los periodistas **se dieron prisa** para dar la noticia.	*The reporters **hurried** to report the news.*

Other verbal expressions with **dar** + *a noun of feeling* convey emotions or reactions to something or someone:

dar alegría a	*to make someone happy*
dar asco a	*to make someone feel sick*
dar ganas de (llorar) a	*to make someone feel like (crying)*
dar miedo a	*to scare, to frighten someone*
dar náuseas a	*to make someone nauseous / nauseated*
dar pánico a	*to make someone panic*
dar pena a	*to make someone feel sorry*
dar risa a	*to make someone laugh*
dar sueño a	*to make someone sleepy*
dar tristeza a	*to make someone sad*
El aburrimiento **da sueño**, y lo ridículo **da risa**.	*Boredom **makes one sleepy**, and silly things **make one laugh**.*
A Lina **le dan miedo** los ratones.	*Mice **frighten** Lina.*
A mí los ratones **me dan náuseas**.	*Mice **make me nauseous**.*
Las campañas llenas de mentiras **nos dan asco**.	*Campaigns full of lies **make us feel sick**.*

EJERCICIO
15·24

En la comunidad. *Create a new sentence using an expression with the appropriate present tense form of the verb.*

1. Carlos conduce rápido. _____

2. Felipe ayuda a Mario. _____

3. Ahora, Ana entiende mi problema. _____

4. Luisa agradece mis consejos. _____

5. Cuando entramos, Ana nos saluda. _____

6. Benita revela los secretos de todos. _____

7. Berta y Alina animan a sus amigos. _____

8. A todos nos encanta pasear. _____

EJERCICIO
15·25

Te toca a ti. *Complete each sentence with the appropriate present tense form of the verb.*

MODELO   la crítica destructiva

         La crítica destructiva no me da risa, me da asco.

dar alegría / dar asco / dar ganas de llorar / dar miedo / dar náuseas / dar pánico / dar pena / dar risa / dar sueño / dar tristeza

1. los comentarios tontos

_____

2. los chistes de mal gusto

_____

3. las biografías de figuras militares

_____

4. los vuelos en avionetas (*small planes*)

_____

5. las películas de horror

_____

6. los animales abandonados

_____

Verbal expressions with hacer

hacer caso	*to heed, to pay attention*
hacer cola	*to stand in line*
hacer de + *noun*	*to work as*
hacer el papel de	*to play the role of*
hacer la vida imposible	*to make someone's life impossible*
hacer preguntas	*to ask, pose questions*
hacer un favor	*to do someone a favor*
hacer un recado	*to run an errand*
hacer(se) daño	*to harm; to hurt oneself*
hacerse + *noun*	*to become*
hacerse pedazos	*to break into pieces*
Juan **hace el papel de** payaso en la fiesta de los niños.	*Juan **plays the role of** a clown at the children's party.*
Siempre **hace favores** a sus amigos.	*He always **does** his friends **favors**.*
Ayer, me **hizo un recado**.	*Yesterday he **ran an errand for me**.*
Marcos me **hace la vida imposible** con sus preguntas.	*Marcos **makes my life impossible** with his questions.*
Marcos quiere **hacerse abogado** pero no está seguro.	*Marcos wants **to become a lawyer** but he is not sure.*
Esta mañana dejé caer el jarrón y **se hizo pedazos**.	*This morning I dropped the vase and **it broke into pieces**.*

A number of expressions that refer to weather conditions use the verbs **haber** (**hay**) and **hacer** (**hace**). Remember to use the third-person singular of the verb tense to describe or talk about the weather:

hacer buen / hacer mal tiempo	*to be good / bad weather*
hacer calor / frío	*to be hot / cold*
hacer fresco	*to be cool*
hacer sol	*to be sunny*
hacer viento	*to be windy*
Pasó la tormenta tropical y **hace calor**.	*The tropical storm passed and **it is hot**.*
Hizo mal tiempo toda la semana pasada.	*All last week **the weather was bad**.*

haber luna	*the moon is out / is shining*
haber niebla	*to be foggy*
haber nubes	*to be cloudy*
haber sol	*to be sunny*
Esta noche **no hay luna** porque **hay muchas nubes**.	*Tonight **there is no moon** because **it is very cloudy**.*
Habrá sol esta tarde. Lleva los lentes de sol.	***It will be sunny** this afternoon. Take your sunglasses.*

EJERCICIO
15·26

*Choose the appropriate verbal expression. Complete each sentence with the appropriate present tense form of **hacer**.*

hacer favores / hacer el papel de / hacer caso / hacer daño / hacer preguntas / hacer la vida imposible

1. ¿Carlos es actor?

   Claro, _____ un loco.

2. ¿Cómo sabes que es curioso?

   Porque siempre _____ .

3. ¿Es amable?

   Sí, a menudo _____ a sus amigos.

4. Entonces, ¿es muy buena persona?

   Por supuesto, jamás _____ a nadie.

5. ¿Es un buen paciente?

   Efectivamente, _____ de los consejos de su médico.

6. Y, ¿también es paciente?

   Sin duda, pues soporta a su suegra, quien le _____ .

Verbal expressions with **perder**

echar a perder	*to spoil, to ruin*
perder cuidado	*not to worry*
perder el autobús, el tren, etc.	*to miss the bus, the train, etc.*
perder la calma	*to lose patience*
perder la razón	*to lose one's mind*
perder de vista	*to lose sight of*
perder el turno	*to miss one's turn*

Verbal expressions with **poner**

poner(se) de acuerdo	*to agree, to come to an agreement*
poner en duda	*to doubt, to cast a doubt*
poner los puntos sobre las íes	*to cross your t's and dot your i's*
ponerle los pelos de punta	*to make your hair stand on end*

Una persona muy especial. *Choose a phrase from column* **B** *to add emphasis to the phrases in column* **A**. *Then create a new sentence.*

modelo   es muy tranquilo y tiene paciencia   (no) perder la calma

Es muy tranquilo y tiene paciencia, no pierde la calma.

A

1. _____ habla con mucha claridad

2. _____ no gasta mucho dinero

3. _____ es convincente

4. _____ no es puntual, no llega a tiempo

5. _____ cuida sus intereses

6. _____ no discute ni pelea con sus hermanos

7. _____ acepta las explicaciones de sus amigos

B

a. (no) salirse con la suya

b. (no) perder el tren

c. (no) poner los puntos sobre las íes

d. (no) poner nada en duda

e. (no) ponerse de acuerdo

f. (no) perder nada de vista

g. (no) tirar la casa por la ventana

1. _____

2. _____

3. _____

4. _____

5. _____

6. _____

7. _____

Verbal expressions with tener

The English verb *to be* translates many of the verbal expressions with **tener**:

tener ansias	*to be anxious*
tener calor	*to be hot, warm*
tener celos	*to be jealous*
tener cuidado	*to be careful*
tener envidia	*to be envious*
tener éxito	*to be successful*
tener frío	*to be cold*
tener hambre	*to be hungry*
tener la culpa	*to be guilty*
tener mala suerte	*to be unlucky*
tener miedo	*to be afraid*
tener nervios	*to be nervous*
tener paciencia	*to be patient*
tener prisa	*to be in a hurry*
tener razón	*to be right*

tener sueño	*to be sleepy*
tener suerte	*to be lucky*

Other verbal expressions with **tener**:

tener escalofríos	*to have the chills*
tener dolor de cabeza	*to have a headache*
tener ganas de	*to feel like*
tener lugar	*to take place*
tener que ver (con)	*to have to do with*

EJERCICIO
15·28

Complete each sentence with the appropriate tense form of the erbal expression with **tener***.*

1. Duerme cuando _____.

2. Corro cuando _____.

3. Están felices si _____.

4. Se puso la chaqueta porque _____.

5. Tomó dos aspirinas porque _____.

6. No se van a la cama aunque _____ de dormir.

7. No nos gusta esperar, no _____.

8. Nunca gano un premio; _____.

9. Margo está equivocada porque _____.

10. Debes pedir perdón porque _____.

Refranes

A saying, **un refrán** in Spanish, states a commonsense observation and applies to certain situations. Like most idiomatic expressions, these phrases are not always easily translated. For example, an adolescent insists on keeping the wrong company. His/her parents are concerned about the consequences of associating with individuals with a bad reputation, and the worried parents give their child a warning:

Dime con quién andas, y te diré quién eres.   *You are judged by the company you keep.*

The message can be interpreted as: *Tell me who your friends are, and I will tell you who you are.* Another example conveys a similar message about keeping bad company. Literally, it says: *God creates them, and they find a way to get together*:

Dios los cría y ellos se juntan.   *Birds of a feather flock together.*

There are many such sayings, proverbs, and sentences in other languages. They vary depending on the region or country where they are popular; some are centuries old. As a cultural note, it is said that there are more than 100,000 **refranes** in Spanish.

The following is a list of commonly used sayings or **refranes** organized by themes or situations where they are used. Some belong to more than one category. Note the equivalents in idiomatic English; only rarely does the English vocabulary "match" the vocabulary in the Spanish saying.

Facing adversity

A mal tiempo, buena cara.	*When life gives you lemons, make lemonade.*
Borrón y cuenta nueva.	*Let bygones be bygones.*
Cuando una puerta se cierra, cien se abren.	*When one door closes, another always opens.*
El amor todo lo puede.	*Love will conquer all.*
El tiempo lo cura todo.	*Time heals all wounds.*
La risa es el mejor remedio.	*Laughter is the best medicine.*
Más vale tarde que nunca.	*Better late than never.*
No hay mal que por bien no venga ni cuerpo que lo resista.	*Nothing lasts forever.*
Nunca es tarde si la dicha es buena.	*Better late than never.*
Ojos que no ven, corazón que no siente.	*Long absent, soon forgotten. / Out of sight, out of mind.*
Peor es nada.	*Half a loaf is better than none.*
Persevera y triunfarás.	*If at first you don't succeed, try, try again.*
Quien espera, desespera.	*Hope deferred makes the heart sick.*
Siempre llueve sobre mojado.	*When it rains, it pours.*

Character and deception

Cría fama y acuéstate a dormir.	*You can rest on your laurels. / Give a dog a bad name and hang it.*
De noche, todos los gatos son pardos.	*All cats are gray in the dark.*
Hierba mala nunca muere.	*The devil looks after himself.*
No es oro todo lo que reluce.	*All that glitters is not gold.*
Poderoso caballero es Don Dinero.	*Money talks.*
Quien mal anda, mal acaba.	*If you live like that, you're bound to come to a bad end.*
Quien roba una vez roba diez.	*Once a thief, always a thief.*
Tanto tienes, tanto vales; nada tienes, nada vales.	*You are what you own.*

Friendship

Amigo en la adversidad es un amigo de verdad.	*A friend in need is a friend indeed.*
Dime con quién andas, y te diré quién eres.	*You are judged by the company you keep.*

Life situations

A la ocasión la pintan calva.	*Strike while the iron is hot.*
Tanto monta, monta tanto.	*It makes no difference.*

Mistakes/consequences

Al que no quiera caldo, dos tazas.	*It never rains, but it pours.*
El hombre propone y Dios dispone.	*Man proposes and God disposes.*
El que la hace, la paga.	*You've made your bed, now you must lie in it.*
El que no trabaje, que no coma.	*No bees, no honey; no work, no money.*
Lo pasado, pasado está.	*Let bygones be bygones.*

Popular wisdom

El mundo es un pañuelo.	*It's a small world.*
El saber no ocupa lugar.	*One can never know too much.*
Hecha la ley, hecha la trampa.	*Every law has its loophole.*
Ladrón que roba a ladrón tiene cien años de perdón.	*It's no crime to steal from a thief.*
Más sabe el diablo por viejo que por diablo.	*There's no substitute for experience.*
No solo de pan vive el hombre.	*Man cannot live by bread alone.*
Sobre gustos, no hay nada escrito.	*Different strokes for different folks.*

EJERCICIO
15·29

Situaciones y refranes. *Review the list of* **refranes** *and create one that applies to the situations given.*

1. Un estudiante se queja porque tiene que estudiar mucho.

   _____

2. Vas a una entrevista pero no te ofrecen el trabajo.

   _____

3. Un buen amigo está enfermo pero no lo sabes.

   _____

4. Compraste un billete de lotería pero sólo ganaste $5.

   _____

5. Un amigo te debe $500 desde hace tres años y ¡por fin te devuelve tu dinero!

   _____

6. Descubres con alegría que un amigo ha pagado una deuda que tenía.

   _____

7. Un colega y tú han tenido problemas pero decides olvidar el pasado.

   _____

8. Un senador va a la cárcel porque ha usado fondos públicos para ayudar a un criminal.

   _____

Colloquial phrases

Most idiomatic expressions are used in colloquial exchanges: dialogues, informal conversations, or situations. However, colloquial phrases may be used in more formal writing to state an idea clearly, and to the point, that can be understood by everyone involved. For example, a political leader may use a phrase to state his/her position in difficult times: **En tiempo de tribulaciones no**

hacer mudanzas. This expression says it is not wise to make hasty decisions during hard times. Other expressions are purely colloquial in nature:

Estás hasta en la sopa.	*There is no getting away from you.*
Te llegó la hora.	*Your time is up.*

Some phrases fall out of fashion and become outdated. It is not easy to keep up with usage. Note the possible English translations for the following example. The second one is more current:

Cada oveja con su pareja.	*Every Jack has his Jill. / Everyone has his soul mate.*

Some phrases are hard to understand if they are part of the jargon or slang of a particular group or consist of a combination of nonstandard vocabulary elements. Remember that the Spanish-speaking world is very large. As a learner, it's best to avoid certain expressions, especially if they convey offensive connotations that might be interpreted as demeaning. A given word or a phrase may be inappropriate in some areas while being completely acceptable in others.

One could create infinitely long lists of colloquial phrases. The following are commonly used. They are listed by groups for easier learning:

Animals

estar loco como una cabra	*to be mad as a hatter*
hacer patas de mosca	*to write like chicken scratching*
no oírse ni una mosca	*to hear a pin drop*
ponérsele a alguien la carne / la piel de gallina	*to get goose bumps*
ser un lince	*to be very very smart*
ser un/a gallina	*to be chicken, a coward*
ser un/a zorra	*to be (like) a fox*
No escribes claro, **haces patas de mosca**.	*You do not write clearly, **it's like chicken scratching**.*
Cuando el juez iba a leer el veredicto no **se oía una mosca**.	*When the judge was going to read the verdict, **you could hear a pin drop**.*
Cantó tan bien que **se me puso la carne de gallina**.	*She sang so well that **it gave me goose bumps**.*

Color

blanco como un papel	*as white as a sheet, as white as a ghost*
como de lo blanco a lo negro	*as different as day and night*
por si las moscas	*just in case*
un chiste verde	*a dirty joke*
un mosca muerta	*a hypocrite*
un viejo verde	*a dirty old man*
Tiene malos atributos: **es un viejo verde y un mosca muerta**.	*He has bad traits: **he is a dirty old man and a hypocrite**.*
Por si las moscas, no lo voy a invitar a la cena.	***Just in case**, I am not inviting him to dinner.*
Oyó la noticia y **se quedó blanco como un papel**.	*She heard the news and **she turned white as a ghost**.*

Food

con su pan se lo coma	*it's his/her own tough luck*
estar hasta en la sopa	*there is no getting away from*
estar más fresco/a que una lechuga	*to be cool as a cucumber*

importar un pepino	not to care
importarle a alguien un rábano/un pepino	he/she could not care less
ser pan comido	to be easy as pie / a piece of cake
Se han equivocado y **con su pan se lo coman**.	They made a mistake and **it is their own tough luck**.
Vas a tomar el examen y te ves **más fresco que una lechuga**.	You are going to take the exam, and you look **as cool as a cucumber**.
Me importa un pepino lo que digan de mí.	**I could not care less** about what they say about me.
¡Ah!, este ejercicio es fácil: **es pan comido**.	This exercise is easy: **a piece of cake**.

Numbers

bajo siete llaves	under lock and key
como que dos y dos son cuatro	as certain as eggs is eggs
seguir en sus trece	to stick to one's guns
igual Pascual	even Steven
Guardo mis secretos **bajo siete llaves**.	I keep my secrets **under lock and key**.
Mi hermano es muy terco; **sigue en sus trece**.	My brother is very stubborn; **he is sticking to his guns**.

Parts of the body

desternillarse de la risa	to be in stitches
estar para chuparse los dedos	to be finger-licking good
la niña de sus ojos	the apple of his/her eye
meter la pata	to put one's foot in one's mouth
patas arriba	upside down
poner los ojos en blanco	to roll one's eyes
Este plato está para **chuparse los dedos**.	This dish is **finger-licking good**.
Su hija es **la niña de sus ojos**.	His daughter is **the apple of his eye**.
Eres muy desordenado y tienes todo **patas arriba**.	You are disorganized, and everything is **upside down**.

Various topics

chitón	mum's the word
de eso nada	my eye
en resumidas cuentas	in a nutshell
eso es otro capítulo	that is another story
estar en un lío	to be in a jam
ir como alma que lleva el diablo	to run like hell
llegarle la hora a alguien	your number is up
no pintar nada	to be out of place
no venir al caso	to be beside / to miss the point
ser un ladrillo	to be extremely boring
tener la sartén por el mango	to have the upper hand, to run the show
Ahora, no hablemos: **chitón**.	Now, let' not talk: **mum's the word**.
No hablemos de mis problemas. **Eso es otro capítulo**.	Let's not talk about my problems. **That is another story**.
Tu crítica y tus comentarios **no vienen al caso**.	Your criticism and your comments **are beside the point**.
Este libro es **un ladrillo**.	This book is **extremely boring**.

EJERCICIO
15·30

Complete each sentence with a colloquial phrase. Be sure to use the appropriate tense form of the verb.

1. Puedes confiar en mí, guardo mis secretos _____.

2. Dices cosas que no tienen sentido, ¡estás _____!

3. ¿Tienes miedo? Estás _____.

4. ¡Es verdad! ¡ _____!

5. Es muy cómico, voy a _____.

6. No hagas lo que no debes hacer porque _____.

7. No hagas comentarios inapropiados, que _____.

8. Pues ahora es tu turno, _____.

EJERCICIO
15·31

Te toca a ti. *For each situation, give a **refrán** or colloquial phrase.*

1. Haces un trabajo difícil y te sientes orgulloso/a.

   _____

2. Quieres ser amigo/a de un/a chico/a pero sabes que tiene mala reputación.

   _____

3. Has encontrado a la pareja perfecta para ti.

   _____

4. Haces un comentario inapropiado, fuera de lugar.

   _____

5. Has esperado mucho tiempo, pero has recibido la respuesta que esperabas.

   _____

6. Sales de casa de prisa, no haces la cama, no lavas los platos.

   _____

7. Preparas una cena y tus amigos dicen que todo está delicioso.

   _____

8. Conociste al hermano de un amigo pero su conversación es aburridísima.

   _____

Using infinitives

The *infinitive*, the name that identifies a verb, is the most basic form of a verb. The infinitive does not indicate a person, or by itself, a notion of time. In English, the infinitive is the *root* of the verb and usually refers to the form *to* + *first person of the verb*. In Spanish, verb infinitives are grouped in three conjugations that have the same infinitive endings: **-ar**, **-er**, and **-ir**.

> **root of the verb + -ar, -er, or -ir → infinitive**

The infinitive is basically a verb, but it performs many functions of a noun. When translated alone, the Spanish infinitive **salir** is the English equivalent of *to leave*. However, in other contexts, the English equivalent may be different. In the first example below, the Spanish infinitive **merendar** (*to snack*) is the *subject* of the sentence and plays the role of a noun. In the second, it also functions as a noun but as the *object* of the sentence:

Merendar es saludable.	*Having a snack is healthy.*
¿Quieres **merendar**?	*Do you want to have a snack?*

Infinitives as nouns

Infinitives acting as nouns belong to the category of *verbals*: words that have the characteristics of a verb (an action) but function in a sentence as a noun.

El errar es humano.	*To err is human.*
Mis padres decidieron **ir**.	*My parents decided to go.*
Me relaja **tocar el piano**.	*Playing the piano relaxes me.*
¡Me encanta **correr**!	*I love to run!*
el ser celoso/a	*being jealous*

Keep in mind the following points:

- Infinitives used as nouns are always masculine and generally appear in the singular form; some are also used in the plural:

los deberes	*homework; duties*
los quehaceres	*duties, work, responsibilities*

Infinitives as nouns may be used with or without a *masculine* article. They may also be modified by *adjectives*, *possessive adjectives*, *demonstrative adjectives*, or *adverbs*:

El comer en exceso es **peligroso**.	*Eating too much is dangerous.*
Los deberes de un ciudadano son **exigentes**.	*The duties of a citizen are demanding.*
Conducir velozmente puede ser **fatal**.	*Driving too fast can be fatal.*
Su melodioso cantar deleita a los pacientes.	*His/her delightful singing pleases the patients.*
Errar es **humano**.	*To err is human.*

- The English present participle (the *-ing* ending), which appears in some of the previous example translations, is frequently used to translate the Spanish infinitive (**-ar**, **-er**, or **-ir**). In English, both the infinitive and the present participle can function as nouns (according to certain rules); in Spanish, the present participle is *never* used as a noun.
- In Spanish, infinitives that refer to actions can be the *subject* of a sentence. Spanish infinitives can also be the *object* of a verb or a predicate nominative, as in the following examples:

¿Te gusta **correr**?   *Do you like **to run**?*
¿Prefiere **trabajar** y no **estudiar**?   *He/she prefers **to work** and not **to study**?*
Es un placer **conocerlo/la**.   *It is a pleasure **to meet you**.*

♦ Split infinitives are possible in Spanish. In English, an infinitive can be split for clarification, although such constructions are often restricted to proverbs and sayings:

... **para verdaderamente saber** la verdad . . . *to truly know the truth*

♦ The infinitive of **haber** (the auxiliary verb in compound tenses) may be combined with a past participle and used as a noun, with or without an article or an adjective. This construction may function as the subject or as the direct object of the main verb or in a subordinate clause. Note the English equivalent, which uses the present participle (or *gerund*, *-ing* form) of *to have*, followed by a past participle or a conjugated form:

El haber aprendido chino me ayudará   *Having learned Chinese will help me to get*
a conseguir esa plaza.   *the position.*
No creo **haber conocido** a ese chico.   *I do not think **I have met** that young man.*

EJERCICIO
15·32

Los beneficios de los deportes. *Translate into Spanish.*

1. Walking is healthy.

   _____

2. Swimming improves your (**el**) appetite.

   _____

3. Running burns a lot of calories.

   _____

4. Playing golf is very relaxing.

   _____

5. Rowing can be hard.

   _____

6. Climbing a mountain is not my favorite activity.

   _____

7. Dancing is almost a sport.

   _____

8. But sleeping is my favorite activity.

   _____

Build each sentence using the infinitive as the subject.

1. no mejora (*improve*) / en exceso / comer y beber / la salud

_____

2. un concierto / a / de música / inspira / a / concierto / personas / muchas / asistir / clásica

_____

3. mensajes / amigos / con / nuestros / email / por / compartir / comunica / nos

_____

4. fortuna / una / invertir / en / la / bolsa / fortuna / aumentar / dinero / puede

_____

5. satisface / contribuir / electoral / una / los / campaña / a / ciudadanos / los / a

_____

6. mérito / tiene / a / desamparados / los / ayudar

_____

EJERCICIO
15·34

Complete each sentence with the article **el** *(if needed) + the infinitive from the list.*

dormir / comer y charlar / trabajar / ahorrar / perder / leer

1. Me encanta _____ el periódico los domingos por la mañana. No tiene

sentido 2. _____ toda la mañana. Además, 3. _____ en

exceso me cansa mucho. 4. Me enoja (*annoys*) _____ cuando juego al tenis.

5. _____ para el futuro, es prudente. 6. Eso sí, _____

con mis amigos me relaja.

Prepositions placed before infinitives

In Spanish, the only form of a verb used after a *preposition* is the infinitive. In English, the present participle (*-ing* form) is used after prepositions. A number of prepositions and prepositional phrases may precede the infinitive in Spanish:

a	*to, at*
al (a + el)	*upon, on*
a condición de	*provided that*
antes de	*before*
después de	*after*
en lugar de	*instead of*

en vez de	instead of
para	in order to
por miedo de	for fear that
por	because of
sin	without

Note that in this construction, the main verb and the following infinitive have the same subject. When the subjects of the two clauses are different, you will need to use the conjunction **que** + a *subjunctive* verb form. (You will learn or review the subjunctive in Chapters 19 and 21.)

main verb + preposition + infinitive

Se levantó + **después de** + tomar el café.	*He got up **after** having coffee.*
Lávate las manos **antes de** comer.	*Wash your hands **before** you eat.*
Descansa **después de** cenar.	*Rest **after** you eat your dinner.*
Estudia **en vez de** dormir.	*Study **instead of** sleeping.*
Me dejó su auto **a condición de** cuidar al perro.	*He lent me his car **provided that** I take care of the dog.*
Salió temprano **por miedo a** perder el avión.	*She left early **for fear (that)** she might miss her flight.*

The following examples are infinitive clauses that cannot stand alone but complete the meaning of the main clause, preceding or following it. An infinitive clause ends with a comma when it precedes the main clause.

| **Para conducir**, necesitas un carnet vigente. | ***In order to drive**, you need a valid license.* |
| **Sin saber la verdad**, acusó a un inocente. | ***Without knowing the truth**, she accused an innocent person.* |

The contraction al + the infinitive

The contraction **al** is made up of the preposition **a** plus the masculine definite article **el: a** + **el** = **al**. The construction **al** + *infinitive* indicates an action or state that is happening at a certain time, present, past, or future. The English equivalent is:

al + infinitive → upon or when + the -ing form of a verb

Vi a Ramona **al llegar** al supermercado.	*I saw Ramona **when I got** to (**upon arriving** at) the supermarket.*
Al salir de casa, te llamo.	***When I leave** (**upon leaving**) the house, I will call you.*
Al entrar, saluda; **al salir**, despídete.	***On entering**, say hello; **upon leaving**, say good-bye.*
Encontramos un perrito **al pasear** por el parque.	*We found a puppy **when (we were) strolling** in the park.*

The most frequently used English equivalent for **al** + *infinitive* in everyday language is *when*. Note that the comma is necessary when the infinitive clause with **al** precedes the main clause in Spanish.

EJERCICIO 15·35

La rutina de mi hermana. *Build each sentence with a preposition + an infinitive. Use the preterit form of the verb and appropriate punctuation.*

1. al / despertarse / mi hermana / llamar por teléfono / a su amiga Loli

2. en vez de / preparar / el desayuno / perder / mucho tiempo

_____

3. antes de / salir / a su trabajo / no apagar / la cafetera

_____

4. en lugar de / ayudar / en la casa / complicar / mi situación

_____

5. sin / despedirse / de mí / salir / de casa

_____

6. después de / llegar / a la oficina / llamar / a mi madre

_____

Los políticos y sus campañas. *Build your own sentences based on your opinion about politicians. Use a preposition + infinitive.*

prometer / mentir / persuadir / construir / engañar / ayudar / recibir

MODELO   después de ganar

   Después de ganar las elecciones, se olvidan de sus promesas.

   or *Se olvidan de sus promesas después de ganar las elecciones.*

1. al empezar

_____

2. en vez de

_____

3. después de

_____

4. por miedo de

_____

5. a pesar de

_____

6. sin

_____

7. para

_____

8. en vez de

_____

Infinitives after verbs

In Spanish and English, there are many verbs that may be directly followed by an infinitive. They can be grouped into verbs of *perception*, *emotion*, *want*, *possibility*, and *movement*, and verbs that emphasize the effect of an action.

Infinitives after verbs of *want, likes and dislikes, opinion, obligation,* and *appearance*

Infinitives are used after the following verbs:

Verbs of want, likes and dislikes

desear	*to desire*
detestar	*to dislike, to detest*
encantar	*to adore, to love*
exigir	*to demand*
gustar	*to like*
querer	*to want*

Susi **prefiere esperar** el autobús.	*Susi **prefers to wait** for the bus.*
Nos **encanta cocinar**.	*We **love to cook**.*
Tú **exiges terminar** con el abuso.	*You **demand to end (an end to)** the abuse.*
Ellos **quieren ir** a Puerto Rico.	*They **want to go** to Puerto Rico.*
Me **gustaría perder** un poquito de peso.	*I **would like to lose** a little weight.*
¿**Te gustaría hacerte** médico?	***Would you like to become** a doctor?*

In the previous examples, the subject of the verb in the infinitive clause is the *same* as the subject—the conjugated verb—of the main clause.

EJERCICIO
15·37

Te toca a ti. *Answer each question according to your opinion. Use the appropriate form of the main verb + the infinitive. Follow the **modelo**.*

MODELO ¿Qué te gusta hacer en tu tiempo libre?

   Me gusta descansar y conversar con mis amigos por teléfono o chatear por Internet.

1. ¿Qué deseas lograr (*accomplish*) en los próximos dos meses?

_____

2. ¿Qué quieres estudiar en el futuro?

_____

3. En tu opinión, ¿qué prefieren hacer los jóvenes?

_____

4. ¿Qué exigen los hijos de sus padres hoy en día?

_____

5. ¿Qué te encanta hacer en tu tiempo libre?

_____

6. ¿Qué detestas, por encima de (*above*) todo?

_____

EJERCICIO
15·38

*For each question read the answer first. Use the present tense form **Ud.** of the main verb +
infinitive.*

MODELO   Deseamos viajar a China estas vacaciones.

qué   *¿Qué desean hacer estas vacaciones?*

1. Prefiero tomar un taxi yo sola al salir del trabajo.

   qué _____

2. Necesito llegar al aeropuerto a las diez en punto.

   a qué hora _____

3. Quiero hacer escala (*stopover*) en Japón antes de llegar a China.

   dónde _____

4. Necesito facturar estas maletas y también estos paquetes.

   qué _____

5. Bueno, me gustaría ir a Corea y Tailandia.

   adónde _____

6. En mi próximo viaje, preferiría viajar con mis amigos al Himalaya.

   con quién _____

Infinitive after verbs of perception

A simple infinitive clause can be used after a verb of *perception*:

ver	*to see*
escuchar	*to listen*

mirar	to watch, to see
oír	to hear
sentir	to feel

Note the word order in the following Spanish and English infinitive clauses. There are two possible word orders for the Spanish infinitive clause, but only one in English.

Veo **el tren salir**.	I see **the train leave/leaving**.
Veo **salir el tren**.	I see **the train leave/leaving**.
Oigo **a los pájaros cantar**.	I hear **birds sing/singing**.
Oigo **cantar a los pájaros**.	I hear **birds sing/singing**.

Also note above that the English equivalent can be in the present tense or the present participle (-*ing* form).

Infinitive after verbs of movement

Infinitives are used after conjugated verbs of movement. The preposition **a**, **de**, or **por** usually follows the verb of movement:

ir a	to go
comenzar a	to start, to begin
empezar	to begin, to start
ponerse a	to begin
volver a	to do (an activity) again
volver de	to return from
venir de	to come from
subir a	to go up
bajar a	to go down
salir de, a, por, etc.	to go out, exit
Voy a comprar una botella de vino.	**I am going to buy** a bottle of wine.
Venimos a cenar contigo.	**We are coming to dine** with you.
Salgo a buscar los vasos en la terraza.	**I am going to get / look for** the drinking glasses on the terrace.
Bajaré a abrir la puerta a los invitados.	**I will go down to open** the door for the guests.

EJERCICIO
15·39

En español. *Use the infinitive.*

1. I saw the plane landing (**aterrizar**).

_____

2. We heard the agent greeting the passengers.

_____

3. Mary started to get ready to receive her family.

_____

4. She went to ask for a wheelchair.

_____

5. Luis started (**empezar**) to look for the suitcases.

_____

6. The children started (**ponerse**) crying when they woke up.

_____

7. Then Luis heard his cell phone ringing.

_____

8. He heard a familiar voice speaking.

_____

9. Then he saw his sister coming.

_____

10. Finally, they all went looking for their car.

_____

Other verbs followed by the infinitive

An infinitive is used after verbs that express authority or influence:

hacer, hacer(se)	to make (someone do something)
dejar	to allow
mandar	to order
impedir	to stop, not to allow
permitir	to allow
prohibir	to forbid
Fernanda **se hizo construir** una piscina.	Fernanda **had** a pool **built**.
Ahora **hace nadar** a sus hijos.	Now she is **making / having** her children **swim**.
Mañana, **hará organizar** los armarios.	Tomorrow she will **make / have someone organize** her closets.

Note below the use of the infinitive after **dejar** (*to allow*), **permitir** (*to let, to allow*), **atreverse a** (*to dare*), and **intentar** (*to try*):

¡**No dejes caer** la torta!	***Do not drop** the cake!*
¡Ay, no! **Dejaste quemar** la carne.	*Oh, no! **You let** the meat **burn**.*
No te atrevas a servirla a los invitados.	***Do not dare (to)** serve it to the guests.*

Infinitives also follow verbs of influence: a verb of *allowing, influencing, prohibiting,* or *obliging*—and similar verbs, such as those involving *requests*—can be followed by an infinitive that represents the action of someone other than the subject of the main verb. An *indirect object* is used to indicate who was asked to perform (or not perform) the action. The indirect object can be *a noun* or *an indirect object pronoun*. These sentences are similar in structure to their English equivalents:

María **me** dejó entrar.	*María allowed **me** to enter.*
Les mandamos escribir la carta.	*We required **them** to write the letter.*
Te prohíbo salir antes de las diez.	*I forbid **you** to leave before ten.*
Lidia **me** hace trabajar en casa.	*Lidia makes **me** work at home.*

Un misterio. *Read the question and give the answer using the verb in parentheses.*

MODELO   ¿<u>Escuchaste</u> la noticia?

(permitir) No, el ruido <u>*no me permitió escuchar la noticia*</u>.

1. ¿<u>Escapó</u> el criminal?

   (dejar) No, la policía _____.

2. ¿El teniente <u>hizo</u> una investigación?

   (mandar) No, el capitán _____.

3. ¿<u>Visitaste</u> a la víctima en el hospital?

   (permitir) No, su familia no _____.

4. ¿<u>Llegaron</u> los periodistas al salón?

   (prohibir) No, los sicólogos _____.

5. ¿<u>Revelaron</u> el nombre de la víctima?

   (dejar) No, las autoridades _____.

6. ¿<u>Llegaron</u> ustedes a recepción en el hospital?

   (impedir) No, un guardia _____.

Infinitives after impersonal expressions

Infinitives are used after *impersonal expressions*. Impersonal sentences do not have a specific subject or person in the main clause. Most impersonal expressions consist of a form of **ser** in the third-person singular, followed by an adjective:

Es aconsejable	*It is advisable to*
Es bueno	*It is good to*
Es importante	*It is important to*
Es imposible	*It is impossible to*
Es indispensable	*It is indispensable to*
Es justo	*It is fair to*
Es malo	*It is bad to*
Es mejor	*It is better to*
Es necesario	*It is necessary to*
Es posible	*It is possible to*
Es preciso	*It is necessary to*
Es preferible	*It is better to*

Impersonal constructions are used to make suggestions and to give general instructions or commands. Note that some of the examples include other elements after the infinitive. English has similar constructions:

Es importante beber mucha agua.	*It is important to drink a lot of water.*
Es bueno practicar deportes.	*It is good to participate in sports.*
Es necesario animar a los jóvenes.	*It is necessary to encourage young people.*
Es mejor no fumar ya en público.	*It is better to no longer smoke in public.*

The word order in this type of construction is flexible. In spoken English, an infinitive with *to* may start a sentence; in written English, starting a sentence with *to* + *infinitive* is usually avoided:

Bailar salsa es divertido.	*To dance (Dancing) salsa is fun.*
No cuidarse la salud es atroz.	*Not to take care of one's health is atrocious.*

Other impersonal expressions are:

Más vale	*It is better to*
Conviene	*It is advisable to*
En el futuro, **más vale evitar** problemas.	*In the future, **it is better to avoid** problems.*
Conviene estar listo para salir.	*It is advisable to be ready to leave.*

If impersonal expressions that communicate *uncertainty, doubt, conjecture, wishes, desires, requests, orders,* or other emotions are followed by a *different* subject, you will need to use the *subjunctive* in the subordinate clause:

impersonal expression + que + a subjunctive form

Es dudoso que el precio **baje.**	*It is doubtful that the price will go down.*

See Chapter 19 to review the use of impersonal expressions followed by the subjunctive.

EJERCICIO
15·41

Te toca a ti. *Build each sentence with an impersonal expression + an infinitve + your thoughts. Follow the* **modelo.**

MODELO   es aconsejable / invertir

Es aconsejable + invertir + en la bolsa de valores con prudencia.

Es aconsejable invertir en la bolsa de valores con prudencia.

1. es bueno / hacer una lista

_____

2. es beneficioso / tener fe

_____

3. es necesario / visualizar

_____

4. mas vale / enfrentar

_____

5. conviene / mantener

_____

6. es mejor / ser

_____

7. es malo / posponer

_____

8. es preferible / imaginar

_____

Infinitive to express the near future

Although it performs many functions as a noun, the infinitive still communicates the idea of an action. The future tense in Spanish is frequently replaced with a form of **ir** followed by the preposition **a** + the infinitive. In this construction, the time the infinitive communicates is *after* (= the future).

ir a + infinitive → action or event in the near future

Vamos a descansar en unos minutos.	*We **will rest** in a few minutes.*
Voy a terminar mis quehaceres.	*I **am going to finish** my chores.*

Note that the English equivalents include either a future tense or a form of *to be* and the gerund or present participle, *going*.

EJERCICIO
15·42

Para el futuro. *First, read the sentence; then, build each sentence with the appropriate form of the verb* **ir** + **a** + *infinitive.*

MODELO   Carlos fue de vacaciones a Europa hace dos años.

probablemente / este verano

Probablemente, Carlos va a ir a Japón este verano.

1. Luisa y Jaco salieron de compras a Nueva York el invierno pasado.

seguramente / el año que viene

_____

2. Miranda y Alejandro no quisieron acompañar a sus padres la semana pasada.

tal vez / la próxima vez

_____

3. Mis sobrinos compitieron en el torneo de golf la primavera pasada.

afortunadamente / este año

_____

4. Cati y Luisa se entrenaron para participar en los Juegos Panamericanos en 1999.

con toda certeza, no / en el futuro

_____

5. Mis hermanos asistieron a la Fiesta de San Fermín hace dos años.

desgraciadamente no / nunca más

_____

6. Tú y yo no nos comunicamos por email desde hace dos años.

desde ahora / con más frecuencia

_____

Building sentences with coordinating conjunctions

A coordinating conjunction connects two words, two phrases, or two clauses. By definition, a *clause* is a group of words containing a subject and a predicate that functions as *part of another sentence*. In this unit, we will build sentences that consist of more than one clause, joined by coordinating conjunctions.

The clause usually consists of a subject followed by a verb, but other elements may be included. If you can understand the idea presented, if the utterance communicates a complete thought and does not depend on any other elements to complete an idea or thought, it is an *independent* clause.

subject + predicate → sentence = independent clause

Each of the following examples of Spanish clauses includes a subject and a verb; each one makes complete sense when it stands alone. Remember that in Spanish the subject is usually understood by the ending of the verb:

Los candidatos no lleg**aron**.	*The candidates did not arrive.*
Viajar**emos** a Buenos Aires.	*We will travel to Buenos Aires.*
¡Termin**en** ahora!	*Finish now!*

The most common coordinating conjunctions are:

y, e	*and*
ni	*nor*
ni... ni	*neither . . . nor*
pero	*but, yet*
sino	*but*
o, u	*or*

Remember that **y** (*and*) changes to **e** when followed by a word that starts with the vowel sounds **i-** and **hi-**:

Luisa **e** Irene son hermanas.	*Luisa **and** Irene are sisters.*
Sofía **e** Hilario son primos.	*Sofía **and** Hilario are cousins.*

Note that **u**, not **o** (*or*), is used when the word following starts with the vowel sounds **o-** and **ho-**:

¿Tienes siete **u** ocho hermanas?   *Do you have seven **or** eight sisters?*

Building sentences with coordinating conjunctions

Coordinating conjunctions can join two or more independent clauses. The result is a *compound sentence*, which means that the new sentence is the result of the combination of separate, independent elements.

> **independent clause + conjunction + independent clause**
>
> Luis juega al fútbol + **y** + Jorge juega al tenis.
> *Luis plays soccer **and** Jorge plays tennis.*

The typical word order for declarative, interrogative, or imperative sentences is used in the clauses that surround a coordinating conjunction:

El Dr. Mena es cardiólogo **y** la Dra. Manfredi es inmunóloga.	*Dr. Mena is a cardiologist **and** Dr. Manfredi is an immunologist.*
¿Quieres descansar **o** quieres ir de compras?	*Do you want to rest **or** do you want to go shopping?*
Devuelve los zapatos **y** regresa a casa inmediatamente.	*Return the shoes **and** come back home immediately.*

In previous units you built *sentences*: affirmative and negative sentences, direct questions, imperatives, and exclamatory sentences. They resemble the examples below:

Me levanto a las cinco todos los días.	*I get up at five o'clock every day.*
Los fines de semana no trabajo.	*On weekends I do not work.*
Salgo de compras.	*I go shopping.*
Regreso al mediodía.	*I come back at noon.*
Quiero un vestido nuevo.	*I want a new dress.*
No tengo mucho dinero.	*I do not have much money.*
¡Préstame el dinero!	*Lend me the money!*
No voy a la fiesta.	*I am not going to the party.*

Coordinating conjunctions can be used to join the simple sentences you just read. Independent clauses are linked with coordinating conjunctions to create longer sentences, each balanced in length:

Me levanto a las cinco todos los días, **pero** los fines de semana no trabajo.	*I get up at five o'clock every day, **but** I do not work on weekends.*
Salgo de compras **y** regreso al mediodía.	*I go out shopping **and** return at noon.*
Quiero un vestido nuevo, **pero** no tengo mucho dinero.	*I want a new dress, **but** I do not have a lot of money.*
¡Préstame el dinero **o** no voy a la fiesta!	*Lend me the money **or** I will not go to the party!*

A comma may be used in Spanish to mark the two clauses when combining sentences with these conjunctions. The comma can be placed *before* **y**, **e**, and **ni**, but only if you need to avoid confusion when linking the two clauses:

Mi jefe trabaja mucho, **y** el descanso le parece absurdo.	*My boss works hard, **and** he thinks resting is absurd.*

Join two independent sentences with the appropriate coordinating conjunction in parentheses.

1. (y / ni) Fui a casa de Laura. Jugué con su perro.

_____

2. (y / pero) Yo quería cenar con ella. Laura tenía una cita con el dentista.

_____

3. (pero / o) Laura no faltará (*miss*) a la cita. No le gusta ir al dentista.

_____

4. (ni / o) Laura no come de día. Duerme por la noche.

_____

5. (sino / o) Va al dentista. Tomará calmantes por mucho tiempo.

_____

6. (o / pero) Tengo mucha paciencia. Laura me enoja (*annoys*).

_____

7. (pero / y) Es una linda persona. Es muy indecisa.

_____

8. (y / o) Regresé a casa. Cené solo.

_____

Omitting the subject and the verb in the second clause

In Spanish, as in English, when the subject of both the first and second clause is the same, it is frequently omitted:

Bertina cerró los ojos y no vio el accidente.	*Bertina closed her eyes and did not see the accident.*
El detective concluyó la investigación y se fue.	*The detective concluded the investigation and left.*

For different reasons, it is also possible to omit the verb of the second clause: for the sake of brevity, to balance the sentence, or as a simple matter of style:

Ni tiene trabajo ni dinero.	*He/she does not have a job or money.*
Se despide de mí y de sus amigos.	*He/she says good-bye to me and his/her friends.*
Preparo una paella de mariscos u otro plato.	*I prepare a seafood paella or another dish.*

EJERCICIO
15·44

Indicate the unnecessary subjects or verbs and reword the sentence. Follow the **modelo**.

MODELO   Fernando y Rosa compraron una casa y <u>ellos</u> vendieron su auto viejo.
        Fernando y Rosa compraron una casa y vendieron su auto viejo.

1. Alicia y yo limpiamos la casa los sábados y los domingos nosotras cenamos con mis padres.

2. Yo no como carne ni como pollo.

3. Alicia prepara la ensalada de lechuga con aguacate y prepara la limonada.

4. Mis padres invitan a mis primos o invitan a sus amigos, los López.

5. A veces, nosotros tomamos una copa de vino o nosotros bebemos un vaso de cerveza.

6. Nos gusta un café con el postre o nos gusta un té de camomila.

7. Después, Alicia y su novio dan un paseo por la ciudad o ellos dan un paseo por la playa.

8. Los domingos no son días buenos ni son días malos.

9. Los domingos yo ceno con mis padres pero yo prefiero una cena con mis primos.

10. Mis primos van al cine conmigo o van al "Café Nostalgia".

Spanish coordinating conjunctions and their functions

At the beginning of this unit you reviewed common coordinating conjunctions. Get acquainted with their use and focus on the message each one communicates, and you will be able to use them correctly as you build sentences in Spanish.

◆ **Y, e** (*and*), and **ni** (*neither, nor*) join independent clauses:

    Marisa canta y yo bailo.   *Marisa sings **and** I dance.*

◆ **O** or **u** (*or*) link independent clauses that exclude each other:

    Loli camina **o** nada en la piscina.   *Loli takes a walk **or** swims in the pool.*

- **Pero** expresses opposition or contrast:

  Estoy cansada, **pero** terminaré la tarea.   *I am tired **but** I will finish the homework.*

- **Ni** (*neither, nor*) means **y no**. It joins two negative independent clauses. For emphasis, **ni** may precede each clause:

  No dormí **ni** estudié.   *I **did not** sleep **or** study. (I neither slept nor studied.)*

  Ni dormí **ni** estudié.   *I **did not** sleep **or** study. (I neither slept nor studied.)*

- **Sino** (*but, rather*) introduces an affirmative idea or concept in the second clause, which has been preceded by a negative idea in the first clause:

  No peleó Pedro **sino** Juan.   *Pedro **did not** fight, Juan **did**.*

EJERCICIO 15·45

Usa la lógica. *Build each sentence with the correct word order.*

1. y / la escritora / su novela / llegó / la oficina / a / se sentó / a / escribir

   _____

2. el / final / escribió / capítulo / pero / no / gustó / le

   _____

3. escribió / otro / muy / capítulo / aburrido / pero / resultó

   _____

4. o / el comienzo / cambiaba / o / el / sería / final / imposible

   _____

5. y / no / ideas / tenía / salió / de / oficina / la

   _____

6. no / ganas / escribir / tenía / de / ni / buscar / más / de / ideas

   _____

7. de / salió / la / oficina / y / fue / librería / a / la

   _____

8. se / en / sentó / una / café / silla / y / un / tomó

   _____

9. la / observó / gente / a / alrededor / su / a / el / inició / capítulo / e

   _____

10. la / autora / inteligente / era / y / el / terminar / capítulo / logró

    _____

Build a new sentence by combining the sentences with the appropriate coordinating conjunction.

o / pero / sino / ni / y

1. Bailas muy bien. Tocas la guitarra mejor.

   _____

2. No habla. No llora.

   _____

3. Entras. Sales.

   _____

4. No eres amable con tus colegas. Tampoco eres cortés con tus amigos.

   _____

5. Es muy caro. Tengo dinero suficiente.

   _____

6. No cerraron la tienda a las nueve. A las diez.

   _____

7. Viajaremos por las montañas. Luego por la costa.

   _____

8. Llévame al aeropuerto ahora. Pierdo mi vuelo a Arizona.

   _____

9. Me gusta esta novela. Es muy larga.

   _____

Punctuation of sentences with more than two independent clauses

In Spanish, a comma is usually not needed with the coordinating conjunctions **y**, **e**, and **ni**. However, when a sentence includes more than two independent clauses, the coordinating conjunction usually precedes the last clause, and a comma separates the previous clauses. Some styles *in English* also include a comma before the conjunction.

independent clause 1 + comma + independent clause 2 + conjunction + independent clause 3 → sentence

Nos levantamos, fuimos al correo **y** regresamos.	*We got up, went to the post office, **and** came back.*
Corro**,** hago gimnasia olímpica **y** levanto pesas.	*I run, practice gymnastics, **and** do weight training.*

Build a new sentence using the conjunction in parentheses. Use a comma if needed.

1. Mi amiga y yo iremos al cine. Compraremos las entradas.

   (y) _____

2. No nos gustan las películas de horror. No preferimos las películas muy dramáticas.

   (ni) _____

3. No llueve mucho. Date prisa.

   (pero) _____

4. Tenemos poco dinero. Tenemos muchas deudas. Nuestro apartamento es muy caro.

   (y) _____

5. Ahorramos (*we save*) mucho. No somos tacaños (*stingy*).

   (pero) _____

6. O ganamos más dinero. Pedimos un aumento de sueldo. Buscamos otro trabajo.

   (o) _____

7. No somos ambiciosos. Cautelosos.

   (sino) _____

8. Somos jóvenes. Tenemos el futuro por delante.

   (y) _____

Building sentences with subordinating conjunctions

Another element to consider when building a complex sentence is the *subordinating conjunction*. A subordinating conjunction links a clause to a *main clause*. A main clause always includes a subject and a verb. The main clause makes complete sense when it stands alone. However, more elements may be needed to add information to such a sentence, with the help of a subordinating conjunction. Subordinating conjunctions introduce *dependent clauses* that cannot stand alone. A dependent clause, also called a *subordinate clause*, depends on the main clause to communicate its full meaning.

main clause + subordinating conjunction + dependent clause → sentence

In the following example, the subordinating conjunction **aunque** (*although*) introduces a subordinate clause. Note that the idea presented in this clause is incomplete:

Aunque tengo miedo.   *Although I am afraid.*

Adding the dependent clause, as follows, to an independent (main) clause results in a complete, complex sentence with a clearer meaning:

| Aunque tengo miedo, **volaré a Cancún**. | *Although I am afraid, **I will fly to Cancún**.* |

The subordinate clause and the main clause may be separated by a comma. The elements or building blocks of a sentence with a subordinate conjunction can be placed in either order:

main clause + subordinating conjunction + clause

Volaré a Cancún, + **aunque** + tengo miedo.

subordinating conjunction + clause + main clause

Aunque + tengo miedo + volaré a Cancún.

Spanish subordinating conjunctions and their functions

A conjunction is a word or a group of words that connect or join parts of a sentence, clauses, or full sentences. A *subordinating conjunction* is placed at the beginning of the clause it introduces. There are a number of subordinating conjunctions. They indicate the nature of the relationship between the main clause and the subordinate clause, such as time, cause, effect, or condition. Some of these clauses behave like adverbs; they are called *adverbial clauses*. Here are some of the most frequently used conjunctions and their relationship to the main clause:

◆ Time

cuando *when*
Juan me llama todos los días **cuando** llega a casa.

*Juan calls me every day **when** he gets home.*

desde que *once*
Desde que empieza el verano, se van a la casa de la playa.

Once summer begins, they go to their beach house.

después (de) que *after, once*
Después que entro, saludo a mis colegas.

After I get in, I greet my colleagues.

hasta que *until, by the time*
Ana me espera todos los días **hasta que** termino mi trabajo.

*Ana waits for me every day **until** I finish work.*

siempre que *whenever*
Ayudo a mis hermanos **siempre que** puedo.

*I help my brothers **whenever** I can.*

◆ Cause and effect

como *because, since*
Como es muy violento, no veo este programa.

***Because** it is very violent, I do not watch this program.*

de modo que *so*
Lucas perdió el partido, **de modo que** pagaré la apuesta.

*Lucas lost the match, **so** now I will pay the bet.*

porque *because*
Salgo ahora mismo **porque** llevo prisa.

*I am leaving right now, **because** I am in a hurry.*

puesto que *since*
Puesto que no tienen dinero, no van de vacaciones.

Since they have no money, they are not going on vacation.

ya que *because, since*
Ya que estás aquí, voy a ayudarte con la tarea.

Since you are here, I will help you with your homework.

◆ Condition

si *if*
Si Uds. están en el museo, iré con mi novio.

If you are at the museum, I will go with my boyfriend.

◆ A difficulty, a concession

aunque *although, even though*
Aunque tiene novia, Felipe no quiere casarse.

Although he has a girlfriend, Felipe does not want to get married.

por más que *even though*
Por más que trabajo duro, no gano mucho dinero.

Even though I work hard, I do not earn a lot of money.

Note that the examples above include a main clause in the indicative mood that states a fact, a certainty, or a good probability; the verb in the dependent clause is also in the indicative.

Another frequently used subordinate conjunction, **que** (*that*), introduces a clause that functions as a direct object of the main clause:

Tomasina dice **que** aprobó el examen de conducir.

*Tomasina says (**that**) she passed the driving test.*

Mi padre sabía **que** yo estaba en Venezuela.

*My father knew (**that**) I was in Venezuela.*

In English, for reasons of style, the conjunction *that* may be omitted. Its presence or absence does not affect the meaning of the sentence. Note that the conjunction **que** cannot be omitted in Spanish.

EJERCICIO
15·48

¿Cuál es la conjunción adecuada? *Complete each sentence with the appropriate conjunction.*

porque / desde que / después que / aunque / si / por más que / ya que / que

1. Antonia es muy tacaña (*stingy*), _____ a veces nos sorprende su generosidad.

2. No compró la chaqueta _____ no le ofrecieron un descuento.

3. _____ se probó varios vestidos, ¡no compró nada!

4. _____ Antonia no cambia su manera de ser, no iré de compras con ella.

5. _____ me gusta salir de casa, no tengo paciencia para ir de compras con Antonia.

6. Antonia ha sido tacaña siempre, _____ era una niña.

7. Estoy convencida de _____ será siempre igual.

8. _____ hablamos de Antonia, ahora sabes que soy chismosa.

Complete each sentence with the appropriate conjunction.

MODELO   (cuando / ya que) ... no vienes conmigo, voy a salir al jardín.
Ya que no vienes conmigo, voy a salir al jardín.

1. (después que / aunque) Necesito trabajar en mi jardín... llueve mucho.

_____

2. (aunque / ya que) Tengo unos guantes... quiero proteger mis manos.

_____

3. (si / después que) ... me pongo los guantes, me pongo mi sombrero.

_____

4. (aunque / si) Tomaremos una limonada... tienes sed.

_____

5. (cuando / desde que) ... empecé a trabajar en el jardín, he rebajado doce libras de peso.

_____

6. (como / desde que) ... tengo mucha paciencia, trabajo lento, despacio.

_____

7. (puesto que / aunque) ... quieres limonada, voy a cortar los limones de mi jardín.

_____

8. (aunque / ya que) Necesitamos hielo ... quieres tomar la limonada fría.

_____

Complete each sentence with your own phrase.

MODELO   Ellos viajarán al espacio porque (confiar) ___confían en los científicos___ .

1. Doce españoles viajarán al espacio porque (ser) _____.

2. Una agencia prepara el viaje porque (querer) _____.

3. Tenemos interés en este viaje ya que (pensar) _____.

4. Como (tú) (tener dinero) _____, no puedes ir al espacio.

5. Los viajeros preparan este viaje que (ofrecer) _____.

6. Si tú (tener) _____ puedes comprar tu billete por $150.000.

7. Aunque (parecer) _____, esta aventura atrae a mucha gente.

8. Es fácil creer esta noticia si (nosotros) (creer) _____.

9. Aunque (los turistas) (estar listos) _____, nos sabemos la fecha de salida.

10. Sueña con un viaje a las estrellas si (tú) (confiar) _____.

Indicative mood in the dependent clause

The verb in the main clause establishes the subject's attitude or mood. In turn, that attitude or mood determines the mood of the verb in the dependent clause. A main clause with a verb that states a fact, a certainty, or a good probability requires the indicative mood in the dependent clause. Note that an adjective such as **seguro** (*sure*) or an adverb, **jamás** (*never, ever*) that leaves no doubt, may appear in the main clause, helping you determine the correct mood for the dependent clause.

In the following examples, the verb in the main clause indicates certainty or probability; thus, the verb in the dependent clause introduced by the conjunction **que** is in the *indicative*. The verb in the dependent clause can be in various tenses of the indicative mood, as required by the context.

Sé **que la Tierra no es el centro del universo**.	*I know **the Earth is not the center of the universe**.*
Se dice **que descubrieron nuevos planetas**.	*They say **they have discovered new planets**.*
Los astrónomos afirman **que se parecen a la Tierra**.	*The astronomers state **that they resemble the Earth**.*
Los pesimistas creen **que jamás llegaremos a Marte**.	*Pessimists think **that we will never get to Mars**.*

Note that the slightest hint of doubt or uncertainty in the main clause requires a *subjunctive* form in the dependent clause:

Dudamos **que el alcalde sea reelegido**.	*We doubt **that the mayor will be reelected**.*

In Chapter 19 you will study more about the subjunctive mood in dependent clauses.

EJERCICIO
15·51

El pronóstico optimista del tiempo. *Complete each sentence in Spanish.*

1. ¡Dios mío! Se anuncia... (*that there will be a snowstorm*).

_____

2. Mi esposo dice... (*that it already snowed a lot during the night*).

_____

3. Yo sé... (*that in winter this is possible*).

_____

4. Creo... (*that we will be able to drive up the mountain*).

_____

5. Pienso... (*that it will be a great day for skiing*).

_____

6. Ah, otro boletín de "El tiempo" dice... (*that the weather conditions are ideal for winter sports*).

_____

7. Sabía... (*that it was going to be a beautiful day*).

_____

8. Mi marido sabe... (*that I am an optimist*).

_____

9. Lo cierto es... (*that I love* [**me encantar**] *snow*).

_____

10. Me siento feliz... (*when I am in a cold place*).

_____

EJERCICIO
15·52

Tu futuro y las condiciones. *Use the indicative future tense + the indicative present tense in the* **yo** *form.*

MODELO   (ser) trilingüe si (estudiar) portugués y español
                Seré trilingüe si estudio portugués y español.

1. (ganar) mucho más dinero si (trabajar) más horas

_____

2. (terminar) mi máster si (tomar) dos cursos en línea este semestre

_____

3. (casarme) en agosto de este año si (convencer) a mi novia

_____

4. (viajar) a Buenos Aires si (ganar) el premio gordo

_____

5. (conseguir) mis metas (*goals*) si (tener) claros mis objetivos

_____

6. (tener) el apoyo de mi familia si (necesitar) ayuda en algún momento

_____

7. (comprar) un apartamento si (tener) un aumento de sueldo

_____

8. (visitar) a mis amigos si (poder) conseguir un billete a buen precio

_____

9. (ir) a Brasil si (aprender) suficiente portugués para hablar con la gente

_____

10. (aumentar) mi fortuna si (invertir) el dinero de manera sensata

_____

Using interrogatives to build subordinate clauses

In Chapter 9 you practiced building interrogative sentences, the word order of interrogatives, and how to answer questions. Now you can use some of that information to build subordinate sentences. Let's start with *yes/no* questions:

¿Está Lucía contigo?	*Is Lucia with you?*
Sí, está conmigo.	*Yes, she is with me.*
No, no está conmigo.	*No, she is not with me.*

Si (*if, whether*) is a subordinating conjunction. A possible answer to a question can be built with **si** as the subordinating conjunction. Note that the adverb **sí** (*yes*) has an accent mark.

¿Tiene Lucía una cita hoy?	*Does Lucia have an appointment today?*
No sé **si** Lucía tiene una cita hoy.	*I don't know if (**whether**) Lucía has an appointment today.*
¿Hay peras y manzanas maduras (*ripe*)?	*Are there any ripe pears and apples?*
No sé **si** hay peras y manzanas maduras.	*I do not know **whether** there are ripe pears and apples.*

Using interrogative words to build subordinate clauses

Interrogative pronouns (**quién**, **cuál**, etc.), adverbs (**dónde**, **adónde**, **cuándo**), and other interrogative words can function as subordinating conjunctions. Here is a quick review of interrogative words:

¿Cómo?	How?
¿Cuál?, ¿Cuáles?	Which?
¿Cuándo?	When?
¿Cuánto?, ¿Cuánta?	How much?
¿Cuántos?, ¿Cuántas?	How many?
¿Dónde?	Where?
¿Adónde?	Where (to)?
¿Por qué?	Why?
¿Qué?	What?
¿Quién?, ¿Quiénes?	Who?
¿A quién?, ¿A quiénes?	(To) Whom?

These words are used to create direct questions with question marks. They are also used without question marks, but with an accent mark, in answers to introduce a *subordinating element*:

—¿**Quién** habla?	—**Who's** speaking?
—No sé **quién** habla.	—*I do not know **who** is speaking.*
—¿**A quién** le pertenece este abrigo?	—**Who(m)** does this coat belong to?
—Pregunta **a quién** le pertenece este abrigo.	—*Ask **to whom** this coat belongs.*
—¿**A qué hora** sale el tren a Madrid?	—***At what time*** does the train leave for Madrid?
—Dime **a qué hora** sale el tren.	—*Tell me **at what time** the train leaves.*

Note that interrogative words in answers retain the interrogative accent mark. When interrogative words function as subordinating conjunctions, the elements of the sentence follow the same order as do clauses with other subordinating conjunctions.

main clause + interrogative word + subordinate clause

No sabemos + quiénes + compraron los regalos.
We do not know who bought the gifts.

Note the use of the indicative mood in the dependent clause introduced by an interrogative adverb. Verb tenses may vary as required by the context:

Yo no sabía **cómo** llegar a tu casa.	*I did not know **how** to get to your house.*
Me preguntó **cuántas** llamadas recibiste ayer.	*He asked me **how many** calls you received yesterday.*
Queremos saber **quiénes** vendrán a la cena.	*We want to know **who** will attend the dinner.*
Explícame **por qué** te enojabas con frecuencia.	*Explain to me **why** you used to get angry so often.*
Pronto sabrán **adónde** iremos.	*Soon you will know **where** we will go.*

EJERCICIO
15·53

Complete each sentence with the appropriate interrogative word.

qué / dónde / quién / si / cómo / por qué / cuándo / quiénes

1. Me pregunto _____ ha llegado al estudio de televisión.

2. Voy a preguntar _____ se llama.

3. Ante todo, quiero que nos explique _____ ha llegado aquí.

4. Le pediré su autógrafo, _____ es una estrella del cine mexicano.

5. Voy a preguntarle _____ hace en esta ciudad.

6. Soy muy chismoso y me pregunto _____ se va a quedar esta noche.

7. Vamos a saber _____ se irá a Ciudad México, ¿tal vez mañana?

8. Ah, y tengo que saber _____ la acompañan.

EJERCICIO

15·54

En la estación de policía. *Answer each question using* **si** *if necessary.*

MODELO   ¿Qué hora es?

Dime ___*qué hora es*___ .

1. ¿Dónde están las joyas robadas?

   Nadie sabe _____.

2. ¿A qué hora llegarán los agentes?

   Me pregunto _____.

3. ¿Quién escribió la nota?

   No recordamos _____.

4. ¿Adónde llevaron a la víctima?

   Dime _____.

5. ¿Cuándo descubrieron el robo?

   Pregúntales _____.

6. ¿Por qué abandonaron la casa de la víctima?

   Ignoro _____.

7. ¿Cómo se llama la sospechosa?

   Nadie sabe con certeza _____.

8. ¿A quiénes vamos a interrogar después?

   Decide tú _____.

9. ¿Asignaron un especialista a este caso?

   Avíseme _____.

10. ¿Desde cuándo no hay un boletín de noticias?

    Olvidé _____.

The conditional tense

You probably have studied the conditional tense in Spanish. It is a simple tense: it does not need an auxiliary verb, unlike the English *would*, as the following examples show.

Carlos **estudiaría** varios idiomas.   *Carlos would study several languages.*

Yo **pintaría** las paredes con   *I would paint the walls with*
un color claro.   *a light color.*

Miguel y Marcos **perderían**   *Miguel y Marcos would miss*
el vuelo.   *the flight.*

Uses of the conditional tense

The conditional tense is used to express the following:

◆ A condition that would or might occur but has not yet been met

¿En qué estado de los EE.UU.   *In which state would you live*
vivirías?   *in the United States?*

Viviría en Texas porque me gusta   *I would live in Texas because*
la ciudad de San Antonio.   *I love San Antonio.*

◆ An action that would or might take place under certain circumstances or situations

Quizás Juan **estudiaría** alemán.   *Perhaps Juan might study German.*

No **compraría** este vestido aunque   *I would not buy this dress even*
me gusta.   *though I like it.*

Cocinaría en casa pero no tengo   *I would cook at home but I do not*
suficiente tiempo.   *have enough time.*

In the previous examples, the words **aunque** and **pero** are followed by the present tense to give an explanation—the reason why the action would or would not be completed. In some cases no reason is given: *I would not buy this dress even though I like it.*

Two reminders about translating the sense of *would* from English to Spanish:

◆ To convey the sense of *would* as *used to*, use the imperfect tense in Spanish.

Yo **corría** a menudo por el parque.   *I often used to run around the park.*

◆ If *would* indicates *to be willing, to want*, use the preterit tense of **querer**.

Luis no **quiso** correr hoy.   *Luis would not run today.*

Other uses of the conditional tense in Spanish are reviewed later in this chapter.

Regular verbs in the conditional tense

If you have reviewed Chapter 14 you will find that the future and the conditional tenses of all three conjugations have a lot in common: most verbs are regular, and the ending is added to the infinitive. The three conjugations have the same ending. Remember that all endings carry a written accent.

-**ar** verbs: -**ía**, -**ías**, -**ía**, -**íamos**, -**íais**, -**ían**

-**er** verbs: -**ía**, -**ías**, -**ía**, -**íamos**, -**íais**, -**ían**

-**ir** verbs: -**ía**, -**ías**, -**ía**, -**íamos**, -**íais**, -**ían**

Here are the full conjugations of the conditional tense.

hablar to *speak*	**comer** to *eat*	**abrir** to *open*
hablar**ía**	comer**ía**	abrir**ía**
hablar**ías**	comer**ías**	abrir**ías**
hablar**ía**	comer**ía**	abrir**ía**
hablar**íamos**	comer**íamos**	abrir**íamos**
hablar**íais**	comer**íais**	abrir**íais**
hablar**ían**	comer**ían**	abrir**ían**

Yo **vendería** mi casa pero me ofrecen muy poco dinero.

I would sell my house but they offer me very little money.

¿Dónde **compraríamos** la lavadora nueva?

Where would we buy the new washing machine?

Vivirías en un pueblo pequeño para disfrutar la belleza de la naturaleza.

You would live in a small town in order to enjoy the beauty of nature.

EJERCICIO
16·1

Y en tu caso, ¿verdadero (V) o falso (F)?

1. _____ Ahorraría más dinero para mi futuro.

2. _____ Pagaría la cena de todos mis amigos.

3. _____ Escribiría una novela histórica.

4. _____ Cambiaría mis costumbres, mis hábitos.

5. _____ Cantaría canciones mexicanas.

6. _____ Visitaría Colombia y Perú.

7. _____ Jugaría ajedrez con un amigo.

8. _____ Llegaría temprano a mi trabajo.

9. _____ Ayudaría a limpiar la casa.

10. _____ Bebería refrescos de dieta.

EJERCICIO
16·2

¿Qué pasaría? *Complete each sentence with the appropriate conditional tense form of the verb in parentheses.*

1. No _____ si la fecha es martes trece, un signo de mala suerte. (viajar, yo)

2. Somos perezosos, vagos, y _____ dormir hasta el mediodía. (preferir)

3. Mis amigas _____ a mi piso para tomar fotos de la ciudad. (subir)

4. Supongo que Uds. _____ juegos de mesa, ajedrez, parchís o dominó. (jugar)

5. Manolo y yo _____ los verbos irregulares del futuro y del condicional. (estudiar)

6. Los vecinos no _____ ruido. (oír)

7. Después Manolo _____ a nadar a la piscina aquí, en el edificio. (ir)

8. Yo no _____ más café si no puedo dormir por la noche. (beber)

9. ¿Y tú, _____ tacos con mucha salsa picante? (comer)

10. A Uds., yo les _____ ayuda para cocinar. (pedir)

EJERCICIO
16·3

Traducción. *Imagine you won one million dollars and a journalist asked you some questions. Use the **tú** form.*

1. Would you spend all the money?

_____

2. Or would you save ten percent at least?

_____

3. What would you buy for your home?

_____

4. Would you help your family?

   _____

5. Would you find another job?

   _____

6. Would you donate some of your money to help your community?

   _____

7. Would you enjoy (**disfrutar**) a few months at home?

   _____

8. Would you travel to other countries?

   _____

9. Would you like to ski in Colorado?

   _____

10. Would you invite your friends to travel with you?

   _____

Irregular verbs in the conditional tense

If you have reviewed the irregular verbs in the future tense in Chapter 14, you will find that the verbs that are irregular in the future are also irregular in the conditional. These verbs are grouped below according to the stem change. Note that the endings for all these verbs are the same throughout.

- ◆ The infinitive drops the **a**, **e**, or **i** from -**ar**, -**er**, -**ir** and the conditional endings are added to the irregular stem.

caber *to fit*	**cabr-**	cabría, cabrías, cabría , cabríamos, cabríais, cabrían
haber *to have (auxiliary)*	**habr-**	habría, habrías, habría, habríamos, habríais, habrían
poder *to be able to*	**podr-**	podría, podrías, podría, podríamos, podríais, podrían
querer *to want*	**querr-**	querría, querrías, querría, querríamos, querríais, querrían
saber *to know*	**sabr-**	sabría, sabrías, sabría, sabríamos, sabríais, sabrían

Remember to use the third person singular only in the impersonal use of **haber**.

¿**Habría** alguna posibilidad de comprar estos billetes?	*Would it be possible to purchase these tickets?*
Habría más o menos cien dólares en la billetera que encontré en la acera.	*There would be about one hundred dollars in the wallet that I found on the sidewalk.*

◆ Replace the final vowel of the infinitive with **d**. Add the conditional endings to this irregular stem.

poner *to place, put*	**pondr-**	pondría, pondrías, pondría, pondríamos, pondríais, pondrían
salir *to leave*	**saldr-**	saldría, saldrías, saldría, **saldríamos**, saldríais, saldrían
tener *to have, hold*	**tendr-**	tendría, tendrías, tendría, tendríamos, tendríais, tendrían
valer *to be worth*	**valdr-**	valdría, valdrías, valdría, valdríamos, valdríais, valdrían
venir *to come*	**vendr-**	vendría, vendrías, vendría, vendríamos, vendríais, vendrían

◆ The verbs **decir** and **hacer** are different; the stems are shortened and the conditional endings added to the irregular stem.

decir *to say, tell*	**dir-**	diría, dirías, diría, diríamos, diríais, dirían
hacer *to do*	**har-**	haría, harías, haría, haríamos, haríais, harían

EJERCICIO
16·4

Traducción.

1. It would be possible to meet our friends in San Juan.

_____

2. I would put your big suitcase in the trunk.

_____

3. Your suitcase would not fit in a seat of the car.

_____

4. Would we be able to arrive at the airport early tomorrow?

_____

5. I would say around (*a eso de*) five o'clock in the afternoon.

_____

6. We would leave at three thirty but we live close to the airport.

_____

7. We would not miss the flight to San Juan.

_____

8. It would be worthwhile to enjoy one long weekend in Puerto Rico.

_____

Posibilidades y decisiones. *Complete each sentence with the appropriate conditional tense form of the verb in parentheses.*

1. Jorge y su esposa Marilú _____ aquí a Alabama a visitarnos. (venir)

2. Ellos dos _____ en nuestra casa. (quedarse)

3. Yo _____ más almohadas en su habitación. (poner)

4. Mi madre _____ varios días si le pido este favor. (cocinar)

5. También nosotros _____ a otros amigos a nuestra casa. (invitar)

6. Eso _____ una sorpresa para Jorge y Marilú. (ser)

7. Esos amigos _____ que llegar antes de Jorge y Marilú. (tener)

8. ¿Quiénes no _____ disfrutar con sus amigos y recordar el pasado? (querer)

9. Yo _____ la verdad: es importante compartir con nuestros amigos. (decir)

10. Creo que _____ la pena pensar en la amistad y disfrutar la vida. (valer)

You may already know some of the verbs in the following **Vocabulario**, especially if you have read and studied the future tense in Chapter 14. These verbs are formed with a prefix that precedes the irregular verbs **tener**, **poner**, **hacer**, **venir**. Some are used with a reflexive pronoun, and a preposition may follow the verb.

VOCABULARIO

abstenerse de	*to abstain from*	**mantener(se)**	*to maintain*
atenerse a	*to depend on*	**obtener**	*to obtain, get*
componer	*to compose*	**oponerse a**	*to be opposed to*
contener	*to contain, hold*	**proponer**	*to propose*
convenir en	*to agree*	**rehacer**	*to remake*
deshacer	*to undo*	**reponer**	*to replace*
detener	*to arrest, detain*	**sostener**	*to hold up, support*
disponer de	*to have (at one's disposal)*	**suponer**	*to suppose*

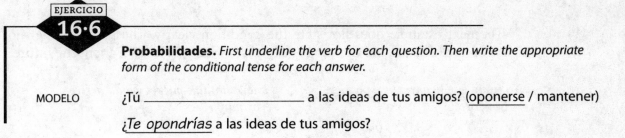

Probabilidades. *First underline the verb for each question. Then write the appropriate form of the conditional tense for each answer.*

MODELO   ¿Tú _____ a las ideas de tus amigos? (<u>oponerse</u> / mantener)

¿Te opondrías a las ideas de tus amigos?

1. ¿Tú _____ otras canciones? (componer / obtener)

2. ¿Ustedes _____ más fama con esta nueva canción? (dispone / obtener)

3. ¿Esta competencia de música _____ ser muy difícil para ustedes?
   (poder / poner)

4. ¿Usted _____ de suficiente tiempo para llegar a su meta?
   (disponer / reponer)

5. ¿Tu canción _____ sentimientos del amor o nostalgia?
   (contener / detenerse)

6. ¿Quiénes _____ ser tus rivales como compositores? (poder / detener)

7. ¿Tú _____ a tus amigos el nombre de un cantante para cantar tu
   melodía? (mantener / proponer)

8. ¿Tú _____ el silencio para no comentar la canción? (reponer / mantener)

More uses of the conditional tense in Spanish

Some of these uses relate to past actions and others relate to the present.

- To express probability or speculation in the past, the equivalent of *could, must, would, probably, I wonder.*

Lila **me llamó** pero no **escuché** el teléfono. ¿A qué hora me **llamaría**?	*Lila called me but I did not hear the phone. I wonder what time she called me.*
Julio **salió** temprano esta mañana. ¿A dónde **iría** antes de llegar a la oficina?	*Julio left early this morning. I wonder where he went before he arrived to the office.*
Pablo **hizo** una cita con su médica. **Se sentiría** enfermo.	*Pablo made an appointment with his doctor. He must have felt sick.*

In the first two examples the verbs in the past tense clearly indicate that the actions happened in the past: **me llamó, escuché, salió.** The speculation is stated in the question that follows each example and the condition is not stated clearly. The third example states that someone made an appointment (**hizo**). **Se sentiría** expresses a possible reason why that happened.

If there is a need to express an action that would happen in the future from the perspective of the past, use the conditional.

Ayer **dijeron** que no **vendrían** hoy.	*Yesterday they said that they would not come here today.*

The next example does not state the condition clearly. The package might or might not have arrived, but the subject expresses what was known about the future.

¡Yo **sabía** que **llegaría** este paquete por correo!	*I knew that this packet would arrive by mail!*

◆ Express politeness or ask for advice

Luis, ¿**podrías** ayudarme a lavar esta ropa?	*Luis, could you please help me to wash these clothes?*
Sr. González, ¿**podría** Ud. decir cuánto cuesta este diamante?	*Mr. Gonzalez, could you please tell me how much this diamond is?*
Perdón, ¿cuál de estos dos anillos me **sugeriría** Ud.?	*Excuse me, which one of these two rings would you suggest?*

One of the uses of the conditional is to express a contrary-to-fact condition, a hypothetical statement that something is in fact not probable.

Si no **estuviéramos** enfermos, **iríamos** al cine.	*If we were not sick we would go to the movies.*
Compraríamos esta lámpara si **tuviéramos** el dinero suficiente.	*We would buy this lamp if we had enough money.*

In the two previous examples, **estuviéramos** and **tuviéramos** show the need for the imperfect subjunctive, a tense that is reviewed in Chapter 21.

EJERCICIO
16·7

Posibilidades en el pasado. *Fill in the blank with the appropriate letter of a sentence from the second column that indicates the probability that caused the action in the first column.*

1. _____ Quería tomar dos aspirinas.
2. _____ Se despertó a las cinco de la mañana.
3. _____ No hizo la tarea.
4. _____ Puso las toallas de baño en la cocina.
5. _____ No usó la tarjeta de crédito.
6. _____ Fue al supermercado.
7. _____ No contestó mi llamada.
8. _____ Hizo una cita con una dentista.
9. _____ No usó su carro para ir a la oficina.
10. _____ Preparó la cena a las once de la noche.
11. _____ No saludó a los vecinos.
12. _____ Se despertó llorando y gritando.

a. No entendería las instrucciones.
b. Tendría dolor de cabeza.
c. Querría ir al gimnasio temprano.
d. Necesitaría comprar vegetales y carne.
e. Tendría un dolor de muela.
f. Tendría suficiente dinero.
g. Se equivocaría de lugar.
h. No tendría suficiente gasolina.
i. No los vería o estaría distraído.
j. No escucharía el teléfono.
k. Llegaría tarde a casa.
l. Tendría una pesadilla (*nightmare*).

The present perfect and past perfect tenses

A compound tense consists of an auxiliary verb and a participle. This chapter reviews two compound tenses: the present perfect and the past perfect.

The present perfect tense

In Spanish the present perfect is used to express actions in the past that continue in the present and to refer to a recently completed action. It is formed with the auxiliary (helping) verb **haber** in the present tense followed by a past participle. English uses a similar construction with a form of *to have* + a past participle: **He** + **hablado** (*I have spoken*).

Muchas personas **han llamado** a la estación de radio para dar su opinión.	*Many people have called the radio station to give their opinion.*
Yo **he enviado** mi carta al banco.	*I have sent my letter to the bank.*

First you must know how to conjugate the auxiliary verb **haber** in the present, and then how to form the past participle. Note that the **vosotros** form **habéis** takes a written accent.

haber *to have* (auxiliary)	
he	hemos
has	habéis
ha	han

Regular past participles

Past participles of regular verbs are formed as follows.

-ar verbs: drop the **-ar** ending and add **-ado**:	comprar	→ **comprado**
-er verbs: drop the **-er** ending and add **-ido**:	beber	→ **bebido**
-ir verbs: drop the **-ir** ending and add **-ido**:	vivir	→ **vivido**

The following examples show the formation of the present perfect in all three conjugations.

comprar *to buy*	**beber** *to drink*	**vivir** *to live*
he comprado	he bebido	he vivido
has comprado	has bebido	has vivido
ha comprado	ha bebido	ha vivido
hemos comprado	hemos bebido	hemos vivido
habéis comprado	habéis bebido	habéis vivido
han comprado	han bebido	han vivido

The past participle is invariable: that is, it remains the same, and does not agree in number and gender with the subject of the sentence.

Word order with the present perfect tense

The rules on correct word order apply to all compound tenses in Spanish. Remember that the auxiliary verb **haber** and the participle cannot be separated.

◆ In a direct statement of fact, the subject usually precedes the compound verb.

Julita ha comprado dos camisas.   *Julita has bought two shirts.*

◆ In an interrogative sentence, the subject follows the compound verb.

¿**Han probado ustedes** el plato de camarones?   *Have you tasted the shrimp dish?*

◆ All object pronouns must be placed before the conjugated form of the auxiliary verb **haber**.

Marta **nos ha pedido** un favor.   *Marta has asked us for a favor.*
Ellos **me lo han llevado** a casa.   *They have brought it to me at home.*

◆ In a negative sentence, the negative word must precede the conjugated verb.

No he comprado el regalo para Lucía.   *I have not bought the present for Lucía.*

◆ In a negative sentence that includes an object pronoun, the negative word precedes both the object pronoun and the conjugated verb.

Ud. **nunca nos ha respondido**.   *You have never answered us.*

EJERCICIO
17·1

Traducción.

1. I have not spoken to my friends today.

_____

2. My cousins have never been with me for two weeks.

_____

3. Rita has showered but she has not washed her hair.

_____

4. Have you (*sing., fam.*) sent me a message to go to a football game?

_____

5. Carla has never answered my question about her age.

_____

6. Has she ever told (**comentar**) you (*pl., fam.*) that she is younger than me?

_____

7. I have never understood why she is so secretive.

_____

8. We have not met before. It has been a pleasure.

_____

Uses of the present perfect

Let's review how the present perfect tense is used in Spanish.

- To indicate an action or something that happened in the past and bears relevance in the present or an action that continues in the present

Elías pensó en mudarse a Nueva York pero no **ha decidido** cuándo.	*Elías thought about moving to New York, but he has not decided when.*

In the next example, the verb **hemos venido** indicates that the action happened many times in the past and it is still happening in the present.

Nosotros **hemos venido** aquí de vacaciones por muchos años.	*We have come here for our vacation for many years.*

- To express a recently completed action

El vuelo **ha aterrizado** y podemos abordar el avión ya.	*The flight has arrived and we may board the plane now.*
Hemos usado la tarjeta de crédito porque la recibimos hoy por correo.	*We have used the credit card because we received it in the mail today.*

In Spanish, to express an action or something that just happened, you may use a form of **acabar de** + an infinitive, the equivalent in English of *has/have just* + a participle.

Acaba de llamar a Manuel.	*He has just called Manuel.*
Acabamos de terminar la tarea.	*We have just finished our homework.*
Mario **acaba de salir** del edificio.	*Mario has just left the building.*

Irregular past participles

Some past participles take a written accent to preserve the stress in pronunciation, or are irregular in their formation.

Past participles of -er and -ir verbs with stems that end in a vowel

When the stem of **-er** and **-ir** verbs ends with **a**, **e**, or **o**, a written accent is needed on the participle ending **-ído** to maintain the stress of the pronunciation. Verbs with infinitives that end in **-uir** need no written accent.

La soprano **ha atraído** al público para esta ópera.	*The soprano has attracted the public for this opera.*
La ciudad **ha reconstruido** esta carretera.	*The city has rebuilt this road.*

Below you will find a list of these verbs with the participle ending **-ído**. This list includes verbs and their compounds that are used frequently in Spanish.

atraer	*to attract*	**atraído**	**recaer**	*to suffer a relapse*	**recaído**
caer	*to fall*	**caído**	**reír**	*to laugh*	**reído**
creer	*to believe*	**creído**	**releer**	*to read again*	**releído**
desoír	*to disregard*	**desoído**	**sonreír**	*to smile*	**sonreído**
leer	*to read*	**leído**	**traer**	*to bring*	**traído**
oír	*to listen*	**oído**			

EJERCICIO
17·2

Y en tu caso, ¿verdadero (V) o falso (F)?

1. _____ Me han atraído las canciones de Shakira.

2. _____ Nunca he sonreído a mis vecinos.

3. _____ He releído varias veces las instrucciones para este ejercicio.

4. _____ He creído lo que dicen las noticias de hoy.

5. _____ He traído pescado para comer esta noche en casa.

6. _____ He desoído las sugerencias de mis amigos.

7. _____ Me he reído hoy con una película tonta y ridícula.

8. _____ He recaído en la gripe otra vez y tengo que descansar en cama.

9. _____ He oído varios chismes esta semana sobre una relación amorosa de dos amigos.

10. _____ He leído las noticias hoy en un periódico en la Internet.

More on irregular past participles

Remember that some common verbs have irregular past participles.

Eli no **ha abierto** la puerta hoy.	*Eli has not opened the door today.*
Ana **ha desenvuelto** el regalo que le di ayer.	*Ana has unwrapped the gift I gave her yesterday.*

Now read this list of irregular participles. It will help to include the appropriate answers for the exercises that follow.

abrir	*to open*	**abierto**
componer	*to compose, write*	**compuesto**
cubrir	*to cover*	**cubierto**
decir	*to say, tell*	**dicho**
descomponer	*to break down*	**descompuesto**
describir	*to describe*	**descrito**
descubrir	*to discover*	**descubierto**
desenvolver	*to unwrap*	**desenvuelto**
deshacer	*to undo*	**deshecho**
devolver	*to return something*	**devuelto**
disolver	*to dissolve*	**disuelto**
encubrir	*to conceal, cover up*	**encubierto**
envolver	*to wrap*	**envuelto**
escribir	*to write*	**escrito**
freír	*to fry*	**frito**
hacer	*to do*	**hecho**
imprimir	*to print*	**impreso**
morir	*to die*	**muerto**
oponer	*to oppose*	**opuesto**
poner	*to place, put*	**puesto**
proveer	*to provide*	**provisto**
reescribir	*to rewrite*	**reescrito**
rehacer	*to redo*	**rehecho**
resolver	*to resolve*	**resuelto**
revolver	*to stir*	**revuelto**
romper	*to break*	**roto**
ver	*to see*	**visto**
volver	*to return*	**vuelto**

Remember that many adjectives in Spanish are actually participles of verbs.

Julia **ha sacado** los platos **rotos** del lavaplatos.   *Julia has taken out the broken dishes from the dishwasher.*

In this example you see the use of a participle following the auxiliary verb, **ha sacado**. This sentence includes the use of an irregular participle, **rotos**, from **romper**. A participle used as an adjective must agree with the noun in gender and number: **platos rotos**.

Una carta sentimental. *Write the appropriate form of the present perfect of the verb that appears in parentheses.*

Querida hermana Nina:

Martina me 1. _____(romper) el corazón. Yo 2. _____

(descubrir) que ella y yo no vamos a continuar nuestra relación amorosa. Martina ya le

3. _____(decir) a uno de nuestros amigos que mis padres

4. _____(oponerse) a nuestra relación, pero eso no es cierto. Martina

5. _____(encubrir) la verdad. Martina no me 6. _____

(devolver) el anillo de diamantes que le regalé. Ella me 7. _____(hacer)

muchas promesas falsas pero no las cumple. Nina, yo te 8. _____(escribir)

esta carta para decirte lo que siento dentro de mi alma. Yo no te 9. _____

(describir) todavía todo el amor que siento por Martina. Yo 10. _____

(poner) el retrato de mi novia Martina en una gaveta para poder olvidarla, ¡pero no puedo!

Ahora mismo yo 11. _____(volver) a poner su retrato aquí, en mi escritorio.

Yo 12. _____(deshacer) varias cartas que le escribí a ella. Siento tanto dolor

que no 13. _____(resolver) otros problemas que tengo ahora.

Un abrazo de tu hermano,

Luis

¿Qué ha pasado? *First choose the verb in parentheses that fits each sentence. Then complete each sentence with the appropriate present perfect tense form of the chosen verb.*

MODELO   El autor _____varias canciones esta semana. (<u>componer</u> / servir)

El autor *ha compuesto* varias canciones esta semana.

1. Los López _____su matrimonio con un divorcio amigable.
   (disolver / proveer)

2. Mis amigos _____mucho con un programa tonto en la tele.
   (oponerse / distraerse)

3. El perro de Paula _____hoy y su esposo le va a traer un gatito. (ver / morir)

4. Raúl _____calamares, pescado y papas para la cena. (revolver / freír)

5. El chico _____varias páginas de respuestas en esta impresora.
   (romper / imprimir)

6. Mi auto _____dos veces esta semana. (oponerse / descomponerse)

7. Yo no _____encontrar un buen mecánico para mi auto.
   (poder / revolver)

8. ¿Qué _____ nosotros? Que no hay buenos productos en esta tienda. (dar / ver)

9. El café está amargo porque tú no _____ el azúcar en la taza. (resolver / disolver)

10. ¿No _____ tú una solución para esos problemas? (resolver / proponer)

The past perfect tense

The past perfect is a compound tense. It therefore needs a form of the auxiliary verb **haber** in the imperfect followed by a past participle: **Yo había** + **salido** (*I had left*). Be aware that some textbooks in Spanish use the term pluperfect rather than past perfect.

These are the forms of the auxiliary verb **haber** in the imperfect.

haber *to have* (auxiliary)	
había	habíamos
habías	habíais
había	habían

Note that the first and third person singular forms are identical. The context will tell you which person is correct.

Reviewing regular past participles

Let's continue to review the formation of the past participle of regular verbs. The participles are used for all compound tenses; they do not change in number or gender. Here are examples of regular verbs in the three conjugations in the past perfect tense.

lavar *to wash*	**comer** *to eat*	**salir** *to leave*
había lavado	había comido	había salido
habías lavado	habías comido	habías salido
había lavado	había comido	había salido
habíamos lavado	habíamos comido	habíamos salido
habíais lavado	habíais comido	habíais salido
habían lavado	habían comido	habían salido

Word order in the past perfect tense

As already noted, the auxiliary verb **haber** and the past participle cannot be separated. The examples below show the required order of the words for the past perfect tense.

- Word order in a direct statement

    Marisa y Lola **habían vivido** en Madrid.   *Marisa and Lola had lived in Madrid.*

- Word order in an interrogative sentence

    ¿**Habías llamado** a tu hermano antes   *Had you called your brother before*
    de llegar aquí?   *you arrived here?*

◆ Word order in negative sentences

No habíamos comprado el sofá en esta tienda. *We had not bought the sofa in this store.*

◆ Placing the object pronouns

Yo **lo había llamado** antes de salir de casa. *I had called him before I left home.*

◆ Placing the object pronouns in a negative sentence

Julián nunca me había invitado a su fiesta de cumpleaños. *Julián had never invited me to his birthday party.*

EJERCICIO
17·5

Y esto es ¿verdadero (V) o falso (F)?

1. _____ Los incas habían creado un sistema de comunicación por carreteras.

2. _____ Una científica francesa había descubierto la cura para la tuberculosis.

3. _____ Los conquistadores españoles habían llegado a las Américas antes del año 1500.

4. _____ Los astronautas norteamericanos habían entrado en órbita antes que los cosmonautas soviéticos.

5. _____ Antes de cumplir Bill Clinton sus sesenta años, el pueblo de los Estados Unidos lo había elegido como presidente.

6. _____ Salvador Dalí y Joan Miró habían visitado París al principio del siglo XX para ver las pinturas de los pintores de Francia.

7. _____ Los Estados Unidos se habían convertido en un imperio al principio del siglo XX.

8. _____ Miguel de Cervantes había publicado *El Quijote* antes de morir.

9. _____ Los experimentos científicos habían creado cura para todo tipo de cáncer en el siglo XX.

10. _____ Las novelas de Harry Potter habían creado ideas para películas.

Reviewing irregular past participles

Remember that in all compound tenses, the participle keeps the same form.

Julia **había vuelto** a la casa antes que yo. *Julia had returned home before me.*
Yo nunca **había visto** los cuadros de Dalí. *I had never seen Dalí's paintings.*
¿Quiénes **habían descubierto** este secreto? *Who had discovered this secret?*
Nosotros **habíamos puesto** la maleta en el maletero. *We had put the suitcase in the trunk.*

You may want to review the earlier list of irregular past participles before completing the following exercise.

¿Qué había pasado? *Complete each sentence with the appropriate form of the past perfect tense of the verb in parentheses.*

1. Mis amigos _____ alimentos a los vecinos que no los tenían. (proveer)

2. Yo les _____ todos los libros a mis amigos. (devolver)

3. Por suerte, los niños _____ mucho con los programas de la tele. (distraerse)

4. Rosa _____ las estrellas muy claras y brillantes en su telescopio. (ver)

5. Mi hermano _____ una copa de cristal en mi casa. (romper)

6. El auto de Lola _____ muchas veces. (descomponerse)

7. ¿Qué _____ Uds. antes de volver a casa? (hacer)

8. Mario mintió y nosotros _____ la verdad. (descubrir)

Uses of the past perfect tense

The past perfect tense in both Spanish and English refers to an action that *had occurred* prior to another action or condition. As you can see in the following example, before buying a new TV, the subject (**nosotros**) had saved the money—that is, someone *had* done this action.

Nosotros compramos un televisor nuevo porque **habíamos ahorrado** el dinero.	*We bought a new TV because we had saved the money.*

Adverbs are often used to indicate that one action preceded another. These adverbs, just like the pronouns and negative words, cannot be placed between the auxiliary verb and the participle.

antes	*before*	**nunca**	*never, ever*
aún	*still, yet*	**todavía**	*still, yet*
después	*after, later*	**ya**	*already*

Cuando llegamos al restaurante, mis amigos **ya habían comido** una ensalada.	*When we got to the restaurant, my friends had already eaten a salad.*
Yo **había llamado** a mis amigos **antes** de verlos en el restaurante.	*I had already called my friends before I saw them in the restaurant.*
Nunca habíamos ido a ese restaurante **antes**.	*We had never gone to that restaurant before.*

The completion of a past action may be implied without the use of an adverb. The following example does not indicate clearly *when* another action had or had not taken place prior to another action.

Jaime me **había contado** algunas noticias de su familia. *Jaime had told me some news about his family.*

EJERCICIO
17·7

Mi educación y mis triunfos. *Complete each sentence with the appropriate past perfect tense form of the verb in parentheses.*

Antes de tener este auto deportivo, yo 1. _____(comprar) uno viejo. Yo nunca 2. _____(tener) la oportunidad de pedir un préstamo al banco. Mis padres ya me 3. _____(ayudar) para pagar las matrículas *(tuition)* para los cursos universitarios. Recuerdo que antes de terminar la escuela secundaria los autos deportivos y las motocicletas me 4. _____(interesar). Yo 5. _____(ver) las carreras de autos en Daytona por la tele. Pero mis padres 6. _____(negarse) *(to deny)* a entender mi pasión por los autos, especialmente mi madre. Antes de yo cumplir cinco añitos, ella me 7. _____(llevar) a museos interactivos para jugar pero también para aprender algo acerca de las ciencias. Pues bien, antes de cumplir mi madre los 60 años, yo le 8. _____(entregar) a ella mi diploma de ingeniería mecánica. Después de graduarme yo 9. _____(recibir) una oferta de una industria automotriz. Pues ahora ya tengo el auto que siempre yo 10. _____(desear) y me encanta mi trabajo.

EJERCICIO
17·8

Boni y yo. Traducción. *Use the words in the **Vocabulario útil** for your translation.*

VOCABULARIO ÚTIL

amazing	**impresionante**	*to impress*	**impresionar**
ancestor	**el antepasado**	*to join*	**ingresar**
aristocrat	**el/la aristócrata**	*outgoing*	**extrovertido/-a**
to face	**enfrentar**	*to realize*	**darse cuenta de**
to find out	**enterarse**		

I had asked a friend of mine, Mario, a favor. I needed a letter of recommendation to join an exclusive and very expensive club. I had not told too many details to Mario. But I had told him that my ancestors were aristocrats and had a lot of money. When I met Boni I always had wanted to visit fabulous places and I had planned to introduce her to my friends in an impressive place, in that exclusive club. I had the impression that Boni was somewhat outgoing. After going out with Boni several times, I had realized that Boni is sincere. Therefore, I decided to face the truth: I do not have to impress anyone.

The passive voice

There are two ways to communicate the passive voice in Spanish. These two forms are reviewed and explained in this chapter.

The active voice vs. the passive voice

A sentence in the active voice indicates that the subject—the agent of the action—performs the action (the verb). The sentence may include a recipient—an object or person that receives the action:

> subject (the agent)+ verb+ object (what/who receives the action)
>
> **Mario Vargas Llosa escribió**   *Mario Vargas Llosa wrote the novel.*
> **la novela**.

In the passive voice, however, the subject is *acted upon*. If the agent—the doer of the action—is mentioned, the preposition **por** is placed before the agent.

> subject (receives the action) + verb + **por** + who/what performs the action
>
> **La novela fue escrita por Mario**   *The novel was written by Mario*
> **Vargas Llosa.**   *Vargas Llosa.*

In a sentence in the passive voice, the agent may be unknown or unspecified. The preceding example does show the agent, **Mario Vargas Llosa**. However, the next two examples in the passive do not specify *who* closed the door, or *who* introduced the writers:

> La librería **fue cerrada**.   *The bookstore was closed.*
>
> Los escritores **fueron presentados**   *The writers were introduced to*
> ante el público.   *the public.*

Formation of the passive

The formation of the passive voice in Spanish is similar to that in English: (subject) + form of the verb **ser** + past participle + **por** + agent. This formation does not change from one tense to another. (You may want to review the list of irregular participles in Chapter 17.) In the following examples you will find the use of the passive voice in the different tenses.

PRESENT	La presidenta del comité **es elegida por** los miembros de su grupo.	*The president of the committee is elected by the group members.*
FUTURE	Estos documentos **serán impresos** por los empleados.	*These documents will be printed by the employees.*
PRETERIT	Las puertas no **fueron instaladas** por un grupo de carpinteros.	*The doors were not installed by a group of carpenters.*
PRESENT PERFECT	El documento para el divorcio **ha sido firmado** por dos abogados.	*The divorce document has been signed by two lawyers.*
PAST PERFECT	El proyecto de la universidad **había sido diseñado** por dos arquitectos.	*The university project had been designed by two architects.*

In the passive voice the past participle must agree in gender and number with the subject of the verb. This is the same form of the participle that we use for certain adjectives.

El nombre del ganador fue **anunciado** ayer.	*The name of the winner was announced yesterday.*
Las noticias habían sido **publicadas**.	*The news had been published.*
Los regalos de Mari fueron **envueltos** en la tienda.	*Mari's gifts were wrapped at the store.*
Unas notas fueron **escritas** en este papel.	*Some notes were written on this paper.*

The passive voice in Spanish is not used frequently in daily conversations, but it tends to appear in newspaper articles and on TV and radio.

Dos bancos **fueron asaltados** ayer.	*Two banks were robbed yesterday.*
Un sospechoso **fue interrogado** por la policía.	*A suspect was interrogated by the police.*
Los candidatos **serán elegidos** mañana.	*The candidates will be elected tomorrow.*

EJERCICIO
18·1

Una feria popular. *Write the appropriate form of the participle of the verb that appears in parentheses. Attention: some participles are irregular.*

1. Las puertas de un parque fueron _____ a las ocho de la mañana. (abrir)

2. Unos loros de Centroamérica han sido _____ en esas jaulas. (traer)

3. Los dibujos de caricaturas fueron _____ por un personaje desconocido. (dibujar)

4. Los objetos de artesanía habían sido _____ en las calles principales. (vender)

5. Los carteles de la protesta serán _____ frente al ayuntamiento esta noche. (distribuir)

6. El plato típico de Perú, ceviche, será _____ en la Tercera Avenida. (preparar)

7. La fiesta de esta ciudad es _____ el 25 de mayo de cada año. (celebrar)

8. Algunos cantantes y guitarristas fueron _____ el año pasado. (invitar)

9. Esta celebración fue _____ por el ayuntamiento años atrás. (aprobar)

10. Muchos artículos típicos de Hispanoamérica serán _____ para decorar las calles. (donar)

EJERCICIO
18·2

La boda. Traducción.

1. The invitations had been sent.

_____

2. The invitations were made by some members of the family.

_____

3. The addresses on the envelopes were written by the bride's sister.

_____

4. A contract had been signed by the band.

_____

5. The menu was created by a Peruvian chef.

_____

6. The ballroom was decorated with many flowers.

_____

7. The day of the wedding was selected by the bride.

_____

8. The presents were sent by the friends of the groom and the bride.

_____

9. Champagne was served for a toast (**el brindis**).

_____

10. Many photographs were taken in the ballroom.

_____

Passive construction with or without an explicit agent

The passive voice construction with **por** + *an explicit agent* emphasizes the agent who does the action:

La congregación fue recibida **por el Papa**.   *The congregation was greeted **by the Pope**.*
La propuesta fue abolida **por el**   *The proposal was abolished **by the**
superintendente.   ***superintendent**.*

The passive voice without an explicit agent has a different purpose, and its message has a different effect. Read the following short paragraph divided into sentences; focus on the *active* and *passive voice* constructions:

Una comisión **ha iniciado** una   *A commission **has started** an investigation.*
investigación.
Varios miembros del Congreso **serán**   *Several members of Congress will **be**
interrogados.   ***interrogated**.*
La comisión **fue creada** debido a protestas   *The commission **was created** due to public
públicas.   protests.*
Ya **han sido reveladas** acusaciones   *Anonymous accusations **have been revealed**.*
anónimas.

In the previous paragraph, the first sentence has an active voice verb, **ha iniciado**, with a subject that is a "doer": **una comisión**. The following example sentences are written in the passive construction, without the agent. This is one way the writer may avoid responsibility for or commitment to the information in the paragraph. This construction is typical of business-related statements, government briefings, or simply when the writer does not want to or need to say who is responsible for the actions.

Such passive constructions are often used in journalistic style. In that context, they often appear in the past or future tense. Note that this construction focuses on the person or thing acted upon:

La identidad de la acusada **no fue revelada**.   *The identity of the accused **was not revealed**.*

EJERCICIO
18·3

Un partido de béisbol. *For each sentence, give the passive construction with the appropriate form of the future tense.*

1. el partido / difundir / por cable

_____

2. el encuentro / televisar / desde San José

_____

3. todos los jugadores / entrenar / para estar en forma

_____

4. el estadio / preparar / para acomodar a la fanaticada

_____

5. el precio de las entradas / controlar / para evitar fraudes

   _____

6. el parqueo / limitar / en los alrededores del estadio

   _____

7. un grupo de niños / invitar / para la ceremonia de apertura

   _____

8. el éxito del partido / asegurar / con los voluntarios

   _____

9. el himno nacional / interpretar / al comienzo del evento

   _____

10. el encuentro / ver / en todo el país

    _____

The passive reflexive

Another way to express the sense of the passive voice in Spanish is the passive reflexive. It is important to understand the passive reflexive construction and its uses because it is used more frequently than the passive voice in everyday conversations in Spanish.

With the passive reflexive an action is performed, yet an agent—the doer of the action—is not stated. The reflexive pronoun **se** appears first and a conjugated verb follows. If a singular noun follows the verb, the verb is conjugated in the third person singular; the third person plural follows a plural noun.

PASSIVE REFLEXIVE, SINGULAR

se + verb (third person singular) + singular noun

Se recicla el papel aquí.	*The paper is recycled here.*
Se abre la oficina a las ocho de la mañana.	*The office is opened at eight in the morning.*
Se necesita un camarero en el restaurante.	*A waiter is needed in the restaurant.*

PASSIVE REFLEXIVE, PLURAL

se + verb (third person plural) + plural noun

Se cierran las puertas a las seis.	*The doors are closed at six.*
Se recogen las botellas vacías en el segundo piso.	*The empty bottles are collected on the second floor.*
Se aceptan los documentos en aquella ventanilla.	*The documents are accepted at that window.*

The passive reflexive is used in all tenses, but the construction does not change from one tense to another. The reflexive pronoun **se** appears in all tenses.

Se vendieron todas las copias de la novela.	*All the copies of the novel were sold.*
Se celebrará el aniversario de bodas de Ana y Paco aquí.	*Ana and Paco's wedding anniversary will be celebrated here.*
No **se habían escrito** estos libros para entretener a los niños.	*These books were not written to entertain the children.*

You may want to review the present perfect tense in Chapter 17 before completing the following exercises.

EJERCICIO
18·4

Comentarios en una reunión en la oficina. *Complete each sentence in the passive reflexive using the present perfect tense form of the verb in parentheses.*

1. _____las puertas ya. (cerrar)

2. No _____las notas de la reunión. (escribir)

3. No _____las reglas todavía. (leer)

4. _____los comentarios negativos aquí. (prohibir)

5. _____botellas de agua al frente de la cafetería. (vender)

6. No _____este problema. (resolver)

7. No _____tus sugerencias. (aceptar)

8. _____los documentos por correo electrónico. (enviar)

9. _____los arbolitos de navidad. (poner)

10. _____la relación de amistad entre Juanita y yo. (romper)

EJERCICIO
18·5

¿Qué opinas, cierto (C) o no (N)?

1. _____Se podía viajar en un avión a finales del siglo XIX.

2. _____En esta época se fabrican muchos autos en Japón y Corea del Sur.

3. _____Se habla más inglés que español en Chile.

4. _____Ahora se usan los teléfonos para enviar fotos a la familia.

5. _____Se habla solamente español en Francia.

6. _____En diez años se descubrirán más soluciones para la salud de muchos individuos.

7. _____Se puede encontrar casi toda la información necesaria a través de la Internet.

8. _____En el futuro se podrá manejar todo tipo de auto sin usar gasolina.

Traducción. *Use the passive reflexive to translate each of the following sentences.*

1. How do you say "thanks" in French?

   _____

2. Where do they sell toys?

   _____

3. When will they raise (**aumentar**) the prices?

   _____

4. Where do they buy books written in Japanese?

   _____

5. What is spoken here at this store?

   _____

6. When do they serve breakfast in the hotel?

   _____

7. Where do they accept coupons for discount?

   _____

8. How do you say "I am sorry" in Portuguese?

   _____

Uses of the impersonal pronoun se

The reflexive pronoun appears in impersonal constructions (see Chapter 11) where the subject of the sentence is indefinite. It is used with the third personal singular of the verb. The impersonal in English is expressed with a subject—*people, they, you, we, one.*

Se comenta mucho acerca del divorcio de estos dos cantantes famosos.	*People are talking about the divorce of these two famous singers.*
Se dice que vale la pena dormir ocho horas cada noche.	*They say that is worthwhile to sleep eight hours every night.*
No **se debe** ir a una fiesta sin una invitación.	*You should not go to a party without an invitation.*
¿**Se puede** encontrar un hotel elegante aquí?	*Can one find an elegant hotel here?*

The next exercise offers you practice with the impersonal pronoun **se**.

EJERCICIO
18·7

Traducción.

1. How can you live without love?

   _____

2. We can live without love but not without money!

   _____

3. Why are people talking a lot about an economic crisis?

   _____

4. They say it is better to think positively and not pessimistically.

   _____

5. Where can one find friends?

   _____

6. They say it is easier to find new friends on a Web page.

   _____

EJERCICIO
18·8

Una entrevista. Traducción. *Use the words in the **Vocabulario útil** for your translation.*

VOCABULARIO ÚTIL

coach	**el entrenador / la entrenadora**
to get used to	**acostumbrarse**
to maintain	**mantenerse**
Olympic Games	**las Olimpiadas**
to promise	**comprometerse**
schedule	**el horario**
self-confidence	**la confianza en sí mismo, -a**
stopwatch	**el cronómetro**
warm-up exercises	**los ejercicios de calentamiento**

—How is a swimmer trained to compete in the Olympic Games?

—Usually, she or he is trained by a professional coach.

—How many days a week?

—It is known that all athletes train six days a week and they rest for one day.

—But how many hours do they swim in a pool?

—Many hours, and they promise to rest and to sleep.

—What is expected from an athlete who wants to swim in the next Olympic Games?

—A lot is expected: to have self-confidence, to persevere, and to maintain himself or herself in good shape, physically and mentally.

—Is it necessary to have a daily schedule?

—Yes, it's needed in order to get used to a daily routine.

—Please, give me (*sing,. form.*) an example of a daily schedule.

—Of course. He/She gets out of bed early, then does warm-up exercises. A stopwatch is used to measure the time and the speed while he/she swims.

—Many thanks, and see you later.

_____

_____

_____

_____

_____

_____

_____

_____

_____

_____

_____

_____

_____

_____

_____

_____

_____

The present subjunctive

In previous chapters we have discussed tenses in the indicative mood. This chapter begins our review of the subjunctive mood.

The word *mood* describes the attitude of the subject. The indicative mood states or indicates certainty: something is real or certain.

> Juan **sabe** que yo **vivo** en Madrid.   *Juan knows that I live in Madrid.*

The subject **Juan** in the main clause knows with certainty something about the subject of the second clause, **yo**. The same tense, the present indicative, appears in both clauses, which are connected with the conjunction **que**.

The next example shows a past indicative tense, the imperfect.

> Julián **sabía** que **íbamos** a viajar a   *Julian knew that we would travel to*
> Ecuador.   *Ecuador.*

The subjunctive mood, on the other hand, expresses uncertainty, something that is not known or will not happen for sure.

> Yo **espero** que **vengas** mañana.   *I hope that you come tomorrow.*

In the first clause, **espero**, itself in the indicative, shows some uncertainty, a wish that something may be completed. In the subsidiary clause the verb **vengas** is in the subjunctive. Note that the conjunction **que** connects the two clauses.

The subjunctive mood is used more frequently in Spanish than in English. Therefore, we need to know and remember the situations where it is used, as in the following examples.

- ◆ Uncertainty

    > **Compraremos** el auto aunque   *We will buy the car even if*
    > **cueste** mucho.   *it costs a lot.*

- ◆ Doubt

    > Nosotros **dudamos** que Marta   *We doubt (It is unlikely) that*
    > **venga** esta noche.   *Marta will come tonight.*

- ◆ Demand

    > **Exigen** que **llamemos** antes de   *They insist that we call before*
    > las ocho.   *eight o'clock.*

- Desire, hope

Julia y yo **deseamos** que **pases** un día feliz.   *Julia and I wish you a nice day.*

¡**Espero** que **ganes** la lotería!   *I hope that you win the lottery!*

- Emotions and feelings

Ellos **temen** que tú **no vuelvas** mañana a casa.   *They are afraid that you won't come back home tomorrow.*

Yo **me alegro** de que Uds. **puedan** cenar conmigo.   *I am happy that you can dine with me.*

- Indefinite, nonexistent person or thing in the subordinate clause

Necesitamos **una secretaria que sea** bilingüe.   *We need a secretary who is bilingual.*

Quiero **un apartamento que tenga** una cocina grande.   *I want an apartment with a big kitchen.*

No conozco **a nadie que quiera** ayudar a esta comunidad.   *I don't know anyone who wants to help this community.*

- Impersonal expressions with opinions and suggestions

Es necesario que Uds. **firmen** esta carta.   *It is necessary that you sign this letter.*

Es posible que **llueva** esta tarde.   *(I think) It may rain this afternoon.*

Formation of the present subjunctive

Most verbs in the present subjunctive are conjugated in the same way, including verbs that have stem changes in the present. Almost all stem-changing verbs in the present indicative have the same changes in the present subjunctive (see Chapter 3 to review stem-changing verbs).

To form the present subjunctive in the three conjugations of regular verbs, take the **yo** form of the present indicative, drop the **-o** ending, and add the endings of the present subjunctive as follows:

-**ar** verbs:	-**e**, -**es**, -**e**, -**emos**, -**éis**, -**en**
-**er** verbs:	-**a**, -**as**, -**a**, -**amos**, -**áis**, -**an**
-**ir** verbs:	-**a**, -**as**, -**a**, -**amos**, -**áis**, -**an**

bailar *to dance*	**beber** *to drink*	**escribir** *to write*
bail**e**	beb**a**	escrib**a**
bail**es**	beb**as**	escrib**as**
bail**e**	beb**a**	escrib**a**
bail**emos**	beb**amos**	escrib**amos**
bail**éis**	beb**áis**	escrib**áis**
bail**en**	beb**an**	escrib**an**

Here now are the present subjunctive conjugations of many familiar verbs.

destruir	*to destroy*	destruya, destruyas, destruya, destruyamos, destruyáis, destruyan
hacer	*to make*	haga, hagas, haga, hagamos, hagáis, hagan
querer	*to want*	quiera, quieras, quiera, queramos, queráis, quieran
salir	*to go out*	salga, salgas, salga, salgamos, salgáis, salgan
tener	*to hold*	tenga, tengas, tenga, tengamos, tengáis, tengan
ver	*to see*	vea, veas, vea, veamos, veáis, vean

From this, you see that the first and third person singular endings are the same. The -**er** and -**ir** verbs have the same endings in all forms. Only the **vosotros** form has a written accent. Of these preceding examples, you will see no stem changes in the first and second person plural forms of **querer**: **queramos**, **queráis**.

◆ Three other verbs make a stem change in the **nosotros** and **vosotros** forms.

mentir	e → i	**mintamos, mintáis**
dormir	o → u	**durmamos, durmáis**
pedir	e → i	**pidamos, pidáis**

You may want to review verbs with spelling changes in the present indicative tense in Chapter 3. These verbs end in -**cer**, -**ger**, -**gir**, and -**guir** in the present indicative. As you can see, **coger**, **conocer**, **dirigir**, and **distinguir** maintain these spelling changes in all persons, singular and plural, in the present subjunctive.

coger	*to take*	coja, cojas, coja, cojamos, cojáis, cojan
conocer	*to know*	conozca, conozcas, conozca, conozcamos, conozcáis, conozcan
dirigir	*to direct*	dirija, dirijas, dirija, dirijamos, dirijáis, dirijan
distinguir	*to distinguish*	distinga, distingas, distinga, distingamos, distingáis, distingan

Verbs with spelling changes in the present subjunctive

In Chapter 7 you reviewed spelling changes in the preterit for verbs that end in -**car**, -**gar**, and -**zar**. These verbs maintain this spelling change in the present subjunctive.

First, go to the **yo** form of the preterit indicative, drop the -**e** ending, and add the present subjunctive endings for -**ar** verbs already given: -**e**, -**es**, -**e**, -**emos**, -**éis**, -**en**:

INFINITIVE	PRETERIT	PRESENT SUBJUNCTIVE STEM
buscar	bus**qué**	**busqu-**
apagar	apa**gué**	**apagu-**
abrazar	abra**cé**	**abrac-**

Here are more examples of verbs with this spelling change in the present subjunctive.

abrazar	*to embrace*	abrace, abraces, abrace, abracemos, abracéis, abracen
apagar	*to turn off*	apague, apagues, apague, apaguemos, apaguéis, apaguen
buscar	*to look for*	busque, busques, busque, busquemos, busquéis, busquen
dedicar	*to dedicate*	dedique, dediques, dedique, dediquemos, dediquéis, dediquen
explicar	*to explain*	explique, expliques, explique, expliquemos, expliquéis, expliquen

llegar	to arrive	llegue, llegues, llegue, lleguemos, lleguéis, lleguen
pagar	to pay	pague, pagues, pague, paguemos, paguéis, paguen
sacar	to withdraw	saque, saques, saque, saquemos, saquéis, saquen
tocar	to touch	toque, toques, toque, toquemos, toquéis, toquen

Irregular verbs in the present subjunctive

There are a few verbs that are irregular in the present subjunctive. These are all verbs we use frequently in daily communication.

dar	to give	dé, dés, dé, demos, deis, den
estar	to be	esté, estés, esté, estemos, estéis, estén
haber	there is, are	haya, hayas, haya, hayamos, hayáis, hayan
ir	to go	vaya, vayas, vaya, vayamos, vayáis, vayan
saber	to know	sepa, sepas, sepa, sepamos, sepáis, sepan
ser	to be	sea, seas, sea, seamos, seáis, sean

Uses of the present subjunctive

In Spanish we use the subjunctive when there is a need to express advice and suggestions, demand and orders, desire and hope, doubt or uncertainty, feelings and emotions, requests and impersonal opinion.

The verb in the main clause, which expresses the advice, suggestion, desire, demand, is in the indicative. The subjunctive form appears in the subordinate clause, usually after the conjunction **que** (*that*).

Mi padre quiere que **yo prepare** la cena.   *My father wants me to prepare dinner.*

The main clause with the indicative **quiere** states a wish of the subject, **mi padre**. He expects that wish to be fulfilled by the subject in the subordinate clause, **yo**. This second clause does not state whether dinner will be prepared or not. In English the equivalent formation includes not a subjunctive form in the subordinate clause but rather an infinitive (*to prepare*) after the pronoun *me*.

If the subjects in the main clause and the subordinate clause are different, use the subjunctive in the subsidiary clause.

Yo necesito que tú compres el billete.   *I want you to buy the ticket.*

If the subject is the same in both clauses, use the infinitive in the subsidiary clause. Note that there is no need for **que** in this case.

Yo necesito comprar el billete.   *I need to buy the ticket.*

In the first example **yo** is the subject of the main clause, **tú** is the subject of the subordinate clause. There is no subject other than **yo** in the second example.

The following lists give you verbs that frequently precede sentences with the subjunctive.

- ◆ Verbs to express advice and suggestions

aconsejar	*to advise, give advice to someone*
insistir en	*to insist*
preferir	*to prefer*
recomendar	*to advise*
sugerir	*to suggest*

Yo **te aconsejo** que **tú firmes** ahora.	*I advise you to sign now.*
Joaquín **insiste en** que **tú vayas** a su casa.	*Joaquin insists that you go to his home.*
Nosotros **preferimos** que los chicos **vean** esta película.	*We prefer that the children watch this movie.*
Ellos **sugieren** que **lleguemos** temprano.	*They suggest that we arrive early.*

- ◆ Verbs that express orders and demands

decir	*to tell, order*
exigir	*to require, call for, demand*
mandar	*to tell, order, give orders*
permitir	*to allow, permit*
prohibir	*to prohibit, forbid*

Alina **dice** que **prepares** la merienda ahora.	*Alina says (orders) that you should prepare the snack now.*
La dueña **exige** que yo **pague** mi alquiler el día primero de cada mes.	*The owner requires that I pay my rent the first day of every month.*
El sargento **manda** que **abras** las puertas.	*The sergeant orders you to open the doors.*
La ley **prohíbe** que ustedes **fumen** cigarrillos aquí.	*The law prohibits smoking (that you smoke) here.*

- ◆ Verbs that express desire, hope

desear	*to wish*
esperar	*to hope, expect*
querer	*to want, expect*

Doris **desea** que Uds. **viajen** con ella.	*Doris wants you to travel with her.*
Yo **espero** que mi hermana **viva** conmigo.	*I hope that my sister will live with me.*
El maestro **quiere** que los chicos **aprendan** español.	*The teacher wants the children to learn Spanish.*

The interjection **ojalá** expresses hope, desire, wish; therefore, the subjunctive mood follows this interjection, which is used very frequently in daily communication.

ojalá (que)	*I wish that, I hope that, God willing*
¡Ojalá puedas ganar!	*I hope that you win!*
Ojalá que no **nieve** esta noche.	*I hope it doesn't snow tonight.*
Ojalá que ganemos este partido.	*God willing, we'll win this game.*

EJERCICIO 19·1

En el teatro. *Complete each sentence with the appropriate form of the present subjunctive of the verb in parentheses.*

1. Espero que Uds. _____ al estreno de la obra de mi amigo Juan. (ir)

2. Les sugiero a Uds. que _____ las entradas en la taquilla del teatro. (comprar)

3. El gerente (*manager*) del teatro exige que nosotros _____ y
_____ cinco minutos antes de las siete y media de la noche.
(entrar, sentarse)

4. Insisto en que todos nosotros _____ mucho y _____
¡«Bravo»! después de cada acto. (aplaudir, gritar)

5. Yo espero que _____ muchas personas en el teatro. (haber)

6. También deseo que esta obra _____ mucho éxito. (tener)

7. Pedro y Luisa dicen que nosotros _____ a Juan al final de la obra.
(abrazar)

8. ¡Ojalá que esta obra _____ por muchos meses en este teatro. (continuar)

9. Ojalá Juan _____ escribir más obras con mucho éxito. (poder)

EJERCICIO 19·2

¿El subjuntivo o el infinitivo? Traducción.

1. I suggest that you (*sing., fam.*) take your dog to the park.

_____

2. Alicia wants to eat with us tonight in the restaurant.

_____

3. Ana hopes that I'll buy the tickets to see a couple of new movies.

_____

4. Let's hope I can win this contest!

_____

5. My sister says that you're (*pl., form.*) not leaving the house now.

_____

6. The manager does not allow me to work on Saturdays.

_____

7. I forbid you (*sing., fam.*) to repeat these lies.

_____

8. The trainer insists that you (*sing., fam.*) run three miles.

_____

9. Does he prefer that I put all these documents on his desk?

_____

10. Why does the doctor recommend that you do not drink sodas?

_____

11. I wish I had a better job and made (**ganar**) more money now!

_____

12. I advise you (*sing., fam.*) to go to the bank today before five o'clock.

_____

13. We hope that you (*pl., form.*) are well and healthy.

_____

14. Louis and Joan want me to write a letter.

_____

15. I hope it does not rain tomorrow.

_____

EJERCICIO
19·3

Y en tu caso, ¿verdadero (V) o falso (F)?

1. _____ Deseo que llueva mañana.

2. _____ Quiero despertarme tarde todos los días de la semana.

3. _____ Necesito que mis amigos rieguen (*water*) el jardín.

4. _____ Prefiero que mis amigos olviden mi cumpleaños.

5. _____ Ojalá mi familia gane la lotería.

6. _____ Espero que nieve mucho mañana para quedarme en casa.

7. _____ Sugiero que mis vecinos no hagan mucho ruido por la noche.

8. _____ Insisto en que mis amigos me acompañen siempre cuando voy a una fiesta.

9. _____ Quiero que pierda mi equipo favorito de fútbol americano.

10. _____ Exijo que mis vecinos sean amables.

♦ Verbs that express doubt and uncertainty

dudar	*to doubt*
no creer	*to not believe*
no estar convencido, **-a de**	*not to be convinced about*
no estar seguro, **-a de**	*to not be sure about*
no pensar	*to not think*
no suponer(se)	*to not suppose*

Dudamos que tú **lleves** estas lámparas para tu sala.	*We doubt that you will take these lamps to your living room.*
Yo **no creo** que **compres** este auto fabuloso.	*I do not believe that you can buy this fabulous car.*
No estoy convencido de que Uds. **sean** miembros de nuestra familia.	*I am not convinced that you are members of our family.*
Lina **no está segura de** que le **devuelvan** su dinero.	*Lina is not convinced that they will return her money.*
El entrenador **no piensa que tú puedas** bajar de peso en dos semanas.	*The coach does not think that you can lower your weight in two weeks.*
No **se supone que** el huracán **afecte** a Puerto Rico.	*It is not thought that the hurricane will affect Puerto Rico.*

Most of the verbs on the previous list are expressed in the negative with **no**. In negative sentences the verb in the subordinate clause is in the subjunctive; otherwise the verb in the subordinate clause is in the indicative.

Ellos **no están seguros** de que Laura **trabaje** aquí.	*They are not sure that Laura works here.*
Ellos **están seguros** de que Laura trabaja aquí.	*They are sure that Laura works here.*
Yo **no creo** que Ud. **pueda** salir del hospital ahora.	*I do not think that you can leave the hospital now.*
Yo **creo** que Ud. **puede** salir del hospital ahora.	*I think that you can leave the hospital now.*

More about doubt, uncertainty, and conjunctions

Conjunctions are invariable: that is, they never change form. Their function is to connect words and phrases. They also connect the main clause to the subordinate clause. If the action in the subordinate clause that follows the conjunction is uncertain or doubtful, use the subjunctive in the subordinate. Some of the conjunctions in this list imply answers to questions such as *how?*, *when?* etc.

a menos que	*unless*	**hasta que**	*until*
antes (de) que	*before*	**mientras que**	*while*
aunque	*although, even if*	**para que**	*in order that, so that*
cuando	*when*	**sin que**	*without*
después (de) que	*after*	**tan pronto como**	*as soon as*
en caso de que	*in case*		

Salimos a las diez de la noche **a menos que tu hermano no llegue** aquí.	We will leave at ten o'clock tonight unless your brother does not get here.
No compraremos el apartamento **antes que el abogado lea** el contrato.	We will not buy the apartment before the lawyer reads the contract.
Tenemos que visitar a Anita **aunque llueva** mucho.	We need to visit Anita even if it rains a lot.
Cenaremos **después que Pedrito termine** la tarea.	We will have dinner after Pedrito finishes his homework.
Te ayudaré a limpiar la casa **para que tú descanses**.	I will help you clean the house so that you can rest.
Yo trabajaré con Ileana **hasta que ella salga** de la oficina.	I will work with Ileana until she leaves the office.
Carlos contestará **tan pronto como pueda**.	Carlos will answer as soon as he can.

In the following examples you see that the conjunctions **cuando** and **aunque** followed by the subordinate clause do not suggest uncertainty or doubt. Therefore, the indicative mood follows the conjunction.

| Juan siempre me contesta **cuando yo lo llamo**. | Juan always answers when I call him. |
| **Aunque** es barato, no vamos a comprar este sofá. | Even though it is not expensive, we are not going to buy this sofa. |

EJERCICIO
19·4

Dudas y posibilidades. *Complete each sentence with the appropriate form of the present subjunctive of the verb in parentheses.*

1. Dudo que tu equipo de fútbol _____el partido hoy. (ganar)

2. No estamos convencidos de que Uds. _____suficiente espacio en el maletero de su auto. (tener)

3. Marta y Rogelio no piensan que nosotros _____llegar temprano a la cena. (poder)

4. Yo dudo que esto _____un platillo volador. (ser)

5. Pedro no está seguro de que tu hermana _____lista para salir conmigo. (estar)

6. Ellas no están convencidas de que estos zapatos _____tanto dinero. (costar)

7. Tus padres no te dejan salir por las noches hasta que tú _____buenas notas en la escuela. (recibir)

8. Luisa explica las palabras para que nosotros _____palabras nuevas en español. (aprender)

9. Yo no voy al cine esta noche a menos que mis amigos _____conmigo. (ir)

10. Regresaremos mañana después que Uds. _____en el restaurante. (cenar)

11. Iré a tu casa este verano cuando mis padres _____una visita a mis abuelos. (hacer)

12. Luis estudia mucho en caso de que _____un examen esta semana. (haber)

Verbs that express feelings and emotions

alegrarse de	*to be glad, happy*
sentir	*to be sorry, regret*
sorprenderse (de)	*to be surprised*
temer	*to fear, suspect*
tener miedo de	*to be afraid of, fear*

Ellos **se alegran de** que tú te **gradúes** este verano.	*They are happy that you will graduate this summer.*
Siento mucho que Uds. no **puedan** cenar conmigo.	*I am sorry that you cannot have dinner with me.*
¡Mi hija **se sorprende de** que sus amigas **estén** aquí!	*My daughter is surprised that her friends are here!*
Temo que no **pases** este examen de matemáticas.	*I am afraid that you may fail this math exam.*
Tengo miedo de que de los ladrones **roben** mi auto.	*I am afraid that the thieves may steal my car.*

More about emotions

To express emotions and feelings, you need a form of **estar** followed by an adjective. These are usually considered temporary conditions. Again, this calls for the subjunctive in the subordinate clause.

estar + adjective + **que** + a subordinate clause

Estamos encantados + **que participes** en esta reunión

We are delighted that you are participating in this meeting.

Estoy feliz que mi novio **venga** esta noche.	*I am happy that my boyfriend is coming tonight.*
Luisa **está preocupada que** tú **pierdas** el vuelo.	*Luisa is worried that you may miss the flight.*

Verbs that express a request

pedir (**e→ i**)	*to ask, request*
rogar (**o → ue**)	*to beg*
suplicar	*to implore*

Juan **pide** que Uds. **traigan** las sábanas a su cuarto.	*Juan requests that you bring the bedsheets to his room.*
Por favor, te **ruego** que **apagues** las luces.	*Please, I beg you to turn off the lights.*
¡Tenemos sueño, te **suplicamos** que no **enciendas** la televisión!	*We are sleepy, we implore you not to turn on the television!*

EJERCICIO
19·5

Las emociones y el subjuntivo. *Complete each sentence with the appropriate form of the present subjunctive of the verb in parentheses.*

1. Te pido que no _____ la hora de la cita mañana. (olvidar)

2. Marcia tiene miedo de que Uds. no _____ las cortinas en su cuarto. (colgar)

3. Yo le ruego a mi novio que no _____ la fecha de nuestra boda. (decir)

4. Juanita se sorprende de que nosotros _____ con ella ahora. (estar)

5. Te suplico que no _____ a ese chico horrible otra vez a la casa. (traer)

6. Los meteorólogos se sorprenden de que _____ venir estas tormentas. (poder)

7. Siento mucho que mis hermanos no _____ la Navidad conmigo el año que viene. (celebrar)

8. Estamos encantados de que Uds. _____ el piano en nuestra sala. (tocar)

9. Te ruego que tú me _____ para la cita con el dentista. (acompañar)

10. Estoy muy preocupado de que tú no _____ en este partido. (jugar)

11. Mis amigos temen que Raúl y Lidia no _____. (casarse)

12. Estamos muy felices de que nuestros hijos _____ sus cursos en la universidad. (terminar)

Impersonal expressions and opinions

Impersonal expressions that express possibility, doubt, uncertainty, necessity, emotion, or a command appear in the main clause. These types of impersonal expressions require the subjunctive in the subordinate clause. The pattern for impersonal expressions requires a form of **ser** + expression + **que** + a subordinate clause: **Es importante que escuches** las noticias (*It is important that you listen to the news*).

es dudoso que	*it is doubtful that*
es importante que	*it is important that*
es imposible que	*it is impossible that*
es (una) lástima que	*it is a shame / a pity that*
es mejor que / más vale que	*it is better that*

es necesario que	*it is necessary that*
es posible que	*it is possible that*
es probable que	*it is probable that*
es fantástico que	*it is fantastic that*
es increíble que	*it is incredible/unbelievable that*
es terrible que	*it is terrible that*

Es dudoso que **escribamos** esta carta esta noche.	*It is doubtful that we will write this letter tonight.*
Es importante que **guardes** una copia de este documento en tu oficina.	*It is important that you keep a copy of this document in your office.*
Es una lástima que no **tengas** acceso a la Internet en casa.	*It is a pity that you don't have access to the Internet at home.*
Es necesario que **aprendamos** otros idiomas.	*It is necessary that we learn other languages.*
Es muy **probable** que **llueva** mañana.	*It is very probable that it will rain tomorrow.*
Es mejor que **estudiemos** para pasar la prueba.	*It is better that we study for the test.*
¡Más vale que manejes (conduzcas) despacio en esta carretera!	*It is better that you drive slowly on this road!*

Some impersonal expressions express certainty in the main clause. In this case the verb in the subordinate clause is in the indicative.

es cierto que	*it is certain*
es verdad que	*it is true*
es obvio que	*it is obvious*

Es cierto que mis padres **vienen** hoy.	*It is certain that my parents come today.*
Es obvio que tú estás alegre.	*It is obvious that you are happy.*

EJERCICIO
19·6

Sugerencias para tener tu éxito en el trabajo. Traducción.

1. It is necessary that you think first and be patient (**tener paciencia**) before answering a question.

_____

2. It is important that you communicate your ideas frequently to your colleagues.

_____

3. It is much better that you attend all the meetings on time.

_____

4. It is fantastic that you take notes to help your group.

_____

5. It is terrible if you do not obey the regulations at work (**reglamento**) even if they are ridiculous.

   _____

6. It is doubtful that you will get (**tener**) a raise unless you follow the rules.

   _____

7. It is not likely that you can help all your colleagues.

   _____

8. But it is better that you continue with your efforts.

   _____

9. It is very likely that you will win the certificate of employee of the year.

   _____

10. It is incredible that you do everything that is on this list!

    _____

11. You are very persistent!

    _____

12. And it is very obvious that you want to be successful.

    _____

Uncertain antecedent

If the subject of the main clause (the antecedent) is vague or uncertain, use the subjunctive in the subordinate clause. If the antecedent is certain and known to exist, use the indicative in the subordinate clause.

Definite antecedent:	**Tengo amigos** que me **ayudan** mucho.	*I have friends who help me a lot.*
Uncertain antecedent:	**No tengo amigos** que me **ayuden** mucho.	*I do not have friends who help me a lot.*
Definite antecedent:	Carlos **encontró a alguien** que **habla** alemán y francés.	*Carlos found someone who speaks German and French.*
Uncertain antecedent:	Carlos **no encontró a nadie** que **hable** alemán y francés.	*Carlos did not find anyone who speaks German and French.*

Remember that the personal **a** needs to be placed before **alguien** (*someone*) and **nadie** (*nobody, no one*), even when their existence is uncertain.

Ellos no conocen **a nadie** que **viva** en Caracas.	*They do not know anyone who lives in Caracas.*
¿Conoce Ud. **a alguien** que **pueda** comprar mi auto?	*Do you know anyone who can buy my car?*

Traducción.

1. I want to buy a home that is far from the city.

   _____

2. We need a car that does not cost too much.

   _____

3. My nephews want a puppy that is mischievous (**travieso**).

   _____

4. We have neighbors who make a lot of noise.

   _____

5. Where can I find a piano that looks like yours?

   _____

6. My friends have a maid who makes excellent enchiladas.

   _____

7. Is there anyone here who can help me now?

   _____

8. No, there is no one here who can open the door to the building.

   _____

Expressing wants and needs

Now we'll look at a conversation that uses the subjunctive to express needs and wants.

Conversation: Looking for a new apartment

AGENTE: Buenos días, señor. ¿En qué puedo ayudarlo?

Good morning, sir. How can I help you?

ALBERTO: Me gustaría alquilar un apartamento **que esté** aquí en la ciudad.

I'd like to rent an apartment here in the city.

AGENTE: Siéntese, por favor, y dígame qué tipo de apartamento quiere. ¿Es sólo para usted?

Have a seat, please, and tell me what kind of apartment you want. Is it just for you?

ALBERTO: Bueno, eso depende de lo que **esté** disponible. Prefiero vivir solo, pero si no veo nada que sea apropiado, podría compartir un apartamento más grande con un amigo mío.

Well, that depends on what's available. I'd rather live alone, but if I don't see anything that works, I could share a bigger apartment with a friend of mine.

AGENTE: Bien. Primero, dígame sus preferencias.

OK. First, tell me what you're looking for.

ALBERTO: **Lo más importante** es la ubicación. **Quiero que** el apartamento **esté** en la ciudad, cerca de la universidad. Por otra parte, **es importante que esté** cerca del metro—pues no tengo carro.	*The most important thing is the location. I want the apartment to be in the city, near the university. Also, it's important that it be near a metro station—I don't have a car.*
AGENTE: Bien, entonces, no le importa si no tiene estacionamiento.	*OK, then you don't mind if there's no parking space.*
ALBERTO: Efectivamente. Pero **quiero** un edificio que tenga **vigilancia**. **Necesito**, además, **que tenga** salón, comedor, un dormitorio y, claro, cocina y baño modernos. Ah, y si es posible, me gustaría tener balcón.	*Exactly. But I want a secure building. I also need it to have a living room, dining room, one bedroom, and, of course, a modern kitchen and bathroom. Oh, and if possible, I'd like to have a balcony.*
AGENTE: ¿Y cuál es su presupuesto? O sea, ¿cuánto piensa pagar mensualmente, **incluyendo** luz, calefacción y agua?	*And what is your budget? I mean, what monthly rent are you thinking about, including utilities?*
ALBERTO: Espero encontrar algo por unos setecientos dólares.	*I'm hoping to find something for about seven hundred dollars.*
AGENTE: Mire, por setecientos dólares, no va a encontrar **nada que sea** decente en el centro de la ciudad. Hay edificios modernos y seguros, que **incluso** están cerca del metro, pero quedan por lo menos seis millas del centro.	*Look, for seven hundred dollars you're not going to find anything decent in the city. There are modern, secure buildings that are actually near the metro, but they're all at least six miles outside the city.*
ALBERTO: ¿Será posible **encontrar algo** más céntrico **que tenga** dos dormitorios por lo doble de esa cantidad, esto es, alrededor de $1,400 al mes?	*Would it be possible to find a two-bedroom place closer in for twice that amount—around $1,400 a month?*
AGENTE: Déjeme averiguarlo. No le voy a decir que sea imposible, pero no le puedo prometer nada. Déme unas horas para ver qué posibilidades hay. Si encuentro algo que **valga la pena**, podemos ir a verlo hoy mismo por la tarde. Mientras tanto, **necesito que** usted **rellene** este **formulario** con sus datos e información de contacto. Por cierto, tanto usted como su amigo tendrán que rellenar una **solicitud** para que los aprueben como inquilinos. Presumo que quieren el alquiler por un año, ¿correcto? **Asegúrense** de traer los documentos relativos a sus finanzas y su crédito.	*Let me have a look. I'm not going to tell you that it's impossible, but I can't promise anything. Give me a couple of hours to see what's out there. If I see anything worthwhile, we can go look at it this afternoon. In the meantime, I need you to fill out this form, so I have your contact information. As a matter of fact, both you and your friend will have to fill out an application in order to be approved as tenants. I'm assuming you are looking for a one-year lease. Is that correct? Be sure to bring your financial and credit information with you.*
ALBERTO: **De acuerdo**. Sí, estamos dispuestos a firmar un contrato por un año. Ahora voy a buscar a mi amigo y reunir la documentación requerida. Regreso con él a mediodía. Muchísimas gracias. **Hasta luego**.	*Fine. Yes, we're willing to sign a one-year lease. Now I'm going to look for my friend and get my papers. I'll be back with him at noon. Thank you very much. See you shortly.*
AGENTE: **Hasta luego**.	*See you later.*

To express *wanting, needing, hoping for,* or *looking for* a person or a thing that fits a certain description—but which you are not certain exists—the subjunctive is used for that description. In other words, if you know what you want but can't take a picture of it, it's still in your imagination, so choose the subjunctive to describe it. Use the following formula:

Conjugated form of **querer/necesitar/esperar encontrar/buscar + una casa/un trabajo/un médico/una pareja/un profesor + que** + subjunctive verb

Quiero una casa **que tenga** piscina.	*I want a house that has a swimming pool.*
Necesita un trabajo **que pague** bien.	*He needs a job that pays well.*
Esperamos encontrar un médico **que sepa** curar esta enfermedad.	*We're hoping to find a doctor who can cure this disease.*
Buscan un profesor **que dé** exámenes fáciles.	*They're looking for a professor who gives easy exams.*

When what is desired is a *person*, no personal **a** is used (because, essentially, it is not yet known who that person might be). However, and not so logically, if you want to express *someone*—**alguien**—you do precede it with **a**.

Busco a alguien que me pueda ayudar.	*I'm looking for someone who can help me.*

If you want, need, or are looking for something that you know exists, or someone you already know (you can take a picture of them!), then you use the indicative and the personal **a**.

Necesito a mi hermana, que sabe solucionar este problema.	*I need my sister, who knows how to solve this problem.*

Compare the following sentences, the first using the subjunctive and the second using the indicative.

Busco una persona que **hable** español.	*I'm looking for somebody who speaks Spanish. (who might practice with me)*
Busco a una persona que **habla** español.	*I'm looking for somebody who speaks Spanish. (she's lost at the shopping mall)*

Buscar, in addition to meaning *to look for,* can also mean *to go get.*

Voy a buscar a mi hija, que me puede ayudar.	*I'm going to get my daughter, who can help me.*
Ve a buscar las llaves, están en la cocina.	*Go get the keys, they're in the kitchen.*

There are other ways to express *get,* all with different meanings. **Conseguir** and **obtener** mean *to get* in a general sense, like *obtain.*

Espero **conseguir** trabajo.	*I hope to get a job.*
Está tratando de **obtener** el dinero.	*He's trying to get the money.*

Ponerse

Ponerse followed by an adjective expresses *to get in that condition.*

La chica **se pone** roja cuando tiene vergüenza.	*The girl gets red when she's embarrassed.*

Me pongo triste cuando pienso en mis padres.		I get sad when I think about my parents.	
Abrígate. **Te vas a poner** enfermo. (used in Spain rather than **enfermarse**)		Put your coat on. You're going to get sick.	

A large number of verbs used with reflexive pronouns can express *to get*. For example:

aburrirse	*to get bored*	emborracharse	*to get drunk*
cansarse	*to get tired*	emocionarse	*to get excited*
casarse	*to get married*	frustrarse	*to get frustrated*
enfadarse (Spain)	*to get angry*	herirse	*to get hurt*
enfermarse	*to get sick*	mejorarse	*to get better*
enojarse (L.A.)	*to get angry*	perderse	*to get lost*
enriquecerse	*to get rich*	preocuparse	*to get worried*

No voy a pedir postre, pues no quiero **ponerme gordo**.	*I'm not going to order dessert—I don't want to get fat.*
Ella no puede caminar esa distancia. **Se cansa.**	*She can't walk that far. She gets tired.*
Siempre usamos el sistema de SPG (Sistema de Posicionamiento Global) porque no queremos **perdernos**.	*We always use the GPS because we don't want to get lost.*
Espero que no **se enojen** conmigo.	*I hope you all don't get mad at me.*

Lo importante

Lo importante means *the important thing*. When it is followed by a known fact, it is stated in the indicative.

Lo importante es que todos están bien.	*The important thing is that everybody is all right.*

When it is followed by something that is hoped for, that is stated in the subjunctive.

Lo importante es que encuentre trabajo.	*The important thing is that I find work.*
Es importante que vengas a clase mañana.	*It's important that you come to class tomorrow.*

Other impersonal expressions that actually state personal opinions are also followed by the subjunctive.

Es ridículo que él no lo trate con más respeto.	*It's ridiculous that he doesn't treat him with more respect.*
Es una lástima que estén enfermos.	*It's a shame that they are sick.*

To indicate that something *needs to be done,* use the subjunctive after an impersonal expression.

Es necesario que practiques.	*It's necessary that you practice./You need to practice.*
Es imprescindible que protejamos los recursos naturales.	*It's absolutely necessary that we protect our natural resources.*

Ir and venir

The verbs that express *coming* and *going* are a little tricky for English speakers. In English, *come* indicates where you are or where the person you are talking to is, or will be, at the time of the expected arrival; and *go* indicates a third place where neither the speaker or the hearer is expected to be. In other words, in English, one can *come here*, *come there*, or *go there*. In Spanish, it's much simpler: **venir** is used with **aquí** (Spain) and **acá** (Latin America); **ir** is used with **allí** and **allá**. It does not matter whether the person will be there or not. Consider the following examples, and you will see that while **venir** is always translated as *to come*, **ir** can be translated as *to come* or *to go*.

Ven a mi casa.	*Come to my house.*
Voy a tu casa.	*I'm coming to your house. (You will be there then.)/I'm going to your house. (You won't be there then.)*
Ve al mercado.	*Go to the market.*
(Suena el timbre)—**¡Voy!**	*(The doorbell rings)—I'm coming!*

Incluyendo

Incluyendo means *including* something that may or may not ordinarily be included:

El alquiler es sólo a quinientos dólares al mes, **incluyendo** luz y agua.	*The rent is only five hundred dollars a month, including electricity and water.*

Incluso can mean *including* or *even* when it refers to something that is not necessarily always considered to be a member of the group mentioned.

Toda la familia, **incluso** el perro, fue a la playa.	*The whole family, including/even the dog, went to the beach.*

Incluso can also be translated as *actually*.

Esta ciudad es muy agradable. Es **incluso** la ciudad que más me gusta de todas.	*This city is very pleasant. It's actually the city I like best of all.*
Esa mujer está siempre con su perro. **Incluso** quiso llevarlo a una boda.	*That woman is always with her dog. She actually tried to take it to a wedding.*

Formulario

A **formulario** is a document with blank spaces that individuals fill in with their personal information.

Es necesario que rellene **este formulario**.	*It's necessary that you fill out this form.*

Forma has several meanings. It can mean *shape*.

¿**De qué forma** es este objeto?	*What shape is this object?*
Es un triángulo.	*It's a triangle.*

It can mean *form*, to refer to elements of grammar.

Las formas del subjuntivo no son difíciles de aprender.	*Subjunctive forms aren't hard to learn.*
Usa **la forma** del infinitivo después de una preposición.	*Use the infinitive form after a preposition.*

To express *to form* use **formar**.

Van a **formar** un grupo de protesta.	*They're going to form a protest group.*

Forma can also refer to the *way* something is or can be done. Alternatives to this meaning of **forma** are **manera** and **modo**.

Debe de haber **alguna forma/alguna manera/algún modo** de hacer esto más rápido.	*There must be a faster way to do this.*
Yo lo hago de **esta forma/de esta manera/de este modo/así.**	*I do it like this.*

De todas formas

De todas formas/De todas maneras/De todos modos can be translated as *anyway*, in the sense that no matter what happened before, what comes next takes precedence.

Hace mucho frío, pero voy a llevar mis nuevas sandalias **de todas formas.**	*It's really cold, but I'm going to wear my new sandals anyway.*
A veces se porta muy mal, pero la quiero **de todos modos.**	*Sometimes she behaves badly, but I love her anyway.*

Solicitud

Solicitud means *application*, in the sense of an appeal for a job or entrance to a school or other organization. The verb for *to apply*, in the same sense, is **solicitar**.

La **solicitud** para la entrada a aquella universidad es muy larga y detallada.	*The application for entrance to that university is long and detailed.*
¿Vas tú a **solicitar** el puesto?	*Are you going to apply for the job?*

Aplicación and aplicar

Aplicación and **aplicar** are only sometimes **falsos amigos**, as they refer to the *application* or *applying* of some kind of liquid or paste to a surface.

Van a **aplicar** tres manos de pintura a las paredes.	*They're going to apply three coats of paint to the walls.*
Deberías **aplicar** protector del sol antes de salir.	*You should apply sunscreen before going out.*

Aplicarse, used with a reflexive pronoun, means *to apply*, in the sense of a law or rule.

La regla **se aplica** a todos los estudiantes, incluso a los que están en su último año.	*The rule applies to all students, including seniors.*

Valer la pena

This expression means *to be worthwhile, worth the time or trouble*, or *to be of great value*.

No gano casi nada. **No vale la pena** seguir trabajando aquí.	*I hardly earn anything. It's not worth the trouble to keep on working here.*
Pon atención a los detalles. **Vale la pena** llenar la solicitud con cuidado.	*Pay attention to the details. It's worthwhile to fill the application form out carefully.*
Su hijo se casa con una chica que realmente **vale la pena.**	*Her son is marrying a girl who is a real treasure.*

Before a word that begins with the letter *i* or the letters *hi*, the word **y** *(and)* changes to **e**.

Esa chica estudia medicina **e ingeniería** a la vez.
That girl is studying medicine and engineering at the same time.

Voy al congreso con Margarita **e Inés.**
I'm going to the conference with Margarita and Inés.

Asegurarse de

Asegurarse de means *to make sure that you do something.* It is followed by a verb in infinitive form.

Tenemos que **asegurarnos de** cerrar la puerta con llave.
We have to make sure we lock the door.

Asegúrate de repasar las formas del subjuntivo.
Make sure you review the subjunctive forms.

EJERCICIO
19·8

Fill in each blank with the subjunctive form of the verb indicated.

1. Necesitamos una secretaria que (ser) _____ bilingüe.

2. Buscan una casa que (tener) _____ una cocina grande.

3. Espero encontrar a alguien que (conocer) _____ a mi hermano.

4. Quiero conseguir un trabajo que me (ofrecer) _____ la oportunidad de viajar.

5. Tú necesitas un amigo que te (comprender) _____.

6. Él busca un profesor que le (aconsejar) _____.

EJERCICIO
19·9

Choose the infinitive, the indicative, or the subjunctive form of each verb indicated, as appropriate.

1. Queremos una persona que (sabe) _____ contabilidad.

2. Están buscando al antiguo contador, que (saber) _____ hacer las cuentas.

3. Mi amiga sabe (hacer) _____ las cuentas.

4. Ella necesita un jefe que la (apreciar) _____.

5. Ellos esperan contratar una persona que (poder) _____ vender sus productos.

6. Mis amigos no quieren (pintar) _____ su casa.

7. Buscan a alguien que (estar) _____ dispuesto a pintar su casa.

8. Él necesita un profesor que (tener) _____ paciencia.

9. Yo quiero mucho a mi profesor, que (tener) _____ mucha paciencia.

10. Esperamos encontrar un restaurante que (servir) _____ comida sana.

¿Cómo se dice en español? *Translate the following sentences into Spanish.*

1. We want a roommate who doesn't smoke.

   _____

2. I'm looking for my cousin, who works here.

   _____

3. She's looking for someone who works here.

   _____

4. They want a car that doesn't use much gas.

   _____

5. We need a salesman who speaks Spanish.

   _____

6. They have a salesman who speaks Spanish.

   _____

Fill in each blank with the most appropriate expression.

1. Él espera (get) _____ un puesto importante.

2. La chica siempre (turns) _____ roja cuando la maestra le hace una pregunta.

3. No queremos (get fat) _____, de modo que no vamos a comer ni pizza ni pasta.

4. Ella siempre (gets) _____ lo que quiere, de alguna manera.

5. Yo (get) _____ triste cuando me despido de mis amigos.

6. Mi amiga compra y vende acciones por Internet, esperando (get rich) _____.

7. Si tú (get sick) _____, te llevo al médico.

8. Si tú (get lost) _____, llama a mi celular.

¿Cómo se dice en español? *Express the following in Spanish.*

1. Don't get sick!

_____

2. I hope he doesn't get mad.

_____

3. He wants to get married.

_____

4. Get better soon!

_____

5. She gets frustrated easily.

_____

6. We get bored in that class.

_____

7. I don't want you to get worried.

_____

8. They get excited when they think about the trip.

_____

Fill in each blank with the subjunctive form of the indicated verb.

1. Es horrible que (haber, una persona singular) _____ guerras.

2. Es ridículo que no (darse cuenta, ellos) _____ del peligro.

3. Es una lástima que (enojarse, él) _____ por tan poca cosa.

4. Es importante que (preservar, nosotros) _____ el medio ambiente.

5. Es necesario que (portarse, tú) _____ bien.

6. Es imprescindible que (perder, usted) _____ peso.

¿Cómo se dice en español? *Express the following in Spanish.*

1. Can you come to my house?

   _____

2. Are you going to the market?

   _____

3. Are you coming to our wedding? It's at the Botanical Garden.

   _____

4. Is he coming to the movies with us?

   _____

5. Do you come here often?

   _____

6. Are you all going to class?

   _____

7. Are you all coming to class tomorrow?

   _____

8. What time are you coming?

   _____

*Answer each of the questions in Exercise 19-14 using a form of **ir** or **venir**, as appropriate.*

1. _____
2. _____
3. _____
4. _____
5. _____
6. _____
7. _____
8. _____

EJERCICIO
19·16

Choose the most appropriate word to fill in each blank.

1. Todo esto nos va a costar $869.32, _____ los impuestos.
   incluyendo   incluso

2. La niña quiere invitar a toda la clase, _____ a la maestra, a su fiesta de cumpleaños.
   incluyendo   incluso

3. Ese actor es muy guapo. Puede ser _____ el actor más guapo de Hollywood.
   incluyendo   incluso

4. Para poder estudiar en la universidad, el primer paso es llenar esta _____.
   forma   aplicación   solicitud   papel

5. ¿Hay algún _____ que tengo que llenar?
   formulario   forma   aplicación   papel

6. La película tiene violencia, pero voy a verla de todas _____.
   aplicaciones   solicitudes   formas   formulario

7. Necesitan meseros en el nuevo restaurante. ¿Quiénes van a _____?
   solicitar   aplicarse   venir   cocinar

8. Esta ley no puede _____ a los niños.
   pertenecer   asegurarse   aplicarse   ponerse

9. Tenemos que _____ de llevar el paraguas, por si llueve.
   aplicarnos   asegurarnos   valer la pena   ponernos

10. En serio, _____ asistir a todas las clases.
    asegura   vale la pena   ponte   solicita

Making requests and offers

Now we'll look at a conversation that utilizes the subjective to make requests and offers.

Conversation: Helping a classmate

FEDERICO: **Oye**, amigo, ¿te puedo **pedir** un favor?

Hey, buddy, can I ask you a favor?

DAVID: **Por supuesto, ¿de qué se trata?**

Of course—what can I do for you?

FEDERICO: **¿Me prestas** tus **apuntes** de la clase de biología? **Es que** estuve enfermo y **perdí** unos días de clase y ahora estoy algo perdido.

Will you lend me your biology notes? When I was sick I missed a couple of classes, and now I'm totally lost.

DAVID: Bueno. Acompáñame a la biblioteca y haremos una fotocopia de mi cuaderno. Luego vamos a tu casa

OK. Come to the library with me and we'll copy my notebook. Then we can go to your house and review the

para repasar las lecciones que **perdiste**. Yo **te las explico** con mucho gusto.

FEDERICO: Pues, muchas gracias. No sé qué haría sin ti.

DAVID: No es nada. **Por cierto**, yo también quiero pedirte un gran favor.

FEDERICO: ¿Ah, sí? ¡No me digas que quieres otro consejo sobre tu novia!

DAVID: No, no es exactamente eso. Lo que pasa es que este fin de semana viene su hermana a verla. ¿Estarías dispuesto a salir con ella el sábado por la noche? Iríamos los cuatro al teatro y luego a comer. ¿Qué te parece?

FEDERICO: Mira, ya **he quedado con** José para ir al cine. Pero, ¿qué te parece si la invito a ir al cine conmigo y con José? Y claro, luego iríamos a comer algo, aunque no sea a un lugar muy elegante.

DAVID: Me parece una buena solución, pero primero la tendré que hablar con mi novia. Mira, **te llamo en cuanto tenga** su respuesta.

FEDERICO: De acuerdo. Y **por cierto**, mil gracias por la ayuda con la biología.

DAVID: No es nada. **No dudes en llamarme** si tienes alguna pregunta.

lessons you missed. I'll be glad to explain them to you.

Man, thanks a lot. I don't know what I'd do without you.

It's nothing. As a matter of fact, I have a favor to ask of you.

Oh yeah? Don't tell me that you want more advice about your girlfriend!

Well, not exactly. It's that her sister is coming to visit this weekend. Would you be willing to go out with her on Saturday night? We'd all four go to the theater and then out to eat. How does that sound?

Look, I already agreed to go to the movies with José. But how about if I invite her to go to the movies with me and José? Of course, afterwards we'd get something to eat, although it won't be a very fancy place.

That sounds like a good solution, but first I'll have to discuss it with my girlfriend. Look, I'll call you as soon as I have her answer.

Good. And by the way, thanks a lot for the help with biology.

No problem. Don't hesitate to call me if you have any questions.

Oye

This is the **tú** command form of **oír**, and it is used to get someone's attention, kind of like *Hey*. The **usted** form is **Oiga**.

Oye, Luis, ¿estás ocupado?
Hey, Luis, are you busy?

Oiga, señor—¿se le cayó este cuaderno?
Excuse me, sir—did you drop this notebook?

Pedir

Pedir is used to make a request or ask someone to do something. To use it in a sentence, follow this pattern:

indirect object pronoun + conjugation of **pedir** + **que** + verb in subjunctive

Te pido que vengas a la oficina ahora mismo.
I'm asking you to come to the office right now.

Él siempre **me pide que hable** más despacio.
He always asks me to speak more slowly.

Other verbs used to make requests—in a more urgent manner—include:

rogar	*beg*
suplicar	*beg (on one knee)*
implorar	*implore/beseech/beg (on both knees!)*

These verbs follow the same pattern as **pedir**.

Le ruego que me ayude.	*I beg you to help me.*
Le suplican que les dé dinero.	*They beg him to give them money.*
Les imploramos que no vayan a la calle.	*We beseech you not to go out into the street.*

Another way to ask a favor is to simply make a question in the present tense, beginning with the indirect object pronoun that indicates the person who is the recipient of the favor. This translates to English as *will you . . . for me/us?*

¿Me ayudas?	*Will you help me?*
¿Me haces un favor?	*Will you do me a favor?*
¿Nos escribe una carta?	*Will you write us a letter?*
¿Nos das las instrucciones?	*Will you give us the directions?*

The most direct way to ask for something is to give a command.

¡Ayúdame!	*Help me!*
Mándame un email.	*Send me an e-mail.*
Escríbanos una carta.	*Write us a letter.*
Danos las instrucciones.	*Give us the directions.*

You could also use the expression **Hazme/Hágame el favor de + infinitive**, which can be a little sarcastic.

Hazme el favor de llamarme esta noche.	*Do me a favor and call me tonight.*

Of course, with any method of asking for something, it's always better to use **Por favor**!

Tratar de

Tratar de means *try to* when it is followed by a verb in infinitive form.

Siempre **trato de** terminar mi trabajo antes de volver a casa.	*I always try to finish my work before I go home.*

It can be used with the impersonal pronoun **se**, giving it the meaning *to be about (something)*.

¿De qué **se trata?**	*What's it about?*
Se trata de un asunto personal.	*It's about a personal matter.*

Ofrecer

When used with reflexive pronouns, this verb indicates an offer to do something for someone else.

La profesora siempre **se ofrece** para ayudarnos.	*The teacher always offers to help us.*

The expression, **¿Qué se te/le/les ofrece?** means *What can I do for you?* Another way to offer a favor to someone is to use the present tense in question form.

¿Te ayudo?	*Can I help you?*
¿Les presto el dinero?	*Can I lend you (plural) the money?*

You could also use **querer que + subjunctive**.

¿Quieres que te ayude?	*Do you want me to help you?*
¿Quieren ustedes que les preste el dinero?	*Do you all want me to lend you the money?*

Por supuesto

Por supuesto indicates *of course/naturally/that goes without saying*.

Por supuesto te acompaño.	*Of course I'll go with you.*
¿Siempre vamos a Cancún para el descanso de primavera?	*Are we still going to Cancún for spring break?*
¡Por supuesto!	*Of course!*

Prestar

Prestar—which means *to lend*—and other verbs that indicate an *exchange* of something from one person to another, need both indirect and direct objects. (See Chapter 12.) The indirect object is always a person—the person who receives something from the subject. The direct object is the thing that is received. The pattern is as follows:

Indirect object pronoun	+	exchange verb (conjugated)	+	direct object noun
↓		↓		↓
Me		presta		el libro.
Te		prestan		el carro.

He lends the book to me. (To me he lends the book.)
They're lending the car to you. (To you they are lending the car.)

To use a direct object pronoun in place of the noun, put it right after the indirect object pronoun.

Me **lo** presta.	*He lends it to me.*
Te **lo** prestan.	*They're lending it to you.*

If the indirect object is **le** (*to her/to him/to you*) or **les** (*to them/to you all*), it changes to **se** when followed by a direct object pronoun.

Se lo presta (a ella).	*He lends it to her.*
Se lo prestan (a ustedes).	*They're lending it to you all.*

Other exchange verbs include:

dar	*give*	explicar	*explain*
decir	*tell*	mandar	*send*
enseñar	*teach/show*	mostrar	*show*
entregar	*deliver*	ofrecer	*offer*
enviar	*send*		

Ella **me da** muchos regalos.	*She gives me a lot of presents.*
Ella **me los da.**	*She gives them to me.*
Ellos **nos dicen** sus secretos.	*They tell us their secrets.*
Ellos **nos los dicen.**	*They tell them to us.*
Ustedes **nos dicen** la verdad.	*You all tell us the truth.*
Ustedes **nos la dicen.**	*You tell it to us.*
Nosotros **te ofrecemos** los boletos.	*We're offering you the tickets.*
Nosotros **te los ofrecemos.**	*We're offering them to you.*

To borrow can be expressed by using **pedir que** + the subjunctive of **prestar**.

Le pido que me preste su libro.	*I'm asking you to lend me your book.*
¿Me lo presta?	*Will you lend it to me?*

When the indirect-direct object combination is used with an infinitive or a gerund, it can be placed before the conjugated verb in the sentence, or it can be attached to the end of the infinitive or gerund.

Te voy a dar las llaves.	*I'm going to give you the keys.*
Te las voy a **dar.**/Voy a **dártelas.**	*I'm going to give them to you.*
Me está prestando su carro.	*He's lending me his car.*
Me lo está **prestando.**/Está **prestándomelo.**	*He's lending it to me.*

As you can see, these exchange verbs have a very different pattern from the one used in English. Another thing that is different from English is that in Spanish when you use an indirect object pronoun, you can also emphasize it by using the preposition **a** followed by the corresponding pronoun. In English this would be redundant.

Te voy a dar las llaves **a ti.** (no a tu hermano)	*I'm going to give the keys to **you.** (not to your brother)*
Me está prestando el carro **a mí.** (no a ti)	*He's lending the car to **me.** (not to you)*

Note that the use of **a** + pronoun is optional, but the indirect object pronoun is necessary.

Apuntes

Apuntes are the *notes* that you take in class. The **nota** that you get at the end of a course is your *grade*.

Mi amigo toma muy buenos **apuntes.**	*My friend takes really good notes.*
Espero sacar una buena **nota** en este curso.	*I hope I get a good grade in this course.*

Es que

Es que and **lo que pasa es que** mean, literally, *It's that . . ./What's happening is that . . .* They are used to indicate that you are about to give an explanation.

Sonia, ¿por qué siempre llegas tarde?	*Sonia, why are you always late?*
Lo siento, señora, **es que** tengo que trabajar antes de venir a clase.	*I'm sorry, Ma'am, it's that I have to work before coming to class.*

Perder

Perder means *to lose*, but it can also mean *to miss* something such as a train, bus, class, or an opportunity.

No me gusta **perder** una clase.	*I don't like to miss a class.*
Apúrate, no quiero **perder** el tren.	*Hurry up, I don't want to miss the train.*

Perderse means *to fail to experience.*

Es una lástima que **te hayas perdido** la fiesta.	*It's a shame that you missed the party.*

To *miss* a person or a place is expressed by **extrañar** (Latin America) or **echar de menos** (Latin America and Spain).

Te extraño mucho.	*I miss you a lot.*
Echo mucho de menos a mis padres.	*I miss my parents a lot.*

When a part is *missing* from a whole, **faltar** is used.

Faltan tres páginas de la revista.	*Three pages are missing from the magazine.*

Faltar a can mean *to miss work or school.*

Nunca **ha faltado** al trabajo.	*He's never missed a day from work.*

To *miss* a goal in a game is expressed with **fallar**.

¡Falló!	*He missed!*

Fallar, when used with an indirect object pronoun, means *to let someone down.*

Trabajo duro porque no quiero **fallarte**.	*I work hard because I don't want to let you down.*

To *miss* an item on a test is expressed with **pasarse (por alto)**.

Se me pasaron (por alto) tres preguntas.	*I missed three questions.*

Quedar con... para

This expression means *to agree to meet someone for.*

Quedé con Alfredo para almorzar.	*I agreed to meet Alfredo for lunch.*

Alternatively, you can use a plural conjugation of **quedar en** + infinitive—*to agree to do something.*

Quedamos en reuinirnos a las ocho.	*We agreed to get together at eight o'clock.*

De acuerdo is a way of saying that you agree to a plan.

Entonces, ¿pasas por mí a las cinco?	*Then will you pick me up at five o'clock?*
De acuerdo.	*OK.*

En cuanto

En cuanto is translated as *as soon as* and is followed by a verb in the subjunctive.

Los llamo **en cuanto** llegue a Bogotá.	I'll call you (all) as soon as I arrive in Bogotá.
Dejaré este trabajo **en cuanto** tenga el dinero que necesito para comprar la casa.	I'll leave this job as soon as I have the money I need to buy the house.

Por cierto

This expression can be used to insert a new topic—or a new aspect of a topic being discussed—into a conversation. It can be translated as *by the way*.

Ayer vi a Olga con un grupo de sus amigas. **Por cierto,** ¿sigues saliendo con ella?	I saw Olga yesterday with a group of her girlfriends. By the way, do you still go out with her?

No dudar en is an expression that means *not to hesitate to*, usually in command form.

No dudes en contactarme si necesitas algo.	Don't hesitate to contact me if you need anything.

EJERCICIO 19·17

Fill in each blank with the appropriate indirect object pronoun.

1. Amigo, _____ pido que me ayudes.

2. Señor González, _____ rogamos que no nos dé el examen hoy.

3. A sus padres _____ suplica que cambien de opinión.

4. A su novia _____ implora que no llore.

5. _____ voy a pedir a la profesora que me explique la lección.

EJERCICIO 19·18

Change each of the following sentences from English to Spanish.

1. I beg you not to drive so fast.

_____

2. We're asking them to go with us.

_____

3. They implore their professor to change the date of the exam.

_____

4. Are you asking me to leave?

_____

Express in Spanish the following favors that you might ask of a friend. Use the question form in the present tense.

1. llamar esta noche (a mí) _____

2. llevar a casa (a nosotros) _____

3. ayudar con las maletas (a nosotras) _____

4. mandar una postal (a mí) _____

5. comprar un helado (a mí) _____

6. traer flores (a mí) _____

*Change the favors requested in Exercise 19-19 to direct commands. Give two commands for each favor, one in the **tú** form and one in the **usted** form.*

1. _____

2. _____

3. _____

4. _____

5. _____

6. _____

Express in Spanish the following offers that you might make to one person or several people, as indicated.

1. Can I help you? (a ti) _____

2. Can I clean the house for you? (a ustedes) _____

3. Can I take you to the airport? (a vosotros) _____

4. Can I wash your car for you? (a usted) _____

Rewrite each of the following sentences, changing the direct object noun (underlined) into a pronoun.

1. Le estoy enviando <u>un email</u>.

_____

2. Te doy <u>el dinero</u> la próxima semana.

_____

3. Nos van a mostrar <u>las fotos</u> de su viaje esta noche.

_____

4. Él le dice <u>todos sus secretos</u> a su amiga.

_____

5. Le tengo que entregar <u>la tarea</u> a la profesora mañana.

_____

6. Les ofrecemos <u>nuestra casa</u> para el verano.

_____

7. ¿Te presto <u>el dinero</u>?

_____

8. Ella le enseña <u>español</u> a mi hijo.

_____

¿Cómo se dice en español? *Express the following in Spanish.*

1. He wants to show you (**tú**) his photos.

_____

2. He wants to show them to you.

_____

3. She's going to teach us the song.

_____

4. She's going to teach it to us.

_____

5. I'm explaining the lesson to her.

_____

6. I'm explaining it to her.

_____

7. I'm going to send him a message.

_____

8. I'm going to send it to him.

_____

EJERCICIO
19·24

¿Cómo se dice en español? *Express the following in Spanish.*

1. Will you lend me your notes?

_____

2. Will you lend them to me?

_____

3. May we borrow your car?

_____

4. May we borrow it?

_____

EJERCICIO
19·25

¿Cómo se dice en español? *Express the following in Spanish.*

1. I miss my friends.

_____

2. You're going to miss the party.

_____

3. I don't want to lose my homework.

_____

4. We're going to miss the bus.

_____

5. Do you miss your country?

_____

6. Two books are missing from the list.

_____

7. She never misses a question.

_____

8. They're going to lose the game.

_____

9. They're going to miss the train.

_____

Indefinite and negative words and expressions

You are probably already familiar with most of the words and expressions in this chapter. Indefinite and negative words can be adjectives (**alguno**[a], *some*), pronouns (**nadie**, *no one, nobody*), or adverbs (**nunca**, *never*).

Algunas personas no viajan por avión.	**Some** people do not travel by plane.
No veo a **nadie**.	I do not see **anyone**.
No sale **nunca**.	He **never** goes out.

Algo and **nada** may be *pronouns* that describe something imprecise and, therefore, indefinite.

Algo puede cambiar.	**Something** may change.

Yet these two words serve as *adverbs* in situations such as:

Marta se siente **algo** mejor ahora.	Marta feels **somewhat** better now.
No me gusta esta situación **nada**.	I do not like this situation **at all**.

Conjunctions may also be used as indefinite and negative words. Note: **O... o...** and **ni... ni...** are always used in pairs:

O salimos **o** nos quedamos.	**Either** we go **or** we stay.
Ni fumo **ni** bebo.	I **neither** smoke **nor** drink.

By grouping these expressions together as indefinite and negative words, we can focus on their uses and contrast them with their English equivalents.

Indefinite and negative words in Spanish

Indefinite and negative words may refer to people or things. You will learn them more easily as contrasting pairs, as they are presented in the following list.

INDEFINITE		NEGATIVE	
algo	*something, somewhat*	**nada**	*nothing*
alguien	*someone, somebody, anyone, anybody*	**nadie**	*no one, not anyone*
algún, -a, -o, -as, -os	*some, somebody*	**ningún, -a, -o, -as, -os**	*no, none*
o... o...	*either . . . or . . .*	**ni... ni...**	*neither . . . nor . . .*
sí	*yes*	**no**	*no*
siempre	*always*	**nunca, jamás**	*never*
también	*also*	**tampoco**	*neither*

En español.

1. No one works in this office. _____

2. Some people (**personas**) are nicer than others. _____

3. I never ask questions. _____

4. I do not talk much either. _____

5. Sometimes I need help. _____

6. Do you (**Ud.**) speak German too? _____

7. She eats either potatoes or rice only. _____

8. Neither you (**tú**) nor I. _____

When are indefinite and negative words used in Spanish?

Here is a summary of the uses of indefinite and negative words in Spanish:

♦ **Alguien** and **nadie** refer only to *people*.

Alguien me manda flores a la oficina todos los viernes.	**Someone** sends me flowers at my office every Friday.
No veo **a nadie** en el salón de fiestas.	I **don't** see **anyone** in the ballroom.

Note the personal **a** in the second example above; **nadie** is the direct object of the verb **veo**.

♦ **Algo** and **nada** refer only to *things or ideas*.

¿Vas a hacer **algo**?	*Are you going to do **anything (something)**?*
Nada va a cambiar.	***Nothing** is going to change.*

♦ The forms **algún/alguna/alguno/algunas/algunos** and **ningún/ninguna/ninguno/ningunas/ningunos** may refer to both *people and things*. A spelling rule requires a written accent mark on **algún/ningún** when the **-o** ending of the adjectives **alguno** and **ninguno** is dropped, and these words (masculine, singular) precede the noun.

Algunos estudiantes no quieren estudiar pero **ningún profesor** está de acuerdo.	***Some students** do not want to study but **none of the professors** agrees.*

Note: The form **alguno(a)**, when used as an adjective, follows the noun and may replace the negative **ninguno(a)**. **Algún** always precedes the noun.

Las leyes no son respetadas por **criminal alguno**.	***No criminal** respects the laws.*
Algún día vamos a viajar al espacio.	***One day** we are going to travel into space.*

Indefinite and negative words and expressions   **391**

- Use the negative adverb **no** before the conjugated verb or before the pronoun if an object pronoun precedes the verb.

No beben vino.	*They **do not (don't)** drink wine.*
No los quieren aquí.	*They **don't** want **them** here.*

- Two or even three negative words may be used in Spanish in the same sentence. Remember that if a negative follows a verb, the verb must also be preceded by a negative.

Nunca viene **nadie** a las fiestas de Mary. ⎫ **Nadie** viene **nunca** a las fiestas de Mary. ⎬	***No one ever*** *comes to Mary's parties.*
¿**No** traes **ni** dinero **ni** tu documento de identidad al trabajo?	*You bring **neither** your money **nor** your ID to work?*

- Use **jamás**, **nada**, **nadie**, **ninguno**, and **nunca** in questions when you expect a negative answer. These words add emphasis to the message.

¿Conoces a **nadie** más cómico que Ramón?	*Do you know **anyone** funnier than Ramón?*

EJERCICIO
20·2

En el partido de fútbol. Choose the appropriate word to complete each sentence.

algo	alguien	nadie	siempre
algunos	nunca	ni	o

1. Ayer, sucedió _____ muy inusual en el estadio.

2. _____ he visto un equipo de fútbol tan desilusionado.

3. No ganamos el partido porque _____ pudo anotar un gol.

4. _____ los jugadores estaban cansados, _____ estaban confundidos.

5. ¡_____ de los fans estaban llorando!

6. _____ sacó un pañuelo para secarse las lágrimas.

7. _____ celebramos en Casa Manolo cuando ganamos el partido.

8. _____ yo _____ mis amigos fuimos a Casa Manolo.

EJERCICIO
20·3

¡No! Answer each question with the appropriate negative words.

1. ¿Hay refrescos en la nevera? _____

2. ¿Quiere Ud. dormir o jugar al fútbol? _____

3. ¿Van ellos a algún lugar interesante este fin de semana? _____

4. ¿Tienen alguna esperanza (*hope*) Uds. de encontrar el anillo perdido? _____

5. ¿Sabes donde están las preguntas y las respuestas para la tarea? _____

6. ¿Tienen tiempo para ayudarme? _____

7. ¿Vas a visitar a tus suegros siempre? _____

8. ¿Vas a saludar a tus tíos también? _____

9. ¿Celebran Uds. algún día especial esta semana? _____

10. ¿Conocen ellos a alguien de nuestra familia? _____

11. ¿Tienes algo que añadir (*add*)? _____

EJERCICIO
20·4

En español. *Remember, it may be necessary to use more than one negative word in Spanish. Use **algo**, **nada**, **nunca**, etc.*

1. I am somewhat preoccupied. _____

2. Is there someone in this room? _____

3. No one wants to do anything. _____

4. Manny neither took the photos nor filmed (**filmar**) the meeting. _____

5. Do we need to find Peter or Sandra? _____

6. Some day we are going to finish this work. _____

7. They do not like this work at all. _____

8. They will never do this. _____

Other negative expressions

Some of the words you have studied in this unit are also used in multiword negative expressions. These expressions serve as adverbs, prepositions, or conjunctions and are common in everyday conversation. They can be memorized as lexical items.

NEGATIVE EXPRESSIONS

ahora no	*not now*	**no importa**	*it does not matter*
de ninguna manera	*no way, certainly not*	**no... más que**	*no more than*
ni hablar	*certainly not*	**todavía no**	*not yet*
ni siquiera	*(not) even*	**ya no**	*no more, no longer*
ni... tampoco	*neither . . .*		

Un poco de sentido común. *Choose the letter that indicates the most appropriate response.*

_____ 1. Yo no sé dónde está tu auto.   a. No puedo, no tengo dinero.

_____ 2. ¿Ha empezado la película?   b. No, la butaca es dura.

_____ 3. ¿Puedes comprar dos refrescos?   c. Todavía no. En unos diez minutos.

_____ 4. Pero, ¿no tienes dinero?   d. Ni siquiera diez centavos.

_____ 5. ¿Quieres salir al baño ahora?   e. Ni yo tampoco.

_____ 6. ¿Estás cómodo en tu asiento?   f. Ahora, no.

The conjunctions **pero** and **sino** and negative expressions

Sino is a conjunction, a word that is used to link words, phrases, and sentences that have the same grammatical function.

No veo a tu hermano **sino** a tu primo.	*I do not see your brother **but (rather)** your cousin.*
Ellos no hablaron **sino** gritaron en la charla.	*They did not speak **but (rather)** screamed at the get-together.*

In the sentence **No veo *a tu hermano* sino a tu primo**, the direct object of **veo** is **a tu hermano** and **sino a tu primo** completes the direct object. The repeated personal **a** indicates the role of the direct object. In the second half of the sentence, **veo** is understood after **sino**: (**veo**) **a tu primo**. In Spanish, **sino** is referred to as a **conjunción adversativa**, always used after negative statements to state a counter position or contrast. **Sino** communicates the idea *on the contrary* or *rather*.

Sino may also indicate a restriction, equivalent to *only* in English in situations such as:

No espera **sino que** tú defiendas tus ideas.	*He wants **only that** you defend your ideas.*
Las hijas de Marsha no compran **sino** camisas de seda.	*Marsha's daughters buy **only** (do not buy **anything but**) silk shirts.*

Pero is another conjunction equivalent to *but* in English. The contrast expressed by **pero** is not as absolute. The meaning of **pero** is closer to *however* or *instead*.

Quieren papas fritas **pero** sin sal.	*They want French fries, **but** without salt.*
Vamos, **pero** no podemos gastar mucho dinero.	*Let's go, **but** we cannot spend much money.*

When are **pero** and **sino** used in Spanish?

Both **pero** and **sino** are used to state contrasts. When in doubt, think of the message you want to communicate to your audience.

- **Pero** communicates the idea of *however, instead.*

Venden buenos productos **pero** son muy caros.

*They sell good products, **but (however)** they are expensive.*

- **Sino** is used only after a negative statement and its meaning is closer to *on the contrary* or *but rather.*

No les gustan las películas de horror **sino** las películas cómicas.
No entraron **sino que** salieron.

*They do not like horror movies, **but (on the contrary)** funny movies.*
*They did not come in **but (instead)** went out.*

Note, in the example above, that if you contrast two conjugated verbs you should use **sino que**.

EJERCICIO
20·6

*Las cosas claras. Complete each sentence with **sino** + the words in parentheses.*

EJEMPLO   La plata no es un vegetal. (un mineral) →

La plata no es un vegetal sino un mineral.

1. El sol no es un planeta. (una estrella) _____

2. Blanca Nieves no es un personaje (*character*) real. (ficticio) _____

3. La astronomía no es un deporte. (una ciencia) _____

4. El inglés no es la lengua oficial de Portugal. (Inglaterra) _____

5. La paella no es un plato típico mexicano. (español) _____

6. El ballet no es un juego. (un arte) _____

7. Un crucigrama no es un problema. (un pasatiempo) _____

8. Un perro no es una persona. (un animal) _____

9. La luna no es una estrella. (un satélite) _____

EJERCICIO
20·7

¿Pero, sino o sino que? Complete each sentence with the appropriate conjunction.

1. Tienen muchos problemas _____ son felices.

2. No pueden caminar _____ correr para llegar a tiempo.

3. Tampoco saben esquiar _____ quieren aprender.

4. No escalaron la montaña _____ descansaron en el río.

5. Pescaron varias truchas (*trout*) _____ no las llevaron a casa.

6. Montaron en bicicleta _____ también nadaron toda la tarde en la playa.

7. Les gusta bucear (*dive*) _____ no tienen el equipo.

8. No ganaron el partido _____ quedaron en segundo lugar.

9. Tú sabes patinar muy bien _____ casi nunca practicas en el parque.

10. No queremos que se vayan _____ nos acompañen al lago.

Expressing doubts and uncertainty

Now we'll look at a conversation about expressing doubt and uncertainty.

Conversation: Advice to a friend

GABI: Ema, Estoy muy deprimida. Necesito hablar contigo. Voy a tu casa, si **no te importa**.

Ema, I'm really depressed. I need to talk to you. I'm coming over, if you don't mind.

EMA: Está bien. Te espero.

That's fine. I'll wait for you.

Más tarde:

EMA: Gabi, ¿qué tienes?

Gabi, what's the matter?

GABI: Es que todo está mal en mi vida. En primer lugar, tengo muchos problemas en el trabajo. Mi jefe se enoja conmigo **cada vez más**. Me regaña por **cualquier** cosa. Estos días no hago nada que le complazca. Me pone tan nerviosa que empiezo a cometer errores innecesarios.

It's just that everything is wrong with my life. In the first place, I have a lot of problems at work. My boss gets madder at me every day. He's on my case for every little thing. Lately I can't do anything that pleases him. He makes me so nervous that I'm beginning to make unnecesary mistakes.

EMA: ¿A qué **se debe** todo eso?

What's the reason for all that?

GABI: **A lo mejor** es porque él tiene problemas en casa. Pero eso no le da derecho a portarse tan mal conmigo, ¿verdad?

It's probably because he has problems at home. But that doesn't give him the right to take it all out on me, does it?

EMA: Al contrario, es en el trabajo donde debería tener un poco de serenidad para poder solucionar sus problemas personales en casa. **Al menos** es lo que pienso yo.

Quite the contrary, it's at work where he ought to seek a little peace so he can solve his personal problems at home. At least that's what I think.

GABI: Tengo la impresión que **no hay nadie** que sea realmente feliz. La situación en mi casa **tampoco** me da motivos para alegrarme. ¿Sabes ? Esos dos hombres con quienes comparto la casa **no tienen ni idea** de cómo mantenerla limpia. **No** hacen **nada**. Anoche estuve dos horas limpiando la cocina mientras que ellos comían pizza y veían la televisión. Ya **estoy harta** de sus malas costumbres. Pero eso no es

I have the impression that nobody is really happy. The situation at my house doesn't exactly cheer me up either. You know what? Those two guys I share the house with have no idea of how to keep it clean. They don't do anything. Last night I spent two hours cleaning the kitchen while they ate pizza and watched TV. I'm sick of their behavior. But that's not the worst! To top it all off, Roberto refuses to talk to me.

lo peor. **Para colmo**, Roberto ya no quiere hablar conmigo. **A veces** pienso que **no hay nada** en mi vida que realmente valga la pena.	*Sometimes I think there's nothing truly worthwhile in my life.*
EMA: Gabi, tranquilízate y veamos las cosas por orden. **No creo que** las cosas **sean** tan malas como las ves ahora. Para empezar, **te sugiero que hagamos** una lista de las cosas positivas de tu vida. Así, **te darás cuenta** de las ventajas que tienes. Luego haremos un plan para empezar a cambiar las cosas que no te convienen. No deberías deprimirte por lo que tiene solución.	*Calm down, Gabi, and let's look at one thing at a time. I don't think things are as bad as they seem right now. For a start, I suggest we make a list of the positive things in your life. That way, you'll realize the advantages that you have. Then we'll make a plan to begin changing the things that aren't working for you. You shouldn't let yourself get depressed.*
GABI: Gracias, Ema. Sabes, ya me siento mucho mejor. Eres una gran amiga.	*Thanks, Ema. You know, I already feel much better. You're a great friend.*
EMA: **Me importas** mucho. También sé que puedo **contar contigo** para un buen consejo **de vez en cuando.**	*I care about you. I also know that I can count on you for good advice from time to time.*

Importar

Importar can have a number of translations into English. When used with an indirect object, in question form, or as a negative answer, it means *to mind* or *to care*, in the sense of *to be a bother to someone.*

¿Te importa si te llamo en la noche?	*Do you mind if I call you at night?*
No **me importa.** Está bien.	*No, I don't mind. It's okay.*

But if it's just a statement, not a response to the question, *Do you mind?*, it means *to not care*, in the sense of *to not be important to someone.*

No me importa si no me llama.	*I don't care if he doesn't call me.*
A él **no le importa** si llueve.	*He doesn't mind if it rains.*

Importar used with an indirect object is also a way to express *to care about/care for something or someone.*

Me importan mucho mis amigos.	*I care a lot about my friends.*
¿Ya no **te importo**?	*Don't you care about me anymore?*

To express *to not matter*, use **importar** without the indirect object.

Está lloviendo.	*It's raining.*
No importa, vamos a jugar de todos modos.	*It doesn't matter. We're going to play anyway.*

To ask someone *what the matter is,* in the sense of *what's wrong,* there are several possible expressions.

¿Qué tiene(s)?
¿Qué te/le pasa?
¿Qué te/le ocurre?

And to tell someone to back off from a private matter, use:

¡Eso **no te/le/les importa**!	*It's none of your business!*

Cada vez más

Cada vez más is a way to express *more and more*, or *gradually getting to be more of a certain quality.*

Me molesta **cada vez más**.	*It bothers me more and more.*
Las lecciones son **cada vez más** complicadas.	*The lessons are more and more complicated.*
El curso es **cada vez más** difícil.	*The course is getting harder and harder.*
La chica es **cada vez más** bonita.	*The girl is getting prettier and prettier.*

Vez is also used in other expressions:

de vez en cuando	*once in a while*
a veces	*sometimes*
una vez	*once*
dos veces	*twice*
tres/cuatro/etc. veces	*three/four/etc. times*
a la vez	*at the same time*
una vez más	*again*
otra vez	*again*
otras veces	*at other times*
la primera vez	*the first time*
la última vez	*the last time*

No nos vemos con mucha frecuencia, pero ella me llama **de vez en cuando**.	*We don't see each other a lot, but she calls me from time to time.*
A veces nos gusta salir.	*Sometimes we like to go out.*
Ella era mi novia **una vez**.	*She was my girlfriend once.*
Voy a hacer esta tarea solamente **una vez**.	*I'm only going to do this assignment one time.*
Comemos **tres veces** al día.	*We eat three times a day.*
Todas las chicas hablan **a la vez**.	*The girls all talk at the same time/at once.*
Por favor, cántala **una vez más**.	*Please sing it again.*
Por favor, cántala **otra vez**.	*Please sing it again.*
A veces dice que sí; **otras veces** dice que no.	*Sometimes he says yes; other times he says no.*
Esta es **la última vez** que te llamo.	*This is the last time that I'm going to call you.*

Cualquier

Cualquier, generally translated as *any*, is an adjective that has the same form for masculine and feminine nouns.

No dudes en llamarme por **cualquier** cosita.	*Don't hesitate to call me for any little thing.*
Voy a comprar **cualquier** libro que encuentre.	*I'm going to buy any/whatever book I find.*

This adjective changes to **cualquiera** when it occurs *after* a masculine or feminine noun, and has the meaning of *just any old*.

Yo no voy a leer **un libro cualquiera**.	*I'm not going to read just any old book.*
A veces se pone **un vestido cualquiera**.	*Sometimes she puts on just any old dress.*

No

No is used in Spanish before other negative words, unless they are placed at the beginning of a sentence. Some common negative words are:

nada	*nothing*
nadie	*nobody*
nunca	*never*
ninguno, -a	*not a single one*
ni	*not even*
ni... ni	*neither. . . nor*
tampoco	*not either*

¿Qué tienes?	*What do you have?*
Nada. No tengo **nada.**	*Nothing. I don't have anything.*

¿Quién sabe esto?	*Who knows this?*
Nadie. No lo sabe **nadie.**	*No one. No one knows it.*

¿Cuándo te vas a casar?	*When are you getting married?*
Nunca. No me voy a casar **nunca.**	*Never. I'm never getting married.*

¿Quiénes saben la respuesta?	*Who knows the answer?*
No la sabe **ninguno** de los chicos. No la sabe **ninguna** de las chicas.	*None of the boys know it. None of the girls know it.*

Ninguno changes to **ningún** when it is placed *before* a masculine noun, but not before a feminine one.

¿Adónde vas?	*Where are you going?*
No voy a **ningún lugar.**/ No voy a **ninguna parte.**	*I'm not going anywhere.*

Ni means *not even.* This can also be expressed with **ni siquiera.**

¿Cuántos amigos tienes en Facebook?	*How many friends do you have on Facebook?*
Ninguno. No tengo **ni** uno. No soy miembro.	*None. I don't have even one. I'm not a member.*
El pobre no tiene **ni siquiera** un lugar donde dormir.	*The poor guy doesn't even have a place to sleep.*

Ni... ni means *neither . . . nor* but can also be translated as *not . . . either.*

El niño no trae **ni lápiz ni cuaderno** a la escuela.	*The child does doesn't bring either a pencil or a notebook to school.*

Tampoco, *not . . . either* is the negative of **también,** *also.*

María no va a la escuela hoy.	*María isn't going to school today.*
Entonces, yo no voy **tampoco.**	*Then I'm not going either.*
Yo **tampoco. Tampoco** va Juan. ¿Va Carlos?	*Me neither. Juan's not going either. Is Carlos going?*
Tampoco.	*(He's not going) either.*

To express *and neither,* use **ni... tampoco.**

Él no baila, **ni su hermano tampoco.**	*He doesn't dance, and neither does his brother.*
Ella no está aburrida, **ni yo tampoco.**	*She's not bored, and neither am I.*

To express that something or somebody does not exist—at least in the opinion of the speaker—the subjunctive is used after a negative expression.

No hay nada en esta tienda que me **guste**.	There's nothing in this store that I like.
No conozco a nadie que **cocine** como mi mamá.	I don't know anybody who cooks like my mother.
En esta ciudad no hay ningún restaurante que **tenga** pizza como la de Chicago.	In this city there's not a single restaurant that has Chicago-style pizza.

Se debe

Se debe indicates *is due to, has been caused by.*

Toda esta destrucción **se debe** al huracán.	All this destruction is due to the hurricane.

Deber has a number of functions. You can use it to express *obligation* or *requirement*.

Debemos pagar los impuestos antes del 15 de abril.	We have to pay our taxes before April 15th.
Los alumnos **deben** hacer las tareas cada noche.	The students are required to do the homework every night.

Speaking of *homework*, remember that both **la tarea** (Latin America) and **el deber** (Spain) refer to *one assignment*. If you have more than one **tarea** or **deber**, then *homework* is expressed as **las tareas** or **los deberes**.

To express *should*, use **deber** in its conditional form, **debería**.

Deberías ir a casa, ya es muy tarde.	You should go home. It's very late.

While **deber** can be translated as *to have to*, it is limited to the sense of *being obligated* or *required to*. Other ways of expressing *to have to* include **tener que**, which is more personal.

Debo estar en casa antes de las ocho. Si no, mi mamá se pone nerviosa.	I have to be home before eight, otherwise my mother gets nervous.
Tengo que llamar a mi hermana. Le tengo que dar una noticia importante.	I have to call my sister. I have to tell her some important news.

Hay que means *have to* or *should* in a very general, impersonal sense.

Hay que tener mucho cuidado en la ciudad por la noche.	One should be very careful in the city at night./ You should be careful in the city at night.

A less direct way of giving advice is to use **sugerir**, **aconsejar**, or **recomendar** with an indirect object, followed by **que** and a verb in the subjunctive. The pattern is as follows:

indirect object	+	conjugation of **sugerir** /aconsejar/recomendar	+	**que**	+	subjunctive clause
↓		↓		↓		↓
(A Juan) le		**sugiero**		**que**		**estudie más.**

(To Juan) to him I suggest that he study more.

Le recomiendo que compre estas acciones.	*I recommend that you buy these stocks.*
Les aconsejo que no hagan tanto ruido.	*I advise you all to not make so much noise.*

Expressing doubt

There are a number of ways to express doubt or not being sure of something.

Lo dudo.	*I doubt it.*
Creo que no.	*I don't think so.*
No le creo.	*I don't believe him.*
No lo creo.	*I don't believe it.*
No es posible.	*It's not possible.*
No estoy seguro, -a.	*I'm not sure.*

To express doubt, use a conjugation of **dudar/no creer/no estar seguro, -a** followed by **que** and a subjunctive clause that tells *what you're not sure of* or what you think is *impossible*.

Dudan que esa chica tenga veintiún años.	*They doubt that that girl is twenty-one.*
No creemos que tu hermano esté aquí.	*We don't think your brother is here.*
No estoy segura que él diga la verdad.	*I'm not sure that he's telling the truth.*

Expressions of possibility, impossibility, and probability are also used with a subjunctive verb phrase.

Es posible **que llame** mi amigo.	*My friend might call.*
Es imposible **que salgamos** ahora.	*It's not possible for us to leave now.*
Es probable **que tenga** la gripe.	*She probably has the flu.*

Remember that you use the indicative, rather than the subjunctive, after the expressions **creer que, estar seguro, -a que, no dudar que** y **no hay duda que**.

¿Dónde está Miguel?	*Where is Miguel?*
Creo que está en Madrid.	*I think he's in Madrid.*
Estoy seguro que está en Madrid.	*I'm sure he's in Madrid.*
No hay duda que esta es la mejor cocina del mundo.	*Without a doubt, this is the best cuisine in the world.*

Darse cuenta and realizar

Darse cuenta de que is a common expression that means *to realize* in English.

Me doy cuenta de que tengo que buscar trabajo.	*I realize that I have to look for a job.*

Realizar, on the other hand, means *to carry out, to effect*, or *to make happen*.

El cirujano **realizó** la operación con mucha destreza.	*The surgeon carried out the operation with great skill.*
Por fin **se realizaron** sus sueños.	*Her dreams finally came true.*

A lo mejor

A lo mejor is an expression that means *probably*, or *most likely*, but it is followed by the indicative rather than the subjunctive.

¿Dónde está Roberto?
A lo mejor está con sus amigos.

Where's Roberto?
He's probably with his friends.

Al menos means *at least*.

Al menos deberías darle la mano.
Ellos no van a ganar. **Al menos** eso es lo que pienso yo.

You should at least shake his hand.
They're not going to win. At least, that's what I think.

When numbers are involved, it's better to use **por lo menos**.

Existen **por lo menos** tres tipos de nieve.
Vas a necesitar **por lo menos** $200 para el viaje.

There are at least three kinds of snow.
You're going to need at least $200 for the trip.

In the least, in the sense of *not at all*, is expressed by **en lo más mínimo**.

Eso no me molesta **en lo más mínimo**.

That doesn't bother me in the least./
I couldn't care less.

Estar harto

Estar harto, -a de algo/de alguien means *to be fed up with something or somebody.*

¡Vámonos! **Estoy harta de** este lugar.
El papá **está harto del** comportamiento de los niños.

Let's go! I'm sick of this place.
The father is fed up with the children's behavior.

Para colmo

Para colmo introduces the element that finally causes everything to collapse, like *the straw that broke the camel's back.*

Tengo la gripe, no tengo ningún medicamento, no hay nadie en la casa y **para colmo,** mi teléfono no funciona.
¡Esto es **el colmo**!

I have the flu, I don't have any medicine, I'm all alone, and as if that weren't enough, my telephone isn't working.
That's the last straw!

Contar

Contar is:

◆ To count

El niño sabe **contar** de uno a cien.

The child can count from one to a hundred.

◆ To tell a story

Cuéntame de tu juventud.

Tell me about when you were young.

◆ And when followed by **con**, *to count on* or *depend on someone or something.*

Cuenta conmigo. Te voy a llevar la medicina.

Count on me. I'm going to bring you the medicine.

Aquí no se puede **contar con** nada.
Ahora ni tenemos agua caliente.

You can't count on anything here. Now we don't even have hot water.

EJERCICIO
20·8

Match the Spanish expressions in the right column with the English ones in the left column.

1. _____ I don't care.
2. _____ It doesn't matter.
3. _____ What's the matter?
4. _____ That's none of your business.
5. _____ Do you mind?
6. _____ I care about you.

a. No me importa.
b. ¿Te importa?
c. No te importa.
d. Me importas.
e. ¿Qué tienes?
f. No importa.

EJERCICIO
20·9

*Choose between **cualquier** and **cualquiera** to fill in each blank appropriately.*

1. Ella no se va a casar con un hombre _____.

2. A mí me gusta _____ regalo que me dé.

3. No te preocupes, me puedes llamar a _____ hora.

4. Para la boda, quiero un vestido que valga la pena, no un vestido _____.

EJERCICIO
20·10

Fill in each blank with the word or expression that most appropriately translates the English words.

1. Estoy completamente solo. No hay _____ aquí. *(anybody)*

2. Vamos al mercado, pues no tenemos _____ de comer. *(anything)*

3. _____ voy a comprender a mi jefe. *(Never)*

4. Yo no estoy de acuerdo, _____ mi hermano _____. *(and, neither)*

5. Hoy no vamos a _____. *(anywhere)*

6. No hay _____ vendedor de chocolate en el mercado. *(a single)*

7. No hay _____ un vendedor de chocolate en el mercado. *(even)*

8. _____ mi mamá _____ mi papá fuma. *(Neither, nor)*

EJERCICIO
20·11

*Using the guidelines below, express the activities that need to be carried out. Use **hay que**, **deber**, **debería**, or **tener que** as appropriate for each category. Ask a Spanish-speaking friend to read your sentences.*

1. What are you obligated or required to do on a regular basis?

   _____

2. What do you have to do every day?

   _____

3. What should you do either now or in the near future?

   _____

4. What is a safety measure required of the general public where you live?

   _____

EJERCICIO
20·12

Complete the following sentences as directed.

1. A mi mejor amigo le aconsejo que se (olvidar) _____ de esa chica.

2. El profesor le sugiere a la estudiante que (pasar) _____ un semestre en el extranjero.

3. Mi amiga me recomienda que (buscar) _____ otro trabajo.

4. La consejera le recomienda a la chica que (solicitar) _____ a varias universidades.

5. El médico le aconseja a la mujer que (tranquilizarse) _____.

EJERCICIO
20·13

Complete the following sentences as directed.

1. El profesor duda que su alumno (poner) _____ atención en la clase.

2. El alumno cree que (sacar) _____ muy buenas notas.

3. Nuestros vecinos no dudan que nuestro barrio (ser) _____ uno de los más seguros de la ciudad.

4. Yo no estoy segura que (ser) _____ cierto.

5. Mis amigas no creen que sus niños (asistir) _____ a las mejores escuelas.

6. Es probable que (haber) _____ mejores escuelas en otras ciudades.

7. A lo mejor el alcalde (estar) _____ haciendo todo lo posible para mejorar las escuelas.

8. Es probable que nosotros (mudarse) _____ en julio o agosto.

EJERCICIO
20·14

¿Cómo se dice en español? Fill in each blank with the Spanish equivalent of the indicated expression.

1. Él _____ de la violencía en esta ciudad. *(is fed up with)*

2. Hay _____ cinco robos cada día. *(at least)*

3. _____ deberíamos saludarlo. *(At least)*

4. Primero, pierdo el bus y llego tarde a la oficina, luego mi jefe me despide del trabajo

   y_____, mi mejor amiga se enoja conmigo. *(to top it all off)*

5. _____ sé que puedo _____ mi esposo. *(At least, count on)*

 **The imperfect subjunctive**

As we saw in Chapter 19, the subjunctive mood is used with ideas that show uncertainty, doubt, demand, desire, emotions, among other feelings. The imperfect subjunctive is used in exactly the same sense, but it refers to the past, not the present.

Let's consider the two sentences below and the tenses that appear in the main and subordinate clauses.

Nosotros **dudamos** que Marta **compre** el piano.	*We doubt that Marta is buying the piano.*
Nosotros **dudábamos** que Marta **comprara** el piano.	*We doubted that Marta would buy the piano.*

The first sentence shows the indicative present tense **dudamos** in the main clause and the present subjunctive **compre** in the subordinate clause. In the second sentence, the indicative imperfect tense **dudábamos** is in the main clause. It refers to the past, so therefore **comprara** in the subsidiary clause is in the imperfect subjunctive. But first we need to review the formation of the imperfect subjunctive and the circumstances in which we need to use it.

Formation of the imperfect subjunctive

The first step is to remember the third person plural of the indicative preterit tense and then drop the **-ron** ending. This will give you the stem for forming the imperfect subjunctive.

comprar	compraron	**compra-**
vender	vendieron	**vendie-**
abrir	abrieron	**abrie-**

The second step is to add the appropriate endings. There are actually two possible sets of endings for the imperfect subjunctive, which apply to all three conjugations.

-ra endings: **-ra, ras, ra, -ramos, -rais, -ran**
-se endings: **-se, -ses, -se, -semos, -seis, -sen**

Either set of endings may be used and both mean the same, but the **-ra** endings are used more frequently in the Spanish-speaking world, and we will be using them from now on, as the following examples from each conjugation of regular verbs show.

-ar verbs: comprar	compraron	comprara, compraras, comprara, compráramos, comprarais, compraran

-er verbs: vender	vendieron	vendiera, vendieras, vendiera, vendiéramos, vendierais, vendieran
-ir verbs: abrir	abrieron	abriera, abrieras, abriera, abriéramos, abrierais, abrieran

Note that a written accent is required in the **nosotros** form of both sets of endings. The stress falls on the vowel before the subjunctive ending.

Querían que nosotros **comiéramos** con ellos.	*They wanted us to eat with them.*
Deseaban que nosotros **llegásemos** pronto.	*They wished that we would arrive soon.*
Ella dudaba que nosotros **estuviéramos** aquí.	*She doubted that we would be here.*

As with the present subjunctive that we reviewed in Chapter 19, verbs that have a change in spelling in the preterit tense maintain that spelling change in the stem of the imperfect subjunctive:

destruir	destruyeron	**destruye-**
dirigir	dirigieron	**dirigie-**
distinguir	distinguieron	**distingui-**
estar	estuvieron	**estuvie-**
ir	fueron	**fue-**
hacer	hicieron	**hicie-**
querer	quisieron	**quisie-**
recoger	recogieron	**recogie-**
tener	tuvieron	**tuvie-**
ver	vieron	**vie-**

Uses of the imperfect subjunctive

In order to use the imperfect subjunctive in the subordinate clause, the main clause must be in a past tense.

◆ Main clause in the preterit

¿No **cenaste** antes de que tus vecinos **llegaran**?	*Did you not eat before your neighbors arrived?*
Tú **sugeriste** que **jugáramos** en el parque.	*You suggested that we play in the park.*
Fue horrible que no **estuvieras** tomando esa medicina.	*It was terrible that you were not taking that medicine.*

◆ Main clause in the imperfect

Era necesario que **practicáramos** antes de jugar.	*It was necessary that we practice before we played.*
Alicia **necesitaba** que le **dieran** una copia de su documento.	*Alicia needed them to give her a copy of her document.*
Ellos **querían** que yo **descansara**.	*They wanted me to rest.*

◆ Main clause in the past perfect

El maestro no **había autorizado** que
los estudiantes **salieran** del aula.

*The teacher did not allow the students to leave
the classroom.*

¡Práctica! *Complete each sentence with the appropriate form of the imperfect subjunctive
(-**ra** ending) of the verb in parentheses.*

1. Queríamos que tú _____ con nosotros. (venir)

2. Nos pidieron que nosotros _____ a sus padres. (acompañar)

3. Mi jefe nunca permitía que los empleados _____ más de una hora para
la hora del almuerzo. (tomar)

4. Yo había salido con mis amigos para que ellos _____ disfrutar su visita
a mi ciudad. (poder)

5. Sentimos mucho que María no _____ a tocar el violín. (aprender)

6. Nosotros nunca queríamos que _____ tanta gente en la playa. (haber)

7. Laurita y Pablito dudaban que la fiesta de mi aniversario de bodas
_____ divertida. (ser)

8. Me dijeron que yo _____ quedarme con ellos en su casa durante mi
visita. (deber)

9. Y también me rogaron que yo _____ a mi hermana Rosa. (traer)

10. Fue una pena que Rosa no _____ con nosotros. (estar)

11. Queríamos que Uds. _____ de una manera apropiada y agradable.
(comportarse)

12. Fue fabuloso que ellos _____ a todos sus amigos el día de su (abrazar)
llegada.

Traducción. *Use the appropriate form of the imperfect subjunctive (-**ra** ending) or an
infinitive, as needed.*

1. I wanted you (*sing., fam.*) to bring two bottles of soda.

_____

2. You (*sing., fam.*) wanted us to cook rice and beans.

_____

3. It was ridiculous that we had so much food for five people.

   _____

4. Alberto and Carlos were not sure that their friends would come.

   _____

5. It was a pity that we spent so much.

   _____

6. They wanted to divide the amount of the expenses by three.

   _____

7. I was not sure that they would pay me.

   _____

8. Carlos begged me to wait until the weekend.

   _____

9. Did he prefer not to pay? Of course!

   _____

10. No one believed that Carlos would return the money to me.

   _____

Y en tu caso, ¿verdadero (V) o falso (F)?

1. _____ Deseaba que mis padres me regalaran un auto nuevo.

2. _____ Quería que mis amigos me ayudaran con las tareas.

3. _____ Prefería que mi novio/novia no supiera mi edad.

4. _____ Necesitaba que mis vecinos dejaran un espacio para aparcar mi auto.

5. _____ Ojalá mi familia ganara mucho dinero en la lotería.

6. _____ Quería que hubiera mucha paz y no más guerras.

7. _____ Quería que mis vecinos no sacaran mi ropa de la lavadora en el sótano.

8. _____ Siempre insistía en que mis colegas llegaran temprano al trabajo todos los días.

9. _____ Yo quería que mi familia se mudara a México.

10. _____ Yo siempre autoricé a mis colegas a que usaran mi computadora en la oficina.

The conditional in the main clause: Contrary-to-fact conditions

As seen in Chapter 16, one of the uses of the conditional is to express a contrary-to-fact action—that is, a hypothetical statement or events that are not probable. In some textbooks they are called hypothetical *if*-clauses. Usually all *if*-clauses with a past tense are considered hypothetical and therefore require the subjunctive, as demonstrated in the following sentences.

Si yo **tuviera** más dinero, no **ahorraría** tanto.	*If I had more money I would not save so much.*
Si tú **estudiaras** más, **tendrías** más oportunidades en el futuro.	*If you studied more, you would have more opportunities in the future.*

These *if*-clauses indicate actions or events that may be possible, yet most probably will not happen.

EJERCICIO
21·4

¡Práctica otra vez! *Complete each sentence with the appropriate form of the imperfect subjunctive (-**ra** ending) of the verb in parentheses.*

1. Serías trilingüe si tú _____ italiano. (estudiar)

2. Nadie te creería si tú no _____ la verdad. (decir)

3. Llamaría a mi madre si yo _____ enfermo. (estar)

4. Podríamos disfrutar más si nosotros _____ un televisor grande. (tener)

5. No esperaría a mis amigos si ellos _____ muy tarde al aeropuerto. (llegar)

6. ¿Qué harías si yo _____ el piano en tu casa? (tocar)

7. María se casaría si su novio le _____ la mano. (pedir)

8. Le pediría ayuda a mis padres si yo no _____ pagar el alquiler. (poder)

9. Nosotros iríamos de compras si no _____ mucha gente. (haber)

10. Estaríamos felices si Uds. nos _____ al cine. (llevar)

EJERCICIO
21·5

Traducción. *Use the -**ra** endings of the imperfect subjunctive.*

1. If I had a friend here now I would be happy.

_____

2. I would not sing a song if you do not play the guitar.

_____

3. I would introduce you to my sister if you were not so shy.

_____

4. I would not answer the question if I did not know the answer.

_____

5. If it weren't raining, we would have dinner on the terrace.

_____

6. This house would be worth (**valer**) one million dollars if it had a pool in the backyard.

_____

7. It would be a miracle if my friends helped me to finish my homework.

_____

8. If you were stronger you would be able to play better.

_____

9. If the suitcase were bigger, I would not take it with me.

_____

10. If I were a liar, who would believe me?

_____

Y en tu caso, ¿verdadero (V) o falso (F)?

1. _____ Si tuviera que trabajar los domingos, yo renunciaría (*resign*).

2. _____ No ayudaría a mis colegas si se rieran de mí.

3. _____ Sería terrible si no aprendiera español.

4. _____ Si alguien pusiera su auto en mi espacio de parqueo, llamaría a la policía.

5. _____ Sería increíble si yo pudiera tocar el violín.

6. _____ Si mis amigos me pidieran un favor, yo lo haría.

7. _____ Si yo pudiera, viviría en Madrid.

8. _____ Si yo tuviera más tiempo, me entrenaría para un maratón en Nueva York.

9. _____ Yo no pudiera correr rápido si no practicara tres veces a la semana.

10. _____ Sería fantástico si yo comprara una computadora nueva.

Sueños son sueños. Traducción. *Use the words in the* **Vocabulario útil** *for your translation.*

VOCABULARIO ÚTIL

broken, broken-down	**descompuesto, -a**
dishes (pl.)	**la vajilla**
happy	**placentero, -a**
in-laws	**los suegros**
fairy tale	**el cuento de hadas**
to achieve, meet	**lograr**
to call, warn	**avisar**
to be lucky	**tener suerte**
to wash (*dishes, clothes*)	**fregar**
unknown	**desconocido, -a**

Everyone would like his/her life to be pleasant. For example, if it had not rained today I would be very happy. If I worked fewer hours in my office, I would have more time to relax and to watch movies on my TV. If my parents lived close to me, they would help me every week to clean the house. If I found one thousand dollars, I would invite my friends to have dinner in a fabulous restaurant. If I had the luck not to have to go back to my job, I would travel to an unknown place. I would not have to open my door if my in-laws were visiting without warning us by telephone. If I were rich I would not have this horrible, old and broken-down car. I would be the queen of the house if I did not have to wash the dishes. It would be a perfect world! It would a fairy tale if I could keep everything under my control. But dreams are dreams, nothing else.

Subordinating clauses

There is one word in Spanish that seems to turn up everywhere—the word **que**. This word has many functions and is translated into English in various ways, depending on the grammatical job it performs in any particular sentence. Sometimes it means *that*, *who*, or *which*. In comparisons, **que** means *than*. Other times, it can't be translated at all, but it has to be in the Spanish phrase, such as in **hacer** *time clauses* or in the formula of obligation formed by **tener** + **que** + infinitive. Last but not least, don't forget that **¿qué?** (note the accent mark!) is the Spanish interrogative meaning *what?*

In this chapter you will see another way that simple sentences can be joined to form more complex ones and how, often, various tenses of the subjunctive mood must be used for verbs in subordinated clauses. This chapter will examine subordinated noun, adjective, and adverbial clauses and make some additional observations about sequence of tense. First, let's review some definitions.

In order for a clause to be subordinated, there has to be some principal clause to introduce it. Another name for the principal clause is *independent clause*; likewise, the subordinated clause is also known as the *dependent clause*. Observe how the following two independent sentences can be combined. In the first combined or more complex sentence, the result is a relative clause. In the second example, the second of the two joined sentences has become a subordinated noun clause.

I saw the boy. The boy climbed the tree.

↓

I saw the boy that/who climbed the tree.

↓

I saw that the boy climbed the tree.

The relative clause *describes* the boy. The portion of the sentence beginning with *that* (or *who*) all the way to the end of the sentence functions as a giant *adjective*. In the third sentence, the portion of the sentence beginning with *that* to the end of the sentence functions as a giant *direct object* of the verb *saw*—the verb in the main clause. Here the relative clause tells the reader or listener *what* the subject of the independent clause (*I*) saw. The phrase *that the boy climbed the tree* can't stand alone as a grammatical sentence; it has been subordinated to the main clause *I saw*, which can stand alone. Notice that each clause in the third sentence has its own subject and its own conjugated verb. Here is an example of a sentence in which all the subjects are implicit since the verb endings clearly tell us who the subjects are. Remember that whereas the word *that* can be omitted in English, the conjunction **que** can never be omitted in Spanish:

Veo **que** escribes una carta.   *I see (that) you're writing a letter.*

The structure of subordinated noun clauses can be stated in formulaic terms. Observe the following formula wherein S = *subject* and V = *verb*. The subscripted numbers remind us that the subjects of the two clauses are different and that each has its own verb.

$$S_1 + V_1 + \textbf{que} + S_2 + V_2$$

This formula is very valuable when we apply one more mnemonic (memory) trick for telling us when a subjunctive form of the verb in the subordinated clause must be used. The mnemonic is W.E.I.R.D.O. and the letters stand for types of verbs in the V_1 position that will require the subjunctive be used for verbs in the V_2 position. Let's unpack what the acronym W.E.I.R.D.O. stands for and then see some examples.

W Wanting, wishing, hoping, expecting
E Emotion
I Impersonal expressions of any of the other letters in this acronym (**es** + adjective)
R Requests, requirements, orders, commands, petitions
D Doubt, denial, negation
O Ojalá

In English, the most frequently used structure that corresponds in meaning to the Spanish in the **W** and **R** categories of the acronym is verb + object + infinitive. This structure makes no sense whatsoever in Spanish, so observe carefully the differences and similarities between the structure of Spanish and the English translations in the following examples. The examples are listed in order of the categories represented by the acronym:

Quieren **que tú les ayudes**.	*They want you to help them.*
Es importante **que ellos vayan al gimnasio**.	*It's important (that) they go to the gym.*

However, if an impersonal expression does not correspond to any of the verb categories of the acronym, the *indicative* is used. In the following first example, the impersonal expression **es obvio** does not express a *wish, emotion, requirement*, or a *doubt*:

Es obvio que ellos van al gimnasio.	*It's obvious (that) they're going/they go to the gym.*
Juana **se alegra de que** su novio tenga un buen trabajo.	*Jane is glad (that) her boyfriend has a good job.*
El capitán **manda que** los tripulantes limpien la cubierta.	*The captain orders the crew to clean the deck.*
Los agnósticos **dudan que** Dios exista.	*Agnostics doubt that God exists.*

Furthermore, if a verb of belief is negated by using **no**, the subjunctive must be used:

No creo que el Sr. Acero **vaya** a admitirlo.	*I don't believe (that) Mr. Acero is going to admit it.*

Likewise, when a verb of doubt is undone by using **no**, the indicative must be used:

No dudo que el Sr. Acero **es** culpable de varios crímenes.	*I do not doubt (that) Mr. Acero is guilty of various crimes.*

Finally, *always* use the subjunctive with **ojalá**. The word **ojalá** is derived from Arabic and means, roughly, *May God (Allah) grant that . . .* or *May it please God (Allah) to. . . .* It is not necessary to use **que** when using **ojalá** because, interestingly, the original Arabic phrase already implied it. When translated into English, it comes out simplest by saying *I hope that. . . .*

Ojalá (que) Juan **venga** esta noche.	*I hope John's coming/John comes tonight.*

You may have been wondering what happens if the subjects of two sentences to be joined are the same person. When there is no change of subject, the new sentence is structured as in English:

I want. I dance.
What do I want to do?—I want to dance.

The structure is the same in Spanish, as the following examples show:

Yo quiero bailar.	*I want to dance.*
Me alegro de estar aquí.	*I'm glad to be here/about being here.*
Es importante bailar.	*It's important to dance.*

However, since a singular subject cannot logically command him- or herself, there is no example of the **R** category in which the subject of the main clause is also the subject of the dependent clause. The nearest one can come to that is the **nosotros** command (always expressed in the present subjunctive):

Cantemos.	*Let's sing.*

When verbs of doubt are involved, the rule about the subjects of the two clauses having to be different *can* be broken. However, the preference of the Royal Academy is to use the structure of the first form in the following example.

Dudo poder ir.	*I doubt I'll be able to go.*
Dudo que (yo) pueda ir.	

Before continuing to examine subordinated adjective clauses, you need to understand the concept of sequence of tense. First, examine the following series of examples that show the temporal logic of the use of the four tenses of the subjunctive mood. Since emotion can be felt now about actions in the present, past, or future, a verb of emotion in the present is used in the main clause to allow you to focus on what is happening in the subordinated clause:

Me alegro de que Juan **venga** esta noche.	*I'm glad John is coming tonight.*
Me alegro de que Juan **haya venido** a esta fiesta.	*I'm glad John has come to this party.*
Me alegro de que Juan **viniera** a la fiesta anoche.	*I'm glad John came to the party last night.*
Me da pena que Juan **no hubiera llegado** a tiempo para conocer a María.	*I'm so sorry John hadn't arrived in time to meet Mary.*

When the main verb in a sentence containing a subordinated clause is in the present, the present or present perfect subjunctive is used. If the main verb is in the past, then the imperfect or the imperfect subjunctive is used.

Juan **espera** que María lo **llame**.	*John hopes Mary will call him.*
Juan **esperaba** que María lo **llamara**.	*John hoped Mary would call him.*
Ellos le **dicen*** que **ponga** la ropa en la maleta.	*The tell him/her/you formal to put the clothes in the suitcase.*
Ellos le **dijeron** que **pusiera** la ropa en la maleta.	*They told him/her/you formal to put the clothes in the suitcase.*
Es raro que **no haya nevado** todavía.	*It's odd that it hasn't snowed yet.*

Subordinated adjective clauses are clauses that describe a noun or pronoun mentioned in the main, or independent clause. In the following example, the clause **que se fabricó en Suiza** is a giant adjective and could be replaced by using the adjective **suizo**. The fact that the whole clause could be replaced by one adjective proves that it is an adjective clause and not a noun clause. It is important to make the distinction, since the rules governing the requirement of the subjunctive in subordinated adjective clauses are different from the rules used with subordinated noun clauses.

Tengo un reloj **que se fabricó en Suiza**.	*I have a watch that was made in Switzerland.*
Tengo un reloj **suizo**.	*I have a Swiss watch.*

*****decir**, as in *to tell* someone to do something.

The subjunctive must be used in a subordinated adjective clause if the antecedent, or previously mentioned noun (**reloj**, in the example), is vague or doesn't exist. Let's change the example to require the subjunctive in the subordinated clause:

Busco un reloj que **sea** suizo.	*I'm looking for a watch that's Swiss.*

Of course, you could simply say **Busco un reloj suizo**—but there are times when one needs subordinated adjective clauses (and the subjunctive as well). This example simply shows how they are constructed. Here are a couple more examples that also show sequence of tense in action:

No hay relojes en esta tienda que **vengan** de Suiza.	*There are no watches in this shop that come from Switzerland.*
No había relojes en esa tienda que **vinieran** de Suiza.	*There were no watches in that shop that came from Switzerland.*
Necesito un reloj que **tenga** una manecilla para marcar los segundos.	*I need a watch that has a hand for showing the seconds.*
Necesitaba un reloj que **tuviera** una manecilla para marcar los segundos.	*I needed a watch that had a hand for showing the seconds.*

Some students have been told that if the indefinite article is used before the antecedent in the main clause, the subjunctive must be used in the adjective clause. This is often true, but as often it is not. Both the verb and the article of the main clause must be taken into account. In other words, pay attention to the meaning of the whole situation as expressed by the whole sentence, as these examples illustrate:

Busco un carro que **tenga** GPS.	*I'm looking for a car that has GPS.*
Buscaba un carro que **tuviera** GPS.	*I was looking for a car that had GPS.*

But:

Tengo un carro que **tiene** GPS.	*I have a car that has GPS.*
Tenía un carro que **tenía** GPS.	*I had a car that had GPS.*
Busco la secretaria que **sabe** alemán.	*I'm looking for the secretary that/who speaks German.*
Buscaba la secretaria que **sabía** alemán.	*I was looking for the secretary that/who spoke German.*

The best way to approach the use of adverbial expressions to form more complex sentences is to observe from the outset that some adverbial expressions are *always* followed by a verb in the subjunctive and others only *sometimes* are followed by a verb in the subjunctive.

The subjunctive is always used after the following expressions:

a menos que, a no ser que	*unless*
antes de que	*before*
como si (+ imperfect subjunctive)	*as if*
con tal de que, siempre y cuando	*provided that, as long as*
en caso de que	*in case that*
el hecho de que	*the fact that*
para que, a fin de que	*in order that*
sin que	*without*

After the following expressions, the subjunctive is sometimes used:

a pesar de que	*despite, in spite of*
acaso, tal vez, quizá	*perhaps*
así que, así como	*such that*
aunque	*although*
cuando	*when*
de modo que, de manera que	*in such a way that*
después de que, luego que	*after*
hasta que	*until*
mientras	*while*
por más que, por mucho que	*no matter how much*
siempre que	*as long as*
tan pronto como, en cuanto	*as soon as*
una vez que	*once you have*

One of the best ways to learn how to use the subjunctive correctly (when faced with an expression on the second list) is to remember the following three examples. Observe that when a time clause is involved, the subjunctive must be used if the action is—or was—anticipated.

Vamos a la tienda **después de que** deje de llover.	*We'll go to the store after it quits raining.*
Fuimos a la tienda **después de que** dejó de llover.	*We went to the store after it quit raining.*
Íbamos a ir a la tienda **después de que** dejara de llover.	*We were going to go to the store after it quit raining.*

The problem then is how to determine whether the subjunctive is needed after the adverbial expressions in the second list. Just as we have the W.E.I.R.D.O. acronym to help us deal with subordinated noun clauses, and the idea of vague or non-existent antecedents to guide our choice with subordinated adjective clauses, the use of the subjunctive after the expressions in the second list of adverbial expressions is decided by whether the action(s) following the expressions are or were anticipated or whether the action is a mere report of an action in the past.

In concrete terms, if the main verb is in the past, the time frame of the whole sentence is in the past. There is no anticipation and, therefore, the subjunctive is not used. When the main verb is in the present, actions following the adverbial expressions are (or were) anticipated and, therefore, verbs following the expressions must be in the subjunctive. Among the expressions in the second list, the expressions **acaso**, **tal vez**, and **quizá** (*perhaps*) and **aunque** (*although*) are the only ones in which the use of the subjunctive or indicative depends on the attitude of the speaker, to show more or less certainty.

It is important to understand the concept of sequence of tense when dealing with the subjunctive generally, but for some students this is particularly tricky when dealing with adverbial expressions. Observe the following contrastive examples, noting how the subjunctive is used when the element of anticipation is present and the indicative is used (second example) when the action following the adverbial expression is a mere report. Note too that the tense of the subjunctive is present if the main verb is in the present, as in the first and third examples, but imperfect subjunctive when the main verb is in the past and the expression requires the subjunctive, as in the last example.

Vamos al parque después de que **deje** de llover.	*We'll go to the park after it quits raining.*
Fuimos al parque después de que **dejó** de llover.	*We went to the park after it quit raining.*

Vamos al parque antes de que	*Let's go the park before it rains.*
empiece a llover.	
Fuimos al parque antes de que	*We went to the park before it started to rain.*
empezara a llover.	

The following translation exercises will challenge you to create various types of subordinated clauses. The first set, from Spanish to English, is intended to sensitize you, to enable you to recognize the various types of subordinated clauses. The second will require you to create them in Spanish. Remember, in English, the conjunction *that* can be omitted! In both, the issue of sequence of tense will be addressed.

EJERCICIO
21·8

Translate the following sentences from Spanish to English.

1. Era dudoso que mis primos hubieran preparado la cena cuando mi papá llegó.

   _____

2. Creo que es posible que llueva mañana.

   _____

3. Buscábamos una escopeta que tuviera dos cañones.

   _____

4. Mi papá tenía un jardín que producía muchos tomates.

   _____

5. Cuando decidas si vas a ir conmigo o no, me llamarás, ¿no?

   _____

6. Venderá el auto con tal de que se le ofrezca por lo menos quinientos dólares.

   _____

7. Los niños esperan que todos nosotros juguemos al fútbol.

   _____

8. Es preciso que tú y yo lleguemos a un acuerdo.

   _____

9. Los tres querían que yo me quedara en casa hasta que dejara de llover.

   _____

10. Es curioso que ella siempre haya insistido en que yo no la llamara los fines de semana.

    _____

11. Por mucho que le rogáramos que nos prestara el dinero, él no quiso prestárnoslo.

    _____

12. Necesitamos un programa que nos permita procesar más datos en menos tiempo.

_____

13. Ella tiene un novio que la quiere mucho.

_____

14. Dudamos que los padres de Enrique hayan olvidado su cumpleaños.

_____

15. Ellos se alegran de que tú no hayas dejado los estudios.

_____

16. Te ruego que me llames antes de que se cierre el mercado.

_____

17. ¿Quieres que te busque una película que no sea de terror?

_____

18. Después de que se bañó, Juan se vistió y se fue.

_____

19. Antes de que saliera de casa, Juan se bañó y se vistió.

_____

20. Es imposible que ella no lo supiera antes de la fiesta.

_____

EJERCICIO
21·9

Translate the following sentences from English to Spanish.

1. Her mother is glad you have seen the play. (**tú**)

_____

2. We went to the store before our father came home.

_____

3. Do you want me to read the story to you? (**tú**)

_____

4. She and I needed to find a car that had a CD player.

_____

5. Are you worried the computer doesn't have enough memory? (**tú**)

_____

6. Did they ask you to bring the report? (**Uds.**)

_____

7. They needed to find a pharmacy that was open twenty-four hours.

_____

8. We know you have written the letters to him. (**tú**)

_____

9. They are sure he had seen the movie before their mother returned home.

_____

10. It was important he finish the race.

_____

11. It is doubtful Catherine has published, or will publish, an article.

_____

12. She required her students to have five written pages by the end of every week.

_____

13. It was a miracle he hadn't drowned.

_____

14. It was obvious that her mother had not wanted her to come to our party.

_____

15. They promised us they would help us, provided we pay them in advance.

_____

16. If you asked me to do you a favor, I would do it for you. (**tú**)

_____

17. After you have finished breakfast, we can go to the zoo. (**Uds.**)

_____

18. It's good you're going to the concert! (**tú**)

_____

19. She entered the house again without her parents' knowing it.

_____

20. We saw the salesman who had sold us the car.

_____

The subjunctive in relative clauses

In this chapter, you will build sentences with relative clauses using the *subjunctive*. If the antecedent of the pronoun is *indefinite*, does not exist, or is not specific, the relative (subordinate) clause requires the subjunctive. The most frequently used indefinite pronouns are:

alguien	*someone*
algo	*something*
nadie	*nobody, no one*
nada	*nothing*
un/a, unos/as	*one, some*

Let us compare the following sentences and examine their clauses:

Tengo **unos** zapatos negros **que son** muy elegantes.	*I have **some** black shoes **that are** very elegant.*
Pero necesito **unos** zapatos **que sean** cómodos.	*But I need **some** shoes **that are** comfortable.*
¿Conoces **alguna** zapatería **que esté** cerca?	*Do you know **any** shoe store **that is** close by?*

The first example sentence above contains a relative clause starting with **que**, preceded by the antecedent **unos zapatos negros**. This pair of shoes is real, specific. In the second example, **necesito unos zapatos** refers to a *desired* pair of shoes. In the last example sentence, **alguna zapatería que esté** is *indefinite* and possibly nonexistent.

EJERCICIO
21·10

¿Indicativo o subjuntivo? *Complete each sentence with the appropriate form of the subjunctive or the indicative of the verb in parentheses.*

1. (ser) Tiene una novia que _____ feísima.

2. (poder) Necesita una peluquera que _____ hacerle un buen corte de pelo.

3. (querer) Conoce a una sicóloga que _____ ayudarla a ganar autoestima (*self-confidence*).

4. (tener) Eso sí, no hay nadie que _____ una novia tan fiel (*loyal*).

5. (comprender) Raúl no ha encontrado a nadie que lo _____ como ella.

6. (costar) Ayer ellos encontraron un apartamento que _____ poco.

7. (compartir) Raúl ha encontrado a alguien que _____ su filosofía de la vida.

8. (lograr) No hay nada que _____ separar a Raúl y su novia.

Te toca a ti. *First, select a theme (your ideal partner, your ideal home, or your ideal salary); then create a sentence using the appropriate form of the subjunctive or indicative of the verbs.*

Mi _____ ideal.

1. buscar

_____

2. necesitar

_____

3. desear

_____

4. es necesario que yo...

_____

5. querer

_____

6. ¿conocer... ?

_____

Talking about future events

Now let's look at a conversation that talks about the future.

Conversation: Seeking a professor's advice

KATY: Profesora Martínez, ¿tiene usted tiempo para hablar un rato conmigo?

Professor Martínez, do you have time to talk to me for a few minutes?

P. MARTÍNEZ: Sí, Katy, **voy a estar** libre hasta mediodía, así que no hay apuro. ¿Qué se te ofrece?

Yes, Katy, I'm going to be free until noon, so there's no rush. What can I do for you?

KATY: Es que me encanta su clase y **estoy pensando especializarme** en la lengua española. ¿Usted cree que tengo el talento suficiente como para **llegar** algún día **a ser** profesora de español?

It's that I love your class, and I'm thinking about majoring in Spanish. Do you think I have the ability to become a Spanish teacher one day?

P. MARTÍNEZ: Claro que lo creo. Me alegra mucho saber que te interesaría especializarte en la lengua española. Te advierto que no te **harás** rica si te dedicas a ser profesora, pero **tendrás** una satisfacción enorme. Para mí, es la mejor profesión.

Of course I think so. I'm so happy to hear that you are interested in majoring in Spanish. I warn you that you probably won't get rich if you devote your life to being a teacher, but you will have enormous satisfaction. I think it's the best profession.

KATY: ¿Qué me recomienda que haga? Estoy en mi segundo año en la universidad y este es mi cuarto semestre de español.

What do you recommend that I do? I'm a sophomore and this is my fourth semester of Spanish.

P. MARTÍNEZ: Mira, después de este semestre, **sabrás** lo básico de la gramática española. Como es imprescindible que estudies por lo menos un semestre en el extranjero, te recomiendo que lo hagas **cuanto antes**, o sea, el próximo semestre. Y si realmente quieres ser profesora de la lengua, te aconsejo que vayas a España durante seis meses y que luego pases otro semestre en uno de los países hispanoamericanos. Así **lograrás ser** completamente bilingüe dentro de un año. Después, **cuando vuelvas**, **completarás** en tu último año los cursos y créditos que hagan falta para tu título.

Look, after this semester, you'll know all the basics of Spanish grammar. Since it's absolutely necessary that you do at least one semester abroad, I recommend that you do it as soon as possible, I mean, next semester. And if you really do want to be a Spanish teacher, I advise you to go to Spain for six months and after that do another semester in one of the Spanish-speaking Latin-American countries. That way, you'll be completely bilingual in just one year. After that, when you come back, you'll finish the courses and credits that you need for your degree in your senior year.

KATY: Todo esto me emociona mucho, pero no sé qué pensarán mis padres sobre estar fuera del país durante un año entero.

I'm so excited about all this, but I don't know what my parents will think about my being out of the country for a whole year.

P. MARTÍNEZ: Deberías hablarlo con ellos. **¿Por qué** no preparas una propuesta formal, en la cual les explicas cuáles son tus **metas** para el futuro y cómo **piensas alcanzar** cada una de ellas? Incluye todos los detalles—lo que **piensas estudiar**, donde e incluso cuánto **va a costar** todo y cómo **vas a ayudar** con los gastos. Eres muy buena estudiante y es probable que consigas una beca.

You should talk it over with them. Why not prepare a formal proposal that explains what your goals are for the future and how you plan to achieve each one? Include all the details—what you're planning to study, where, and even how much it's going to cost, and how you're going to help pay for it. You're an excellent student and you can probably get a scholarship.

KATY: Eso sería fantástico. No se imagina lo emocionada que estoy. Ahora mismo **voy a hablarlo** con mi consejero y luego con la Oficina de Study Abroad. Y **cuando tenga** más información, me gustaría hablar otra vez con usted. Muchísimas gracias por todo.

That would be fantastic. You can't imagine how excited I am. I'm going right now to discuss this with my advisor and then to the Study Abroad Office. And when I have more information, I'd like to talk to you more. Thank you so much for everything.

El futuro (the future)

There are a number of ways to talk about the future in Spanish. Since no one knows for sure what the future will bring, the different ways of expressing it reflect the speaker's opinion on how probable it is that something will happen. When it is certain (as certain as it can be) that something is going to happen, then the present tense is used. (This is similar to English.)

La película **empieza** a las 8:10.	*The movie starts at 8:10.*
Las clases **terminan** en mayo.	*Classes end in May.*

| Roberto **llega** mañana. | *Roberto arrives tomorrow.* |
| Nos **vamos** el domingo. | *We're leaving on Sunday.* |

Likewise, when you want to make a promise or a commitment to do something, use the present tense. (Look how different this is from English!)

Estoy en tu casa a las ocho.	*I'll be at your house at eight o'clock.*
Te **llamo** esta noche.	*I'll call you tonight.*
Le **prestamos** el dinero.	*We'll lend you the money.*
No se lo **digo** a nadie.	*I won't tell anyone.*

When someone has decided or has made plans to do something, a conjugation of **ir** + **a** + infinitive is used.

Voy a ir a la casa de Antonio a las ocho.	*I'm going to go to Antonio's at eight o'clock.*
Voy a llamar a mi mamá esta noche.	*I'm going to call my mother tonight.*
Ellos **van a prestarnos** el dinero.	*They're going to lend us the money.*
Vamos a cenar juntos el viernes.	*We're going to have dinner together Friday.*

When someone has not yet decided to do something, but is still thinking about it, a conjugation of **pensar/estar pensando** + infinitive is used.

| ¿Qué **piensas hacer**? | *What are you planning to do?* |
| **Estoy pensando invitar** a Ana a cenar. | *I'm thinking about inviting Ana to dinner.* |

The negative of this construction is more decisive, and is equivalent to **no ir** + **a** + infinitive.

| **No pienso cenar** con él. | *I'm not going to eat with him.* |
| **No pensamos hacer** el viaje. | *We're not going to take the trip.* |

Note that in English it is common to use the present progressive to express plans for the near future. This is not done in Spanish (except in Argentina, where it is!).

| ¿Qué **vas a hacer** mañana? | *What are you doing tomorrow?* |
| **Voy a trabajar** todo el día mañana. | *I'm working all day tomorrow.* |

When the activity is too far ahead to plan for, or if someone is a bit ambivalent or uncertain about doing something, the future tense is used. (You may want to review Chapter 14.)

¿Qué piensas hacer esta noche?	*What are you planning to do tonight?*
No sé, **iré** al cine o a algún club.	*I don't know, maybe I'll go to the movies or to a club.*
Leeré un libro.	*I'll probably read a book.*
Algún día, **llamaré** a Ángela.	*One of these days I'll call Ángela.*

The future tense can also be used to make predictions—definitely the tense that would be used by the fortune-teller reading your palm or telling you what the crystal ball says—but it is also used for just ordinary feelings we might have about what will happen in the future.

Se casará y **tendrá** cuatro hijos.	*You will get married and have four children.*
Su hijo mayor **será** médico.	*Your eldest son will be a doctor.*
Se eliminarán muchas enfermedades.	*Many diseases will be eliminated.*
Habrá diversas fuentes de energía.	*There will be many different sources of energy.*

A question put in the future tense is the best way to express *I wonder . . .*

¿Qué hora **será**?	*I wonder what time it is?*
¿Cuántos años **tendrá** esa mujer?	*I wonder how old that woman is?*
¿Dónde **estará** mi antigua profesora?	*I wonder where my former teacher is?*

The future tense is also used to express *probably/must be/I guess.*

Juan ya **estará** en su casa.	*Juan must be home by now.*
Ustedes **tendrán** hambre.	*You all must be hungry./I guess you're hungry.*
Mis padres **estarán** preocupados.	*My parents must be worried. /I guess my parents are worried.*

Any of these ways to talk about the future can be used in combination with a subjunctive clause that indicates *when* that future action might happen. Common words that introduce these subjunctive clauses include:

cuando	*as soon as/when*
en cuanto	*as soon as/when*
tan pronto como	*as soon as/when*
siempre y cuando	*if and when*

There are two patterns for these sentences. The subjunctive clause can occur:

◆ After the future clause.

Te llamo **cuando llegue tu hija.**	*I'll call you as soon as your daughter arrives.*
Pensamos ir a la universidad **tan pronto como nos graduemos de la escuela secundaria.**	*We're planning to go to college as soon as we graduate from high school.*
Van a salir **en cuanto termine el programa.**	*They're going to leave as soon as the show is over.*
Los visitaré **cuando vuelva al Perú.**	*I'll visit them when I go back to Perú.*

◆ Before the future clause.

Cuando llegue tu hija, te llamo.	*As soon as your daughter arrives, I'll call you.*
Tan pronto como nos graduemos de la escuela secundaria, pensamos ir a la universidad.	*As soon as we graduate from high school, we plan to go to college.*
En cuanto termine el programa, van a salir.	*As soon as the program ends, they're leaving.*
Cuando vuelva al Perú, los visitaré.	*When I go back to Perú, I'll visit them.*

Be very careful not to confuse the **cuando** that indicates a future activity (followed by a subjunctive clause) with the **cuando** that indicates *every time that/whenever,* or simultaneous action (followed by an indicative clause.)

Future activity (subjunctive clause)	**Simultaneous activities (indicative clause)**
Te llamo **cuando llegue al trabajo.**	Te llamo **cuando llego al trabajo.**
I'll call you when I get to work.	*I (always) call you when I get to work.*
Cuando esté en México voy a comprar ese libro.	**Cuando estoy en México** compro libros.
When I'm in Mexico I'm going to buy that book.	*When (Every time that) I'm in Mexico I buy books.*
Cuando vuelva a casa, ella estará contenta.	**Cuando vuelve a casa,** ella está contenta.
When/As soon as she comes back home, she'll be happy.	*When/Whenever she comes back home, she's (always) happy.*

Si

Si without a written accent mark is unstressed, and usually translates to English as *if*. However, to the English speaker, *if* represents *doubt*, while **si** to the Spanish speaker can represent probability—it really does have a relationship with stressed **sí**—or *yes*! Perhaps this is why **si** is followed by the indicative rather than the subjunctive when it refers to possible future action.

Voy a tu casa **si** no apareces.	*I'm coming to your house if you don't show up.*
Pediremos frijoles **si** no hay carne.	*We'll order beans if there's no meat.*

Unstressed **si** is followed by the *imperfect subjunctive* when it means *if something were true*.

Si tú supieras la verdad...	*If you knew the truth . . .*
Si mi papá estuviera aquí...	*If my dad were here . . .*
Si yo tuviera dinero...	*If I had money . . .*

Unstressed **si** is also followed by the imperfect subjunctive to express *if something were to happen*.

Si yo fuera a Argentina...	*If I went to Argentina . . .*
Si ellos nos dieran permiso...	*If they gave us permission . . .*
Si consiguiera ese puesto...	*If I got that job . . .*

These clauses are normally used with a clause using the *conditional* (you may want to review Chapter 16.):

Si tú supieras la verdad, **comprenderías.**	*If you knew the truth, you would understand.*
Si mi papá estuviera aquí, me **enseñaría** a hacerlo.	*If my dad were here, he would show me how to do it.*
Si yo tuviera dinero, **compraría** un coche.	*If I had money, I would buy a car.*
¿Qué **harías** si fueras a Argentina?	*What would you do if you went to Argentina?*
Si yo fuera a Argentina, **hablaría** español todo el tiempo.	*If I went to Argentina, I would speak Spanish all the time.*
Si ellos nos dieran permiso, nos **quedaríamos** un año.	*If they gave us permission, we would stay for a year.*
Si consiguiera ese puesto, **podríamos** comprar una casa.	*If I got that job, we could buy a house.*

Meta

A **meta** is a *goal*—it can even be a *soccer goal*—something we dream about achieving and work hard to reach. *Reaching a goal* is expressed with the verb **alcanzar**.

Voy a trabajar muy duro para alcanzar todas mis **metas.**	*I'm going to work hard to achieve all my goals.*
Su **meta** es ser arquitecto. Lo alcanzará porque es un joven decidido.	*His goal is to be an architect. He'll achieve it because he's a determined young man.*

Alcanzar

Alcanzar can also mean *to reach* a person you've been trying to communicate with, *to reach* something that's up high, or *to catch up with* somebody.

Voy a invitar a Marta si la puedo **alcanzar.**	*I'm going to invite Marta if I can reach her.*

| Necesito un libro que está arriba, pero no lo puedo **alcanzar.** | *I need a book that's up there, but I can't reach it.* |
| Jacinto está bastante alto. Muy pronto **alcanzará** a su papá. | *Jacinto is pretty tall. Soon he'll be as tall as his father.* |

Lograr

Lograr is another verb that indicates *achieving*, usually with some struggle.

| Espero que **logre** convencerlos. | *I hope she is able to convince them.* |
| Voy a **lograr** que me paguen el dinero que me deben. | *I'm going to make sure they pay me the money they owe me.* |

It can be followed by an infinitive and then means *to manage to.*

| **Logramos** llegar a San Antonio en tres días. | *We managed to get to San Antonio in three days.* |

Llegar a ser

Llegar a ser means *to become*, involving a good deal of effort and/or time.

| Si te dedicas al trabajo, **llegarás a ser** presidente de la compañía. | *If you devote yourself to the job, you'll become the president of the company.* |

Another way to express *become* is **hacerse**, which is more general. It could require effort, but it could also be just what naturally happens.

| El hombre **se hizo** rico y famoso. | *The man became rich and famous.* |
| El hombre **se hizo** viejo. | *The man got old.* |

Cuanto antes

Cuanto antes means *as soon as possible.* Other expressions that indicate urgency of action are **lo antes posible** and **en seguida** *(as soon as possible/right away).*

| Deberías denunciarlos a la policía **cuanto antes**. | *You should report them to the police as soon as possible.* |
| Ven a casa **en seguida**. | *Come home right away.* |

Por

Por has many functions. It can indicate an exchange of something for something else.

| Te doy seis dólares **por** el cuadro. | *I'll give you six dollars for the picture.* |

Remember that *please* uses **por**, and *thank you* is followed by **por**:

| **Por favor**, ayúdenos. | *Please help us.* |
| Gracias **por ayudarnos**. | *Thank you for helping us.* |

Por qué

Por qué asks for the *reason* or *motive* of an action (something that has already happened), and **por** indicates the answer.

¿Por qué llegaste tan tarde?	*Why were you so late?*
Por la lluvia.	*Because of the rain.*

Para

Para also has many functions, which usually indicate something that is *ahead*, either in time or location.

¿Vas a estudiar **para** un título?	*Are you going to study for a degree?*
Voy **para** la biblioteca.	*I'm going toward the library.*

In the same vein, **para** followed by an infinitive means *in order to.*

Voy a estudiar **para** aprender todo lo que pueda.	*I'm going to study in order to learn everything I can.*

EJERCICIO
21·12

Write the Spanish future tense forms for the following verbs.

1. estar (yo) _____

2. ser (él) _____

3. ir (ellos) _____

4. querer (nosotros) _____

5. decir (tú) _____

6. aparecer (ella) _____

7. escribir (nosotros) _____

8. poner (ellos) _____

9. pensar (yo) _____

10. salir (nosotros) _____

11. hacer (vosotros) _____

12. volver (ustedes) _____

13. venir (él) _____

14. comer (tú) _____

15. tener (yo) _____

Match the English expressions in the left column with the most appropriate Spanish expressions in the right column.

1. _____ Help me.

2. _____ I help you (every day).

3. _____ I'm going to help you (tomorrow).

4. _____ I'll help you (one of these days).

5. _____ I'll help you (tomorrow).

a. Te ayudaré.

b. Ayúdame.

c. Te voy a ayudar.

d. Te ayudo.

EJERCICIO

21·14

Express the following sentences in Spanish.

1. You will get married and have twins.

_____

2. The party is at three o'clock.

_____

3. We're leaving tomorrow.

_____

4. I'll buy a car one day.

_____

5. I'll call you tonight.

_____

6. They're going to move to this building next week.

_____

7. What are you planning to do?

_____

8. I'm thinking about sending him an e-mail.

_____

9. I wonder what she's doing.

_____

10. She's probably working at a hospital.

_____

Choose between the indicative and the subjunctive to complete the following sentences.

1. Veremos la película en cuanto los niños (estar) _____ dormidos.

2. Ella siempre me llama si (tener, ella) _____ un problema.

3. ¿Qué harás si el profesor nos (dar) _____ un examen mañana?

4. Voy a estudiar tan pronto como (llegar, yo) _____ a la biblioteca.

5. Los contactaré tan pronto como (salir, yo) _____ del avión.

6. Te compro un helado si (portarse, tú) _____ bien.

7. La niña se pone roja cuando la maestra le (hacer, ella) _____ una pregunta.

8. No vamos en el metro cuando (llover) _____.

9. Iremos en el carro si (llover) _____.

10. Abriré el paraguas cuando (empezar) _____ a llover.

Write the Spanish imperfect subjunctive forms of the following verbs.

1. abrir (ellos) _____

2. saber (yo) _____

3. correr (tú) _____

4. enseñar (ella) _____

5. dormirse (él) _____

6. volver (nosotros) _____

7. traer (yo) _____

8. ser (usted) _____

9. ir (ustedes) _____

10. pensar (tú) _____

11. poder (ellos) _____

12. querer (vosotros) _____

13. leer (yo) _____

14. comprender (ella) _____

15. sentirse (él) _____

Write the Spanish conditional forms of the following verbs.

1. dar (él) _____

2. decir (ella) _____

3. vender (nosotros) _____

4. venir (ustedes) _____

5. poder (yo) _____

6. hacer (vosotros) _____

7. ir (yo) _____

8. bailar (tú) _____

9. encontrarse (ellos) _____

10. conocer (ellas) _____

11. deber (nosotros) _____

12. pagar (ella) _____

13. invitar (él) _____

14. enojarse (yo) _____

15. aburrirse (él) _____

Use the conditional and the imperfect subjunctive to fill in the blanks.

1. Si (tener, yo) _____ tiempo, te (ayudar, yo) _____.

2. Si (saber, tú) _____ la verdad, (enojarse, tú) _____.

3. Si (estar, nosotros) _____ en clase, (estar, nosotros) _____ haciendo el examen.

4. Si (hacer, yo) _____ un esfuerzo, (ser, yo) _____ mejor estudiante.

5. Si el profesor (ser, él) _____ más simpático, no nos (asignar, él) _____ tanta lectura para el fin de semana.

*Fill each blank with **por** or **para**, as appropriate.*

1. _____ favor, enséñame a bailar salsa.

2. Gracias _____ acompañarnos.

3. _____ alcanzar sus metas, tendrá que trabajar duro.

4. Ella pagó cien dólares _____ los zapatos.

5. ¿_____ qué pagaste tanto?

6. ¿_____ qué quieres ir al banco?

7. Vamos _____ Filadelfia _____ ver la Campana de Libertad.

Write down a possible conversation you might have with a teacher, friend, or relative in which you tell your ideas about your future. Include what is already established (a date of graduation, perhaps), what you are thinking about doing, what you have already planned to do, and what you might do one day. You might add that if something else were true or possible, your plans would be different. You may want to ask this person to help you in some way, and at the end, make a promise to him or her. Be careful not to translate from English, but rather use the guidelines suggested in this chapter for expressing the likelihood of different aspects of your future. Ask a Spanish-speaking friend to read your conversation and comment on your expression.

_____

_____

_____

_____

_____

_____

_____

_____

Relative pronouns

Reviewing a few points of grammar will help you understand the role played by relative pronouns in everyday communication. A relative pronoun always refers back to its *antecedent*, a noun or a pronoun previously mentioned in a sentence. In other words, relative pronouns serve as links or connectors between sentences or clauses. *That, those, which, who, whom,* and *whose* are used to introduce relative clauses in English.

Juan es el profesor **que**
    enseña filosofía.

*Juan is the professor **who***
    teaches philosophy.

Antecedent means previous or prior. The antecedent in the above example, **el profesor**, is immediately followed by **que**, a relative pronoun that introduces a relative clause (**que enseña filosofía**). Relative clauses are always subordinate (dependent) clauses.

Velázquez es el autor de
    Las Meninas, **el cual** es
    mi cuadro favorito.

Velázquez is the creator of
    Las Meninas, ***which** is*
    my favorite painting.

The main (independent) clause in this case, **Velázquez es el autor de *Las Meninas***, makes complete sense; it stands on its own. The subordinate clause, **el cual es mi cuadro favorito**, embellishes the sentence; it adds meaning to the main sentence, but cannot stand on its own. This type of clause is called *nonrestrictive* because it does not act upon or limit the content of the main clause.

However, in other sentences, the information in a dependent clause is necessary to understand the main clause. In this case, it is called a *restrictive* clause, because its presence limits the content of the main clause.

Las manzanas **que están**
    podridas no son saludables.

*The apples **that are rotten** are not*
    healthful. (Rotten apples are not
    healthful.)

Apples are considered a healthful fruit. If we take out the relative clause, **que están podridas**, the utterance would not make much sense.

Relative pronouns may refer to people, things, actions, events, or ideas. However, the correct pronoun must be used to convey the proper message. Observe the relative pronouns **que** and **quien** in the following sentences:

El libro **que está en la mesa** es mío.
El autor, **quien acaba de llegar de**
    Francia, firmó muchos libros.

*The book **that is on the table** is mine.*
*The author, **who has just arrived from***
    ***France**, signed many books.*

The antecedent of the relative pronoun **quien** is always a person. Note that in English, relative pronouns (*that, which, who, whom*) are not necessarily included in a complex sentence. Note the English equivalent of the following example:

La playa **que nosotros visitamos** estaba desierta.

*The beach **we visited** was deserted.*

Que: When is the relative pronoun que used in Spanish?

The most common relative pronoun in Spanish, especially in conversational exchanges, is **que**, the equivalent of *that*. The antecedent of **que** is never omitted in Spanish. Use **que** in a relative clause:

- that refers to people, animals, things, ideas, or events in the singular and plural.

  El hombre **que sale del banco ahora** lleva una maleta.

  *The man **who is leaving the bank now** carries a suitcase.*

  El pájaro **que canta** es mi regalo para ti.

  *The bird **that is singing** is my gift to you.*

  No queremos ir a la fiesta **que organizan los estudiantes**.

  *We do not want to attend the party **(that) the students are organizing**.*

  ¿No vas a usar los zapatos **que compraste ayer**?

  *Aren't you going to wear the shoes **that you bought yesterday**?*

- where it functions as the subject of a clause.

  In the following example, **que**, referring back to **el guía**, functions as the subject of the verb (**llevó**) in the relative (dependent) clause.

  Éste es el guía **que lo llevó al museo**.

  *This is the guide **who took him to the museum**.*

- where it functions as the object of a clause.

  In the example below, **que** refers back to the direct object (**al técnico**) of the verb (**reco-miendo**) in the main clause. **Que** functions as the direct object of the verb (**llamamos**) in the relative (dependent) clause. (**Nosotros** [implied] is the subject of the relative clause.)

  Te recomiendo al técnico **que llamamos ayer**.

  *I recommend to you the technician **whom we called yesterday**.*

EJERCICIO
22·1

En mi ciudad. Complete each sentence by combining the two sentences with the relative pronoun.

EJEMPLO   El libro dice "Romance nocturno". Es aburridísimo. →
           El libro que dice "Romance nocturno" es aburridísimo.

1. La casa está cerca del puente. Es de María. _____

2. Vimos los tigres en el zoo. Son de la India. _____

3. La escuela está cerrada. Es una institución privada. _____

4. Los policías cuidan el banco. Están dormidos. _____

5. Los árboles son más altos. Están en el parque. _____

6. En la catedral hay unos turistas. Esperan ver unos cuadros de El Greco. _____

_____

EJERCICIO
22·2

Un poco de geografía. ¿Verdadero (V) o falso (F)?

_____ 1. La ciudad de Quito, que está en el hemisferio sur, es la capital de Perú.

_____ 2. Chile, un país que está en la costa del Pacífico, exporta muchas frutas.

_____ 3. En la ciudad de San Antonio, que está en Texas, hay poca herencia hispana.

_____ 4. La ciudad de Barcelona, que es famosa por las obras del arquitecto Antoni Gaudí, está en Cataluña, España.

_____ 5. La selva del Amazonas es parte de varios países hispanos que están en Suramérica.

_____ 6. La isla de Cuba, que atrae a muchos turistas, está a pocas millas de Cayo Hueso.

EJERCICIO
22·3

*En español. Use the relative pronoun **que**.*

1. While Jackie goes to the market, which is next to the movie theater, we watch a movie.

_____

2. The child who is with me is Jackie's son. _____

3. The movie that we watch is not too interesting. _____

4. Matt saw two women who did not pay for their tickets. _____

5. Mark came to see a movie that is a foreign (**extranjero**) film. _____

6. I bought the things that the children want, chocolates and refreshments. _____

_____

Quien: When is the relative pronoun quien used in Spanish?

The English pronouns *who* and *whom* are the equivalents of **quien** and the plural form **quienes**. This relative pronoun, which refers only to people, is not used as frequently as **que**. It may appear in written language, to clarify the identity of the antecedent. Sometimes it is the equivalent of *whoever*.

Use **quien/quienes** instead of **que** when the antecedent is a person, in a dependent clause where it functions as:

- the subject of a verb.

    In the following example, **Fernando** is the subject of the verb **invita**. The relative pronoun **quien** in the dependent clause is the subject of **es**.

    Fernando, **quien es un viejo amigo**, me invita a su boda.   *Fernando, **who is an old friend**, is inviting me to his wedding.*

- the object of a verb.

    In the following example, **quienes** is preceded by the preposition **a**: **a quienes**. This construction parallels the antecedent in the main clause, **al Dr. Salama** (which contains the contraction of the preposition **a** plus the definite article **el**). **A quienes** is the object of the verb **vimos**.

    Saludamos al Dr. Salama y su esposa, **a quienes vimos ayer**.   *We said hello to Dr. Salama and his wife, **whom we saw yesterday**.*

The clause introduced with **quien** or **quienes** is separated from the main clause with commas. It is normally nonrestrictive.

EJERCICIO
22·4

En el baile de máscaras. Combine all the words in each sentence with the appropriate relative pronoun **quien** *or* **quienes**.

EJEMPLO   Amelia | cumple años hoy | va a una fiesta de disfraces (*costume*) →
    Amelia, quien cumple años hoy, va a una fiesta de disfraces.

1. El hombre | tiene un traje de Arlequín | es muy gordo. _____

2. El chico | trae un disfraz de Frankenstein | es muy bajo. _____

3. Los hombres | se visten como los siete enanitos (*dwarves*) | son muy viejos. _____

    _____

4. Una señora | parece la Bella Durmiente | está durmiendo en el sofá _____

5. Un señor | viene con un traje de príncipe | no tiene aspecto aristocrático. _____

    _____

6. Las niñas | se ponen un disfraz de bruja (*witch*) | son muy simpáticas. _____

    _____

¿Quién o quiénes? Complete each sentence with the appropriate relative pronoun.

1. Vimos a los camarógrafos (*cameramen*), _____ filmaron el documental.

2. Ésta es la narradora, _____ va a grabar la información del documental.

3. Los ayudantes, a _____ van a pagar un sueldo (*salary*), empiezan a trabajar mañana.

4. Un profesor de biología, _____ es el investigador del grupo, escribió el guión (*script*).

5. Saludamos al productor, a _____ conocen como el rey de los documentales.

6. Las actrices, _____ tienen un papel (*role*) muy corto, tienen miedo de los osos.

En español. Use the relative pronoun *quien* or *quienes*.

1. The man who is sitting to my right is from San Diego. _____

2. The people who bought the tickets today paid a high price. _____
   _____

3. The women whom you (**tú**) invited are dancing the rumba. _____
   _____

4. But I do not see their husbands, who were here. _____

5. Marlo, who is a good friend (*f.*), plays the piano. _____

6. Do you (**tú**) know the woman who is singing now? _____

El que and el cual: When are the relative pronouns el que and el cual and their forms used in Spanish?

The relative pronoun forms of **que** with a definite article, **el que**, **los que**, **la que**, and **las que** and the set of forms **el cual**, **los cuales**, **la cual**, and **las cuales** are interchangeable. Their English equivalents are *that*, *which*, *who*, and *whom*.

If you understand when to use **que** and **quien** (**quienes**), you are ready to use the alternate forms **el que**, **los que**, **la que**, and **las que** and **el cual**, **los cuales**, **la cual**, and **las cuales**. They add variety to a context that requires the use of many relative pronouns. Use these forms in dependent clauses where they:

- function as the subject of a verb.

El autor de Don Quijote es Cervantes,
el cual escribió otras novelas.

The author of Don Quixote is Cervantes,
***who wrote other novels**.*

- function as the object of a verb.

In the following example, **el que** is preceded by the preposition **a** (**al que**), paralleling **a Eduardo** in the main clause.

Saludamos a Eduardo, el hermano
de Ali, **al que vimos ayer**.

We said hello to Eduardo, Ali's brother,
***whom we saw yesterday**.*

- have two antecedents.

In this use, these forms refer to the person or thing physically farther away from the pronoun in the sentence.

Hay una foto de mis nietos,
la cual es muy simpática.

There is a photo of my grandchildren,
***which is very nice**.*

Note that **quien** (**quienes**), and **el que**, **los que**, **la que**, or **las que** may be used as the indefinite subject of a verb. Their equivalents are: *he who, those who,* etc.

Quien espera, desespera. ⎫
El que espera, desespera. ⎬   ***He who** waits, loses hope.*
⎭

EJERCICIO
22·7

*Práctica. Complete each sentence with the appropriate relative pronoun **el cual, los cuales, la cual, las cuales**.*

1. Los hijos de Juan, _____ son mis colegas, viajarán al Oriente pronto.

2. Ellos viven en una casa muy bonita, _____ está al lado del río.

3. En la casa hay un salón, _____ está al lado de la escalera (*stairway*).

4. Juan también tiene dos hijas gemelas (*twins*), _____ hablan japonés.

5. Tienen libros en japonés, _____ solamente ellas pueden leer.

6. En esa casa hay dos colecciones de perlas orientales, _____ son muy valiosas.

Lo que and lo cual: When are the relative pronouns lo que and lo cual used in Spanish?

The antecedents of **lo que** and **lo cual** (interchangeable forms) are always ideas. They are neuter relative pronouns, more frequently used in writing than in speech. Their English equivalents are *that, which, which, what,* or *whatever*. Follow these guidelines when using **lo que, lo cual**:

- Use **lo que** or **lo cual** to refer to a statement, concept, or idea previously mentioned.

  Siempre llama después de las once
  de la noche, **lo que nos irrita**.

  He always calls after eleven at night,
  which irritates us.

The idea of calling after a certain, inappropriate hour is understood or summed up in **lo que**. Remember that **lo cual** could also be used here.

- Use **lo que** to refer to a statement, concept, or idea that is understood because it has been discussed previously.

  Lo que te avisó, no va a suceder.

  ***What** he announced to you is not going to happen.*

EJERCICIO
22·8

¿Y en tu caso? Complete each sentence with a phrase that explains your reaction. Note that more than one answer may be acceptable.

| me aburre | me enoja | me fascina | me gusta |
| me hace falta | me importa | me irrita | me interesa |

1. No tengo dinero para comprar el auto que quiero, lo cual _____.

2. Voy a ir al gimnasio todos los días esta semana, lo cual _____.

3. Tengo que ir a casa de mi suegra (*mother-in-law*), lo que _____.

4. Hay una venta especial de zapatos esta semana, lo que _____.

5. Veo películas en mi computadora, lo cual _____.

6. Mis amigos me regalaron cien dólares para mi cumpleaños, lo que _____

   _____.

7. Este verano gané un viaje gratis a Cancún, lo cual _____.

8. Mañana es un día feriado (*holiday*), lo cual _____.

EJERCICIO
22·9

En español.

1. The columnist reveals the actor's secrets, which is interesting. _____

   _____

2. What you (**tú**) want to know is in today's paper. _____

   _____

3. I always eat what I want. _____

4. The nutritionist recommends eating what is healthy. _____

5. My friends do not go to the gym often, which is not good. _____

_____

6. Leonardo is not here, which worries me. _____

7. Do you (**Ud.**) see what I see now? _____

8. You (**Uds.**) are very generous, which is fabulous! _____

Relative pronouns after prepositions

When relative pronouns are used after prepositions, they function as objects of a verb. In the example that follows, **al niño** is replaced in the relative clause by **a quien**, which is the direct object of **descubrieron**. Remember that a direct object answers the question *what*, *who*, or *whom*.

Castigaron al niño, **a quien descubrieron rompiendo la ventana.** | *They punished the boy, **whom they discovered breaking a window.***

- **El que, los que, la que, las que** and **el cual, los cuales, la cual,** and **las cuales** may be used after any preposition.

Abrimos la ventana, **desde la cual vemos el valle.** | *We opened the window **from which we see the valley.***
La escuela **en la que ellos estudian** ganó el campeonato. | *The school **that they attend** won the championship.*
Daniela es una persona **en la cual se puede confiar.** | *Daniela is a person **whom you can trust.***

- **Que** may follow the prepositions **a**, **de**, **en**, and **con** if **que** does not refer to a person.

Éste es el auto **en que chocaron**. | *This is the car **in which they crashed**. (They crashed in this car.)*

- **Que** may follow the preposition **de** when the antecedent is a person.

Aquí entra el señor **de que hablamos**. | *Here comes the gentleman **about whom we talked**.*

- **Quien (quienes)** and **el que** refer to people and may follow any preposition.

El hombre **con quien se casó Vera** es de Marruecos. | *The man **whom Vera married** is from Morocco.*

*En la montaña. Use the appropriate relative pronoun **el cual, los cuales, la cual, las cuales, quien** or **quienes**.*

1. Los jóvenes subieron una montaña desde _____ vieron un río.

2. Ellos vieron un puente muy viejo, por _____ pasaron.

3. Caminaron hasta una casa al lado de _____ había unos perritos.

4. La abuela preparó el almuerzo para _____ visitan su casa en el campo.

5. Los chicos buscan los cuchillos (knives), con _____ cortan la carne.

6. Comen todos excepto _____ no tienen hambre.

7. Después, llegó Pedro, con _____ todos quieren jugar al tenis.

8. También jugaron con las chicas, _____ no ganaron el partido de tenis.

Cuyo, cuya: When are the relative adjectives cuyo, cuya used in Spanish?

Cuyo (**cuyos**), **cuya** (**cuyas**) mean *whose*. These are forms of a relative adjective referring to persons and things. They precede the noun they modify and must agree in gender and number with that noun.

Ésta es la señora **cuya tienda robaron anoche**.	*This is the lady **whose store was robbed (they robbed) last night**.*
Lazlo es un artista **cuyos cuadros se venden bien**.	*Lazlo is an artist **whose paintings are selling well**.*

Note that **cuyo** and its forms establish a relationship of possession. Each example sentence could be divided into two parts. If you delete **cuya** and **cuyos** and replace them with a possessive adjective, the sentences become: **Robaron *su* tienda anoche** and *Sus* **cuadros se venden bien**.

*Práctica. Complete each sentence with the appropriate relative pronoun **cuyo, cuyos, cuya** or **cuyas**.*

1. El autor, de _____ libro te he hablado, ha ganado un premio literario.

2. Éste es el arquitecto _____ creación es la torre (*tower*) más alta de la ciudad.

3. ¿No es Ud. la persona _____ abogado ganó el caso?

4. Aquí está el congresista _____ palabras aparecen en el periódico.

Numbers

Cardinal numbers

Here is a list of Spanish cardinal numbers (**los números cardinales**). Note alternative spellings for some numbers under 30.

0	**cero**
1	**uno**
2	**dos**
3	**tres**
4	**cuatro**
5	**cinco**
6	**seis**
7	**siete**
8	**ocho**
9	**nueve**
10	**diez**
11	**once**
12	**doce**
13	**trece**
14	**catorce**
15	**quince**
16	**dieciséis, diez y seis**
17	**diecisiete, diez y siete**
18	**dieciocho, diez y ocho**
19	**diecinueve, diez y nueve**
20	**veinte**
21	**veintiuno, veinte y uno**
22	**veintidós, veinte y dos**
23	**veintitrés, veinte y tres**
24	**veinticuatro, veinte y cuatro**
25	**veinticinco, veinte y cinco**
26	**veintiséis, veinte y seis**
27	**veintisiete, veinte y siete**
28	**veintiocho, veinte y ocho**
29	**veintinueve, veinte y nueve**
30	**treinta**

31	**treinta y uno**	100	**ciento (cien)**
32	**treinta y dos**	101	**ciento uno, una**
33	**treinta y tres**	200	**doscientos/doscientas**
34	**treinta y cuatro**	300	**trescientos/trescientas**
35	**treinta y cinco**	400	**cuatrocientos/cuatrocientas**
36	**treinta y seis**	500	**quinientos/quinientas**
37	**treinta y siete**	600	**seiscientos/seiscientas**
38	**treinta y ocho**	700	**setecientos/setecientas**
39	**treinta y nueve**	800	**ochocientos/ochocientas**
40	**cuarenta**	900	**novecientos/novecientas**
50	**cincuenta**	1.000	**mil**
60	**sesenta**	2.000	**dos mil**
70	**setenta**	100.000	**cien mil**
80	**ochenta**	1.000.000	**un millón**
90	**noventa**	1.000.000.000	**mil millones**

Cardinal numbers may be used as adjectives or pronouns. If they precede a noun, they function as an adjective. Note the following rules for the use of cardinal numbers in Spanish:

- Instead of commas, Spanish uses periods to indicate the value of units, and commas instead of periods to indicate decimals.

  Recibimos **12.532** votos.   *We got **12,532** votes.*
  Este libro cuesta **$22,30**.   *This book costs **$22.30**.*

- If a number ending in **uno** (*one*) precedes a noun, it agrees with that noun in gender. The masculine form drops the **-o** and the feminine changes to **una**. All other numbers are invariable.

  No tengo **veintiún** dólares.   *I do not have **twenty-one** dollars.*
  Hay **treinta y una** señoras esperando.   *There are **thirty-one** women waiting.*

  Note the accent mark on **veintiún** in the first example above.

- The numbers 16 to 19 and 21 to 29 may be spelled in two ways: in one word or with three words, as in **dieciséis** or **diez y seis**. The one-word spelling requires an accent mark and reflects contemporary spelling preference.

  El **dieciocho** es mi número favorito.   *Eighteen* is my favorite number.

- Use **y** to separate tens and units only. Note the different construction in the English equivalent.

  Tienes **treinta y siete** años solamente.   *You are only **thirty-seven** years old.*
  Pagaron **cuatrocientos cuarenta y**   *They paid **four hundred and forty-five** dollars.*
  cinco dólares.

- If a noun does not follow the number, a number ending in **uno** does not change to **un**. The noun omitted is understood from previous information.

  ¿Cuántos chicos hay en esta clase?   *How many boys are there in this class?*
  Treinta y uno.   *Thirty-one.*

- Compounds that end in **-ciento** also agree with the noun that follows them.

  Trajeron **doscientas esmeraldas**   *They brought **two hundred** Colombian **emeralds**.*
  colombianas.

♦ **Cien** indicates the number, quantity, or amount before **mil** and **millones**.

Hay **cien mil dólares** para tu proyecto.

*There is **one hundred thousand dollars** for your project.*

Dicen que el dictador tiene **cien millones de dólares** en el banco.

*They say the dictator has a **hundred million dollars** in the bank.*

Note that the preposition de follows **millón** or **millones** in Spanish, preceding a noun.

En español. Spell out the number that appears in parentheses.

1. _____ personas (35)

2. _____ habitantes (2.341)

3. _____ castillos (322)

4. _____ lápices (16)

5. _____ billetes (67)

6. _____ caballeros (71)

7. _____ maletas (100)

8. _____ copias (502)

9. _____ alumnas (26)

10. _____ soldados (100.000)

11. _____ días (31)

12. _____ millas (miles) (700)

13. _____ de dólares (1.000.000)

14. _____ tarjetas (51)

When do we use cardinal numbers?

Cardinal numbers are used:

♦ to count.

Veinticuatro, veinticinco...

Twenty-four, twenty-five . . .

♦ to indicate arithmetic problems.

dividido por, entre divided by (÷)

Sesenta **entre** tres son veinte.
Ochenta **dividido por** diez son ocho.

*Sixty **divided by** three is twenty.*
*Eighty **divided by** ten is eight.*

más, y plus (+)

Dos **y** once son trece.
Cinco **más** cuatro son nueve.

*Two **plus** eleven is thirteen.*
*Five **plus** four is nine.*

menos minus (−)

Cien **menos** veinticinco son setenta y cinco.

*One hundred **minus** twenty-five is seventy-five.*

por multiplied by (×)

Nueve **por** tres son veintisiete.   *Nine **multiplied by** three is twenty-seven.*

◆ to tell time (**la hora**). The third-person singular form of **ser** (**es, era**) is used for *one o'clock* and any time that includes la una: **la una y diez minutos**. The third-person plural of **ser** (**son, eran**) is used for all other times.

Es **la una** en punto.	*It's exactly **one o'clock**.*
Son **las cuatro y diez**.	*It is **four ten**.*
Eran **las cinco y veinte** cuando salieron de clase.	*It was **five twenty** when they left the classroom.*

The arithmetic expressions **menos** (*minus*) and **y** (*and, plus*) are also used to tell time. The fraction **media** (*half*) is used to indicate the half hour. For telling time in English **menos** = *to* and **y** = *past*.

Son las dos **y** cuarto. Salimos a las tres **menos** cuarto.	*It is a quarter **past** two. We leave at a quarter **to** three.*
¿Podemos irnos a las dos **y media**?	*May we leave at **half past** two?*

As in English, cardinal numbers are also used to tell time in Spanish: **las dos y quince** (*two fifteen*), **dos y cuarenta y cinco** (*two forty-five*), and **dos y treinta** (*two thirty*).

Note that the preposition **a** + **la** or **a** + **las** + the time is the equivalent for *at* + time in English. Use the expressions of time **de la mañana** (*in the morning*), **de la tarde** (*in the afternoon*), and **de la noche** (*at night*) to indicate a more precise time. They translate as A.M. and P.M. in English.

◆ to indicate dates. Note the use of **ser**:

¿Qué día **es** hoy? Hoy **es** el 3 de noviembre.	*What day **is** today? Today **is** November 3.*
Mi cumpleaños no **es** el primero de mayo.	*My birthday **is** not on May first.*

All days of the month are indicated with cardinal numbers except **el primero** (*the first*). In English, the preposition *on* is used where Spanish uses the definite article **el** to indicate when an event takes place. To tell the date, the order of the words in Spanish is different from English. **Hoy es el cinco de mayo** is the equivalent of *Today is May 5*. However, it is also possible to use an expression with **estar a** + the day of the month:

Estamos a quince de marzo.	*It is March 15.*

Here are the months of the year in Spanish:

enero	*January*	**julio**	*July*
febrero	*February*	**agosto**	*August*
marzo	*March*	**septiembre**	*September*
abril	*April*	**octubre**	*October*
mayo	*May*	**noviembre**	*November*
junio	*June*	**diciembre**	*December*

EJERCICIO
23·2

¿Qué hora? ¿Qué fecha? Translate into Spanish. Spell all the numbers in Spanish.

1. March 15, 1898 _____

2. It is 3:30 p.m. _____

3. July 14, 1770 _____

4. June 1, 2002 _____

5. It is 10:15 p.m. _____

6. January 31, 1999 _____

7. At 9:30 a.m. _____

8. November 30 at 7 p.m. _____

EJERCICIO
23·3

Preguntas personales.

1. ¿Cuántos años tienes? _____

2. ¿Qué día celebras tu cumpleaños? _____

3. ¿Cuál es tu número de la suerte (lucky)? _____

4. Escribe el número de tu distrito postal (zip code). _____

5. ¿Qué hora tienes? _____

6. ¿Cuánto dinero quieres ganar a la semana? _____

EJERCICIO
23·4

Aritmética. Spell the numbers in Spanish.

EJEMPLO   13 + 45 = __58__ *Trece más cuarenta y cinco son cincuenta y ocho.*

1. 100 − 45 = _____ _____

2. 25 + 12 = _____ _____

3. 30 × 3 = _____ _____

4. 12 + 16 + 15 = _____ _____

5. 200 ÷ 4 = _____ _____

6. 77 × 3 = _____ _____

¿Verdadero (V) o falso (F)?

_____ 1. El primero de enero es la celebración de Año Nuevo.

_____ 2. El mes de abril tiene treinta y un días.

_____ 3. Veinticinco más treinta son setenta.

_____ 4. Hay más de treinta millones de hispanos en los Estados Unidos.

_____ 5. En un año bisiesto (*leap*) febrero tiene veintisiete días.

_____ 6. Cincuenta es el número de estados de los Estados Unidos.

_____ 7. Celebramos el Día de las madres el catorce de febrero.

_____ 8. Vivimos en el siglo (*century*) veintiuno.

_____ 9. Hay 102 senadores en el senado de los Estados Unidos.

_____10. Hay doce rosas en una docena.

En español.

1. There are more than one hundred television channels. _____

2. Many American families have only one child (**hijo**). _____

3. Many American households (**hogares,** *m.*) have three television sets. _____

4. One cannot buy much with twenty-five dollars. _____

5. There are thirty-two pieces (**pieza**) in a chess set (**juego de ajedrez**). _____

6. We work fifty weeks every year. _____

7. Lincoln's birthday is February 12. _____

Ordinal numbers

Ordinal numbers (**números ordinales**) are used to assign a place in a series. They may function as adjectives or as pronouns. The following are the ordinal numbers used in Spanish:

primero(a)	*first*	**sexto(a)**	*sixth*
segundo(a)	*second*	**séptimo(a)**	*seventh*
tercero(a)	*third*	**octavo(a)**	*eighth*
cuarto(a)	*fourth*	**noveno(a)**	*ninth*
quinto(a)	*fifth*	**décimo(a)**	*tenth*

Ordinal numbers in Spanish are used in the following ways:

- After the ordinal number **décimo** (*tenth*), cardinal numbers are used to indicate the order in a series, and they usually follow the noun.

  Éste es el Congreso **15** de esta organización.

  *This is the **15th** Convention of this organization.*

- Ordinals can function as adjectives and nouns.

  El segundo día, fueron a la playa.
  Es **la segunda vez** que llamo.
  Marcos es **el tercero**.

  *The **second day**, they went to the beach.*
  *This is **the second time** I'm calling.*
  *Marcos is **the third** (**one**).*

- When **primero** and **tercero** are used as adjectives and precede a masculine noun, they drop the **-o**.

  En primer lugar, tú debes hacer tu trabajo.
  Ellos viven en **el tercer piso**.

  ***In the first place**, you should do your work.*
  *They live on **the third floor**.*

Ordinal numbers in English are often printed with *-th* following the number as in: *5th*. Spanish printed equivalents are: **1º, 2ª, 3er, 5ta**, etc. Note that the suffixes of the abbreviations reflect the final letter or letters of the ordinal number written out.

EJERCICIO

23·7

Los ordinales. *Spell out the ordinal number in parentheses.*

1. la _____ vez (1)

2. el _____ grado (5)

3. el _____ día (10)

4. la _____ sesión (8)

5. el _____ lugar (1)

6. la _____ lección (3)

7. la _____ pregunta (7)

8. el siglo (*century*) _____ (20)

9. la _____ estación (4)

10. la _____ salida (2)

EJERCICIO

23·8

Preguntas personales.

1. ¿Quién era tu maestra(o) en el tercer grado? _____

2. ¿Dónde vivías cuando estabas en el grado 11? _____

3. ¿Qué equipo de fútbol americano está en primer lugar en la Liga Nacional? _____

_____

4. ¿Cuándo fue la primera vez que tomaste una clase de español? _____

5. ¿Cuándo terminaste el quinto ejercicio de esta lección? _____

6. ¿Qué haces el primero de enero? _____

En español.

1. This is my third visit to the museum. _____

2. But it is the first time I take (am taking) pictures. _____

3. The tenth chapter is difficult. _____

4. Daisy always arrives second, after Julia. _____

5. They are betting (**apostar**) in the fifth race (**carrera**). _____

6. Picasso lived in the 20th century. _____

7. Today is the first day of the rest of my life. _____

8. December is the twelfth month of the year. _____

9. Fortunately, today is the seventh day of the week. _____

10. We live on the fourth floor. _____

Fractions

In order to express fractions in Spanish, the cardinal numbers are used for the numerator. This is the same as English. For fractions beginning with 1/4 to 10/10, the cardinal numbers are used as denominators, except for *half*, which is called **medio** and *thirds*, which are **tercio(s)**.

un medio	1/2
un tercio	1/3
dos tercios	2/3
un cuarto	1/4
tres quintos	3/5
dos sextos	2/6
seis séptimos	6/7
tres octavos	3/8
cuatro novenos	4/9
cuatro décimos	4/10

Beginning with 1/11, numerators continue being cardinals, but the denominators are formed by adding the suffix -**avo** to the cardinal number. They can be a bit cumbersome to say; for example:

dos diecisieteavos	2/17
tres veinteavos	3/20

But:

un centavo (*not* cientavo)	1/100

There is a way to avoid these tongue-twisters (evidently even Spanish speakers need a way out). One can use the word **parte(s)** (*part[s]*), which is feminine, with the ordinal forms in the feminine, to agree with it. The only disadvantage is that this structure leaves unsaid the idea of "parts of *what* whole." Therefore, it is more common in cooking or when giving instructions for mixing diverse ingredients such as fertilizer:

las dos terceras partes	*two thirds*
tres quintas partes	*three fifths*

Finally, remember that as an adjective **medio** is *half* (and agrees with any noun it modifies) and **mitad** is the noun for *a half*:

Ella me vendió **media** docena de huevos.	*She sold me half a dozen eggs.*
El proyecto se atrasó **medio** mes por la lluvia.	*The project was half a month behind due to rain.*
Juan se comió **la mitad** de la torta.	*John gobbled up half the cake.*

Percentages, rates, and fees

One common error is that of confusing the words **por ciento** (*percent*) and **el porcentaje** (*percentage*). The distinct usages are identical in both languages. One convention should be observed when writing or speaking of *percentages* expressed numerically as a *percent*: always use the indefinite article **el** in front of the number. Note that the article **el** also makes the verb **ser** singular, since the group of 5% is considered collectively: **El 5%** (expressed aloud as **el cinco por ciento**) **de la población es analfabeta.**

When the English word *rate* is used with the meaning of *index* or *frequency*, the usual Spanish word is **tasa**. When rate refers to a *fee* or other financial *charge*, it is **tarifa** or **cuota**. A *fine*, closely related in the transactional sense, is called **una multa**. The verb phrase for *to fine* is **poner(le) una multa**. When *rate* is used in the sense of *exchange rate*, the Spanish word is **el tipo de cambio**. For engineers, the word *rate* usually involves **la velocidad** (*velocity*) or **el volumen** (*volume*). Additionally, the concept of *per* is often expressed using **por**, but also by **el, al** or **la, a la**, depending on the type and gender of the unit of measurement. Observe the following examples:

La agencia tomó medidas para reducir **la tasa** de analfabetismo en la región.	*The agency took measures to lower the illiteracy rate in the region.*
Los aduaneros me cobraron **una tarifa** de 20 pesos **por** la importación de estos bienes.	*The customs officers charged me a 20 peso fee to import these goods.*
¿Cuánto es **la cuota** de ingreso para el gimnasio?	*How much is the membership (joining) fee for the health club?*
El policía le dio una multa de $50 **por** exceso de velocidad.	*The police gave him a $50 fine for speeding.*
¿Cuál es **el tipo de cambio** hoy?	*What is today's exchange rate?*
El volumen del derrame excedió **los** 2 millones de barriles al/por mes.	*The spill rate exceeded 2 million barrels per month.*
El petróleo salía del tubo de perforación a **una velocidad** de 50 kilómetros **la/por** hora.	*The gas was spilling from the bore tube at 50 km. per hour.*

Forms, charts, and graphs

In order to discuss what numbers actually mean, you need to know vocabulary related to their contexts. In other words, you need to know a handful of terms commonly used to refer to the types of documents, figures, and diagrams in which statistics and numbers are recorded. The English word for a *form*, as in something to fill out, is either **un formulario** or **una planilla**. The choice is mostly a regional preference. The little *boxes* that have to be filled in also can be called either **los encasillados** or **las casillas**.

The word for a *table* (as in a *diagram*) can be **un cuadro** or **una tabla**. As for how to express *graphics*, the choice depends on the design of the visual. For a *pie chart*, use **un gráfico de sectores**; for *a bar graph*, use **un gráfico de barras**. Keep in mind that in most of these common words or phrases, one choice is masculine, the other feminine, so be prepared if you need to use a direct object pronoun or other pronominal forms to refer to them.

¿La planilla? Ah, la puse ahí.	*The form? Oh, I put it there.*
Entre **los cuadros** a continuación, quiero llamar su atención a éste.	*Among the following tables, I wish to draw your attention to this one.*

Statistics

Among the many statistical terms, *range* is one of the most frequently encountered. The best translations for this concept that will work in nearly every use, except golf and ballistics, is **la gama** (the *spread*, as in from one point through others to an end point) or **el abanico** (literally, *fan*, like the ones found in Asia). These two terms also have a close affinity to **la variabilidad** (*variability*), although they are not synonymous.

The term *standard deviation* is **la desviación normal** (or **estándar**). Other words any statistician or responsible citizen will need include **el promedio** (*average*), **la mediana** (*median*), **el valor medio** (*mean*), **el modo** (mode), **el eje-x** and **el eje-y** (*x-* and *y-axis*), and of course **máximo/mínimo** (*minimum/maximum*) and **límite superior/inferior** (*upper/lower limit*). These are probably all the terms anyone would need to know (and understand) in order to talk about news items written and broadcast for the general public.

Según este gráfico, **el valor medio** es 45.	*According to this graph, the median is 45.*
El límite superior en la prueba fue de 300 partes por millón.	*The upper limit in the test was 300 parts per million.*

The stock market

Let's start with that: **La Bolsa de Valores**. Beyond that, it is important to realize that the English world's lingo of high finance is colorful in the extreme. In it you can find animals: *bears* and *bulls*, and acronyms that spell or are pronounced as animal names: *TIGR*, comes to mind. The Spanish-speaking world of high finance, when it is not borrowing freely from English, is drab and matter-of-fact by comparison. This is because Spanish tends to focus on verbs—the action—while English focuses on nouns.

Thus a *bear market* is said to be **un mercado de tendencia bajista** (from the verb **bajar**, *to go down*), while a *bull market* is **un mercado de tendencia alcista** (from the verb **alzar**, *to rise*). Likewise, one hears and reads of **el alza** or **la baja del mercado** (*the rising* or *the falling of the market*). **Stock brokers** are called **corredores de acciones** or **corredores de valores** (from the verb **correr**—because they do a lot of running, figuratively and literally).

Options are, well, **opciones**. In Spanish, *a put option* is called by a name that almost makes it understandable to non-brokers: **una opción a vender**. The same is true of *a call option*, which is **una opción a comprar**. As is true in any business, *the profits* are **las ganancias** or **los beneficios** and *the margin* is **el margen**. Armed with these terms, a good ear, and a decent general verb vocabulary, you should be able to read the financial section of the newspaper with relative confidence.

El inversionista se puso nervioso a causa del **mercado de tendencia bajista**.	*The investor got nervous because of the bear market.*
Algunos vieron la tendencia bajista y decidieron comprar **una opción a vender**.	*Some saw the downward trend and decided to buy a put action.*

EJERCICIO
23·10

Match the English with the Spanish.

_____ 1.	un cuadro	a.	standard deviation
_____ 2.	el tipo de cambio	b.	a bull market
_____ 3.	la bolsa de valores	c.	average
_____ 4.	la tasa	d.	form
_____ 5.	una opción a vender	e.	margin
_____ 6.	un gráfico de sectores	f.	percent
_____ 7.	el porcentaje	g.	the spread/range
_____ 8.	un mercado de tendencia alcista	h.	index/frequency
_____ 9.	el eje-*x*	i.	divided by
_____ 10.	la desviación normal	j.	variability
_____ 11.	un formulario	k.	table
_____ 12.	dividido por	l.	percentage
_____ 13.	el por ciento	m.	a call option
_____ 14.	el promedio	n.	upper limit
_____ 15.	por año	o.	pie chart
_____ 16.	el margen	p.	mean
_____ 17.	el valor medio	q.	stock market
_____ 18.	la variabilidad	r.	*x*-axis
_____ 19.	límite superior	s.	exchange rate
_____ 20.	el abanico	t.	per annum

EJERCICIO
23·11

Write out how you would express aloud the following basic mathematical operations and express the following values.

1. 3 + 5 = 8 _____

2. 42 × 34 = 1,428 _____

3. 89 ÷ 7 = 12, r5 _____

4. 77 − 52 = 25 _____

5. 93 × 7 = 651 _____

6. 2/3 _____

7. 2/7 _____

8. 3/4 _____

9. 1/2 _____

10. 4/5 _____

11. 3/4 + 1/2 = 1 1/4 _____

12. 5,3 − 4,1 = 1,2 _____

13. 6 − 5 = 1 _____

14. 97% _____

15. 101 − 1 = 100 _____

16. 10 × 100 = 1000 _____

17. 1000 + 1 = 1001 _____

18. 777 + 555 = 1,332 _____

19. 3/7 _____

20. 23% _____

EJERCICIO
23·12

Translate the following sentences from Spanish to English.

1. Se cree que la tendencia bajista de la bolsa seguirá a menos que la Reserva tome medidas.

_____

2. Se ha calculado que la tasa de mortalidad por la peste bubónica fue del 30% de la población.

_____

3. La secretaria me mostró un panfleto con un gráfico de barras.

_____

4. El corredor de valores tiene una opción a comprar que caduca a la hora del cierre de operaciones.

_____

5. La tasa de crecimiento de la economía se ha disminuido debido a las guerras civiles en la región.

_____

6. La cuota de ingreso es $187 y desde entonces es $140 al año.

_____

7. La junta de directores anunció que reinvertirá el 5% de las ganancias en campañas publicitarias.

_____

8. La cantidad dedicada a la educación es el 4% menos este año con respecto al año pasado.

_____

9. Un estudio de las condiciones económicas reveló que hay un abanico de posibilidades para resolver la crisis.

_____

10. Los acreedores han propuesto un aumento del 4% en el tipo de interés.

_____

11. Por una semana, el precio del valor vaciló entre $40 y $50.

_____

12. El Congreso aprobó un aumento del 2% para los bienes de consumo importados.

_____

13. Para poner de manifiesto su oposición a la postura anti-sindicalista del gobernador, los obreros salieron en huelga.

_____

_____

14. El personal a cargo de investigación y desarrollo recibió un aumento de sueldo del 4%.

_____

15. Debido a que la tasa de inflación está al 9% al año y a que la del desempleo se acerca al 12%, es dudoso que en las próximas elecciones el partido en el poder vaya a permanecer en control ni de los cuerpos legislativos ni de los puestos ejecutivos.

_____

_____

_____

Calendar dates, time, and phone numbers

This chapter deals with the conventions for expressing dates, the time, phone numbers, and addresses. Knowing these conventions will enable you to function socially with less confusion.

When analog clocks became available in wristwatch size, more variety began to appear in how people would report what time it was. For instance, when looking at an analog display reading of 1:15, it makes more sense to say *one-fifteen* than *a quarter-past one*, although both are correct. This usage is also more common today since cell phones are now our primary mode of finding out the time.

Likewise, when the year 2000 rolled around, there was discussion in the English-speaking world about how we would express the year after 2010. Would we say *twenty-ten* or *two-thousand ten*? The matter is not settled for English speakers, but it seems likely that beginning in 2020, English speakers will revert to the two-digit manner of stating the year and we will say *twenty twenty*, *twenty twenty-one*, and so forth. There was no such discussion in the Spanish-speaking world about how to express the year because in Spanish, the year has always been stated just as any other number (e.g., **dos mil**, **dos mil uno**). So, in the year 2020, Spanish speakers will simply say **dos mil veinte** and not **veinte-veinte**—*unless* the latter becomes briefly fashionable because of the digital and verbal symmetry of that particular year.

Let's begin with the days of the week, hours of the day, months, and seasons—all of which you certainly already know as vocabulary items. Knowing the gender of these nouns is important in order to correctly express more detailed data, whether in speech or when doing something simple such as filling out a form or recording the date.

The days of the week are:

lunes	*Monday*
martes	*Tuesday*
miércoles	*Wednesday*
jueves	*Thursday*
viernes	*Friday*
sábado	*Saturday*
domingo	*Sunday*

The months of the year are:

enero	*January*
febrero	*February*
marzo	*March*
abril	*April*
mayo	*May*
junio	*June*
julio	*July*
agosto	*August*
septiembre*	*September*
octubre	*October*
noviembre	*November*
diciembre	*December*

Keep in mind that the days and months are masculine because the words **día** and **mes** are masculine: **el día**, **el mes**. Unlike English, the names of the days of the week and the months are not capitalized in Spanish, except on a wall calendar or in a heading. One trick for remembering that days and months both are masculine is to visualize a calendar because it displays the *days* of each *month*. The use of the article **el** before the name of a day of the week means *on* that day; when used in the plural, it means *on* all the days of that same name. However, the article **el** is not used before the names of months to mean "in" that month; to say *in March*, Spanish says, like English,

---

*An alternate spelling of *September* in Spanish is **setiembre**.

en marzo. When referring to a month more remote in time, use **en el mes de** … .This also is important when speaking of the past, since the preterit and imperfect are involved:

Mi tía vino **el lunes**.	*My aunt came on Monday.*
Mi tía venía **los lunes**.	*My aunt would come (habitually) on Mondays.*
En marzo, volvieron las golondrinas.	*In March, the swallows returned.*
En diciembre, Amanda cumplirá treinta años.	*In December, Amanda will turn thirty.*
Ese año, **en el mes de abril**, comenzó la guerra.	*That year, in the month of April, the war began.*

The hours of the day, on the other hand, are *feminine*, because the word **hora** is feminine: **la hora**. There are four things that English-speaking students of Spanish need to keep in mind when dealing with the time of day.

First, all times of the day are expressed as plurals, except when the point of reference is one o'clock, morning or afternoon. Secondly, many students seem to have difficulty distinguishing between telling what the hour is and telling at what time something takes place. Examine the following examples of questions and answers:

¿Qué hora es?	*What time is it?*
Son **las cuatro** y veinte.	*It's four twenty.*

But:

Es **la una** menos cuarto.	*It's quarter to one.*
Es **la una** y media.	*It's one-thirty.*
¿A **qué hora** te acuestas?	*What time do you go to bed?*
Me acuesto a **las once** y media.	*I go to bed at eleven-thirty.*

With analog clocks and military time, used in some Latin American countries (most notably in Argentina), the following example shows how one displayed military time could be expressed verbally. In American military parlance, the word *hours* is often expressed as a singular in *casual* speech. Rapid speech in Spanish could also result in the suppression of the **y** or **con**:

13:25	Son las trece (y/con) veinticinco horas	*Thirteen hundred (and) twenty-five hour(s)*

Radio DJs, sports announcers, and others who work in live media are often creative with how they express the hour. The spontaneous variations are unpredictable and sometimes, just as in English, they can be mildly amusing. However, one will often hear the following, particularly when a new hour is drawing nigh:

Son seis (minutos) pa'(ra) las cuatro de la tarde.	*It's six t' four in the afternoon.*

The abbreviations A.M. and P.M. are used in print but the letters are not spoken. (Spanish tends to avoid speaking acronyms.) Instead, as appropriate or needed for clarity, you can append the phrases **de la mañana** (*in the morning*), **de la tarde** (*in the afternoon*), and **de la noche** (**at night**). Also, don't forget the grammatical genders of *morning*, *afternoon*, and *night* so you can properly greet people:

Buenos días, señor.	*Good morning, sir.*

But:

Buenas tardes/noches, señorita.	*Good afternoon/evening/night, Miss.*

When reporting time in the past, just as when telling someone's age in the past, always use the imperfect:

Era la una.	*It was one.*
Eran las cinco de la tarde.	*It was five in the afternoon.*
Mi hermana mayor **tenía** cinco años cuando nací.	*My older sister was five years old when I was born.*

Finally, while the word for *season* is feminine (**la estación**), the individual seasons vary in grammatical gender. When speaking of seasons, the articles or demonstrative adjectives are used:

la primavera	*spring*
el verano	*summer*
el otoño	*fall*
el invierno	*winter*

En la primavera, espero viajar a San Francisco en tren.	*In the spring, I hope to travel to San Francisco by train.*
Ese otoño llovió mucho.	*It rained a lot that fall.*
Este verano, mis amigos van a Oregon.	*This summer, my friends are going to Oregon.*

Compare the formatting conventions for the printed form for recording the date. Note that in Spanish the date comes before the month (**lunes** is capitalized only because it is the first word in the line). The word **de** before the year can also be replaced by a comma:

Lunes, 16 de enero de 2018	*Monday, January 16, 2018*

Compare how this date would be expressed in full sentences in English and Spanish, such as in the opening of a national news program on television or radio:

Hoy es lunes, dieciséis de enero del año dos mil doce.	*Today is Monday, the sixteenth of January, two thousand twelve.*

When speaking or writing of the first day in a month, the ordinal is used: **primero** (*first*), abbreviated as 1°. After the first of the month, the cardinal numbers are used to write and say the date:

Es el primero de mayo.	*It's May first.*
Mañana es el dos de mayo.	*Tomorrow is May second.*

On a form, such as a job application, the formula in English is *month/day/year*. In Spanish, it is *day/month/year*. Here's one way that the date could appear in a form in the Spanish-speaking world and in an American form (the abbreviations for the months are almost the same as in English, except for January):

16/ene/2018	01/16/2018

Most students learn that when verbally expressing address and phone numbers in Spanish, the number is broken into two-digit parts as much as possible. Where to break up an odd series seems to depend more on the relative ease of pronouncing the result. There is no hard-and-fast rule, but zeroes cause one or more numbers to be stated separately. Observe in the following that (206) 284–7960 in English becomes 2-0-6; 2-84; 79-60 in Spanish. Likewise, a number in an English address changes from 1608 Avenida Cuatro Oeste to 16-0-8 Avenida Cuatro Oeste.

Match the English words and phrases with their corresponding Spanish translations.

____ 1.	fall	a.	la temporada
____ 2.	season (of the year)	b.	el verano
____ 3.	January	c.	jueves
____ 4.	season (for a sport)	d.	la estación
____ 5.	winter	e.	sábado
____ 6.	On Mondays	f.	miércoles
____ 7.	On Friday	g.	el invierno
____ 8.	Saturday	h.	la primavera
____ 9.	Wednesday	i.	enero
____ 10.	spring	j.	los lunes
____ 11.	summer	k.	el viernes
____ 12.	Thursday	l.	el otoño

Write out how you would say the following sentences in Spanish that include numbers in addresses, telephone numbers, time of day, days of the week, and month and year.

1. On Saturday, March 12, 2011, I finished writing this book.

_____

2. The soccer game began at 1:15 P.M. on Saturday, January 8, 2018.

_____

3. Last year, March 1st was on a Monday.

_____

4. By 4 P.M. today, I will have worked for ten hours.

_____

5. On Monday, I have an appointment at 3 P.M.

_____

6. What time did the movie begin?

_____

7. He lived at 305 N. Eighth Street from June 1978 until August 1980.

    _____

8. Don't forget to call me some evening at 235–1102. (**tú**)

    _____

9. In Spanish-speaking countries, Tuesday, not Friday, the 13th is considered unlucky.

    _____

10. Do you know what happened on Friday, October 12, 1492? (**Ud.**)

    _____

11. The White House is at 1600 Pennsylvania Avenue.

    _____

12. I think her number is 247–9538, but don't call her on Sundays. (**Ud.**)

    _____

13. She was born on 01/22/98 at 9:44 A.M. It was a Thursday.

    _____

14. 11/22/63 was a Friday.

    _____

15. It's 12:01 A.M.

    _____

16. On Thursdays, I go to bed at 12:45 A.M., which means that on Wednesdays, I don't go to bed!

    _____

17. The library is on 4th Avenue. Beginning in March, it opens at 9 A.M. every day except Sundays.

    _____

18. It's 22:45 hrs.

    _____

19. (Write out your birthday, including as much information as you know).

    _____

20. (Write your phone number, dividing it into as many two-digit combinations as are easy to say).

    _____

More writing

Letter writing

Some say writing letters is a lost art. In our busy lives, e-mailing and text messaging have replaced letter writing to a great extent. But the art is not all lost. We still receive hand-written, typed, and printed letters and need to master the written conventions needed to communicate effectively. Moreover, e-mails are often in the form of letters. You already know that spelling and punctuation rules are an essential part of written language. These rules apply to writing letters and many types of e-mail messages. Here are the terms used to identify the parts of a letter:

el encabezamiento	*heading*
la fecha	*date*
el/la destinatario/a	*addressee*
el saludo	*greeting*
la redacción de la carta	*body of the letter*
la despedida	*closing*
la firma	*signature*
la carta	*letter*

The heading includes the writer's contact information. In Spanish, greetings and closings are various formulas or set phrases used in different contexts.

Writing a letter

The formats of Spanish and English letters are somewhat similar, but there are some differences, especially in punctuation. When you write a letter in Spanish, in order to avoid misunderstandings, it is important to identify your reader, to choose formal (polite) or informal (familiar) verb forms, to select the corresponding letter format, and to follow the conventions of written language. First, let's consider formal letters.

Formal letters

Use the appropriate format for all letters. Formal letters include correspondence regarding legal matters, business, and trade. A letter addressed to a person who is not familiar to you, or to individuals you would normally address with polite verb forms because of their position, age, or status are also formal letters.

    A business letter is usually written on letterhead paper which provides the sender's information: name, title, business department, address, etc. A personal letter is sometimes written on personalized stationery that provides the writer's contact information. If you use plain paper to write a formal letter, include your full name above your address at the top of the letter, or in the center, if you choose block style.

At the beginning of this unit, we listed the parts of a letter. You may wish to review them before you start the following exercise.

EJERCICIO
24·1

Una carta formal en español. *Provide the appropriate terms for a formal letter.*

1. _____

   _____

                                                  2. _____

3. _____

   _____

   _____

4. _____ :

5. _____

   _____

   _____

6. _____ ,

7. _____

Place and date

In the heading of the letter, the sender's city or town (usually at the top right) appears, separated from the date by a comma. Note the order of the date in Spanish: day, the preposition **de**, month, and year.

Quito, 12 de diciembre de 2018	*Quito, December 12, 2018*
Caracas, 15 de agosto de 2020	*Caracas, August 15, 2020*

Remember that names of the months of the year are not capitalized in Spanish. Note that, in Spanish, the ordinal number **primero** (*first*) is used to refer to the first day of the month.

Siempre celebramos el Año Nuevo **el primero de enero**.	*We always celebrate the New Year **on January first**.*

Las fechas de las cartas. *Translate into Spanish.*

1. Havana, November 13, 1988 _____

2. Santo Domingo, July 31, 2000 _____

3. Bogotá, January 1, 2018 _____

4. San Fernando, February 28, 2005 _____

5. Los Angeles, March 16, 2023 _____

6. Barcelona, April 23, 1995 _____

Formal greetings

In Spanish and in English, one difference between formal and informal greetings or salutations is the use of a title in formal letters. Good letter writing uses formal and informal salutation phrases and closing phrases appropriately. With a title you also use polite verb forms (**usted, ustedes**). Don't forget their abbreviations: **Ud.** and **Uds.**

The following greetings are used to address a formal letter to a person or persons you do not know, or to a person you must address with polite verb forms. The greeting may include only the addressee's last name, his or her full name, or no name, depending on how well you know the person:

Estimada Sra. López:	*Dear Mrs. López:*
Estimada Srta. Urrutia:	*Dear Miss Urrutia:*
Estimadas Sras. Lucía Aragón y Marta Felipe:	*Dear Mmes. Lucía Aragón and Marta Felipe:*
Estimado Sr. Bermúdez:	*Dear Mr. Bermúdez:*
Estimados Sres. Alberto Correa y Luis Correa:	*Dear Messrs. Alberto Correa and Luis Correa:*
Estimada señora:	*Dear Madam:*
Estimado señor:	*Dear Sir:*

The English abbreviation *Ms.* does not have a Spanish equivalent. Use **Sra.**, a title of courtesy, even if you do not know a woman's marital status. Note the Spanish punctuation for greetings. A colon (:) follows a formal salutation, both in English and Spanish.

Use the following salutations only to address a person you do not know:

Muy señor mío:	*Dear Sir:*
Muy señora mía:	*Dear Madam:*
Muy señores míos:	*Dear Sirs:*
Muy señoras mías:	*Dear Mesdames:*

With individuals who have a professional title, use the title if you know it:

Estimada señora Directora:	*Dear Director:*
Estimado Dr. Aranguren:	*Dear Dr. Aranguren:*
Estimada Dra. Bernal:	*Dear Dr. Bernal:*

Body of the letter

Here are a number of set phrases that appear frequently in the body of a formal letter:

A través de la presente	*The purpose of this letter*
De acuerdo con su solicitud	*In regard to your request*
Deseo comunicarle	*I would like to tell you*
He recibido su atenta carta	*I have received your letter*
Lamento informarle	*I am sorry to tell you*
Por medio de esta carta	*The purpose of this letter*
Tengo el gusto de comunicarle que	*I have the pleasure to inform you that*

Remember that the *conditional* and the *imperfect subjunctive* verb forms are used to indicate politeness:

Quisiera pedirle	***I would like*** *to request*
Nos gustaría recibir	***We would like*** *to receive*

Formal closings

In Spanish, formal closing formulas are often more elaborate than English closings and do not translate literally into English. Here are a few frequently used examples. Note that they are followed by a comma (,):

Atentamente,	*Respectfully yours,*
Con mi más cordial saludo,	*Sincerely,*
Con todo mi respeto,	*Yours truly,*
Cordialmente,	*Truly yours,*
Muy agradecido/a por su atención,	*With gratitude,*
Le saluda atentamente,	*Truly yours,*
Respetuosamente,	*Very truly yours,*
Su servidor,	*Yours truly,*
Un saludo afectuoso,	*Sincerely,*

Avoid using **sinceramente** at the end of a letter. It does *not* have the same meaning that it does in English.

The final closing of your letter is your signature. A postscript may be added. The abbreviation of the Latin phrase in English is *P.S.*, *postscriptum*. The corresponding phrase in Spanish is **P.D.**, **postdata**.

P.D. No olvide enviarme la cuenta.	**P.S.** *Do not forget to send me the bill.*

EJERCICIO 24·3

Práctica. *Use the information provided to give the date, a formal greeting, and a formal closing.*

MODELO   Santiago de Compostela / March 12, 2018 / la presidenta de Asturias, S.A.

     Santiago de Compostela, 12 de marzo de 2018

     Estimada Sra. Presidenta:

     Atentamente,

1. Madrid / May 3, 2001 / Doctor Blanco (tu médico)

_____

_____

_____

2. Guadalajara / July 19, 2018 / Berta Rodríguez (la abuela de uno de tus amigos)

_____

_____

_____

3. San Diego / January 13, 2019 / Pedro Vázquez (capitán de la policía)

_____

_____

_____

Informal letters

An informal letter is written to those familiar to you. A personal letter is sometimes written on personalized stationary that provides the writer's contact information.

Place and date

In an informal letter, the date may appear in numbers only. In Spanish, the first number refers to the day of the month. For a friendly letter, your address and the addressee's are not needed as part of the heading.

Lima, 21-12-2018   *Lima, 12-21-2018*

Informal greetings

If you know the person to whom you are writing, use the correct form of the adjectives and nouns in the following formulas, with or without a first name. Note that a colon (:) is also used after an informal greeting in Spanish:

Querida amiga:	*Dear friend,*
Querida Ana:	*Dear Ana,*
Queridísimas hermanas:	*My dear sisters,*
Queridos Julio y Rosario:	*Dear Julio and Rosario,*

Informal closings

In English and in Spanish the closing of the letter will depend on the degree of intimacy between the intended reader and the person who writes the letter. Sometimes the closing is an entire sentence (ending with a period); sometimes it is just a phrase or a word (usually ending with a comma or an exclamation mark). These expressions cannot be translated literally. Note that many include the word **amistad** (*friendship*) or a reference to the relationship:

Abrazos y besos cariñosos,	*Hugs and kissses,*
Cariñosamente,	*Warm regards,*
Tu amigo/a,	*Your friend,*

The closing can be a full sentence in the first or third person, ending with a period:

Cuenta conmigo. *You have all my support. (Count on me.)*
Te envío un abrazo cariñoso. *My warmest regards,*
Te envío todo mi cariño. *With all my love,*

EJERCICIO
24·4

Escribe la fecha en español.

1. 03-27-2000 _____

2. 05-05-1999 _____

3. 12-12-2008 _____

4. 08-08-2018 _____

5. 10-10-2020 _____

6. 02-10-1980 _____

EJERCICIO
24·5

Práctica. *Use the information to give the date, an informal greeting, and an informal closing.*

MODELO   Buenos Aires / March 25, 2019 / tu hermana Lucía
    Buenos Aires, 25 de marzo de 2019
    Mi querida (hermana) Lucía:
    Un abrazo,

1. Barcelona / May 10, 2017 / Anita (tu novia)

_____

_____

_____

2. Managua / June 9, 2018 / Úrsula Domínguez (tu tía)

_____

_____

_____

3. Guayaquil / August 3, 2019 / Pablo Duval (tu amigo de la infancia)

_____

_____

_____

Addressing an envelope

The following are the Spanish terms for addressing an envelope:

el/la remitente	*sender*
el/la destinatario/a	*addressee*
la dirección	*address*
el sobre	*the envelope*

When writing a person's address on an envelope, the lines follow a similar order in English and in Spanish. However, the order of the information in these lines varies. Your name and address appear at the top left corner of the envelope. The addressee's full name appears on the envelope. Courtesy titles may be used. Note the abbreviations; you may want to review the list under the section "Formal greetings" earlier in this chapter:

Sr. D. (Don)	*Mr.*
Sra. Dña. (Doña)	*Miss, Ms., Mrs.*

In many Spanish-speaking countries, addresses are longer; they may include numbers and letters that indicate streets and/or apartment numbers, even the floor numbers in a building, the name of a neighborhood within a city, and the zip code numbers (**distrito postal**). In some countries, the name of a province or state may also appear. Note that the name of the country must appear on international letters, as in the second example below:

Sr. Martín López Calvo
Calle Moratines, 25, 2° A
14225 Gijón, Asturias

Dr. A. López Iriarte
Calle de la Victoria, 30
Colonia "La Colmena"
Quito, Ecuador

Note that in Spanish-speaking countries, a street may be called **Callejón** (*alley*), **Camino** (*path*), or **Paseo** (*promenade*). Those names may be capitalized. The word **Avenida** (*avenue*) is usually abbreviated (**Ave.**):

Sra. María Pastor de González
Ave. de la Reina Victoria, 13, 4°, A
07882, Madrid

Note that the zip code consists of five digits and appears before the name of the town or city in most addresses throughout the Hispanic world.

When writing to a company, write the company's name on the first line, then the department and the name of the person (if applicable) on the second line, the street address on the third line, the zip code followed by the city on the fourth line, and the country on the fifth line. See the following example:

Aseguradora del Norte S.A.
Sra. Vallejo, Departamento de Reclamaciones
Avenida del Puerto, 118 Entresuelo
75009 Pontevedra (Galicia)

Escribe el sobre. *Use the information to give the name and title (if neccessary) of the addressee, the address, and the zip code.*

MODELO   Una carta para tu abuela Margarita López-Rivas / Paseo de la Victoria / 27 / 1ᵉʳ Piso / Badajoz / 25667

      Sra. Margarita López

      Paseo de la Victoria, 27, Primer Piso

      25667 Badajoz

1. Una carta para tu amiga Lidia Gómez / Avenida del Norte / 27 / Barcelona / 00087

_____

_____

_____

2. Una carta para el alcalde Raúl Benítez / Alcaldía de Pueblo Nuevo / 305 / Torreón / 27250 / México D.F.

_____

_____

_____

3. Una carta para tus tíos Dolores y José Antonio Bermúdez / Calle C, 17111 / Apart. D / La Habana / 00891

_____

_____

_____

Text messaging and e-mails

E-mail and text messaging have become the fastest ways to communicate all over the world. In Spanish, e-mail is most commonly called by an adaptation of its English name, **el email**, but it is also called **un correo**, **el correo electrónico**. The acronym **SMS** stands for both *Short Message Service* and **servicio de mensaje corto**. The acronym is used in text messaging, since it fits in a small screen.

Text messages use characters, letters, and numbers that can be read to reproduce sound (**bbr**, **beber** *to drink*) that imitates a word, abbreviations that reproduce sound to create a word (**bb**, **bebé** *baby*), and acronyms. It is a changing language, and there are variations throughout the Hispanic world. The following list is for your reference:

a2	adiós	*good-bye*	pco	poco	*a little*
ac	hace	*form of* hacer, *to do*	pf	por favor	*please*
aki	aquí	*here*	pq	porque	*because, why*
amr	amor	*love*	q	que	*that, what*
aora	ahora	*now*	q acs?	¿Qué haces?	*What are you doing?*
bb	bebé	*baby*	qand	cuando	*when*
bbr	beber	*to drink*	qdms	quedamos	*we're staying*
bs	besos	*kisses*	q qrs?	¿Qué quieres?	*What do you want?*
bye	adiós	*good-bye*	q risa!	¡Qué risa!	*What a laugh!*
chao	adiós	*good-bye*	q sea	qué sea	*whatever*
d2	dedos	*fingers*	q tal?	¿qué tal?	*What's happening?*
dfcl	difícil	*difficult*	sbs?	¿sabes?	*Do you know?*
dnd	dónde	*where*	salu2	saludos	*hello, good-bye*
exo	hecho	*act*	sms	mensaje	*message*
grrr	enfadado	*angry*	spro	espero	*I hope*
finde	fin de semana	*weekend*	tq	te quiero	*I love you*
hl	hasta luego	*see you later*	tqi	tengo que irme	*I have to leave*
k	que, qué	*that, what*	tb	también	*also*
kls	clase	*class*	tas OK?	¿Estás bien?	*Are you OK?*
KO	estoy muerto/a	*I'm in big trouble*	tqm	te quiero mucho	*I love you a lot*
msj	mensaje	*message*	tb	también	*also*
mxo	mucho	*a lot*	zzz	dormir	*sleeping*
npn	no pasa nada	*nothing's happening*			

E-mail messages are mostly used for informal communication. In the business world, though, they often must respect some of the formal conventions of the written language. A person's full name, business title, phone, and fax number appear at the bottom of the message. Accents are often avoided so as not to interfere with e-mail systems. No added dates are needed for e-mail messages.

Remember to use the appropriate format to write an e-mail to a friend: use an informal register for the greeting, the body of the message, and the closing. Use polite verb forms, a formal salutation, and a formal closing when sending a message to a person you do not know. Don't forget to use the appropriate punctuation.

EJERCICIO
24·7

Te toca a ti.

1. Escríbele un correo electrónico a un(a) amigo/a a.) salúdalo/la; b.) invítalo/la a tu fiesta el día de tu cumpleaños; c.) despídete.

_____

_____

_____

_____

2. Escríbele un correo electrónico al/la gobernador/a de tu estado o provincia a.) salúdalo/la; b.) felicítalo/la por su trabajo; c.) despídete.

_____

_____

_____

_____

Let's write!

Now it's time for you to become more independent in your writing. You've practiced writing different types of sentences. Learning to write effectively takes time and practice, especially in a second language. You are now aware of your weaknesses and, most of all, your strengths. You have studied and practiced how to convey ideas with both simple and complex sentences, strengthening your abilities to better communicate in Spanish.

We will start this unit with simple exercises and then move on to more complex sentences and paragraphs and more challenging activities. Study the model answers in each exercise. You will find examples of possible answers for most exercises in the Answer key.

EJERCICIO
24·8

Vamos a escribir oraciones. *For each sentence, use the appropriate verb tense, nouns, adjectives, and articles, and add the appropriate punctuation.*

MODELO   (*preterit*) mi / vecino / ir / a / el / Perú

         Mi vecino fue al Perú.

1. (*preterit*) mis / hermano / visitar / ese / región / vario / vez

_____

2. (*preterit, passive voice*) el / idea / sugerir / por / la agencia / de viajes

_____

3. (*imperfect*) el / proyecto / de / el / viaje / ser / interesante

_____

4. (*preterit*) un / grupo / local / compartir / el / trayectoria / con / el / viajeros

_____

5. (*preterit, passive voice*) el / turistas / recibir / por / un / banda / de música

_____

6. (*imperfect*) el / cantante / no / cantar / en / español

_____

7. (*present*) ahora / hacer / planes / para / viajar / a / el / sur / de / Bolivia

_____

8. (*future*) el / próximo / vacaciones / mi / sobrinas / venir a / mi / casa

_____

EJERCICIO
24·9

Entrevistas cortas. *Complete each sentence with interrogative words and question marks.*

MODELO   Voy a ver una película.

¿qué? / ¿quién? / ¿por qué? / ¿dónde? / ¿cuándo? / ¿cómo?

¿Qué película quieres ver?

¿Quién es el protagonista?

¿Dónde filmaron la película?

¿Cuándo quieres ver la película?

¿Cómo es la película, corta o larga?

1. El vuelo Barcelona-Madrid tiene dos horas de retraso (*delay*).

¿por qué? / ¿quién?, ¿quiénes? / ¿dónde? / ¿cuándo? / ¿qué?

_____

_____

_____

_____

_____

2. Hoy es el aniversario de bodas de mis padres.

¿qué? / ¿quién?, ¿quiénes? / ¿dónde? / ¿cuándo? / ¿cómo?

_____

_____

_____

_____

_____

3. Vamos a cenar.

¿dónde? / ¿cuál? / ¿quién?, ¿quiénes? / ¿por qué? / ¿cuánto?

_____

_____

_____

_____

4. Mi amigo está en el hospital.

¿cómo? / ¿qué? / ¿quién?, ¿quiénes? / ¿dónde? / ¿cuándo?

_____

_____

_____

_____

5. Hay una venta especial en la tienda de productos electrónicos.

¿qué? / ¿dónde? / ¿cuánto/a?, ¿cuántos/as? / ¿cómo?

_____

_____

_____

_____

6. Hoy es mi cumpleaños.

¿cuántos?, ¿cuántas? / ¿qué? / ¿con quién?, ¿con quiénes? / ¿dónde? / ¿cómo?

_____

_____

_____

_____

_____

EJERCICIO

24·10

Mis experiencias. _Complete each sentence with the indicative imperfect tense of the verb in parentheses and add the appropriate words in parentheses._

MODELO   hace mucho tiempo (querer) escribir (vario) libros ya que (gustar) contar anécdotas

Hace mucho tiempo, quería escribir varios libros ya que me gustaba contar anécdotas.

1. en otra época (ser) (más / menos) paciente porque (tener) (más / menos) tiempo.

   _____

2. a menudo (estudiar) español ya que (querer) hablar (claro) con mis amigos (mexicano)

   _____

3. con frecuencia (aprender) a escribir (mucho) tipos de oraciones más (complejo)

   _____

4. siempre (poder) contar con mi (bueno) amigo Pablito

   _____

5. a veces no (tener) la constancia (necesario) ni la disciplina (preciso) para estudiar

   _____

6. día tras día (ser) difícil escribir en dos idiomas (diferente) y a veces con palabras no (similar)

   _____

7. en ocasiones (ir) al cine para ver películas (mexicano) y (colombiano) y eran (divertido)

   _____

8. con frecuencia (reflexionar) sobre la (poco) capacidad de los seres humanos para ser
   (constante) y (dedicado)

   _____

EJERCICIO
24·11

Te toca a ti. *Go back to Ejercicio 24-10. Choose the adverbial phrase that indicates the need for the imperfect tense. Use these phrases + verb to describe your own experience. Follow the **model**.*

MODELO   frase + tener

   En otra época, yo tenía más tiempo para escribir cartas a mis
   amigos en varios estados de EE.UU.

1. frase + poder

   _____

2. frase + querer

   _____

3. frase + poder

   _____

4. frase + ir

   _____

5. frase + comprar

_____

6. frase + practicar

_____

_____

¿Cómo eres? El poder de las palabras. _Create a paragraph to describe yourself, your family, your traditions, your achievements, your education, and your expectations. Use adjectives, adverbs, and verb tenses to communicate your ideas._

MODELO

Me llamo Julián y tengo veintidós años. Soy alto, delgado y tengo el pelo rubio. Soy trabajador y quiero escribir bien en español.

Así soy yo.

_____

_____

_____

_____

_____

_____

Comparación y contraste. _Create a paragraph to compare and contrast your ideas._

MODELO

La tecnología avanza muy rápido. Antes, los teléfonos celulares eran más grandes y caros. Ahora, son pequeños y más baratos.

La tecnología y el futuro.

_____

_____

_____

_____

_____

_____

Si pudieras cambiar algo en tu vida, ¿qué harías? *Create a paragraph using the subjunctive or conditional to indicate what you would do if you could change your life.*

MODELO

Si yo pudiera, no viviría en Estados Unidos por un año. Yo viviría en México para aprender español. Después, yo viajaría a Chile para conocer a los padres de mi amigo Felipe Cerdeña.

Si pudiera cambiar algo en mi vida,

_____

_____

_____

_____

_____

_____

_____

Una carta. *Create a short letter to a friend describing your profession, books you have read, and plans for the future.*

MODELO

Los Angeles, 25 de marzo de 2014

Querida Martica:

¿Cómo estás? Quiero compartir contigo mis ideas.

Una carta a un(a) amigo/a:

_____

_____

_____

_____

_____

_____

_____

_____

_____

More conversations

Making dates and appointments

Let's look at a conversation about making a date.

Conversation: Making an informal date

Suena el teléfono.

INÉS: **¿Bueno?**

Hello?

SERGIO: Hola, Inés, **soy Sergio**. **Te llamo** para ver si quieres acompañarme al cine **el viernes por la noche**. Están dando una nueva película **mexicana** en el cine de Shirlington.

Hi, Inés, this is Sergio. I'm calling to see if you'd like to go to the movies with me on Friday night. They're showing a new Mexican film at the Shirlington theater.

INÉS: Uuy, sí, **me encantaría** ir contigo. Es la película basada en la novela de Ángeles Mastretta, ¿verdad?

Ooh, yes, I'd love to go with you. It's the movie based on Ángeles Mastretta's novel, right?

SERGIO: **Efectivamente**. Yo también **tengo ganas** de verla.

Yes, exactly. I really want to see it, too.

INÉS: Sí, dicen que es muy buena. ¿A qué hora empieza?

Yeah, they say it's very good. What time does it start?

SERGIO: Bueno, la película empieza a las ocho, pero estaba pensando que podríamos **cenar** algo antes, en uno de los restaurantes del mismo barrio. **¿Estás de acuerdo?**

Well, the movie starts at eight o'clock, but I was thinking that we could eat dinner beforehand, in one of those restaurants in the same neighborhood. Is that OK with you?

INÉS: Ay, qué pena, es que el viernes no salgo del trabajo hasta las seis, y con el tráfico no llegaré a casa hasta las siete. Creo que sería mejor que nos encontráramos en el cine a eso de las ocho menos cuarto. ¿Qué te parece?

Oh, what a shame—on Friday I don't leave work until six o'clock, and with the traffic I won't get home until seven o'clock. I think it would be better if we met at the theater at around a quarter to eight. Does that sound OK?

SERGIO: **Está bien. Entonces**, nos vemos en la entrada del cine el viernes un poco antes de las ocho. Y **después**, si quieres, podemos ir a un café por ahí para charlar de la película.

Good. I'll see you at the theater entrance on Friday, then, a little before eight o'clock. Then, if you like, we can go to a nearby café to discuss the movie.

INÉS: **Bien**, Sergio. Me dará mucho gusto verte el viernes. Hasta **entonces**.

OK, Sergio. I'll look forward to seeing you on Friday. Bye.

SERGIO: Chao, hasta el viernes.

Bye, see you Friday.

Bueno

This is what you say in Mexico when you answer the phone, but only in Mexico. In other countries the typical answers when the phone rings are as follows:

Diga/Dígame	Spain
Hola	Argentina
Aló	Other countries

Soy [Sergio]

The most common way to identify yourself on the telephone is **Soy** _____. Another common way to say this is **Habla Sergio**, or **Te habla Sergio**. (*Sergio calling/Sergio calling you.*)

Te llamo

Either **Te llamo** or **Te estoy llamando** can be used here. The present tense is often used in Spanish where only the present progressive (*be* + *-ing* form of verb) is used in English.

> Be careful with the pronunciation of **Te llamo**. The *ll* (and also *y* at the beginning of a word or syllable) is a strong consonant, not as relaxed as the English *y* but more like the double *y* of *Say yes!* Some effort is required to lengthen this *y*, and many Spanish speakers often let their tongues touch the palate, making a sound exactly like English *j*. In Argentina and Uruguay, this sound is more like a *sh* (as in *sugar*) or a *zh* (as in *pleasure*). It's better to make the *j* sound than to make the *y* too weak: this would produce **Te amo** (*I love you*)—probably not what Inés was expecting when she answered the phone.

El viernes

When used with a present or future tense verb, **el viernes** means *on Friday*, or *this coming Friday*. You could also use **el próximo viernes** or **el viernes que viene**. If you use a past tense verb, **el viernes** would mean *this past Friday/last Friday*. You could also use **el viernes pasado**.

Mañana es **viernes**.	*Tomorrow is Friday.*
Te veo **el viernes**.	*I'll see you (on) Friday.*
Lo vi **el viernes**.	*I saw him last Friday.*

Por la noche

Por la noche or **en la noche**, following the name of a day, indicate *night* or *at night*. *On Saturday night*, then, would be **el sábado por la noche/el sábado en la noche**. Use the same pattern for morning and afternoon.

el lunes por la mañana	*on Monday morning*
el martes en la tarde	*on Tuesday afternoon*

> Note that the days of the week are not capitalized (in case you're texting your conversation).

Tonight can be **esta noche** or **hoy en la noche**. Also:

esta tarde/hoy en la tarde	*this afternoon*
mañana por la mañana	*tomorrow morning*

So, when do you use **de la noche, de la mañana,** and **de la tarde**? Only after a specific time, for example, **las diez de la noche** (10:00 P.M.). Think of **de la mañana** as A.M. and **de la tarde** and **de la noche** as P.M.

Estudio **por la noche/en la noche**.	*I study at night.*
Tengo una clase a las ocho **de la noche**.	*I have a class at eight P.M.*

Also remember to use **son las tres, son las cuatro**, and so on, only when telling the current time. Use **a las tres, a las cuatro,** and so on, when giving the time of an event.

Son las nueve.	*It's nine o'clock.*
Es a las nueve.	*It's at nine o'clock.*

When giving the *place* of an event, you also use the verb **ser**.

¿Dónde **es** la fiesta?	*Where's the party?*
Es en la casa de Marta.	*It's at Marta's house.*
¿Dónde **es** el concierto?	*Where is the concert?*
Es en el Centro Cultural.	*It's at the Cultural Center.*

Note that this is different from all the other ways of telling where something is, which use **estar**.

¿Dónde **estás**?	*Where are you?*
Estoy en casa.	*I'm at home.*
¿Dónde **está** tu país?	*Where is your country?*
Está en Centroamérica.	*It's in Central America.*
¿Dónde **están** mis gafas?	*Where are my glasses?*
Están en la mesa.	*They're on the table.*

Mexicana

Again, for the texters—be sure to write nationalities (and religious affiliations) in lowercase letters.

una mujer **española**/una **española**	*a Spanish woman*
dos muchachos **católicos**	*two Catholic boys*

Pay attention to the gender and number of the nouns you are describing, and reflect them in the adjective.

las costumbres **peruanas**	*Peruvian customs*
el vino **chileno**	*Chilean wine*

Both singular and plural nouns need an article when used as the subject of a sentence.

El vino chileno es barato aquí.	*Chilean wine is cheap here.*
Las verduras son un componente importante en una dieta sana.	*Vegetables are an important part of a healthy diet.*
Me gustan **las verduras**.	*I like vegetables. (Vegetables appeal to me.)*

Singular and plural nouns used as direct objects require an article when they refer to something specific.

Compra **el vino chileno**.	*Buy the Chilean wine (rather than the Argentinean).*
No compres **las verduras** aquí.	*Don't buy the vegetables here (the ones we need for tonight).*

Singular and plural nouns used as direct objects do not need an article when they refer to the whole category in general.

Siempre trae **vino chileno**.	*He always brings Chilean wine.*
Ella no come **verduras**.	*She doesn't eat vegetables.*

En el cine

En el cine means *at the movies*. **En** in Spanish indicates *in, on,* or *at*. **Al cine**, on the other hand, indicates where you are going: *to the movies*.

Sara está **en el aeropuerto**.	*Sara is at the airport.*
Vamos **al aeropuerto** a buscar a Sara.	*Let's go to the airport to get Sara.*
Vamos a comer **al restaurante**.	*Let's go to the restaurant to eat.*

Remember:
 ♦ To use **en** to indicate a location, and **a** to indicate a destination.
 ♦ That **a** followed by **el** is always contracted to **al**.

Me encantaría

Me encantaría (ir al cine) means *I would love to (go to the movies)*. Literally, *It would enchant me (to go to the movies)* or *Going to the movies would enchant me*. The subject of this sentence is **ir al cine**, and when an infinitive such as **ir** is used as a subject, it is considered singular; this is why the main verb, **encantaría,** has a singular conjugation. Note the difference between *Me encanta* and *me encantaría*.

Me encanta ver películas.	*I love watching movies./I love to watch movies.*
Me encantaría ver una película.	*I would love to watch a movie.*

Remember that both people and objects can **encantar,** but you can **amar** only people you know.

Me encantan las telenovelas.	*I love soap operas.*
Me encanta el actor principal.	*I love the main actor.*
Amo a mi esposo.	*I love my husband.*

Querer can also mean *to love*—in the sense of "to care about"—as you would say this to a member of your family or a good friend as well as to a boyfriend, girlfriend, or spouse. **Te quiero** does not mean *I want you*. Physical attraction is better expressed by the verb **gustar**.

Me gustas mucho.	*I'm really attracted to you./I like you.* (Literally: *You please me a lot.*)
Le gusta Sonia.	*He has a crush on Sonia./He likes Sonia.*
Es mi mejor amiga y **la quiero** mucho.	*She's my best friend and I like her a lot.*

Efectivamente/en efecto

These are real **falsos amigos**, as they do not mean *effectively* or *in effect*. **Efectivamente** and **en efecto** are interchangeable, and are used to comment that what was just said is correct, kind of like *exactly* or *that's true*.

Dicen que ustedes han invitado a más de 200 personas a la boda.	*I hear that you invited more than 200 people to the wedding.*

En efecto. Es que los dos tenemos muchos familiares y muchos amigos y además, casi todos viven aquí en la ciudad.	*Yeah, that's right. We both have a lot of relatives and friends, plus almost all of them live here in the city.*

When **en efecto** or **efectivamente** occur in the middle of a sentence, they are better translated as *indeed* or *as was just pointed out.*

El próximo semestre vamos a tener clases más grandes, pues más de 300 estudiantes nuevos ya se han matriculado.	*Next semester we're going to have bigger classes, as more than 300 new students have already registered.*
El número de estudiantes matriculados, **efectivamente,** es mucho mayor de lo que hemos experimentado en los últimos años.	*The number of new students already registered, indeed, is much larger than what we've seen in recent years.*

Remember that **en efecto** and **efectivamente** are used to answer a yes-or-no question affirmatively or to confirm a previous statement. *Effectively,* and *in effect,* on the other hand, mean *essentially.*

efectivamente/en efecto esencialmente/casi como si fuera	*exactly/yes, that's correct/indeed effectively/in effect*
Ella lleva seis años dirigiendo la compañía y es ahora **esencialmente/casi como si fuera** su presidente.	*She's been in charge of the company for six years, and is now effectively its president.*

Tener ganas de (+ infinitive)

Literally, *to have desires to (do something),* this expression is better translated as *to feel like (doing something)* or *to really want to (do something).*

Tengo ganas de ir de compras.	*I feel like going shopping.*
Mi esposo **no tiene ganas de acompañarme**.	*My husband doesn't want to go with me.*
Mi esposo **tiene muy pocas ganas de ir** de compras.	*My husband really doesn't feel like going shopping.*

Cenar

Cenar means literally—and elegantly in English—*to dine.* But in Spanish, it's just eating dinner, even a plain, boring one. The point here is that you don't *eat* **la cena**; you can **planear la cena**, **prepararla**, or **servirla**—but to eat it is **cenar**. And it's the same with breakfast—**desayunar**—and lunch—**almorzar**.

¿A qué hora **cenan** ustedes?	*What time do you (all) eat dinner?*
Hoy no **almorcé**.	*I didn't eat lunch today.*
Vamos a desayunar en casa.	*We're going to eat breakfast at home.*

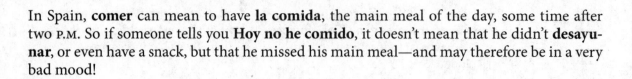

In Spain, **comer** can mean to have **la comida**, the main meal of the day, some time after two P.M. So if someone tells you **Hoy no he comido**, it doesn't mean that he didn't **desayunar**, or even have a snack, but that he missed his main meal—and may therefore be in a very bad mood!

Bien

Bien (*Fine*) is the perfect answer to **¿Cómo está?** (*How are you?*). You can also use it to agree to a suggestion—one translation of *OK* or *Good*. An alternative to this **Bien** is **De acuerdo.** In Spain, **Vale** is commonly used for this purpose.

Te llamo mañana a las 5.	*I'll call you tomorrow at 5.*
Bien./Está bien./De acuerdo./Vale.	*OK/Good. I'll wait for your call.*
Esperaré tu llamada.	

Always think of the function of the word rather than the translation. While **bueno** often translates as *good*, in this case it doesn't work. **Bien** is the best answer here.
Estar de acuerdo means *to agree with someone*.

No me gusta este restaurante. No quiero volver.	*I don't like this restaurant. I don't want to come back.*
Estoy de acuerdo contigo. La próxima vez iremos a otro lugar.	*I agree with you. The next time we'll go someplace else.*

Entonces

One function of **entonces** translates as *then* in the sense of *so* or *therefore*.

No voy a poder salir contigo de ahora en adelante.	*I'm not going to be able to go out with you anymore.*
Entonces, ¿es cierto? ¿ Te vas a casar con Julio?	*Then/So it's true? You're going to marry Julio?*

Alternatively, **entonces** can also mean *then* as in *at that time*. *So* cannot be used here.

Me dijiste hace dos meses que te ibas a casar con Julio.	*You told me two months ago that you were going to marry Julio.*
Sí, pero **entonces** pensé que estaba enamorada de él.	*Yes, but back then I thought I was in love with him.*

In the following example, **entonces** is translated by *so* but not by *then*.

Entonces, ¿vienes o no vienes?	*So, are you coming or not?*

Después/Luego

Después and **luego** are the best translations of *then* when it means *after that*.

Estuvieron dos semanas en Chile y **después/luego** fueron a Argentina.	*They were in Chile for two weeks and then they went to Argentina.*

Hasta luego

This is a very common way of saying *See you later* in Spanish—easy—but watch the pronunciation! Just as **hasta** has two syllables, so does **luego**. That is, the combination of *u* and *e* (when there's no written accent mark) is pronounced as one syllable: *ue* = weh. Granted, it's a little hard to say when it follows the letter *l*. Try putting the *l* on the end of **hasta:** "ah stahl WEH goh." And in Spain, you often hear just "staluego" (stahl WEH goh).

Adiós

Adiós can indicate a long time before you expect to see someone again. Literally, it means, (*I leave you) to God*. And, especially in Mexico and Central America, it's followed by **Que te/le/les vaya bien**—*May all go well for you*. In English, people say *Hi* when passing in a car (or bus full of kids) going in the other direction, but in Spanish you would call out, "**¡Adiós!**"

Adiós, like **luego**, is pronounced in two syllables: "ah dyos." The combination of *i* and *o* in Spanish (when there's no written accent) is pronounced as one syllable. Again, you might find it easier to say if you put the *d* at the end of the first syllable: "ad YOHS." But be careful here, too, as the *d* (between two vowels) is pronounced like English *th* (as in *brother*). So you have "ath YOHS."

But **adiós** has a written accent! This is because of another convention: when a word ends in *s* (or *n, a, e, i, o, u*), it is pronounced with emphasis on the next-to-last syllable. Any exception to this rule requires a written accent. Compare *Dios* (one syllable) with *Adiós* (two syllables). If there were no accent mark, it would be mispronounced as "AH thyohs," which would probably be worse than the *gringo* "ah dee OHS."

EJERCICIO
25·1

Fill in the blanks with the most appropriate words.

1. ¿Quieres ir a una fiesta _____?

   los sábados   el sábado   en el sábado   en sábado

2. La fiesta es _____.

   por la noche   a la noche   a noche   anoche

3. Voy a tu casa _____.

   a ocho   en las ocho   son las ocho   a las ocho

4. Fíjate que ya son las diez _____.

   a la noche   por la noche   de la noche   a noche

5. Me gusta salir a bailar _____.

   los jueves   el jueves   a la mañana   anoche

6. Me gustaría salir a bailar _____.

   el jueves   anoche   en domingo   son las once

EJERCICIO
25·2

¿Cómo se dice en español? *Translate each sentence into Spanish.*

1. This is Margarita (calling). _____

2. I'm calling you . . . _____

3. The party is on Sunday night. _____

4. It's at eight P.M. _____

5. Where's the party? _____

6. It's at my house. _____

EJERCICIO
25·3

Fill in the blanks with the most appropriate words.

1. Voy a tomar agua porque no me gusta _____.

   cerveza   vino   la cerveza   las cervezas

2. Queremos ver esa película porque _____ el actor principal.

   no me gusta   amo   amamos   nos encanta

3. Por favor, espérame _____.

   al cine   a la película   por mi casa   en el cine

4. _____ mucho a todos mis amigos.

   Me gusta   Me encanta   Quiero   Amo

5. ¿Me acabas de llamar? _____.

   En efecto   Bueno   Bien   Adiós

6. No tengo ganas de _____.

   estudiando   estudiar   estudio   estudiamos

7. Quiero _____ mañana a las seis.

   comer el desayuno   comer desayuno   desayunar   desayuno

¿Cómo se dice en español? *Translate each sentence into Spanish.*

1. I love Peruvian food.

   _____

2. Do you love me?

   _____

3. You have a crush on my sister, don't you?

   _____

4. Exactly.

   _____

5. Would you like to talk to her?

   _____

6. Yes, I'd love to.

   _____

7. Do you feel like going to the movies?

   _____

8. No, I don't feel like going.

   _____

Match each situation with the most appropriate remark in Spanish. Note: there may be more than one answer for certain situations.

1. _____ Introducing a friend   a. a las ocho

2. _____ Saying who is calling   b. Adiós

3. _____ Saying you'll meet the day after Wednesday   c. al aeropuerto

4. _____ Naming the day after Wednesday   d. Bien

5. _____ Giving the actual time   e. Bueno

6. _____ Telling the time of an event   f. el jueves

7. _____ Saying which dress you like   g. el vestido rojo

8. _____ Saying what kind of dress you are looking for   h. Ella es

9. _____ Saying where you are going   i. En efecto

10. _____	Saying where you are	j.	en el aeropuerto
11. _____	Saying you love chocolate	k.	Entonces
12. _____	Saying you love your sister	l.	hasta entonces
13. _____	Saying you love your wife	m.	Hola
14. _____	Saying you have a crush on someone	n.	jueves
15. _____	Acknowledging that something is correct	o.	La amo
16. _____	Saying you're not in the mood	p.	La quiero
17. _____	Prefacing an answer that requires a little explanation	q.	hasta luego
18. _____	Agreeing to a suggestion	r.	Me encanta
19. _____	Prefacing a conclusion	s.	Me gusta
20. _____	Saying you'll see someone later	t.	No tengo ganas
21. _____	Saying you'll see someone at an appointed time	u.	Son las ocho
22. _____	Greeting someone on the phone	v.	Soy
23. _____	Waving to a bunch of kids on a bus	w.	un vestido rojo

EJERCICIO 25·6

Write questions that ask where the following are.

1. la biblioteca

2. José y Carlos

3. Uruguay

4. los conciertos

5. nosotros

6. la reunión

7. yo

8. la fiesta

EJERCICIO
25·7

¿Cómo se dice en español? *Translate each sentence into Spanish.*

1. It's me.

   _____

2. Do you feel like eating lunch?

   _____

3. Um, I'm busy now.

   _____

4. Fine. I'll call you on Saturday.

   _____

5. Then you're not mad?

   _____

6. No. I'll see you later.

   _____

EJERCICIO
25·8

¿Cómo se dice en español? *Translate each sentence into Spanish.*

1. What do you want?

   _____

2. I'd love to see you tonight.

   _____

3. I'm going to the movies with Sara.

   _____

4. Then you can't have dinner with me?

   _____

5. Exactly.

   _____

6. OK, bye.

   _____

¿Cómo se dice en español? *Translate each sentence into Spanish.*

1. Hi, this is Miguel.

_____

2. I'm calling to see if you can eat dinner with me tonight.

_____

3. OK. What time?

_____

4. At seven?

_____

5. Fine.

_____

At the restaurant . . .

6. Marta doesn't love me.

_____

7. Then why don't you go out with Patricia? She has a big crush on you!

_____

8. Well, then—why not?

_____

Write an original conversation in which you call someone and invite him or her to do something with you.

_____

_____

_____

_____

_____

_____

_____

Narrating a story

Let's look at a conversation about telling a story.

Conversation: A traffic accident

PABLO: Amigo, ¿qué te **pasó**? ¿**Se te rompió** la pierna?

JESÚS: Hola, Pablo. No, no es tan dramático. Sólo **me torcí** el tobillo. **Sin embargo**, me duele bastante y es muy incómodo andar con estas muletas.

PABLO: ¿Cuándo te **pasó** eso?

JESÚS: **Fue** la noche del campeonato de **básquetbol**. Y **lo peor** es que **perdimos** el partido y las esperanzas de recuperar el título.

PABLO: **Sentémonos** aquí un rato y cuéntame cómo **sucedió** todo.

JESÚS: Bueno, todo **ocurrió el jueves pasado**. **Era** un día lluvioso y además **hacía** mucho frío. Yo **quería** llegar temprano al gimnasio para estar bien preparado para el partido. **Estaba** un poco preocupado por el partido cuando **salía** de casa, pero **subí** al **carro** y **empecé** a manejar hacia el gimnasio. **De repente sonó** mi celular—**era** mi novia. Ella **estaba** muy entusiasmada por el partido y me **quería** desear buena suerte. **Empecé** a **sentirme** fuerte y preparado para el partido. Mi novia y yo **seguíamos conversando** cuando **de repente me di cuenta** que los carros que **iban** delante **estaban** parados y yo **iba manejando** un poco rápido. **Frené** fuerte, pero ya **era** demasiado tarde. La carretera **estaba** mojada y **choqué** con el carro que **estaba** parado delante. Por la fuerza del frenazo, **se me torció** el tobillo. Me **costó** mucho trabajo salir del carro para hablar con el conductor del otro **carro**, pues me **dolía** mucho el tobillo. La verdad, en ese momento, no **sabía** qué hacer. **Estaba pensando** en el partido, en mi novia, en mis compañeros de equipo, **era** imposible **darme cuenta de que** no **iba a poder** jugar esa noche. Pero **por fin llegó** un policía, me **hizo** firmar unos documentos y **luego** una ambulancia me **llevó** al hospital. Allí me **hicieron**

Hey buddy, what happened to you? Did you break your leg?

Hi Pablo. No, it's not that drastic. I just twisted my ankle. Still, it hurts a lot and walking with these crutches is so uncomfortable.

When did it happen?

It was the night of the basketball championship. And the worst thing is that we lost the game and all hopes of winning our title back.

Let's sit down for a minute and tell me how it all happened.

Well, it all happened last Thursday. It was a rainy day and it was also freezing. I wanted to get to the gym early to be ready for the game. I was a little worried about the game when I left home, but I got in the car and started to drive toward the gym. All of a sudden my phone rang—it was my girlfriend. She was all excited about the game and wanted to wish me good luck. I started to feel strong and ready for the game. My girlfriend and I kept on talking when I suddenly realized that the cars in front of me were stopped and I was going a little fast. I slammed on the brakes, but it was too late. The street was wet and I hit the car that was stopped in front of me. That hard braking caused me to twist my ankle. I could hardly get out of the car to talk to the other driver because my ankle hurt so much. To tell you the truth, I didn't know what to do. I was thinking about the game, about my girlfriend, my teammates—it never occurred to me that I wouldn't be able to play that night. But a policeman finally came and made me sign some documents, and then an ambulance took me to the hospital. They took some X-rays to see if my ankle was broken or not. Thank goodness it wasn't broken, but at any rate I wasn't going to play that night. And now I have to use these crutches.

una radiografía para averiguar si el tobillo **estaba** roto o no. Gracias a Dios no **estaba** roto, pero **de todos modos** no **iba** a jugar esa noche. Y ahora tengo que usar estas muletas.

PABLO: Hombre, ¡qué mala suerte! Lo siento mucho, de verdad.

Man, what bad luck! I'm sorry, really.

Narrating in the past

Both the imperfect tense and the preterite tense are used in telling what happened in the past. Each tense has a specific purpose. It is easier to use these tenses correctly if you think about their purposes rather than try to translate from English. Note that the use of the imperfect tense to describe a special period of the past has a very different set of translations into English from those used in a narration. This is reflected in the fact that in a narration (but not in a description) the imperfect progressive tense can be used as an alternative to the imperfect.

Hablaba/Estaba hablando.	*He was talking.*
Comíamos/Estábamos comiendo.	*We were eating.*

Time expressions used with the past tenses:

ayer	*yesterday*
la semana pasada	*last week*
hace dos días	*two days ago*
anteayer	*the day before yesterday*
el año pasado	*last year*
hace diez minutos	*ten minutes ago*
anoche	*last night*
el viernes pasado	*last Friday*
hace cinco años	*five years ago*

To form the imperfect progressive tense, use the following formula:

IMPERFECT OF **ESTAR** + GERUND OF MAIN VERB

(yo) estaba trabajando *I was working*	(nosotros, -as) estábamos pensando *we were thinking*
(tú) estabas durmiendo *you were sleeping*	(vosotros, -as) estabais jugando *you all were playing*
(él/ella/usted) estaba soñando *he/she/you were dreaming*	(ustedes/ellos, -as) estaban escribiendo *you all/they were writing*

Setting the scene with the imperfect tense

To tell the time and place, to describe the weather, and to tell what was already happening when your story began, use the imperfect tense.

Estábamos en San Antonio.	*We were in San Antonio.*
Hacía mucho calor.	*It was hot.*
Eran las dos de la tarde.	*It was two o'clock in the afternoon.*
Yo **nadaba/estaba** nadando.	*I was swimming.*

Telling what happened with the preterite tense

To tell the events of the story, use the preterite tense. Events are often preceded by expressions that indicate the sequence of the action, the time of the action, or that something triggered the action. These are considered preterite signals.

primero	*first*
después/luego	*after that*
de repente/de pronto/súbitamente	*suddenly*
a las ocho	*at eight o'clock*
finalmente	*finally*

Adding details

There are three patterns in a narration:

- Simultaneous actions: imperfect + imperfect
    To tell that two actions were going on at the same time, put both verbs in the imperfect.

Mientras **manejaba, hablaba** por celular.	*While she was driving, she was talking on her cell phone.*
Cuando yo **estudiaba,** mi amigo **veía** la televisión.	*When I was studying, my friend was watching television.*

- Interrupted action: imperfect + preterite
    To tell that one action was already in progress and that another interrupted it, put the first verb—the action in progress—in the imperfect, and the second verb—the action that interrupts—in the preterite.

Mientras **manejaba, sonó** el celular.	*While she was driving, her cell phone rang.*

- A sequence of uninterrupted actions: preterite + preterite
    To tell actions that happened without relating them to any other actions, put all the verbs in the preterite.

Ella **tomó** un vaso de leche y **fue** a la cama.	*She drank a glass of milk and went to bed.*

Querer, saber, poder, tener, and entender

Certain verbs can be tricky to use in the past, simply because they are not used in a progressive form in English. However, when they indicate simultaneous or interrupted action (or feeling) in Spanish, they require the imperfect tense.

Ella no **quería** ir a la fiesta hasta que Juan la invitó.	*She didn't want (wasn't wanting) to go to the party until Juan invited her.*
Sabíamos que él le gustaba.	*We knew (we were knowing) that she liked (was liking) him.*
No **podía** abrir la puerta de mi cuarto así que fui a buscar ayuda.	*I couldn't (wasn't being able to) open the door to my room, so I went to look for help. (The situation wasn't resolved.)*
Tenía que volver a casa y llamé a mi hermano.	*I had (was having) to go home and I called my brother.*

Since the preterite tense indicates that an action occurred all of a sudden, or that it resolved the question at hand, it can translate into English as a different word.

Quise llamarte, pero mi celular no funcionaba.	*I tried (wanted to and failed) to call you, but my cell didn't work (wasn't working).*
¡Yo la invité y ella no **quiso** ir!	*I invited her and she refused to go (did not want to go, period)!*
Él era muy pequeño cuando **supo** la verdad.	*He was (was being) very young when he found out (suddenly knew) the truth.*
El asistente en el hotel **pudo** abrir la puerta de mi cuarto.	*The assistant at the hotel was able (finally managed) to open the door to my room. (The situation was resolved.)*
Mi hermano vino por mí y **tuve** que volver a casa.	*My brother came to get me and I had to go home.*

Rompérsele la pierna

Since no one breaks a bone on purpose, this phrase is used to indicate that *someone's leg got broken*. The construction is as follows:

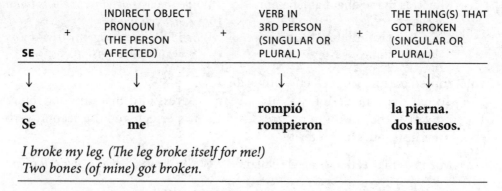

SE	+	INDIRECT OBJECT PRONOUN (THE PERSON AFFECTED)	+	VERB IN 3RD PERSON (SINGULAR OR PLURAL)	+	THE THING(S) THAT GOT BROKEN (SINGULAR OR PLURAL)
↓		↓		↓		↓
Se		**me**		**rompió**		**la pierna.**
Se		**me**		**rompieron**		**dos huesos.**

I broke my leg. (The leg broke itself for me!)
Two bones (of mine) got broken.

Other verbs that blame the accident on the thing rather than on the person include:

◆ **Quebrársele**, also *to get broken*

(A mí) **se me quebró** el brazo.	*My arm got broken.*

◆ **Olvidársele**, *to have slipped someone's mind/be forgotten*

(A él) **se le olvidó** la cita.	*The appointment slipped his mind./He forgot the appointment.*

◆ **Quemársele**, *to get burned*

(A ella) **se le quemaron** los dedos.	*Her fingers got burned./She burned her fingers.*

◆ **Caérsele**, *to fall from one's hands*

(A nosotros) **se nos cayó** la caja.	*The box fell from our hands./We dropped the box.*

◆ **Perdérsele**, *to lose something*

(A usted) ¿**se le perdió** la tarjeta de crédito?	*Did you lose your credit card?*

- **Quedarse**, *to be left somewhere by mistake*

> **(A mí) se me quedaron** las cartas en el carro.
> *The letters were left in the car./I left the letters in the car.*

- **Acabársele**, *to run out of something*

> **Se me acabó** la gasolina.
> *I ran out of gas.*

Coche/carro

In Spain, individual automobiles are called **coches**, while in Latin America they are called **carros**. In Spain, *to drive* is **conducir**, while in Latin America **manejar** is used. In Spain, you should never **conducir** while talking on your **móvil**, while in Latin America this wonderful invention is called a **celular**.

Another word in this chapter is different between the two areas: In Spain, they play **baloncesto**. In Latin America, it's **básquetbol**.

Solo

Solo can be used as an alternative for **solamente**, which means *only*.

> **Solo** quería ayudarlo.
> *I only wanted to help him.*

Solo can also be a masculine singular adjective. The feminine form is **sola**, and the plural forms are **solos** and **solas**. It can be used to express *only one*, by placing **un solo/una sola** before a noun.

> Tenemos **una sola pregunta**.
> *We have only one question.*

It can be used to express *all alone/all by oneself*.

> El niño está **solo**.
> *The little boy is alone.*
> Los chicos se fueron y nos dejaron **solas**.
> *The boys left and left us alone.*

The expression **dejar (-le a uno) en paz**, literally to leave someone in peace, is usually translated as *to leave someone alone*.

> **Déjame en paz.** Solo quiero estar sola.
> *Leave me alone. I just want to be alone.*

When used with the verb **sentir**, **solo** means *lonely*.

> **Me sentía muy solo.**
> *I felt really lonely.*

Sin embargo

This expression introduces a statement that is surprising after what was said previously, but takes over in importance. It can be translated as *nevertheless,* or *still*.

> No estaba listo para el examen. **Sin embargo,** lo aprobé.
> *I wasn't ready for the exam. Still, I passed it.*

Lo peor

This is translated as *the worst thing*. **Lo** can precede an adjective to make it into a noun.

Lo peor de esta clase es que la profesora es terrible.	*The worst thing about this class is that the teacher is terrible.*
Solucionar el problema es **lo importante**.	*Solving the problem is the important thing/ what is important.*

Lo before an adjective can also indicate its strength, and is translated as *how*.

¡No te imaginas **lo contenta** que estoy!	*You can't imagine how happy I am!*

Un rato

This looks like it might be a nasty rodent, but that's actually **una rata**! (And the little one is **un ratón**—which is also the name for the computer mouse.) **Un rato** means *a short period of time, a while.*

Charlamos **un rato** anoche.	*We talked for a while last night.*

Other ways to express time include:

◆ Una **época**, which isn't an epoch, but rather a period of time where things are or were different from those of other **épocas**. For example, *when I was in high school* is an **época**. When describing an **época** in the past, the imperfect is used.

Cuando estaba en la escuela secundaria, no estudiaba mucho.	*When I was in high school, I didn't study very much.*

◆ **La hora**, which means *time* in the sense of *time to do something*.

Es **la hora** de comer.	*It's time to eat.*

◆ **La vez**, which means *the incidence*, as in *the first/second/only/last/etc. time*:

Es **la primera vez** que estoy en esta ciudad.	*It's the first time I've ever been in this city.*
Fue **la única vez** que lo visité.	*It was the only time I visited him.*
La última vez que lo vi fue en octubre.	*The last time I saw him was in October.*

◆ **A la (misma) vez** means *at the same time*.
◆ **A veces** means *sometimes*.
◆ **El tiempo**, which can refer to *time* in general:

El tiempo vuela.	*Time flies.*
No tengo mucho **tiempo**.	*I don't have much time.*

El **tiempo** can also refer to the weather:

Hace muy buen **tiempo** aquí.	*The weather is great here.*

And *to have a good time* is **divertirse** or **pasarla/pasarlo bien**.

Nos divertimos mucho.	*We had a good time.*
La pasamos muy bien.	

De repente

This means *all of a sudden*, and is a true signal that the verb that follows should be in the preterite tense (if you are telling the story in the past tense).

Estaba caminando por la calle cuando **de repente** oí un sonido muy raro.

I was walking down the street when all of a sudden I heard a strange noise.

Other expressions with the same meaning include: **súbitamente/de pronto/de buenas a primeras**.

Sentirse

Sentirse, used with a reflexive pronoun, is followed by an adjective to tell *how someone feels*.

Me **siento** enfermo.
De repente, **se sintió** mejor.

I feel sick.
Suddenly, she felt better.

Sentir is used with a direct object to tell *what someone feels*.

Siento un dolor en la espalda.

I feel a pain in my back.

A common expression is **lo siento**—literally *I feel it,* but better translated as *I'm sorry.*

Seguir

Seguir, which means *to follow,* can also mean *to keep on doing something* when the verb that follows it is in the gerund (**-ndo**) form.

Seguí manejando.
Ella **siguió** hablando.

I kept on driving.
She kept on talking.

Continuar can also mean *to keep on doing something*, and it is also followed by a verb in gerund form.

Continuamos discutiendo.

We kept on arguing.

Darse cuenta de

This is a very common expression that means *to realize/to suddenly become aware of.*

Ya **me doy cuenta de** que tengo que buscar trabajo.

Now I realize that I have to look for a job.

Nos dimos cuenta de que era muy tarde para llegar.

We realized it was very late to be arriving.

Es tarde

This means that *the time is late.*

Es muy tarde. Tienes que ir a la cama.
El examen es mañana y ya **es demasiado tarde** para estudiar.

It's very late. You have to go to bed.
The test is tomorrow and now it's too late to study.

Llegar tarde means *to be late* in the sense of *to arrive late.*

¿Llego tarde?	*Am I late?*
Tu amigo **llegó tarde** y nos perdimos la primera parte de la película.	*Your friend was late and we missed the first part of the movie.*

Estar atrasado means *to be late* in the sense of *to be behind schedule*.

Lo siento, el informe no está listo. **Estoy muy atrasada.**	*I'm sorry, the report isn't ready. I'm really behind.*

Tardar en means *to be late in doing something, to delay*.

No tardes en enviarme la carta.	*Don't be late in sending me the letter.*
Tardé en mandar la solicitud y no me aceptaron en la universidad.	*I was late in sending my application and they didn't accept me at the university.*

Por fin

Por fin indicates relief that something finally happened.

¡**Por fin** estás aquí!	*You're finally here!*

De todos modos

This is an expression that indicates a conclusion that doesn't seem logical in view of what was previously said. It is usually translated as *anyway*.

Yo no invité a Marta a la fiesta, pero vino **de todos modos.**	*I didn't invite Marta to the party, but she came anyway.*

Express in Spanish the following setting for a story.

1. It was three P.M. _____

2. It was raining. _____

3. I was driving home. _____

4. Two friends were with me. _____

5. We were all tired. _____

Express in Spanish the following simultaneous actions.

1. While I was sleeping, my friends were celebrating. (dormir/celebrar)

_____

2. She was listening to music while she was studying. (escuchar/estudiar)

_____

3. He was cleaning the house while the children played outside. (limpiar/jugar)

_____

4. I was worried when I was taking the test. (estar preocupado/hacer)

_____

5. The teacher wasn't watching when he was texting his friends. (ver/textear)

_____

EJERCICIO

25·13

Express in Spanish the following interrupted actions.

1. While I was sleeping, my mother called. (dormir/llamar)

_____

2. She was listening to music when the phone rang. (escuchar/sonar)

_____

3. We were having fun when the teacher came in. (divertirse/entrar)

_____

4. He was talking on his cell when he hit the other car. (hablar/chocar con)

_____

5. They were playing baseball when it started to rain. (jugar/empezar)

_____

EJERCICIO

25·14

Express in Spanish the following uninterrupted actions.

1. I got up and got dressed. (levantarse/vestirse)

_____

2. We went back home and looked for our books. (volver/buscar)

_____

3. He studied a lot and passed the test. (estudiar/aprobar)

_____

4. She came to class and sat down. (venir/sentarse)

_____

5. They went to the supermarket and bought drinks. (ir/comprar)

_____

Circle the appropriate verb form for each blank.

1. No _____ el problema de matemáticas y fui a hablar con el profesor.
   entendí   entendía

2. El profesor me explicó cómo solucionarlo y luego _____ completar mi tarea.
   pude   podía

3. ¿Cuándo _____ que ella mentía?
   supiste   sabías

4. El chico _____ mucha hambre cuando llegó al restaurante.
   tuvo   tenía

5. _____ contactarte, pero no contestaste tu celular.
   Quise   Quería

Fill in each blank with the most appropriate form.

1. Ayer, a Antonio _____ rompió el brazo.

2. A mí no _____ quemaron los dedos.

3. Al profesor _____ olvidaron los exámenes.

4. A mis amigos _____ perdió la llave.

5. A Sarita se le _____ (olvidar) el nombre del profesor.

6. A Rosita y Mariana se les _____ (quedar) las tareas en casa.

7. ¿A ti se te _____ (caer) esta bufanda?

Choose the most appropriate word to fill in each blank.

1. Vamos afuera. Hoy hace muy buen _____.

   hora   tiempo   época   vez

2. No puedo acompañarte, pues no tengo _____.

   tiempo   rato   vez   hora

3. Te lo dije muchas _____.

   épocas   veces   tiempos   horas

4. ¿Qué _____ es?

   tiempo   hora   horas   rato

5. Mis padres se conocieron en otra _____.

   tiempo   vez   época   hora

6. _____ me frustraba mucho.

   A veces   Un rato   La época   Ahora

Fill in each blank with the correct form of the gerund.

1. Estábamos (trabajar) _____ duro.

2. El padre siguió (caminar) _____.

3. Los chicos continuaron (correr) _____.

4. Yo estaba (dormir) _____.

5. La mesera siguió (servir) _____ la cena.

6. La niña estaba (pedir) _____ información.

7. Seguimos (divertirse) _____.

8. ¿Seguiste (mentir) _____?

Match the words or expressions in the left column with their meanings in the right column.

1. _____ Tardé en entregárselo.   a. *Don't be late.*

2. _____ Estaba atrasada.   b. *I was behind schedule.*

3. _____ ¡No tardes!   c. *It was too late.*

4. _____ Ya era demasiado tarde.   d. *It's very late.*

5. _____ Llegué tarde.   e. *I handed it in late.*

6. _____ Es muy tarde.   f. *I was late.*

Complete each sentence with an appropriate message.

1. Ella estaba soñando y de repente _____.

2. Quería comprar la casa, pues era bonita, estaba en una vecindad cómoda y ademas, _____

    _____.

3. No me gustaba este carro, pero de todos modos _____

    _____.

4. Esperé a mi amigo dos horas y por fin _____.

5. Este apartamento no es perfecto, sin embargo _____.

Put each verb in parentheses in either the imperfect tense or the preterite tense, as appropriate.

Ayer, cuando (1. entrar, yo) _____ en la clase, (2. ser) _____ las dos.

(3. llover) _____. (4. querer, yo) _____ hablar con mi amiga. No (5. estar,

yo) _____ preparada para la clase, pues no me (6. interesar) _____ el

tema. Gracias a Dios, el profesor no (7. estar) _____ en clase cuando (8. entrar,

yo) _____, y (9. poder, yo) _____ encontrar un asiento al lado de mi

amiga. (10. Empezar, nosotras) _____ a hablar. (11. hablar, nosotras) _____

cuando el profesor me (12. hacer) _____ una pregunta sobre la lección.

(13. sentirse, yo) _____ muy avergonzada. (14. levantarse, yo) _____ y

(15. salir, yo) _____ del aula. Más tarde, (16. arrepentirse, yo) _____ y le

(17. mandar, yo) _____ un email al profesor. (18. querer, yo) _____

disculparme, pero el profesor no me (19. contestar) _____. Él no (20. querer)

_____ hablar conmigo.

Write a paragraph of eight or nine sentences in which you tell a friend something that happened to you recently. Describe what was going on before the action started, and include at least one example of simultaneous actions, one of interrupted action, and one of uninterrupted action. Use **primero**, **después**, **luego**, **de repente**, *and* **finalmente**. *Ask a Spanish-speaking friend to read your story and comment on your use of the past tenses.*

_____

_____

_____

_____

_____

_____

_____

_____

Retelling a conversation

Now let's look at some conversations about retelling a story.

Conversation 1: Conversation between mother and kindergarten teacher

SRA. MARTÍNEZ: Buenos días, Srta. Sánchez. Es un placer verla de nuevo.

Good afternoon, Miss Sánchez. It's nice to see you again.

SRTA. SÁNCHEZ: Buenos días, Sra. Martínez. Igualmente. El año escolar ha pasado tan rápido, parece mentira que **estemos a punto de** terminar. Creo que Sam ha tenido un buen año y que disfrutará mucho del primer grado.

Good afternoon, Mrs. Martínez. Same here. The school year went so fast, I can't believe it's almost over. I think Sam has had a good year and that he'll enjoy first grade.

SRA. MARTÍNEZ: Me alegro mucho que usted lo diga. Nosotros también creemos que ha hecho muy bien en el kindergarten.

I'm glad to hear you say that. We think he's done well in kindergarten, too.

SRTA. SÁNCHEZ: Sam es un niño que atiende muy bien, algo que me parece muy importante, **ya que** hoy en día hay muy pocos niños—ni hablar de los adultos—que realmente sepan atender. Ustedes lo han educado muy bien, le puedo decir que es **el niño más cortés y considerado de toda** la clase.

Sam is a boy who listens very well, something I think is very special, since these days not very many kids—and few adults—really know how to listen. You have raised him very well; I can tell you he's the best-mannered child in the whole class.

SRA. MARTÍNEZ: Me alegra mucho oírlo, Srta. Sánchez. Nosotros pensamos que Sam lee, escribe y trabaja con los números muy bien **para** su edad. ¿Está usted de acuerdo?

That's music to my ears, Miss Sánchez. We think Sam reads, writes, and works with numbers very well for his age. Do you agree?

SRTA. SÁNCHEZ: Sí, Sra. Martínez. Los exámenes indican que Sam está dentro de los parámetros **para** su edad en lectura, escritura y aritmética. Dibuja bien y es bastante creativo. Y le gusta cantar.

Yes, Mrs. Martínez. The tests show that Sam is within the norms for his age in reading, writing, and arithmetic. He draws well, and he's quite creative. And he likes to sing.

SRA. MARTÍNEZ: Entonces, todo está bien.

Then everything is fine.

SRTA. SÁNCHEZ: La verdad, Sra. Martínez, Sam **sí tiene** un problema bastante serio.

Actually, Mrs. Martínez, Sam has a rather serious problem.

SRA. MARTÍNEZ: ¿Sí? ¿Cuál problema?

Oh? What problem?

SRTA. SÁNCHEZ: Es que no es nada agresivo.

He's not at all aggressive.

SRA. MARTÍNEZ: Pero, ¡eso es una buena noticia! Nosotros no somos gente agresiva.

That's great! We're not aggressive people.

SRTA. SÁNCHEZ: Nada de bueno, Sra. Martínez. Si no aprende a ser más decidido, a tener más iniciativa, nunca conseguirá un trabajo, ni una pareja. Cuando hago preguntas a toda la clase, Sam nunca levanta la mano, como los otros niños. Si quiero que conteste, tengo que hacerle las preguntas a él en particular.

There's nothing good about it, Mrs. Martínez. If he doesn't learn to assert himself voluntarily, he'll never get a job, or even a partner in life. When I ask questions to the whole class, Sam never raises his hand like the other children do. If I want him to answer, I have to call on him individually.

SRA. MARTÍNEZ: Y en ese caso, ¿contesta correctamente?

And when you do that, does he answer correctly?

SRTA. SÁNCHEZ: Pues, sí, siempre.

Well, yes, always.

SRA. MARTÍNEZ: Eso es todo lo que necesito saber. Muchas gracias, Srta. Sánchez. Que tenga un buen día.

That's all I need to know. Thank you very much, Miss Sánchez. Have a nice day.

Conversation 2: Gossip between a mother and daughter

ELENA: Mamá—¡aquí estoy! Tengo que contarte algo sobre la conversación que tuve con la maestra de Sam.

Mom—here I am! I have to tell you about the conference I had with Sam's teacher.

MAMÁ: Soy toda oídos. ¿Qué te dijo?

I'm all ears. What did she say?

ELENA: Bueno, empezó felicitándome por tener un hijo tan **bien educado** y simpático. Y destacó que era un niño que sabía atender.

Well, she started off by congratulating me for a boy so well-mannered and nice. She emphasized that he was a child who knew how to listen.

MAMÁ: ¿Y luego?

And after that?

ELENA: Luego dijo que su lectura, escritura y comprensión de aritmética estaban «dentro de los parámetros **para** su edad».

Then she said that his reading, writing, and math skills were "within the norms for his age."

MAMÁ: Entonces, no hubo ninguna sorpresa.	*So there were no surprises.*
ELENA: ¡Sí, sí que la hubo! No vas a creer esto. Me dijo que había algo muy importante que tenía que decirme. Cuando le pregunté cuál era el problema, me dijo que Sam no era lo suficientemente agresivo. Yo me quedé aliviada y le contesté que para mí eso era bueno. Pero ella respondió que no era bueno, sino todo lo contrario. Y yo le dije que no éramos gente agresiva y que estaba muy orgullosa de lo que había dicho sobre el comportamiento de Sam. Luego me explicó que él nunca levantaba la mano como los otros niños para contestar una pregunta, que si quería que respondiera Sam, tenía que dirigirle la pregunta a él individualmente. Y que si él no cambia, nunca conseguirá un trabajo o una pareja.	*Yes, there were! You're not going to believe this. She told me that there was something really important that she had to tell me. When I asked her what the problem was, she told me that Sam wasn't aggressive enough. I was so relieved and I told her that I thought that was good. But she said there was nothing good about it, just the opposite. So I said that we weren't aggressive people and that I was really proud about what she had told me about Sam's behavior. Then she explained to me that he never raised his hand to answer a question like the other kids, and that if she wanted him to answer, she had to call on him individually. And that if he doesn't change, that he'll never get a job or a girlfriend!*
MAMÁ: Esto es increíble.	*This is unbelievable.*
ELENA: ¿Sabes lo que hice? Le pregunté si Sam respondía correctamente cuando le hacía las preguntas a él. Me contestó que sí. Entonces le di las gracias y le dije que eso era todo lo que necesitaba saber.	*You know what I did? I asked her if Sam answered correctly when she asked him a question, and she said yes. So I thanked her and told her that was all I needed to know.*
MAMÁ: Bien hecho, hija.	*Good for you, Sweetie.*

Direct quotations

Just as in English, in Spanish a conversation can be repeated by quoting exactly what was said using quotation marks (which, as illustrated here, are different from English quotation marks) when the conversation is written. This kind of reported speech is excellent for telling a children's story, and it is also effective for telling the most exciting or dramatic part of something that happened.

Nos escondimos en la cocina y cuando entró Sara, gritamos: «**¡Sorpresa!**»	*We hid in the kitchen and when Sara came in, we shouted, "Surprise!"*

The interlocutor's words are often indicated by placing a dash before the quote, instead of using the quotation marks.

«Tengo mucho miedo», dijo el niño. —No te preocupes, estoy aquí contigo— respondió el padre.	*"I'm really scared," said the child. "Don't worry, I'm here with you," replied the father.*

Indirect quotations

A longer story, on the other hand, would save the quoted speech (direct discourse) for the most exciting parts, and use reported speech (indirect discourse) to retell all the other things that people said. In reported speech you do not quote a person's exact words, but rather paraphrase what he or she said.

DIRECT QUOTATION	INDIRECT QUOTATION
«Tengo mucho miedo», dijo el niño.	El niño **dijo que tenía mucho miedo.**
"I'm really scared," said the child.	*The child said that he was really scared.*

Formula for indirect quote, or reported speech

subject	+	verb in preterite or imperfect tense	+	**que**	+	verb in imperfect tense
↓		↓		↓		↓
El niño		**dijo/decía**		**que**		**tenía mucho miedo.**

The child said/was saying (that) he was really scared.

There are two ways to report a question. For a yes-or-no question, use the same formula as shown previously, with **si** instead of **que**.

DIRECT QUESTION	INDIRECT QUESTION
«¿Estudias español?» me preguntó la señora.	La señora **me preguntó si estudiaba español.**
"Are you studying Spanish?" the woman asked me.	*The woman asked me if I was studying Spanish.*

To report an answer to a yes-or-no question, use **que sí** or **que no**.

Le contesté **que sí/que no**.	*I told her yes/no.*

For an information question, use the same formula as shown, with the question word instead of **que**.

DIRECT QUESTION	INDIRECT QUESTION
«¿Cuándo estudias?» me preguntó la señora.	La señora **me preguntó cuándo estudiaba.**
"When do you study?" the woman asked me.	*The woman asked me when I (usually) studied.*
«¿Adónde van ustedes?» nos preguntó el señor.	El señor **nos preguntó adónde íbamos.**
"Where are you going?" the man asked us.	*The man asked us where we were going.*

Quoted requests and commands

La niña me pidió: «**Ayúdame con mi tarea, por favor**».	*The little girl asked me: "Help me with my homework, please."*
Los turistas nos rogaban, «**Llévenos a la estación de trenes, por favor**».	*The tourists were begging us, "Please take us to the train station."*
Mi mamá me advirtió: «**No llegues tarde esta noche**».	*My mom warned me: "Don't be late tonight."*
El policía me dijo: «**Baje del auto**».	*The policeman told me: "Get out of the car."*

Formula for reported requests and commands

subject	+	indirect object	+	verb in preterite /imperfect	+	**que**	+	verb in imperfect subjunctive
↓		↓		↓		↓		↓
La niña		**me**		**pidió**		**que**		**la ayudára con su tarea.**
Los turistas		**nos**		**rogaban**		**que**		**los lleváramos a la estación.**

Mi mamá	me	advirtió	que	no llegara tarde.
El policía	me	dijo	que	bajara del auto.

The little girl asked me to help her with her homework.
The tourists were begging us to take them to the station.
My mom warned me not to be late.
The policeman told me to get out of the car.

Advanced reported speech

The previous guidelines are for reporting conversations that are in the present indicative tense. When the conversations are in other tenses, use the following formulas. (See the Verb Tables for conjugations.)

Quoted verb	Reported verb
PRESENT SUBJUNCTIVE	IMPERFECT SUBJUNCTIVE
Nos avisó, «**No creo que el director venga**».	Nos avisó **que no creía que el director viniera**.
She informed us, "I don't think the director is coming."	*She informed us that she didn't think the director was coming.*
FUTURE	CONDITIONAL
Él me dijo, «**Te llamaré**».	Él **me dijo que me llamaría**.
He told me, "I'll call you."	*He told me (that) he would call me.*
PRETERITE	PRETERITE PERFECT
Isabel dijo, «**Fui a una fiesta**».	Isabel **dijo que había ido a una fiesta**.
Isabel said, "I went to a party."	*Isabel said that she had gone to a party.*

Ya que

This expression translates to English as *since*, in the sense of *considering the fact that*.

Ya que su hermano está aquí en la oficina, le daré los documentos personalmente.	*Since your brother is here in the office, I'll give him the documents personally.*

Educar

Educar means *to teach good manners to,* and a person who is **bien educado** is one who *has good manners.* A *well-educated person* is **una persona culta**.

La chica es **muy bien educada**.	*The girl has very good manners.*
La chica es **muy culta**.	*The girl is very well educated.*

El más... de todo el grupo

The pattern for expressing a superlative in Spanish is different from the English pattern. Note that the noun is placed before the superlative adjective, and the preposition *in* is expressed as **de**.

Ella es **la chica más alta de la clase**.	*She's the tallest girl in the class.*
Es **el senador más conservador del partido**.	*He's the most conservative senator in the party.*

Sí

When **sí** comes directly after a noun or pronoun, it is translated as an auxiliary verb, such as *does* or *is*, emphasizing contrast to the previous negative statement.

Nadie va a clase hoy.	*Nobody's going to class today.*
¡Nosotros sí!	*We are!*
El chico no habla español.	*The boy doesn't speak Spanish.*
El chico **sí lo habla,** pero es muy tímido.	*The boy does speak it, but he's very shy.*

Estar a punto de

Estar a punto de followed by an infinitive means *to be about to do something.*

Estamos a punto de salir.	*We're about to leave.*
El niño **está a punto de empezar** el primer grado.	*The child is about to start first grade.*

Para

Para can be used to compare someone or something with others of the same category.

Pablo es muy alto **para** su edad.	*Pablo es very tall for his age.*
Para una extranjera, habla muy bien el idioma.	*For a foreigner, she speaks the language very well.*

Por ser

Por ser is used to show that being in a particular category is the reason for a reality.

Por ser tan alto, Pablo fue escogido para el equipo de básquetbol.	*Because he's so tall, Pablo was chosen for the basketball team.*
Por ser extranjera, comete algunos errores cuando habla.	*Because she's a foreigner, she makes some mistakes when she speaks.*

Aconsejar que

Aconsejar que means *to advise* in the sense of *to give advice* and is followed by a verb in the subjunctive.

La profesora **me aconseja que estudie** en el extranjero.	*The teacher advises me to study abroad.*
Le aconsejé que estudiara química.	*I advised her to study chemistry.*

Avisar

Avisar means *to advise* in the sense of *to inform,* usually of something important.

El policía **me avisó** que el registro de mi carro se había caducado.	*The policeman informed me that my car registration had expired.*
La vecina de mi mamá **nos avisó** que mi mamá había salido.	*My mother's neighbor informed us that my mother had gone out.*

Advertir

Advertir is a little stronger than **avisar**, more like *to warn*.

Mi papá **me advirtió** que no manejara
si bebía cerveza.

*My dad warned me not to drive if I
drank beer.*

Anunciar

Anunciar is *to advertise*.

Hoy **anunciaron** un puesto para un
profesor de matemáticas.

*Today they advertised an opening for a
math teacher.*

Anunciar can also mean *to announce*.

El jefe **anunció** que se iba a jubilar.

The boss announced that he was going to retire.

EJERCICIO
25·23

Change the following direct quotes to indirect (reported) speech.

1. El niño dijo: «Estoy contento».

_____

2. Mi amigo dijo: «Tengo hambre».

_____

3. Las chicas dijeron: «Nos gusta la clase».

_____

4. Les dijimos: «Vivimos en esta calle».

_____

5. Nos dijeron: «Esta es la calle más bonita de toda la ciudad».

_____

EJERCICIO
25·24

Change the following reported speech to direct quotes.

1. Su mamá me dijo que él no estaba en casa.

_____

2. Los directores nos dijeron que no había suficiente dinero para el proyecto.

_____

3. La novia de mi hermano me dijo que ella quería casarse en abril.

_____

4. Mi hermano me dijo que él no estaba de acuerdo con ese plan.

_____

5. Su jefe le avisó que no iba a conseguir una subida de sueldo.

_____

Change the following direct questions to indirect (reported) questions.

1. Nos preguntaron: «¿Ustedes van al cine esta noche?»

_____

2. Me preguntó: «¿Cuánto cuesta un vuelo de ida y vuelta a México?»

_____

3. Le preguntó, «¿Cuándo te gradúas de la escuela secundaria?»

_____

4. Me preguntaron: «¿Qué quieres hacer hoy?»

_____

5. Te preguntó, «¿Comes con frecuencia en este restaurante?»

_____

Change the following indirect questions to direct (quoted) questions.

1. Él le preguntaba si quería acompañarlo.

_____

2. Me preguntó a qué hora comía.

_____

3. Nos preguntó dónde estudiábamos.

_____

4. Te preguntó con quién andabas.

_____

5. Me preguntaron si tenía miedo.

_____

Change the following direct requests or commands to indirect (reported) requests or commands.

1. Le pedimos: «Por favor, díganos la verdad».

_____

2. Le pedí: «Traiga este sobre al director de la compañía».

_____

3. Le dije: «Venga temprano al trabajo el viernes».

_____

4. Les dijo: «No lleguen tarde».

_____

5. Me pidió: «Cómprame un helado, por favor».

_____

Change the following indirect requests or commands to direct (quoted) requests or commands.

1. Ella le dijo que no la llamara.

_____

2. Él le pidió que lo pensara.

_____

3. Yo te aconsejé que vieras esa película.

_____

4. Me advirtió que no bebiera demasiado.

_____

5. Ellos le dijeron que saliera temprano.

_____

EJERCICIO
25·29

*Choose **por** or **para** to fill in the blanks in the following sentences.*

1. _____ un estudiante del cuarto año de la universidad, no es muy maduro.

2. _____ no ser muy maduro, tendrá problemas en su trabajo.

3. Lo despideron _____ no ser miembro del partido.

4. _____ un miembro del partido conservador, es bastante liberal.

5. _____ una película _____ niños, era buena.

EJERCICIO
25·30

¿Cómo se dice en español? *Translate the following sentences into Spanish.*

1. She's the best student in the class, since she studies all the time.

   _____

2. He's not well educated, but he has good manners.

   _____

3. He *is* well educated, since he reads constantly.

   _____

4. He has good manners, since his parents were very strict.

   _____

5. She is the best-educated one in her family.

   _____

6. For a well-educated woman, she doesn't seem very bright.

   _____

7. She *is* bright, it's that she doesn't listen.

   _____

8. She lost her job for being late every day.

   _____

¿Cómo se dice en español? *Translate the following sentences into Spanish.*

1. She announced that she was getting married.

   _____

2. The doctor warned her not to smoke.

   _____

3. She advised him that she was going on vacation.

   _____

4. The boss advised her not to leave.

   _____

5. They advertised the position.

   _____

Listen to a conversation (in English or Spanish) and write down exactly what the two people say. If the conversation is in English, translate it into Spanish. Then change the direct quotes to indirect (reported) discourse. Ask a Spanish-speaking friend to check your work.

_____

_____

_____

_____

_____

_____

_____

_____

Conversation: Meeting at a party

MARIO: Hola, **soy** Mario, el primo de Ana.

Hi, I'm Mario, Ana's cousin.

CECILIA: **Encantada**, Mario. También eres **del Perú**, **¿verdad?**

I'm glad to meet you, Mario. You're from Perú too, aren't you?

MARIO: No, no soy **del Perú**, **sino** de Chile. Mi papá, que es peruano, fue a Chile a estudiar y **conoció** allí a mi mamá, que es chilena, y se quedó allí.

No, I'm not from Perú, I'm from Chile. My dad, who is Peruvian, went to Chile to study, and stayed there after he met my mother, who's Chilean.

CECILIA: **¿Desde cuándo** estás aquí?

How long have you been here?

MARIO: **A ver**, llegué el 14 de este mes, **así que ya** llevo casi dos semanas aquí.

Let's see, I got here on the 14th of this month, so I've been here almost two weeks.

CECILIA: ¿Y qué te parece nuestra ciudad?

And what do you think of our city?

MARIO: Me encanta. Es preciosa. En comparación con las ciudades de mi país, me parece muy grande y espaciosa, muy verde. Y tú, ¿de qué parte eres?

I love it. It's beautiful. Compared to the cities in my country, it seems really spacious and green. And where are you from?

CECILIA: **Bueno**, nací aquí en esta ciudad. He viajado bastante y he vivido en Sudamérica, pero soy de aquí.

Well, I was born right here in this city. I've travelled quite a bit and I've lived in South America, but I'm from here.

MARIO: Viviste en Buenos Aires, ¿verdad?

You lived in Buenos Aires, right?

CECILIA: Sí. Y ¿cómo lo sabías?

Yes. How did you know?

MARIO: Porque hablas como una auténtica porteña. **Parece mentira** que seas **norteamericana**.

Because you talk like a true "Porteña." It doesn't seem possible that you're a North American.

Soy Mario

The most common way of introducing yourself or others is to use the verb **ser** plus your name or the name of the person you're introducing. You can then add something else about the person.

Hola, soy Mario.	Hi, I'm Mario.
Ella es Susana, mi esposa/novia/ amiga/hermana/mamá.	This is Susana, my wife/girlfriend/friend/ sister/mother.
Ellas son Ana, Sonia y Gladys, mis amigas/hermanas/primas.	These are Ana, Sonia, and Gladys, my friends/ sisters/cousins.
Él es Jaime, mi esposo/novio/amigo/ hermano/papá.	This is Jaime, my husband/boyfriend/friend/ brother/father.
Ellos son Miguel y Martín, mis amigos/ hermanos/primos.	These are Miguel and Martín, my friends/ brothers/cousins.

Remember to use subject pronouns only if you're changing the subject of the conversation. If it is clear whom you are talking about, leave off the subject pronoun (**yo, usted, tú, él, ella, nosotros, nosotras, ustedes, vosotros, vosotras, ellos, ellas**).

¿Eres Jaime?	Are you Jaime?
No, no **soy** Jaime.	No, I'm not Jaime.

But if someone walks into a room and says, **¿Quién es Jaime?** (*Who is Jaime?*), he would identify himself by saying, **Soy yo./Yo soy Jaime.** (*It's me./I'm Jaime.*)

Encantada

This is a nice way of saying you are delighted or charmed to meet someone. Of course, a male would say **Encantado**. You could also say:

Mucho gusto.	*I'm glad to meet you.*
Es un placer (conocerlo/conocerla).	*It's a pleasure (to meet you [male/female]).*

And if the other person says **Mucho gusto** or **Encantado** or **Es un placer** first, you can answer, **Igualmente** (*Me, too*) or **El gusto es mío** (*The pleasure is mine*).

Conocer

Conocer means *to meet someone for the first time*, and also *to know*, in the sense of *already having met* someone or *having visited* a place.

Es un placer **conocerte**.	*It's a pleasure to meet you.*
Ya **conozco** a tu hermana.	*I already know your sister.*
Desafortunadamente, no **conozco** tu país.	*Unfortunately, I've never been to your country.*

Encontrarse

To meet, in the sense of running into people you already know, is **encontrarse**.

Siempre se **encuentran** en la biblioteca.	*They always run into each other at the library.*

Encontrarse can also mean *to arrange to meet* someone somewhere.

Entonces, **nos encontramos** aquí a las seis.	*Then we'll meet here at six.*

To meet, in the sense of *having a meeting or a get together*, is **reunirse**.

Nos vamos a reunir el viernes por la tarde.	*We're going to meet on Friday afternoon.*
Hace tiempo que no **nos reunimos**.	*It's been a while since we got together.*

To know, in the sense of *being aware of information*, is **saber**.

¿Quién **sabe** la respuesta a esa pregunta?	*Who knows the answer to that question?*
La **sé** yo, Srta. Jiménez.	*I know it, Miss Jiménez.*

Llamarse

Use this verb to ask for or to tell names. The verb, **llamar**—*to call*—is used with a reflexive pronoun here, and literally means *to call oneself*. It is perfectly all right to use the alternative expression, **¿Cuál es su nombre?** (*What is your name?*), which is more like English.

Remember that a reflexive pronoun always refers to the same person as the conjugated verb.

(yo)	me _____o		(nosotros/as)	nos _____amos/emos/imos
(tú)	te _____as/es		(vosotros/as)	os _____áis/éis
(usted/él/ella)	se _____a/e		(ustedes/ellos/ellas)	se _____an/en

¿Cómo se llama usted?/¿Cuál es su nombre?	*What's your name?* (to someone older, or someone completely unfamiliar)
¿Cómo te llamas?/¿Cuál es tu nombre?	*What's your name?* (to someone obviously near your age or your social circle)

¿Cómo se llama (él/ella)?/¿Cuál es su nombre?	*What's his/her name?*
¿Cómo se llaman (ellos/ellas)?	*What are their names?*
¿Cómo se llaman (ustedes)?	*What are your names?*
¿Cómo os llamáis (vosotros/vosotras)?	*What are your names? (used only in Spain, to two or more people)*

Me llamo...

The same verb is used for telling names.

Me llamo Sara./Soy Sara./Mi nombre es Sara.	*I call myself Sara./I'm Sara./My name's Sara.*
Se llama Martín./Es Martín./Su nombre es Martín.	*He calls himself Martín./He's Martín./ His name's Martín.*
Se llama Elena./Es Elena./Su nombre es Elena.	*She calls herself Elena./She's Elena./ Her name's Elena.*
Se llaman Jaime y Martín./Son Jaime y Martín./Sus nombres son Jaime y Martín.	*They call themselves Jaime y Martín./ They're Jaime and Martín./Their names are Jaime and Martín.*
Se llaman Ana e Isabel./Son Ana e Isabel./Sus nombres son Ana e Isabel.	*They call themselves Ana and Isabel./ They're Ana and Isabel./Their names are Ana and Isabel.*

¿Verdad?

Adding this or one of the following expressions to a statement is a way of affirming that your listener agrees with you.

¿Verdad?/¿Verdad que sí?/¿No es así?/¿No?	*Right?/Isn't it?/Aren't you?*

del Perú

The names of the following countries are traditionally used with a definite article.

el Perú	la Argentina
el Ecuador	el Uruguay

Remember that **de** followed by **el** is always contracted to **del**.

Son **del** Ecuador.	*They're from Ecuador.*
Soy **de la** Argentina.	*I'm from Argentina.*

It is becoming common, however, to omit the article.

Son de Ecuador.
Soy de Argentina.

The article is always used with El Salvador, as that is part of the name of the country.

When referring to the United States, the use of **los** is optional.

Son de Estados Unidos.	*They're from the United States.*
Son de **los** Estados Unidos.	*They're from the United States.*

Sino

This is a great word for correcting a negative statement or impression. It implies *but rather* in English. First, state what isn't true; then add **sino** and give the correction.

> ¿Eres Mario? No, no soy Mario, **sino** Jaime.

> *Are you Mario? No, I'm not Mario, I'm Jaime. (I'm not Mario but rather Jaime.)*

If there is a preposition in the construction, repeat it.

> ¿Vas al cine? No, no voy al cine, **sino** al teatro.

> *Are you going to the movies? No, I'm not going to the movies, I'm going to the theater.*

If you are correcting a verb, or repeating the verb in the correction, use **sino que**.

> ¿Vas a estudiar esta noche? No, no voy a estudiar, **sino que** voy a trabajar.

> *Are you going to study tonight? No, I'm not going to study, I'm going to work.*

> ¿Salen a las cinco? No, no salimos a las cinco, **sino que** salimos a las seis.

> *Are you leaving at five? No, we're not leaving at five, we're leaving at six.*

Que y quien

Qué is used to ask the question *what*. **Quién** is used to ask the question *who* when the answer is expected to be one person. If the answer is expected to be more than one person, **quiénes** is used. To indicate more specifically which person has been mentioned, **que**—without a written accent mark—is used:

> Mi hermana que vive en Chicago viene a visitarnos este fin de semana.

> *My sister who lives in Chicago is coming to visit us this weekend.*

To further describe a person, in an appositive phrase, either **que** or **quien** (both without accent marks) can be used:

> Mi hermana, que/quien es la madre de mis sobrinas, viene a visitarnos este fin de semana.

> *My sister, who is the mother of my nieces, is coming to visit us this weekend.*

Remember that if there is a comma between the named person and *who*, you can use *quien*, but not otherwise. It's always safest to use *que*.

¿Desde cuándo... ?

To find out how long something has been going on, instead of using the present perfect tense, as in English, use the following expressions with the present or present progressive tense in Spanish.

> ¿**Desde cuándo** estudias/estás estudiando español?

> *How long have you been studying Spanish?*

> ¿**Hace cuánto tiempo que** estudias/estás estudiando español?

> *How long have you been studying Spanish?*

Or use the present tense of **llevar** + the gerund of the following verb.

> ¿Cuánto tiempo **llevas estudiando** español?

> *How long have you been studying Spanish?*

> Vivo/Estoy viviendo aquí desde febrero.

> *I've been living here since February.*

Vivo/Estoy viviendo aquí desde hace
  dos meses.
Hace dos meses que vivo/estoy viviendo } *I've been living here for two months.*
  aquí.
Llevo dos meses viviendo aquí.

Similar expressions indicate the length of time that something has not occurred.

Hace mucho tiempo que no hablo
  español. } *I haven't spoken Spanish in a long time.*
Llevo mucho tiempo sin hablar español.

Ya

Ya can mean *now* or *already*, but its meaning is usually expressed in English by rising intonation.

Llevo **ya** tres horas esperándote.   *I've been waiting for you for three hours.*
Hace **ya** veinte años que vivimos en   *We've been living here for twenty years.*
  este país.

A ver

This is used to indicate that you are making a calculation and implies "Let's see/Let me see/Let me think."

¿Hace cuánto tiempo que conoces a mi   *How long have you known my brother?*
  hermano?
A ver, nos conocimos en la escuela   *Let's see, we met in high school, so I've*
  secundaria, así que lo conozco desde   *known him for six years.*
  hace seis años.

Así que

This indicates a logical conclusion, and can be translated as *so,* with the meaning of *therefore.*

Tus padres son mis tíos, **así que** tú eres   *Your parents are my aunt and uncle, so*
  mi primo hermano.   *you're my first cousin.*

Bueno

This is often used as a lead-in to a response that requires a little explanation. In this case it does not mean *good,* but more like *Well . . .* or *Actually . . .*

No estás casada, ¿verdad?   *You're not married, are you?*
Bueno, no, pero sí estoy comprometida.   *Well, no, but I am engaged.*

Parece mentira

This expression—literally, *It seems a lie*—is better translated as *It doesn't seem possible.* If you go on to say what doesn't seem possible, add **que** + a verb in the subjunctive.
Following are examples of the subjunctive used with **parece mentira**:

Hace mucho calor. **Parece mentira** que   *It's so hot. It doesn't seem possible that*
  estemos en pleno otoño.   *we're in the middle of fall.*
El tiempo pasa rápido. **Parece mentira**   *Time goes by so fast. It doesn't seem possible*
  que ya tengas doce años.   *that you are already twelve years old.*

Norteamericano, -a

While people from the United States often refer to themselves as *Americans*, **americano** in Spanish refers to someone from any part of the Western Hemisphere. In fact, in Spain, **americano** usually refers to someone from Latin America. **Norteamericano** is someone from Canada or the United States (Mexicans are **mexicanos**), while **estadounidense** literally means *United States citizen*. It is common for people to use nicknames for certain nationalities or groups of people. For example:

porteño, -a	someone who lives in Buenos Aires, Argentina
nuyorican	someone of Puerto Rican descent who lives in New York
chicano, -a	someone of Mexican descent who lives in the southwestern United States
hispano, -a	someone from a Spanish-speaking country
latino, -a	someone from a Spanish- or Portuguese-speaking country
gringo, -a	someone from the United States, especially in Mexico; it's not exactly a compliment, but isn't necessarily offensive.

Tú/Usted/Ustedes/Vosotros

All of these mean *you*—so easy in English! The choice of **tú** or **usted** can be tricky, as different regions, even within the same country, often have different customs regarding this. **Tú** is used more freely in Spain than in Latin America, where it is generally reserved to address children or people whom you consider your social peers. There are exceptions, however, as in the case of parts of Colombia where **usted** can be used for your closest friends and family members!

A rule of thumb is to use **usted** until you are asked to please **"¡Tutéame, que no soy tan viejo!"** (*Use "tu" with me, I'm not that old!*) Also, pay attention to what the natives say, or even ask for advice if you're not sure.

The choice between **vosotros** and **ustedes** is simpler, especially in Latin America, where **vosotros** is not used, so **ustedes** is the plural of both **tú** and **usted**. In Spain, **vosotros** is the plural form of **tú**, and **ustedes** is the plural form of **usted**.

EJERCICIO

25·33

*Fill in the blanks with the appropriate forms of the verb **ser**.*

1. María _____ preciosa.

2. Yo _____ tu mejor amigo.

3. Tú y yo ya _____ viejos.

4. Tú no _____ de aquí.

5. Juan y José no _____ ingenieros.

6. Tú y Luisa _____ muy listas. [form used in Spain]

7. Tú y Luisa _____ muy listas. [form used in Latin America]

8. Víctor _____ un actor muy bueno.

Choose the most appropriate word or expression to fill in each blank.

1. Conozco a Roberto, pero no _____ el nombre de su hermano.

   conozco   encuentra   sé   se

2. ¿_____ usted a qué hora se van a reunir?

   Sabe   Conoce   Se   Encuentra

3. ¿_____ Bolivia?

   Reune   Conoces   Sabes   Sabe

4. Nos _____ en el Bistro a las seis y media.

   conocemos   sabemos   encontramos   conozco

5. Mi familia siempre _____ los domingos.

   se reúne   se encuentra   se conoce   sabe

*Answer each question with the appropriate form of **llamarse**.*

1. ¿Cómo te llamas? _____ Carolina.

2. ¿Cómo se llama tu hermano? _____ Claudio.

3. ¿Cómo os llamáis? _____ Margarita y Eva.

4. ¿Cómo se llaman ustedes? _____ Sonia y Marta.

5. ¿Cómo se llama ella? _____ Susana.

*Choose **qué, quién, quiénes, que,** or **quien** to complete the following sentences.*

1. Quiero invitar a la chica _____ vive en la esquina.

2. ¿_____ es el profesor _____ viene de España?

3. El profesor, _____ acaba de mudarse a nuestra vecindad, se llama Juan Díaz.

4. ¿_____ son los actores que te gustan más?

5. ¿_____ es esto?

Answer each question in a complete sentence.

1. ¿Hace cuánto tiempo que viven ustedes en este país? (cuatro años)

   _____

2. ¿Desde cuándo trabajan ustedes juntos? (el once de febrero)

   _____

3. ¿Cuánto tiempo llevas nadando? (treinta minutos)

   _____

4. ¿Hace cuánto tiempo que no ve a su familia? (tres meses)

   _____

5. ¿Cuánto tiempo llevas sin fumar? (dos semanas)

   _____

Circle the most appropriate word or expression for the blank space.

1. ¿Quién es esa chica? _____ mi amiga.

   Ella es   Ellas son   Es   Eres

2. ¿Cómo se llaman tus hermanos? _____ Germán y Javier.

   Te llaman   Se llaman   Su nombre es   Lo llamo

3. ¿Cómo te llamas? _____ Pepe.

   Mi nombre es   Me llama   Se llama

4. Amiga, te presento a mi primo, Juan. _____.

   Encantada   Me gustas mucho   Encantado   El gusto es mío

5. ¿_____? Somos de la Argentina.

   Dónde estás   De dónde es   De dónde son   Dónde es

6. Tú eres de aquí, ¿_____?

   desde cuándo   así que   no es así   ya

7. No soy de aquí _____ México.

   pero   pero de   sino   sino de

8. Es tu novio, ¿verdad? No, no es mi novio _____ mi esposo.

   pero   pero es   sino que   sino

9. ¿Hace cuánto tiempo que estudias español? _____ cuatro años _____ español.

Hace... estudio   Estudio... el   Llevo... estudiando   Desde... estudiando

10. Vivimos aquí desde hace veinte años. Sí, _____.

parece mentira   a ver   ya   mucho gusto

EJERCICIO
25·39

Match the questions or statements in the left column with the most appropriate responses in the right column.

1. _____ ¿De dónde son ustedes?

2. _____ ¿Por qué no te gusta esta película?

3. _____ Tu hermano trabaja aquí también, ¿verdad?

4. _____ Hace ya veinte años que estamos casados.

5. _____ ¿Cómo te llamas?

6. _____ Soy Marcos Jiménez.

7. _____ ¿Qué te parece este vestido?

8. _____ ¿Desde cuándo vives aquí?

9. _____ ¿De dónde es su esposo?

10. _____ Tu hermana vive aquí, ¿no es así?

a. Sí, vive aquí.

b. Es de Bolivia.

c. No, no trabaja, sino que estudia.

d. Es muy feo.

e. Somos estadounidenses.

f. A ver. Ya llevo seis meses viviendo aquí.

g. Parece mentira.

h. Soy Marcos Jiménez.

i. Es un placer.

j. Bueno, me parece un poco violenta.

EJERCICIO
25·40

Fill in each blank with the present subjunctive form of the verb indicated.

1. Parece mentira que (ser, nosotros) _____ vecinos.

2. Parece mentira que (estar, tú) _____ aquí.

3. Parece mentira que (tener, él) _____ dieciséis años.

4. Parece mentira que (hacer, el tiempo) _____ 80 grados.

5. Parece mentira que (trabajar, tú y yo) _____ juntos.

6. Parece mentira que (correr, nuestros esposos) _____ el maratón.

7. Parece mentira que (escribir, ella) _____ una carta tan larga.

8. Parece mentira que (pensar, ustedes) _____ así.

9. Parece mentira que (conocer, vosotras) _____ a mi papá.

10. Parece mentira que (dormir, ellos) _____ durante todo el día.

Choose the most appropriate expression for each blank space.

1. No tenemos dinero, _____ no podemos comprar flores.

   sino   a ver   así que   sino que

2. Francisco no es mi primo, _____ mi novio.

   sino   sino que   no es así   así que

3. ¿Por qué te vas? _____, tengo que irme porque mis padres me están esperando.

   A ver   Parece mentira   Bueno   Ya

4. Parece mentira que _____ aquí.

   estás   eres   son   estén

¿Cómo se dice en español? *Translate each sentence into Spanish.*

1. What are your names?

   _____

2. You're from Ecuador, right?

   _____

3. No, we're not from Ecuador, we're from El Salvador.

   _____

4. How long have you been here?

   _____

5. We've been living here for two years.

   _____

6. You know our sister, right?

   _____

7. It doesn't seem possible that I don't know her.

   _____

Write a dialogue in which you introduce yourself and some friends to a new neighbor. Be sure to include as many of the new expressions as possible. Ask a Spanish speaker if your dialogue needs any corrections.

_____

_____

_____

_____

_____

_____

_____

_____

Conversation: Running into a friend

ALEJANDRA: Hola, amiga, **¿qué tal?** **(besos)**

Hi, how are you? (kisses)

GABRIELA: Todo bien, gracias. Y tú, ¿cómo va todo?

Everything's fine, thanks. How's everything with you?

ALEJANDRA: Bien. Estoy ocupada, como siempre. Pero, ¿qué te parece un **cafecito?**

Good. I'm busy, as usual. But how about a cup of coffee?

GABRIELA: Encantada. Hace tiempo que no hablamos. Ahora, **cuéntame, ¿qué hay de nuevo?**

I'd love that. It's been a while since we've talked. Now, tell me, what's new?

ALEJANDRA: Bueno, hay mucho que contar. Primero, he aceptado un nuevo trabajo.

Well, there's a lot to tell. First, I've just accepted a new job.

GABRIELA: **¿En serio?** ¿Dónde? ¿Qué vas a hacer?

Really? Where? What are you going to do?

ALEJANDRA: Es fantástico. Voy a ser profesora de matemáticas en una escuela de arte cerca de aquí, que **se dedica** a preparar sus alumnos para una carrera en diseño interior, diseño de ropa, dibujo—cualquier tipo de arte comercial.

It's wonderful. I'm going to be a math teacher at an art school near here that prepares students for a career in interior design, fashion design, drawing—any kind of commercial art.

GABRIELA: ¿Matemáticas? ¿En una escuela de arte?

Math? At an art school?

ALEJANDRA: Así es, **aunque** suene raro. Los alumnos, **aunque** son muy inteligentes y han enfocado bien sus estudios, necesitan tener una base en matemáticas, **pues** casi todos algún día tendrán su propio negocio.	That's right, even though it sounds odd. The students, even though they're smart and focused on their studies, need basic math—almost all of them will have their own business one day.
GABRIELA: Claro, ya entiendo. **¡Qué bueno!** Me parece perfecto para ti—y para tus futuros alumnos. **Fíjate** que yo también tengo una noticia emocionante.	Of course, now I get it. That's great! I think it's perfect for you—and for your future students. Actually, I have exciting news, too.
ALEJANDRA: Ah, ¿sí? Pero, **¡cuéntame!**	Yeah? Tell me about it!
GABRIELA: **Acabo de** comprarme un condominio en la ciudad. **Me mudo** el próximo lunes.	I just bought a condo in the city. I'm moving next Monday.
ALEJANDRA: **¡Qué bueno!** ¿Dónde está? ¿Cómo es?	That's great! Where is it? What's it like?
GABRIELA: Está en el centro, cerca de todo. Podré ir andando de compras, a los restaurantes, **incluso** al trabajo. El apartamento no es muy grande, pero está en un edificio antiguo que han convertido en modernos apartamentos. Está muy bien planeado. ¡Estoy contentísima!	It's downtown, near everything. I'll be able to walk to the shops, restaurants, even to work. The apartment isn't very big, but it's in an old building that they've converted to modern units. It's very well designed. I'm just thrilled.
ALEJANDRA: ¡Qué suerte tenemos las dos! Mira, tendremos que vernos con más frecuencia, para hablar de nuestra nueva vida. (besos) **¡Chao**, amiga! Nos vemos pronto.	We're both lucky. Look, we have to see each other more often, to talk about our new lives. Bye, I'll see you soon. (kisses)

Besos

When women greet or say good-bye to a friend, male or female, they usually touch right cheeks and "kiss the air"; in Spain, this is done with both cheeks, right first, then left. Men greet each other with a handshake or an **abrazo**: with right cheeks facing, but not touching, they give each other a pat on the back.

¿Qué tal?

This is another way of saying **¿Cómo está?**, *How are you?* You may also hear **¿Quiúbole?/¿Qué hubo?/¿Quiú?**, which are more informal, like *What's up?* The answer is usually **Bien, gracias, ¿y usted?/¿y tú?**

¿Qué hay de nuevo?

This is a way to ask *What's new?* Other expressions for the same purpose are:

¿Qué noticias tienes?	What's new?
¿Qué hay de tu vida?	What's new?

Cafecito

It is common, more in some areas than others, and sometimes as a characteristic of an individual's speech, to add **-it** before the final **o** or **a** to nouns or adjectives. This **-ito** or **-ita** indicates that the objects or people described are small, unimportant, cute, ridiculous, dear, slightly naughty or illegal, just informal, or something else! Obviously, the meaning denoted can be tricky, so it's best to learn the ropes while listening to others.

casita	*a small house/cabin/cottage*
perrito	*small dog/puppy*
ojitos	*beautiful eyes*
pequeñito, -a	*tiny*
bajito, -a	*very short*

When the noun or adjective ends in an **e**, an **n**, or an **r**, **-cito** is added instead.

cafecito	*a quick cup of coffee*
vallecito	*a little valley*
rinconcito	*an intimate corner*
mujercita	*a small woman/an adolescent girl*

The ending **-ecito** is used with one-syllable words and with words with two vowels in the stem.

redecita	*a small net*
pececito	*a little fish*
pueblecito	*a small town*

Also, there are automatic spelling changes if the original word ends with the following letters.

co/ca	quito/quita	chico → chiquito	chica → chiquita
go/ga	guito/guita	luego → lueguito	
guo/gua	güito/güita		agua → agüita
zo/za	cito/cita		plaza → placita

There are some exceptions to these guidelines, for example:

mamacita/mamita	*mommy*
papacito/papito	*daddy*
Carlitos	*little Carlos*

Cuéntame

This is the **tú** command form of the verb **contar**, and it means *Tell me all about it.* You could also use **dime** from **decir**.

¿En serio?

This is a way to react to something surprising, equivalent to *Seriously?* Other ways to express this include:

¿De verdad?	*Really?*
¿De veras?	*Is that so?*
¿Sí?	*Are you sure?*
¡No!	*No way!*
¡No me lo puedo creer!	*I can't believe it!*
¡Increíble!	*Unbelievable!*

Dedicarse

This verb, used with reflexive pronouns, indicates the purpose of an institution or organization.

La organización **se dedica** a enseñar a leer a los adultos analfabetos.	*The organization teaches illiterate adults to read.*

It is also used to tell what someone devotes a lot of time to.

Esa mujer **se dedica** a mantener limpia su casa.	*That woman spends her life cleaning her house.*

And it is the verb used to ask what someone does for a living.

¿A qué **se dedica** su esposo?	*What does her husband do?*
¿A qué **te dedicas**?	*What do you do?*

But instead of using **dedicarse** in the answer, use the verb **ser**. Note that in telling what somebody does for a living, you do not use an article.

Es ingeniero.	*He's an engineer.*
Soy estudiante.	*I'm a student.*

However, if you want to tell *how* someone does his job by adding an adjective, you do need the article.

Es un ingeniero bueno.	*He's a good engineer.*
Soy una estudiante seria.	*I'm a serious student.*

Aunque

Aunque means *even though/although*. It is followed by a verb in the indicative if the information that it introduces is new to the listener.

Voy a prepararte algo de comer, **aunque** no soy experto en la cocina.	*I'm going to make you something to eat, although I'm no expert in the kitchen.*

Aunque is followed by a verb in the subjunctive when the information it introduces is already known by the listener.

Aunque no seas experto en la cocina, el sándwich que me preparaste estuvo muy rico.	*Although you're not an expert in the kitchen, the sandwich you made for me was delicious.*

Pues

Pues has a number of different meanings. One of them is to indicate a reasoning for what was previously said. You could use **porque** instead here.

Lleva el paraguas—**pues** parece que va a llover.	*Take your umbrella—it looks like it's going to rain.*
Voy a salir temprano—**pues** no me siento bien.	*I'm leaving early—I feel a little sick.*

Claro

This indicates that you agree with something, or that it goes without saying, like *of course*.

¿Me ayudas con estos paquetes?	*Will you help me with these packages?*
¡Claro (que sí)! Con mucho gusto.	*Of course! I'll be glad to.*

¿Vas a comprar esta casa?   *Are you going to buy this house?*
¡**Claro**! Es perfecta para mí.   *Of course! It's perfect for me.*

¡Qué bueno!

This indicates that you are happy with the news, either for yourself or for somebody else.

Me acaban de aceptar en la Facultad   *I just got accepted to law school.*
    de Leyes.
¡**Qué bueno**!   *That's great!*

You could also use:

¡Fantástico!   *Fantastic!*
¡Super!   *Great!*
¡Fenomenal!   *Wonderful!*
¡Qué bien!   *That's terrific!*

Fíjate que

This expression is used to introduce information that you think may slightly surprise your listeners, or at least get their attention. You could alternatively use **Imagínate que**.

¡Vamos a comer!   *Let's go eat!*
Fíjate que no tengo hambre.   *Actually I'm not hungry.*

Ese chico es guapo pero, ¿es simpático?   *That boy is cute, but is he nice?*
Imagínate que sí!   *He actually is!*

¡**Fíjate/Imagínate** que me caso en   *Just imagine—I'm getting married in*
    septiembre!   *September!*

Acabar de

When this verb is conjugated, it indicates that the subject has recently done something. This is expressed in English as *to have just*.

Acabo de hablar con mi mamá.   *I (have) just talked to my mom.*
Acabamos de ver esa película.   *We just saw that movie./We have just seen*
           that movie.

No acabar de indicates that something *just seems impossible*.

No acabo de entender lo que escribe   *I just don't understand what this author*
    este autor.   *writes.*

Mudarse

This verb, used with reflexive pronouns, means *to move* (to a new residence). (In Spain, it is more common to use **trasladarse** for this purpose.)

El próximo mes **nos mudamos** a otro   *Next month we're moving to another state.*
    estado.

Moverse, used with a reflexive pronoun, means *to move your body.*

No me gusta bailar porque no sé
  moverme.

*I don't like to dance because I don't know
  how to do the movements.*

Cada vez que intento sacar una foto,
  ¡te mueves!

*Every time I try to take a photograph,
  you move!*

Mover, without a reflexive pronoun, means *to move a part of your body.*

Trata de **mover** los dedos.

Try to move your fingers.

To express moving something from one place to another, use **poner**.

Vamos a **poner** el sofá allí.

We're going to move the sofa over there.

Incluso

Incluso indicates that you are including something or someone in a category that seems surprising.

Todos, **incluso** mi papá, bailamos en
  la fiesta.

*Everybody, including/even my dad, danced
  at the party.*

Chao

This is a common way of saying good-bye. It can also be spelled the Italian way, **ciao**. Or you could say any of the following:

Hasta luego.   *See you later.*
Hasta pronto/prontito.   *See you soon/very soon.*
Nos vemos.   *See you.*
Cuídate.   *Take care.*

 And in Mexico, *Bye* is very common.

EJERCICIO
25·44

Fill in the blanks with appropriate words or phrases.

1. ¿Cómo estás? _____ bien.

2. ¿Cómo está tu mamá? _____ mejor, gracias.

3. Y tus hermanos, ¿cómo _____?

4. ¿Cómo están ustedes? _____ muy cansados.

5. Mi amiga tiene que ir al hospital, pues _____ _____.

6. Los muchachos quieren descansar, pues _____ _____.

7. Hoy tengo una fiesta y _____ _____.

8. Tenemos un examen mañana, así que _____ _____.

Fill in the blanks with the correct words or phrases.

1. Su mamá _____ dedica a preparar comida sana.

2. ¿A qué _____ dedicas?

3. ¿A qué _____ dedican ustedes?

4. Las maestras se _____ a enseñar a los niños.

5. _____ mudamos en junio.

6. ¿Por qué te mud_____?

7. Me mud_____ porque no estoy contenta aquí.

8. ¿Cuándo _____ mud_____ tu compañero de cuarto?

Give the following commands.

To a good friend:

1. Tell me   _____

2. Don't tell me   _____

3. Listen!   _____

4. Don't move!   _____

To your boss:

5. Tell him . . .   _____

6. Write a letter   _____

To three friends:

7. Wait for me.   _____

8. Don't forget!   _____

Rewrite each word, adding **-ito, -ita, -cito,** *or* **-cita,** *as appropriate. Make spelling changes as necessary.*

1. suave _____   *very soft*

2. chica _____   *very small*

3. loco _____   *a little crazy*

4. boca _____   *a small mouth*

5. animal _____   *a small animal*

6. casa _____   *a small house*

7. pájaro _____   *a small bird*

8. flor _____   *a small flower*

9. Diego _____   *little Diego*

10. Carmen _____   *little Carmen*

Choose the most appropriate responses.

1. ¿Qué tal? _____

   ¡Claro!   Bien.   ¿En serio?   ¡Qué bien!

2. ¿Qué hay de nuevo? _____

   Pues.   ¡Qué bueno!   Acabo de comprar   Cuéntame.
                 un carro.

3. Mañana me mudo. _____

   ¿En serio?   Claro.   Somos amigos.   Está peor.

4. Acabo de comprar un carro. _____

   ¡Qué bueno!   Pues.   Bueno.   ¡Claro!

5. ¿Te gusta mi nuevo carro? _____

   ¡Bueno!   ¡Claro!   ¡Fíjate!   Nos vemos.

Match the situation in the column on the left with an expression in the column on the right.

1. _____ You run into a girlfriend at the mall.   a. pues

2. _____ You ask your friend how she is.   b. incluso

3. _____ You tell what you have just done.   c. ¿Qué tal?

4. _____ You are about to tell your friend something surprising.   d. ¿Qué hay de nuevo?

5. _____ You indicate that something is true in spite of another fact.   e. ¡Fantástico!

6. _____ You include someone in an unusual category.   f. ¡Cuéntame!

7. _____ You explain why a situation exists.   g. Fíjate que...

8. _____ You ask about your friend's news.   h. (Besos)

9. _____ Your friend has told you something unbelievable.   i. Acabo de...

10. _____ You want to know the whole story.   j. aunque...

11. _____ You indicate that you are happy about your friend's news.   k. ¿De verdad?

12. _____ You indicate that there's no question about it.   l. ¡Claro!

¿Cómo se dice en español? *Translate each sentence into Spanish.*

1. What does your boyfriend do?

_____

2. He's a teacher.

_____

3. He's an excellent teacher.

_____

4. Elena spends all her time cleaning the house.

_____

5. Please don't move away.

_____

6. Don't move! I want to take a picture of you.

_____

7. We (have) just finished the exam.

_____

8. What did you just say?

_____

9. Just imagine! I'm moving next week.

_____

Complete each of the following sentences with the verb in the present indicative, indicating that what you write is new information to your reader.

1. Quiero invitar a ese chico a la fiesta aunque *he doesn't know my other friends.*

_____

2. No voy a estudiar informática este semestre aunque *the teacher is very good.*

_____

3. Carlos va a ver esa película aunque *he's already seen it twice.*

_____

4. Nos mudamos a Springfield aunque *we love this city.*

_____

5. Vivo en una ciudad grande aunque *I prefer small towns.*

_____

Complete each of the following sentences with the verb in the present subjunctive, indicating that what you write is information already known by your reader.

1. Quiero invitar a ese chico a la fiesta aunque *he doesn't attend our school.*

_____

2. No voy a estudiar informática este semestre aunque *the teacher is excellent.*

_____

3. Carlos va a ver esa película aunque *nobody wants to go with him.*

_____

4. Nos mudamos a Springfield aunque *it's a long way from here.*

_____

5. Vivo en una ciudad grande aunque *there's more traffic here than in a small town.*

_____

EJERCICIO
25·53

Write a conversation between yourself and a friend when you run into each other unexpectedly. Use as many as possible of the expressions that are new to you. Ask a Spanish-speaking friend to read and correct it for you.

_____

_____

_____

_____

_____

_____

_____

Conversation: Selecting a company officer

JAVIER: Hoy estamos aquí para hablar de la selección del nuevo director del Departamento de Información y Reclamaciones. Como bien saben ustedes, **actualmente** hay dos candidatas, Marta Gutiérrez e Yvonne Piñeiro. Primero hablaremos de Marta. ¿Qué **opinan** ustedes de su candidatura?

We're here today to talk about the selection of a new director for the Customer Service Department. As you know, at present there are two candidates, Marta Gutiérrez and Yvonne Piñeiro. First, we'll talk about Marta. What do you think of her candidacy?

BELÉN: Yo creo que Marta es la persona perfecta para este puesto. Lleva ya veinte años trabajando aquí, **de modo que** conoce bien los negocios de la empresa. Es una persona formal y seria y **además**, se lleva bien con todos los empleados.

Marta seems to me to be the perfect person for this position. She's been with the company for twenty years, so she knows the business well. She's conservative and serious, plus she gets along well with all the employees.

CATI: Bueno, **para mí**, si ella es la nueva directora, nada cambiará. Es decir, no veríamos ninguna idea nueva, **por el contrario**, seguiríamos aplicando los mismos programas de siempre. **Es más**, perderíamos clientes que tenemos, simplemente porque nuestros competidores tienen gente dinámica y programas innovadores.

DAVID: Yo estoy de acuerdo con Cati. **Por una parte**, Marta es demasiado conservadora **y por otra**, no despertaría el entusiasmo de los empleados.

JAVIER: Bien. Ahora díganme qué piensan de Yvonne para este puesto.

BELÉN: Miren ustedes, si le damos este puesto a Yvonne, sería un desastre para la empresa. En primer lugar, **aunque** ella **tenga** un título de una universidad prestigiosa, no tiene la experiencia necesaria para un puesto tan importante. **Además**, no la conocemos bien, pues sólo trabaja aquí desde febrero de este año. Y **por si fuera poco**, bien saben ustedes que la **despidieron** de su trabajo anterior.

CATI: **Por cierto**, he oído que sus colegas piensan que es bastante presumida, que se cree la reina de la oficina. No es muy popular, **que digamos**, entre los empleados. No creo que la acepten como jefa.

DAVID: Pues, como la nominé yo, les tengo que decir que la veo como una persona muy inteligente y competente. No obstante, reconozco que le falta experiencia. Y ahora que me dicen que su personalidad podría causar fricciones entre los empleados, apoyaré su decisión en este caso.

JAVIER: **Evidentemente** no hemos encontrado todavía **la persona indicada** para este puesto. Es posible que tengamos que buscar fuera de la empresa, algo que **en el fondo** no quisiera hacer. Nos reuniremos aquí mañana a la misma hora. Esperaré sus propuestas—¡y **que** sean más esperanzadoras!

Well, in my opinion, if she becomes director, nothing will change. I mean, we wouldn't see any new ideas— just the opposite—we'd keep on implementing the same programs as always. Even more than that, we'd lose our current customer base, simply because our competitors have enthusiastic new people and innovative programs

I agree with Cati. In the first place, Marta is too conservative, and furthermore, she wouldn't inspire any enthusiasm among the employees.

OK. Now tell me what you think of Yvonne for this position.

Look, if we give the job to Yvonne, it will be a disaster for the company. In the first place, even though she has a fancy degree, she doesn't have the experience necessary for such an important job. Besides, we don't even know her very well, I mean, she's only been here since last February. And to top it all off, you all know that she was fired from her last job.

As a matter of fact, I've heard that her coworkers think she's a bit too sure of herself, that she thinks she's the queen of the office. She's not exactly popular with the other employees. I don't think they'll be happy with her as the boss.

Well, since I put her name up, I have to say that I see her as a very bright and competent person. But I do recognize that she lacks experience. And now that you tell me that her personality could cause friction among the employees, then I'll go along with your decision in this case.

Obviously we haven't found the ideal person for this position yet. We may have to look outside the company, which I don't particularly want to do. We'll meet here tomorrow at the same time. I'll expect your suggestions—and they'd better be more promising!

Actualmente

This is a true **falso amigo**, as it does not mean *actually*, but rather *right now*, *at the moment*, or *currently*.

Actualmente, tenemos ciento setenta y cinco empleados.	*Currently, we have a hundred and seventy-five employees.*

Opinar que

Opinar que means *to be of the opinion that*.

Opino que no es una buena idea.	*In my opinion, it's not a good idea.*

Another way to express an opinion is by introducing it with **para** + personal pronoun: **mí/ti/usted/él/ella/nosotros, -as/vosotros, -as/ellos, -as**.

Para mí, no es una buena idea.	*In my opinion, it's not a good idea.*

You could also use **pensar que** or **creer que**.

Pienso que/Creo que es una buena candidata.	*I think she's a good candidate.*

If you use either of these expressions after **no**, the next verb should be in the subjunctive.

No pienso/No creo que **sea** una buena candidata.	*I don't think she's a good candidate.*

De modo que

De modo que is an expression that means *so much so, that*.

Tenía frío, **de modo que** me puse un suéter.	*I was cold, so I put a sweater on./I was so cold that I put a sweater on.*
Era un tipo bastante estudioso, **de modo que** quiso ir a una universidad prestigiosa.	*He was a pretty studious fellow, so he wanted to go to a prestigious university.*

Por una parte... y por otra

This combination is a common way to give two reasons to back up your point. It can be translated as *for one thing . . . and for another* or *in the first place . . . and furthermore/also*.

Debemos ascenderlo. **Por una parte,** lleva años trabajando aquí **y por otra,** es el sobrino del presidente de la empresa.	*We have to promote him. For one thing, he's been working here for years, and for another—he's the nephew of the president of the company.*

Además

This word is used to introduce additional information that helps get a point across. It is usually translated as *plus, in addition,* or *besides*.

Quiero contratarlo. Es inteligente, preparado y **además,** muy trabajador.	*I want to hire him. He's smart, educated, and, in addition, a hard worker.*

No quiero ver esa película. Tiene mucha violencia, es larga y **además,** no tiene ningún actor conocido.

I don't want to see that movie. It has a lot of violence, it's long, and besides, it doesn't have a single well-known actor.

Es más

Es más is used to add information to an argument that is more important than the previous information.

Tengo muchas ganas de ver la película. Es una comedia romántica y tiene mi actor favorito. **Es más,** fue nominada para un Óscar.

I really want to see the movie. It's a romantic comedy and it has my favorite actor. Plus, it was nominated for an Oscar.

Por si fuera poco

This expression introduces the final, and strongest, reason to support an argument. It can be used for either a positive or a negative argument.

Voy a aceptar el puesto. El trabajo es interesante, paga bien y **por si fuera poco,** me darán seis semanas de vacaciones al año.

I'm going to take the position. The work is interesting, it pays well, and as if that weren't enough, they'll give me six weeks of vacation every year.

In Spain it is also common to use **encima** for the same purposes.

El trabajo es interesante y paga bien. **Encima,** ¡es en París!

The work is interesting and it pays well. To top it all off—it's in Paris!

To introduce a superlative like this for a negative argument, you can use **para colmo.**

Él no es un caballero, que digamos. Llegó tarde para la cita, no se disculpó, pasó todo el tiempo hablando por su celular y **para colmo,** ni se ofreció para llevarme a mi casa después de la fiesta.

He's not exactly a gentleman. He was late for the date, he didn't apologize, he spent the whole time talking on his cell, and to top it all off, he didn't even offer to take me home after the party.

Por el contrario

This expression indicates that what follows is the opposite of what was said before.

No es un buen jugador, **por el contrario,** ni sabe las reglas del juego.

He's not a good player—just the opposite, he doesn't even know the rules of the game.

Bien

Bien is used here to mean *OK* or *understood*—as an acknowledgement of what was previously said. In Spain, **vale** is often used instead.

La decisión está hecha. Ya no hay nada más que hacer.
Bien/Vale. Vámonos, entonces.

The decision is made. Nothing else can be done.

OK. Then let's go.

En primer lugar

En primer lugar introduces a first reason to support an argument, like *in the first place*, or *first of all*.

No voy a quedarme aquí. **En primer lugar,** no hay trabajo para mí aquí.

I'm not staying here. In the first place, there's no work for me here.

Aunque

Remember that **aunque**, which means *even though/although*, is followed by the subjunctive when it introduces information that is already known to the listeners.

Aunque no haya trabajo aquí para ti, yo te puedo mantener.

Although there's no work for you here, I can support you.

Aunque is followed by the indicative when the information is news to the listeners.

Aunque te agradezco la oferta, que es muy generosa, voy a volver a la ciudad.

Although I appreciate your offer, which is very generous, I'm going back to the city.

Ni

This word means *not even*, to point out an unusual example.

Y ¿qué va a hacer José?
Ni José sabe la respuesta a esa pregunta.

So what's José going to do?
Not even José knows the answer to that question.

Ni siquiera can be used with the same meaning.

Ni siquiera José sabe la respuesta.

Not even José knows the answer.

Ni... ni means *neither . . . nor*.

Ni Susana ni su hermana aparecieron en la fiesta.

Neither Susana nor her sister showed up at the party.

Despedir

When used without a reflexive pronoun, this verb means *to fire/let go* (from a job). An alternative verb is **correr**, but this is more like *to kick out*—not only from a job, but also from a place.

Me despidieron por faltar tantos días cuando estaba enfermo.
Y ¿qué haces tú por aquí?
Me corrió Lisa.

They fired me for missing so many days when I was sick.
And what are you doing here?
Lisa kicked me out.

Despedirse, used with a reflexive pronoun, means *to say good-bye*.

Ahora tengo que **despedirme** de ti.
Me sentí muy triste cuando **nos despedimos.**

Now I have to say good-bye to you.
I felt really sad when we said good-bye.

Por cierto

Por cierto is used when you want to insert new information about the topic into the conversation.

Vamos a San Juan para el descanso de primavera.	*We're going to San Juan for spring break.*
Por cierto, yo fui allá el año pasado, y me encantó.	*As a matter of fact, I went there last year, and I loved it.*

Creerse

Creerse, used with a reflexive pronoun, indicates that someone is a little *stuck* on himself or herself.

Ella es simpática, pero su hermano **se cree** mucho.	*She's nice, but her brother is really conceited.*
Ese tipo **se cree** irresistible para las mujeres.	*That guy thinks he's God's gift to women.*

Que digamos

This expression can be inserted after a negative statement to mean *not exactly* in a sarcastic way. It could also be translated as *you might say that*.

Esa profesora no es un genio, **que digamos.**	*That teacher isn't exactly a genius./You might say that that teacher is no genius.*

No obstante

No obstante is an expression that the obstacle to a conclusion that was just stated has been overcome. It is usually translated as *nevertheless* or *still*.

Hacía mal tiempo y llovía durante todo el trayecto. **No obstante,** llegamos a tiempo.	*The weather was awful and it rained throughout the whole trip. Nevertheless, we made it on time.*

Faltar

Faltar (like **gustar**), when used with an indirect object pronoun, indicates *what is lacking to someone*. It is better translated as *to need* or *to not have what's necessary*.

No puedo continuar estudiando, pues **me falta** el dinero.	*I can't keep on studying—I don't have the money (the money is lacking to me).*

Hacerle falta a uno is used in the same way, with the same meaning.

Me hace falta el dinero necesario para seguir estudiando.	*I don't have the money I need to keep on studying.*

Faltar without an indirect object is used to indicate a period of time or an amount of something needed to make up a whole entity.

No podemos participar en el partido, pues **faltan** tres jugadores.	*We can't play the game—we need three more players.*
Tenemos que seguir luchando. Sólo **faltan** dos semanas para las elecciones.	*We have to keep working. There are only two weeks left until the election.*

Evidentemente

Evidentemente is a little bit of a **falso amigo**, as its meaning is closer to *obviously* than *evidently*.

Faltan dos jugadores, así que no vamos a poder jugar.	*We're lacking two players, so we're not going to be able to play.*
¡Evidentemente!	*Obviously!*

Evidently is better translated as **por lo visto**.

Por lo visto, Carlos y Sergio no van a aparecer.	*Evidently, Carlos and Sergio aren't going to show up.*

La persona indicada

La persona indicada is a way of saying *the ideal person for a specific purpose*. It could also be **la mujer indicada**, **el hombre indicado**, **el profesor indicado**, and so on.

El pianista tiene mucha paciencia. Parece ser **el maestro indicado** para mi hijo.	*The pianist is very patient. He seems to be the ideal teacher for my son.*

This could also refer to an object or a place that is perfect for a specific purpose.

Este club es muy elegante. Creo que es **el lugar indicado** para la recepción.	*This club is so elegant. I think it's the perfect place for the reception.*

Es posible que

Es posible que as well as **es probable que** are followed by a verb in the subjunctive.

Es posible que llueva mañana.	*It might rain tomorrow.*
Es probable que llueva mucho este mes.	*It will probably rain a lot this month.*

En el fondo

En el fondo can be translated as *basically*, *as a matter of principle*, or as *down deep*, when it refers to a gut feeling.

En el fondo, no quisiera viajar mucho en el trabajo porque tengo niños pequeños.	*Basically, I'd rather not travel a lot in my job because I have small children.*
En el fondo, creo que es el hombre indicado para ti.	*Down deep, I think he's the right man for you.*

¡Que... !

An expression with **que...** plus a verb in the subjunctive is often used as a final blessing or warning.

Que le vaya bien.	*May all go well with you.*
Que tenga un buen día.	*Have a nice day.*
Que la pases bien./**Que te diviertas.**	*Have a good time.*
¡Que encuentres trabajo!	*I hope you get a job!*

Circle the correct verb to complete each sentence.

1. Ahora tenemos que _____.

   despedir   despedirnos

2. Como Pablo no trabaja bien, lo tenemos que _____.

   despedir   despedirse

3. Él es muy presumido, _____ mucho.

   cree   se cree

4. Él es muy presumido, _____ que es el único chico guapo en toda la escuela.

   cree   se cree

5. No puedo terminar la tesis. _____ el tiempo para hacer la investigación.

   Me falta   Falta

6. Es muy tarde para estudiar. _____ una hora para el examen.

   Me falta   Falta

Circle the most appropriate expression for each blank.

1. Creo que es muy listo y _____, muy simpático.

   no obstante   además   por una parte   es más

2. Sólo queda un minuto en el partido. _____, vamos a ganar.

   Por cierto   Aunque   Es más   Evidentemente

3. El curso fue muy difícil para él, _____, pasó con una buena nota.

   no obstante   por el contrario   por lo visto   de modo que

4. El curso fue muy difícil para él, _____ no sacó una buena nota.

   no obstante   por el contrario   por lo visto   de modo que

5. En matemáticas ella es un desastre, pues _____ sabe sumar y restar.

   por cierto   evidentemente   aunque   ni

6. Él no es un experto, _____, pues no sabía solucionar el problema.

   que digamos   no obstante   de modo que   por otra parte

7. _____, es un experto _____, está listo para trabajar.

   por una parte... y por otra   ni... ni

8. _____ es un experto, _____ está listo para trabajar.

    por una parte... y por otra   ni... ni

9. Vamos a contratarla, _____ no tenga experiencia.

    aunque   por el contrario   además   es más

EJERCICIO 25·56

Fill in each blank with the most appropriate of the following expressions.

actualmente   de modo que   es más   por el contrario   no obstante

1. Todos estamos muy impresionados con la nueva candidata, _____ le vamos a ofrecer el puesto.

2. Estamos muy impresionados con la nueva candidata, _____, no le vamos a ofrecer el puesto.

3. Yo lo apoyo incondicionalmente. Es un hombre responsable y honrado. _____, es mi mejor amigo.

4. Yo no quiero ascenderlo, _____, creo que lo deberíamos despedir.

5. Ese señor es _____ el presidente de la empresa, pero se va a jubilar *(retire)* el próximo mes.

EJERCICIO 25·57

¿Qué opinas de la dieta vegetariana? *Complete the following sentences with your opinion. Ask a Spanish-speaking friend to read your answers.*

1. Opino que _____.

2. No pienso que _____.

3. Creo que _____.

4. Para mí, _____.

¿Cómo se dice en español? *Translate the following sentences into Spanish.*

1. Basically, I think it's a mistake.

   _____

2. We think he's the perfect person for the job.

   _____

3. To be honest with you, I don't think she's the girl for you.

   _____

4. I don't know anybody in this city, I don't have a job or a place to live, and as if that weren't enough, I don't speak the language.

   _____

   _____

5. This isn't exactly the best job in the world.

   _____

6. Have a good day!

   _____

Complete the following sentences in your own words, thinking of a topic about which you care a lot. Do not worry about the order of the sentences at this point, but rather think of them as individual sentences.

1. Opino que _____.

2. Para mí, _____.

3. Por una parte, _____.

4. y por otra, _____.

5. Además, _____.

6. Es más, _____.

7. Aunque _____.

8. Por cierto, _____.

9. No obstante, _____.

10. Por lo visto, _____.

11. Evidentemente, _____.

12. Por el contrario, _____.

13. Ni _____, ni _____.

14. _____ de modo que _____.

EJERCICIO
25·60

Now arrange at least eight of your sentences from Exercise 25-59 into a cohesive paragraph, placing them in a logical order. Make a convincing argument for your cause! Ask a Spanish speaker to comment on the result.

_____

_____

_____

_____

_____

_____

_____

_____

Problem solver

This chapter tackles common problems that students of Spanish experience on their way to mastering the language.

Social conventions

The best and most traditional place to begin when introducing the topic of forms of address is with the well-known distinction of the use of the two singular forms of address, **tú** and **usted**, commonly abbreviated **Ud.**, and sometimes as **Vd.** As you already know, the use of the **tú** form is reserved for family and friends in most places in the Spanish-speaking world.

In terms of its cultural usage, this distinction is a big deal in many places. While we in the United States tend to throw the word *friend* around rather loosely, for most Latinos, **amigo** or **amiga** is generally taken more seriously, and thus the **tú** form is reserved for people who truly are special. I have heard people being rebuked for using the **tú** form without really knowing the person. Use **Ud.** until you are given permission, or you are invited to use the **tú** form (you'll probably be told **tutéame, por favor**—meaning *use the tú form with me, please*). The only exception is that among young people, **tú** tends to be used automatically, but these same young people likely would not dare to use it when speaking to strangers who are older.

Most students have no problem with the concept of having a polite and a familiar form of address. Using **tú** is somewhat comparable to being on a first-name basis with someone, while using **usted** is more like using Mr. or Ms. in the English-speaking world.

Many students encounter a stumbling block when they first encounter **tú** and **usted** and any residual confusion often continues into the intermediate level, resulting in imperfect mastery of the verb forms and even patterned errors. Part of the problem is that **usted** and **ustedes** are *second-person in meaning but require the third-person forms of verbs*. Let's examine this problem in more detail.

The personal pronoun **usted** is derived from **Vuestra Merced**, meaning *Your Mercy* or *Your Grace*, which, because it is an indirect way of speaking to someone, requires the third-person form of verbs.

There are four ways to say *you* in Spanish: formal and familiar, singular and plural, and all refer to a second-person. Keep in mind that the second person is defined as the person or persons *to whom* one is speaking when that person is the subject of a statement or question. The two singular forms are **tú** and **usted**; the two plural forms are **vosotros** and **ustedes**. **Vosotros** is used almost exclusively in Spain and is simply the plural of the familiar **tú** with its corresponding verb form. In the Americas, **ustedes** is used for any situation when the plural of *you* is used, a fact that comes as a bit of relief for English-speaking students of Spanish.

If the same statement or question is expressed using any of the other Spanish forms of *you*, the English "translation" remains the same. However, keep in mind that the verb form changes, since it must agree with the subject in person and number. Observe these examples in which all the other forms of *you* are used. Note also that the following sentences and questions are great examples of how "translation" requires more than the mere rendering of words. For our immediate purposes, however, two things should be noted in comparing them. First, the parentheses indicate the subject pronoun the speaker has in mind. Secondly, since there is no other subject associated with the **tú** and the **vosotros** form of verbs, this pronoun would not need to be used; however, since **usted** and **ustedes** employ the third-person form of the verb, these subject pronouns might need to be used in order to avoid misunderstanding:

(Tú) **estudias** por la tarde.	*You study in the afternoon.*
¿**Estudias** (tú) por la tarde?	*Do you study in the afternoon?*
(Usted) **estudia** por la tarde.	*You study in the afternoon.*
¿**Estudia** (usted) por la tarde?	*Do you study in the afternoon?*
Estudiáis por la tarde.	*You study in the afternoon.*
¿**Estudiáis** por la tarde?	*Do you study in the afternoon?*
(Ustedes) **estudian** por la tarde.	*You study in the afternoon.*
¿**Estudian** (ustedes) por la tarde?	*Do you study in the afternoon?*

EJERCICIO
26·1

Indicate how you should address the following people as either **tú**, **Ud.**, **vosotros**, *or* **Uds.**, *according to the situation described.*

1. A un juez, que es su amigo, en un tribunal de justicia. _____

2. Al mismo juez, que es su amigo, en una fiesta familiar. _____

3. A su tío. _____

4. A un desconocido, mayor de edad, en la calle. _____

5. A dos niños, en España. _____

6. A tres personas, en Latinoamérica. _____

7. A sus abuelos, en España. _____

8. A las amigas de sus padres, a quienes Ud. no conoce. _____

9. A un compañero de clase. _____

10. A unas compañeras de clase, en España. _____

Select the sentence or question with the correct form of address and correspondingly proper verb form, according to the situational cues.

1. A un amigo, en una fiesta.

    a. ¿Cómo está usted, Tomás?

    b. Me gustan tus zapatos.

    c. ¡Qué elegantes son!

2. A un profesor, en la clase.

    a. ¿Le puedo hacer una pregunta, señor?

    b. ¿Nos vas a dar un examen mañana?

    c. ¿Qué hacen Uds. este fin de semana?

3. A varios amigos, en una fiesta en Madrid.

    a. Espero que puedan venir a casa este fin de semana.

    b. ¿Queréis tomar una copa conmigo en el balcón?

    c. ¿Han visto a Jaime?

4. Al público, en una conferencia.

    a. El discurso que voy a presentarles...

    b. El discurso que voy a presentarte...

    c. El discurso que voy a presentaros...

5. A su padre.

    a. ¿Quiere ir a pescar este fin de semana?

    b. ¿Quieres jugar al tenis esta tarde?

    c. ¿Desean ir a la playa mañana?

6. A varios jugadores en su equipo de fútbol, en Málaga.

    a. Pasan la pelota muy despacio.

    b. Tienes que correr un kilómetro o dos todos los días.

    c. Podéis ganar si practicáis más.

7. A sus compañeros de trabajo, en Latinoamérica.

    a. El jefe quiere hablar con Ud.

    b. ¿No van a participar en la conferencia la semana que viene?

    c. No me habléis de asuntos personales, por favor.

8. A una cajera, en el banco, a quien no conoce.

    a. ¿Podría darme un sobre para este cheque?

    b. Dame un sobre en el que pueda guardar este cheque.

    c. Espero que tengáis un sobre para este cheque.

9. A sus profesores.

    a. Yo los admiro mucho por lo que me han enseñado.

    b. Quiero felicitarte por la publicación de tantos artículos.

    c. ¿Tenéis tiempo disponible para explicar las notas que me habéis dado?

10. A su mamá y su hermana gemela, en Sevilla.

    a. Su cumpleaños es este fin de semana. ¡Qué emoción!

    b. Quiero daros una fiesta de cumpleaños.

    c. ¿No vienen con sus primas?

11. A su hermano.

    a. ¿No oye lo que dice en la radio?

    b. Si tienen sed, tomen agua.

    c. Oye, ¡no me pidas dinero todo el tiempo!

12. A su padre y un tío, en España.

    a. ¿No podéis acompañarme a comer unas tapas?

    b. Sé que desean ir a Pamplona este verano.

    c. Préstenme unos euros para que pueda comprar un coche.

13. A su nuevo jefe, mayor de edad, en México.

    a. Gracias por la oficina tan amplia que me dio.

    b. Son muy amables por haberme contratado.

    c. ¿Deseáis ir a ver una película esta noche?

14. Una mamá, en una consulta con el pediatra.

    a. Por favor, quiero que me dé una receta para quitarle el dolor a mi bebe.

    b. ¿Qué me recomiendan para bajarle la fiebre a mi bebé?

    c. ¿Crees que mi bebé tiene la gripe?

15. Un esposo a su esposa.

    a. ¡Dame un besito, mi amor!

    b. ¿Quiere ver la tele o prefiere salir a dar un paseo?

    c. Le doy cien dólares para comprar un nuevo suéter.

Prepositions and translating English phrasal verbs

Prepositions comprise a small group of tiny words that do a great deal of heavy lifting in both English and Spanish. To begin, it is important to know what prepositions are and what they do.

First of all, prepositions are *relater* words. They express the relationship between two nouns (or pronouns) in time or space, or in metaphorical interpretations of temporal and spatial relationships. There are two types of prepositions found in Spanish: *simple* (one-word forms) and *compound*. Prepositional phrases, which are easily identified because they begin with a preposition, function both as adjectives and adverbs.

Simple forms

The following is a complete list of all the simple prepositions in Spanish. English and Spanish often use different prepositions for the same verb, as the example below the list shows.

a	*at, to*
ante	*before, in front of*
bajo*	*under, beneath*
con	*with*
contra	*against*
de	*of, from*
desde	*from, since*
durante	*during*
en	*in, into, at, on*
entre	*among, between*
excepto	*except*
hacia	*toward*
hasta	*until, to, up to*
mediante	*be means of*
para	*for, toward*
por	*for, by, through, along, around, around in, across, within*
salvo	*except, save for*
según	*according to*
sin	*without*
so	*under (now exclusively legal, e.g.,* so pena de*—under pain of)*
sobre	*on, about, concerning*
tras	*after*

El libro está **en** la mesa.	*The book is **on** the table.*
Juan no está **en** casa.	*John is not **at** home.*

Compound

Many of the compound prepositions are synonymous with some of the simple forms. The following list of useful, high-frequency expressions involving multiple prepositions is a starting point for your emerging mastery of compound prepositions. To perfect your skill in using these, note when you come across them in articles or when you hear them. In this way, you can distinguish the various situations in which one is more appropriate than another, whose dictionary meaning may be identical.

a causa de	*on account of*
a excepción de	*with the exception of*
a fuerza de	*by virtue/dint of*
a menos que	*unless*

---

*__Bajo__ is an adjective serving as a preposition.

a pesar de	*in spite of*
acerca de	*about, concerning*
además de	*besides, in addition to*
adversamente a	*adversely to*
alrededor de	*around*
antes de	*before (time, order)*
a través	*across*
con tal de que	*provided that*
concerniente a	*concerning*
conforme a	*according to*
congruente con	*consistent with*
contrario a	*contrary to*
correspondiente a	*corresponding to*
debajo de	*under, underneath, beneath*
delante de	*before (place), in front of*
dentro de	*within*
después de	*after (time, order)*
detrás de	*behind, after (place)*
encima de	*over, on top of*
en cuanto a	*as for*
en frente de	*in front of*
en vez de	*instead of*
en virtud de	*by virtue of*
frente a	*opposite to*
junto a	*close to*
lejos de	*far from*
por causa de	*on account of*
por razón de	*by reason of*
relativo a	*in relation to*
respecto a	*with respect to*
sin embargo	*notwithstanding*
tocante a	*in (or with) regard to*

La farmacia está **frente al** banco.	*The pharmacy is **opposite** the bank.*
Vamos al cine **en vez del** teatro.	*Let's go to the movies **instead of** the theater.*

Often, prepositional usage in Spanish makes perfect sense to English-speaking learners, but when it is baffling, it can be maddening. There are three major reasons for this. First, quite simply, people tend to take these words for granted—that is, they don't give them much thought, unless they are, for example, reading legal contracts or giving directions for assembling a piece of equipment.

Secondly, prepositional usage is confusing because learners are unaware of the way verbs are "built." Following are three common examples. **Casarse** and **soñarse** both require the preposition **con** to indicate the English *to get married to* and *to dream about*. **Enamorarse** requires **de** for the English *to fall in love with*. Consider how the use of **con** with **casarse** makes sense when you realize that the verb is built from the noun **casa** turned into the verb **casar** (*to house*). Then realize that when two people get married, they make their house *with* each other!

The third reason English speakers find Spanish prepositional usage baffling is that English has a vast number of phrasal verbs—verbs whose meaning changes completely depending on the preposition used with them. In the introduction, reference was made to these verbs. As a point of departure for exploring how these verbs complicate verb choice in Spanish, experiment with how the meanings of the English verbs *get* and *put* change radically by appending different prepositions to them. One of the exercises at the end of this chapter will expose you to a handful of common phrasal verbs involving *get* and *put*.

Since there are thousands of phrasal verbs in English, the best way to deal with the problem of learning their Spanish counterparts is to be careful when using a dictionary. If you want the proper Spanish verb to express *Get down!* (when this is meant as a warning of danger), you will find solutions in **bajarse** or **agacharse**, depending on the physical parameters of the situation.

Observe the following two examples. The first might be what a mother says to her son when he climbs too high in a tree. The second could happen on a battlefield, where the more likely English expression upon perceiving incoming fire would be "Duck!" and even more problematic if you looked in a dictionary and carelessly picked the noun for the bird.

¡**Bájate** de allí, Juanito!	*Get down from there, Johnny!*
¡Fuego! ¡**Agáchense**!	*Fire! Get down!*

Por and para

The pair of prepositions **por** and **para** cause English speakers more trouble than perhaps any other word pair in Spanish for which English has only one word. Let's begin at the most abstract level. **Para** is dynamic, as the following three examples show. In the first example, **para** is operating in a spatial way. The speaker is observing the flight of the plane as a vector—its flight path is in a certain direction. The second example shows **para** functioning in a temporal way, pointing toward a deadline. The third example simply shows that **para** is the preposition that must be used before an infinitive when you want to say *in order to*; that is, you cannot simply use the infinitive to do this as is possible in English and as is shown by the second translation of the third example.

El avión vuela **para** Alaska.	*The plane is flying to/toward/for Alaska.*
El artículo es **para** la edición de mañana.	*The article is for tomorrow's edition.*
Estudiamos español **para** poder hablarlo bien.	*We study Spanish in order to be able to speak it well.*
	We study Spanish to be able to speak it well.

The preposition **para** also is used to express an unexpected or surprise comparison. Observe the following examples.

Juanito sabe mucho de matemáticas **para** un niño de ocho años.	*Johnny knows a lot about math **for** a boy of eight.*
Para administrador, el Sr. Acero es bien bobo.	***For** an administrator, Mr. Acero is really dumb.*
¡Vaya!, **Para** un equipo de colegio, juegan como profesionales.	*Wow! **For** a high school team, they play like pros!*

The preposition **para** also shows the purpose for something:

Un martillo no sirve **para** eso.	*A hammer is no good **for** that.*
Es una copa **para** cognac.	*It is a cognac snifter.*

The preposition **por** is rendered in English by many prepositions, for instance: *through, around, within, by, along, per,* and of course, *for,* as in many stock phrases such as **por Dios** (*for the love of God*). You can see how many of these prepositions are used spatially simply by their meaning:

Caperucita Roja caminó **por** el bosque.	*Little Red Riding Hood walked through the forest.*
El perro corría **por** el río.	*The dog was running along the river.*

The preposition **por** can also be used in a figurative way, just as many of its English counterparts can.

Fue **por** sus estudios que llegó a ser médico.	*It was **through** his studies that he became a doctor.*

Now that you see how **por** works *spatially*, it will be easy to see that its *temporal* uses are analogous. For instance, one function of **por** is to show duration of time (e.g., **por tres días**). In comparison to **para**, **por** is static. The action of the verb with which **por** is associated takes place *across, along, around, by, in, through* or *within* some space where **por** is relating two nouns, as the following examples show.

Los novios caminaron **por** el parque por dos horas.	*The couple walked around in the park for two hours.*
El pájaro volaba **por** las ramas.	*The bird was flying around/amid/through/ among the branches.*
Pasé **por** tu casa pero no estabas.	*I went by your house but you weren't there.*

By now, it should be becoming clear that the problem of **por** and **para** is best solved by concluding two things. First, the English preposition *for* is not used in one way—to mean one thing—in English, as the previous examples show. Second, **por** and **para** don't simply mean *for* (whatever meaning you wish to give it). Think about the following examples and substitute each of the English prepositions just cited, one at a time, and you'll see just how **por** works as a spatial preposition. Note that the two nouns being related in the first example are the *dog* and the *room*, and the preposition **por** shows how the dog's action happened in that space. English has some advantage over Spanish because English has a number of prepositions that can be more specific about the dog's movement with respect to the room.

El perro corrió **por** la sala.	*The dog ran around the room.*
Juan estuvo **por** aquí ayer a las tres.	*John was around here yesterday at three.*

As a temporal preposition, **por** means **during**, or *for* in the sense of *duration of time*. It also corresponds exactly to the uses of *per*, which is the Latin word it evolved from. Other meanings of **por** include *for the sake of* and *because*, when used in the sense of *on account of*. It is also used to mark a noun as the *object of an errand*. In addition, there are many, stock phrases using **por**, most of which will come easily.

Estuvimos en Guanajuato **por** varios días.	*We were in Guanajuato for a few days.*
No lo van a hacer, **por** ahora.	*They aren't going to do it, for now.*
El carro iba a cien kilómetros **por** hora.	*The car was traveling at a sixty miles an hour.*
Hidalgo murió **por** la Patria.	*Hidalgo died for the country.*
Por cobarde, no quiso contestarme.	*Because he's a coward, he refused to answer me.*
Mi hermana fue a la tienda **por** pan.	*My sister went to the shop for bread.*

But:

Mi hermana fue a la tienda **para** comprar pan.	*My sister went to the shop to buy bread.*

The differences between **por** and **para** account for why these two questions are so different:

¿**Por qué** quieres ser médico?	*Why do you want to be a physician?*
¿**Para qué** quieres ser médico?	*What [on earth] do you want to be a physician for?*

Finally, I offer you one final, general comment about prepositions. You may have heard it said that in English you shouldn't end a sentence (or a clause) with a preposition. First, that isn't so. Winston Churchill is often quoted (rightly or wrongly) for observing that such a rule was *a lot of poppycock up with which he would not put* (!). There is no such rule in English, as anyone can prove by picking up a volume of Shakespeare. However, in Spanish, it is an absolute rule. In Spanish, you must never end a sentence or clause with a preposition. Note the following examples.

No tengo **con quién** hablar allí.	*I have no one to speak with there.*
¿**De quién** fue la llamada?	*Who was the call from?*
¿**De qué** sabor es esto?	*What flavor is this (of)?*

EJERCICIO
26·3

Match the following English prepositions with their Spanish counterparts—remember, though, that usage is not as simple as matching them!

_____ 1. with	a. en
_____ 2. against	b. hacia
_____ 3. to, at	c. sobre
_____ 4. close to	d. a
_____ 5. under, underneath, beneath	e. por
_____ 6. on, in, at	f. hasta
_____ 7. on, about, concerning	g. desde
_____ 8. with respect to	h. entre
_____ 9. for, by, around	i. contra
_____ 10. within	j. frente a
_____ 11. of, from	k. detrás de
_____ 12. from	l. debajo de
_____ 13. opposite to	m. tras
_____ 14. among, between	n. respecto a
_____ 15. toward	o. con
_____ 16. after	p. lejos de
_____ 17. behind, after (place)	q. para
_____ 18. until	r. junto a
_____ 19. for, toward	s. dentro de
_____ 20. far from	t. de

*Match the following English phrasal verbs involving the verbs **get** and **put** with their corresponding Spanish solutions.*

_____ 1. to get even

_____ 2. to become (e.g., a doctor)

_____ 3. to get bored

_____ 4. to put on (e.g., clothes)

_____ 5. to put up with

_____ 6. to get on (e.g., a bus)

_____ 7. to put down (e.g., jot a note)

_____ 8. to get tired

_____ 9. to get going

_____ 10. to get it (e.g., a joke).

_____ 11. to get over (e.g., a problem)

_____ 12. to put down (e.g., a personal affront)

_____ 13. to put back (e.g., an object)

_____ 14. to get married

_____ 15. to get sick

_____ 16. to fall in love with

_____ 17. to put away (e.g., jail)

_____ 18. to get lost

_____ 19. to put out (e.g., a fire)

_____ 20. to get better (e.g., from illness)

a. casarse

b. subir

c. cansarse

d. sobreponerse

e. devolver

f. enamorarse de

g. enfermarse

h. aguantar

i. encarcelar

j. aburrirse

k. darse prisa

l. extraviarse

m. vengarse

n. llegar a ser

o. mejorarse

p. apuntar

q. apagar

r. ponerse

s. insultar

t. comprender

¿Por *or* **para?**

1. Le voy a ofrecer mil dólares _____ su auto.

2. El helicóptero pasó velozmente _____ encima del edificio sin chocar con nada.

3. El avión volaba a mil kilómetros _____ hora.

4. La niña fue a la tienda _____ arroz.

5. _____ esto he venido: ayudarte a pintar la casa.

6. El Sr. José Martí y el Dr. José Rizal dieron sus vidas _____ sus patrias.

7. Y, _____ colmo, el Sr. Acero es mentiroso.

8. ¿_____ qué no vamos a San Francisco de vacaciones?

9. A lo mejor, ese avión va _____ San Francisco.

10. Este regalo es _____ mi mamá.

11. Su amigo estaba enfermo, así que Juan asistió a la reunión _____ él.

12. Sé que dejé mi billetera _____ aquí.

13. Necesito el informe sobre la contaminación del río _____ el viernes.

14. Juan y Tomás iban al centro comercial _____ buscar un regalo.

15. Si quieres, amigo, yo se lo diré _____ respaldarte.

16. ¿_____ qué sirve esta herramienta?

17. El Sr. Acero debe ir a la cárcel _____ razón de su corrupción.

18. Te digo que fue _____ eso que no lo puedo ver ni en pintura.

19. Mi amigo estudió mucho _____ llegar a ser profesor.

20. Los novios pasaron una hora caminando _____ el parque.

Translate the following sentences from Spanish to English.

1. Esa familia pasaba por el pueblo en marzo todos los años.

_____

2. Por poco, el héroe de guerra da la vida por la liberación de su país.

_____

3. Debido a sus nociones limitadas sobre la política, yo intenté convencerle con las mías.

_____

4. Las aguas se precipitaban por un lecho de piedras entre dos montañas.

_____

5. Se fundó la aldea a orillas del río.

_____

6. Un hombre se cayó por el techo cuando intentó robar la casa.

_____

7. La anciana de pelo rizado enterró una figura llena de oro debajo de la cama.

   _____

8. Por dondequiera que fuera, se oía una música suave.

   _____

9. El hermano menor, con sus esfuerzos y talento, trabajó por años para arreglar la casa.

   _____

10. Llovió por varios días.

   _____

11. Un hombre subió al tren que no iba hacia ninguna parte, sin rumbo cierto ni destino.

   _____

12. La señora que vive en el piso de abajo fue la única que le tuvo lástima.

   _____

13. Los perros corrieron tras el conejo.

   _____

14. La ruta del correo de mulas pasaba por las montañas.

   _____

15. El músico estuvo sentado en medio de las piezas desarmadas de un clavicordio.

   _____

16. Las palomas, asustadas por el grito de la mujer, volaron hacia las nubes.

   _____

17. Debido a su locura, varios hombres lo tuvieron que refrenar con cuerdas.

   _____

18. La lanza que arrojó el héroe voló hasta que pasó por el pecho del general enemigo.

   _____

19. El acusado tuvo que comparecer ante el juez.

   _____

20. La ciudad se hundió en el lodo.

   _____

Translate the following sentences from English to Spanish.

1. The dog almost ran under the bus.

   _____

2. The house is within five miles of the city.

   _____

3. Mr. Acero made accusations not only without evidence but contrary to it.

   _____

4. He didn't tell us anything about it.

   _____

5. She got angry with him when he came into the house.

   _____

6. When I left the movie, I saw the girl I had fallen in love with.

   _____

7. She told me that she dreamed about me.

   _____

8. They weren't sure if they should get married or not.

   _____

9. The story, according to which he was from Italy, turned out to be false.

   _____

10. The children ran through the house, getting mud all over the carpet.

    _____

11. Don't betray the king, under pain of death! (**Ud.**)

    _____

12. They looked until they found everything they wanted to sell.

    _____

13. As for me, give me Liberty or give me Death. (**tú**)

    _____

14. Not withstanding their differences, they agreed to sign the treaty.

    _____

15. Whose book is this?

    _____

16. Instead of complaining, you should work. (**tú**)

_____

17. The library is close to the building I work in.

_____

18. Does she expect to speak with him?

_____

19. Despite what she said, she is interested in him.

_____

20. They marched across the desert.

_____

Using verbs to show politeness

I'm sure you've learned to say **por favor**. This expression is generally sufficient to show courtesy to your listener, but it isn't the only means to indicate various degrees of earnestness when making a request. Compared with Spanish, English is relatively poor in terms of verbs or phrases for expressing politeness without seeming sarcastic. The word _please_ is pretty much all that English speakers have at hand to verbally express politeness without adding verbiage that makes the speaker seem "over the top."

The use of **deber**, **querer**, and **poder** as helping verbs is progressively more polite in the present, conditional, and imperfect subjunctive. While they convey no difference in meaning, they display a great difference in tone for indicating three degrees, or gradations, of politeness in Spanish. In other words, the increasing gradations of politeness are shown by means of the tenses and moods used. Learning the forms in this chapter will place you beyond the bare territory of **por favor** and show that you are more socially functional than those who cannot manage these forms properly.

Like all helping verbs, these three verbs are used to introduce an infinitive (without any preposition between them). It is worth noticing that they have to do with the three aspects of the human mind: **poder** shows ability, capacity, or power (_can, could_): **querer** expresses volition or the will (_want_ or _desire_); and **deber** indicates a moral obligation (_ought, should,_ and _owe_).

Other auxiliary verbs or verb phrases that indicate moral obligation or necessity cannot be used as **deber** is to express degrees of politeness. The moral obligation expressed by **deber** is not as strong as that conveyed by **tener que** + infinitive, **necesitar** + infinitive, or the impersonal **hay que** + infinitive. Thus, unlike what many dictionaries indicate, **deber** is not the best translation for _must_, when _must_ really means business.

Tenemos que pagar los impuestos cada año.	_We have to pay taxes every year._
Necesitan ponerse loción o se van a quemar.	_They need to put on lotion or they will get a sunburn._
Deben escribir una carta a su abuela.	_They should write a letter to their grandmother._

In the present tense, **deber**, **querer**, and **poder** create unadorned statements and questions. They are neither polite nor impolite (of course, spoken tone could incline them either way). Consider the following examples:

Alejandra, **debes** practicar la flauta si quieres tocar en la sinfonía.	*Alexandra, you should practice the flute if you want to play in the symphony.*
¿**Puedes** acompañarme a la playa este fin de semana?	*Can you go to the beach with me this weekend?*
¿**Quieres** preparar la cena esta noche?	*Do you want to fix dinner tonight?*

When the verb tenses or moods in these same examples are changed to the conditional (technically a mood, not a tense), the statements and questions become more polite:

Alejandra, **deberías** practicar la flauta si quieres tocar en la sinfonía.	*Alexandra, you ought to practice the flute if you want to play in the symphony.*
¿**Podrías** acompañarme a la playa este fin de semana?	*Could you go to the beach with me this weekend?*
¿**Querrías** preparar la cena esta noche?	*Would you like to fix dinner tonight?*

The English language is incapable of adequately expressing just how much more polite these statements and questions become when the helping verb is in the imperfect subjunctive because any attempt to reflect this gradation would sound obsequious or even sarcastic. It isn't that English speakers can't be as polite, it is because our tonal and verbal arsenals are different from those of Spanish. Nevertheless, in the following examples, I have tried to approximate this degree of politeness by augmenting them with an intensifying adverb or some other expression.

Alejandra, **debieras** practicar la flauta si quieres tocar en la sinfonía.	*Alexandra, you really ought to practice the flute if you want to play in the symphony.*
¿**Pudieras** acompañarme a la playa este fin de semana?	*Could you, would you please, go to the beach with me this weekend?*
¿**Quisieras** preparar la cena esta noche?	*Would you mind fixing dinner tonight, please?*

Since the conditional form of **querer** (**querrías** in the example sounds so close to the imperfect forms of this verb (**quería**, **querías**), even native speakers of Spanish tend to not use it, preferring to use the imperfect subjunctive—**quisiera**, **quisieras**—which is the most polite form. Why not? It never hurts to be civil.

Due to the difficulty of expressing this most polite degree in English, many Spanish speakers are mistakenly labeled as impolite or sarcastic by English speakers who are unaware of this feature of Spanish. Consider how the last question could come off if a Spanish speaker, who has not mastered the wide range of tones in spoken English, were to attempt embellishing English in an attempt to reflect the politeness of Spanish.

¿Quisieras preparar la cena esta noche?	*Would you really be so kind as to fix dinner tonight, please?*

It's a good lesson in cultural sensitivity at the most basic level—language—where culture is inextricably embedded.

Give the proper form of the three helping verbs for the given subject pronouns in the tense and mood indicated.

1. (deber) él/imperfect subjunctive _____

2. (poder) tú/present indicative _____

3. (querer) ella/conditional _____

4. (querer) nosotros/imperfect subjunctive _____

5. (poder) Ud./imperfect subjunctive _____

6. (deber) Uds./conditional _____

7. (poder) yo/conditional _____

8. (deber) tú/imperfect subjunctive _____

9. (poder) yo/present indicative _____

10. (deber) ella/conditional _____

11. (querer) Ud./present indicative _____

12. (querer) vosotros/conditional _____

Translate the following sentences from Spanish to English.

1. Juan no debería manejar tan rápido.

_____

2. Por favor, ¿podría Ud. ayudarme con esta maleta?

_____

3. Creo que ella quisiera salir con Juan.

_____

4. Pues, deberías ir al baile.

_____

5. ¿Pudieran esperar hasta que lleguemos?

_____

6. Yo querría probar este postre.

_____

7. ¿Puedes echar una mano a esta tarea?

_____

8. Es obvio—Ella debe dejar de fumar.

_____

9. Por mucho que quisiéramos prestarle el dinero, no tenemos tanto.

_____

10. ¿Quieres comprar la ensalada si yo compro la carne?

_____

11. Si de veras quieren aprender la lección, deberían apagar la tele.

_____

12. Es cierto que quiero hacer la tarea, pero no dispongo de tiempo ahora.

_____

13. Ellos quisieran contribuir más a la organización.

_____

14. Mis hermanos podrían ayudarte mañana.

_____

15. ¿Pudieras tener la bondad de pedirle que venga a la reunión?

_____

16. Juanito, no debieras dejar de asistir a las lecciones de música.

_____

17. Mis primas quieren manejar ahora.

_____

18. ¡Con mucho gusto pudiéramos respaldarle en la campaña!

_____

19. Yo sé lo que debo hacer; es cuestión de no perder el ánimo.

_____

20. ¿Pueden Uds. enviarnos las herramientas dentro de un par de días?

_____

Translate the following sentences from English to Spanish. For the sake of eliciting the various degrees of politeness, the word really is used in regular type to show the middle degree of politeness. When really is italicized, it indicates the most polite degree. For the forms of **poder**, could indicates the middle degree of politeness and really or kindly, when used with could and italicized, indicate the most polite degree.

1. I *really* would like to go with you, but I can't. (**tú**)

   _____

2. She really ought to bring her friend.

   _____

3. We ought to read more.

   _____

4. Can you come help me fix dinner? (**tú**)

   _____

5. His friends *really* could do more for him.

   _____

6. They ought to have returned the correct key to me.

   _____

7. We *really* want to go to the movies with you (**tú**).

   _____

8. She wants to invite John to the party.

   _____

9. They *really* would like to bring their dog.

   _____

10. My sister really ought to practice the violin more.

   _____

11. Could you *kindly* turn off the radio? (**Uds.**)

   _____

12. She and Ana *really* ought to thank their mother.

   _____

13. He would like to loan you the money if you can pay him soon. (**Ud.**)

   _____

14. His friend really should stop smoking.

   _____

15. Could you bring me the chair? (**tú**)

_____

16. Wouldn't you and your friends *really* like to go to the beach?

_____

17. She would come, but she can't.

_____

18. He and I ought to fix the car.

_____

19. You really ought to go to school. (**Ud.**) (use **asistir a**)

_____

20. I *really* would like to invite you to lunch. (**tú**)

_____

Translating *ago* with **hacer** clauses

If you look up the word *ago* in most bilingual dictionaries, you'll discover that Spanish has no one-word equivalent for it. English speakers make handy and concise use of it all the time. The word *ago* enables English speakers to refer to actions in the past, measuring backward from the present. Logically, both English and Spanish use a verb in the past tense to do this. But Spanish commonly uses a construction that baffles English speakers—until they learn to accept it as a whole. This chapter will teach you how to use the verb **hacer** to ask and answer more complex questions about the temporal relationship between events—putting them on a time line that is every bit as clear as English, and quite formulaic.

There is no English structure to guide English-speaking students of Spanish and enable them to grasp the ways Spanish routinely frames the temporal notions that the **hacer** time clauses refer to. Thus, it is important to know what these Spanish structures mean in English, and not merely what the individual words mean.

The verb **hacer** is used in three ways. While each one follows the same structure, the use of the tenses of **hacer** and another verb render different meanings. Each structure denotes distinct relationships between the moment of speaking and an event, events, or situations in the past.

Present perfect meaning

The first structure we will examine shows *how long* something has been going on relative to the moment of speaking. It shows how an action that began in the past is either still going on or whose influence or impact is still being felt. This should sound familiar if you have learned the present perfect in Spanish or know the verb tense this grammatical term refers to. The difficulty for English speakers is that when when one wishes to express *how long* something has been going on, the present perfect tense is rarely used in Spanish. Observe the following example and notice that the translation into English uses, as it must, the present perfect, but in Spanish the verb **hacer** is used.

Hace una hora que **escribo** esta carta.　　*I have been writing this letter for an hour.*

Notice the structure: the present indicative, third-person singular form of the verb **hacer**, followed by a measure of time, then **que**, then the sentence finishing with another verb in the present. This structure shows what action began in the past and continues into the present and can be summarized as follows:

present indicative of **hacer** (third-person singular) +
measure of time + **que** + verb (present tense)

The sentence could also be structured like this:

Escribo esta carta **desde hace** una hora.   *I've been writing this letter since an hour ago/for an hour.*

Just as an English speaker would understand, so too the Spanish speaker grasps immediately that the person making this statement began writing a letter an hour ago and still is writing it.

How to express the concept of *ago*

An action that began in the past doesn't have to be going on still, in the literal sense, in order for its impact to be felt at the moment of speaking. Notice the following example, supposing the speaker is turning down an invitation to eat lunch. This is a sentence whose English translation requires *ago*:

Hace una hora que **comí.**   *I ate an hour ago.*

Notice that the structure of this sentence is identical to the first example. The verb **hacer** is still in the same form as before and is followed by a measure of time, then the conjunction **que**; but the verb that ends the thought is in the preterit.

present indicative of **hacer** (third-person singular) +
measure of time + **que** + verb (preterit tense)

It is this whole structure and the relationship of the tenses that combine to create the equivalent of the notion expressed by the English word *ago*. It could also be structured as follows:

Comí hace una hora.   *I ate an hour ago.*

Pluperfect in meaning

The third way **hacer** is used in a time clause expresses how long something *had been going on* but does not tell us how long ago the action was happening. As the following model shows, Spanish uses the imperfect indicative of the two verbs in the **hacer** time clause and a verb in the preterit outside the **hacer** time clause; its English translation requires a combination of the pluperfect and another in the past tense.

Hacía cinco meses que María **estudiaba**   *Mary had been studying French for five*
   francés cuando decidió cambiar   *months when she decided to switch*
   al español.   *to Spanish.*

Notice that the structure, up to the adverb **cuando**, is the same as in the previous examples. What is different is that both **hacer** and the verb completing the time-clause structure are in the imperfect indicative.

imperfect indicative of **hacer** (third-person singular) +
measure of time + **que** + verb (imperfect indicative tense)

This structure establishes the sequence of how, at some time in the past (we are not informed how long ago), Mary began studying French, continued for five months, then switched to Spanish—three neat facts strung on a verbal time line.

You may also encounter the following structure, which is useful for providing background information. Notice that it too translates as pluperfect and that, as in the previous example, we do not know how long ago John followed his routine.

Juan **hacía** ejercicios todos los miércoles **desde hacía** años.	*John had been working out every Wednesday for years.*
Hacía años que Juan **hacía** ejercicios todos los miércoles.	

Asking questions

The **hacer** time clauses are also used to ask questions. Here are the two types of question structures that could have been asked to elicit the previous examples. The word **tiempo** is in parentheses to indicate that it is optional.

¿**Cuánto (tiempo) hace** que **escribes** la carta?	*How long have you been writing the letter?*
¿**Hace cuánto (tiempo)** que **escribes** la carta?	
¿**Cuánto (tiempo) hace** que **comiste**?	*How long ago did you eat?*
¿**Hace cuánto (tiempo)** que **comiste**?	
¿**Cuánto (tiempo) hacía** que María **estudiaba** francés cuando decidió cambiar al español?	*How long had Mary studied French when she decided to switch to Spanish?*
¿**Hacía cuánto (tiempo)** que María **estudiaba** francés cuando decidió cambiar al español?	

Ways to say *I wonder*

It frequently happens that not long after Spanish learners have begun to take baby steps to converse with native Spanish speakers, they realize just how often the word *wonder* comes to mind and find themselves at a loss to express it. Consultations with bilingual dictionaries usually leave English speakers unsatisfied. As it turns out, there are five principal ways in which this word is used in English and, as it happens with phrasal verbs, so too do these various usages have as many solutions in Spanish. Since Spanish only has nouns (e.g., **maravilla**, **prodigio**), but no verbs for this word, the solutions do not involve any translation of *wonder* itself, but instead use ways to express what the English word intends.

The first usage of *wonder* is to express a *polite request*, such as:

Me gustaría si pudieras cenar conmigo.	*I was wondering if you could have dinner with me. (Literally: It would please me if you could dine with me.)*

This usage of *wonder* is accomplished in Spanish by the use of the conditional plus the imperfect subjunctive. There are other simpler solutions that do not involve the subjunctive—by avoiding a change of subject:

Me gustaría cenar contigo.	Literally: *It would please me to dine with you.*

The second use of *wonder* is to express *curiosity*. For instance, you may wonder if something has happened yet:

A ver si me ha llegado el cheque en el correo.

I wonder if my check has come in the mail. (Literally: Let's see if the check for me has arrived in the mail.)

Another solution for expressing this aspect of *wonder* is to employ the *future of probability*, a usage of the simple future tense in Spanish that defies translation into English:

¿Me **habrá** llegado el cheque?

Literally: *Will the check for me have arrived?*

The third way that English speakers use *wonder* is to suggest *mentally weighing* something, or turning something over in one's mind. A handy way to remember this usage is to note that the verbs both for *turning* and *to ask oneself* can be used in Spanish when this is what is meant in English.

Hacía varios días que yo **le daba muchas vueltas** a esto.
Me preguntaba si debería comprar ese auto.

I had been wondering about this for a few days.
I was wondering if I should buy that car. (Literally: I was asking myself if I should buy that car.)

The fourth way English uses *wonder* is to express *uncertainty*:

Ella **no sabía** si debiera solicitar ese trabajo.

She was wondering if she should apply for that job.

Finally, the fifth use of *wonder* is to show a *lack of surprise*:

No me extraña/sorprende que no me haya llamado—está todavía en el trabajo.
Con razón no me habías llamado, ¡estabas todavía en el trabajo!

No wonder he didn't call me—he's still at work.
No wonder you hadn't called me—you were still at work!

EJERCICIO
26·11

Select the translation that best reflects the meaning of the following sentences in English.

1. She has lived in Mexico for two years.

   a. Ella vivió en México por dos años.

   b. Ella ha vivido en México por dos años.

   c. Hace dos años que ella vive en México.

2. I wonder where my dog is.

   a. ¿Dónde está el perro?

   b. ¿Dónde está mi perro?

   c. ¿Dónde estará mi perro?

3. They had been in Buenos Aires for a week when they decided to buy a car.

   a. Estaban en Buenos Aires por una semana cuando decidieron comprar un auto.

   b. Habían estado en Buenos Aires por una semana y decidieron comprar un auto.

   c. Hacía una semana que estaban en Buenos Aires cuando decidieron comprar un auto.

4. I started cooking an hour ago.

   a. He cocinado por una hora.

   b. Empecé a cocinar hace una hora.

   c. Hace una hora que cocino.

5. How long has it been since you've been to the dentist?

   a. ¿Desde cuándo no has ido al dentista?

   b. ¿Cuánto tiempo hace que no has ido al dentista?

   c. ¿Cuándo fue la última vez que fuiste al dentista?

6. How many days were you lost in the woods?

   a. ¿Hace cuánto tiempo que te perdiste en el bosque?

   b. ¿Cuántos días hacía que andabas perdido en el bosque?

   c. ¿Por cuántos días estuviste perdido en el bosque?

7. We were wondering if you'd like to go shopping tomorrow.

   a. Queremos saber si quieres ir de compras mañana.

   b. Nos gustaría saber si quisieras ir de compras mañana.

   c. Nos dará gusto si quieres ir de compras mañana.

8. I was wondering if the package had arrived.

   a. Me preguntaba si el paquete había llegado.

   b. Me preguntó si el paquete había llegado.

   c. ¿Me habrá llegado el paquete?

9. No wonder he didn't run. He had a broken foot.

   a. No es una sorpresa que no corriera. Se le había roto el pie.

   b. No me sorprende que no corriera. Tenía una rotura del pie.

   c. Con razón no corrió. Se rompió el pie.

10. I was wondering if I should accept the job.

    a. Yo no sé si deba aceptar el puesto.

    b. Yo no sabía si debía aceptar el puesto.

    c. Me pregunto si es un puesto bueno para mí.

11. They opened the store two hours ago.

    a. Hacía dos horas que habían abierto la tienda.

    b. Ellos abren la tienda a las dos.

    c. Hace dos horas que abrieron la tienda.

12. He and I had been friends for years when he moved away.

    a. Él y yo somos amigos desde hace años, pero se mudó hace tiempo.

    b. Cuando él se mudó, hacía años que él y yo éramos amigos.

    c. Él se mudó cuando hacía años que éramos amigos.

13. Arnold had been driving the bus for an hour when he got sick.

    a. Arnold se enfermó después de manejar el autobús por una hora.

    b. Hacía una hora que Arnold manejaba el autobús cuando se enfermó.

    c. Arnold estuvo enfermo por una hora después de manejar el autobús.

14. John was working at the newspaper for years.

    a. Juan trabajaba para el periódico desde hacía años.

    b. Juan ha trabajado para el periódico por muchos años.

    c. Juan estuvo trabajando para el periódico por años y años.

15. How long had you (**tú**) been sleeping when I called?

    a. ¿Cuántas horas habías dormido cuando yo te llamé?

    b. ¿Por cuánto tiempo dormiste antes de que te llamara?

    c. ¿Hacía cuánto tiempo que dormías cuando te llamé?

16. When she met her boyfriend, she had been traveling in Europe for a month.

    a. Conoce a su novio desde cuando estuvo viajando por Europa por un mes.

    b. Cuando conoció a su novio, hacía un mes que viajaba por Europa.

    c. Ella viajaba por Europa por un mes cuando conoció a su novio.

17. I wonder what will happen tomorrow.

    a. ¿Qué pasa mañana?

    b. ¿Qué pasó esta mañana?

    c. Me pregunto qué pasará mañana.

18. No wonder he gained weight—all he has been eating for weeks is pizza.

    a. No me sorprende que esté más gordo—lo único que ha comido en semanas es pizza.

    b. Con razón aumentó de peso—hace semanas que no come sino pizza.

    c. Gran cosa que se está engordando—no come nada excepto pizza.

19. When he left work, Arnold had been on the phone for an hour.

    a. Cuando salió del trabajo, hacía una hora que Arnold hablaba por teléfono.

    b. Arnold habló por una hora en el teléfono y luego salió del trabajo.

    c. Arnold salió del trabajo e hizo una llamada por teléfono.

20. They lived in Mazatlán three years ago.

    a. Hacía tres años que vivían en Mazatlán.

    b. Hace tres años que vivieron en Mazatlán.

    c. Vivieron en Mazatlán por tres años.

EJERCICIO 26·12

*Recompose these dehydrated sentences about **hacer** time clauses, ways to express wonder, and probability in the present and the past. Watch for when you'll need to add articles, nouns, prepositions—and **que**.*

1. tú/preguntarse/qué nota/sacar/en último examen.

   _____

2. ahora/hacer/dos horas/ellos/correr/en el parque.

   _____

3. hacer/dos años/él/jugar al fútbol/cuando/romperse la pierna.

   _____

4. ayer/a las tres/yo/estar/en la biblioteca/,¿dónde/estar/Juan?

   _____

5. ¿cuántos/años/hacer/tú/conocer/tu novia/cuando/casarse?

   _____

6. hacer/una hora/yo/comer

   _____

7. no te sorprende/María y Juan/casarse

   _____

8. le gustar (a él)/si/ellos/acompañarle/cine

   _____

9. ayer/ellos/esperar/tú/llegar/pero (tú) no/llegar/¿dónde/estar (tú)?

_____

10. ¿quién/saber/dónde/estar/llaves/ahora/? Él/perder (llaves)/todo/tiempo.

_____

Translate the following sentences from Spanish to English.

1. Nos mudamos a este pueblo hace un par de años, cuando mi hija tenía tres años.

_____

2. No le sorprendió que su hermano ganara la carrera, ya que hacía un año que se entrenaba.

_____

3. A ver si no hay un cheque en mi buzón.

_____

4. Con razón ha sido detenido el Sr. Acero—hace años que defrauda a los empleados.

_____

5. Juan se preguntaba por qué hacía tiempo que María no le contestaba cuando la llamaba.

_____

6. Mis padres vivían allí desde hacía años.

_____

7. ¿Cuánto hace que no ves a tus padres?

_____

8. Hice muchos ejercicios hace una hora.

_____

9. ¿Cuánto hacía que Teresa ponía la mesa? Me pregunto si no se distrae mucho.

_____

10. Nos gustaría si tuvieras la bondad de devolvernos el libro que te prestamos hace una semana.

_____

11. ¿Hace cuánto que el sastre te arregló el abrigo?

_____

12. Hacía tiempo que el mecánico se tardaba en inspeccionar el auto.

13. Cuando detuvieron al Sr. Acero, hacía meses que lo vigilaban las autoridades.

   _____

14. Cinco de mis amigos y yo fuimos testigos de un evento paranormal hace tres semanas.

   _____

15. Duró sólo un minuto o menos, pero nos pareció que hacía una hora que lo veíamos.

   _____

16. Hacía una hora que ensayábamos cuando Jorge hizo que se apagara la luz.

   _____

17. ¿Mi amigo le habrá dejado un mensaje de voz a Juan?

   _____

18. Cuando se les rompió la ventana hace un mes, ellos no sabían si debían llamar a la policía.

   _____

19. A ver si mi padre no me haya llamado.

   _____

20. Me pregunto qué me hubiera sucedido si no me hubiera casado con ella.

   _____

EJERCICIO
26·14

*Translate the following sentences from English to Spanish. Use **hacer** time clauses when dealing with time frames, not perfect or pluperfect tenses.*

1. Who knows how he got that job a year ago.

   _____

2. She wondered whether he would call her or not.

   _____

3. They had worked for an hour when the boss came in.

   _____

4. Mr. Acero hadn't told the truth for years.

   _____

5. When the play ended, she realized that she had been sleeping for twenty minutes.

   _____

6. He had been trying to borrow money from his brother for a month.

   _____

7. We have been the owners of the business for a year.

_____

8. The flowers dried up because she had not watered them for a week.

_____

9. The dog has been sleeping for three hours.

_____

10. I had lived in Mazatlán for four years when I decided to return to the USA.

_____

11. The bread had been baking for twenty minutes when the power went out.

_____

12. Her cousin went to Europe for two weeks about six months ago.

_____

13. How many years ago was your grandfather born?

_____

14. How long had you been shopping when you realized that you had lost your credit card? (**tú**)

_____

15. The clothes had been hanging out to dry for only ten minutes when it started to rain.

_____

16. She's been in her room studying for two hours.

_____

17. When the submarine surfaced, it had been under the polar ice cap for over two months.

_____

18. He has been snoring in the rocking chair for at least an hour.

_____

19. We woke him up after he had slept for two hours.

_____

20. No wonder you're tired: these sentences are hard! (**tú**)

_____

The gustar verb family

There is no Spanish verb that corresponds to the English verb *to like*. This should not cause as many problems as it seems to. In this chapter, you'll discover a few tricks that will dispel any confusion you might have about the verb **gustar** and other verbs of the **gustar** family.

Gustar

Textbooks try to get students to use this verb correctly by resorting to a bit of subterfuge: they introduce it in a preliminary lesson, including it in some short, model dialogues, using questions such as **¿Te gusta...?** and a reply of **Sí, me gusta...** or **No, no me gusta...** to condition students to use the verb correctly. It seems like a good idea to introduce this structure of indirect object + **gustar** in the third-person singular as if it were a vocabulary item to be learned whole. Unfortunately, the translations of **gustar** in the dialogues often are *Do you like . . .* and *Yes, I do like . . .* or *No, I don't like. . . .* These translations soon cause confusion when students learn to conjugate verbs and discover that the first-person singular (in the present indicative) ends in **-o** and not in **-a**. Later, when students encounter the lesson about **gustar** and the **gustar** family of verbs, usually in conjunction with indirect object pronouns, confusion about the one often is compounded by confusion about the other.

Another problem in learning how to use the verb **gustar** is that when students move on to intermediate or advanced study, they discover that **gustar** can be used in more than just the third-person singular and plural. The earlier problems resurface at this point for some students because they were improperly conditioned. If you have experienced these sorts of confusions, then this chapter will resolve them.

Let's start with English, but not with the verb *to like* (since we know it is the source of the problem). The English verb *disgust* works grammatically just like the Spanish verb **gustar**. Happily, too, its root is quite obviously from the same Latin root as the Spanish verb. The English verb *disgust* expresses a stronger emotion than the Spanish verb **disgustar**, but let's examine the following example:

Me disgustan las anchoas.	*Anchovies disgust me. (More accurately: Anchovies displease me).*

From this sentence, we need only make a short hop in order to see how the verb **gustar** really works—and how its meaning requires it to work as it does! For the sake of example, recognize that *dis-* negates the verb it is prefixed to, and let's remove it and pretend for a moment that English has a verb *gust*, which means the opposite of *disgust*. In the following example, note that although the word orders of English and Spanish are different, the grammatical relationships between subject (**anchoas**/*anchovies*), object (**me**/*me*) and verb (**gusta**/*gust*) in both languages are the same.

Me gustan las anchoas.	*Anchovies gust me.*

The verb **gustar**, in a way, makes more sense than *to like*. Consider this: although an English speaker says *I like pizza*, the only thing the subject does is *eat* the pizza. It's the pizza that does the *pleasing*.

Doler

The verb **doler** causes similar confusion because, just as **gustar** means *to please* instead of *to like*, **doler** means *to be painful* instead of *to hurt*. However, having seen the grammatical relationship by some creative manipulation of the verb *disgust*, the following examples reveal how its meaning requires it to be used in the same way:

Me duelen los pies.	*My feet hurt (me).*
A Juan **le duele** una muela.	*John's molar hurts (him).*

Other members of the **gustar** family

The English counterparts of the rest of the verbs in the **gustar** family work grammatically in English in the same way as they do in Spanish. Examine the following sentences using **fascinar**, **encantar**, and **interesar**. Note that the second English translation in each example is the most common way English speakers express these ideas—and the reason why they often have difficulty using the Spanish verbs correctly: Spanish prefers verbs in the active voice to express these ideas whereas English prefers adjectives and passive constructions.

Nos fascinan historias sobre extraterrestres.	*Stories about extraterrestrials fascinate us.* *We are fascinated by stories about extraterrestrials.*
Les encanta escuchar óperas.	*Listening to operas enchants them.* *They're enchanted by the opera.* Or: *They just love operas.*
¿**Te interesan** las películas de espionaje?	*Do spy movies interest you?* *Are you interested in spy movies?*

As an example of how **gustar** can be used in forms other than the third person, consider this short and amusing dialogue between two young people who have just started dating. She is a native speaker of Spanish; he is an English speaker who doesn't know that **gustar** can be in the first- or second-person forms.

In his first reply, he simply mumbles her question aloud, trying to figure it out. She, of course, understands it perfectly! Remember: **gustar** means *to please*; it does not mean *to like*.

Juana:	¿**Te gusto?**	*Do you like me? (Literally: Do I please you?)*
John:	¿**Te gusto?**	*Do you like me?* [puzzled: talking to himself]
Juana:	¡Claro que **me gustas**, pero quiero saber si yo te gusto a ti.	*Of course I like you, but I want to know if you like me.*
John:	Sí.	*Yes.*

EJERCICIO
26·15

Translate the following sentences from Spanish to English.

1. Me fascina la geometría pero no me gusta estudiar estadísticas.

    _____

2. A mis padres, no les gustaba nada que yo hiciera travesuras en la escuela.

    _____

3. ¿Qué te parece si vamos a Cancún de vacaciones?

    _____

4. Esta mañana, me dolía la cabeza hasta que tomé una aspirina.

    _____

5. Cuando la conocí, les conté a mis amigos en seguida cómo ella me encantaba.

_____

6. ¿Te interesa estudiar conmigo?

_____

7. A ese chico no le importó que su hermana no se sintiera bien.

_____

8. Espero que estos ejercicios les gusten a mis lectores.

_____

9. Juana tenía dolor de cabeza pero no le dolía el estómago.

_____

10. Yo sé que si fueras a España, te encantarían las tapas.

_____

11. De niño, le fascinaba observar a los insectos.

_____

12. Ese Sr. Acero no me ha caído bien nunca.

_____

13. Le pareció raro que a la niña no le gustara nada en la escuela.

_____

14. Antes, me interesaba la literatura, pero ahora me llaman más la atención la historia y las biografías.

_____

15. Al joven, yo le impresiono con lo que sé sobre la historia local.

_____

16. ¿No te importa nada la política? Pues, tal vez porque no les importamos mucho a los políticos.

_____

17. María, yo sé que le gustas a Enrique.

_____

18. Las plantas carnívoras le fascinan a mi amiga.

_____

19. ¿No te repugna el olor del humo de tabaco?

_____

20. Me duelen los oídos cuando oigo cantar a esa mujer.

_____

Translate the following sentences from English into Spanish.

1. I like you. (**tú**)

   _____

2. Does she like me?

   _____

3. Are you fascinated by classical music? (**vosotros**)

   _____

4. Doesn't the way he writes seem strange to you? (**tú**)

   _____

5. I think you like me. (**tú**)

   _____

6. They used to be interested in playing chess, but not anymore.

   _____

7. After she quit smoking, she gained weight.

   _____

8. They don't like them (e.g., apples).

   _____

9. Aren't you repulsed by violent movies? (**Uds**.)

   _____

10. Money and power seemed to not matter to him after he returned from the war.

    _____

11. We really like making ice cream.

    _____

12. He was charmed by her smile.

    _____

13. You don't impress me, Mr. Acero. (**tú**)

    _____

14. My foot hurts.

    _____

15. What most matters to you in life, Alexandra? (**tú**)

    _____

16. Her mother's hands were hurting.

_____

17. It seemed strange to him that you liked asparagus. (**tú**)

_____

18. I hope you'll still be interested in studying Spanish after you finish this chapter! (**Uds.**)

_____

19. I'll be interested in the news.

_____

20. She likes me!

_____

Verb tables

Regular Verbs

Simple tenses

Indicative mood

PRESENT

hablar	hablo	hablas	habla	hablamos	habláis	hablan
comer	como	comes	come	comemos	coméis	comen
vivir	vivo	vives	vive	vivimos	vivís	viven

PRETERIT

hablar	hablé	hablaste	habló	hablamos	hablasteis	hablaron
comer	comí	comiste	comió	comimos	comisteis	comieron
vivir	viví	viviste	vivió	vivimos	vivisteis	vivieron

IMPERFECT

hablar	hablaba	hablabas	hablaba	hablábamos	hablabais	hablaban
comer	comía	comías	comía	comíamos	comíais	comían
vivir	vivía	vivías	vivía	vivíamos	vivíais	vivían

FUTURE

hablar	hablaré	hablarás	hablará	hablaremos	hablaréis	hablarán
comer	comeré	comerás	comerá	comeremos	comeréis	comerán
vivir	viviré	vivirás	vivirá	viviremos	viviréis	vivirán

CONDITIONAL

hablar	hablaría	hablarías	hablaría	hablaríamos	hablaríais	hablarían
comer	comería	comerías	comería	comeríamos	comeríais	comerían
vivir	viviría	vivirías	viviría	viviríamos	viviríais	vivirían

AFFIRMATIVE AND NEGATIVE COMMANDS

hablar (tú)	habla	no hables	**vivir (tú)**	vive	no vivas
hablar (Ud.)	hable	no hable	**vivir (Ud.)**	viva	no viva
hablar (vosotros)	hablad	no habléis	**vivir (vosotros)**	vivid	no viváis
hablar (Uds.)	hablen	no hablen	**vivir (Uds.)**	vivan	no vivan

comer (tú)	come	no comas
comer (Ud.)	coma	no coma
comer (vosotros)	comed	no comáis
comer (Uds.)	coman	no coman

Subjunctive mood

hablar	hable	hables	hable	hablemos	habléis	hablen
comer	coma	comas	coma	comamos	comáis	coman
vivir	viva	vivas	viva	vivamos	viváis	vivan

IMPERFECT -*RA* FORMS

hablar	hablara	hablaras	hablara	habláramos	hablarais	hablaran
comer	comiera	comieras	comiera	comiéramos	comierais	comieran
vivir	viviera	vivieras	viviera	viviéramos	vivierais	vivieran

IMPERFECT -*SE* FORMS

hablar	hablase	hablases	hablase	hablásemos	hablaseis	hablasen
comer	comiese	comieses	comiese	comiésemos	comieseis	comiesen
vivir	viviese	vivieses	viviese	viviésemos	vivieseis	viviesen

Compound tenses

Use a form of auxiliary **haber** plus the past participle of a verb (**hablado, comido, vivido**).

Indicative mood

PRESENT PERFECT

hablar	he	has	ha	hemos	habéis	han	**hablado**
comer	he	has	ha	hemos	habéis	han	**comido**
vivir	he	has	ha	hemos	habéis	han	**vivido**

PLUPERFECT

hablar	había	habías	había	habíamos	habíais	habían	**hablado**
comer	había	habías	había	habíamos	habíais	habían	**comido**
vivir	había	habías	había	habíamos	habíais	habían	**vivido**

PRETERIT PERFECT

hablar	hube	hubiste	hubo	hubimos	hubisteis	hubieron	**hablado**
comer	hube	hubiste	hubo	hubimos	hubisteis	hubieron	**comido**
vivir	hube	hubiste	hubo	hubimos	hubisteis	hubieron	**vivido**

FUTURE PERFECT

hablar	habré	habrás	habrá	habremos	habréis	habrán	**hablado**
comer	habré	habrás	habrá	habremos	habréis	habrán	**comido**
vivir	habré	habrás	habrá	habremos	habréis	habrán	**vivido**

CONDITIONAL PERFECT

hablar	habría	habrías	habría	habríamos	habríais	habrían	**hablado**
comer	habría	habrías	habría	habríamos	habríais	habrían	**comido**
vivir	habría	habrías	habría	habríamos	habríais	habrían	**vivido**

Subjunctive mood

PRESENT PERFECT

hablar	haya	hayas	haya	hayamos	hayáis	hayan	**hablado**
comer	haya	hayas	haya	hayamos	hayáis	hayan	**comido**
vivir	haya	hayas	haya	hayamos	hayáis	hayan	**vivido**

PLUPERFECT -RA FORMS							
hablar	hubiera	hubieras	hubiera	hubiéramos	hubierais	hubieran	**hablado**
comer	hubiera	hubieras	hubiera	hubiéramos	hubierais	hubieran	**comido**
vivir	hubiera	hubieras	hubiera	hubiéramos	hubierais	hubieran	**vivido**

PLUPERFECT -SE FORMS							
hablar	hubiese	hubieses	hubiese	hubiésemos	hubieseis	hubiesen	**hablado**
comer	hubiese	hubieses	hubiese	hubiésemos	hubieseis	hubiesen	**comido**
vivir	hubiese	hubieses	hubiese	hubiésemos	hubieseis	hubiesen	**vivido**

Verbs with spelling changes

-**ger** or -**gir** infinitives change **g** to **j** before -**o** and -**a**:

PRESENT INDICATIVE						
escoger	escojo	escoges	escoge	escogemos	escogéis	escogen

PRESENT SUBJUNCTIVE						
escoger	escoja	escojas	escoja	escojamos	escojáis	escojan

-**guir** infinitives change **gu** to **g** before -**o** and -**a**:

PRESENT INDICATIVE						
extinguir	extingo	extingues	extingue	extinguimos	extinguís	extinguen

PRESENT SUBJUNCTIVE						
extinguir	extinga	extingas	extinga	extingamos	extingáis	extingan

-**cer** and -**cir** infinitives change **c** to **z** before -**o** and -**a**:

PRESENT INDICATIVE						
vencer	venzo	vences	vence	vencemos	vencéis	vencen

PRESENT SUBJUNCTIVE						
vencer	venza	venzas	venza	venzamos	venzáis	venzan

-**car** infinitives change **c** to **qu** before -**e**:

PRETERIT INDICATIVE						
explicar	expliqué	explicaste	explicó	explicamos	explicasteis	explicaron

PRESENT SUBJUNCTIVE						
explicar	explique	expliques	explique	expliquemos	expliquéis	expliquen

-**gar** infinitives change **g** to **gu** before -**e**:

PRETERIT INDICATIVE						
llegar	llegué	llegaste	llegó	llegamos	llegasteis	llegaron

PRESENT SUBJUNCTIVE						
llegar	llegue	llegues	llegue	lleguemos	lleguéis	lleguen

-**zar** infinitives change **z** to **c** before -**e**:

PRETERIT INDICATIVE						
cruzar	crucé	cruzaste	cruzó	cruzamos	cruzasteis	cruzaron

| **cruzar** | cruce | cruces | cruce | crucemos | crucéis | crucen |

Verbs with stem changes

Infinitives in **-ar** change stem **e** to **ie**, **o** to **ue**, and **u** to **ue**:

CERRAR

Present indicative	cierro	cierras	cierra	cerramos	cerráis	cierran
Present subjunctive	cierre	cierres	cierre	cerremos	cerréis	cierren

CONTAR

Present indicative	cuento	cuentas	cuenta	contamos	contáis	cuentan
Present subjunctive	cuente	cuentes	cuente	contemos	contéis	cuenten

JUGAR

Present indicative	juego	juegas	juega	jugamos	jugáis	juegan
Present subjunctive	juegue	juegues	juegue	juguemos	juguéis	jueguen

Infinitives in **-er** change stem **e** to **ie** and **o** to **ue**:

PERDER

Present indicative	pierdo	pierdes	pierde	perdemos	perdéis	pierden
Present subjunctive	pierda	pierdas	pierda	perdamos	perdáis	pierdan

MOVER

Present indicative	muevo	mueves	mueve	movemos	movéis	mueven
Present subjunctive	mueva	muevas	mueva	movamos	mováis	muevan

Infinitives in **-ir** change stem **e** to **i**, **e** to **ie** and **i**, and **o** to **ue** and **u**:

PEDIR

Present indicative	pido	pides	pide	pedimos	pedís	piden
Preterit indicative	pedí	pediste	pidió	pedimos	pedisteis	pidieron
Present subjunctive	pida	pidas	pida	pidamos	pidáis	pidan
Imperfect subjunctive	pidiera	pidieras	pidiera	pidiéramos	pidierais	pidieran

MENTIR

Present indicative	miento	mientes	miente	mentimos	mentís	mienten
Preterit indicative	mentí	mentiste	mintió	mentimos	mentisteis	mintieron
Present subjunctive	mienta	mientas	mienta	mintamos	mintáis	mientan
Imperfect subjunctive	mintiera	mintieras	mintiera	mintiéramos	mintierais	mintieran

MORIR

Present indicative	muero	mueres	muere	morimos	morís	mueren
Preterit indicative	morí	moriste	murió	morimos	moristeis	murieron
Present subjunctive	muera	mueras	muera	muramos	muráis	mueran
Imperfect subjunctive	muriera	murieras	muriera	muriéramos	murierais	murieran

Infinitives in **-uir** add **y** to the stem before the endings:

HUIR

Present indicative	huyo	huyes	huye	huimos	huís	huyen
Preterit indicative	huí	huiste	huyó	huimos	huisteis	huyeron
Present subjunctive	huya	huyas	huya	huyamos	huyáis	huyan
Imperfect subjunctive	huyera	huyeras	huyera	huyéramos	huyerais	huyeran

Irregular verbs

Indicative mood

PRESENT

caber	quepo	cabes	cabe	cabemos	cabéis	caben
caer	caigo	caes	cae	caemos	caéis	caen
dar	doy	das	da	damos	dais	dan
decir	digo	dices	dice	decimos	decís	dicen
estar	estoy	estás	está	estamos	estáis	están
haber	he	has	ha	hemos	habéis	han
hacer	hago	haces	hace	hacemos	hacéis	hacen
ir	voy	vas	va	vamos	vais	van
oír	oigo	oyes	oye	oímos	oís	oyen
poner	pongo	pones	pone	ponemos	ponéis	ponen
saber	sé	sabes	sabe	sabemos	sabéis	saben
salir	salgo	sales	sale	salimos	salís	salen
ser	soy	eres	es	somos	sois	son
tener	tengo	tienes	tiene	tenemos	tenéis	tienen
traer	traigo	traes	trae	traemos	traéis	traen
valer	valgo	vales	vale	valemos	valéis	valen
venir	vengo	vienes	viene	venimos	venís	vienen
ver	veo	ves	ve	vemos	veis	ven

PRETERIT

andar	anduve	anduviste	anduvo	anduvimos	anduvisteis	anduvieron
caber	cupe	cupiste	cupo	cupimos	cupisteis	cupieron
dar	di	diste	dio	dimos	disteis	dieron
decir	dije	dijiste	dijo	dijimos	dijisteis	dijeron
estar	estuve	estuviste	estuvo	estuvimos	estuvisteis	estuvieron
haber	hube	hubiste	hubo	hubimos	hubisteis	hubieron
hacer	hice	hiciste	hizo	hicimos	hicisteis	hicieron
ir	fui	fuiste	fue	fuimos	fuisteis	fueron
poder	pude	pudiste	pudo	pudimos	pudisteis	pudieron
poner	puse	pusiste	puso	pusimos	pusisteis	pusieron
querer	quise	quisiste	quiso	quisimos	quisisteis	quisieron
saber	supe	supiste	supo	supimos	supisteis	supieron
ser	fui	fuiste	fue	fuimos	fuisteis	fueron
tener	tuve	tuviste	tuvo	tuvimos	tuvisteis	tuvieron
traducir	traduje	tradujiste	tradujo	tradujimos	tradujisteis	tradujeron
traer	traje	trajiste	trajo	trajimos	trajisteis	trajeron
venir	vine	viniste	vino	vinimos	vinisteis	vinieron
ver	vi	viste	vio	vimos	visteis	vieron

IMPERFECT

ir	iba	ibas	iba	íbamos	ibais	iban
ser	era	eras	era	éramos	erais	eran
ver	veía	veías	veía	veíamos	veíais	veían

FUTURE

caber	cabré	cabrás	cabrá	cabremos	cabréis	cabrán
decir	diré	dirás	dirá	diremos	diréis	dirán
haber	habré	habrás	habrá	habremos	habréis	habrán
hacer	haré	harás	hará	haremos	haréis	harán

poder	podré	podrás	podrá	podremos	podréis	podrán
poner	pondré	pondrás	pondrá	pondremos	pondréis	pondrán
querer	querré	querrás	querrá	querremos	querréis	querrán
saber	sabré	sabrás	sabrá	sabremos	sabréis	sabrán
salir	saldré	saldrás	saldrá	saldremos	saldréis	saldrán
tener	tendré	tendrás	tendrá	tendremos	tendréis	tendrán
valer	valdré	valdrás	valdrá	valdremos	valdréis	valdrán
venir	vendré	vendrás	vendrá	vendremos	vendréis	vendrán

CONDITIONAL

caber	cabría	cabrías	cabría	cabríamos	cabríais	cabrían
decir	diría	dirías	diría	diríamos	diríais	dirían
haber	habría	habrías	habría	habríamos	habríais	habrían
hacer	haría	harías	haría	haríamos	haríais	harían
poder	podría	podrías	podría	podríamos	podríais	podrían
poner	pondría	pondrías	pondría	pondríamos	pondríais	pondrían
querer	querría	querrías	querría	querríamos	querríais	querrían
saber	sabría	sabrías	sabría	sabríamos	sabríais	sabrían
salir	saldría	saldrías	saldría	saldríamos	saldríais	saldrían
tener	tendría	tendrías	tendría	tendríamos	tendríais	tendrían
valer	valdría	valdrías	valdría	valdríamos	valdríais	valdrían
venir	vendría	vendrías	vendría	vendríamos	vendríais	vendrían

Subjunctive mood

PRESENT SUBJUNCTIVE

caber	quepa	quepas	quepa	quepamos	quepáis	quepan
caer	caiga	caigas	caiga	caigamos	caigáis	caigan
dar	dé	des	dé	demos	deis	den
estar	esté	estés	esté	estemos	estéis	estén
haber	haya	hayas	haya	hayamos	hayáis	hayan
hacer	haga	hagas	haga	hagamos	hagáis	hagan
ir	vaya	vayas	vaya	vayamos	vayáis	vayan
poner	ponga	pongas	ponga	pongamos	pongáis	pongan
saber	sepa	sepas	sepa	sepamos	sepáis	sepan
salir	salga	salgas	salga	salgamos	salgáis	salgan
ser	sea	seas	sea	seamos	seáis	sean
traer	traiga	traigas	traiga	traigamos	traigáis	traigan
valer	valga	valgas	valga	valgamos	valgáis	valgan
ver	vea	veas	vea	veamos	veáis	vean

IMPERFECT SUBJUNCTIVE

andar	anduviera	anduvieras	anduviera	anduviéramos	anduvierais	anduvieran
caber	cupiera	cupieras	cupiera	cupiéramos	cupierais	cupieran
dar	diera	dieras	diera	diéramos	dierais	dieran
decir	dijera	dijeras	dijera	dijéramos	dijerais	dijeran
estar	estuviera	estuvieras	estuviera	estuviéramos	estuvierais	estuvieran
haber	hubiera	hubieras	hubiera	hubiéramos	hubierais	hubieran
hacer	hiciera	hicieras	hiciera	hiciéramos	hicierais	hicieran
ir	fuera	fueras	fuera	fuéramos	fuerais	fueran
poder	pudiera	pudieras	pudiera	pudiéramos	pudierais	pudieran
poner	pusiera	pusieras	pusiera	pusiéramos	pusierais	pusieran
querer	quisiera	quisieras	quisiera	quisiéramos	quisierais	quisieran
saber	supiera	supieras	supiera	supiéramos	supierais	supieran

ser	fuera	fueras	fuera	fuéramos	fuerais	fueran
tener	tuviera	tuvieras	tuviera	tuviéramos	tuvierais	tuvieran
traducir	tradujera	tradujeras	tradujera	tradujéramos	tradujerais	tradujeran
traer	trajera	trajeras	trajera	trajéramos	trajerais	trajeran
venir	viniera	vinieras	viniera	viniéramos	vinierais	vinieran
ver	viera	vieras	viera	viéramos	vierais	vieran

Spanish-English glossary

A

abismo (*m.*) abyss
abogado/a (*m./f.*) lawyer
abrazar to embrace, hug
abril (*m.*) April
abrir to open
abuelo/a (*m./f.*) grandfather/ grandmother
aburrido/a bored; boring
aburrir to bore; **aburrirse** to get bored
accidente (*m.*) accident
aceite (*m.*) oil (*cooking; motor*)
aceituna (*f.*) olive
aceptar to accept
acerca de about
aconsejar to advise
acordarse (**o > ue**) (**de**) to remember
acostar (**o > ue**) to put to bed; **acostarse** to go to bed
acostumbrarse (**a**) to get used (to)
actitud (*f.*) attitude
actuar to act; to behave
acuerdo (*m.*) agreement; **estar de acuerdo** to agree
adelgazar to lose weight
adentro inside
adivinar to guess
adolescente (*m./f.*) teenager; adolescent
¿adónde? where to?
aduana (*f.*) customs
advertir (**e > ie**) to advise, warn
aerolínea (*f.*) airline
aeropuerto (*m.*) airport
afeitarse to shave
aficionado/a (*m./f.*) fan
afuera outside; **afueras** (*f. pl.*) suburbs
agente de viajes (*m./f.*) travel agent
agosto (*m.*) August
agradable (*m./f.*) pleasant
agregar to add (up)
aguacero (*m.*) downpour, shower
aguinaldo (*m.*) bonus; Christmas gift
ahora now

ahorrar to save (up)
aire (*m.*) air; **al aire libre** outdoors
ajedrez (*m.*) chess
ajo (*m.*) garlic
alcalde (*m.*) mayor
alcanzar to reach
alegría (*f.*) happiness
alejarse to walk away
alemán (*m.*) German (*language*); **alemán (alemana)** German (*person*)
alfombra (*f.*) rug; carpet
algo something; anything
algodón (*m.*) cotton
alguien someone, somebody; anybody
allí there
almohada (*f.*) pillow
almorzar (**o > ue**) to eat lunch
almuerzo (*m.*) lunch
alquilar to rent
alquiler (*m.*) rent
alrededor (**de**) around
amable (*m./f.*) nice, kind
amar to love
amarillo/a yellow; (*m.*) yellow (*color*)
ambiente (*m.*) environment; **medio ambiente** (*m.*) environment
ambos/as both
amistad (*f.*) friendship
amistoso/a friendly
amor (*m.*) love
ancho/a wide
andar to walk
anfitrión (anfitriona) (*m./f.*) host/hostess
anillo (*m.*) ring
anoche last night
anónimo/a anonymous
anteojos (*m. pl.*) eyeglasses
antes (**de**) before; beforehand
antipático/a unpleasant
anuncio (*m.*) commercial; advertisement
añadir to add
año (*m.*) year
apagar to turn off

aparcamiento (*m.*)   parking lot, parking space
aparcar   to park
aparecer   to appear
apenas   hardly
aprender   to learn
aprobar (**o > ue**)   to approve
aquí   here
arañar   to scratch
árbol (*m.*)   tree
archivo (*m.*)   file
arena (*f.*)   sand
arete (*m.*)   earring
armario (*m.*)   closet; cabinet
arquitecto/a (*m./f.*)   architect
arreglar   to fix; to repair
arreglo (*m.*)   repair
arroz (*m.*)   rice
arruga (*f.*)   wrinkle
artículo (*m.*)   item; article
ascensor (*m.*)   elevator
así   in this way
asistente (*m./f.*)   assistant; **asistente de vuelo** flight attendant
asistir (**a**)   to attend
aspiradora (*f.*)   vacuum cleaner; **pasar la aspiradora** to vacuum
astronauta (*m./f.*)   astronaut
asunto (*m.*)   matter
asustar   to scare; **asustarse** to get scared
atacar   to attack
aterrizar   to land
atleta (*m./f.*)   athlete
atraer   to attract
aumento (*m.*)   raise; increase
aunque   although
autobús (*m.*)   bus
autopista (*f.*)   expresssway; **autopista de peaje** (*f.*) turnpike
ave (*f.*)   bird
avergonzado/a   embarrassed
averiguar   to find out
avión (*m.*)   airplane
avisar   to let know
ayer   yesterday
ayuda (*f.*)   help
ayudar   to help
azúcar (*m.*)   sugar

B

bailar   to dance
baile (*m.*)   dance
bajo/a   short; low
ballena (*f.*)   whale; **observar ballenas** (*f.*) whale watching
baloncesto (*m.*)   basketball
banco (*m.*)   bank
bandera (*f.*)   flag
bañar   to bathe; **bañarse** to take a bath

baño (*m.*)   bath; bathroom
baraja (*f.*)   deck of cards
barato/a   inexpensive
barco (*m.*)   boat; ship
barrer   to sweep
barrio (*m.*)   neighborhood
bastante   enough
bastar   to suffice
basura (*f.*)   garbage; trash
baúl (*m.*)   trunk
bebé (*m.*)   baby
beber   to drink
béisbol (*m.*)   baseball
belleza (*f.*)   beauty
bendecir (**e > i**)   to bless
beso (*m.*)   kiss
biblioteca (*f.*)   library
bicicleta (*f.*)   bicycle
bien   well
bienestar (*m.*)   well-being
bilingüe (*m./f.*)   bilingual
billete (*m.*)   ticket
billetera (*f.*)   wallet
billón (*m.*)   billion
boca (*f.*)   mouth
boda (*f.*)   wedding
boleto (*m.*)   ticket
bolígrafo (*m.*)   pen
bolsa (*f.*)   purse; pocketbook; bag
bolsillo (*m.*)   pocket
bombero/a (*m./f.*)   firefighter
bombilla (*f.*)   light bulb
bosque (*m.*)   woods; forest
botón (*m.*)   button
bravo/a   brave
breve (*m./f.*)   brief
brillar   to shine
broma (*f.*)   joke
bronceador (*m.*)   suntan oil
bruja (*f.*)   witch
bueno/a   good
burbuja (*f.*)   bubble
buscar   to look for, search for
butaca (*f.*)   armchair
buzón (*m.*)   mailbox

C

caballo (*m.*)   horse
cabello (*m.*)   hair
caber   to fit
cabeza (*f.*)   head
cada (*m./f.*)   every; each
caer   to fall; **caerse** to fall down
café (*m.*)   coffee; brown
cafetería (*f.*)   cafeteria; coffee shop
caja (*f.*)   box
cajero/a (*m./f.*)   cashier

calcetines (*m.*)   socks
cálido/a   warm
callarse   to be quiet
calle (*f.*)   street
calor (*m.*)   heat; warmth
calvo/a   bald
cama (*f.*)   bed
cámara (*f.*)   camera
cambiar   to change
cambio (*m.*)   change; exchange rate; **en cambio** on the other hand
camino (*m.*)   road
camisa (*f.*)   shirt
camiseta (*f.*)   T-shirt
campaña (*f.*)   campaign
campeón (campeona) (*m./f.*)   champion
campeonato (*m.*)   championship
canción (*f.*)   song
candidato/a (*m./f.*)   candidate
cansado/a   tired
cansar   to tire; **cansarse** to get tired
cantante (*m./f.*)   singer
cantar   to sing
cantidad (*f.*)   amount
capital (*f.*)   capital city; **capital** (*m.*) capital wealth
capítulo (*m.*)   chapter
carácter (*m.*)   character; temper
cárcel (*f.*)   jail; prison
carne (*f.*)   meat
caro/a   expensive
carrera (*f.*)   career
carretera (*f.*)   highway
carta (*f.*)   letter; card
casado/a   married
casarse (**con**)   to marry, get married (to)
casi   almost
caso (*m.*)   case
castillo (*m.*)   castle
catálogo (*m.*)   catalogue
cazar   to hunt
cebolla (*f.*)   onion
celebrar   to celebrate
celoso/a   jealous
cena (*f.*)   dinner
cenar   to eat dinner
centro (*m.*)   center; downtown
centro comercial (*m.*)   shopping mall/ center
cepillar(se)   to brush (oneself) (*hair, teeth*)
cepillo (*m.*)   brush
cerebro (*m.*)   brain
ceremonia (*f.*)   ceremony
cerrado/a   closed
cerrar (**e > ie**)   to close
cerveza (*f.*)   beer
césped (*m.*)   lawn

chaqueta (*f.*)   jacket
charlar   to chat
cheque (*m.*)   check
chico/a (*m./f.*)   small; boy/girl
chimenea (*f.*)   fireplace
chisme (*m.*)   gossip
chiste (*m.*)   joke
chocar   to crash
cielo (*m.*)   sky
ciencia (*f.*)   science
cierto/a   certain; true
cigarro (*m.*)   cigar
cine (*m.*)   movie theater; movies
cinta (*f.*)   tape
cinturón (*m.*)   belt
cita (*f.*)   date; appointment
clase (*f.*)   class
clasificar   to classify
cliente/clienta (*m./f.*) client; customer
clima (*m.*)   climate
cocinar   to cook
cocinero/a (*m./f.*)   cook; chef
coger   to catch, grab
cohete (*m.*)   rocket
cola (*f.*)   line; tail
colchón (*m.*)   mattress
colgar (**o > ue**)   to hang (up)
collar (*m.*)   necklace
comedor (*m.*)   dining room
comenzar (**e > ie**)   to begin, start
comer   to eat
cometa (*m.*)   comet; (*f.*) kite
cómico/a   funny
comida (*f.*)   food; meal
comisión (*f.*)   commission
como   as
¿cómo?   how?
cómodo/a   comfortable
compañero/a (*m./f.*)   classmate; colleague; **compañero/a de cuarto** roommate
compañía (*f.*)   company
competir (**e > i**)   to compete
componer   to compose
comportarse   to act, behave
compra (*f.*)   purchase; **ir de compras** to go shopping
comprar   to buy, purchase
comprender   to understand, comprehend
compromiso (*m.*)   commitment; engagement
con   with
con tal (de) que   provided that
conceder   to grant
concierto (*m.*)   concert
concluir   to conclude
concurso (*m.*)   contest
conducir   to drive; to conduct, lead
confesar (**e > ie**)   to confess
confianza (*f.*)   trust

congelar to freeze

congreso (*m.*) convention; congress

conjugar to conjugate

conocer to know, be acquainted with

conquistar to conquer

conseguir (**e** > **i**) to get; to succeed in

consejo (*m.*) advice

consentir (**e** > **ie**) to consent, allow

constituir to constitute, make up

construir to construct, build

consultorio (*m.*) doctor's office

contado (**al contado**) (for) cash

contaminación (*f.*) contamination; pollution

contar (**o** > **ue**) to count

contener to contain

contestar to answer

contra against

contraseña (*f.*) password

contribuir to contribute

convencer to convince

convenir (**en**) to agree (to)

convertir (**e** > **ie**) to turn into

convidar to invite

copa (*f.*) stem glass

corazón (*m.*) heart

corbata (*f.*) necktie

corregir (**e** > **i**) to correct

correo (*m.*) mail; **echar al correo** to mail (*a letter*)

correr to run

cortar to cut

corte (*m.*) cut; **corte de pelo** (*m.*) haircut

cortés (*m./f.*) polite

cortina (*f.*) curtain

cosa (*f.*) thing

cosecha (*f.*) harvest

costar (**o** > **ue**) to cost

costumbre (*f.*) custom, habit

crecer to grow

creer to believe

criar to raise

crimen (*m.*) crime

cristal (*m.*) crystal

cruzar to cross

cuadra (*f.*) city block

cuadro (*m.*) painting

cualquier(a) any

cuando when; **cuando quiera** whenever

cuanto/a whatever; **¿cuánto?** how much?; **¡cuánto!** how!

cuarto (*m.*) room

cubrir to cover

cuchara (*f.*) spoon

cuchillo (*m.*) knife

cuenta (*f.*) bill

cuento (*m.*) story; **cuento de hadas** fairy tale

cuestión (*f.*) issue; matter

cuidado (*m.*) care

cuidadosamente carefully

cuidadoso/a careful

cuidar to care for; **cuidarse** to take care of oneself

culpa (*f.*) blame; **tener la culpa** to be to blame

culpar to blame

cultivar to grow plants

cumpleaños (*m.*) birthday

cuñado/a (*m./f.*) brother-in-law/sister-in-law

curso (*m.*) class, course

cuyo/a whose

D

dama (*f.*) lady, woman; **damas** checkers

dañar to break; to damage

daño (*m.*) injury; damage; **hacer daño** to hurt, do damage

dar to give; **dar un paseo** to take a walk; **darse cuenta de** to realize

debajo de under

deber ought to; must

decidir to decide

decir (**e** > **i**) to say, tell

defender (**e** > **ie**) to defend

dejar to leave (out); to allow

delgado/a thin; slim

demasiado too much

demostrar (**o** > **ue**) to demonstrate

dentro de inside

dependiente (*m./f.*) clerk

depositar to deposit

deprimido/a depressed

derecha (*f.*) right; **a la derecha** to the right

derecho (*m.*) right (*privilege*)

desaparecer to disappear

desastre (*m.*) disaster

desayunar to have breakfast

desayuno (*m.*) breakfast

descansar to rest

descortés impolite

describir to describe

descubrir to discover

desde from

deseo (*m.*) wish; desire

desfile (*m.*) parade

deshacer to undo

desierto (*m.*) desert

desmayarse to faint

despedirse (**e** > **i**) to say good-bye

despertar(se) (**e** > **ie**) to wake up

después later; **después de** afterwards

destacar(se) to stand out

destruir to destroy

desvestirse (**e** > **ie**) to undress (oneself)

detener to stop; to arrest

devolver (**o** > **ue**) to return

día (*m.*)   day; **día feriado** (*m.*) holiday
diamante (*m.*)   diamond
diario (*m.*)   diary; newspaper
dibujo (*m.*)   drawing
diciembre (*m.*)   December
diente (*m.*)   tooth
dieta (*f.*)   diet; **estar a dieta** to be on a diet
difícil (*m./f.*)   hard, difficult
dificultad (*f.*)   difficulty
dinero (*m.*)   money
Dios; dios (*m.*)   God; god
diploma (*m.*)   diploma
dirección (*f.*)   address
dirigir   to direct
disculparse   to excuse oneself
discutir   to discuss; to argue
diseñador(a) (*m./f.*)   designer
diseño (*m.*)   design
disfraz (*m.*)   disguise, costume
distancia (*f.*)   distance
distinto/a   different
diversión (*f.*)   amusement, fun; **parque de diversiones** (*m.*) amusement park
divertirse (**e > ie**)   to have fun
doblar   to turn
docena (*f.*)   dozen
documento (*m.*)   document
dólar (*m.*)   dollar
doler (**o > ue**)   to hurt
dolor (*m.*)   ache; pain
domingo (*m.*)   Sunday
donde   where; **¿dónde?** where?
dondequiera   wherever
dormir (**o > ue**)   to sleep; **dormirse** to fall asleep
dormitorio (*m.*)   bedroom
drama (*m.*)   play
ducha (*f.*)   shower
ducharse   to take a shower
dudar   to doubt
dulce (*m./f.*)   sweet
durante   during
durar   to last
duro/a   hard

E

echar   to pour; **echarse** to rest; **echar de menos** to miss someone, something
edad (*f.*)   age
edificio (*m.*)   building
educar   to educate
egoísta (*m./f.*)   selfish
ejército (*m.*)   army
elección (*f.*)   election
elegir (**e > i**)   to elect
embajador(a) (*m./f.*)   ambassador

emboscada (*f.*)   ambush
emisora (*f.*)   radio station
emocionante (*m./f.*)   exciting
empacar   to pack
empezar (**e > ie**)   to begin
empleado/a (*m./f.*)   employee
empleo (*m.*)   job; work
empresa (*f.*)   enterprise
enamorado/a (*m./f.*)   lover; **estar enamorado/a** to be in love
encantador(a)   charming
encender (**e > ie**)   to light; to kindle
encima de   on top of
encontrar (**o > ue**)   to find; **encontrarse con** to meet with
enemigo/a (*m./f.*)   enemy
energía (*f.*)   energy
enero (*m.*)   January
enfermarse   to get sick
enfermedad (*f.*)   illness
enfermero/a (*m./f.*)   nurse
enfermo/a   sick
enfrente (de)   in front (of)
engañar   to deceive
enigma (*m.*)   enigma; puzzle
enojado/a   angry
enojarse   to get angry
ensalada (*f.*)   salad
ensayar   to rehearse
ensayo (*m.*)   rehearsal
enseñar   to teach
entender (**e > ie**)   to understand
entero/a   entire
entonces   then
entrada (*f.*)   entrance; admission
entrar   to enter
entre   between
entregar   to deliver
entrenar   to train
entrevista (*f.*)   interview
enviar   to send
envolver (**o > ue**)   to wrap
equipaje (*m.*)   equipment; luggage
equipo (*m.*)   team; gear
equivocarse   to make a mistake
error (*m.*)   error; mistake
escalera (*f.*)   staircase; stairs; ladder
escena (*f.*)   scene
escenario (*m.*)   stage
escoger   to select
esconder   to hide
escrito/a   written; **por escrito** in writing
escritorio (*m.*)   desk
escuchar   to listen

escuela (*f.*)   school; **escuela secundaria** high school
esmeralda (*f.*)   emerald
espacio (*m.*)   space; room
espalda (*f.*)   back
espejo (*m.*)   mirror
esperar   to hope; to wait
espía (*m./f.*)   spy
esposo/a (*m./f.*)   husband/wife
esquiar   to ski
esquina (*f.*)   corner
establecer   to establish
estación (*f.*)   season; station
estacionar   to park
estado (*m.*)   state
Estados Unidos (*m.*)   United States
estampilla (*f.*)   stamp
estante (*m.*)   shelf
estar   to be; **estar a dieta** to be on a diet
estómago (*m.*)   stomach
estornudar   to sneeze
estrella (*f.*)   star; **estrella de cine** movie star
estudiante (*m./f.*)   student
estudios (*m.*)   studies
estupendo/a   great
examen (*m.*)   exam
excursión (*f.*)   day trip
exigir   to demand
éxito (*m.*)   success; **tener éxito** to be successful
exitoso/a   successful
exposición (*f.*)   exhibit
extinguir   to extinguish
extranjero/a   foreign
extraño/a   strange; odd

F

fábrica (*f.*)   factory
falda (*f.*)   skirt
faltar   to be lacking, be absent
fama (*f.*)   fame
fantasía (*f.*)   fantasy
fantasma (*m.*)   ghost
farmacia (*f.*)   pharmacy
fascinar   to fascinate
fastidiar   to bother
favor (*m.*)   favor
febrero (*m.*)   February
felicidad (*f.*)   happiness
feliz (*m./f.*)   happy
ferrocarril (*m.*)   railroad
fiebre (*f.*)   fever
fiesta (*f.*)   party
fin (*m.*)   end; **fin de semana** weekend
financiero/a   financial
fingir   to pretend
firma (*f.*)   signature
firmar   to sign
flan (*m.*)   custard

flor (*f.*)   flower
florero (*m.*)   vase
flotar   to float
fondo (*m.*)   bottom
forma (*f.*)   shape; **en buena forma** in good shape
foto (*f.*)   photo
francés (*m.*)   French (*language*); **francés (francesa)**
   French (*person*)
frase (*f.*)   sentence; phrase
frecuencia (*f.*)   frequency;
   con frecuencia frequently, often
fregar (**e > ie**)   to wash (*dishes*)
freír (**e > i**)   to fry
fresa (*f.*)   strawberry
fresco/a   cool
frío/a   cold
frontera (*f.*)   border
fuego (*m.*)   fire
fuera   outside
fumar   to smoke
funcionar   to work, run (*machinery*)
fútbol (*m.*)   soccer
fútbol americano (*m.*)   football

G

gafas de sol (*f.*)   sunglasses
gana (*f.*)   desire; **tener ganas de**
   to feel like
ganador(a) (*m./f.*)   winner
ganar   to win; to earn
ganga (*f.*)   bargain
gasolina (*f.*)   gasoline
gastar   to spend
gato (*m.*)   cat
gente (*f.*)   people
gigante (*m.*)   giant
gimnasio (*m.*)   gym; gymnasium
girar   to turn
gobernador(a) (*m./f.*)   governor
goma (*f.*)   glue; **goma de borrar** eraser
gota (*f.*)   drop
gozar   to enjoy
grabadora (*f.*)   recorder
grabar   to record
graduarse   to graduate
gran (*m./f.*)   great; grand
grande (*m./f.*)   big; large
grave (*m./f.*)   serious
gravedad (*f.*)   gravity
griego (*m.*)   Greek (*language*); **griego/a** Greek (*person*)
guante (*m.*)   glove
guapo/a   handsome; good-looking
guardar   to keep; **guardar cama**
   to stay in bed
guerra (*f.*)   war
guía (*m./f.*)   guide; **guía de turismo**
   (*f.*) travel guide

guitarra (*f.*)   guitar
gustar   to like; to be pleasing
gusto (*m.*)   taste

H

habitación (*f.*)   room
hablar   to speak, talk
hacer   to make; to do; **hacer ejercicio** to exercise;
　hacer una pregunta to ask a question
hamaca (*f.*)   hammock
hambre (*f.*)   hunger
hamburguesa (*f.*)   hamburger
hasta   until
hecho (*m.*)   fact
helado (*m.*)   ice cream
herido/a   wounded
hermano/a (*m./f.*)   brother/sister
hervir (**e > ie**)   to boil
hidrante de incendios (*m.*)   fire hydrant
hielo (*m.*)   ice
hierba (*f.*)   grass
hipoteca (*f.*)   mortgage
hogar (*m.*)   home
hoja (*f.*)   leaf
hombre (*m.*)   man
hombro (*m.*)   shoulder
honrado/a   honest
horario (*m.*)   schedule
horno (*m.*)   oven
hotel (*m.*)   hotel
hoy   today
huelga (*f.*)   strike
hueso (*m.*)   bone
huésped (*m./f.*)   guest
huevo (*m.*)   egg
huir   to flee
humano/a   human
humilde   humble
humor (*m.*)   humor
huracán (*m.*)   hurricane

I

idioma (*m.*)   language
iglesia (*f.*)   church
igual (*m./f.*)   equal; same
imaginarse   to imagine
impedir (**e > i**)   to prevent
impermeable (*m.*)   raincoat
imponer   to enforce
importante (*m./f.*)   important;
　importarle a alguien to be important
importar   to import
impuesto (*m.*)   tax
incendio (*m.*)   fire
incluir   to include
incluso   including
incómodo/a   uncomfortable

influir   to influence
información (*f.*)   information
ingeniero/a (*m./f.*)   engineer
Inglaterra (*f.*)   England
inglés (*m.*)   English (*language*); **inglés**
　(inglesa)   English (*person*)
insistir   to insist
intentar   to try
interés (*m.*)   interest
interesar   to interest
introducir   to present
inundación (*f.*)   flood
inundar   to flood
invertir (**e > ie**)   to invest
investigar   to investigate
invierno (*m.*)   winter
invitación (*f.*)   invitation
invitado/a (*m./f.*)   guest
invitar   to invite
ir   to go; **irse** to go away; **ir de compras** to go shopping
izquierda   left; **a la izquierda** to the left

J

jamás   never; not ever
jardín (*m.*)   garden
jaula (*f.*)   cage
jefe/a (*m./f.*)   boss; employer
jirafa (*f.*)   giraffe
joven (*m./f.*)   young
joya (*f.*)   jewel
joyas (*f.*)   jewelry
joyería (*f.*)   jewelry store
juego (*m.*)   game
jueves (*m.*)   Thursday
juez(a) (*m./f.*)   judge
jugar (**o > ue**) **(a)**   to play (*a game or sport*)
juguetería (*f.*)   toy store
juicio (*m.*)   trial
julio (*m.*)   July
junio (*m.*)   June
juntos/as   together
justificar   to justify
justo/a   fair; just
juventud (*f.*)   youth

L

lado (*m.*)   side; **al lado de** next to
ladrar   to bark
ladrón (ladrona) (*m./f.*)   thief
lago (*m.*)   lake
lágrima (*f.*)   tear
lámpara (*f.*)   lamp
lana (*f.*)   wool
langosta (*f.*)   lobster
lanzador(a) (*m./f.*)   pitcher (*baseball*)
lanzar   to throw
largo/a   long

lástima (*f.*)   pity; shame
lavaplatos (*m.*)   dishwasher
lavar   to wash; **lavarse** to wash oneself
leche (*f.*)   milk
lechuga (*f.*)   lettuce
lectura (*f.*)   reading
leer   to read
legumbre (*f.*)   vegetable
lejos   far; **lejos de** away from
lenguaje (*m.*)   language
lentes (*m. pl.*)   eyeglasses
lento/a   slow
león (*m.*)   lion
letra (*f.*)   letter (*of the alphabet*); **letra mayúscula** capital
   letter; **letra minúscula** lowercase letter
levantarse   to stand up; to get up
ley (*f.*)   law
leyenda (*f.*)   legend
libertad (*f.*)   freedom; liberty
libra (*f.*)   pound
libre   free
librería (*f.*)   bookstore
libro (*m.*)   book
líder (*m./f.*)   leader
limonada (*f.*)   lemonade
limpiar   to clean
limpio/a   clean
línea (*f.*)   line; **línea aérea** (*f.*) airline; **en línea** online
listo/a   ready; smart
llamada (*f.*)   call; **llamada telefónica** phone call
llamar   to call
llave (*f.*)   key
llegar   to arrive; **llegar a ser** to become
llenar   to fill
lleno/a   full
llevar   to carry; to wear
llorar   to cry
llover (**o > ue**)   to rain
lluvia (*f.*)   rain
lluvioso/a   rainy
loco/a   crazy
lograr   to achieve, succeed
lotería (*f.*)   lottery
lucha (*f.*)   fight; struggle
luego   later; then
lugar (*m.*)   place
luna (*f.*)   moon
luna de miel (*f.*)   honeymoon
lunes (*m.*)   Monday
luz (*f.*)   light

M

madera (*f.*)   wood
maduro/a   ripe
maestro/a (*m./f.*)   teacher
mago/a (*m./f.*)   magician
maldecir (**e > i**)   to curse

maleta (*f.*)   suitcase
maletero (*m.*)   trunk
malo/a   bad; evil
mancha (*f.*)   spot
manejar   to drive; to manage
manga (*f.*)   sleeve
mano (*f.*)   hand; **dar una mano** to give a hand
manta (*f.*)   blanket
mantel (*m.*)   tablecloth
mantener   to maintain
mantequilla (*f.*)   butter
manzana (*f.*)   apple
mañana (*f.*)   morning; (*adv.*) tomorrow
maratón (*m.*)   marathon
maravilloso/a   wonderful
marcharse   to leave
marido (*m.*)   husband
mariposa (*f.*)   butterfly
marrón (*m.*)   brown
martes (*m.*)   Tuesday
martillar   to hammer
martillo (*m.*)   hammer
marzo (*m.*)   March
más   more
máscara (*f.*)   mask
materia (*f.*)   matter; (school) subject
mayo (*m.*)   May
mayor (*m./f.*)   older; larger
mecánico/a (*m./f.*)   mechanic
media (*f.*)   stocking
medianoche (*f.*)   midnight
medio/a   half; (*m.*) middle
mediodía (*m.*)   noon
medir (**e > i**)   to measure
mejor (*m./f.*)   better
menor (*m./f.*)   younger
menos   less
mensaje (*m.*)   message; **mensaje de texto** (*m.*) text
   message
mentir (**e > ie**)   to lie, tell a lie
mentira (*f.*)   lie
mentiroso/a (*m./f.*)   liar
merecer   to deserve
mes (*m.*)   month
mesero/a (*m./f.*)   waiter, waitress
meta (*f.*)   goal
meter   to put
metro (*m.*)   meter; subway
mezclar   to blend
mientras   while
miércoles (*m.*)   Wednesday
mil (*m.*)   thousand
milla (*f.*)   mile
mirar   to watch, look at
mismo/a   same; **lo mismo** the same thing
misterio (*m.*)   mystery
mitad (*f.*)   half

modales (*m. pl.*) manners
modelo (*m./f.*) model
mojado/a wet
molestar to bother
moneda (*f.*) coin; change
mono (*m.*) monkey
monstruo (*m.*) monster
montar to ride (*horseback*); **montar en bicicleta** to ride a bike
monumento (*m.*) monument
morder (**o > ue**) to bite
mordida (*f.*) bite
morir (**o >ue**) to die
mosca (*f.*) (house)fly
mosquito (*m.*) mosquito
mostrar (**o > ue**) to show
mover (**o > ue**) to move
mucho/a much; many; a lot
mudarse to move, change residence
mueble (*m.*) piece of furniture; **muebles** furniture
muela (*f.*) tooth; molar; **muela del juicio** wisdom tooth
muerte (*f.*) death
muerto/a dead
mujer (*f.*) woman
multa (*f.*) fine; traffic ticket
mundo (*m.*) world; **todo el mundo** everybody
muñeca (*f.*) doll; wrist
museo (*m.*) museum
música (*f.*) music

N

nacer to be born
nada nothing; **de nada** you are welcome
nadar to swim
nadie nobody; no one
naranja (*f.*) orange
nariz (*f.*) nose
naturaleza (*f.*) nature
navaja (*f.*) razor
Navidad (*f.*) Christmas
necesitar to need
negar (**e > ie**) to deny
negociante (*m./f.*) businessman/ woman
negocio (*m.*) business; **empresa de negocios** (*f.*) company
nervioso/a nervous
nevada (*f.*) snowfall
nevar (**e > ie**) to snow
niebla (*f.*) fog
nieto/a (*m./f.*) grandson/ granddaughter
nieve (*f.*) snow
ninguno/a (ningún) none; not any
noche (*f.*) night; **por la noche** at night
nombre (*m.*) name
nota (*f.*) note
notas (*f.*) grades

noticias (*f.*) news
novia (*f.*) girlfriend; fiancée; bride
noviembre (*m.*) November
novio (*m.*) boyfriend; fiancé; groom
nube (*f.*) cloud
nublado/a cloudy
nuevo/a new; **de nuevo** again
número (*m.*) number
nunca never

O

o... o... either . . . or . . .
obedecer to obey
octubre (*m.*) October
ocupado/a busy
odiar to hate
odio (*m.*) hatred
odontología (*f.*) dentistry
ofrecer to offer
oír to hear
ojalá God willing
ojo (*m.*) eye
oler (**o > ue**) to smell; to (have a) smell
olimpiadas (*f.*) Olympics
oliva (*f.*) olive
olvidar to forget
oponer to oppose
ordenado/a neat
organizar to organize
orgulloso/a proud
oro (*m.*) gold
oscuridad (*f.*) darkness
oscuro/a dark
oso (*m.*) bear
otoño (*m.*) autumn
otro/a another
OVNI (*m.*) UFO

P

pagar to pay
página (*f.*) page
pájaro (*m.*) bird
palabra (*f.*) word
palacio (*m.*) palace
pálido/a pale
pan (*m.*) bread
panadería (*f.*) bakery
panadero/a (*m./f.*) baker
pantalla (*f.*) screen
pantalones (*m.*) pants
papa (*f.*) potato
papá (*m.*) father; dad
papel (*m.*) paper; role
papelería (*f.*) stationery store
paquete (*m.*) package
par (*m.*) pair

parada (*f.*) (bus) stop
paraguas (*m.*) umbrella
parecer to seem; **parecerse a** to look like
pared (*f.*) wall
pariente (*m./f.*) relative
parrilla (*f.*) grill; **a la parrilla** grilled
partido (*m.*) game
pasajero/a (*m./f.*) passenger
pasar to pass
pasatiempo (*m.*) hobby
pasillo (*m.*) hallway
pastel (*m.*) cake
patata (*f.*) potato
patinar to skate
pato (*m.*) duck
pavo (*m.*) turkey
payama (*f.*) pajamas
payaso/a (*m./f.*) clown
paz (*f.*) peace
pedazo (*m.*) piece
pedir (**e > i**) to ask for
pegar to glue; to hit
peinar(se) to comb (one's hair)
peine (*m.*) comb
película (*f.*) movie
peligro (*m.*) danger
peligroso/a dangerous
pelo (*m.*) hair
peluquería (*f.*) hairdresser's shop; barber shop
pensar (**e > ie**) to think; **pensar en** to think about; **pensar de** to have an opinion
peor (*m./f.*) worse
pequeño/a small, little
percha (*f.*) hanger
perder (**e > ie**) to lose; **perder el tiempo** to waste time
perezoso/a lazy
periódico (*m.*) newspaper
periodista (*m./f.*) journalist
perla (*f.*) pearl
permiso (*m.*) permission; **con permiso** excuse me
permitir to permit, allow
perseguir (**e > i**) to pursue
personaje (*m.*) character
pertenecer to belong
pesadilla (*f.*) nightmare
pesado/a annoying
pesar to weigh
pescado (*m.*) fish (*to eat*)
peso (*m.*) weight
pez (*m.*) fish (*in water*)
pie (*m.*) foot; **estar de pie** to be standing
piel (*f.*) skin
pierna (*f.*) leg
pijama (*m.*) pajamas
píldora (*f.*) pill

pintor(a) (*m./f.*) painter
pintura (*f.*) paint
pirámide (*f.*) pyramid
piscina (*f.*) swimming pool
piso (*m.*) floor; apartment
pista (*f.*) clue; track; **pista de hielo** (*f.*) ice-skating rink
plancha (*f.*) (clothes) iron
planchar to iron
planeta (*m.*) planet
plata (*f.*) silver
plátano (*m.*) banana
playa (*f.*) beach
población (*f.*) population
poco/a little; **hace poco** a short time ago
poder (**o > ue**) to be able to
policía (*m./f.*) police officer; (*f.*) police force
política (*f. sing.*) politics
político/a (*m./f.*) politician
poner to put; **ponerse** to become; to put on clothing; **ponerse a dieta** to go on a diet
porque because
portero/a goalkeeper; goalie
poseer to possess, own
postre (*m.*) dessert
precio (*m.*) price
preferir (**e > ie**) to prefer
premio (*m.*) prize
preocupado/a worried
preocuparse to worry
preparar to prepare
presentación (*f.*) presentation; introduction
préstamo (*m.*) loan
prestar to loan, lend
primavera (*f.*) spring
primero/a first
primo/a (*m./f.*) cousin
prisa (*f.*) hurry; **de prisa** quickly
probar (**o > ue**) to prove; to taste
probarse (**o > ue**) to try on
problema (*m.*) problem
producir to produce
profesión (*f.*) profession
profesional (*m./f.*) professional
programa (*m.*) program
progreso (*m.*) progress
prohibido/a prohibited
promesa (*f.*) promise
prometer to promise
pronóstico (*m.*) forecast
pronto soon
pronunciación (*f.*) pronunciation
propina (*f.*) tip
proponer to propose
proteger to protect

próximo/a next
prueba (*f.*) quiz
publicar to publish
publicidad (*f.*) publicity; advertisement
público (*m.*) public; audience
pueblo (*m.*) town
puente (*m.*) bridge
puesto (*m.*) place; job
pulgada (*f.*) inch
pulsera (*f.*) bracelet
punto (*m.*) point; **punto de vista** point of view; **en punto** on the dot
puro/a pure

Q

que that; than; **¿qué?** what?
quedar(se) to stay, remain
quehacer (*m.*) chore, task
queja (*f.*) complaint
quejarse (de) to complain (about)
quemar to burn
querer (e > ie) to want; **querer decir** to mean
querido/a dear
queso (*m.*) cheese
quien who; **¿quién?** who?
quienquiera whoever
química (*f.*) chemistry
quitar(se) to take off, remove
quizás perhaps

R

rabia (*f.*) rage
radio (*m./f.*) radio
rama (*f.*) branch (*tree*)
ramo (*m.*) bouquet (*of flowers*)
rana (*f.*) frog
rápidamente quickly
rápido/a fast
raqueta (*f.*) (tennis) racket
raro/a odd
rato (*m.*) while; **pasar un buen rato** to have a good time
razón (*f.*) reason; **tener razón** to be right
realizar to achieve; to fulfill
rebaja (*f.*) special sale
rebajar de peso to lose weight
recepción (*f.*) reception
receta (*f.*) recipe; prescription
recetar to prescribe
rechazar to reject
recibir to receive
reciclar to recycle
recoger to pick up, gather
reconocer to recognize
recordar (o > ue) to remember

recuerdo (*m.*) memory; souvenir; **recuerdos** regards
recurso (*m.*) resource
reducir to reduce, cut down
referir (e > ie) to refer
refresco (*m.*) refreshment; soft drink
refrigerador (*m.*) refrigerator
regalar to give a present
regalo (*m.*) gift
regar (e > ie) to water
regla (*f.*) rule; ruler
rehacer to redo, remake
reina (*f.*) queen
reír(se) (e > i) to laugh
relajarse to relax
relámpago (*m.*) lightning
reloj (*m.*) watch; clock
renunciar to quit (*a job, etc.*)
reñir(se) (e > i) to quarrel
repetir (e > i) to repeat
reportaje (*m.*) report
resfriado (*m.*) (head) cold; **tener un resfriado** to have a cold
resolver (o > ue) to solve, resolve
respirar to breathe
respuesta (*f.*) answer
restaurante (*m.*) restaurant
reunión (*f.*) meeting
reunir(se) to gather, meet
revista (*f.*) magazine
rey (*m.*) king
rezar to beg; to pray
rico/a rich; tasty
ridículo/a ridiculous
riqueza (*f.*) wealth
risa (*f.*) laughter
robar to rob, steal
robo (*m.*) robbery
robótica (*f.*) robotics
rodilla (*f.*) knee; **de rodillas** kneeling
rogar (o > ue) to pray; to beg
rompecabezas (*m.*) puzzle
romper to break
ropa (*f.*) clothing
ropero (*m.*) closet
roto/a broken
rubí (*m.*) ruby
rubio/a blond(e)
rueda (*f.*) wheel
ruido (*m.*) noise
ruso (*m.*) Russian (*language*); **ruso/a** (*m./f.*) Russian (*person*)

S

sábado (*m.*) Saturday
saber to know; **saber de** to know about
sabio/a wise
sabor (*m.*) flavor

sabroso/a delicious

sacar to take out; **sacar una foto** to take a picture

sacudir to shake; **sacudir el polvo** to dust (*furniture*)

sal (*f.*) salt

sala (*f.*) living room; **sala de juntas** boardroom

salchicha (*f.*) sausage

salida (*f.*) exit

salir to come out; to leave

saltar to jump

salud (*f.*) health

saludable (*m./f.*) healthy

saludar to greet

saludo (*m.*) greeting

sangre (*f.*) blood

sano/a healthy

secadora (*f.*) (clothes) dryer

secar(se) to dry (oneself)

seco/a dry

secreto (*m.*) secret

secundaria (*f.*) high school

sed (*f.*) thirst

seda (*f.*) silk

seguir (**e** > **i**) to follow, continue

seguro/a safe

sello (*m.*) stamp

selva (*f.*) jungle; **selva tropical** rain forest

semáforo (*m.*) traffic light

semana (*f.*) week

semilla (*f.*) seed

sentado/a sitting; seated

sentarse (**e** > **ie**) to sit down, be seated

sentir (**e** > **ie**) to regret; **sentirse** to feel

septiembre (*m.*) September

Serie Mundial (*f.*) World Series

servilleta (*f.*) napkin

servir (**e** > **i**) to serve

siempre always

siglo (*m.*) century

siguiente (*m./f.*) next; following

silla (*f.*) chair

sillón (*m.*) armchair

sin without

sobrar to be left over

sobre (*m.*) envelope

sociedad (*f.*) society; company

sofá (*m.*) sofa, couch

sol (*m.*) sun

solamente only

soldado (*m./f.*) soldier

solicitud (*f.*) application

solo/a alone; (*adv.*) **solo** only; just

sombra (*f.*) shade; shadow

sombrero (*m.*) hat

sonar (**o** > **ue**) to ring; **sonar a** to sound like

sonreír (**e** > **i**) to smile

sonrisa (*f.*) smile

soñar (**o** > **ue**) (**con**) to dream (of)

sopa (*f.*) soup

sostener to sustain; to support

sótano (*m.*) basement

subir to climb, go up

subrayar to underline

sucio/a dirty

suegro/a (*m./f.*) father-in-law/mother-in-law

sueldo (*m.*) salary

suelo (*m.*) floor

sueño (*m.*) dream

suéter (*m.*) sweater

suficiente (*m./f.*) enough

sufrir to suffer

sugerir (**e** > **ie**) to suggest

supersticioso/a superstitious

suponer to suppose

sur (*m.*) south

sustituir to substitute

T

tabaco (*m.*) tobacco; cigar

taladrar to drill

talla (*f.*) size (*for clothing*)

tamaño (*m.*) size

también also, too

tampoco neither, not either

tanto/a so much

taquilla (*f.*) box office

tardar to take time

tarde late

tarjeta (*f.*) card; **tarjeta de crédito** credit card

taza (*f.*) cup; mug

té (*m.*) tea

teatro (*m.*) theater

tela (*f.*) cloth; fabric

teléfono (*m.*) telephone

televisión (*f.*) television; television (set)

tema (*m.*) theme; topic

temblar (**e** > **ie**) to tremble; to shake

temer to fear

temor (*m.*) fear

temprano early

tenedor (*m.*) fork

tener to have; **tener que** to have to

terminar to finish

terremoto (*m.*) earthquake

tesoro (*m.*) treasure

tiempo (*m.*) time; weather; **a tiempo** on time

tienda (*f.*) store

tierra (*f.*) land; earth

tijeras (*f.*) scissors

toalla (*f.*)   towel

tocar   to touch; to play (*an instrument*)

todavía   still; yet

todo (*m.*)   all; everything

tolerar   to tolerate

tomar   to take; to drink; **tomar una decisión** to make a decision

tomate (*m.*)   tomato

tonto/a   silly; ridiculous

tormenta (*f.*)   storm

torta (*f.*)   cake

tostada (*f.*)   toast

tostar (**o > ue**)   to toast

trabajar   to work

trabajo (*m.*)   work; job

traducir   to translate

traer   to bring; to carry

tráfico (*m.*)   traffic

trágico/a   tragic

traje (*m.*)   suit; **traje de baño** bathing suit

tranquilo/a   peaceful, calm

tratar   to treat; **tratar de** +*inf.* to try to (*do something*)

tren (*m.*)   train

triste (*m./f.*)   sad

tristeza (*f.*)   sadness

tropezar (**e > ie**)   to stumble; **tropezar con** to bump into

trueno (*m.*)   thunder

U

último/a   last

único/a   only; unique

unir   to unite

uva (*f.*)   grape

V

vaca (*f.*)   cow

vacaciones (*f. pl.*)   vacation

vacío/a   empty

valer   to be worth; **valer la pena** to be worthwhile

valor (*m.*)   value

variedad (*f.*)   variety

varios/as   several

vaso (*m.*)   glass

vecindario (*m.*)   neighborhood

vecino/a (*m./f.*)   neighbor

vehículo (*m.*)   vehicle

vela (*f.*)   candle

vencer   to conquer

vendedor(a) (*m./f.*)   salesperson

vender   to sell

venir   to come

venta (*f.*)   sale

ventana (*f.*)   window

ventanilla (*f.*)   box office; car window

ver   to see

verano (*m.*)   summer

verdad (*f.*)   truth

vestido (*m.*)   dress

vestir(se) (**e > i**)   to dress

vez (*f.*) (*pl.* **veces**)   time; **de vez en cuando** from time to time

viajar   to travel

viaje (*m.*)   trip

vida (*f.*)   life

vidrio (*m.*)   glass

viejo/a   old

viento (*m.*)   wind

viernes (*m.*)   Friday

vigilar   to watch over; to guard

vino (*m.*)   wine; **vino tinto** red wine

vista (*f.*)   view

vitamina (*f.*)   vitamin

vivir   to live

vivo/a   alive

volar (**o > ue**)   to fly

voleibol (*m.*)   volleyball

volver (**o > ue**)   to return

voz (*f.*)   voice

vuelo (*m.*)   flight

W

web (*f.*)   Web; **página web** (*f.*) Web page

Y

ya   already

Z

zapatería (*f.*)   shoe store

zapatilla (*f.*)   slipper

zapato (*m.*)   shoe

English-Spanish glossary

A

a un, una

a lot mucho/a

about acerca de

accept aceptar

accident accidente (*m.*) **by accident** por casualidad

ache dolor (*m.*)

achieve lograr; realizar

acquire adquirir (e > ie)

across a través (de); por

act actuar; comportarse

action movie una película de acción

actor actor (*m.*)

actress actriz (*f.*)

add agregar; añadir

address dirección (*f.*)

admire admirar

advice consejo (*m.*)

advise advertir (e > ie); aconsejar

afraid asustado/a; **to be afraid of** tener miedo de

after; afterwards después (de)

afternoon tarde (*f.*)

again otra vez; de nuevo

against contra

agent agente (*m./f.*)

agree (*to do something*) convenir (en); **to agree with** estar de acuerdo con

air aire (*m.*)

airline aerolínea (*f.*)

alive vivo/a

all todo (*m.*); **all day long** todo el día

allow consentir (e >ie); dejar; permitir

already ya

also también

although aunque

always siempre

ambassador embajador(a) (*m./f.*)

ambush emboscada (*f.*)

among entre

amount cantidad (*f.*)

amusement diversión (*f.*); **amusement park** parque de atracciones, parque de diversiones(*m.*)

and y; e (*preceding a word starting with* **i** *or* **hi**)

anecdote anécdota (*f.*)

angry enfadado/a, enojado/a

anniversary aniversario (*m.*)

annoy molestar

annoying pesado/a

anonymous anónimo/a

another otro/a

answer respuesta (*f.*); contestar; responder

any; anything algo; cualquiera; cualquier cosa

anyway de cualquier forma

anywhere; not anywhere en cualquier parte; en ninguna parte

apparently al parecer; por lo visto

appear aparecer

apple manzana (*f.*)

application solicitud (*f.*); formulario (*m.*)

appointment cita (*f.*)

approve aprobar (o > ue)

April abril (*m.*)

architect arquitecto/a (*m./f.*)

armchair butaca (*f.*); sillón (*m.*)

army ejército (*m.*)

around alrededor (de)

arrange arreglar

arrest detener

arrive llegar

article artículo (*m.*)

as como; **as much as** tanto como; **as soon as** tan pronto como

ask preguntar

ask (for) pedir (e > i)

asleep dormido/a

assignment tarea (*f.*)

astronaut astronauta (*m./f.*)

athlete atleta (*m./f.*)

attack atacar
attend asistir a
attitude actitud (*f.*)
attract atraer
audience público (*m.*)
August agosto (*m.*)
aunt tía (*f.*)
autumn otoño (*m.*)
away from lejos de; **to go away** irse (*irr.*)

B

baby bebé (*m.*)
back (*adv.*) atrás
backyard jardín; patio (*m.*)
bad malo/a
bad mood mal humor (*m.*)
bag bolsa (*f.*)
baker panadero/a (*m./f.*)
bakery panadería (*f.*)
bald calvo/a
ball pelota (*f.*)
banana plátano (*m.*)
bank banco (*m.*)
bargain ganga (*f.*)
bark ladrar
baseball béisbol (*m.*)
baseball field campo de pelota (*m.*)
basement sótano (*m.*)
basketball baloncesto (*m.*)
bath; bathroom baño (*m.*)
bathe bañar(se)
bathing suit traje de baño (*m.*)
be ser; estar
beach playa (*f.*)
bear oso (*m.*)
because porque
become ponerse; hacerse
bed cama (*f.*)
bedroom dormitorio (*m.*)
beer cerveza (*f.*)
before antes (de)
beg rogar (o > ue); rezar
begin comenzar; empezar (e > ie)
beginning principio (*m.*)
behave comportarse
believe creer
belong pertenecer
belt cinturón (*m.*)
best mejor (*m./f.*)
better mejor (*m./f.*)
between entre
bicycle bicicleta (*f.*)
big grande; gran (*m./f.*)
bilingual bilingüe (*m./f.*)
bill cuenta (*f.*)
billion billón (*m.*)
bird pájaro (*m.*); (el) ave (*f.*)

birthday cumpleaños (*m.*)
bite mordida (*f.*); morder (o > ue)
blame culpa (*f.*); culpar; **to be blamed** tener la culpa
blanket manta (*f.*)
blend mezclar
block (*city*) manzana; cuadra (*f.*)
blond(e) rubio/a
blood sangre (*f.*)
boardroom sala de juntas (*f.*)
boat barco (*m.*)
boil hervir (e > ie)
bomb bomba (*f.*)
bone hueso (*m.*)
book libro (*m.*)
bookstore librería (*f.*)
border frontera (*f.*)
bored; boring aburrido/a
born (to be) nacer
boss jefe/a (*m./f.*)
bother fastidiar; molestar
bottom fondo (*m.*)
bouquet ramo de flores (*m.*)
box caja (*f.*)
box office taquilla (*f.*); ventanilla (*f.*)
boy chico (*m.*)
boyfriend novio (*m.*)
bracelet pulsera (*f.*); brazalete (*m.*)
brain cerebro (*m.*)
branch (*tree*) rama (*f.*)
brave valiente (*m./f.*)
bread pan (*m.*)
break romper; quebrar
breakfast desayuno (*m.*); **to have breakfast** desayunar
breathe respirar
brick ladrillo (*m.*)
bride novia (*f.*)
bridge puente (*m.*)
bring traer
bring back devolver (o > ue)
broken roto/a; dañado/a
brother hermano (*m.*)
brother-in-law cuñado (*m.*)
brown marrón (*m.*), *adj.* (*m./f.*)
brush cepillo (*m.*)
brush (oneself) cepillar(se)
build construir
building edificio (*m.*)
bump into tropezar(se) con (e > ie)
burn quemar
bury enterrar (e > ie)
bus autobús (*m.*)
business negocio (*m.*); **businessman/ woman** negociante (*m./f.*)
busy ocupado/a
butter mantequilla (*f.*)
butterfly mariposa (*f.*)

button botón (*m.*)

buy comprar

by por; **by accident** por casualidad

C

cabinet armario (*m.*)

café café (*m.*)

cafeteria cafetería (*f.*)

cage jaula (*f.*)

cake torta (*f.*); pastel (*m.*)

call llamada (*f.*)

call (oneself) llamar(se)

calorie caloría (*f.*)

camera cámara (*f.*)

candidate candidato/a (*m./f.*)

candle vela (*f.*)

candy caramelos (*m. pl.*)

capital (*city*) capital (*f.*)

capital (*wealth*) capital (*m.*)

card tarjeta (*f.*); carta (*f.*)

cards (*deck of*) baraja (*f.*)

care cuidado (*m.*); cuidar; **to care for** (*a person*) cuidar a; **to care for oneself** cuidarse

career carrera (*f.*)

careful cuidadoso/a

carefully con cuidado, cuidadosamente

carpet alfombra (*f.*)

case caso (*m.*)

castle castillo (*m.*)

cat gato (*m.*)

catalogue catálogo (*m.*)

catch agarrar; coger

celebrate celebrar

center centro (*m.*)

century siglo (*m.*)

ceremony ceremonia (*f.*)

chair silla (*f.*)

champion campeón (campeona) (*m./f.*)

championship campeonato (*m.*)

change cambio (*m.*); cambiar

chapter capítulo (*m.*)

character personaje (*m.*); carácter (*m.*)

charming encantador(a)

check cheque (*m.*)

checkers damas (*f. pl.*)

cheese queso (*m.*)

chemistry química (*f.*)

chess ajedrez (*m.*)

choose elegir (e > i); escoger

chore tarea (*f.*)

Christmas Navidad (*f.*)

cigar puro (*m.*); cigarro (*m.*)

class clase (*f.*)

classify clasificar

classmate compañero/a de clase (*m./f.*)

clean limpio/a; limpiar

clerk dependiente (*m./f.*)

client cliente (*m.*); clienta (*f.*)

climate clima (*m.*)

climb subir

clock reloj (*m.*)

close cerca

close cerrar (e > ie)

closed cerrado/a

closet armario (*m.*)

clothes, clothing ropa (*f.*)

cloudy nublado/a

clown payaso/a (*m./f.*)

clue pista (*f.*)

coffee café (*m.*)

coffee-colored marrón (*m./f.*)

coffee shop cafetería (*f.*)

coin moneda (*f.*)

cold resfriado (*m.*) (*illness*); frío (*m.*) (*temperature*); **to have a cold** tener un resfriado

colleague compañero/a (*m./f.*)

comb peine (*m.*)

comb (one's) hair peinar(se)

come venir

comet cometa (*m.*)

comfortable cómodo/a

commercial anuncio (*m.*); aviso (*m.*)

company compañía (*f.*); sociedad (*f.*); empresa de negocios (*f.*)

compete competir (e > i)

complain quejar(se) de

complaint queja (*f.*)

complete acabar; terminar

compose componer

concert concierto (*m.*)

confess confesar (e > ie)

conjugate conjugar

constitute constituir

construct construir

contain contener

contamination contaminación (*f.*)

contest concurso (*m.*)

continue continuar; seguir (e > ie)

contract contrato (*m.*)

convince convencer

cook cocinero/a (*m./f.*); cocinar

corner esquina (*f.*); rincón (*m.*)

cost costar (o > ue)

cotton algodón (*m.*)

count contar (o > ue)

counter mostrador (*m.*)

couple par (*m.*); **a couple of** un par de

coupon cupón (*m.*)

course curso (*m.*), clase (*f.*); **of course** por supuesto

courteous cortés (*m./f.*)

cover   cubrir
cow   vaca (*f.*)
crazy   loco/a
credit card   tarjeta de crédito (*f.*)
crime   crimen (*m.*)
cross   cruz (*f.*); **cross** (*the street*) cruzar; pasar
cry   llorar
crystal   cristal (*m.*)
cup   taza (*f.*)
curtain   cortina (*f.*)
custom   costumbre (*f.*)
customer   cliente (*m./f.*)
customs   aduana (*f.*)
cut   cortar

D

dance   baile (*m.*); bailar
danger   peligro (*m.*)
dangerous   peligroso/a
dark   oscuro/a
darkness   oscuridad (*f.*)
date   fecha (*f.*); cita (*f.*)
day   día (*m.*)
daybreak   al amanecer
dead   muerto/a
dear   querido/a
death   muerte (*f.*)
deceive   engañar
December   diciembre (*m.*)
decide   decidir
defend   defender (e > ie)
delicious   delicioso/a, sabroso/a, rico/a
deliver   entregar
demand   exigir
demonstrate   demostrar (o > ue)
dentistry   odontología (*f.*)
deny   negar(se) (e > ie)
depend   depender (de)
deposit   depositar
depressed   deprimido/a
describe   describir
desert   desierto (*m.*)
deserve   merecer
desire   deseo (*m.*)
desk   escritorio (*m.*)
dessert   postre (*m.*)
destroy   destruir
diamond   diamante (*m.*)
diary   diario (*m.*)
die   morir (o > ue)
diet   dieta (*f.*); ponerse a dieta
different   diferente (*m./f.*); distinto/a
difficult   difícil (*m./f.*)
difficulty   dificultad (*f.*)
dine   cenar
dining room   comedor (*m.*)

dinner   cena (*f.*); **to have dinner** cenar
dirty   sucio/a
disappear   desaparecer
disaster   desastre (*m.*)
discover   descubrir
discuss   discutir
dish   plato (*m.*)
dishwasher   lavaplatos (*m. sing.*)
dissolve   disolver (o > ue)
do   hacer; **to have nothing to do with** no tener nada que ver con
document   documento (*m.*)
dollar   dólar (*m.*)
doubt   duda (*f.*); dudar
down   abajo
downtown   centro (*m.*)
dozen   docena (*f.*)
draw   dibujar
dream   sueño (*m.*); soñar (o > ue); **to dream of** soñar con
dress   vestido (*m.*); vestir(se) (e > i)
drill   taladro (*m.*); taladrar
drink   bebida (*f.*); beber; tomar
drive   conducir; manejar
drop   gota (*f.*)
drugstore   farmacia (*f.*)
drunk   borracho/a
dry   seco/a; secar(se)
dryer   secadora (*f.*)
duck   pato (*m.*)
during   durante
dust   polvo (*m.*); sacudir (*clean*)

E

each   cada (*m./f.*)
early   temprano
earn   ganar
earring   pendiente (*m.*), arete (*m.*)
earth   tierra (*f.*)
earthquake   terremoto (*m.*)
eat   comer; **to eat lunch** almorzar (o > ue)
education   educación (*f.*)
effort   esfuerzo (*m.*)
egg   huevo (*m.*)
either (**neither**)   tampoco
either . . . or . . .   o... o...
elect   elegir (e > i)
election   elección (*f.*)
elevator   ascensor (*m.*)
embarrassed   avergonzado/a
employee   empleado/a (*m./f.*)
employer   jefe/a (*m./f.*)
empty   vacío/a; vaciar
end   fin (*m.*); acabar; terminar
enemy   enemigo/a (*m./f.*)
energy   energía (*f.*)

engagement compromiso (*m.*)
England Inglaterra (*f.*)
English inglés (*m.*) (*language*)
enigma enigma (*m.*)
enjoy gozar de; disfrutar de
enough bastante; suficiente (*m./f.*)
enter entrar
enterprise empresa (*f.*)
entire entero/a
entrance entrada (*f.*)
envelope sobre (*m.*)
environment medio ambiente (*m.*)
equal igual (*m./f.*)
equipment equipaje (*m.*)
error error (*m.*)
establish establecer
evening noche (*f.*); **in the evening** por la noche
every cada (*m./f.*)
everybody, everyone todos; todo el mundo
everything todo (*m.*)
everywhere en (por) todas partes
exam examen (*m.*)
exciting emocionante (*m./f.*)
exercise hacer ejercicio
exhibit exposición (*f.*)
exit salida (*f.*)
expensive caro/a
explain explicar
express expresar(se)
extinguish extinguir
eye ojo (*m.*)
eyeglasses anteojos (*m. pl.*); lentes (*m. pl.*)

F

face cara (*f.*)
fact hecho (*m.*)
fair justo/a
fairy tale cuento de hadas (*m.*)
fall (*season*) otoño (*m.*)
fall (*down*) caer(se)
familiar familiar; **to be familiar with** conocer
fan aficionado/a (*m./f.*)
fantasy fantasía (*f.*)
far lejos
fast rápido/a
father padre (*m.*); papá (*m.*)
father-in-law suegro (*m.*)
favorite favorito/a
fear temor (*m.*); tener miedo de
February febrero (*m.*)
feel sentir(se) (e > ie); **to feel like** tener ganas de
fever fiebre (*f.*)
few pocos; **a few** unos cuantos
fiancé/fiancée prometido/a (*m./f.*); novio/a (*m./f.*)
fight lucha (*f.*); pelear; reñir
file archivo (*m.*)
fill (**up, out**) llenar

film película (*f.*)
finally al fin; por fin
finance finanzas (*f. pl.*)
financial financiero/a
find encontrar (o > ue); **to find out** averiguar
fine bien
fine (*traffic ticket*) multa (*f.*)
fingernail uña (*f.*)
finish terminar
fire fuego (*m.*); incendio (*m.*)
fire (*dismiss*) despedir (e > i)
fire hydrant hidrante de incendios (*m.*)
firefighter bombero/a (*m./f.*)
fireplace chimenea (*f.*)
first primero/a
fish pescado (*m.*) (*for eating*);
  pez (*m.*)
fit caber
fix arreglar
flag bandera (*f.*)
flan (*custard*) flan (*m.*)
flavor sabor (*m.*)
flee huir
float flotar
flood inundación (*f.*); inundar
floor suelo (*m.*); piso (*m.*)
  (*level*)
flower flor (*f.*)
fly mosca (*f.*); volar (o > ue)
fog niebla (*f.*)
foggy nublado/a
follow seguir (e > i)
following siguiente (*m./f.*)
food comida (*f.*)
fool tonto/a (*m./f.*); engañar
foot pie (*m.*); **on foot** a pie
football fútbol americano (*m.*)
for para; por
forecast pronóstico (*m.*)
foreign extranjero/a
forest bosque (*m.*); selva (*f.*)
forever para siempre
forget olvidar
fork tenedor (*m.*)
fortunately por suerte
free libre (*m./f.*)
freedom libertad (*f.*)
freeway autopista (*f.*)
freeze congelar
French francés (*m.*) (*language*)
frequently con frecuencia; frecuentemente
Friday viernes (*m.*)
friendly amistoso/a
friendship amistad (*f.*)
frighten asustar
frog rana (*f.*)
from de; **from time to time** de vez en cuando

fry   freír (e > i)
fulfill   realizar
full   lleno/a
fun   diversión (f.); **to have fun** divertirse (e > ie)
funny   cómico/a; chistoso/a
furious   furioso/a
furniture   mueble (m.) (*one piece*); muebles (m. pl.)

G

gain weight   engordar
game   juego (m.); partido (m.)
garbage   basura (f.)
garden   jardín (m.)
garlic   ajo (m.)
gasoline   gasolina (f.)
generally   por lo común, por lo general, generalmente
genuine   auténtico/a
German   alemán (m.) (*language*)
get   obtener; conseguir (e > i)
ghost   fantasma (m.)
giant   gigante (m.)
gift   regalo (m.)
giraffe   jirafa (f.)
girl   chica (f.); niña (f.)
girlfriend   novia (f.)
give   dar
glass   vaso (m.); vidrio (m.)
glove   guante (m.)
glue   goma de pegar (f.); pegar
go   ir; **to go away** ir(se); **to go to bed** acostarse (o > ue)
goal   gol (m.); meta (f.)
goalkeeper   portero/a (m./f.)
God; god   Dios (m.); dios (m.)
God willing   ojalá
gold   oro (m.)
good   bueno/a
gossip   chisme (m.); chismorrear
governor   gobernador(a) (m./f.)
grab   agarrar; coger
grades   notas (f. pl.)
grand   gran; grande (m./f.)
granddaughter   nieta (f.)
grandfather   abuelo (m.)
grandmother   abuela (f.)
grandson   nieto (m.)
grape   uva (f.)
grass   hierba (f.)
great   gran, grande (m./f.); estupendo/a
Greek   griego (m.) (*language*)
greet   saludar
greeting   saludo (m.)
grill   parrilla (f.); asar a la parrilla
groom   novio (m.)
grow   crecer; cultivar (*plants*)
guest   invitado/a (m./f.)
guide   guía (m./f.); **travel guide** guía de turismo (m./f.)

guitar   guitarra (f.)
guy   chico (m.)
gym   gimnasio (m.)

H

hair   cabello (m.); pelo (m.)
haircut   corte de pelo (m.)
hallway   pasillo (m.)
hamburger   hamburguesa (f.)
hammer   martillo (m.); martillar
hammock   hamaca (f.)
hand   mano (f.); **to give a hand** dar una mano
handsome   guapo/a
hang (up)   colgar (o > ue)
hanger   percha (f.); perchero (m.)
happen   pasar; suceder
happiness   felicidad (f.)
happy   feliz (m./f.)
hard   duro/a; difícil (m./f.)
hardly   apenas
harvest   cosecha (f.)
hat   sombrero (m.)
hate   odiar
have   tener; **to have fun** divertirse; **to have something to do with** tener que ver con
head   cabeza (f.)
health   salud (f.)
healthy   saludable (m./f.); sano/a
hear   oír
heart   corazón (m.)
help   ayuda (f.); ayudar
here   aquí
hide   esconder
highway   autopista (f.); carretera (f.)
hold   sostener
holiday   fiesta (f.), día feriado (m.)
home   hogar (m.)
honest   honrado/a
honeymoon   luna de miel (f.)
hope   esperanza (f.); esperar
horse   caballo (m.)
host   anfitrión (m.)
hostess   anfitriona (f.)
hotel   hotel (m.)
how?   ¿cómo?; **how much?** ¿cuánto?; **how!** ¡cuánto!
hug   abrazo (m.); abrazar
human   humano/a (m./f.)
humble   humilde
humor   humor (m.)
hunger   (el) hambre (f.); **to be hungry** tener hambre
hunt   cazar
hurricane   huracán (m.)
hurry   prisa (f.); **to be in a hurry** tener prisa
hurt   doler (o > ue); hacer daño
husband   esposo (m.)

I

ice hielo (*m.*)
ice cream helado (*m.*)
ice skating patinar
ice-skating rink pista de hielo (*f.*)
ill enfermo/a
illness enfermedad (*f.*)
imagine imaginar(se)
immediately en seguida, inmediatamente
impede impedir (e > i); dificultar
import importar
important importante (*m./f.*); **to be important** importarle a alguien
inch pulgada (*f.*)
include incluir
increase aumentar
influence influencia (*f.*); influir (en)
information información (*f.*)
innocent inocente (*m./f.*)
insane loco/a
inside adentro; dentro (de)
insist (on) insistir (en)
instead of en vez de
interest interés (*m.*); interesar
interpreter intérprete (*m./f.*)
introduce presentar
introduction presentación (*f.*)
invest invertir (e > ie)
investigate investigar
invitation invitación (*f.*)
invite invitar
iron plancha (*f.*); planchar
item artículo (*m.*)
itinerary itinerario (*m.*)

J

jaguar jaguar (*m.*)
jail cárcel (*f.*)
jam mermelada (*f.*)
January enero (*m.*)
jealous celoso/a
jewel joya (*f.*)
jewelry joyas (*f.*); **jewelry store** joyería (*f.*)
job empleo (*m.*); trabajo (*m.*)
joke broma (*f.*); chiste (*m.*)
joy alegría (*f.*); felicidad (*f.*)
judge juez(a) (*m./f.*)
July julio (*m.*)
jump brincar; saltar
June junio (*m.*)
jungle selva (*f.*)
just justo/a; (*adv.*) sólo; solamente
justice justicia (*f.*)
justify justificar

K

keep guardar
key llave (*f.*)
king rey (*m.*)
kiss beso (*m.*)
kitchen cocina (*f.*)
knee rodilla (*f.*)
kneel arrodillarse, estar de rodillas
knife cuchillo (*m.*)
know saber; conocer; **to know about** saber de; **to know how** saber; **to let know** avisar

L

lack carecer; **to be lacking** hacer falta
ladder escalera (*f.*)
lake lago (*m.*)
lamp lámpara (*f.*)
land tierra (*f.*); aterrizar
language idioma (*m.*); lenguaje (*m.*)
large grande (*m./f.*)
last último/a; **last night** anoche; **to last** durar
late tarde
later más tarde; luego
laugh reír(se) (e > i)
law ley (*f.*)
lawn césped (*m.*)
lawyer abogado/a (*m./f.*)
lazy perezoso/a
leader líder (*m./f.*)
leaf hoja (*f.*)
learn aprender
leave salir; irse; **to leave behind** dejar
left izquierda (*f.*); **to the left** a la izquierda
leftovers sobras (*f. pl.*)
leg pierna (*f.*)
legend leyenda (*f.*)
lemonade limonada (*f.*)
lend prestar
less menos
lesson lección (*f.*)
let dejar; permitir
letter carta (*f.*); letra (*of alphabet*) (*f.*)
lettuce lechuga (*f.*)
liar mentiroso/a (*m./f.*)
liberty libertad (*f.*)
library biblioteca (*f.*)
lie mentira (*f.*); **to tell a lie** mentir (e > ie)
lie down acostarse (o > ue)
life vida (*f.*)
light luz (*f.*); encender (e > ie)
light bulb bombilla (*f.*)
lightning relámpago (*m.*)
like gustarle a uno; **to feel like** tener ganas de

line   cola (*f.*); línea (*f.*); **online** en línea
lion   león (*m.*)
listen (to)   escuchar
little   pequeño/a; un poco
live   vivir
lively   animado/a
living room   sala (*f.*); sala de
   estar (*f.*)
loan   préstamo (*m.*); prestar; **home loan** hipoteca (*f.*)
lobster   langosta (*f.*)
lock   cerradura (*f.*); candado (*m.*); encerrar (e > ie)
long   largo/a; **a long time** mucho tiempo; **how long?**
   ¿cuánto tiempo?
look (at)   mirar; **to look for** buscar;
   to look like someone parecerse a alguien
lose   perder (e > ie); **to lose weight** adelgazar; bajar de
   peso
lot   mucho/a
lottery   lotería (*f.*)
love   amor (*m.*); amar, querer; **to be in love with** estar
   enamorado de; **to fall in love with** enamorarse de
lucky   afortunado/a; **to be lucky** tener suerte
luggage   equipaje (*m.*)
lunch   almuerzo (*m.*); almorzar
   (o > ue)

M

mad (*angry*)   enojado/a
magazine   revista (*f.*)
magician   mago/a (*m./f.*)
mail   correo (*m.*); echar al correo
mailbox   buzón (*m.*)
maintain   mantener
make   hacer; **to make a decision**
   tomar una decisión
male   varón (*m.*)
mall   centro comercial (*m.*)
man   hombre (*m.*)
manager   gerente (*m./f.*)
manners   los modales (*m. pl.*)
many   muchos/as
marathon   maratón (*m.*)
March   marzo (*m.*)
married   casado/a
marry   casarse (con); **to get married** casarse (con)
mask   máscara (*f.*)
matter   asunto (*m.*); **to matter** importar
mattress   colchón (*m.*)
May   mayo (*m.*)
mayor   alcalde (*m.*)
meal   comida (*f.*)
meanwhile   mientras tanto
measure   medida (*f.*); medir (e > i)
meat   carne (*f.*)
mechanic   mecánico/a (*m./f.*)
medicine   medicina (*f.*)

meet   conocer; **to meet with** encontrarse con (o > ue)
meeting   reunión (*f.*)
merit   merecer
message   mensaje (*m.*)
messy   desordenado/a
meter   metro (*m.*)
midday   mediodía (*m.*)
middle   medio (*m.*); **in the middle**
   en medio de
midnight   medianoche (*f.*)
mile   milla (*f.*)
milk   leche (*f.*)
minute   minuto (*m.*)
mirror   espejo (*m.*)
miss   echar de menos
mistake   error (*m.*); **to make a mistake** equivocarse
model   modelo (*m./f.*)
Monday   lunes (*m.*)
money   dinero (*m.*)
monkey   mono (*m.*)
monster   monstruo (*m.*)
month   mes (*m.*)
moon   luna (*f.*)
more   más
morning   mañana (*f.*)
mortgage   hipoteca (*f.*)
mosquito   mosquito (*m.*)
mother   mamá (*f.*); madre (*f.*)
mother-in-law   suegra (*f.*)
mouth   boca (*f.*)
move   mover(se) (o > ue); **to change residence**
   mudarse
movie   película (*f.*)
movies   cine (*m. sing.*)
much   mucho/a; **too much** demasiado
multiply   multiplicar
museum   museo (*m.*)
music   música (*f.*)
must   deber de; tener que; **one must** hay que
mystery   misterio (*m.*)

N

name   nombre (*m.*); llamar(se)
nap   siesta (*f.*)
napkin   servilleta (*f.*)
nature   naturaleza (*f.*)
near   cerca
neat   ordenado/a
necklace   collar (*m.*)
need   necesidad (*f.*); necesitar
neighbor   vecino/a (*m./f.*)
neighborhood   barrio (*m.*);
   vecindario (*m.*)
neither   tampoco
nephew   sobrino (*m.*)
nervous   nervioso/a

never   nunca; jamás; **never ever** nunca más

new   nuevo/a

news   noticias (*f. pl.*)

newspaper   diario (*m.*); periódico (*m.*)

next   al lado de; próximo/a; siguiente (*m./f.*)

nice   amable (*m./f.*); simpático/a

niece   sobrina (*f.*)

night   noche (*f.*); **at night** por la noche

nightmare   pesadilla (*f.*)

nobody; no one   nadie

noise   ruido (*m.*)

none   ningún; ninguno/a

noon   mediodía (*m.*)

nose   nariz (*f.*)

not any; not a single one   ningún; ninguno/a

not anything   nada

not ever   jamás

note   nota (*f.*)

nothing   nada

novel   novela (*f.*)

November   noviembre (*m.*)

now   ahora

nowhere   en ninguna parte

number   número (*m.*)

numerous   muchos/as; numerosos/as

O

obey   obedecer

occur   ocurrir; pasar

October   octubre (*m.*)

odd   extraño/a; raro/a

of   de; **of course** por supuesto

offer   oferta (*f.*); ofrecer

often   a menudo; frecuentemente; muchas veces

oil   aceite (*m.*); **suntan oil** bronceador (*m.*)

old   viejo/a

older   mayor (*m./f.*)

olive   oliva (*f.*); aceituna (*f.*)

Olympics   olimpiadas (*f.*)

once   una vez; **once in a while** de vez en cuando

onion   cebolla (*f.*)

only   sólo, solamente; único/a

open   abrir

orange   naranja (*f.*)

organize   organizar

otherwise   de lo contrario; de otro modo

outside   fuera

oven   horno (*m.*)

owe   deber

own   tener

owner   dueño/a (*m./f.*)

P

pack   empacar

package   paquete (*m.*)

page   página (*f.*)

pain   dolor (*m.*)

painful   doloroso/a; **to be painful** doler (o > ue)

paint   pintura (*f.*); pintar

painter   pintor(a) (*m./f.*)

painting   cuadro (*m.*)

pajamas   pijama (*m.*); payama (*f.*)

palace   palacio (*m.*)

pale   pálido/a

pants   pantalones (*m. pl.*)

paper   papel (*m.*); informe (*m.*)

parade   desfile (*m.*)

park   parque (*m.*); aparcar; estacionar

parking space   aparcamiento (*m.*)

partner   socio/a (*m./f.*)

party   fiesta (*f.*)

passenger   pasajero/a (*m./f.*)

passport   pasaporte (*m.*)

password   contraseña (*f.*)

pay   pagar

peace   paz (*f.*)

pearl   perla (*f.*)

pen   bolígrafo (*m.*); pluma (*f.*)

people   gente (*f.*); personas (*f. pl.*)

perhaps   quizás

permit   permitir; dejar

pet   animal doméstico (*m.*)

pharmacy   farmacia (*f.*)

phone call   llamada telefónica (*f.*)

photo   foto (*f.*); fotografía (*f.*)

pick   escoger; **to pick up** recoger

picture   pintura (*f.*); cuadro (*m.*)

piece   pedazo (*m.*)

pillow   almohada (*f.*)

pitcher (*baseball*)   lanzador(a) (*m./f.*)

pity   lástima (*f.*)

place   lugar (*m.*); poner

planet   planeta (*m.*)

play   drama (*m.*); jugar (u > ue); **to play an instrument** tocar un instrumento; **to play a game** jugar un juego; **to play a joke** gastar una broma

please   por favor; agradar

pleasant   agradable (*m./f.*)

pleasing   agradable (*m./f.*)

pocket   bolsillo (*m.*)

point   punto (*m.*); **point of view** punto de vista

police force   policía (*f.*); cuerpo de policía (*m.*)

policeman   policía (*m.*)

policewoman   policía (*f.*)

polite   cortés (*m./f.*); educado/a

politician   político/a (*m./f.*)

politics   política (*f. sing.*)

pollution   contaminación (*f.*)

pool   piscina (*f.*); alberca (*f.*)

population   población (*f.*)

possess   poseer; tener

poster   cartel (*m.*); poster (*m.*)

potato   patata (*f.*); papa (*f.*)

pound   libra (*f.*)

pray   rezar; rogar (o > ue)

prefer   preferir (e > ie)

prepare   preparar

prescription   receta médica (*f.*)

present   regalo (*m.*); presentar

pretend   fingir

price   precio (*m.*)

prince   príncipe (*m.*)

princess   princesa (*f.*)

principal (*school*)   director(a) (*m./f.*)

prison   prisión (*f.*); cárcel (*f.*)

prize   premio (*m.*)

problem   problema (*m.*)

produce   producir

profession   profesión (*f.*); carrera (*f.*)

professional   profesional (*m./f.*)

program   programa (*m.*)

progress   progreso (*m.*)

prohibited   prohibido/a

promise   promesa (*f.*); prometer

pronunciation   pronunciación (*f.*)

propose   proponer

protect   proteger

proud   orgulloso/a

prove   probar (o > ue)

provided that   con tal que

public   público (*m.*); audiencia (*f.*)

publicity   publicidad (*f.*)

publish   publicar

purchase   compra (*f.*); comprar

pure   puro/a

purse   bolsa (*f.*)

pursue   perseguir (e > i)

put   poner; **to put on oneself** ponerse;
   to put into meter en

puzzle   enigma (*m.*); rompecabezas (*m. sing.*);
   crossword puzzle crucigrama (*m.*)

pyramid   pirámide (*f.*)

Q

quality   calidad (*f.*)

quarrel   pelea (*f.*), riña (*f.*); reñir, pelear

queen   reina (*f.*)

question   pregunta (*f.*); (*issue*) cuestión (*f.*)

quick   rápido/a

quickly   rápidamente

quiet   tranquilo/a; callar(se)

quit   renunciar a

quite   bastante

quiz   prueba (*f.*)

R

racket (*tennis*)   raqueta (*f.*)

radio   radio (*m./f.*); **radio station** emisora (*f.*)

railroad   ferrocarril (*m.*); tren (*m.*)

rain   lluvia (*f.*)

raincoat   impermeable (*m.*)

rain forest   selva tropical (*f.*)

rainy   lluvioso/a

raise   aumento (*m.*); (*a child*) criar; levantar

rate   velocidad (*f.*); **exchange rate**
   cambio (*m.*)

razor   navaja de afeitar (*f.*)

reach   llegar a; alcanzar (*un objetivo*)

read   leer

ready   listo/a

real   verdadero/a

realize   darse cuenta de

really   de veras

receive   recibir

reception   recepción (*f.*)

recipe   receta (*f.*)

recognize   reconocer

recommend   recomendar (e > i)

record   grabar

recorder   grabadora (*f.*)

recycle   reciclar

redo   rehacer

reduce   reducir

refrigerator   refrigerador (*m.*)

regret   sentir (e > i)

rehearsal   ensayo (*m.*)

rehearse   ensayar

reject   rechazar

relax   relajarse

remain   quedarse

remake   rehacer

remember   acordarse (o > ue) de; recordar

remove   quitar(se)

rent   alquiler (*m.*); alquilar

repair   arreglo (*m.*), reparación (*f.*); arreglar, reparar

repeat   repetir (e > i)

report   informe (*m.*);
   reportaje (*m.*)

request   pedir (e > i)

resolve   resolver (o > ue)

resource   recurso (*m.*)

respect   respetar

rest   descansar

restaurant   restaurante (*m.*)

retire   jubilar(se)

return   regresar; (*something*) devolver (o > ue)

rice   arroz (*m.*)

rich   rico/a

riddle   enigma (*m.*)

ride (*horseback*)   montar; **to ride a bike** montar en
   bicicleta

ridiculous   ridículo/a; tonto/a
right   derecha (*f.*); **to the right**
   a la derecha; **to be right**
   tener razón; **right** (*privilege*)
   derecho (*m.*)
right now   ahora mismo
ring   anillo (*m.*); sortija (*f.*); sonar
   (o > ue)
ripe   maduro/a
river   río (*m.*)
road   camino (*m.*)
rob   robar
robotics   robótica (*f.*)
rocket   cohete (*m.*)
role   papel (*m.*); **to play the role of** hacer el papel de
room   cuarto (*m.*); habitación (*f.*)
roommate   compañero/a (*m./f.*)
routine   rutina (*f.*)
ruby   rubí (*m.*)
rug   alfombra (*f.*)
rule   regla (*f.*)
ruler   regla (*f.*)
run   correr; (*machine*) funcionar
run away   huir
Russian   ruso (*m.*) (*language*)

S

sad   triste (*m./f.*)
sadness   tristeza (*f.*)
safe   seguro/a
salad   ensalada (*f.*)
salary   sueldo (*m.*)
sale   venta (*f.*); **special sale** rebaja (*f.*)
salesperson   vendedor(a) (*m./f.*)
salt   sal (*f.*)
same   mismo/a; **the same** lo mismo; igual
sand   arena (*f.*)
Saturday   sábado (*m.*)
save   ahorrar; **to save a life** salvar una vida
say   decir (e > i); **to say good-bye** despedirse (e > i)
scare   asustar; **to get scared** asustarse
scene   escena (*f.*)
schedule   horario (*m.*)
school   escuela (*f.*); **high school** secundaria (*f.*)
science   ciencia (*f.*)
scissors   tijeras (*f. pl.*)
scratch   arañar
scream   gritar
screen   pantalla (*f.*)
scrub   fregar (e > ie)
search   busca (*f.*); búsqueda (*f.*); buscar
season   estación (*f.*)
seat   asiento (*m.*); sentar(se)
   (e > ie)
seated   sentado/a
secret   secreto (*m.*)

see   ver
seem   parecer
seldom   rara vez
select   escoger
selfish   egoísta (*m./f.*)
sell   vender
send   mandar; enviar
sentence   frase (*f.*); oración (*f.*)
separately   por separado
September   septiembre (*m.*)
serious   grave (*m./f.*)
serve   servir (e > i)
server   camarero/a (*m./f.*);
   mesero/a (*m./f.*)
set   juego (*m.*); poner(se)
several   varios/as
shade   sombra (*f.*)
shadow   sombra (*f.*)
shame   lástima (*f.*); pena (*f.*)
shape   forma (*f.*); **in good shape** en buena forma
shave   afeitar(se)
shelf   estante (*m.*)
shine   brillar
ship   barco (*m.*)
shoe   zapato (*m.*)
shop   ir de compras
shopping mall/center   centro comercial (*m.*)
short   corto/a
shoulder   hombro (*m.*)
shovel   pala (*f.*)
show   mostrar (o > ue)
shower   aguacero (*rain*) (*m.*);
   ducha (*f.*); ducharse
shut   cerrar (e > ie)
shy   tímido/a
sick   enfermo/a; **to get sick** enfermarse
sign   anuncio (*m.*); letrero (*m.*);
   firmar
signature   firma (*f.*)
silly   ridículo/a, tonto/a
silver   plata (*f.*)
sing   cantar
sister   hermana (*f.*)
sister-in-law   cúnada (*f.*)
sit down   sentarse (e > ie)
size   talla (*f.*); tamaño (*m.*)
skate   patín (*m.*); patinar
ski   esquiar
sky   cielo (*m.*)
sleep   dormir (o > ue)
sleepy   soñoliento/a; **to be sleepy** tener sueño
sleeve   manga (*f.*)
slim   delgado/a
slipper   zapatilla (*f.*)
slow   lento/a
small   pequeño/a

smart   listo/a
smell   oler (o > ue)
smile   sonrisa (f.); sonreír (e > i)
smoke   humo (m.); fumar
snake   culebra (f.); serpiente (f.)
sneeze   estornudar
snow   nieve (f.); nevar
snowfall   nevada (f.)
snowstorm   nevada (f.)
Snow White   Blanca Nieves
so   tan
so many   tantos/as
so much   tanto/a
so that   para que
soap   jabón (m.)
soccer   fútbol (m.)
society   sociedad (f.)
socks   calcetines (m. pl.)
sofa   sofá (m.)
soldier   soldado (m./f.)
some   algunos/as
somebody; someone   alguien
something   algo
sometimes   a veces
song   canción (f.)
soon   pronto
sorry (I'm)   lo siento
sound   sonar (o > ue)
soup   sopa (f.)
south   sur (m.)
souvenir   recuerdo (m.)
space   espacio (m.)
speak   hablar
spend   gastar
spoon   cuchara (f.)
spring   primavera (f.)
spy   espía (m./f.)
stage   escenario (m.)
stain   mancha (f.)
stairway   escalera (f.)
stamp   sello (m.); estampilla (f.)
stand up   levantar(se)
star   estrella (f.); movie star estrella de cine (f.)
start   empezar (e > ie)
state   estado (m.)
stay   quedarse
steal   robar
still   todavía
stomach   estómago (m.)
stop   parada (f.); dejar de; impedir (e > i)
store   tienda (f.)
storm   tormenta (f.)
story   cuento (m.)
stove   cocina (f.)
strange   extraño/a, raro/a

strawberry   fresa (f.)
street   calle (f.)
strict   estricto/a
strike   huelga (f.)
strong   fuerte (m./f.)
student   estudiante (m./f.)
studies   estudios (m. pl.)
study   estudiar
stumble   tropezar (e > ie)
subtract   restar
suburbs   afueras (f. pl.)
subway   metro (m.)
success   éxito (m.)
successful   exitoso/a; to be successful tener éxito
such   tal; such a thing tal cosa
suddenly   de repente
suffer   sufrir
suffering   sufrimiento (m.)
sugar   azúcar (m./f.)
suggest   sugerir (e > ie)
suit   traje (m.); bathing suit traje de baño (m.)
suitcase   maleta (f.)
summer   verano (m.)
sun   sol (m.)
Sunday   domingo (m.)
sunglasses   gafas de sol (f. pl.)
superstitious   supersticioso/a
support   mantener
suppose   suponer
sweater   suéter (m.)
sweep   barrer
sweet   dulce (m./f.)
swim   nadar
swimming pool   piscina (f.)
swing   columpio (m.); columpiarse

T

table   mesa (f.)
tablecloth   mantel (m.)
take   tomar; to take off despegar;
    to take off clothing quitar(se) ropa
tale   cuento (m.)
talk   hablar
tape   cinta (f.)
task   tarea (f.)
taste   gusto (m.); probar (o > ue)
tax   impuesto (m.)
tea   té (m.)
teach   enseñar
teacher   maestro/a (m./f.)
tear   lágrima (f.)
teenager   adolescente (m./f.)
telephone   teléfono (m.); on the telephone por teléfono
television   televisión (f.);
    televisor (m.)
tell   decir (e > i)

tennis tenis (*m.*)

test examen (*m.*); probar (o > ue)

text message mensaje de texto (*m.*)

theater teatro (*m.*)

theme tema (*m.*)

then entonces

theory teoría (*f.*)

therefore por lo tanto

thief ladrón (ladrona) (*m./f.*)

thin delgado/a; flaco/a

thing cosa (*f.*)

think pensar (e > ie); **to think of** pensar en

thirst sed (*f.*); **to be thirsty** tener sed

thousand mil (*m.*)

through por; a través de

throw lanzar; tirar

thunder trueno (*m.*)

Thursday jueves (*m.*)

ticket boleto (*m.*); **round-trip ticket** billete de ida y vuelta; multa (*f.*)

time tiempo (*m.*); vez (*f.*); **on time** a tiempo; **from time to time** de vez en cuando

tip propina (*f.*)

tired cansado/a; **to be tired** estar cansado/a

toast tostada (*f.*); tostar (o > ue)

together juntos/as

tolerate tolerar

tomato tomate (*m.*)

tomorrow mañana

ton tonelada (*f.*)

tonight esta noche

too también

tooth diente (*m.*); muela (*f.*); **wisdom tooth** muela del juicio (*m.*)

toothpaste pasta de dientes (*f.*)

top (of) encima de

touch tocar

tour excursión (*f.*)

towel toalla (*f.*)

town pueblo (*m.*); población (*f.*)

toy juguete (*m.*)

traffic tráfico (*m.*); **traffic light** semáforo (*m.*)

tragic trágico/a

train tren (*m.*), entrenar(se)

translate traducir

trash basura (*f.*)

travel viajar

travel agent agente de viajes (*m./f.*)

tray bandeja (*f.*)

treasure tesoro (*m.*)

tree árbol (*m.*)

trial juicio (*m.*); proceso (*m.*)

trip viaje (*m.*); **day trip** excursión (*f.*)

truck camión (*m.*)

true cierto/a; verdadero/a

trunk baúl (*m.*); maletero (*m.*)

truth verdad (*f.*)

try intentar; tratar de; **to try on clothing** probar(se) (o > ue)

T-shirt camiseta (*f.*)

Tuesday martes (*m.*)

tunnel túnel (*m.*)

turkey pavo (*m.*)

turn doblar; **to turn off** apagar; girar

turnpike autopista de peaje (*f.*)

U

UFO OVNI (*m.*)

umbrella paraguas (*m. sing.*)

uncle tío (*m.*)

uncomfortable incómodo/a

under debajo de

underline subrayar

understand comprender; entender (e > ie)

undo deshacer

undress desvestir(se) (e > i)

unfortunately por desgracia, desgraciadamente

unite unir

United States Estados Unidos (*m. pl.*)

university universidad (*f.*)

unless a menos que

unpleasant antipático/a

until hasta

up arriba

use usar

usually por lo general; generalmente

V

vacation vacaciones (*f. pl.*)

variety variedad (*f.*)

various varios/as

vase florero (*m.*); jarrón (*m.*)

vegetable vegetal (*m.*)

vehicle vehículo (*m.*)

videotape grabar, filmar

view vista (*f.*)

visit visita (*f.*)

vitamin vitamina (*f.*)

voice voz (*f.*)

volleyball voleibol (*m.*)

vote votar

W

wait esperar

waiter camarero (*m.*); mesero (*m.*)

waitress camarera (*f.*); mesera (*f.*)

wake despertar(se) (e > ie)

wake up despertarse (e > ie)

walk andar; caminar; **to walk away** alejarse

wall pared (*f.*)

wallet billetera (*f.*)

want querer (e > ie)

war guerra (*f.*)

warm cálido/a, tibio/a; **to be warm** tener calor; **warm-up exercise** ejercicio de calentamiento (*m.*)

warn advertir (e > ie)

wash lavar(se); **to wash dishes** fregar (e > ie)

waste malgastar; **to waste time** perder (e > ie) el tiempo

watch (*time*) reloj (*m.*)

watch mirar

water (el) agua (*f.*); regar (e > ie)

wealth riqueza (*f.*)

wealthy rico/a

wear llevar; usar

Web web (*f.*); red informática (*f.*)

wedding boda (*f.*)

Wednesday miércoles (*m.*)

week semana (*f.*)

weekend fin de semana (*m.*)

weigh pesar

weight peso (*m.*)

welcome bienvenido/a; **you're welcome** de nada

well bien

well-being bienestar (*m.*)

wet mojado/a; **to get wet** mojarse

whale ballena (*f.*); **whale watching** observar las ballenas

what? ¿qué?, ¿cómo?

whatever cuanto/a

whenever cuando quiera

where donde; **where?** ¿dónde?

wherever dondequiera

while mientras; rato (*m.*)

who quien; **who?** ¿quién?

whoever quienquiera

wide ancho/a

wife esposa (*f.*)

win ganar

wind viento (*m.*)

window ventana (*f.*); **car window** ventanilla (*f.*)

wine vino (*m.*); **red wine** vino tinto

winner ganador(a) (*m./f.*)

winter invierno (*m.*)

wise sabio/a

wish deseo (*m.*); desear; querer (e > ie)

witch bruja (*f.*)

with con; **with me** conmigo; **with you** contigo

within dentro de

without sin

woman mujer (*f.*)

wonderful maravilloso/a

wood madera (*f.*)

woods bosque (*m.*)

word palabra (*f.*)

work trabajo (*m.*); empleo (*m.*); trabajar; (*machine*) funcionar

world mundo (*m.*)

World Series Serie Mundial (*f.*)

worry preocupación (*f.*); preocuparse

worse peor (*m./f.*)

worth valor (*m.*); **to be worth** valer

wounded herido/a

wrap envolver (o > ue)

wrinkle arruga (*f.*)

wrist muñeca (*f.*)

write escribir

written escrito/a

wrong equivocado/a; **to be wrong** no tener razón

Y

year año (*m.*)

yellow amarillo/a

yesterday ayer

yet todavía

young joven

younger menor (*m./f.*)

Answer key

1 Spelling, pronunciation, and punctuation

1·1 *The stressed vowels are underlined.* 1. missing; organización 2. missing; cónsul 3. correct, no accent mark; lealtad 4. superfluous; animal 5. correctly used; camión 6. missing; tecnología 7. superfluous; hablas 8. missing; teórico 9. correct, no accent mark; temeraria 10. correct, no accent mark; primorosa 11. missing; carácter 12. incorrectly placed; avión 13. correct, no accent mark; caracteres 14. missing; vendió 15. superfluous; ventana 16. correct, no accent mark; vecino 17. correct, no accent mark; frijoles (Note: in Colombia: **fríjoles**) 18. correct, no accent mark; proyector 19. correct, no accent mark; cortinas 20. correctly used; teoría

1·2 1. El Sr. Jiménez viaja a los EE.UU. 2. Encontró artefactos del 200 a.C. 3. La Dra. Melissa Marcos es una experta en civilizaciones antiguas. 4. La Srta. Marcos, su hija, ayuda a su madre. 5. Darán una conferencia en la UE.

1·3 1. Alicia, Luisa e Irene son disciplinadas, trabajadoras, pacientes y eficientes. 2. Hacen ejercicios, montan en bicicleta, levantan pesas y corren siete u ocho millas. 3. Estas chicas también hacen yoga, trabajos comunitarios y sirven a la comunidad. 4. Hacen campañas en EE.UU. para recoger fondos para niños e indigentes. 5. Han recibido premios, certificados e innumerables homenajes de varias organizaciones.
6. Ellas demuestran que la rutina es esencial para ser disciplinado, cumplir metas y triunfar.

1·4 1. Carmen regresa esta noche a las ocho. Regresa esta noche a las ocho, Carmen. 2. Al llegar a casa, decidimos escuchar los mensajes. Decidimos escuchar los mensajes al llegar a la casa. 3. De hecho, no tienes paciencia porque te enojas mucho. 4. Recibieron una carta de San Antonio, Texas. 5. Necesitaba tu ayuda, tu amistad y tu compañía. 6. Este documento dice que eres de Lima, Perú.

1·5 1. Vamos a mudarnos a una casa más grande; no tenemos suficiente espacio. 2. Los muebles de la sala, los cuadros, los platos de la cocina: todo está listo. 3. Compramos cuatro aparatos nuevos: una computadora, un televisor HD, un teléfono móvil y una aspiradora. 4. Cómoda, amplia, fresca y acogedora: así es la casa nueva. 5. Una cocina debe ser lo mejor de una casa: espaciosa, bien equipada y llena de luz. 6. Ahora podemos quitar el letrero que dice: "Se vende casa".

1·6 1. El primer día del verano (21 de junio en el hemisferio norte) nos trae alegría. 2. Mi madre (mujer muy sabia) siempre me hablaba de sus experiencias cuando era niña. 3. Uno de sus consejos era: "El tiempo es oro". 4. Pensaba que mi madre era invencible (¡qué ilusión!) cuando yo era niño. 5. Todas las mañanas cantábamos una canción: "La cucaracha". 6. ¡Qué risa me da ahora (han pasado tantos años) porque mi madre era divertida! 7. Y le gustaba en especial un poema: "La rosa blanca". 8. Raras veces era dura, pero su amenaza siempre era: "¡A la cama!" 9. Cuando no estaba de buen humor, yo sabía que estaba ocupada. 10. Y puedo repetir las palabras que decía mi padre para recordarla: "Corazón de oro".

1·7 En, Universidad, Sevilla, En, Mario Vargas Llosa, Isabel Allende, Al, Casa Belisa

1·8 Marcia, lunes, California, África, ella, suroeste, Estados Unidos

1·9 Answers will vary.

2 Subject pronouns and the present tense

2·1 1. Ella 2. ellas 3. Él 4. Ellos 5. Nosotros / Nosotras 6. Ustedes 7. ellos
8. Ustedes

2·2 1. canto 2. escucha 3. bailan 4. descansan 5. preparamos 6. lavas
7. compartes 8. confío 9. deciden 10. responden 11. entra 12. recibe

2·3 1. Necesitas descansar. 2. Él habla, yo escucho. 3. Estudia chino y español también.
4. Nosotros gastamos mucho dinero. 5. Ustedes compran camisas caras.
6. Trabajo cinco días a la semana. 7. Ellas bailan todos los sábados. 8. Mi hermana toca el piano, pero
yo toco la guitarra.

2·4 1. vive 2. trabaja 3. estudia 4. planean 5. sube 6. saca 7. conversas 8. necesita

2·5 1. Yo preparo la cena. 2. Los niños suben la escalera. 3. Mis gatos beben leche. 4. El cliente suma la
cuenta. 5. La mamá de Carli habla al reportero a la reportera. 6. La actriz teme a los críticos. 7. Tus
amigos comen fajitas.

2·6 Answers will vary.

2·7 1. Hoy Martha y Linus celebran su aniversario. 2. Sus parientes llegan a tiempo. 3. Varios amigos
conversan en la sala. 4. En el patio, los chicos escuchan música latina. 5. El olor a enchiladas circula por
toda la casa. 6. Los niños beben limonada.

2·8 Answers will vary.

2·9 1. Hace... que estudio español. 2. Uso la computadora desde hace... 3. Hace... años que los Estados
Unidos son una nación independiente. 4. Usamos la Internet desde hace... años. 5. Escucho música
clásica desde hace... / No escucho música clásica.

2·10 Answers will vary.

2·11 1. V 2. F 3. F 4. F 5. V

2·12 1. doy 2. ponen 3. ven 4. cabemos 5. traigo 6. caigo 7. haces 8. salgo

2·13 1. Compongo canciones para mis amigos. 2. Propongo un brindis. 3. Reponen el dinero en mi
cuenta. 4. Ud. distrae al público. 5. Las niñas deshacen el rompecabezas.

2·14 1. b 2. a 3. h 4. c 5. f 6. g 7. e 8. d

2·15 1. conduzco 2. salen 3. conozco 4. ofrece 5. merezco 6. obedecen

2·16 1. Merezco un aumento de sueldo. 2. ¿Salgo ahora? 3. Agradezco tu amistad. 4. No pertenezco a este
grupo. 5. Traduzco las instrucciones. 6. ¡Rara vez impongo mis ideas! 7. Permanezco callado/a.

2·17 1. está 2. hay 3. llegan 4. es; digo 5. vienen 6. tiene 7. oyes 8. van

2·18 1. exijo 2. escojo 3. extingo 4. recojo 5. venzo 6. protejo 7. convenzo 8. finjo

2·19 1. No hay neblina esta mañana. 2. El reloj da las diez y media. 3. Hace sol ahora./Hay sol ahora. 4. El
público da gritos en el estadio. 5. El capitán le da un abrazo al portero.

2·20 Answers will vary.

2·21 Answers will vary.

2·22 1. ¿Tienes hambre? 2. Tenemos sed. 3. Lori hace una visita a su primo. 4. Mario le da un abrazo a su
amigo. 5. Tienen prisa. 6. Tienes razón esta vez. 7. No tengo miedo. 8. ¿Tiene Ud. frío?

2·23 1. e 2. b 3. h 4. a 5. d 6. f 7. c 8. g

3 Present tense irregular verbs

3·1 1. desciende 2. despierta 3. enciende 4. Empieza 5. hierve 6. Friega
7. atraviesa 8. Comienza 9. sienta 10. cierra

3·2 1. comenzar; comienza 2. divertir; divierte 3. sentir; sienten 4. defender; defienden 5. recomendar;
recomiendan 6. empezar; empieza 7. advertir; advierte 8. cerrar; cierran

3·3 1. Bernardo y José suelen ayudar a sus amigos. 2. Cuando llueve, José me recoge en mi oficina.
3. Bernardo recuerda mi cumpleaños todos los años. 4. Almuerzo con José frecuentemente. 5. Juegan al
golf los domingos. 6. Cuando juego con ellos, yo cuento los puntos para el resultado. 7. José vuela a
Costa Rica todos los veranos / cada verano. 8. Usualmente vuelve a Albuquerque después de una semana.

3·4	1. h 2. i 3. c 4. d 5. f 6. e 7. b 8. g 9. j 10. a

3·4   1. h 2. i 3. c 4. d 5. f 6. e 7. b 8. g 9. j 10. a

3·5   1. consigue 2. pide 3. sonríen 4. siguen 5. sirve 6. compite 7. impide 8. huye 9. despide 10. concluye

3·6   Answers will vary.

3·7   1. digo 2. tiene 3. pongo 4. sé 5. viene 6. doy 7. es 8. estoy 9. traigo 10. oímos 11. hace 12. propongo

3·8   Answers will vary.

3·9   1. Conozco 2. Sé 3. conozco 4. Conozco 5. sé 6. Sé 7. Conozco 8. conozco

4 The near future, nouns, and articles

4·1   1. Mañana por la mañana vamos a visitar un museo en Madrid. 2. Más tarde voy a caminar por la ciudad. 3. Mañana por la tarde Laurita va a ver a sus amigos de Barcelona. 4. La semana que viene Laurita y yo vamos a viajar a Sevilla. 5. La semana siguiente tú y Laura vais/van a regresar a California. 6. Mis padres van a mudarse de Los Ángeles a Miami el año que viene.

4·2   Answers will vary.

4·3   1. M 2. M 3. M 4. M 5. X 6. M 7. M 8. X 9. M 10. X 11. M 12. X

4·4   1. N 2. Y 3. N 4. N 5. Y 6. Y 7. N 8. N 9. Y 10. N 11. Y 12. N 13. Y 14. Y 15. Y 16. Y 17. N 18. Y 19. N 20. N

4·5   1. la 2. la 3. la 4. la 5. la 6. la 7. el 8. el 9. la 10. la

4·6   1. La dermatitis 2. la dosis 3. El tenor 4. el equipaje 5. la estación 6. La fealdad

4·7   1. El arpa 2. El hacha 3. La campeona 4. La gerente 5. El águila 6. La estrella 7. El marqués 8. El mes

4·8   1. el portugués 2. El rojo, el blanco y el azul 3. el lunes 4. el lavaplatos 5. el sacacorchos 6. el paraguas 7. el alemán

4·9   1. la profesora 2. la maestra 3. la periodista 4. la reina 5. la pintora 6. la actriz 7. la madre 8. la gerente 9. la yegua 10. la comandante 11. la artista 12. la bailarina

4·10   Answers will vary.

4·11   1. la estudiante 2. el león 3. la abogada 4. el manzano 5. la pera 6. la emperatriz 7. el marido, el esposo 8. el yerno 9. la heroína 10. la turista 11. la víctima 12. la papa

4·12   1. los señores 2. las reinas 3. las almas 4. los aviones 5. las leonas 6. las flores 7. las cárceles 8. los restaurantes 9. las carnes 10. las aguas 11. las guías 12. los padres 13. los temores 14. los domingos

4·13   1. las sopas 2. las residencias 3. los pasajes 4. las mujeres 5. los relojes 6. las españolas 7. los bebés 8. los manteles 9. los rubís, los rubíes 10. las canciones 11. las luces 12. las regiones

4·14   1. Mis vacaciones terminan el domingo. 2. Voy a ver las panteras en el zoológico mañana. 3. Ahora Lina y yo nos ponemos las gafas de sol. 4. Este hotel está en las afueras de Madrid. 5. Viajamos de noche y descansamos en un coche cama. 6. Lina nunca trae el paraguas/la sombrilla.

4·15   1. los gemelos 2. los domingos 3. los binoculares 4. las tesis 5. las tijeras 6. las gafas

4·16   1. Los, la 2. Los, los 3. Los, los 4. El, la 5. Los, las 6. Las, los 7. Los, el

4·17   1. La 2. los 3. los 4. blank 5. los 6. blank 7. la 8. las 9. la 10. las 11. el

4·18   1. Hoy tengo una cita a las nueve y media de la mañana. 2. El/La asistente del/de la dentista habla portugués y español. 3. Me duele la muela del juicio. 4. Las caries pueden causar dolor/dolores. 5. Los viernes siempre llego a casa tarde. 6. Yo voy a ir a casa a eso de las diez. 7. ¡Necesito descansar!

4·19   1. diez centavos la docena 2. los Goya de hoy 3. los López 4. los Estados Unidos 5. doce dólares la yarda 6. (el) trabajar duro 7. las (islas) Galápagos 8. el presidente Roosevelt 9. (el) comer y (el) beber

4·20   1. la 2. la 3. la 4. Los 5. la 6. X 7. X 8. la

4·21   1. una 2. un 3. una 4. un 5. un 6. una 7. un 8. un 9. una 10. un 11. un 12. una

4·22   1. unas veces 2. unos temblores 3. unas verdades 4. unos pasajes 5. unos hospitales 6. unas crisis 7. unos rubís, unos rubíes 8. unos sofás 9. unas escaleras 10. unos manatís, unos manatíes 11. unos capitanes 12. unas pensiones

4·23   Answers will vary.

4·24   1. Unos   2. una   3. unas   4. X   5. un   6. un   7. X   8. X   9. un   10. X

5 Gustar, ser, and estar and expressing opinions

5·1   1. le gustan   2. Le fascinan   3. nos interesa   4. os encantan   5. Les agrada   6. Te disgusta   7. nos molestan   8. les apasionan

5·2   1. duelen   2. preocupa   3. quedan   4. sobra   5. toca   6. hacen falta   7. importa   8. bastan

5·3   le encantan; le fascina; le importa; le aburre; le molestan; le bastan; le quedan; le duele; le hace falta

5·4   1. Le gustan los deportes y las actividades al aire libre.   2. A Pablo le fascina esquiar y patinar sobre hielo.   3. No, a Miguel no le importa si hace frío o calor.   4. A Julia le aburre quedarse en casa.   5. Hoy le duele la cabeza.

5·5   1. F   2. F   3. V   4. V   5. F   6. V

5·6   1. Este es Manuel Ortiz.   2. Es de Puerto Rico.   3. Esta es su asistente, Leticia.   4. Ella es ecuatoriana.   5. Ellos son nuestros amigos.   6. Manuel es un atleta excelente.

5·7   1. e   2. a   3. f   4. b   5. c   6. d

5·8   1. Son, está   2. está   3. está   4. es   5. son   6. es

5·9   1. telling time; present progressive form   2. temporary condition   3. temporary physical condition   4. characteristic   5. time an event takes place   6. occupation

5·10   1. está   2. está   3. estar   4. Están   5. están   6. Es

5·11   1. Estoy deprimido/a pero no estoy loco/a.   2. Estos no son mis zapatos.   3. ¿Por qué están Uds. aquí?   4. ¡Uds. no están seguros!   5. Bueno, tengo hambre y estoy cansado/a.   6. ¿Estamos listos para salir?   7. El partido es en el estadio de la universidad.

5·12   1. f   2. a   3. b   4. e   5. d   6. c

5·13   1. h   2. i   3. e   4. m   5. j   6. f   7. l   8. d   9. k   10. a   11. c   12. b   13. g

5·14   1. My Russian friend knows a lot about physics and astronomy.   2. That book was printed in Barcelona.   3. The shopping center isn't exactly in the center of the city.   4. At this moment, I am sitting in front of my computer, writing this.   5. I have a letter written for the boss.   6. Are you okay, guy? You look worried / preoccupied.

5·15   1. ¿Conoces bien a María? (*note the use of the personal* **a**)   2. Él es cansado.   3. José es mexicano.   4. Este vestido es de seda.   5. La fiesta es en la playa. (*Events use* **ser**, *not* **estar**.)   6. Éste es el carro de mi papá.   7. ¿Están cansados?   8. Julio César está muerto.   9. Acabas de hacer este ejercicio. (**acabar** *contains the idea of* finishing, *so there is no need to use* **terminar**).

5·16   1. desde   2. Como   3. como   4. Cómo   5. Desde   6. cómo   7. como   8. Desde   9. Como   10. como

5·17   1. hoy o mañana   2. aquí o en tu país   3. con un hombre o con una mujer   4. para ti o para tu amiga

5·18   1. de hecho   2. para serte sincero   3. por otra parte   4. A propósito   5. o sea

5·19   1. me   2. te   3. les   4. nos   5. les   6. os   7. les   8. le

5·20   1. encantan   2. parece   3. gustan   4. parecen   5. gustan   6. gustas   7. importas   8. importo

5·21   1. a, b, c, e, j, l   2. d, i   3. d, i   4. a, b, c, e, h, j, l   5. g   6. d, i   7. a, b, c, e, h, j, l   8. k   9. f

5·22   1. His attitude bothers me.   2. They love to play basketball.   3. What do you think?/How do you like it?   4. Do you like to go to the movies?   5. Children annoy him.   6. The news makes me sad/The news saddens me.   7. The class bores us.   8. You're important to me./I care about you.

5·23   1. Me encanta ir a la playa.   2. Le fascinan sus ideas.   3. No le gusta el ruido.   4. Le gustas tú.   5. Le aburren sus clases.   6. Me encanta la música de la guitarra.   7. Nos gustan las películas de horror.   8. Les encanta ir de compras.   9. Me parece feo.   10. Nos gusta.

5·24   1. mantienen   2. sostienen   3. apoyan   4. soporto

6 Adjectives, adverbs, and comparisons

6·1 1. agudo 2. grande 3. viejo 4. fabulosa 5. interminable 6. profundo 7. redonda 8. malicioso

6·2 1. elegante 2. raras 3. violentos 4. populares 5. azules 6. preferida 7. cálido 8. feas

6·3 1. un día bonito 2. una mañana triste 3. una mano grande 4. un aroma (un perfume) agradable 5. una canción larga 6. un sueño profundo 7. una amiga sincera 8. una enfermera dedicada/un enfermero dedicado 9. una ciudad interesante 10. un idioma/lenguaje, una lengua difícil 11. una explosión terrible 12. un soldado valiente

6·4 1. h 2. j 3. f 4. i 5. g 6. c 7. e 8. a 9. d 10. b

6·5 1. algunos informes 2. temas filosóficos 3. muchas decisiones 4. ningunas zapatillas 5. ningún premio 6. proyecto difícil

6·6 1. ¡Esta comedia es única, fuera de serie! 2. Mi viejo amigo, Manolito, escribe el guión. 3. Un antiguo colega vine al teatro para ver la comedia. 4. El protagonista es un hombre simple. 5. Manolito siempre usa ideas nuevas. 6. Cualquier persona que viene al teatro paga cinco dólares.

6·7 Answers will vary.

6·8 1. El viajero <u>portugués</u> trae un pasaporte <u>vencido</u>. 2. El <u>tercer</u> año en la universidad es <u>difícil</u> y <u>largo</u>. 3. Han pasado <u>tres</u> meses. 4. Pablo Neruda, el <u>gran</u> poeta <u>chileno</u>, es un personaje <u>curioso</u> en una película <u>italiana</u>. 5. ¿Quién es el cantante <u>famoso</u> de San Juan?

6·9 Answers will vary.

6·10 1. Es cortés y generoso. 2. Escuchamos un ruido alto y claro. 3. Esta silla cuesta trescientos dólares. 4. Un vaso de leche fría, por favor. 5. Su oficina está en una calle larga y estrecha. 6. Hay algunas tiendas nuevas en el primer piso de este centro comercial. 7. Elly quiere una bicicleta nueva.

6·11 1. los pendientes/los zarcillos de diamantes 2. la puerta abierta 3. un vestido de verano 4. los discos rotos 5. algunas bolsas de plástico 6. tres cestas (cestos) de papel 7. un plato de cristal 8. la carta escrita 9. mi anillo de oro 10. los hombres perdidos.

6·12 Answers will vary.

6·13 1. lejos 2. nunca 3. bien 4. cerca 5. todavía 6. debajo 7. mal 8. poco

6·14 Answers will vary.

6·15 1. Siempre hay una razón para ser feliz. 2. Nunca tengo suficiente dinero. 3. Todavía tengo esperanzas de ganar la lotería. 4. Bueno, sueño mucho. 5. Espero demasiado de mis amigos. 6. También tengo dolores de cabeza frecuentemente. 7. Además, no me quejo a menudo. 8. Luego voy a tomar dos aspirinas. 9. Pero todavía no, quiero esperar. 10. Entonces continuaré hablando de mi personalidad.

6·16 1. ansiosamente 2. definitivamente 3. lentamene 4. tímidamente 5. ágilmente 6. fácilmente 7. dulcemente 8. desgraciadamente 9. profundamente 10. inmediatamente 11. totalmente 12. obviamente 13. claramente 14. hábilmente 15. alegremente 16. desafortunadamente 17. violentamente 18. completamente 19. fuertemente 20. rápidamente

6·17 Answers will vary.

6·18 1. Hacemos los ejercicios lentamente. 2. ¿Siguen Uds. las instrucciones cuidadosamente? 3. Usualmente no nos gusta trabajar los fines de semana. 4. Evidentemente este perro no protege su casa. 5. Desafortunadamente, Uds. no tienen muchas joyas. 6. Uds. pueden proteger fácilmente su casa con una alarma. 7. Lisa habla despacio y claramente. 8. También habla brevemente. 9. Francamente, no me gusta esperar. 10. Afortunadamente, no tengo mucha tarea.

6·19 1. de noche 2. de día 3. al mismo tiempo 4. Por suerte 5. con frecuencia/a menudo 6. A veces 7. Sin duda 8. de nuevo

6·20 Answers will vary.

6·21 1. Por lo visto, queremos una vida mejor. 2. De vez en cuando tenemos que considerar que la vida es corta. 3. ¡ De veras, no puedo encontrar un apartamento! 4. De ahora en adelante vamos a cambiar nuestro estilo de vida. 5. No nos vamos a levantar al salir el sol. 6. Al anochecer podemos relajarnos y olvidarnos de mañana. 7. Desde aquí, tenemos una vista del río. 8. Hasta aquí, este plan es muy aburrido. 9. ¿De veras tenemos que cambiar nuestro estilo de vida? 10. De ahora (hoy) en adelante no podemos quejarnos más.

6·22 1. Tú eres más alto que Tomás. 2. Mi hermano corre tan rápido como ellos. 3. Su hermana tiene tanto dinero como yo. 4. Hoy hace menos frío que ayer. 5. Llueve más aquí que en Arizona. 6. El Sr.

Acero es tan malo como el diablo.   7. Juana es la alumna más lista de la clase.   8. Hay menos de cinco libros en la mesa.   9. ¡Los padres siempre son mayores que sus hijos!   10. Pedro es el químico más preparado del equipo.   11. María y Teresa bailan mejor que yo.   12. Estos dos son los peores platos del menú.   13. Me gusta este postre más que el otro.   14. ¡Es un jugador de baloncesto altísimo!   15. Juanito tiene tantos juguetes como su hermanita.   16. Hay menos nieve en esta montaña que en la otra.   17. Este carro es más costoso que el otro.   18. Ella lee tantas revistas como yo.   19. Esa muchacha es la más interesante de todas.   20. La oveja no bebe tanta agua como el camello.

6·23   1. The children don't sleep as many hours as I do.   2. My girlfriend has hair as long as her mother. / My girlfriend's hair is as long as her mother's.   3. That girl is drop-dead gorgeous.   4. Are you as popular as he is?   5. Do you have as many friends as I do?   6. I don't believe (that) John is younger than you.   7. What's your oldest sibling's name? (sibling, *because it could be a brother or a sister*)   8. There are no more than five (*i.e., five, no more, no less*) on a basketball team.   9. She is as much of a crybaby as her aunt.   10. Which is the biggest country in the world?   11. Puerto Rico is not as big as Cuba.   12. New York doesn't have as many people as Mexico City.   13. There are fewer than four pizzas in the refrigerator.   14. You're as friendly as my sister tells me.   15. George likes to play tennis as much as he does to watch movies.   16. I love to swim in the ocean more than in lakes.   17. These two are the most athletic ones in the group.   18. She doesn't have as much energy as we hoped.   19. On the table there are as many ballpoint pens as there are pencils.   20. More than anything, he is interested in making little gold fish.

6·24   1. ¿Quién es / será la persona más importante de tu vida?   2. ¿Qué quieren hacer sus amigos más que nada?   3. Ella es la mujer más rica del mundo.   4. ¿Tienen tantas camisas como calcetines / medias?   5. Ella es la mejor nadadora del equipo.   6. Ella pinta tanto como él.   7. No hay menos de mil libros en esta colección.   8. Su mamá vende más que yo.   9. ¿Cuál es el lago más profundo de los Estados Unidos?   10. El Atlántico es más pequeño que el Pacífico.   11. Su hermano es más joven que tú.   12. No somos los jugadores más altos del equipo.   13. Este reloj cuesta tanto como ése / aquél.   14. ¿Quién tiene / tendrá tantos zapatos como ella?   15. Somos los mejores cocineros del pueblo.   16. Venus puede brillar tanto como el foco de un avión.   17. Hay más peces en este lago que en ése / aquél.   18. Él es el peor jugador de ajedrez de la escuela.   19. Él va al cine tanto como yo.   20. Ella escribe tan bien como canta.

6·25   1. irresponsable   2. buenos   3. amistosa   4. exigente

6·26   1. estoy   2. está   3. están   4. son   5. son   6. es   7. son   8. son

6·27   1. más alto que Diego   2. más bajo que Arturo   3. tan alto como Arturo   4. más de   5. menos de   6. mas... que   7. tan... como   8. más libros que Ana   9. tantos libros como Berta

6·28   1. bastante   2. demasiado   3. muy/bien   4. muy/bien

6·29   1. tan... como   2. la más lista de todas   3. tan lista como   4. más lista que

6·30   1. dejar   2. sales   3. dejes   4. se van/se marchan   5. parte/sale   6. deja

6·31   1. Mira   2. es decir   3. La verdad   4. Vamos   5. ni hablar   6. Con razón   7. todo lo contrario

6·32   Individual answers will vary. Sample answer: 1. ¡Con razón está tan orgullosa su mamá!

6·33   Individual answers will vary.

7   The preterit tense

7·1   1. robaron   2. perdió   3. corrí   4. dispararon   5. sospechamos   6. Escuchaste   7. salió   8. Compraron

7·2   1. Anteanoche Ana regresó a casa.   2. Esta mañana, Pilar envió tres mensajes electrónicos al banco.   3. Roberto viajó a San Antonio el mes pasado.   4. Hace diez años me mudé a este edificio.   5. El detective Rojas y su asistente resolvieron el caso la semana pasada.   6. Esta mañana a las ocho el doctor visitó a su nuevo paciente.

7·3   Answers will vary.

7·4   1. 2   2. 4   3. 5   4. 1   5. 3

7·5   1. compramos un televisor para ver películas.   2. comimos comida mexicana, tomamos un refresco y lavamos los platos.   3. visitamos a mi tía Matilde.   4. llegamos a las tres y charlamos con mi tía.   5. nos dimos cuenta de que el perro de Matilde es feísimo.

7·6   Answers will vary.

7·7   1. Ayer perdí un anillo de oro y lo busqué en mi apartamento.   2. Me equivoqué.   3. ¿Dónde coloqué mi anillo?   4. Empecé a buscar mi anillo en la sala.   5. Recé por/durante unos minutos.   6. Entonces apagué la luz y salí de la sala.   7. Saqué un traje y un par de pantalones de mi auto /carro.   8. Más tarde los colgué en un armario/closet.   9. Entonces tropecé con una maleta grande.   10. Toqué algo en el suelo/piso y encontré mi anillo.   11. Empecé a sentirme mucho mejor.   12. Entonces desempaqué mi maleta.

7·8   Answers will vary.

7·9   1. Alfonso leyó una novela gótica de Ruiz Zafón.   2. Su hermano se cayó de la silla.   3. ¡Oímos sus gritos!   4. Sus perros ladraron y contribuyeron al ruido.   5. El gato huyó de la casa.   6. Alfonso construyó esa casa hace muchos años.   7. Yo intuí que esta familia está loca.

7·10   1. leyó   2. incluyó   3. intuyó   4. distribuyeron   5. contribuyó   6. concluyeron

7·11   1. consiguieron   2. prefirió   3. durmieron   4. sonrió   5. pidieron   6. sirvió   7. se rió   8. se vistió   9. pidieron   10. se divirtieron, disfrutaron

7·12   1. En el gimnasio, Marisa consiguió terminar sus ejercicios temprano.   2. Se vistió y llegó al cine a las seis de la tarde.   3. Compró su entrada y pidió un refresco.   4. Una chica joven le sirvió la bebida y sonrió.   5. En el teatro, Marisa se sentó y miró los comerciales.   6. ¡Cuántos comerciales! ¡Pagó para ver una película, no anuncios comerciales aburridos!   7. Marisa durmió por una hora.   8. Se despertó veinte minutos antes del final de la película.

7·13   1. Alberto no pudo.   2. Anoche Rita puso las llaves sobre la mesa.   3. La maleta no cupo en el maletero.   4. Ayer hubo una reunión.   5. Estuvieron aquí.   6. Puse el tenedor en la gaveta.   7. Tuvimos que ir a la tienda.   8. ¿Estuvieron Uds. en la fiesta?   9. Mis amigos tuvieron un accidente.

7·14   1. No dije una mentira.   2. Trajo un pastel.   3. Tradujeron los ejercicios.   4. Hicimos el trabajo.   5. Tú viniste tarde.   6. Tim hizo la tarea.   7. ¿Vinieron ellos?

7·15   1. hizo   2. trajo   3. dio   4. fuimos   5. puse   6. vino   7. produjeron   8. propusimos   9. pude   10. supuso

7·16   1. Ayer conocí a Lily, la nueva secretaria.   2. Supe que habla tres idiomas.   3. Pero ella no pudo terminar su primera tarea a tiempo.   4. Ella no quiso trabajar después de las cinco.   5. Lily tradujo tres documentos.   6. Hizo un trabajo estupendo.   7. Yo leí los documentos.   8. Supimos la noticia al día siguiente.   9. Lily se fue antes de las cinco y no regresó al día siguiente.   10. No quise creerlo. ¡Necesitamos una nueva secretaria!

8   The progressive tenses

8·1   1. está patinando   2. están bebiendo   3. estamos esquiando   4. está aplaudiendo   5. estás jugando   6. estoy sacando   7. están discutiendo   8. están compartiendo

8·2   1. oyendo   2. huyendo   3. destruyendo   4. construyendo   5. atrayendo   6. contribuyendo

8·3   1. sirviendo   2. hirviendo   3. siguiendo   4. riñendo   5. compitiendo   6. diciendo

8·4   1. está escondiendo   2. está dando   3. están gritando   4. están esperando   5. Está durmiendo   6. está viviendo

8·5   1. Los fanáticos están viendo un buen juego.   2. Ahora no está lloviendo.   3. El equipo está jugando bien.   4. El entrenador está animando a sus jugadores.   5. Un vendedor de cerveza está subiendo las escaleras.   6. Él está gritando: "¡Cacahuates, cerveza!"   7. Ahora, la banda está tocando música.   8. Los fanáticos están divirtiéndose.   9. El otro equipo está perdiendo el juego.

8·6   1. está buscando   2. están rellenando   3. está escribiendo   4. están respondiendo   5. está recibiendo   6. están haciendo   7. estoy cambiando   8. está tomando   9. está leyendo

8·7   Answers will vary.

8·8   1. Miriam sigue cantando la misma canción.   2. Mi hijo anda buscando trabajo.   3. ¿Quién continúa haciendo ruido?   4. Iremos buscando una respuesta.   5. No siguen mintiendo.   6. (Ella) Está perdiendo la esperanza.

8·9   1. buscando   2. ir   3. Nadar   4. encontrar   5. disfrutando   6. bronceándose   7. flotando   8. durmiendo

9 Questions, answers, and exclamations

9·1 1. ¿Llegas tarde? 2. ¿María ya está lista? 3. ¿Tiene poca paciencia? 4. ¿Esperamos hasta las cinco? 5. ¿Hay un taxi en la esquina? 6. ¿Hace calor en la calle? 7. ¿Lloverá esta noche? 8. ¿Llegaremos al cine a tiempo?

9·2 1. ¿No te gusta tu trabajo? 2. ¿Todavía no ganas mucho dinero? 3. ¿Ya no estudias en una universidad? 4. ¿No estás listo/a para un ascenso? 5. ¿Todavía no tienes novio/a? 6. ¿Ya no estás enamorado/a?

9·3 1. ¿Es ella tu profesora de matemáticas? 2. ¿Aprecian los alumnos los conocimientos de la profesora? 3. ¿Tiene ella un hermano en esta facultad? 4. ¿Eres su alumna preferida? 5. ¿Admira a sus colegas de otras disciplinas? 6. ¿Responde ella tus preguntas? 7. ¿Explicó la profesora la teoría?

9·4 1. ¿Necesita Ud. ayuda? 2. ¿Ven ustedes a los niños? 3. ¿Ya llegaron Uds.? / ¿Llegaron ya Uds.? 4. ¿Hizo Ud. una donación? 5. ¿Entregaron Uds. el auto? 6. ¿Quiere/Desea Ud. un asiento cerca de la ventana?

9·5 1. ¿Quiere/Desea Ud. este vestido? 2. ¿Prefiere Ud. este par de zapatos? 3. ¿Necesita Ud. lentes nuevos? 4. ¿Está Ud. cansado/a? 5. ¿Está Ud. listo/a para pagar? 6. ¿Pagó Ud. con una tarjeta de crédito?

9·6 1. ¿Prefieres un refresco de limón, una cola o una cerveza? 2. ¿Llegáis esta tarde o mañana? 3. ¿Desean ir a la playa o nadar en la piscina? 4. ¿Compramos la corbata, el sombrero o un libro? 5. ¿Quieren ver una película o cenar conmigo? 6. ¿Duerme en la hamaca o en el sillón? 7. ¿Vive en la ciudad o en el campo?

9·7 1. Lucía ve muchos programas dramáticos, ¿no? 2. Pedro prefiere los documentales del canal de cable, ¿no es verdad? 3. Carla y Marcos van a un concierto de un grupo mexicano, ¿no es cierto? 4. En el concierto venderán copias del último CD, ¿verdad? 5. Después del concierto irán a cenar todos juntos, ¿no es cierto? 6. Celebran la ocasión especial del cumpleaños de Lucía, ¿no es verdad?

9·8 *Possible answers:* 1. ¡Qué va! 2. ¡Qué va! 3. ¡Naturalmente! / ¡Claro que sí! 4. ¡Naturalmente! / ¡Claro que sí! 5. ¡Qué va!

9·9 *Possible answers:* 1. ¿Cómo se llama? 2. ¿Dónde vive? 3. ¿Cuándo es su cumpleaños? 4. ¿Qué limpia / Qué hace Nora el viernes por la tarde? 5. ¿Qué estudia Nora? 6. ¿Dónde quiere trabajar Nora? 7. ¿Quiénes son sus amigas? 8. ¿Cuándo van de vacaciones?

9·10 1. Qué 2. Cuál 3. Cuáles 4. Cuál 5. Qué 6. Qué

9·11 1. ¿De dónde eres? 2. ¿Adónde vas? 3. ¿Desde cuándo estudias español? 4. ¿Cuándo vas a terminar / acabar este ejercicio? 5. ¿Hasta cuándo vas a esperar? 6. ¿A quién le escribes la mayoría de tus mensajes electrónicos? 7. ¿Quién toca a la puerta? 8. ¿Dónde estás (tú)?

9·12 1. ¿Cuántos países ha visitado? 2. ¿Cuándo decidió que quería ser cantante? 3. ¿Dónde será su próximo concierto? 4. ¿Cómo ensaya la voz para los conciertos? 5. ¿Por qué decidió dedicarse a la música? 6. ¿Cuáles son sus cantantes favoritos? 7. ¿Qué quiere hacer en el futuro? 8. ¿Cuándo serán sus próximas vacaciones?

9·13 1. ¿Cuántos años tiene Abel? 2. ¿A qué jugaba Abel? 3. ¿Quién lo llevaba? 4. ¿Qué quiere Abel? 5. ¿Dónde quiere jugar? 6. ¿Para qué equipo juega Abel? 7. ¿Cómo es Abel? 8. ¿Qué hace Abel para mantenerse en buena forma física? 9. ¿Qué será Abel? / ¿Quién será Abel? / ¿Cómo será Abel? 10. ¿Cuándo será famoso Abel?

9·14 1. Qué 2. Adónde 3. Cuándo 4. qué 5. qué 6. cuál 7. Qué 8. Qué / Cómo

9·15 1. ¡Hay una luna linda (bella)! 2. ¡Nosotras vamos a caminar por la playa! 3. ¡Hace mucho calor afuera! 4. ¡La limonada está fría! 5. ¡Lucy está muy cansada! 6. ¡Ahora nosotras estamos listas para descansar! 7. ¡No voy a dormir! 8. ¡Estoy de acuerdo!

9·16 Answers will vary.

9·17 1. ¡Cuánto cuestan estos zapatos! 2. ¡Qué largo es el vestido! 3. ¡Cómo ha subido el precio de la vida! 4. ¡Cuánto ganan! 5. ¡Qué amable es el camarero! 6. ¡Cuántas entradas vendieron para el concierto! 7. ¡Qué bien hacen la paella en este restaurante! 8. ¡Cuánta belleza hay en este lugar!

9·18 1. e 2. d 3. c 4. b 5. a

9·19 1. ¡Chitón, hay demasiado ruido! 2. ¡Cielos, la conferencia empieza a las ocho en punto! 3. ¡Pst / Chst / Eh, estamos aquí! 4. ¡Pobre de mí / Ay de mí, no tengo tiempo! 5. ¡Ojalá, necesito ganar! 6. ¡Ah, el reloj es bonito!

9·20 1. b / c 2. a 3. d 4. b / c 5. e

10 The imperfect tense

The imperfect tense

10·1 1. ibais / iban 2. se despertaba 3. iba 4. vivían 5. éramos 6. veían 7. llevaba 8. se ponía 9. sentía 10. podía, padecía 11. conocíamos 12. querían 13. era 14. sabía, querían

10·2 1. Cuando tenía dieciséis años, vivía en un pueblo pequeño. 2. Mi hermano y yo corríamos a un lago cerca de nuestra casa. 3. Durante el verano muchos de nuestros amigos nadaban en el lago. 4. El lago era bello / bonito pero el agua siempre estaba fría. 5. Yo siempre quería dormir debajo de un árbol. 6. Me sentía cómodo/a y seguro/a allí. 7. Mi hermano y yo siempre queríamos disfrutar un verano largo y delicioso.

10·3 1. b 2. a 3. c 4. e 5. e 6. d 7. c 8. a 9. b 10. e

10·4 1. tenía 2. dibujaba 3. iba 4. hacía 5. tenía 6. había 7. entraba 8. escuchaba 9. veía 10. leía 11. quería 12. pensaba 13. era

10·5 1. Mis padres y yo generalmente visitábamos varias ciudades en los Estados Unidos cuando era una jovencita. 2. Cada año viajábamos a lugares como Fresno, St. Augustine y otras ciudades. 3. Muchas veces mi padre alquilaba un auto / carro grande. 4. En aquellos días me encantaba quedarme por unos días en ciudades diferentes. 5. A veces conocía a nuevos amigos como Fernando. 6. Todas las semanas yo quería hablar con Fernando. 7. ¡Era tan cómico! Varias veces yo escribí su nombre y dibujé un corazón en un papel. 8. Fernando me enviaba muchas cartas. 9. Yo siempre me sentía feliz leyendo sus cartas. 10. Fernando y no nos casamos y ahora recordamos aquellos días cuando éramos jóvenes.

10·6 1. miraba 2. comías 3. tenía 4. veía 5. habíamos 6. hacían 7. trabájabais 8. quería 9. podían 10. debían 11. era 12. veía 13. ibas 14. podía 15. era 16. iba 17. establecían 18. leíamos 19. escribía 20. creías

10·7 1. vi 2. sentiste 3. supo 4. cupieron 5. di 6. viajó 7. vivieron 8. traje 9. trabajamos (*the* **nosotros** *form of* -ar *verbs is the same in present indicative and preterit*) 10. quiso 11. entretuve (*compounds of irregular verbs are irregular in the same pattern*) 12. condujiste 13. tuve 14. hubisteis 15. hablaron 16. puse 17. estuvo 18. comiste 19. pudieron 20. hiciste

10·8 1. While my sisters were talking, I was playing the guitar. 2. When *Star Wars* came out, I was 22 years old. 3. There were several men on the corner when the car skidded and crashed into the wall. 4. When we were on vacation, my friends and I would go skiing and to restaurants. 5. Where were you and what were you doing when the total eclipse of the sun happened? 6. We ate, rested, and watched TV for a while, then decided to go to the beach. 7. I didn't like it that the phone rang while I was fixing dinner. 8. The children were playing on the porch / patio when their grandmother arrived. 9. Elena was waking up when her father called. 10. It was four in the afternoon and raining when I left the movie theater. 11. My sister was four years old when I was born. 12. What was the weather like while you were going to the lake to ski? 13. My parents moved into another house when I was two years old. 14. The dog took off running after the rabbit as soon as he saw it. 15. At three o'clock sharp, I was waiting at the library entrance. 16. When it quit raining, we went back to the tent. 17. The dinner turned out well and the food was delicious. 18. That year, it snowed a lot in the city. 19. When I realized (that) I didn't have Web access, I decided to take off / leave / get out of there. 20. The band was playing and the people were dancing, but I felt alone.

10·9 1. Cuando llegué, el perro dormía / estaba dormido / estaba durmiendo. 2. Mientras comías, nuestro hermano trabajaba. 3. Ella salió / se fue cuando él llegó. 4. Alexandra tenía tres años cuando nos mudamos a Seattle. 5. Después de que subimos al taxi, empezó a llover. 6. Ayer fue un día muy frío para Seattle. (*the day is considered as a completed time period, hence preterit;* **día** *is masculine.*) 7. Él arreglaba la mesa cuando se lastimó la mano. (*don't use possessive with parts of the body*) 8. ¿Quisiste llamarme ayer? 9. Eran las cinco de la tarde, y llovía, cuando mis amigos decidieron visitarme. 10. Yo preparaba el rosbif mientras escribía este ejercicio. 11. Cuando yo ponía la mesa, mi amigo estaba abajo haciendo las maletas para su viaje. 12. Tres pájaros se posaban / estaban posados en un alambre cuando, de repente, el gato quiso subir para comerse uno. 13. Su mamá se sentó cuando oyó las noticias. 14. El Sr. Acero chismeaba, todos le escuchaban, pero sólo unos pocos le creían. 15. Quería acostarse pero tenía demasiado trabajo a entregar el día siguiente. 16. El avión aterrizó mientras nevaba. 17. Cuando paró el tren, los pasajeros bajaron. 18. Mientras el buque entraba en el puerto, los aduaneros lo detuvieron. 19. Mientras mi abuela tejía a punto de aguja, nosotros y el perro jugábamos. 20. Sus amigos de ella le trajo / llevó el regalo mientras ella almorzaba / comía el almuerzo.

10·10   1. eran   2. vivía   3. aceptó   4. exigió   5. sabía   6. pareció   7. aceptó   8. se preparaban   9. hacían   10. empacaban   11. llegaron   12. se alegraron   13. Llegó   14. Llovía   15. Salió (**Salía** *is acceptable if the idea is* while they were on their way out.)   16. estaban   17. iban   18. Eran   19. abordaron   20. tuvieron   21. aterrizó   22. bajaron   23. se sorprendieron   24. hacía   25. estaban   26. era

10·11   Esta mañana me desperté tarde. Bostecé muchas veces, estaba feliz, me sentía optimista. Entonces abrí la ventana de mi habitación y estiré los brazos. Los semáforos no funcionaban. Por suerte no había mucho tráfico en la calle y veía pocos peatones. Salí a recoger mi periódico. No lo abrí. No leí las noticias horribles. Fui a la cocina y preparé mi desayuno. Quería dormir y roncar. De repente sonó el despertador y me desperté. ¡Ay, Dios mío! No era sábado, domingo. No era día feriado. ¡Qué mala suerte! Era un sueño.

11   Reflexive verbs and reflexive pronouns

11·1   1. se levanta   2. se ducha   3. se cepillan   4. nos maquillamos   5. se desvisten / os desvestís   6. se secan

11·2   1. Me acuesto temprano todas las noches.   2. Antes de acostarme me desvisto.   3. Después me pongo el pijama / piyama.   4. Me duermo a eso de las diez de la noche.   5. A las seis de la mañana me despierto.   6. Pero me levanto media hora más tarde.   7. Después me ducho con agua fría.   8. Me seco el pelo.   9. No me afeito.   10. Me cepillo los dientes por la mañana en casa.   11. Me maquillo un poco.   12. Me miro en el espejo.   13. Me visto antes de las ocho de lunes a viernes.   14. Al final / Por fin me lavo las manos y estoy listo/a.

11·3   Answers will vary.

11·4   1. se aburre   2. se parecen   3. va   4. duermen   5. parece   6. pone   7. duerme   8. se pone   9. va   10. lleva

11·5   1. Tus comentarios me aburren.   2. Me aburro cuando estoy solo/a.   3. Voy a ir dormir ahora.   4. Molestas a mi perro.   5. El dinero no cae del cielo.   6. Mi amigo Alex despierta a sus hijos.   7. Voy a llevar a mi mamá al dentista.   8. Usualmente / Por lo general yo no me despierto tarde los fines de semana.   9. Me enojo si no duermo bien.   10. Me quito los zapatos y me pongo las zapatillas / pantuflas.   11. Me llevo muy bien con mi jefe/a.   12. ¿Cuándo te vas?   13. Creo que vas a visitar a Mila.   14. Pongo mis toallas en el baño.   15. Llevo a mis perros al parque todos los días.

11·6   1. se burla, se ríe   2. se da cuenta   3. nos negamos   4. se queja   5. se atreven   6. nos olvidamos   7. me sorprendo

11·7   1. ¿Te acuerdas de mi amigo Carlos?   2. ¡Me burlo del novio de mi hermana!   3. No me arrepiento de mis comentarios.   4. Ahora nos enteramos de tus mentiras.   5. No me quejo de tus preguntas.   6. ¡Me sorprendo porque estás aquí!   7. Me doy cuenta de que mi auto / mi carro no está en el garaje.   8. ¡Me muero de sed!   9. No me atrevo a jugar golf con tu padre.   10. ¡Me olvido de todo!   11. Nos negamos a mudarnos a otra ciudad.

11·8   De acuerdo a mi nutricionista, nosotros necesitamos escribir dos listas.

Una lista de los buenos hábitos: acostarse temprano y dormir ocho horas, levantarse temprano y dar gracias por un nuevo día, atreverse a cambiar la rutina diaria, olvidarse del pasado y pensar en el futuro, enterarse de las necesidades de nuestros amigos, negarse a ser haragán / vago y acordarse de que la vida es corta.

Y una lista corta de malos hábitos: quejarse de todo, no darse / no darnos cuenta de nuestra buena fortuna, burlarse de los hábitos de otras personas y olvidarse que mañana es otro día.

11·9   1. q   2. s   3. t   4. o   5. i   6. l   7. b   8. r   9. n   10. c   11. d   12. p   13. g   14. j   15. k   16. h   17. a   18. e   19. f   20. m

11·10   1. Do you know if there's an apartment for rent in this building?   2. John and Mary took off running when they heard the bomb blast.   3. Nothing was heard for several hours after the incident.   4. My homework? The dog ate it. *(the English possessive achieves what* **me** *does in Spanish)*   5. Geez! Just take the medicine already / and be done with it!   6. A friend of mine gave me this antique ring as a gift.   7. Mr. Martinez got up, took the proposal from the table, and took it with him.   8. You told them that? But, man—it was a secret!   9. Our car broke down on the road and we had to call my uncle.   10. The postcard? I sent it to our parents yesterday.   11. How do you make a salad, Mom? *(you, as in* one: how does one *or even* how is *a salad prepared?)*   12. The gift is for you. I went with my brother to buy it for you.   13. The boss needs the hammer. So, loan it to him then.   14. The mechanic's hands are dirty. He's going to wash them before using the phone.   15. What do I do day in and day out? Well, nothing less than what you / one has to do.   16. Thomas's bill? I'm preparing it for him now.   17. Do you want to see that movie with me or with him?   18. The couple was looking at each other all the time.   19. That guy seems crazy—he talks to himself all the time.   20. Mr. Acero doesn't get embarrassed even when his lies are exposed.

11·11   1. ¿Cómo se prepara una buena ensalada?   2. El bebé se cayó.   3. Se rompió el plato.   4. Ella se puso un par de zapatos nuevos.   5. El perro se lamió las patas.   6. Se recuperó / se mejoró rápidamente.   7. ¡Subieron / escalaron la montaña inmediatamente / en seguida / directamente / sin demora!   8. El sweater se deshizo antes de que ella pudiera terminar de tejerlo.   9. Se prometieron amarse.   10. Nos buscábamos el uno al otro todo el día.   11. Se los dimos (a ellos).   12. Llegaron a ser / se hicieron maestros.   13. Ella se peinó y se puso maquillaje.   14. Se lo vendí (a ellos).   15. Se colgó la camisa en una percha.   16. Ella se alegró de que la hubieras llamado.   17. En Macondo, no se pintaron las casas de rojo.   18. Él se asustó con el ruido / El ruido lo asustó.   19. Se escribió esta carta en el siglo diecinueve.   20. Se colgaron las medias con cuidado junto a la chimenea.

11·12   1. Él se miró en el espejo ayer.   2. Ellos se compraron regalos anoche.   3. Los zapatos se perdieron esta mañana en la playa.   4. Anoche el vino se derramó en la mesa.   5. Ese día las campanas se repicaban para celebrar la paz.   6. El Sr. Acero se condenará pronto.   7. Ellas se creían lo máximo.   8. Los niños se durmieron a las ocho ayer.   9. Ella se levanta a las siete de la mañana.   10. Ellos se enojaron de que tú no hicieras / no hubieras hecho la tarea ayer.   11. El bebé se toma / se está tomando / está tomándose la leche ahora.   12. Juan y María se abrazaron anoche en el parque.   13. Mientras ella se vestía anoche, ellos se durmieron en el sofá.   14. Anoche, se la escribí.   15. Juan se enojó al irse.   16. Hansel no se perdía en el / bosque nunca.   17. La mantequilla se derrite si no se pone en la nevera.   18. Se perdió el juicio Don Quijote.   19. ¿Cómo se escribe / su nombre?   20. Él fue a esquiar ayer y se le rompió la pierna.

12   Direct and indirect object pronouns, commands, and double object pronouns

12·1   1. los; Rosa los recita.   2. las; Manolita está componiéndolas / Manolita las está componiendo.   3. le; Mari no le lleva los cuadernos.   4. los; Almodóvar los hace reír.   5. la; Yo la llevo para Marcela.   6. la; Martín no quiere conocerla. Martín no la quiere conocer.   7. los; Gustavo los toca.   8. nos; ¿Vas a incluirnos en la lista? / ¿Nos vas a incluir en la lista?

12·2   1. les; Ángel está comprándoles creyones. Ángel les está comprando creyones.   2. les; Ali está llevándoles regalos. Ali les está llevando regalos.   3. les; Raquel va a distribuirles la comida. Raquel les va a distribuir la comida.   4. les; Lalo y María no van a cantarles canciones mexicanas. Lalo y María no les van a cantar canciones mexicanas.   5. le; Lola nunca puede prestarle atención. Lola nunca le puede prestar atención.   6. le; Margarita no quiere recitarle sus poemas en el ayuntamiento. Margarita no le quiere recitar sus poemas en el ayuntamiento.

12·3   1. las, les; Carmen se las compra.   2. los, les; Ella se los prepara.   3. la, le; Pedrito se la da.   4. las, nos; Raúl nos las plancha.   5. les, los; Carmen y Raúl están dándoselos. Carmen y Raúl se los están dando.   6. los, les; Marta se los compra.   7. las, les; ¿Marcos se las envió?   8. las, me; Manuel me las trae.   9. las, le; Yo se las compro.   10. las, les; Martín está enviándoselas. Martín se las está enviando.

12·4   1. cambia; no cambies   2. pide; no pidas   3. viaja; no viajes   4. vuelve; no vuelvas   5. duerme; no duermas   6. piensa; no pienses   7. corre; no corras   8. sufre; no sufras   9. lee; no leas   10. vende; no vendas

12·5   1. Usa la computadora nueva.   2. No borres mis notas.   3. Pon el papel en la impresora.   4. Por favor, no contestes el teléfono.   5. ¡Ve a tu oficina ahora!   6. Guarda estos papeles, por favor.   7. No uses estas llaves viejas.

12·6   1. Pon la maleta / la bolsa en el piso / el suelo.   2. Sal a las ocho y media hoy.   3. Ten cuidado porque está lloviendo.   4. Ven temprano a la clase.   5. Sé amable / cortés.   6. Ve al mercado y compra pan.   7. Di la verdad ahora.   8. Haz tu trabajo con cuidado / cuidadosamente.

12·7   1. No pongas tu maleta en mi asiento.   2. No dejes los papeles en el suelo / el piso.   3. No tengas problemas con tus amigos.   4. No vengas tarde al teatro.   5. ¡No seas ridículo/a!   6. No vayas ahora a la playa.   7. ¡No digas mentiras!   8. No hagas comentarios inapropiados.

12·8   1. lea / no lea   2. conteste / no conteste   3. use / no use   4. reciba / no reciba   5. asista / no asista   6. vaya / no vaya   7. sea / no sea   8. descanse / no descanse

12·9 1. Doblen a la derecha. 2. Sigan las instrucciones. 3. Busquen la salida 45 en la autopista de peaje. 4. Manejen dos millas después de la salida. 5. Lleguen a la calle Olmedo, número 114. 6. Aparquen al frente de nuestro edificio de apartamentos. 7. Toquen el timbre a la entrada del edificio.

12·10 1. leed, no leáis 2. dormid, no durmáis 3. sufrid, no sufráis 4. pensad, no penséis 5. viajad, no viajéis 6. vivid, no viváis 7. caminad, no caminéis 8. conseguid, no consigáis 9. haced, no hagáis

12·11 1. lo, les; Léeselo. 2. la, le; Anita, escríbesela. 3. lo, le; Dáselo. 4. los, me; No me los compren. 5. los, le; Díganselos. 6. los, le; Sra. Blanco, cuénteselos. 7. la, les; Ábransela. 8. la, les; No se la envíen.

12·12 1. t 2. i 3. g 4. j 5. k 6. a. 7. l 8. b 9. m 10. f 11. c 12. d 13. r 14. s 15. e 16. n 17. o 18. h 19. p 20. q

12·13 1. Ella le lava las manos de él. 2. Se lo queremos comprar / Queremos comprárselo. 3. ¡Tráemelo! 4. Ella esperaba encontrárselos. 5. ¡No me la mandes / envíes! 6. Él debe grabárselas. 7. Me los dan / Me los están dando / Están dándomelos. 8. Nos lo dio para la Navidad. 9. Se la mandaron ayer. 10. Se la mandará / Se la va a mandar / Va a mandársela (*or, with* **enviar**). 11. Queremos hacérsela / Se la queremos hacer. 12. Ella no quería tejérselo / no se lo quería tejer. (**no quiso** *would mean* she refused). 13. Nos los trajeron. 14. Ella se la preparó. 15. Queremos comprártelo / Te lo queremos comprar. 16. Ellos están construyéndosela / Ellos se la están construyendo. 17. ¡No me la compres! 18. Se lo debo dar / Debo dárselo. 19. ¿Quieres mandársela? / ¿Se la quieres mandar? 20. No se la vamos a mandar / No vamos a mandársela.

12·14 1. Tú se los quieres mandar / Tú quieres mandárselos ahora. 2. Yo se la tuve que comprar anoche / Yo tuve que comprársela anoche. 3. Se lo íbamos a vender la semana pasada. / Íbamos a vendérselo la semana pasada. 4. Ellos no se la deben servir. / Ellos no deben servírsela. 5. Tú se lo estás escribiendo en este momento. / Tú estás escribiéndoselo en este momento. 6. ¡Arréglanosla! 7. Él me lo trajo ayer. 8. Yo se la voy a poner pronto. / Voy a ponérsela pronto. 9. Ella me la hizo esta mañana. 10. Uds. se los querían dar el fin de semana pasado. / Ellos querían dárselos el fin de semana pasado. 11. Los niños me la rompieron el domingo pasado. 12. Ella se lo va a pedir mañana. / Ella va a pedírselo mañana. 13. ¡No se la manden! 14. Nosotros no te lo podemos mandar ahora. / Nosotros no podemos mandártelo ahora. 15. Ella se lo quería dar anoche. / Ella quería dárselo anoche. (**quiso** means *she tried*). 16. Tú nos la debes mostrar ahora. / Tú debes mostrárnosla ahora. 17. ¡Déselo! 18. Yo se los quería pedir. / Yo quería pedírselos. (**quise** means *I tried*.) 19. Ella se las va a enviar esta tarde. / Ella va a enviárselas esta tarde. 20. Él se la quería escribir la semana pasada. / Él quería escribírsela la semana pasada. (**quiso** means *he tried*.)

12·15 1. Cambiemos 2. Recitemos 3. Hablemos 4. Repasemos 5. Tomemos 6. enojemos 7. Compremos 8. olvidemos

12·16 1. Naveguemos 2. Investiguemos 3. Empecemos 4. Busquemos 5. hagamos

12·17 1. Alquilémoslo. 2. Dibujémoslos. 3. Compongámoslas. 4. Incluyámosla. 5. Vendámoslas.

12·18 1. ¡Usemos el diccionario! 2. ¡Hagamos /Hagámosle preguntas a la maestra! 3. ¡Viajemos a México! 4. ¡Veamos telenovelas colombianas! 5. ¡Repasemos la gramática! 6. ¡Escuchemos las canciones españolas!

12·19 1. Preparen el salón. 2. Limpien las mesas. 3. Compren las bebidas. 4. Envíen las invitaciones. 5. Envuelvan los regalos. 6. Traigan las flores.

12·20 1. Marta, ponga la carne en la nevera. 2. Corte la cebolla. 3. Abra la botella de aceite. 4. Felipe, lave los platos en la fregadora. 5. Sirva las cervezas a los invitados. 6. Prepare el café, Mario.

12·21 1. la; ¡Llámala! 2. los; ¡Recógelos! 3. nos; ¡Cómpranoslas! 4. me, lo; ¡Dímelo! 5. me, lo; ¡Léemelo! 6. me; ¡Espérame!

12·22 1. ¿La ventana? ¡Ciérrala ahora mismo! 2. ¿Tus zapatos? ¡No los tires al suelo! 3. ¿El perro? ¡No lo molestes! 4. ¿Tus amigos? ¡Llámalos a su casa! 5. ¿Las toallas? ¡Búscalas en el dormitorio! 6. ¿El auto? ¡Llévalo al mecánico! 7. ¿Las manzanas? ¡Lávalas antes de comerlas! 8. ¿Las luces? ¡No las apagues! 9. ¿Los vegetales? ¡Cómpralos en el mercado! 10. ¿Los ejercicios? ¡No los entregues!

12·23 1. Despiértense 2. Levántense 3. Prepárense 4. Lávense 5. Cepíllense 6. se desanimen 7. se miren 8. Pónganse 9. Siéntense 10. Quédense

12·24 1. Marcos, él es el hermano de Marta. 2. Trabaja con Marta. 3. Él es el chef, no Marta. 4. Conozco bien a Marta. 5. Yo quiero ir al cine esta noche; no Marta. 6. ¿Quieres ir al cine?

12·25 1. usted 2. usted 3. tú 4. usted 5. usted 6. ustedes 7. ustedes 8. tú

12·26   1. Ellos querían comer.   2. Tú cantas pero ella toca la guitarra.   3. ¡Ellas pueden terminar la tarea!   4. Ustedes empezaron a las diez pero nosotros terminamos temprano.   5. Ahora, tú descansas mientras yo lavo la ropa.

12·27   1. lo; La policía lo encontró.   2. la; La llevaron al hospital.   3. lo; La víctima no lo reveló.   4. le; El médico le diagnosticó un trauma leve.   5. le (se), lo; La enfermera se lo llevó.   6. le (se), lo; El noticiero local se lo comunicó.   7. los; Al día siguiente la policía los investigó.   8. la; El criminal la recibirá.

12·28   1. Le di una nota a ella.   2. Le pedimos un favor a su hermano.   3. Nos trajeron una computadora nueva a nosotros.   4. Luis y Ana le pidieron un aumento a su jefe.   5. Marcela les mandó flores a ellos / ellas.   6. Tú nos preparaste la recepción a nosotros.   7. Cindy le dijo varios chistes a mi hermano.   8. Roberto les anunció su jubilación a sus amigos.

12·29   1. Los clientes le devolvieron los zapatos   2. El empleado les mostró otro modelo   3. Le compraron ese par de zapatos.   4. La tienda les dio un descuento   5. Los clientes gastaron más dinero.   6. El jefe le dio una comisión   7. Los clientes les agradecieron la amabilidad

12·30   *Possible answers:*   1. ¿Le gusta el té?   2. ¿Les gusta la comida mexicana?   3. ¿Le gusta correr por la playa?   4. ¿Les gusta nadar en la piscina?   5. ¿Le gustan los programas cómicos o dramáticos?   6. ¿Les ha gustado esta encuesta?

12·31   1. Me fascinan las novelas de misterio.   2. No me interesan las biografías, son aburridas.   3. Me duele la cabeza y tomo una aspirina.   4. Me hace falta dinero y voy al banco.   5. Me basta con poco, soy modesto/a.   6. Me cae mal Carolina; es antipática.   7. Me cae bien Nina porque es agradable.   8. Me faltan diez dólares.   9. Me toca descansar porque he terminado el ejercicio.   10. Me encanta estudiar español.

12·32   1. se   2. nos   3. se   4. se   5. me   6. te   7. os   8. me

12·33   Eduardo Benítez dirige una agencia de publicidad. Eduardo la dirige con éxito. El año pasado dobló las ganancias. Y las logró con su esfuerzo. Los inversionistas le agradecen su perseverancia. Eduardo les asegura que al año próximo doblará las ganancias: más dinero. Y van a ganarlo / lo van a ganar porque hay una gran demanda en el mercado internacional. Eduardo lo conoce muy bien.

12·34   1. Estoy admirándola.   2. Van a encontrarlas.   3. Vas a pedirlo.   4. No va a tenerla.   5. ¿Quieren dejarlo?   6. Vamos a terminarlo.

13   Demonstrative and possessive adjectives and pronouns

13·1   1. Este   2. esos   3. aquellos   4. esos   5. Aquellos   6. este   7. aquellos   8. aquellas   9. Estas   10. Estos

13·2   1. Esta joyería está vacía.   2. ¡Ah, estos anillos de diamantes deben costar una fortuna!   3. Esos aretes no son baratos.   4. Usen / usad aquel elevador/ascensor para ir al segundo piso.   5. En ese escaparate tienen perlas y esmeraldas.   6. A aquellos caballeros les encantan los relojes de Suiza.   7. Estoy listo/a para comprar ese brazalete de oro.

13·3   1. mi carro / mi auto   2. tu bicicleta   3. sus patines   4. su taxi   5. nuestra motocicleta   6. sus cercas   7. sus / vuestros vecinos / sus, vuestras vecinas   8. su / vuestro jardín   9. mis árboles   10. nuestro edificio

13·4   1. el mapa mío   2. el calendario tuyo   3. el boleto suyo   4. la mochila suya   5. los asientos nuestros   6. las maletas suyas   7. El auto nuestro   8. los sombreros vuestros

13·5   1. estos   2. aquellas   3. esos   4. estas   5. aquel   6. aquella   7. esa   8. estos   9. aquel   10. estas

13·6   1. ¿Por qué quieres esto?   2. Esta es mi sombrilla y esa es la sombrilla de Manuel.   3. Tengo un impermeable pero me gusta este.   4. Molly no tiene un sombrero. Ella necesita aquel.   5. Y aquello, ¿qué es?

13·7   1. las nuestras.   2. la tuya   3. las nuestras   4. el suyo   5. el suyo   6. los vuestros   7. las suyas   8. la nuestra

13·8   1. estas dos alumnas   2. este sombrero   3. esta primera montaña   4. esos cuadros / esas pinturas   5. aquella luz   6. este museo   7. esos libros antiguos / viejos   8. este espejo antiguo   9. aquella caja de libros   10. este perro amable   11. esta camisa roja   12. esa mujer delgada   13. esa clase   14. estos vestidos bonitos   15. estos zapatos pardos   16. esos jugadores de fútbol (*or* esas jugadoras de fútbol)   17. aquel hombre   18. aquel barco de vela   19. estos seis carros nuevos   20. esta casa antigua

13·9   1. a   2. b   3. b (*the placement of* **ese** *makes it the best choice*)   4. b (*the placement of* **esa** *makes it the best choice*)   5. b   6. b (**aquella** *conveys remoteness while* **época** *expresses a time period*)   7. b (**señor**, *in option* a, *is too formal as a translation for* guy, *while the position of* **grande** *in option* c *makes its meaning literal*)   8. a (b *assumes too much, i.e., that something has to be accomplished after studying the subject*)   9. c.   10. a   11. b   12. c (**decir** *expresses the idea of telling something to others, while* **lo de ayer** *expresses* that business about)   13. b   14. a   15. a

13·10   famosos, bellas, elevadas, africanas, vegetarianos, compleja, jóvenes, ágiles, curiosa, inteligentes, simpáticos, enormes, tropicales

13·11   1. fieles; incapacitadas   2. habladoras   3. tropicales   4. agresivos; inteligentes   5. cariñosa; simpática   6. humanas   7. rápidas   8. anfibio

13·12   Answers will vary.

13·13   1. f; largo pelo   2. a; bellas flores   3. d; dulce bebida   4. b; fuerte dolor   5. e; destructivo huracán   6. c; suave piel

13·14   Answers will vary.

13·15   1. buen   2. algún   3. gran   4. mal   5. ningún   6. primer   7. tercer   8. cien

13·16   1. Ayer mi hermano fue a visitar a su viejo amigo Mario.   2. Mario mismo me dijo que admira a mi padre.   3. Él cree que nuestro padre es una gran influencia en su propia vida.   4. El padre de Mario es muy viejo y está enfermo.   5. El padre de Mario vivía en una casa vieja en Guatemala.   6. Un día decidió mudarse a Nuevo México.   7. La familia de Mario no era pobre.   8. Una vieja amiga mía conoció a Mario y a su padre, Don Julián.   9. Pobre Don Julián, está demasiado enfermo para regresar a Guatemala.

13·17   1. abiertas   2. muertas   3. desechos   4. desenvueltos   5. impreso   6. reescrito   7. revuelta   8. rotas

13·18   1. F   2. O   3. O   4. F   5. F   6. O

13·19   1. Mi hermano Marcos estuvo en Buenos Aires.; Mi hermano Marcos estará en Buenos Aires.   2. Él vivió en Argentina.; Él vivirá en Argentina.   3. Tuvo un apartamento en el centro de la ciudad.; Tendrá un apartamento en el centro de la ciudad.   4. Trabajó en una oficina del gobierno.; Trabajará en una oficina del gobierno.   5. Marcos viajó a Santiago también.; Marcos viajará a Santiago también.

13·20   1. Pedro Gómez vive en ese edificio.   2. Lucía es la esposa de Pedro.   3. Leímos la noticia de su boda en el periódico.   4. Tienen una casa en la playa.   5. Lucía y su esposo salieron de luna de miel.   6. Pedro y Lucía nacieron en Barcelona.   7. Mis hermanos estudiaron con ellos.   8. Recibimos un email de Pedro anoche.

13·21   *Some examples; other answers are possible:*   1. cuando necesito comunicarme   2. día tras día   3. cuando hago mucho ejercicio   4. en la piscina olímpica   5. en diez minutos   6. con sólo un billete   7. con frecuencia   8. en el autobús camino a casa

13·22   1. el cumpleaños de Laura   2. una fiesta   3. none   4. a Laura   5. la cena   6. mi guitarra   7. dos rancheras   8. none   9. su nombre

13·23   1. una reacción   2. un presidente   3. un problema   4. un recuento   5. una pregunta   6. una campaña   7. una solución

13·24   1. X   2. X   3. a   4. X   5. a   6. a   7. a   8. a

13·25   1. Melisa trabaja en la librería.   2. Ella ve a su jefe en la parada del autobús todas las mañanas.   3. Yo conozco a su jefe.   4. Él bebe cuatro tazas de café por la mañana.   5. Melisa prefiere el té.   6. Yo vi a su jefe la semana pasada.   7. Él lleva / usa ropas viejas.   8. El jefe de Melisa necesita una chaqueta nueva.

13·26   1. Paula alquiló un apartamento a su hermana Ana.   2. Ella tiene la llave del apartamento.   3. La hermana necesita ayuda.   4. Ana estudia inglés en la universidad.   5. Ella encontrará un trabajo mejor.   6. Ana y su hermana envían saludos a sus amigos.   7. Invitan a sus primos a su apartamento.

13·27   *Possible answers:*   1. Jamás digo mentiras.   2. Nunca falto a mi trabajo.   3. Nunca duermo hasta tarde.   4. Jamás termino el desayuno.   5. Tampoco ahorro agua.   6. Nunca gasto todo mi salario en la tienda.   7. Ni recibo un bono por Navidad.

13·28   1. Los políticos no mienten nunca.; Los políticos no mienten jamás.   2. Los periodistas no redactan noticias optimistas nunca.; Los periodistas no redactan noticias optimistas jamás.   3. Los vendedores no respaldan sus productos nunca.; Los vendedores no respaldan sus productos jamás.   4. Los camareros no sirven a los clientes con amabilidad nunca.; Los camareros no sirven a los clientes con amabilidad jamás. 5. Los maestros no asignan poca tarea a sus estudiantes nunca.; Los maestros no asignan poca tarea a sus estudiantes jamás. 6. Los marineros no tienen miedo al mar nunca.; Los marineros no tienen miedo al mar jamás.

13·29 1. Nunca 2. nada 3. no / nunca 4. nunca / jamás 5. nadie 6. nada

14 The future tense

14·1 Answers will vary.

14·2 1. empezará 2. será 3. bajará 4. destruirá 5. mostrará 6. oirán 7. caerá 8. deberán 9. protegerán 10. mejorará

14·3 Answers will vary.

14·4 1. estará 2. tendremos 3. costarán 4. harán 5. vendrán 6. hará 7. pondrá 8. querrán 9. tendrán 10. Habrá 11. Valdrá

14·5 1. deberás 2. Tendrás 3. Conocerás 4. ganarás 5. encontrarás 6. Recibirás 7. Podrás 8. ahorrarás 9. perderás

14·6 1. Te opondrás 2. obtendrán 3. dispondré 4. supondrán 5. mantendremos 6. repondrá 7. detendrá 8. obtendrá

14·7 1. estará 2. será 3. se llamará 4. podrá 5. tendrá 6. pertenecerá 7. costará 8. Lloverá 9. se sentirán 10. querrán 11. dejará

14·8 Mila cumplirá cinco años pronto. Esta noche su abuela Alina leerá el cuento de hadas favorito de Mila: Cenicienta. Mila se dormirá y soñará con Cenicienta. Mila sabe este cuento de memoria. Cenicienta ayudará a sus hermanastras miserables y seguirá las órdenes de su madrastra. Después sus hermanastras irán a la sala de baile en el palacio. Afortunadamente, Cenicienta tendrá la ayuda de su hada madrina: con una varita mágica hará un vestido bello, un par de zapatillas de cristal y un carruaje de lujo para ir al palacio. Cenicienta conocerá al príncipe y bailará con él. A las doce menos cuarto, regresará a casa. Cenicienta dejará caer una de las zapatillas de cristal. Y después el príncipe la encontrará y se casarán.

15 Prepositions, phrases, and conjunctions

15·1 1. entre 2. con 3. ante 4. por 5. sobre 6. hacia 7. desde 8. sin 9. en 10. Según

15·2 1. F 2. F 3. V 4. V 5. V 6. F 7. F

15·3 1. Luisa no puede vivir sin Jacob. 2. Jacob le envió una tarjeta a Luisa desde Lima. 3. Jacob viajaba a/hacia/para Ecuador. 4. Desde el aeropuerto, llamó a Luisa. 5. Él no llegó a Quito hasta la medianoche. 6. Jacob encontró una moneda debajo de la almohada. 7. Según Luisa, él es supersticioso. 8. Con suerte, Jacob venderá muchos de sus productos en Quito.

15·4 1. en una semana 2. en vez de 3. a cargo de 4. En cambio 5. además de 6. de ahora en adelante 7. a pie 8. a tiempo

15·5 Answers will vary.

15·6 1. Las tiendas están lejos de nuestra casa. 2. Mi auto está fuera del garaje. 3. En vez de azúcar, la receta dice miel. 4. De vez en cuando corro diez millas. 5. Esta reunión termina dentro de una hora. 6. Hay alrededor de quince pájaros en ese árbol.

15·7 1. por 2. antes de 3. dentro del 4. a través de 5. al lado de 6. en vez de 7. alrededor de 8. hacia 9. hasta 10. sobre

15·8 Answers will vary.

15·9 1. T 2. M 3. L 4. T 5. O 6. L 7. O 8. O 9. M 10. L

15·10 1. Esta casa huele a pescado. 2. ¿Llamas a Rosa o a Manuel? 3. ¡Yo amo a mi canario! 4. Ellos no invitan a nadie a su aniversario. 5. Mi sopa sabe a perejil. 6. ¿Conocen Uds. a alguien en esta clase? 7. Las flores son a tres dólares la docena. 8. La estación de trenes está a diez millas de mi casa 9. Luisa cuida a mi gato.

15·11   1. en lugar de/en vez de caminar   2. Después de entrar   3. Al terminar   4. sin hacer   5. con rapidez   6. en paz   7. al llegar   8. En lugar de/En vez de lavar

15·12   1. e   2. h   3. f   4. g   5. a   6. c   7. d   8. b

15·13   1. Para ser un liberal tiene ideas tradicionales.   2. ¿Te entrenas para los juegos olímpicos?   3. Necesito una lámpara para mi dormitorio.   4. Deben estar aquí para las cuatro.   5. Este café es para nosotros.   6. Lucille lee el periódico para encontrar un apartamento.   7. ¿Es para Susan esta carta?   8. Vamos para San Francisco.   9. ¿Para qué necesitas este dinero?   10. Necesito el dinero para una computadora nueva.

15·14   1. ¿Vas al trabajo por tren o por carro/auto?   2. ¿Estás por terminar tu trabajo ahora?   3. ¿Envías tus saludos por correo electrónico?   4. ¿Corres por el parque a menudo?   5. ¡Caramba!, ¿compraste esos zapatos por trescientos dólares?   6. ¿Conduces/Manejas en la autopista a sesenta y cinco millas por hora?   7. ¿Regresas a casa por la tarde o por la noche?   8. Y por último, ¿estás por los liberales o los conservadores?

15·15   1. por ahí   2. Por favor   3. Por supuesto   4. Por lo visto   5. Por cierto   6. Por Dios   7. Por lo menos   8. por favor   9. Por fin   10. por eso

15·16   1. para   2. por   3. por   4. Para   5. Por   6. Para   7. por   8. por

15·17   1. Trabajamos por Lidia.   2. Ellos pasan por el túnel.   3. Él tiene por lo menos dos autos.   4. Por su enfermedad no está aquí.   5. Mi amigo pasa por mi oficina.   6. Viene por tren.   7. Él estará aquí para las cuatro (en punto).

15·18   Answers will vary.

15·19   1. destination   2. "by means of"   3. deadline, time in the future   4. exchange   5. comparison   6. purpose or goal   7. moving through   8. reason, because of   9. duration of time   10. idiomatic expression with **por**

15·20   1. huele a   2. suenan a   3. inspira a   4. se atreven a   5. montar a   6. se oponen a

15·21   1. de   2. con   3. con   4. en   5. de   6. de   7. en   8. de

15·22   Bajo las escaleras, entro a la sala, pongo la tele y escucho las noticias. Sueño con un día lleno de buenas noticias. Por ejemplo, los líderes extranjeros no amenazan con un nuevo conflicto internacional, los expertos financieros no reportan detalles horribles acerca de la economía y yo dejo de pensar en los problemas del mundo. No soy egoísta, por Dios. Yo solamente quiero un día de paz y pensamientos felices. ¿Qué noticias quiero escuchar? Por ejemplo, que todos estamos por la paz y en contra de la guerra, y que nos alegramos de las cosas simples de la vida. Hoy voy a apagar la televisión y voy a buscar mi pala para trabajar en el jardín.

15·23   1. k; El detective llevó a cabo un excelente trabajo.   2. e; Pasó la noche en blanco.   3. b; Afuera, llovía a cántaros.   4. a; Ató cabos.   5. f; No quería dejar pasar la ocasión.   6. c; Sacó una foto del sospechoso.   7. g; Para el detective, el caso valía la pena.   8. i; El sospechoso guardaba cama.   9. j; Pero el sospechoso era hombre muerto.   10. d; El detective iba a salirse con la suya.   11. g; El trabajo valió la pena.

15·24   1. Carlos se da prisa.   2. Felipe da una mano a Mario. Felipe le da una mano a Mario.   3. Ahora, Ana se da cuenta de mi problema.   4. Luisa me da gracias por mis consejos.   5. Cuando entramos, Ana nos da la mano.   6. Benita da a conocer los secretos de todos.   7. Berta y Alina dan ánimo a sus amigos.   8. A todos nos encanta dar una vuelta.

15·25   Answers will vary.

15·26   1. hace el papel de   2. hace preguntas   3. hace favores   4. hace daño   5. hace caso   6. hace la vida imposible

15·27   1. c; Habla con mucha claridad, pone los puntos sobre las íes.   2. g; No gasta mucho dinero, no tira la casa por la ventana.   3. a; Es convincente, se sale con la suya.   4. b; No es puntual, no llega a tiempo, pierde el tren.   5. f; Cuida sus intereses, no pierde nada de vista.   6. e; No discute ni pelea con sus hermanos, se pone de acuerdo.   7. d; Acepta las explicaciones de sus amigos, no pone nada en duda.

15·28   1. tiene sueño   2. tengo prisa   3. tienen éxito   4. tenía frío   5. tenía dolor de cabeza   6. tienen ganas   7. tenemos paciencia   8. no tengo suerte / tengo mala suerte   9. no tiene razón   10. tienes la culpa

15·29   1. El saber no ocupa lugar.   2. Cuando una puerta se cierra, cien se abren. / Quien espera, desespera. / Persevera y triunfarás.   3. Ojos que no ven, corazón que no siente.   4. Peor es nada.   5. Más vale tarde que nunca.   6. Amigo en la adversidad es un amigo de verdad.   7. El tiempo lo cura todo. / Lo pasado, pasado está. / Borrón y cuenta nueva.   8. El que la hace, la paga. / Quien mal anda, mal acaba.

15·30   1. bajo siete llaves   2. loco como una cabra   3. blanco como un papel   4. ¡Como que dos y dos son cuatro!   5. desternillarme de la risa   6. te vas a meter en un lío   7. no vienen al caso   8. te llegó la hora

15·31   *Some examples; other answers are possible:*   1. Vale la pena.   2. Dime con quién andas y te diré quién eres.   3. Cada oveja con su pareja.   4. No viene al caso.   5. Nunca es tarde si la dicha es buena.   6. La casa está patas arriba.   7. Para chuparse los dedos.   8. Es un ladrillo.

15·32   1. Caminar es saludable.   2. Nadar abre el apetito.   3. Correr quema muchas calorías.   4. Jugar al golf es muy relajante.   5. Remar puede ser difícil.   6. Subir una montaña no es mi actividad preferida.   7. Bailar es casi un deporte.   8. Pero dormir es mi actividad favorita.

15·33   1. Comer y beber en exceso no mejora la salud.   2. Asistir a un concierto de música clásica inspira a muchas personas.   3. Compartir mensajes por email nos comunica con nuestros amigos.   4. Invertir dinero en la bolsa puede aumentar una fortuna.   5. Contribuir a una campaña electoral satisface a los ciudadanos.   6. Ayudar a los desamparados tiene mérito.

15·34   1. el leer   2. el dormir   3. el trabajar   4. el perder   5. el ahorrar   6. el comer y charlar

15·35   1. Al despertarse, mi hermana llamó por teléfono a su amiga Loli.   2. En vez de preparar el desayuno, perdió mucho tiempo.   3. Antes de salir a su trabajo, no apagó la cafetera.   4. En lugar de ayudar en la casa, complicó mi situación.   5. Sin despedirse de mí, salió de casa.   6. Después de llegar a la oficina, llamó a mi madre.

15·36   Answers will vary.

15·37   Answers will vary.

15·38   *Possible answers:*   1. ¿Qué prefiere hacer al salir del trabajo?   2. ¿A qué hora necesita llegar al aeropuerto?   3. ¿Dónde quiere hacer escala?   4. ¿Qué necesita facturar?   5. ¿Adónde le gustaría ir?   6. ¿Con quién preferiría viajar la próxima vez?

15·39   1. Vi el avión aterrizar.   2. Escuchamos al agente (de vuelo) saludar a los pasajeros.   3. Mary empezó a prepararse para recibir a su familia.   4. Ella fue a pedir una silla de ruedas.   5. Luis empezó a buscar las maletas.   6. Los niños se pusieron a llorar cuando se despertaron.   7. Entonces Luis oyó sonar su celular.   8. Escuchó hablar una voz familiar.   9. Entonces vio venir a su hermana.   10. Por fin, todos fueron a buscar el auto.

15·40   1. no dejó escapar al criminal   2. mandó hacer una investigación   3. permitió visitar a la víctima en el hospital   4. prohibieron llegar a los periodistas al salón   5. no dejaron revelar el nombre de la víctima   6. nos impidió llegar a recepción en el hospital

15·41   Answers will vary.

15·42   *Possible answers:*   1. Seguramente van a salir de compras a Nueva York el año que viene.   2. Tal vez Miranda y Alejandro van a querer acompañar a sus padres la próxima vez.   3. Afortunadamente mis sobrinos van a competir en el torneo de golf este año.   4. Con toda certeza, Cati y Luisa no se van a entrenar para participar en los Juegos Panamericanos en el futuro.   5. Desgraciadamente mis hermanos no van a asistir a la Fiesta de San Fermín nunca más.   6. Desde ahora, tú y yo nos vamos a comunicar por email con más frecuencia.

15·43   1. Fui a casa de Laura y jugué con su perro.   2. Yo quería cenar con ella, pero Laura tenía una cita con el dentista.   3. Laura no faltará a la cita, pero no le gusta ir al dentista.   4. Laura no come de día ni duerme por la noche.   5. Va al dentista o tomará calmantes por mucho tiempo.   6. Tengo mucha paciencia pero Laura me enoja.   7. Es una linda persona pero es muy indecisa.   8. Regresé a casa y cené solo.

15·44   1. nosotras; Alicia y yo limpiamos la casa los sábados y los domingos cenamos con mis padres.   2. Yo, como; No como carne ni pollo.   3. prepara; Alicia prepara la ensalada de lechuga con aguacate y la limonada.   4. invitan; Mis padres invitan a mis primos o a sus amigos, los López.   5. nosotros; A veces, tomamos una copa de vino o bebemos un vaso de cerveza.   6. nos gusta; Nos gusta un café con el postre o un té de camomila.   7. ellos dan un paseo; Después, Alicia y su novio dan un paseo por la ciudad o por la playa.   8. son días; Los domingos no son días buenos ni malos.   9. yo; Los domingos ceno con mis padres pero prefiero una cena con mis primos.   10. van; Mis primos van al cine conmigo o al "Café Nostalgia".

15·45 1. La escritora llegó a la oficina y se sentó a escribir su novela.   2. Escribió el capítulo final pero no le gustó.   3. Escribió otro capítulo pero resultó muy aburrido.   4. O cambiaba el comienzo o el final sería imposible.   5. No tenía ideas y salió de la oficina.   6. No tenía ganas de escribir ni de buscar más ideas.   7. Salió de la oficina y fue a la librería.   8. Se sentó en una silla y tomó un café.   9. Observó a la gente a su alrededor e inició el capítulo.   10. La autora era inteligente y logró terminar el capítulo.

15·46 1. Bailas muy bien pero tocas la guitarra mejor.   2. No habla ni llora. / Ni habla ni llora.   3. Entras y sales. O entras o sales.   4. No eres amable con tus colegas ni tampoco eres cortés con tus amigos.   5. Es muy caro pero tengo dinero suficiente. / Es muy caro y tengo dinero suficiente.   6. No cerraron la tienda a las nueve sino a las diez. / No cerraron la tienda a las nueve ni a las diez.   7. Viajaremos por las montañas y luego por la costa.   8. Llévame al aeropuerto ahora o pierdo mi vuelo a Arizona.   9. Me gusta esta novela pero es muy larga.

15·47 1. Mi amiga y yo iremos al cine y compraremos las entradas.   2. No nos gustan las películas de horror ni (preferimos) las películas muy dramáticas.   3. No llueve mucho, pero date prisa.   4. Tenemos poco dinero, (tenemos) muchas deudas y nuestro apartamento es muy caro.   5. Ahorramos mucho, pero no somos tacaños.   6. O ganamos más dinero, pedimos un aumento de sueldo o buscamos otro trabajo.   7. No somos ambiciosos, sino cautelosos.   8. Somos jóvenes y tenemos el futuro por delante.

15·48 1. aunque / por más que   2. porque   3. Después que   4. Si   5. Por más que / Aunque   6. desde que   7. que   8. Ya que

15·49 1. Necesito trabajar en mi jardín aunque llueve mucho.   2. Tengo unos guantes ya que quiero proteger mis manos.   3. Después que me pongo los guantes, me pongo mi sombrero.   4. Tomaremos una limonada si tienes sed.   5. Desde que empecé a trabajar en el jardín, he rebajado doce libras de peso.   6. Como tengo mucha paciencia, trabajo lento, despacio.   7. Puesto que quieres limonada, voy a cortar los limones de mi jardín.   8. Necesitamos hielo ya que quieres tomar la limonada fría.

15·50 Answers will vary.

15·51 1. ¡Dios mío! Se anuncia que habrá / va a haber una tormenta de nieve.   2. Mi esposo dice que ya había nevado mucho durante la noche.   3. Yo sé que en (el) invierno esto es posible.   4. Creo que podremos / vamos a poder subir la montaña en auto.   5. Pienso que será / va a ser un día magnífico para esquiar. 6. Ah, otro boletín de "El tiempo" dice que las condiciones del tiempo son ideales para los deportes de invierno.   7. Sabía que iba a ser un día bonito.   8. Mi marido sabe que soy optimista.   9. Lo cierto es que me encanta la nieve.   10. Me siento feliz cuando estoy en un lugar frío.

15·52 1. Ganaré mucho más dinero si trabajo más horas.   2. Terminaré mi máster si tomo dos cursos en línea este semestre.   3. Me casaré en agosto de este año si convenzo a mi novia.   4. Viajaré a Buenos Aires si gano el premio gordo.   5. Conseguiré mis metas si tengo claros mis objetivos.   6. Tendré el apoyo de mi familia si necesito ayuda en algún momento.   7. Compraré un apartamento si tengo un aumento de sueldo. 8. Visitaré a mis amigos si puedo conseguir un billete a buen precio.   9. Iré a Brasil si aprendo suficiente portugués para hablar con la gente.   10. Aumentaré mi fortuna si invierto mi dinero de manera sensata.

15·53 1. quién / cómo / por qué   2. cómo   3. por qué / cómo   4. si   5. qué   6. dónde   7. cuándo   8. quiénes

15·54 1. dónde están las joyas robadas   2. a qué hora llegarán los agentes   3. quién escribió la nota   4. adónde llevaron a la víctima   5. cuándo descubrieron el robo   6. por qué abandonaron la casa de la víctima   7. cómo se llama la sospechosa   8. a quiénes vamos a interrogar después   9. si asignaron un especialista a este caso   10. desde cuándo no hay un boletín de noticias

16 The conditional tense

16·1 Answers will vary.

16·2 1. viajaría   2. preferiríamos   3. subirían   4. jugarían   5. estudiaríamos   6. oirían   7. iría   8. bebería   9. comerías   10. pediría

16·3 1. ¿Gastarías todo el dinero?   2. ¿O ahorrarías el diez por ciento por lo menos?   3. ¿Qué comprarías para tu casa?   4. ¿Ayudarías a tu familia?   5. ¿Buscarías otro tipo de trabajo?   6. ¿Donarías un poco de tu dinero para ayudar a tu comunidad?   7. ¿Disfrutarías unos meses en casa?   8. ¿Viajarías a otros países?   9. ¿Te gustaría esquiar en Colorado?   10. ¿Invitarías a tus amigos para viajar contigo?

16·4 1. Sería posible encontrar a nuestros amigos en San Juan.   2. Pondría tu maleta grande en el maletero.   3. Tu maleta no cabría en un asiento del auto/carro.   4. ¿Podríamos llegar al aeropuerto temprano mañana?   5. Yo diría a eso de las cinco de la tarde.   6. Saldríamos a las tres y media pero vivimos cerca del aeropuerto.   7. No perderíamos el vuelo a San Juan.   8. Valdría la pena disfrutar un largo fin de semana en Puerto Rico.

16·5 1. vendrían 2. se quedarían 3. pondría 4. cocinaría 5. invitaríamos 6. sería 7. tendrían 8. querrían 9. diría 10. valdría

16·6 1. <u>componer</u>; compondrías 2. <u>obtener</u>; obtendrían 3. <u>poder</u>; podría 4. <u>disponer</u>; dispondría 5. <u>contener</u>; contendría 6. <u>poder</u>; podrían 7. <u>proponer</u>; propondrías 8. <u>mantener</u>; mantendrías

16·7 1. b. 2. c 3. a 4. g 5. f 6. d 7. j 8. e 9. h 10. k 11. i 12. l

17 The present perfect and past perfect tenses

17·1 1. No he hablado con mis amigos hoy.   2. Mis primos / Mis primas nunca han estado conmigo por dos semanas.   3. Rita se ha duchado pero no se ha lavado el pelo / el cabello.   4. ¿Me has enviado un mensaje para ir a un partido de fútbol?   5. Carla jamás/nunca me ha contestado/respondido una pregunta acerca de su edad.   6. ¿Les ha comentado a ustedes / a vosotros(as) que ella es más joven que yo?   7. Nunca he entendido/comprendido por qué ella es tan reservada.   8. No nos hemos conocido antes. Ha sido un placer.

17·2 Answers will vary.

17·3 1. ha roto 2. he descubierto 3. ha dicho 4. se han opuesto 5. ha encubierto 6. ha devuelto 7. ha hecho 8. he escrito 9. he descrito 10. he puesto 11. he vuelto 12. he deshecho 13. he resuelto

17·4 1. disolver; han disuelto 2. distraerse; se han distraído 3. morir; ha muerto 4. freír; ha frito 5. imprimir; ha impreso 6. descomponerse; se ha descompuesto 7. poder; he podido 8. ver; hemos visto 9. disolver; has disuelto 10. proponer; has propuesto

17·5 1. V 2. F 3. V. 4. F 5. F 6. V 7. F 8. V 9. F 10. V

17·6 1. habían proveído 2. había devuelto 3. se habían distraído 4. había visto 5. había roto 6. se había descompuesto 7. habían hecho 8. habíamos descubierto

17·7 1. yo había comprado 2. había tenido 3. habían ayudado 4. habían interesado 5. había visto 6. se habían negado 7. había llevado 8. había entregado 9. había recibido 10. había deseado

17·8 Yo le había pedido un favor a un amigo mío, Mario. Necesitaba una carta de recomendación para ingresar en un club muy exclusivo y carísimo. No le había dicho muchos detalles a Mario. Pero le había dicho que mis antepasados eran aristócratas y tenían mucho dinero. Cuando conocí a Boni siempre había querido visitar lugares fabulosos y había pensado presentarla a mis amigos en un lugar impresionante, en ese club exclusivo. Yo había tenido la impresión de que Boni era algo extrovertida. Después de salir varias veces con Boni, me había dado cuenta de que Boni es sincera. Por eso, decidí enfrentar la verdad: no tengo que impresionar a nadie.

18 The passive voice

18·1 1. abiertas 2. traídos 3. dibujados 4. vendidos 5. distribuidos 6. preparado 7. celebrada 8. invitados 9. aprobada 10. donados

18·2 1. Las invitaciones habían sido enviadas.   2. Las invitaciones fueron hechas por algunos de los miembros de la familia.   3. Las direcciones de los sobres fueron escritas por la hermana de la novia.   4. Un contrato ha sido firmado por la banda de música.   5. El menú fue creado por un chef peruano.   6. El salón de baile fue decorado con muchas flores.   7. El día de la boda fue elegido por la novia.   8. Los regalos fueron enviados por los amigos del novio y la novia.   9. El champán fue servido para un brindis.   10. Muchas fotos fueron sacadas en el salón de baile.

18·3 1. El partido será difundido por cable.   2. El encuentro será televisado desde San José.   3. Todos los jugadores serán entrenados para estar en forma.   4. El estadio será preparado para acomodar a la fanaticada.   5. El precio de las entradas será controlado para evitar fraudes.   6. El parqueo será limitado en los alrededores del estadio.   7. Un grupo de niños será invitado para la ceremonia de apertura.   8. El éxito del partido será asegurado con los voluntarios.   9. El himno nacional será interpretado al comienzo del evento.   10. El encuentro será visto en todo el país.

18·4   1. Se han cerrado   2. se han escrito   3. se han leído   4. Se han prohibido   5. Se han vendido   6. se ha resuelto   7. se han aceptado   8. Se han enviado   9. Se han puesto   10. Se ha roto

18·5   Answers will vary.

18·6   1. ¿Cómo se dice «gracias» en francés?   2. ¿Dónde se venden juguetes?   3. ¿Cuándo se aumentarán los precios?   4. ¿Dónde se compran libros escritos en japonés?   5. ¿Qué se habla aquí en esta tienda?   6. ¿Cuándo se sirve el desayuno en el hotel?   7. ¿Dónde se aceptan cupones de descuento?   8. ¿Cómo se dice «lo siento» en portugués?

18·7   1. ¿Cómo se puede vivir sin amor?   2. ¡Podemos vivir sin amor pero no sin dinero!   3. ¿Por qué se habla tanto de / acerca de una crisis económica?   4. Se dice que es mejor pensar de una manera positiva y no pesimista.   5. ¿Dónde se puede encontrar amigos/as?   6. Se dice que es más fácil encontrar amigos/as nuevos/as en una página de la Web.

18·8   —¿Cómo se entrena un nadador / una nadadora para competir en natación en las Olimpiadas?

—Por lo general, se entrena con un entrenador / una entrenadora profesional.

—¿Cuántos días a la semana?

—Se sabe que todos los atletas se entrenan seis días a la semana y descansan un día.

—Pero, ¿cuántas horas se nada en la piscina?

—Muchas horas y se debe comprometer a descansar y dormir.

—¿Qué se espera de un/una atleta que quiere nadar en las próximas Olimpiadas?

—Se espera mucho: tener confianza en sí mismo/misma, ser perseverante y mantenerse en buena forma, físicamente y mentalmente.

—¿Se debe tener un horario todos los días?

—Sí, se necesita para acostumbrarse a una rutina diaria.

—Por favor, deme un ejemplo de un horario diario.

—Por supuesto. Se levanta temprano, después los ejercicios de calentamiento. Se usa un cronómetro para medir el tiempo y la rapidez cuando nada.

—Muchas gracias y hasta pronto.

19   The present subjunctive

19·1   1. vayan   2. compren   3. entremos, nos sentemos   4. aplaudamos, gritemos   5. haya   6. tenga   7. abracemos   8. continúe   9. pueda

19·2   1. Yo sugiero que tú lleves a tu perro al parque.   2. Alicia quiere cenar con nosotros esta noche en el restaurante.   3. Ana espera que yo compre las entradas para ver un par de películas nuevas.   4. ¡Ojala yo pueda ganar este concurso!   5. Mi hermana dice que no salgan Uds. de la casa ahora.   6. El gerente no me permite trabajar los sábados.   7. Te prohíbo que repitas estas mentiras.   8. El entrenador insiste en que tú corras tres millas.   9. ¿Él prefiere que yo ponga todos los documentos en su escritorio?   10. ¿Por qué el doctor / la doctora te recomienda que no tomes refrescos?   11. ¡Yo deseo tener un trabajo mejor y ganar más dinero ahora!   12. Te aconsejo que vayas al banco hoy antes de las cinco en punto.   13. Ojalá / Espero que todos Uds. estén bien y saludables.   14. Louis y Joan quieren que yo escriba una carta.   15. Ojalá / Espero que no llueva mañana.

19·3   Answers will vary.

19·4   1. gane   2. tengan   3. podamos   4. sea   5. esté   6. cuesten   7. recibas   8. aprendamos   9. vayan   10. cenen   11. hagan   12. haya

19·5   1. olvides   2. cuelguen   3. diga   4. estemos   5. traigas   6. puedan   7. celebren   8. toquen   9. acompañes   10. juegues   11. se casen   12. terminen

19·6   1. Es necesario que pienses primero y que tengas paciencia antes de contestar una pregunta.   2. Es importante que comuniques tus ideas a menudo con tus colegas.   3. Es muchísimo mejor que asistas a todas las reuniones a tiempo.   4. Es fantástico que tomes notas para ayudar a tu grupo.   5. Es terrible que no obedezcas los reglamentos en el trabajo aunque sean ridículos.   6. Es dudoso que tengas un aumento a menos que sigas las reglas.   7. No es probable que puedas ayudar a todos tus colegas.   8. Pero más vale / Es mejor que continúes con tus esfuerzos.   9. Es muy posible que ganes el certificado del empleado del año.

10. ¡Es increíble que hagas todo lo que aparece en esta lista!   11. ¡Eres muy persistente!   12. Y es muy obvio que tú quieres tener éxito.

19·7   1. Quiero comprar una casa que esté lejos de la ciudad.   2. Necesitamos un auto que no cueste demasiado.   3. Mis sobrinos quieren un perro que sea travieso.   4. Tenemos vecinos que hacen mucho ruido.   5. ¿Dónde puedo encontrar un piano que se parezca al tuyo?   6. Mis amigos tienen una criada que hace enchiladas excelentes.   7. ¿Hay alguien / una persona aquí que me pueda ayudar ahora?   8. No, no hay nadie aquí que pueda abrir la puerta del edificio.

19·8   1. sea   2. tenga   3. conozca   4. ofrezca   5. comprenda   6. aconseje

19·9   1. sepa   2. sabe   3. hacer   4. aprecie   5. pueda   6. pintar   7. esté   8. tenga   9. tiene   10. sirva

19·10   1. Queremos un(a) compañero(a) de cuarto que no fume.   2. Busco a mi primo, que trabaja aquí.   3. Ella busca a alguien que trabaje aquí.   4. Quieren un carro/coche que no use mucha gasolina.   5. Necesitamos un vendedor que hable español.   6. Ellos tienen un vendedor que habla español.

19·11   1. conseguir/obtener   2. se pone   3. engordar   4. consigue/obtiene   5. me pongo   6. enriquecerse   7. te enfermas/te pones enfermo(a)   8. te pierdes

19·12   1. ¡No te enfermes!/¡No te pongas enfermo(a)!   2. Espero/Ojalá que no se enoje/enfade.   3. Quiere casarse.   4. ¡Mejórate/Mejórese/Mejoraos pronto!   5. Ella se frustra fácilmente.   6. Nos aburrimos en esa clase.   7. No quiero que te preocupes/se preocupe.   8. Se emocionan cuando piensan en el viaje.

19·13   1. haya   2. se den cuenta   3. se enoje   4. preservemos   5. te portes   6. pierda

19·14   1. ¿Puedes venir a mi casa?   2. ¿Vas al mercado?   3. ¿Vas a nuestra boda? Es en el Jardín Botánico.   4. ¿Va él al cine con nosotros?   5. ¿Vienes acá/aquí mucho/frecuentemente/a menudo?   6. ¿Van ustedes a clase?/¿Vais a clase?   7. ¿Vienen ustedes a clase mañana/¿Venís a clase mañana?   8. ¿A qué hora viene/vienes/vienen/venís?

19·15   1. Sí, voy./No, no puedo ir.   2. Sí, voy./No, no voy.   3. Sí, voy./No, no voy.   4. Sí, va./No, no va.   5. Sí, vengo a menudo/frecuentemente/mucho./No, no vengo...   6. Sí, vamos./No, no vamos.   7. Sí, venimos./No, no venimos.   8. Venimos a las _____.

19·16   1. incluyendo   2. incluso   3. incluso   4. solicitud   5. formulario   6. formas   7. solicitar   8. aplicarse   9. asegurarnos   10. vale la pena

19·17   1. te   2. le   3. les   4. le   5. Le

19·18   1. Te ruego que no manejes/conduzcas tan rápido.   2. Les pedimos que vayan con nosotros.   3. Le imploran a su profesor(a) que cambie la fecha del examen.   4. ¿Me pides/estás pidiendo que me vaya?

19·19   1. ¿Me llamas esta noche?   2. ¿Nos llevas a casa?   3. ¿Nos ayudas con las maletas?   4. ¿Me mandas una postal?   5. ¿Me compras un helado?   6. ¿Me traes flores?

19·20   1. Llámame/Llámeme esta noche.   2. Llévanos/Llévenos a casa.   3. Ayúdanos/Ayúdenos con las maletas.   4. Mándame/Mándeme una postal.   5. Cómprame/Cómpreme un helado.   6. Tráeme/Tráigame flores.

19·21   1. ¿Te ayudo?   2. ¿Les limpio la casa?   3. ¿Os llevo al aeropuerto?   4. ¿Le lavo el carro/coche?

19·22   1. Se lo estoy enviando./Estoy enviándoselo.   2. Te lo doy la próxima semana.   3. Nos las van a mostrar./Van a mostrárnoslas.   4. Se los dice a su amiga.   5. Se la tengo que entregar mañana./Tengo que entregársela mañana.   6. Se la ofrecemos para el verano.   7. ¿Te lo presto?   8. Ella se lo enseña a mi hijo.

19·23   1. Quiere mostrarte sus fotos.   2. Te las quiere mostrar./Quiere mostrártelas.   3. Ella nos va a enseñar la canción.   4. Nos la va a enseñar./Va a enseñárnosla.   5. Le estoy explicando la lección.   6. Se la estoy explicando./Estoy explicándosela.   7. Voy a enviarle un mensaje.   8. Se lo voy a enviar./Voy a enviárselo.

19·24   1. ¿Me presta(s) sus/tus apuntes?   2. ¿Me los presta(s)?   3. ¿Nos presta(s) su/tu carro/coche?   4. ¿Nos lo presta(s)?

19·25   1. Extraño/Echo de menos a mis amigos.   2. Te vas a perder la fiesta.   3. No quiero perder mi tarea.   4. Vamos a perder el autobús.   5. ¿Extrañas/Echas de menos tu país?   6. Faltan dos libros de la lista.   7. Nunca se le pasa (por alto) una pregunta.   8. Van a perder el juego.   9. Van a perder el tren.

20   Indefinite and negative words and expressions

20·1   1. Nadie trabaja en esta oficina.   2. Algunas personas son más agradables que otras.   3. Nunca hago preguntas.   4. No hablo mucho tampoco.   5. A veces necesito ayuda.   6. ¿Habla Ud. alemán también?   7. Ella come o papas/patatas o arroz solamente.   8. Ni tú ni yo.

20·2 1. algo 2. Nunca 3. nadie 4. O, o 5. Algunos 6. Alguien 7. Siempre 8. Ni, ni

20·3 1. No hay refrescos en la nevera. 2. No quiero ni dormir ni jugar al fútbol. 3. No van a ningún lugar interesante este fin de semana. 4. No tenemos ninguna esperanza de encontrar el anillo perdido. 5. No sé dónde están ni las preguntas ni las respuestas para la tarea. 6. No tenemos tiempo para ayudarte. 7. Nunca voy a visitar a mis suegros. 8. No voy a saludar a mis tíos tampoco. 9. No celebramos ningún día especial esta semana. 10. No conocen a nadie de nuestra familia. 11. No tengo nada que añadir.

20·4 1. Estoy algo preocupado/a. 2. ¿Hay alguien en esta habitación? 3. Nadie quiere hacer nada. 4. Manny ni sacó las fotos ni filmó la reunión. 5. ¿Tenemos que encontrar a Peter o a Sandra? 6. Algún día vamos a terminar este trabajo. 7. No les gusta nada este trabajo. 8. Nunca harán esto.

20·5 1. e 2. c 3. a 4. d 5. f 6. b

20·6 1. El sol no es un planeta sino una estrella. 2. Blanca Nieves no es un personaje real sino ficticio. 3. La astronomía no es un deporte sino una ciencia. 4. El inglés no es la lengua oficial de Portugal sino de Inglaterra. 5. La paella no es un plato típico mexicano sino español. 6. El ballet no es un juego sino un arte. 7. Un crucigrama no es un problema sino un pasatiempo. 8. Un perro no es una persona sino un animal. 9. La luna no es una estrella sino un satélite.

20·7 1. pero 2. sino 3. pero 4. pero, sino que 5. pero 6. pero 7. pero 8. sino que 9. pero 10. sino que

20·8 1. a 2. f 3. e 4. c 5. b 6. d

20·9 1. cualquiera 2. cualquier 3. cualquier 4. cualquiera

20·10 1. nadie 2. nada 3. Nunca 4. ni... tampoco 5. ninguna parte/ningún lugar 6. ningún 7. ni/ni siquiera 8. Ni... ni

20·11 Individual answers will vary. Sample answer: 1. Debo sacar la basura cada día.

20·12 1. olvide 2. pase 3. busque 4. solicite 5. se tranquilice

20·13 1. ponga 2. saca 3. es 4. sea 5. asistan 6. haya 7. está 8. nos mudemos

20·14 1. está harto 2. por lo menos 3. Al menos 4. para colmo 5. Al menos... contar con

21 The imperfect subjunctive

21·1 1. vinieras 2. acompañáramos 3. tomaran 4. pudieran 5. aprendiera 6. hubiera 7. fuera 8. debiera 9. trajera 10. estuviera 11. se comportaran 12. abrazaran

21·2 1. Yo quería que tú trajeras dos botellas de refrescos. 2. Querías que cocináramos arroz y frijoles. 3. Era ridículo que tuviéramos tanta comida para cinco personas. 4. Alberto y Carlos no estaban seguros de que sus amigos vinieran. 5. Fue una pena que gastáramos tanto. 6. Querían dividir la cantidad de los gastos entre tres. 7. No estaba seguro/a que ellos me pagaran. 8. Carlos me suplicó que yo esperara hasta el fin de semana. 9. ¿Él prefería no pagar? ¡Por supuesto! 10. Nadie creía que Carlos me devolviera el dinero a mí.

21·3 Answers will vary.

21·4 1. estudiaras 2. dijeras 3. estuviera 4. tuviéramos 5. llegaran 6. tocara 7. pidiera 8. pudiera 9. hubiera 10. llevaran

21·5 1. Si tuviera un amigo aquí ahora estaría feliz. 2. Yo no cantaría una canción si tú no tocaras la guitarra. 3. Te presentaría a mi hermana si tú no fueras tan tímido. 4. No contestaría la pregunta si no supiera la respuesta. 5. Si no lloviera, cenaríamos en la terraza. 6. Esta casa valdría un millón de dólares si tuviera una piscina en el patio. 7. Sería un milagro si mis amigos me ayudaran a terminar mi tarea. 8. Si tú fueras más fuerte, podrías jugar mejor. 9. Si la maleta fuera más grande no la llevaría conmigo. 10. Si fuera mentiroso/a, ¿quien me creería?

21·6 Answers will vary.

21·7 Todo el mundo querría / quisiera que su vida fuera placentera. Por ejemplo, si no lloviera hoy, yo estaría muy feliz. Si trabajara menos horas en la oficina tendría mucho más tiempo para descansar y ver películas en mi tele. Si mis padres vivieran cerca de mí, me ayudarían todas las semanas a limpiar la casa. Si encontrara mil dólares invitaría a mis amigos a cenar en un restaurante fabuloso. Si tuviera la suerte de no tener que regresar a mi trabajo, viajaría a un lugar desconocido. No tendría que abrir la puerta de la casa si mis suegros nos visitaran sin avisarnos por teléfono. Si fuera rica no tendría este auto horrible, viejo y descompuesto.

Yo sería la reina de la casa si no tuviera que fregar la vajilla. ¡Sería un mundo perfecto! Sería un cuento de hadas si pudiera tener todo bajo mi control. Pero los sueños son sueños, nada más.

21·8 1. It was doubtful (that) my cousins had prepared dinner when my father arrived.   2. I think it is possible that it will rain tomorrow. (*The verb* **llover** *is governed by the notion of possibility, while the verb* **ser** *is governed by a verb of belief.*)   3. We were looking for a shotgun that had two barrels.   4. My father had a garden that produced / used to produce a lot of tomatoes.   5. When you decide if you're going to go with me or not, you'll call me, won't you?   6. He / She / You will sell the car provided at least five hundred dollars is offered (to him / her / you).   7. The children hope (that) we'll all play soccer.   8. It is essential that you and I come to an agreement.   9. The three of them wanted me to stay home until it quit raining.   10. It's odd that she always has insisted that I not call her on weekends. (*There are two subordinated clauses, both governed by verbs that make the subjunctive necessary.*)   11. No matter how much we asked him to lend us the money, he refused to lend it to us.   12. We need a program that will allow us to process more data in less time.   13. She has a boyfriend who loves her a lot.   14. We doubt (that) Henry's parents have forgotten his birthday.   15. They are glad that you haven't abandoned your studies.   16. I ask that you call me before the market closes. (**rogar** *is a very polite verb for asking, corresponding to the formal, and now seldom encountered, use of* to beg)   17. Do you want me to find a movie that isn't a horror film?   18. After he bathed, John got dressed and took off (left).   19. Before he left the house, John bathed and got dressed.   20. It's impossible (that) she didn't find out about it before the party. (*or* know about it)

21·9 1. Su mamá se alegra de que tú hayas visto el drama.   2. Fuimos a la tienda antes de que nuestro papá viniera / regresara / llegara a casa.   3. ¿Quieres que te lea el cuento?   4. Ella y yo tuvimos que buscar un carro que tuviera un reproductor de CDs.   5. ¿Te preocupas de que la computadora no tenga suficiente memoria?   6. ¿Les pidieron que trajeran el informe?   7. Tuvieron que hallar una farmacia que estuviera / permaneciera abierta las veinticuatro horas.   8. Sabemos que le has escrito las cartas.   9. Están seguros de que él había visto la película antes de que su mamá regresara / volviera a casa.   10. Fue importante que él terminara la carrera.   11. Es dudoso que Catherine haya publicado o que publique un artículo.   12. Ella les exigía a sus alumnos que tuvieran escritas cinco páginas al final de cada semana.   13. Fue un milagro que él no se hubiera ahogado.   14. Fue obvio que su mamá no hubiera querido / deseado que ella viniera a nuestra fiesta.   15. Ellos nos prometieron que nos ayudarían, con tal de que les pagáramos por adelantado.   16. Si tú me pidieras que te hiciera un favor, te lo haría.   17. Después de que Uds. se hayan desayunado, podemos ir al zoológico.   18. ¡Es bueno / Qué bueno que vayas al concierto!   19. Ella entró en la casa de nuevo sin que sus padres lo supieran.   20. Vimos al vendedor que nos vendió el carro.

21·10 1. es 2. pueda 3. quiere 4. tenga 5. comprenda 6. cuesta 7. comparte 8. logre

21·11 Answers will vary.

21·12 1. estaré 2. será 3. irán 4. querremos 5. dirás 6. aparecerá 7. escribiremos 8. pondrán 9. pensaré 10. saldremos 11. haréis 12. volverán 13. vendrá 14. comerás 15. tendré

21·13 1. b 2. d 3. c 4. a 5. d

21·14 1. Te casarás/Se casará/Se casarán/Os casaréis y tendrás/tendrá/tendrán/tendréis gemelos.   2. La fiesta es a las tres.   3. Nos vamos mañana.   4. Compraré un carro/coche algún día.   5. Te llamo esta noche.   6. Van a mudarse/Se van a mudar a este edificio la próxima semana.   7. ¿Qué piensas/piensa hacer?   8. Pienso/Estoy pensando mandarle un email.   9. ¿Qué estará haciendo (ella)?   10. Estará trabajando en un hospital.

21·15 1. estén 2. tiene 3. da 4. llegue 5. salga 6. te portas 7. hace 8. llueve 9. llueve 10. empiece

21·16 1. abrieran 2. supiera 3. corrieras 4. enseñara 5. se durmiera 6. volviéramos 7. trajera 8. fuera 9. fueran 10. pensaras 11. pudieran 12. quisiérais 13. leyera 14. comprendiera 15. se sintiera

21·17 1. daría 2. diría 3. venderíamos 4. vendrían 5. podría 6. haríais 7. iría 8. bailarías 9. se encontrarían 10. conocerían 11. deberíamos 12. pagaría 13. invitaría 14. me enojaría 15. se aburriría

21·18 1. tuviera... ayudaría 2. supieras... te enojarías 3. estuviéramos... estaríamos 4. hiciera... sería 5. fuera... asignaría

21·19 1. Por 2. por 3. Para 4. por 5. Por 6. Para 7. por... para

21·20 Answers will vary.

22 Relative pronouns

22·1 1. La casa que está cerca del puente es de María. 2. Los tigres que vimos en el zoo son de la India. 3. La escuela que está cerrada es una institución privada. 4. Los policías que cuidan el banco están dormidos. 5. Los árboles que son más altos están en el parque. 6. En la catedral hay unos turistas que esperan ver unos cuadros de El Greco.

22·2 1. F 2. V 3. F 4. V 5. V 6. V

22·3 1. Mientras Jackie va al mercado que está al lado del cine, nosotros vemos una película. 2. El niño que está conmigo es el hijo de Jackie. 3. La película que vemos no es muy interesante. 4. Matt vio a dos mujeres que no pagaron sus entradas. 5. Mark vino a ver una película que es extranjera. 6. Compré las cosas que los niños quieren: chocolates y refrescos.

22·4 1. El hombre, quien tiene un traje de Arlequín, es muy gordo. 2. El chico, quien trae un disfraz de Frankenstein, es muy bajo. 3. Los hombres, quienes se visten como los siete enanitos, son muy viejos. 4. Una señora, quien parece la Bella Durmiente, está durmiendo en el sofá. 5. Un señor, quien viene con un traje de príncipe, no tiene aspecto aristocrático. 6. Las niñas, quienes se ponen un disfraz de bruja, son muy simpáticas.

22·5 1. quienes 2. quien 3. quienes 4. quien 5. quien 6. quienes

22·6 1. El hombre quien está sentado a mi derecha es de San Diego. 2. La gente quien compró/Las personas quienes compraron los boletos hoy pagaron un precio alto. 3. Las mujeres a quienes invitaste están bailando la rumba. 4. Pero no veo a sus esposos, quienes estaban aquí. 5. Marlo, quien es una buena amiga, toca el piano. 6. ¿Conoces a la mujer quien está cantando ahora?

22·7 1. los cuales 2. la cual 3. el cual 4. las cuales 5. los cuales 6. las cuales

22·8 Answers will vary.

22·9 1. El/La columnista revela los secretos del actor, lo cual es interesante. 2. Lo que tú quieres saber está en el periódico de hoy. 3. Siempre como lo que quiero. 4. El/La nutricionista recomienda comer lo que es saludable. 5. Mis amigos no van al gimnasio con frecuencia, lo cual no es bueno. 6. Leonardo no está aquí, lo cual me preocupa. 7. ¿Ve Ud. lo que yo veo ahora? 8. ¡Ustedes son muy generosos, lo cual es fabuloso!

22·10 1. la cual 2. el cual 3. la cual 4. quienes 5. los cuales 6. quienes 7. el cual, quien 8. las cuales, quienes

22·11 1. cuyo 2. cuya 3. cuyo 4. cuyas

23 Numbers

23·1 1. treinta y cinco 2. dos mil trescientos cuarenta y un 3. trescientos veintidós 4. dieciséis 5. sesenta y siete 6. setenta y un 7. cien 8. quinientas dos 9. veintiséis 10. cien mil 11. treinta y un 12. setecientas 13. un millón 14. cincuenta y una

23·2 1. el quince de marzo de mil ochocientos noventa y ocho 2. Son las tres y media de la tarde. 3. el catorce de julio de mil setecientos setenta 4. el primero de junio de dos mil dos 5. Son las diez y quince de la noche./Son las diez y cuarto de la noche. 6. el treinta y uno de enero de mil novecientos noventa y nueve 7. A las nueve y media de la mañana. 8. el treinta de noviembre a las siete de la tarde

23·3 Answers will vary.

23·4 1. 55; Cien menos cuarenta y cinco son cincuenta y cinco. 2. 37; Veinticinco más doce son treinta y siete. 3. 90; Treinta por tres son noventa. 4. 43; Doce más dieciséis/diez y seis más quince son cuarenta y tres. 5. 50; Doscientos entre/dividido por cuatro son cincuenta. 6. 231; Setenta y siete por tres son doscientos treinta y uno.

23·5 1. V 2. F 3. F 4. V 5. F 6. V 7. F 8. V 9. F 10. V

23·6 1. Hay más de cien canales de televisión. 2. Muchas familias americanas tienen solamente un hijo. 3. Muchos hogares norteamericanos tienen tres televisores. 4. Uno no puede comprar mucho con veinte y cinco (veinticinco) dólares. 5. Hay treinta y dos piezas en un juego de ajedrez. 6. Trabajamos cincuenta semanas cada año/al año. 7. El cumpleaños de Lincoln es el 12 de febrero.

23·7 1. primera 2. quinto 3. décimo 4. octava 5. primer 6. tercera 7. séptima 8. veinte 9. cuarta 10. segunda

23·8   Answers will vary.

23·9   1. Esta es mi tercera visita al museo.   2. Pero es la primera vez que saco fotos.   3. El décimo capítulo es difícil.   4. Daisy siempre llega la segunda, después de Julia.   5. Ellos/Ellas apuestan en la quinta carrera.   6. Picasso vivió en el siglo veinte.   7. Hoy es el primer día del resto de mi vida.   8. Diciembre es el mes doce del año.   9. Afortunadamente, hoy es el séptimo día de la semana.   10. Vivimos en el cuarto piso.

23·10   1. k.   2. s.   3. q.   4. h.   5. m.   6. o.   7. l.   8. b.   9. r.   10. a.   11. d.   12. i.   13. f.   14. c.   15. t.   16. e.   17. p.   18. j.   19. n.   20. g.

23·11   1. tres y / más cinco son ocho   2. cuarenta y dos (multiplicado) por treinta y cuatro son mil cuatrocientos veintiocho   3. ochenta y nueve dividido por siete son doce con cinco restantes / y quedan (*or* restan) cinco.   4. setenta y siete menos cincuenta y dos son veinticinco   5. noventa y tres (multiplicado) por siete son seiscientos cincuenta y uno   6. dos tercios / dos terceras partes   7. dos séptimos / dos séptimas partes   8. tres cuartos / tres cuartas partes   9. un medio   10. cuatro quintos / cuatro quintas partes   11. tres cuartos / cuartas partes más / y un medio igual a uno y cuarto / una cuarta parte (*using* **igual a** *avoids the potencial confusion even native speakers of Spanish can feel when faced with whether to use* **es** *or* **son** *when the result is one* plus *a fraction*)   12. cinco coma tres menos cuatro coma uno igual a uno coma dos (or use **punto** instead of **coma**, depending on notation system of the country).   13. seis menos cinco es uno   14. el noventa y siete por ciento   15. ciento y uno menos uno son cien   16. diez (multiplicado) por cien son mil (**un** *is not used before* **mil**)   17. mil más uno son mil y uno / mil y uno son mil y uno   18. setecientos setenta y siete más / y quinientos cincuenta y cinco son mil trescientos treinta y dos   19. tres séptimos / tres séptimas partes   20. el veintitrés por ciento

23·12   1. It is believed that the bear market will continue unless the Reserve takes measures.   2. It has been calculated that the death rate from the bubonic plague was 30% of the population.   3. The secretary showed me a pamphlet with a bar graph.   4. The stock broker has a call option that expires at close of business.   5. The economy's growth rate has slowed due to civil wars in the region.   6. The initiation fee is $187 and thereafter it is $140 per year.   7. The board of directors announced that it will reinvest 5% of profits in publicity campaigns.   8. The amount dedicated to education is 4% less this year compared to last year.   9. One study of economic conditions revealed that there is a range of possibilities for resolving the crisis.   10. The creditors have proposed an increase in interest rates of 4%.   11. For a week, the price of the stock fluctuated between $40 and $50.   12. Congress approved a 2% increase on imported consumer goods.   13. In order to show their opposition to the anti-union sentiments of the governor, the workers went on strike.   14. The personnel in charge of research and development received a salary increase of 4%.   15. Due to the fact that the inflation rate is at 9% per year and that the unemployment rate is approaching 12%, it is doubtful that the ruling party is going to remain in control after the coming elections, whether in the legislative bodies or in executive positions.

23·13   1. l.   2. d.   3. i.   4. a.   5. g.   6. j.   7. k.   8. e.   9. f.   10. h.   11. b.   12. c.

23·14   1. El sábado, doce de marzo del año dos mil once, terminé de escribir este libro.   2. El partido de fútbol comenzó a la una y quince / cuarto de la tarde, el sábado, ocho de enero del año dos mil dieciocho.   3. El año pasado, el primero de marzo fue un lunes.   4. Para las cuatro de la tarde hoy, habré trabajado diez horas.   5. El lunes, tengo una cita a las tres de la tarde.   6. ¿A qué hora empezó la película?   7. Él vivió en la Calle Ocho Norte, en el número tres cero cinco, desde junio del año mil novecientos setenta y ocho hasta agosto del año mil novecientos ochenta.   8. No te olvides de llamarme una noche de éstas al dos treinta y cinco, once cero dos.   9. En los países de habla española, los martes trece, no los viernes, se consideran días de mala suerte.   10. ¿Sabe Ud. lo que / qué pasó el viernes, doce de octubre del año mil cuatrocientos noventa y dos?   11. La Casa Blanca se ubica en la Avenida Pennsylvania, en el número mil seiscientos.   12. Creo que su número de ella es dos cuarenta y siete, noventa y cinco, treinta y ocho, pero no le llame los domingos.   13. Ella nació el veintidós de enero del año mil novecientos noventa y ocho a las nueve y cuarenta y cuatro de la mañana. Fue un jueves.   14. El veintidós de noviembre del año mil novecientos sesenta y tres, fue un viernes.   15. Son las doce y uno de la mañana.   16. Los jueves, me acuesto a la una menos quince / cuarto de la mañana, ¡lo que quiere decir que los miércoles no me acuesto!   17. La biblioteca se ubica en la Avenida Cuatro. A partir de marzo, se abre a las nueve de la mañana todos los días, excepto los domingos.   18. Son las veintidós y cuarenta y cinco.   19. *Answers will vary, but the formats are in this chapter and in this answer key.*   20. *Answers will vary.*

24   More writing

24·1   1. el encabezamiento   2. la fecha   3. el destinatario   4. el saludo   5. la redacción de la carta   6. la despedida   7. la firma

24·2   1. La Habana, 13 de noviembre de 1988   2. Santo Domingo, 31 de julio de 2000   3. Bogotá, 1 de enero de 2018   4. San Fernando, 28 de febrero de 2005   5. Los Ángeles, 16 de marzo de 2023   6. Barcelona, 23 de abril de 1995

24·3   *There may be other possible closing formulas.*

1. Madrid, 3 de mayo de 2001
   Estimado Dr. Blanco:
   Atentamente,
2. Guadalajara, 19 de julio de 2018
   Querida Sra. Rodríguez:
   Le saluda cordialmente,
3. San Diego, 13 de enero de 2019
   Estimado Capitán Vázquez:
   Con todo mi respeto,

24·4   1. 27 de marzo de 2000   2. 5 de mayo de 1999   3. 12 de diciembre de 2008   4. 8 de agosto de 2018   5. 10 de octubre de 2020   6. 10 de febrero de 1980

24·5   1. Barcelona, 10 de mayo de 2017
   Mi queridísima Anita:
   Con todo mi amor,
2. Managua, 9 de junio de 2018
   Mi querida tía Úrsula:
   Con todo mi cariño,
3. Guayaquil, 3 de agosto de 2019
   Mi querido amigo:
   Un abrazo cariñoso,

24·6   1. Sra. Lidia Gómez
   Avenida del Norte, 27
   00087 Barcelona
2. Sr. Alcalde Raúl Benítez
   Alcaldía de Pueblo Nuevo
   Torreón, 305
   27250 México D.F.
3. Sres. Dolores y Antonio Bermúdez
   Calle C, 17111, Apart. D
   00891 La Habana

24·7   Answers will vary.

24·8   1. Mis hermanos visitaron esa región varias veces.   2. La idea fue sugerida por la agencia de viajes   3. El proyecto del viaje era interesante.   4. Un grupo local compartió la trayectoria con los viajeros.   5. Los turistas fueron recibidos por una banda de música.   6. El cantante no cantaba en español.   7. Ahora hacen planes para viajar al sur de Bolivia.   8. Las próximas vacaciones, mis sobrinas vendrán a mi casa.

24·9   *Some examples; other answers are possible.*   1. ¿Por qué vas a Madrid? ¿Quiénes van a Madrid contigo? ¿Dónde está tu pasaporte? ¿Cuándo regresas a Barcelona? ¿Qué vas a hacer en Madrid mañana?   2. ¿Qué regalo has comprado? ¿Quiénes van a celebrar el aniversario? ¿Dónde van a celebrar el aniversario? ¿Cuándo se casaron tus padres? ¿Cómo van a celebrar el aniversario?   3. ¿Dónde quieres cenar? ¿Cuál es tu plato favorito? ¿Quiénes van a cenar? ¿Por qué no invitas a tus amigos? ¿Cuánto cuesta la cena?   4. ¿Cómo está tu amigo? ¿Qué le pasa a tu amigo? ¿Quién es el médico de tu amigo? ¿Dónde está el hospital? ¿Cuándo vas a visitar a tu amigo?   5. ¿Qué productos quieres comprar? ¿Dónde está la tienda? ¿Cuánto dinero vas a gastar? ¿Cuántas veces has ido a esa tienda? ¿Cómo vas a pagar, con tarjeta de crédito?   6. ¿Cuántos años cumples? ¿Qué regalos quieres recibir? ¿Con quién vas a celebrar tu cumpleaños? ¿Dónde va a ser la fiesta? ¿Cómo quieres celebrar tu cumpleaños?

24·10   1. En otra época, era más paciente porque tenía más tiempo.   2. A menudo estudiaba español, ya que quería hablar claro con mis amigos mexicanos.   3. Con frecuencia, aprendía a escribir muchos tipos de oraciones más complejas.   4. Siempre podía contar con mi buen amigo Pablito.   5. A veces, no tenía la constancia necesaria ni la disciplina precisa para estudiar.   6. Día tras día, era difícil escribir en dos idiomas diferentes y a veces con palabras no similares.   7. En ocasiones, iba al cine para ver películas mexicanas y colombianas y eran divertidas.   8. Con frecuencia reflexionaba sobre la poca capacidad de los seres humanos para ser constantes y dedicados.

24·11   1. En otra época, yo podía...   2. A menudo quería...   3. Con frecuencia podía...   4. Siempre iba...   5. A veces compraba...   6. Día tras día practicaba...

24·12   *Some examples; other answers are possible:*   Me llamo Julián y tengo veintidós años. Soy alto, delgado y tengo el pelo rubio. Soy trabajador: me levanto a las seis de la mañana y siempre llego a tiempo a mi trabajo. Mi familia es muy cariñosa y siempre me ayuda en mis momentos difíciles. Me llaman por teléfono los fines de semana. He aprendido a hablar y escribir en francés y puedo hablar ruso con mis vecinos. Eso para mí es un gran logro. Ahora quiero terminar mis estudios universitarios y ser meteorólogo. Estudié en Los Ángeles y voy a continuar estudiando cursos en línea (*online*).

24·13   *Sample answer:*   La tecnología avanza muy rápido. Antes, los teléfonos celulares eran más grandes y caros. Ahora, son pequeños y más baratos. Las computadoras también son más rápidas. Hoy usamos el ratón para hacer un clic y escribir un documento. O hacemos un clic para entrar en una página de la Internet. En cambio, en el futuro, no necesitaremos el ratón. Solamente usaremos un dedo para tocar la pantalla.

24·14   *Sample answer:*   Si yo pudiera, no viviría en Estados Unidos por un año. Yo viviría en México para aprender español. Después, yo viajaría a Chile para conocer a los padres de mi amigo Felipe Cerdeña. Quisiera visitar la costa chilena y compararla con la costa de California. Me gustaría ser ingeniero civil y construir puentes. Si pudiera conseguir una beca, podría ir a una buena universidad y cambiar mi vida.

24·15   *Sample answer:*

Los Angeles, 25 de marzo de 2014

Querida Martica:

    ¿Cómo estás? Quería saludarte y decirte que tengo un nuevo trabajo. Ayer comencé a trabajar en la Clínica del Puerto, una clínica dental en Oviedo. La clínica se especializa en la ortodoncia y en los tratamientos para blanquear (bleach) los dientes. Ahora soy la recepcionista. Este verano voy a terminar mi entrenamiento como asistenta dental, y luego el semestre que viene, como higienista.

    ¿Has terminado tus estudios? Cuando termine mi entrenamiento visitaré a mi familia en Miami. Quiero verte entonces. Podemos hacer planes para cenar una noche, ¿no crees?

Con un saludo cariñoso,

Felicia

25   More conversations

25·1   1. el sábado   2. por la noche   3. a las ocho   4. de la noche   5. los jueves   6. el jueves

25·2   1. Soy Margarita./Habla Margarita./Te llama Margarita.   2. Te llamo   3. La fiesta es el domingo por la noche.   4. Es a las ocho de la noche.   5. ¿Dónde es la fiesta?   6. Es en mi casa.

25·3   1. la cerveza   2. nos encanta   3. en el cine   4. Quiero   5. En efecto   6. estudiar   7. desayunar

25·4   1. Me encanta la cocina/comida peruana.   2. ¿Me quieres?/¿Me amas?   3. Te gusta mi hermana, ¿verdad?/¿no?/¿no es así?   4. En efecto./Efectivamente.   5. ¿Te gustaría/Quisieras hablar con ella?   6. Sí, me encantaría.   7. ¿Tienes ganas de ir al cine?   8. No, no tengo ganas de ir.

25·5   1. h   2. v   3. f   4. n   5. u   6. a   7. g   8. w   9. c   10. j   11. r   12. p   13. o,p   14. s   15. i   16. t   17. e   18. d   19. k   20. q,l   21. a   22. e,m   23. b

25·6   1. ¿Dónde está?   2. ¿Dónde están?   3. ¿Dónde está?   4. ¿Dónde son?   5. ¿Dónde estamos?   6. ¿Dónde es?   7. ¿Dónde estoy?   8. ¿Dónde es?

25·7   1. Soy yo.   2. ¿Tienes ganas de almorzar?   3. Bueno, estoy ocupado(a) ahora.   4. Bien/Vale. Te llamo el sábado.   5. Entonces, ¿no estás enojado(a)?   6. No. Hasta luego/Nos vemos luego.

25·8   1. ¿Qué quieres?   2. Me encantaría verte esta noche.   3. Voy al cine con Sara.   4. Entonces, ¿no puedes cenar conmigo?   5. En efecto/Efectivamente.   6. Bien/Vale/De acuerdo. Hasta luego.

25·9   1. Hola, soy Miguel.   2. Te llamo a ver si puedes cenar conmigo esta noche.   3. Bien/Vale. ¿A qué hora?   4. ¿A las siete?   5. Bien. /Vale.   6. Marta no me quiere.   7. Entonces, ¿por qué no sales con Patricia? ¡(A ella) le gustas mucho!   8. Bueno, entonces, ¿por qué no?

25·10   Individual answers will vary.

25·11 1. Eran las tres de la tarde. 2. Llovía/Estaba lloviendo. 3. Yo manejaba/estaba manejando/conducía/estaba conduciendo a casa. 4. Dos amigos estaban conmigo. 5. Todo estábamos cansados.

25·12 1. Mientras yo dormía/estaba durmiendo, mis amigos celebraban/estaban celebrando. 2. Ella escuchaba/estaba escuchando música mientras estudiaba/estaba estudiando. 3. Él limpiaba/estaba limpiando la casa mientras los niños jugaban/estaban jugando afuera. 4. Yo estaba preocupado(a) mientras hacía/estaba haciendo el examen. 5. El profesor/La profesora no veía cuando él texteaba/estaba texteando a sus amigos.

25·13 1. Mientras yo dormía/estaba durmiendo, mi mamá/madre llamó. 2. Ella escuchaba/estaba escuchando música cuando sonó el teléfono. 3. (Nosotros) nos divertíamos/nos estábamos divirtiendo cuando entró la profesora/el profesor. 4. Él hablaba/estaba hablando por celular/móvil cuando chocó con el otro carro/coche. 5. Jugaban/Estaban jugando (al) béisbol cuando empezó a llover.

25·14 1. (Yo) me levanté y me vestí. 2. Volvimos a casa y buscamos nuestros libros. 3. Estudió mucho y aprobó el examen. 4. Vino a clase y se sentó. 5. Fueron al supermercado y compraron bebidas.

25·15 1. entendía 2. pude 3. supiste 4. tenía 5. Quise

25·16 1. se le 2. se me 3. se le 4. se les 5. olvidó 6. quedaron 7. cayó

25·17 1. tiempo 2. tiempo 3. veces 4. hora 5. época 6. A veces

25·18 1. trabajando 2. caminando 3. corriendo 4. durmiendo 5. sirviendo 6. pidiendo 7. divirtiéndonos 8. mintiendo

25·19 1. e 2. b 3. a 4. c 5. f 6. d

25·20 Individual answers will vary.

25·21 1. entré 2. eran 3. Llovía/Estaba lloviendo 4. quería 5. estaba 6. interesaba 7. estaba 8. entré 9. pude 10. Empezamos 11. Hablábamos/Estábamos hablando 12. hizo 13. Me sentía (if that's how she felt/was feeling when the next action occurred)/Me sentí (if that's how she suddenly felt) 14. Me levanté 15. salí 16. me arrepentí 17. mandé 18. Quería 19. contestó 20. quería (if that's how he was feeling when the phone rang)/quiso (if he simply refused to answer it)

25·22 Individual answers will vary.

25·23 1. El niño dijo que estaba contento. 2. Mi amigo dijo que tenía hambre. 3. Las chicas dijeron que les gustaba la clase. 4. Les dijimos que vivíamos en esa calle. 5. Nos dijeron que esta era la calle más bonita de toda la ciudad.

25·24 1. Su mamá me dijo: «Él no está en casa». 2. Los directores nos dijeron: «No hay suficiente dinero para el proyecto». 3. La novia de mi hermano me dijo: «Quiero casarme en abril». 4. Mi hermano me dijo: «No estoy de acuerdo con ese plan». 5. Su jefe le avisó: «No vas a conseguir una subida de sueldo».

25·25 1. Nos preguntaron si íbamos al cine esta/esa noche. 2. Me preguntó cuánto costaba un vuelo de ida y vuelta a México. 3. Le preguntó cuándo se graduaba de la escuela secundaria. 4. Me preguntaron qué quería hacer hoy/ese día. 5. Te preguntó si comías con frecuencia en ese restaurante.

25·26 1. Él le preguntaba: «¿Quieres acompañarme?» 2. Me preguntó: «¿A qué hora comes?» 3. Nos preguntó: «¿Dónde estudian/estudiáis?» 4. Te preguntó: «¿Con quién andas?» 5. Me preguntaron: «¿Tienes miedo?»

25·27 1. Le pedimos que nos dijera la verdad. 2. Le pedí que trajera ese sobre al director de la compañía. 3. Le dije que viniera temprano al trabajo el viernes. 4. Les dijo que no llegaran tarde. 5. Me pidió que le comprara un helado.

25·28 1. Ella dijo: «No me llames». 2. Él le pidió: «Piénsalo». 3. Yo te aconsejé: "Ve esta/esa película". 4. Me advirtió: «No bebas demasiado». 5. Ellos le dijeron: «Sal temprano».

25·29 1. Para 2. Por 3. por 4. Para 5. Para, para

25·30 1. Ella es la mejor estudiante de la clase, ya que estudia todo el tiempo. 2. No es culto, pero es bien educado. 3. Él sí es culto, ya que lee constantemente. 4. Es bien educado, ya que sus padres eran muy exigentes. 5. Ella es la más culta de su familia. 6. Para una mujer culta, no parece muy lista. 7. Ella sí es lista, es que no escucha. 8. Ella perdió su trabajo por llegar tarde todos los días.

25·31 1. Ella anunció que se iba a casar/que iba a casarse. 2. El médico le advirtió que no fumara. 3. Ella le avisó que se iba de vacaciones. 4. El jefe le aconsejó que no se fuera. 5. Anunciaron el puesto.

25·32 Individual answers will vary.

25·33 1. es 2. soy 3. somos 4. eres 5. son 6. sois 7. son 8. es

25·34	1. sé 2. Sabe 3. Conoces 4. encontramos 5. se reúne
25·35	1. Me llamo 2. Se llama 3. Nos llamamos 4. Nos llamamos 5. Se llama
25·36	1. que 2. Quién; que 3. que/quien 4. Quiénes 5. Qué

25·37   1. Hace cuatro años que vivimos en este país./Llevamos cuatro años viviendo en este país.   2. Trabajamos juntos desde el once de febrero.   3. Llevo treinta minutos nadando./Hace treinta minutos que estoy nadando.   4. Hace tres meses que no veo a mi familia./Llevo tres meses sin ver a mi familia.   5. Llevo dos semanas sin fumar./Hace dos semanas que no fumo.

25·38   1. Es   2. Se llaman   3. Mi nombre es   4. Encantada   5. De dónde son   6. no es así   7. sino de   8. sino   9. Llevo... estudiando   10. parece mentira

25·39   1. e   2. j   3. c   4. g   5. h   6. i   7. d   8. f   9. b   10. a

25·40   1. seamos   2. estés   3. tenga   4. haga   5. trabajemos   6. corran   7. escriba   8. piensen   9. conozcáis   10. duerman

25·41   1. así que   2. sino   3. Bueno   4. estén

25·42   1. ¿Cómo se llaman ustedes?/¿Cómo os llamáis?   2. Son/Sois de/l Ecuador, ¿verdad?/¿no es así?/¿no?   3. No, no somos de/l Ecuador, sino de El Salvador.   4. ¿Hace cuánto tiempo que están aquí?/¿Cuánto tiempo llevan (viviendo) aquí?   5. Hace dos años que vivimos aquí./Llevamos dos años viviendo aquí.   6. ¿Conoce/s a nuestra hermana, ¿verdad?/¿no es así?/¿no?   7. Parece mentira que no la conozca.

25·43   Individual answers will vary.

25·44   1. Estoy   2. Está   3. están   4. Estamos   5. está enferma   6. están cansados   7. estoy contento, -a/ emocionado, -a   8. estamos nerviosos, -as

25·45   1. se   2. te   3. se   4. dedican   5. Nos   6. -as   7. -o   8. se... -a

25·46   1. Dime   2. No me digas   3. ¡Escucha!   4. ¡No te muevas!   5. Dígale   6. Escriba una carta   7. Espérenme/Esperadme   8. ¡No olviden!/¡No olvidéis!

25·47   1. suavecito(a)   2. chiquita   3. loquito   4. boquita   5. animalito   6. casita   7. pajarito   8. florecita   9. Dieguito   10. Carmencita

25·48   1. Bien.   2. Acabo de comprar un carro.   3. ¿En serio?   4. ¡Qué bueno!   5. ¡Claro!

25·49   1. h   2. c   3. i   4. g   5. j   6. b   7. a   8. d,f   9. k   10. f   11. e   12. l

25·50   1. ¿A qué se dedica tu novio?   2. Es profesor.   3. Es un profesor excelente.   4. Elena se dedica a limpiar la casa.   5. Por favor, no te mudes.   6. ¡No te muevas! Quiero sacar una foto.   7. Acabamos de hacer el examen.   8. ¿Qué acabas de decir?   9. ¡Imagínate!/¡Fíjate que me mudo la próxima semana!

25·51   1. no conoce a mis otros amigos.   2. el profesor es muy bueno.   3. ya la ha visto dos veces.   4. nos encanta esta ciudad.   5. prefiero los pueblos pequeños.

25·52   1. no asista a nuestra escuela.   2. el profesor sea excelente.   3. nadie quiera ir con él.   4. esté muy lejos de aquí.   5. haya más tráfico aquí que en un pueblo pequeño.

25·53   Individual answers will vary.

25·54   1. despedirnos   2. despedir   3. se cree   4. cree   5. Me falta   6. Falta

25·55   1. además   2. Evidentemente   3. no obstante   4. de modo que   5. ni   6. que digamos   7. Por una parte... y por otra   8. ni... ni   9. aunque

25·56   1. de modo que   2. no obstante   3. Es más   4. por el contrario   5. actualmente

25·57   Individual answers will vary. Sample answer: 1. Opino que sería difícil vivir sin carne.

25·58   1. En el fondo creo que es un error.   2. Pensamos/Creemos que es la persona indicada para el puesto.   3. Para serte sincero(a), no creo que sea la chica indicada para ti.   4. No conozco a nadie en esta ciudad, no tengo trabajo ni dónde vivir y por si fuera poco no hablo el idioma/la lengua.   5. Este no es el mejor trabajo del mundo, que digamos.   6. Que tengas un buen día.

25·59   Individual answers will vary.

25·60   Individual answers will vary.

26   Problem solver

26·1   1. Ud.   2. tú   3. tú   4. Ud.   5. vosotros   6. Uds.   7. vosotros   8. Uds.   9. tú
10. vosotras

26·2   1. b   2. a   3. b   4. a   5. b   6. c   7. b   8. a   9. a   10. b   11. b   12. b   13. a
14. a   15. a

26·3   1. o   2. i   3. d   4. r   5. l   6. a   7. c   8. n   9. e   10. s   11. t   12. g   13. j   14. h
15. b   16. m.   17. k   18. f   19. q   20. p

26·4   1. m   2. n   3. j   4. r   5. h   6. b   7. p   8. c   9. k   10. t   11. d   12. s   13. e
14. a   15. g   16. f   17. i   18. l   19. q   20. o

26·5   1. por (*exchange*)   2. por (*along; across*)   3. por (*per*)   4. por (*object of errand*)   5. Para (*purpose, refers to* **a pintar**) *or* Por (*cause:* **por eso** = *for that reason*)   6. por (*for the sake of*)   7. para (*purpose:* **para colmo** = *to top it off*)   8. Por (*why*)   9. para (*direction*)   10. para (*recipient*)   11. por (*in place of*)   12. por (*around here*)   13. para (*deadline*)   14. para (*purpose: in order to*)   15. para (*purpose: in order to*)   16. Para (*purpose*)   17. Por (*cause*)   18. por (*for that reason*)   19. para (*purpose: in order to*)   20. por (*around;* **para** *would indicate they spent an hour walking toward the park*)

26·6   1. That family went through the town / village in March every year.   2. The war hero nearly gave his life for the freedom of his country. (**Por poco** *is an idiomatic expression used with verbs in the present, but its meaning is past*).   3. Due to his limited notions about politics, I tried to convince him with mine.
4. The water flowed over a bed of rocks between two mountains.   5. The hamlet was founded on the banks of the river.   6. A man fell through the roof when he tried to rob the house.   7. The old woman with curly hair buried a figurine full of gold under the bed.   8. Wherever he / she went, soft music could be / was heard.   9. The younger brother, by effort and talent, worked for years to fix up the house.
10. It rained for several days.   11. A man got on / boarded the train that was going nowhere, without any particular route and no destination.   12. The woman who lives on the floor below was the only one who felt pity for him / her.   13. The dogs ran after the rabbit.   14. The overland / mule-train mail route ran / passed through the mountains.   15. The musician was sitting in the middle of / surrounded by the disassembled pieces of a harpsichord.   16. The doves, frightened by the woman's cry, flew up toward the clouds.   17. Due to his insanity, several men had to restrain him with ropes / cords.   18. The spear the hero hurled flew until it pierced the chest of the enemy general.   19. The accused had to appear before the judge.   20. The city sank in the mud.

26·7   1. Por poco el perro corrió debajo del autobús.   2. La casa está / queda / se ubica / dentro de cinco millas de la ciudad.   3. El Sr. Acero no sólo hizo acusaciones sin evidencia, sino contra ella.   4. No nos dijo nada al respecto / sobre eso.   5. Ella se enojó con él cuando él entró en la casa.   6. Cuando salí del cine, vi a la muchacha de quien me había enamorado.   7. Ella me dijo que soñó conmigo.   8. No sabían si deberían casarse o no.   9. Resultó ser falsa la historia, según la cual él era de Italia.   10. Los niños corrieron por la casa, enlodando toda la alfombra.   11. ¡No traicione al rey, so pena de la muerte!
12. Buscaron hasta que encontraron todo lo que querían vender.   13. Por mi parte, dame la Libertad o la Muerte.   14. A pesar de sus diferencias, convinieron en firmar el tratado.   15. ¿De quién es este libro? (**¿Cuyo libro es?** *is admissible, but archaic*.)   16. En vez de quejarte, debes trabajar.   17. La biblioteca está cerca del edificio en que trabajo.   18. ¿Espera ella hablar con él?   19. A pesar de lo que ella dijo, él le interesa a ella.   20. Marcharon por el desierto.

26·8   1. debiera   2. puedes   3. querría   4. quisiéramos   5. pudiera   6. deberían   7. podría
8. debieras   9. puedo   10. debería   11. quiere   12. querríais

26·9   1. John ought not / shouldn't drive so fast.   2. Could you please help me with this suitcase?   3. I think she'd like very much to go out with John.   4. Well, you *should / ought to* go to the dance.   5. Could you kindly wait until we arrive / get there?   6. I would like to try this dessert.   7. Can you give me a hand with this job / task / homework?   8. It's obvious: she should quit smoking.   9. As much as we'd really like to loan you / him / her the money, we don't have that much.   10. Do you want to buy the salad if I buy the meat?   11. If you / they truly want to learn the lesson, you / they should / ought to turn off the TV.
12. It's true / certain (that) I want to do the homework, but I don't have time right now.   13. They really, truly would like to contribute more to the organization.   14. My brothers (and sisters) could / would be able to help you tomorrow.   15. Could you so kindly ask him to come to the meeting?   16. Johnny, you really, really shouldn't quit taking / going to your music lessons.   17. My (female) cousins want to drive now.   18. With gusto / much pleasure / most gladly we could support you in your campaign!
19. I know what I should / ought to do; it's a question of not losing heart / becoming discouraged.
20. Can you send us the tools within a couple of days?

26·10   1. Yo quisiera acompañarte, pero no puedo.   2. Ella debería llevar a su amigo/a.   3. Debemos leer más.   4. ¿Puedes ayudarme a preparar la cena?   5. Sus amigos pudieran hacer más para él.   6. Deben haberme devuelto la llave correcta.   7. Quisiéramos ir contigo al cine.   8. Ella quiere invitar a Juan a la fiesta.   9. Ellos quisieran llevar su perro.   10. Mi hermana debería practicar el violín más.   11. ¿Pudieran apagar la radio?   12. Ella y Ana debieran agradecerle a su mamá.   13. Él querría prestarle el dinero si se lo puede reembolsar pronto / con tal de que se lo pueda reembolsar pronto.   14. Su amigo debería dejar de fumar.   15. ¿Podrías traerme la silla?   16. Tú y tus amigos, ¿no quisieran ir a la playa?   17. Ella vendría, pero no puede.   18. Él y yo debemos arreglar el coche.   19. Ud. debería asistir a la escuela.   20. Yo quisiera invitarte a almorzar.

26·11   1. c   2. c   3. c   4. b   5. b   6. b   7. b   8. a   9. b   10. b   11. c   12. b   13. b   14. a   15. c   16. b   17. c   18. a   19. a   20. b

26·12   1. Te preguntas qué nota sacaste en el último examen.   2. Ahora hace dos horas que ellos corren en el parque.   3. Hacía dos años que él jugaba al fútbol cuando se rompió la pierna.   4. Ayer a las tres yo estuve en la biblioteca, ¿dónde estaría Juan?   5. ¿Cuántos años hacía que tú conocías a tu novia cuando se casaron?   6. Hace una hora que yo comí.   7. No te sorprende que María y Juan se casen / se hayan casado / se casaran / se hubieran casado.   8. Le gustaría que ellos le acompañaran al cine.   9. Ayer ellos esperaban que tú llegaras, pero no llegaste. ¿Dónde estarías? (**estabas** *is used to ask a direct question, expecting an answer*; **estarías** *is used if the questioner is just wondering*)   10. ¿Quién sabe dónde estarán las llaves ahora / ? Él las pierde todo el tiempo.

26·13   1. We moved to this town a couple of years ago, when my daughter was three years old.   2. It didn't surprise him / He wasn't surprised that his brother won the race, since he had been training for a year.   3. Let's see / I wonder if there isn't a check in my mailbox.   4. No wonder Mr. Acero has been arrested—he's been cheating the employees for years.   5. John was wondering why María had not been answering him when he called her.   6. My parents had been living there for years.   7. How long has it been since you haven't / that you haven't seen your parents?   8. I exercised a lot an hour ago.   9. How long was Teresa setting the table? I wonder if she doesn't get distracted a lot.   10. We'd be very pleased if you would kindly return the book we loaned you a week ago.   11. How long ago did the tailor mend your overcoat?   12. The mechanic had been putting off the car inspection for some time. (**tardar** *can also mean* to take a long time doing something)   13. When / By the time (that) they arrested Mr. Acero, the authorities had been watching him for months.   14. Three weeks ago, five of my friends and I were witnesses to a paranormal event.   15. It lasted only a minute or less, but it seemed to us (that) we had been watching it for an hour.   16. We had been practicing for an hour when George made the lights go out.   17. I wonder if my friend has left a voice message for John.   18. When their window was broken a month ago, they didn't know / weren't sure if they should call the police.   19. Let's see / I wonder if my father hasn't called me.   20. I wonder what would have happened to me if I had not married her.

26·14   1. Quién sabe cómo él consiguió ese trabajo hace un año.   2. Ella se preguntaba si él le llamaría o no.   3. Hacía una hora que trabajaban cuando entró el jefe.   4. Hacía años que el Sr. Acero no decía la verdad.   5. Cuando terminó el drama, ella se dio cuenta de que hacía veinte minutos que dormía / estaba dormida.   6. Hacía un mes que él intentaba pedirle prestado dinero a su hermano.   7. Hace un año que somos los dueños del negocio.   8. Las flores se secaron porque hacía una semana que no las regaba.   9. Hace tres horas que duerme el perro.   10. Hacía cuatro años que yo vivía en Mazatlán cuando decidí volver a los EE. UU.   11. Hacía veinte minutos que se horneaba el pan cuando se apagó la luz. (**Luz** *is often used generically to refer to electric power.*)   12. Hace cerca de seis meses que su primo fue a Europa por dos semanas.   13. ¿Hace cuántos años que nació su abuelo?   14. ¿Cuánto tiempo hacía que ibas de compras cuando te diste cuenta de que habías perdido la tarjeta de crédito?   15. Hacía sólo diez minutos que se colgaba la ropa para secarla cuando empezó a llover.   16. Hace dos horas que ella estudia en su cuarto.   17. Cuando el submarino volvió a la superficie, hacía más de dos meses que estaba debajo del casquete glaciar polar.   18. Hace una hora por lo menos / cuando menos que él ronca en la mecedora.   19. Lo despertamos después de que hacía dos horas que dormía.   20. Con razón / No me extraña / sorprende que estés cansado/a: ¡estas oraciones son difíciles!

26·15   1. Geometry fascinates me but I don't like to study statistics.   2. My parents didn't (used to) like it at all when I got into mischief at school.   3. What do you say (*literally*: what does it seem like to you) if we go to Cancún for vacation?   4. This morning, my head hurt / was hurting until I took an aspirin.   5. When I met her, I told my friends right away how much she enchanted me.   6. Are you interested in studying with me?   7. It didn't matter to that guy if his sister didn't feel good.   8. I hope my readers like these exercises. (*Literally*: I hope these exercises please my readers.)   9. Jane had a headache but her stomach didn't hurt.   10. I know that if you went to Spain, you'd love *tapas*.   11. As a boy, watching insects was fascinating to him.   12. I've never liked that Mr. Acero.   13. It seemed odd that the little girl didn't like anything at school.   14. Before, I was interested in literature, but now I'm drawn to history and biographies.   15. I impress the young man with what I know about local history.   16. Politics doesn't matter to you? Well, perhaps it's because we don't matter much to the politicians.   17. Mary, I know (that) Henry likes you.   18. My (female) friend is fascinated by carnivorous plants. (*or* Carnivorous plants fascinate my friend.)   19. Aren't you repulsed by the smell of tobacco smoke?   20. My ears hurt when I listen to that woman sing.

26·16   1. Me gustas.   2. ¿Le gusto a ella?   3. ¿Os fascina la música clásica?   4. ¿No te parece raro su manera de escribir?   5. Creo que te gusto.   6. Antes les gustaba jugar al ajedrez, pero ya no.   7. Después de que ella dejó de fumar, aumentó de peso.   8. No les gustan.   9. ¿No les repugnan las películas violentas?   10. Después de que él volvió de la guerra, parecía que ni el dinero ni el poder le importaban.   11. Nos gusta mucho / encanta hacer helado.   12. (A él,) la sonrisa de ella le encantó / encantaba.   13. Sr. Acero, no me impresionas.   14. Me duele el pie.   15. ¿Qué cosa en la vida más te importa, Alexandra?   16. Le dolían las manos a su mamá.   17. A él le pareció raro que te gustaran los espárragos.   18. ¡Espero que todavía les interese estudiar español después de terminar este capítulo!   19. Las noticias me interesarán.   20. ¡(A ella) le gusto!

Put Your Spanish Language into Practice!

At busuu, you can practice your Spanish skills through graded courses and a broad range of engaging activities. And as you study, busuu encourages direct interaction with native speakers through video and audio chat.

With busuu, you can:

• Practice with exercises that hone all four skills (reading, writing, speaking, listening).
• Enjoy flexible language learning—anytime, anywhere—to fit into your busy schedule.
• Receive personalized feedback on your exercises, talk with native speakers via an integrated chat, and get to know people from all over the world.

With over 55 million registered users, busuu is the largest social network for language learning in the world!

Special Offer: 30% off Premium membership

McGraw-Hill Education has partnered with busuu to provide an exclusive discount on busuu's award-winning Premium service.

Discount: 30% off any plan
Access code: BUSUUSPA30
Code expiry date: June 30, 2019

Or Try A New Language!

busuu offers courses in eleven other languages, specially designed by educational experts. With programs ranging from Beginning to Upper Intermediate, you'll quickly find the level that works for you!

Sign up or log in on **www.busuu.com** and enter your discount code on the payment page to get your exclusive discount!